Lecture Notes in Control and Information Sciences

For further listing of published volumes please turn over to inside of back cover.

Lecture Notes in Control and Information Sciences

Edited by A.V. Balakrishnan and M. Thoma

53

Liu Chen Hui

General Decoupling Theory of Multivariable Process Control Systems

Springer-Verlag
Berlin Heidelberg GmbH 1983

Author
Liu Chen Hui, Associate Professor
Department of Electric Power Systems Engineering
Wuhan Institute of Hydraulic and Electric Engineering
Wuhan, China

ISBN 978-3-540-12496-2   ISBN 978-3-540-44416-9 (eBook)
DOI 10.1007/978-3-540-44416-9

2061/3020-543210

FOREWORD

The process control engineering has got remarkable progress in both theory and practice since sixties. A lot of complicated and successful control projects now have been applied in industries and they are the convincible embodement of some sophisticated design ideas.

Professor Cecil. Smith pointed out that now five kinds of control systems can be regarded as advanced systems in process control engineering . They are :

(1) Cascade control,

(2) The combination of feedforward control with feedback control,

(3) The Smith predictor,

(4) Adaptive control,

(5) Decoupling control.

Most advanced process control systems , although their practical structures are different, are related to the above systems. The process control engineering is certainly under continuous development, but, at least at present time, the above statement is in accordance with practice.

Among them, the decoupling control of multivariable systems is with special meaning. The practical industrial application experience shows that in the multivariable process control systems, a very important and valuable research problem is to analyze the coupling situation among system variables and to determine whether the decoupling design is necessary ; and, logically, if the decoupling design is needful, then how should we do so ? This problem now is very attractive in both process control theory and practice. Recently, Professor K.V. Waller said in a report: " One of the subjects of great research activity in chemical process control in the U.S. today is interaction analysis , in which coupling between inputs and outputs in multi-input multi-output systems is studied. Interestingly enough the topic is studied by consultants and industrial researchers as well as university people. " (81)

We should point out that both the interacting analysis and the decoupling design research are not new ideas. The earliest work on this subject of Boksenbom and Hood was published in 1949. But, however, only during the previous decade or more, this idea got great attention and application in process control engineering and now we can say that several years ago , the research of decoupling design was only a kind of sophisticated design ideas and now it has become a quite perfect and systematic theory in the field of process control engineering.

By the opinion of theorists of modern control theory, the coupling analysis and decoupling control are not the most important problems in the multivariable control system analysis. Certainly, we can not oppose this opinion. But, by the opinion of most theorists and engineers of process control engineering, the coupling analysis and the decoupling design now are the most important and interesting problem in multivariable process control systems.

Obviously, I belong to the latter and so this book is certainly an advanced lecture in process control theory but not in modern control theory. That means that all contents in this book are closely related to the practical needs of process control.

This book is written for doctor candidates in process control engineering, so the readers are expected to have a good background of basic regulation theory. The author´s aim is to introduce them entering this very important and interesting field. Some young researchers, who have not systematic and comprehensive knowledge of process control theory, often have a quite wrong idea that the process control theory were classical and very simple and so they are only interested in the modern control theory. Now, the author provides such a book to them. This book shows although the decoupling control is only an individual subject in process control engineering , yet it contains so abundant contents and is still under further development. Then, can we say that the process control theory is simple?

This book is a try to give a systematic description of the recent decoupling design theory of multivariable process control systems. Some excellent ideas of pioneer books, such as the books of Mesarović, Schwarz, etc, are still kept in this book.

The author should express his honest thanks to Professor. Janis Bubenko , the head of the Energy Research Laboratory of The Royal Institute of Technology, Sweden . From Sept. 1981 to Sept. 1983, I have the honour to work with him as a guest researcher. He provides very good working conditions to me and gives me a lot of help and encouragement. This book is finished under his personal concern and assistance which are so valuable to me that I must say that without his support it certainly would not be able for me to finish it. We have a very good co-operation in different fields, especially in modern electric power system engineering his heuristic ideas and very comprehensive knowledge impress me very much and under his prominent leading, the author has finished several research reports in electric power system engineering. His valuable support to this book shows that he is really a far-seeing scholar in science and certainly I deem that all my research results here are the embodement of friendship between us.

The author also should express his sincere acknowledge to professor K.V.Waller (Finland), professor T.J. McAvoy (U.S.) and associate professor P.Scholander (Sweden), all are famous scholars in process control engineering, for their generous sending me their valuable research works.

Energy Research Laboratory   Liu Chen Hui
The Royal Institute of   Associate professor of Wuhan
Technology. Stockholm. Sweden.   Institute of Hydraulic & Electric
September , 1982.   Engineering, China.

CONTENTS

CHAPTER   ONE

DESCRIPTION OF MULTIVARIABLE COUPLED SYSTEMS

CHAPTER   TWO

DESIGN OF REJECTION TO DISTURBANCES FOR SINGLE VARIABLE

CONTROL   SYSTEMS

CHAPTER   THREE

DIFFICULTY OF ANALYSIS OF MULTIVARIABLE COUPLED SYSTEMS

CHAPTER   FOUR

SOME GENERAL PRINCIPLES FOR DECOUPLING DESIGN

CHAPTER   FIVE

SOME SPECIAL DECOUPLING DESIGN METHODS

CHAPTER   SIX

SOME REALIZATION PROBLEMS IN DECOUPLING DESIGN

CHAPTER   SEVEN

THE   BRISTOL-SHINSKEY   METHOD

CHAPTER   EIGHT

DISTILLATION   COLUMN   CONTROL

CHAPTER ONE

DESCRIPTION OF MULTIVARIABLE COUPLED SYSTEMS

§ 1-1 Introduction

It has been confirmed by engineers and theorists in control engineering field that multivariable control systems belong to the scope of advanced and complicated process control systems. The term " advanced" means that it can successfully execute the unitive control to some production processes containing many coupled variables and this function is always beyond the reach of single variable control systems. The term " complicated" means that the realization of such a system requires more complicated equipments than a single variable system does. On the other hand, from the view-poimt of control theory , the terms " advanced" and " complicated" means that such a system can satisfy higher control requirements or indices and the depth and the extent of theory analysis exceed those of the conventional analysis theory of single variable control systems. Twenty years ago, the process control theory mainly dealt with the problems of single variable and single loop control systems. Even sometimes multiloop systems were met, but in general they were able to be transferred into single variable systems and for such systems, quite abundant experience has been gathered, no matter on analysis theory , synthesis theory or on practice. A very important conclusion of the past research experience is that the frequency method, based on the Laplace transform and with the transfer functions as its main analysis objects, is widely considered as a very effective method for system analysis and synthesis in control theory.

But, however, as the industry develops steadily, the production scale becomes larger and larger and the process complexity grows more and more at the meantime. Especially, in some production processes, the controlled variables are related to each other. For example , a very common multivariable production process is distillation. For a distillation column, all the top product,bottom product, reflux flow, feed rate and temperature distribution are interacted in the whole process. But process control systems always control the variables one by one , so in such a case it is inevitable that interaction should be taken into consideration when some variable is under control. Because the interactions are mutual, so there must be some coupling channels among the single variable control systems. Consequently, the control system being treated is no longer a single variable system.

Thus, from sixties of this century, the multivariable process control theory has got very wide development and many research results have been successfully applied in practice. In chemical engineering process, the control of distillation columns is a typical example of the application of multivariable process control theory in practice. Now, this theory has become a very important field in process control theory and by the depth of its contents, it has been admitted in general that it is one of the most difficult fields in process control theory.

There are a lot of contents with multivariable control theory. For example, the synthesis theory according to some indices, the optimization theory with some restraints, the analytical theory of different models, etc, but, however, there is an important problem in both analysis and synthesis theory, namely how to research and to realize the decoupling control. This means to discuss what measures should be adopted to reduce a multivariable control system containing some interacted variables into some single-variable systems without coupling. If we can reach so, then the decoupled system will be able to be treated by the well-known theory of single-variable systems and the theory to deal with such problems is called as the decoupling theory of multivariable process control systems.

Certainly, decoupling is not the unique problem in multivariable control system analysis, by the view of some theorists of modern control theory, it is not the principal problem and a system with realization of decoupling control in general is not an optimum system. All these are true indeed, but, however, we must point out that from the view-point of general process control engineering practice, not from the view-point of general control theory, now to realize the decoupling control is still the main problem in the application of multivariable control theory in practice.

The decoupling idea was proposed by Boksenbom,A.S. , R.Hood and Tsien, H.S. at first. They introduced the matrix analysis method in the analysis of multivariable control systems and proposed the idea of non-interacting control, namely decoupling control, at the beginning of fifties. The problem they discussed is how to control speed and power of an engine by varying fuel and propeller blade angle. If two controls interacted, then this could cause difficulty to the pilot and they found a method to eliminate the interaction between them. From then on, Kavanagh and others applied this idea in different control systems, including process control systems. The basic idea of this method is: Appropriate design must be taken in order to make the transfer function matrix which expresses the corresponding relations between outputs and inputs of the researched system be a diagonal matrix.Thus, it is also called as the diagonal matrix method. In this method, the dynamic characteristics of control systems, plants and every element in these systems are expressed by their transfer functions, thus this method essentially belongs to the frequency method.

In the development of this method, many excellent scholars offered their valuable contributions.Among them, Mesarović, M.D. is worth being mentioned especially. He proposed several very important and famous analysis principles . One of them is : Only by the measurements

at the two sides of a plant, namely by the measurements of its outputs
and inputs , we can not determine what type of multivariable plants
this plant is. According to different coupling manners, he divided the
plants with equal outputs and inputs into P-canonical and V-canonical
plants, and then he pointed out: In a multivariable control system ,
better decoupling effects will be reached if V-canonical structures
are adopted with feedback decoupling design.

These two ideas of Mesarović demonstrate some essential properties
of decoupling design of multivariable control systems.But,it is a pity,
he discussed these ideas from quite abstracted systems and theory and
did not give explicit proof to his second idea.

But, what we want to discuss here is process control systems, or
more exactly, multivariable process control systems, so we should discuss in detail how to embody the above Mesarović's ideas in multivariable process control systems and show what practical results can be
obtained.

Although many papers were published in different magazines during
the past twenty years, no special book was written to explain the decoupling design of multivariable process control systems systematically.

Naturally ,if we want to explain the decoupling design theory systematically, then a series of problems should be discussed in detail.

For example:

What methods can be used to realize decoupling design? What are
their theory bases?

What are the merits and defects of each method?

What problems can be solved by using these methods and what conclusions are reached?

What are the applied conditions?

What is the practical application value in multivariable process
control system design?

etc.

Because of these, many famous theorists of process control, such as Niederlinsk , Bristol, etc, suggest once more to research the decoupling theory of multivariable process control systems in assortment; not only the research methods should be assorted, but the researched contents for each method should be assorted as well. Their basic idea is that the contents of this theory are very abundant and **under** further development, so it is necessary to do some careful work to make this theory more systematical.

There are many methods which can be used to solve the decoupling design problems of multivariable process control systems indeed. Among them, the follwing several methods are considered to be successful and effctive:

(1) The diagonal matrix method proposed and developed by Boksenbom, Hood, Tsien, Mesarović, Schwarz and others[1][2][3][5],

(2) The relative gain method suggested and developed mainly by Bristol, Shinskey, Nisenfeld, MaCvoy and others[42][7][8][51][70],

(3) The inverse Nyquist array method proposed by Rosenbrock[16] and the characteristic locus method proposed by MacFarlane and Belletrutti[19],

(4) The state variable method proposed by Falb, Wolovich, Gilbert and others[20][22].

Certainly, there are other methods (for example, the sequential return difference method due to Mayne,Chuang and Daly, etc[18]) in references but they are not so popular as those mentioned before.

A problem may arise here logically : Which method is the best?

It is difficult to give an exact answer to this problem. This is simply because different man who uses one of these methods to solve his own problem has different demands and intents. For example, modern control theorists appreciate the state variable method very much and there are a lot of papers and books to discuss this method. But the process control theorists and engineers prefer to use the diagonal matrix method and the relative gain method since these two methods are very convenient to be applied in the decoupling design of multivariable process control systems and the conclusions from the application of these methods are not very difficult to be realized in practice. Therefore, these two methods are the most popular methods applied now in process control engineering practice. The inverse Nyquist array method and the characteristic locus method can be also used in process control practice indeed, but these two methods are of some complicated theory concepts and arduous computation work, so they do not get very popular application. As for the state variable method, up to now its application to the process control practice is still under try.

This book is mainly to discuss the practical demands of process control engineering, so the application of the diagonal matrix method and the relative gain method is the guideline throughout this book.

These two methods will be expounded here and the discussions on some important characters will be given in detail. Especially, emphasis is given to discuss how to use them in process control engineering practice. We will see that the contents of these two methods are so broad that they may be beyond what somebody imagines.

Let us start our discussion from the description of plants.

This problem seems very simple but many theory problems are just derived from it.

§ 1-2 Illustration of Multivariable Process Control Systems

In order to research multivariable process control systems, or simply MPCS, we must know how to express them.

We should point out that to know how to express a MPCS does not mean to know the practical structure of it. In fact, when we know the practical structure of a MPCS, it is not certainly that we can derive a mathematical model from it for analysis; on the contrary, when we know the illustration and the mathematical model of a MPCS, in general we do not know its practical structure either.

It is not strange.

As well-known, even for a simplest single loop, single variable control system, when we research its control characteristics, from the view-point of control theory, we need not and do not restrict our research work only on the practical structure of such a system, but widely apply the transfer function analysis method to get the transfer functions of all elements of this system and then to determine the relative relations and connections among them. Just because there are some dynamic and static connection relations among them, especially some of these relations can be arranged by people, so it is possible to form some theoretically satisfactory systems by suitable arrangements of such relations, for example by introducing some compensation elements or channels. Then we return to practice to find a suitable structure to realize the researched arrangement. It would be better to realize it without any difficulty. If any, then some revision to the theoretical research arrangement should be done and in general meaning some theory sacrifice is necessary.

The development of single variable control system theory has denoted that analysis by using block diagrams is an effective method.

From the view-point of control theory, the connection of different elements and the introduction of some inputs or disturbances or the extraction of outputs all can be shown in the block diagrams. Although the block diagrams can not include all characteristics of practical control systems, they can embody the principal properties of them. This is because there are two very important properties with any control system block diagram.The first is that the transfer function of each block is determinate(for linear constant coefficient systems) and expresses the dynamic characteristics of some practical element;at the meantime the one direction connection between two blocks expresses the interconnection of these two elements. The second is that the block diagram of a control system is capable of being calculated. Just because of these, we can say that not only a control system may be represented by its block diagram,but also theory analysis to this system can be done by using block diagram.

Just like the single variable control systems, block diagrams are also widely applied to analyze MPCS. It is quite logically since any MPCS, in fact, consists of many single variable control systems, but some channels among them are intercrossed,i.e. interactions exist, so certainly a MPCS could be expressed by block diagrams.

But, there are some differences between the two. For MPCS, there are two kinds of block diagrams. The first is a block diagram system composed from transfer functions of all elements; the second is block diagram composed from the matrices of transfer functions of diverse elements. Both these block diagrams are of same characteristics, only the representation manner is different and for the latter, the calculation is certainly carried out by matrices. For the former, it can be also calculated by using matrices. So, we can say that the application of matrices is the main mathematical method in the analysis of MPCS.

For the former,just like the construction of the block diagrams of single variable control systems, in the block diagram, each ele-

ment and each channel should be illustrated.Though it is very intuitive,
it will be very complicated and intricate when there are many variables
and channels in the systems and sometimes it is difficult to draw such
a block diagram.

The application of block diagrams of transfer function matrices can
avoid this problem. The transfer function matrix means to arrange the
transfer functions with analogous property in this system into matrices.
These matrices may be square or not.For a square matrix,the elements on
the main diagonal are the transfer functions of intrinsical channels and
the elements away from the main diagonal are the transfer functions of
interconnection elements,i.e.the elements of interactions.Therefore, a
diagonal matrix means a system without interactions.

In general, transfer function matrices can be included into four
catalogues :

(1) The transfer function matrix of plants,

(2) The transfer function matrix of regulators,

(3) The transfer function matrix of decoupling elements,

(4) The transfer function matrix of feedback elements.

We must point out that the forms of transfer function matrices expressed in block diagrams may be different from those of calculation.

This is because the transfer function matrices in a block diagram
must undertake the restrictions of illustrations.

For example, for the system shown in Fig 1-2-1, its calculation
form is:

$$\begin{pmatrix} m_1 \\ m_2 \end{pmatrix} = \begin{pmatrix} R_{11} & R_{12} \\ R_{21} & R_{22} \end{pmatrix} \begin{pmatrix} u_1 \\ u_2 \end{pmatrix}$$

Obviously, the arrangements of them
may be different, but the practical relations
and properties are the same. About this , we
should know it well.

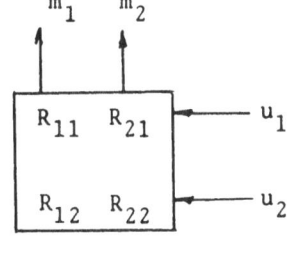

Fig 1-2-1

In the above description, only transfer functions are concentrated and arranged into different kinds of matrices, but the variables of the system still remain separately. In fact, the analogous variables can be also arranged into vectors. Thus, using transfer function matrices and variable vectors, we get the representation of a MPCS fully by matrices.

For example, for a two-variable control system, three kinds of block diagrams can be used to express it as shown in Fig 1-2-2.

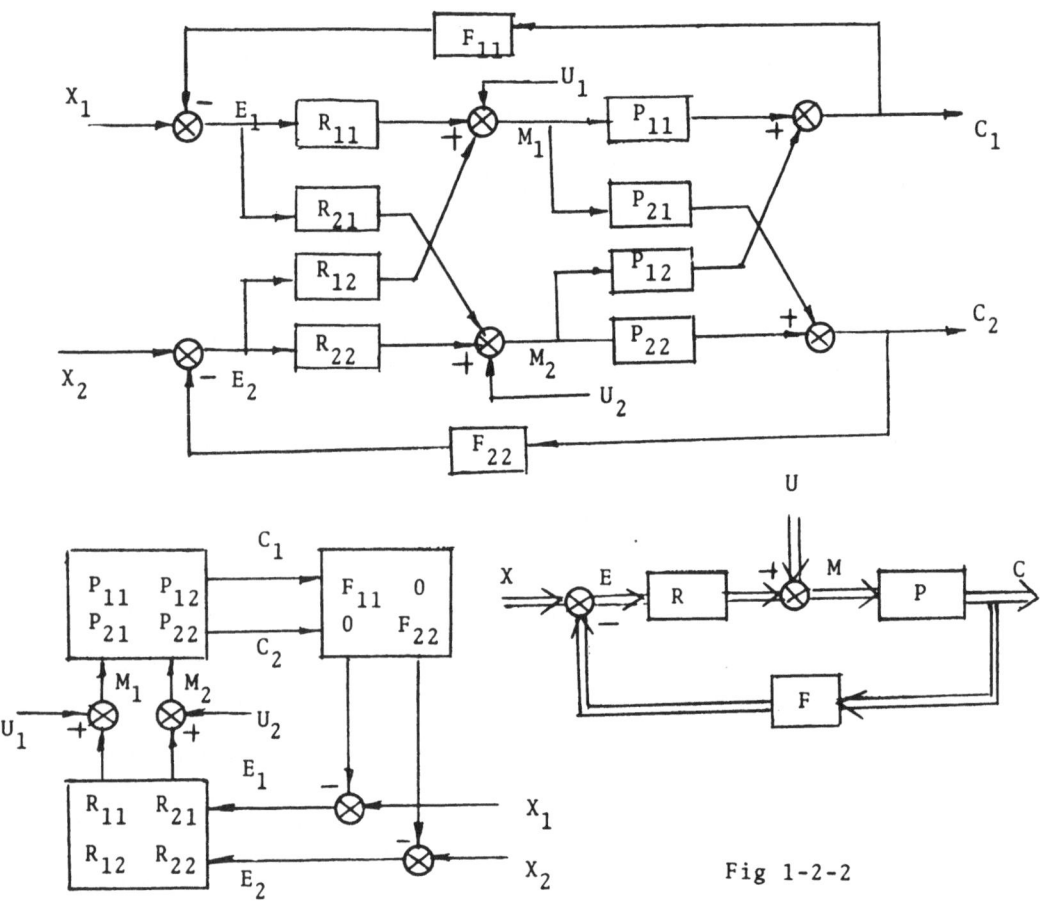

Fig 1-2-2

Where:

X_1 and X_2 are the given inputs,

X is the input vector,

C_1 and C_2 are the outputs,

C is the output vector,

U_1 and U_2 are disturbances,

U is the disturbance vector,

P_{11} and P_{22} are transfer functions of intrinsical channels of plants,

P_{12} and P_{21} are transfer functions of interaction channels of plants,

P is the transfer function matrix of the plant,

R_{12} and R_{21} are the transfer functions of decoupling elements which should be designed,

R_{11} and R_{22} are transfer functions of intrinsical channel regulators. But these transfer functions are related to decoupling design,

R is the transfer function matrix of regulators,

F_{11} and F_{22} are transfer functions of intrinsical feedback channels.

F is the transfer function matrix of feedback.

In this book, all of three kinds of representation will be used.

But we must notice, taking Fig 1-2-2 as an example,though there are many elements in the diagram, it will not be a two-variable system owing to the different connection manners. For instance,the four cases of Fig 1-2-3 all are single variable control systems indeed.

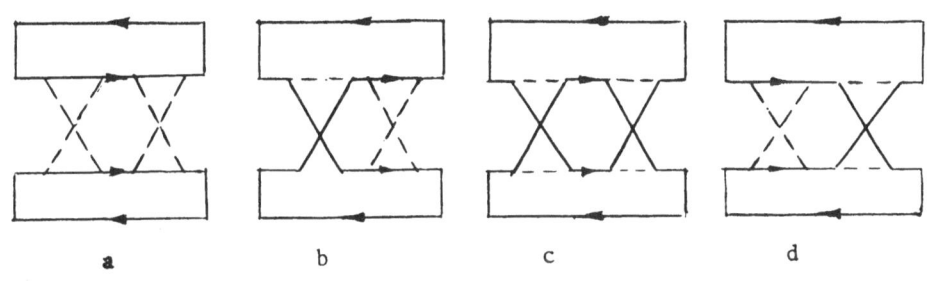

a   b   c   d

Fig 1-2-3

Fig 1-3-1a is an obvious single variable control system, so is Fig 1-2-3c. Both are two separate single variable systems.

Fig 1-2-3b and Fig 1-2-3d both are single variable systems indeed. Where either X_1 or X_2 may be considered as reference input , while the other is the disturbance.

Besides the block diagrams mentioned above, in references some authors use the signal flow diagram to express a MPCS.

For instance, the above example can be expressed by the signal flow diagram as shown in Fig 1-2-4.

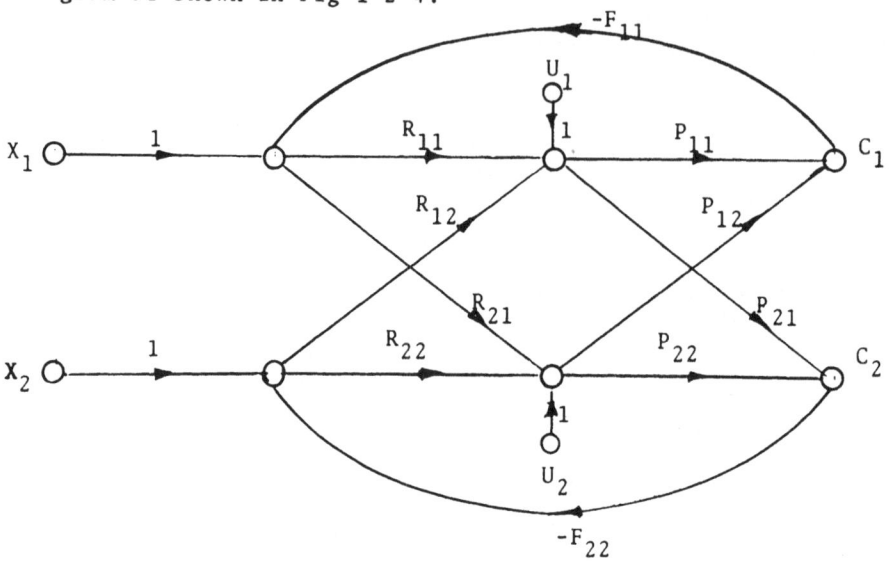

Fig 1-2-4

Certainly, this is also an applicable expression. Perhaps, from the view-point of process control theory, when we analyze the multitray distillation columns, the application of signal flow diagrams may simplify the analysis. And in most other cases, the application of signal   diagrams has no striking advantages over the other expression manners. In addition, most readers are not familiar with the calculation rules of signal flow diagrams, so in this book, in general we do not adopt this diagram.

§ 1-3 Representation of Multivariable Control Systems by State Variables

A multivariable control system can be also expressed by using state variables. Although we do not adopt this expression manner in this book, we introduce it here for theory perfection.

Suppose that the discussed system is with linear constant coefficients and can be described by a set of linear differential equations of first order:

$$
\left.
\begin{array}{l}
\dot{X}_1 = a_{11}X_1 + a_{12}X_2 + \cdots\cdots\cdots + a_{1n}X_n + b_{11}U_1 + \cdots\cdots\cdots + b_{1p}U_p \\[2mm]
\dot{X}_2 = a_{21}X_1 + a_{22}X_2 + \cdots\cdots\cdots + a_{2n}X_n + b_{21}U_1 + \cdots\cdots\cdots + b_{2p}U_p \\[2mm]
\cdots\cdots\cdots\cdots\cdots\cdots\cdots\cdots\cdots\cdots\cdots\cdots \\[2mm]
\dot{X}_n = a_{n1}X_1 + a_{n2}X_2 + \cdots\cdots\cdots + a_{nn}X_n + b_{n1}U_1 + \cdots\cdots\cdots + b_{np}U_p
\end{array}
\right\} \quad (1\text{-}3\text{-}1)
$$

Where X_i denotes a state variable and U_i denotes an input.

If it is written in matrices, then it becomes:

$$
\dot{X} = AX + BU \tag{1-3-2}
$$

Notice that both (1-3-1) and (1-3-2) are defined in the time domain.

A is a nxn matrix. It denotes the intrinsical connection relations of this system. B is a nxp matrix and it denotes how the inputs exert influence on the system.

$$
\dot{X} = \begin{pmatrix} \dot{X}_1 \\ \dot{X}_2 \\ \cdot \\ \cdot \\ \cdot \\ \dot{X}_n \end{pmatrix}
\qquad
X = \begin{pmatrix} X_1 \\ X_2 \\ \cdot \\ \cdot \\ \cdot \\ X_n \end{pmatrix}
\qquad
U = \begin{pmatrix} U_1 \\ U_2 \\ \cdot \\ \cdot \\ \cdot \\ U_p \end{pmatrix}
$$

$\dot{X}$ and X are n-dimensional and U is p-dimensional. They are state variable derivative vector, state variable vector and input vector, respectively. Notice that state variable X_i and state variable derivative $\dot{X}_i$ may be not the variables which are practically and directly researched.

A simple RC circuit is taken as an example.

Two equations can be obtained for two nodes:

$$\frac{V_1 - V_2}{R_3} + \frac{V_1 - U_1}{R_1} + C_1 \frac{dV_1}{dt} = 0$$

$$\frac{V_2 - V_1}{R_3} + \frac{V_2 - U_1}{R_2} + C_2 \frac{dV_2}{dt} = 0$$

(1-3-2)

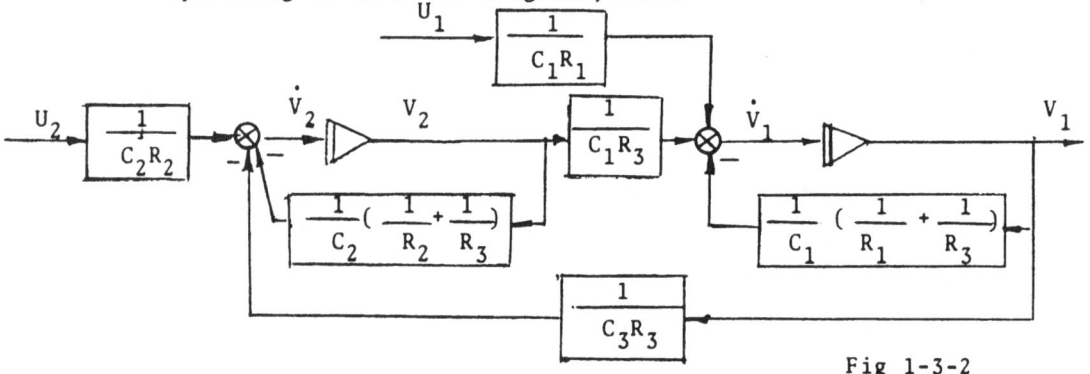

Fig 1-3-1

Then we get:

$$\begin{Bmatrix} \dot{V}_1 \\ \dot{V}_2 \end{Bmatrix} = \begin{bmatrix} -\frac{1}{C_1}\left(\frac{1}{R_1} + \frac{1}{R_3}\right) & \frac{1}{C_1 R_3} \\ \frac{1}{C_2 R_3} & -\frac{1}{C_2}\left(\frac{1}{R_3} + \frac{1}{R_2}\right) \end{bmatrix} \begin{Bmatrix} V_1 \\ V_2 \end{Bmatrix} + \begin{bmatrix} \frac{1}{C_1 R_1} & 0 \\ 0 & \frac{1}{C_2 R_2} \end{bmatrix} \begin{Bmatrix} U_1 \\ U_2 \end{Bmatrix}$$

(1-3-3)

Expressing it in block diagram yields:

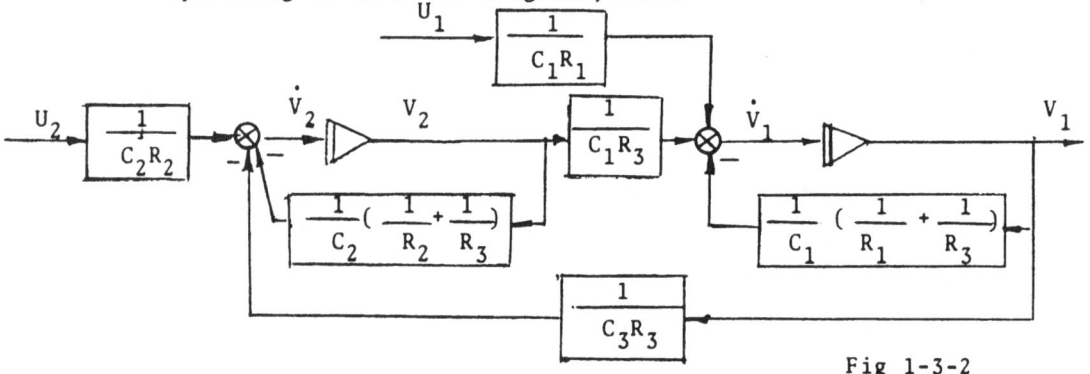

Fig 1-3-2

Notice that there are some essential differences between this block diagram and those we described in §1-2.

The first is : All the variables in this diagram are state variables and the connections are among state variables.

The second is: This diagram is defined in time domain, so only state variables and their derivatives can be expressed and besides the integrators all other connections are coefficients.

Thus, sometimes, circles and triangles are used to replace the blocks in this diagram.

Suppose what we want to know is the relation between V_1 and U_1 .

This means that V_1 is the variable being practically researched and V_2, $\dot{V}_1$, $\dot{V}_2$ are not variables with direct meaning.

In fact , this is a single variable system since V_2 can be eliminated from (1-3-2) and we get:

$$a_2\frac{d^2V_1}{dt^2} + a_1\frac{dV_1}{dt} + a_0V_1 = b_0U_2 \qquad (1-3-4)$$

Thus, it is a single variable system of second order.

For a single variable system with an input and an output, the output observed may be a simple state variable as shown in the previous example, but sometimes it may also be a combination of some state variables with a term directly related to the input. Namely:

$$
\begin{aligned}
y &= C_1x_1 + C_2x_2 + \cdots\cdots\cdots + C_nx_n + du \\
&= (\; C_1 \; C_2 \cdots\cdots \; C_n)X + du \qquad (1-3-5)
\end{aligned}
$$

So, the general form of a single variable system expressed in state variables is:

$$
\left.
\begin{aligned}
X &= AX + BU \\
y &= C^TX + du
\end{aligned}
\right\} \qquad (1-3-6)
$$

Where C^T is the transpose of vector C and B is a vector.

If both inputs and outputs are multivariables, for instance p inputs, m outputs and n states, then the general equations for the system is:

$$
\left.
\begin{aligned}
\dot{X} &= AX + BU \\
Y &= CX + DU
\end{aligned}
\right\} \qquad (1-3-7)
$$

Where, A is a nxn matrix; B is a nxp matrix ;

C is a mxn matrix; D is a mxp matrix.

For a two-variable system, if D is neglected, then its general form is shown as follows:

$$\begin{pmatrix} \dot{X}_1 \\ \dot{X}_2 \end{pmatrix} = \begin{bmatrix} a_{11} & a_{12} \\ a_{21} & a_{22} \end{bmatrix} \begin{pmatrix} X_1 \\ X_2 \end{pmatrix} + \begin{bmatrix} b_{11} & b_{12} \\ b_{21} & b_{22} \end{bmatrix} \begin{pmatrix} U_1 \\ U_2 \end{pmatrix}$$

$$\begin{pmatrix} Y_1 \\ Y_2 \end{pmatrix} = \begin{bmatrix} C_{11} & C_{12} \\ C_{21} & C_{22} \end{bmatrix} \begin{pmatrix} X_1 \\ X_2 \end{pmatrix}$$

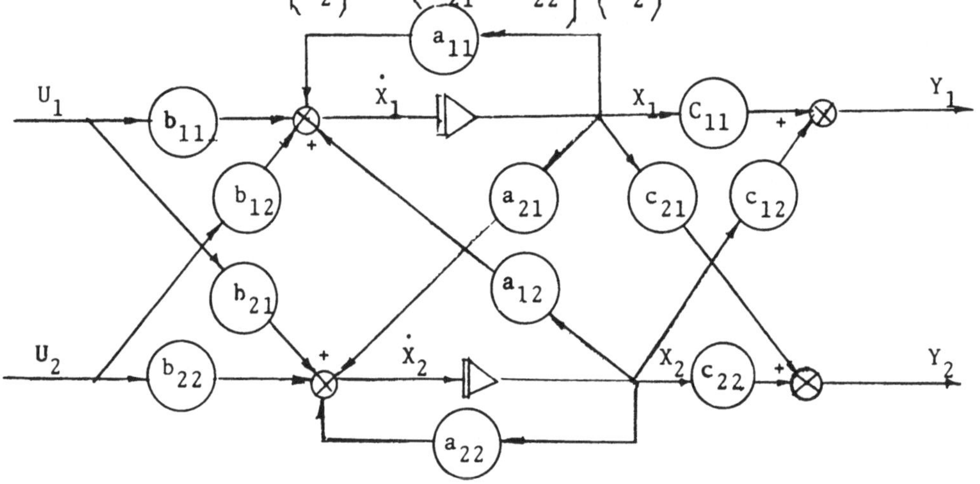

Fig 1-3-3

Because all variables in this diagram are state variables and they may be not the physical variables existing in the control system, so the interaction connections in this system in general do not embody the practical connections among the physical variables.

But what we want to know or we know is always the relations among the system physical variables, i.e. its transfer functions. In such cases, how to express a system in state variables?

In order to do so, at first we must transfer the relations of transfer functions into the relations in time domain since state variables are defined in time domain and then suitable state variables should be chosen. Notice that the state equations may be different for different state variables chosen. For a given system, the choice of state variable set is not unique. For example, if $(X_1, X_2 \cdots X_n)$

is a set of state variables of this system, then $(\bar{X}_1 , \bar{X}_2 , \cdots \cdots \bar{X}_n)$ may also be a set of state variables of the same system if the following relation is held:

$$\bar{X} = PX \tag{1-3-8}$$

where P is a nonsingular matrix.

We consider an example.

A heat exchanger is shown in Fig 1-3-4. The manipulated variables are the strokes of three control valves M_1, M_2 and M_3. The controlled variables are the temperature Y_2 , pressure Y_1 in the vessel and the flow Y_3 through the vessel.

Suppose that by theory and experience research , all the transfer functions of the channels are known and the transfer function matrix is:

$$P = \begin{pmatrix} P_{11} & P_{12} & 0 \\ P_{21} & P_{22} & 0 \\ P_{31} & P_{32} & P_{33} \end{pmatrix} \tag{1-3-9}$$

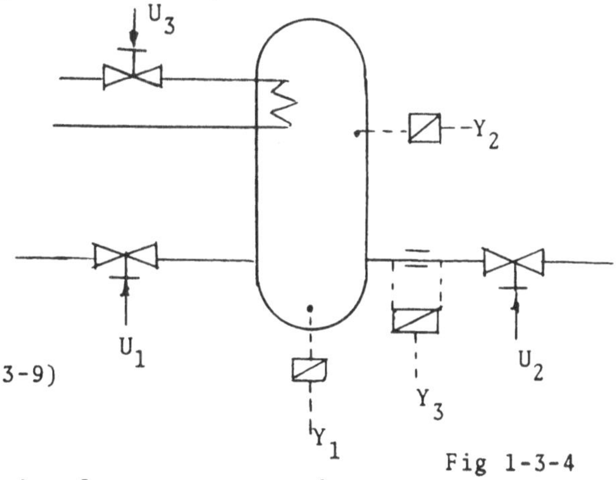

Fig 1-3-4

and the following transfer function forms are assumed:

$$P_{11} = K_{11} \qquad P_{21} = K_{21} \qquad P_{31} = \frac{K_{31}}{1 + T_{31}S}$$

$$P_{12} = K_{12} \qquad P_{22} = K_{22} \qquad P_{32} = \frac{K_{32}}{1 + T_{32}S}$$

$$P_{33} = \frac{K_{33}}{1 + \dfrac{T_{33}}{a} S + T_{33}^2 S^2}$$

Here, K_{ij} is the static gain and T_{ij} is the time constant.

The block diagram of this plant is shown in Fig 1-3-5.

The output equations are:

$$\left. \begin{array}{l} Y_1 = K_{11}U_1 + K_{12}U_2 \\ Y_2 = K_{21}U_1 + K_{22}U_2 \\ Y_3 = X_1 + X_2 + X_3 \end{array} \right\} \tag{1-3-10}$$

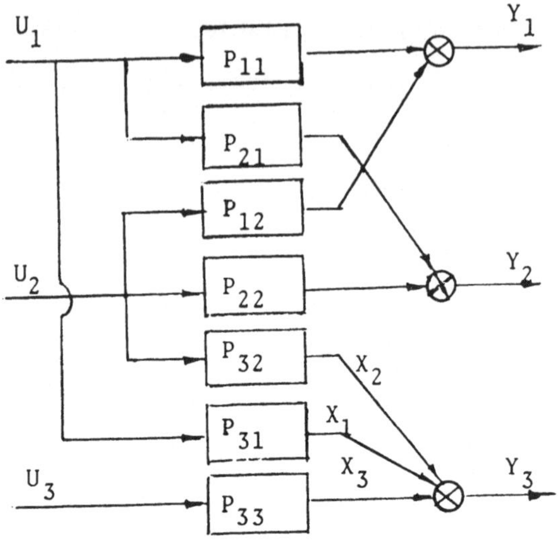

Here X_1 , X_2 and X_3 are a set of state variables as shown in Fig 1-3-5.

Because the state variables have been chosen, then we can return to the time domain from the transfer functions and state variables equations can be obtained.

Fig 1-3-5

From P_{31}, we get:

$$\dot{X}_1 = -\frac{1}{T_{31}}X_1 + \frac{K_{31}}{T_{31}}U_1 \tag{1-3-11}$$

From P_{32}, we get:

$$\dot{X}_2 = -\frac{1}{T_{32}}X_2 + \frac{K_{32}}{T_{32}}U_2 \tag{1-3-12}$$

From P_{33}, we get:

$$T_{33}\dot{X}_3 = X_4 \tag{1-3-13}$$

$$\dot{X}_4 = -\frac{1}{a}X_4 - \frac{1}{T_{33}}X_3 + \frac{K_{33}}{T_{33}}U_3 \tag{1-3-14}$$

Combining the above equations into matrix form, we get:

$$
\begin{pmatrix} \dot{X}_1 \\ \dot{X}_2 \\ \dot{X}_3 \\ \dot{X}_4 \end{pmatrix}
=
\begin{pmatrix}
-\frac{1}{T_{31}} & 0 & 0 & 0 \\
0 & -\frac{1}{T_{32}} & 0 & 0 \\
0 & 0 & 0 & \frac{1}{T_{33}} \\
0 & 0 & -\frac{1}{T_{33}} & -\frac{1}{a}
\end{pmatrix}
\begin{pmatrix} X_1 \\ X_2 \\ X_3 \\ X_4 \end{pmatrix}
+
\begin{pmatrix}
\frac{K_{31}}{T_{31}} & 0 & 0 \\
0 & \frac{K_{32}}{T_{32}} & 0 \\
0 & 0 & 0 \\
0 & 0 & \frac{K_{33}}{T_{33}}
\end{pmatrix}
\begin{pmatrix} U_1 \\ U_2 \\ U_3 \end{pmatrix}
$$

$$\tag{1-3-15}$$

$$\begin{pmatrix} Y_1 \\ Y_2 \\ Y_3 \end{pmatrix} = \begin{bmatrix} 0 & 0 & 0 \\ 0 & 0 & 0 \\ 1 & 1 & 1 \end{bmatrix} \begin{pmatrix} X_1 \\ X_2 \\ X_3 \end{pmatrix} + \begin{bmatrix} K_{11} & K_{12} & 0 \\ K_{21} & K_{22} & 0 \\ 0 & 0 & 0 \end{bmatrix} \begin{pmatrix} U_1 \\ U_2 \\ U_3 \end{pmatrix} \qquad (1\text{-}3\text{-}16)$$

What do the state variables mean? In fact, it is a set of variables with the least number and by these variables the states of the system can be determined. The determination of the system states means:When the inputs of the system at $t > t_0$ are given and the initial conditions of $t = t_0$ are also known, then all the states of the system from then on can be known. Thus, if at least n state variables $X_1(t)$, $X_2(t)$,.....$X_n(t)$ are needed to determine the system states, then these n state variables form a set of state variables. Although the state variables may be either measurable or unmeasurable physically, we had better choose the measurable variables as state variables.

By state variables , a MPCS is expressed in Fig 1-3-6.

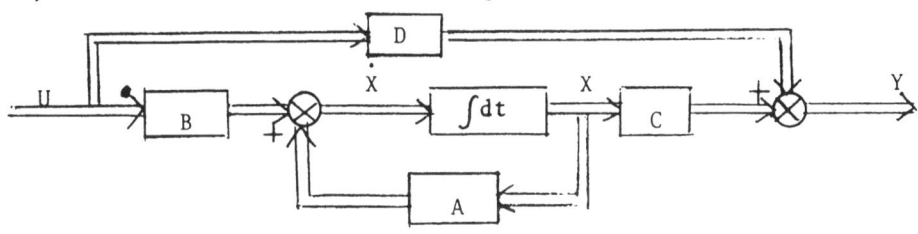

Fig 1-3-6

In order to show how to get such a model, we discuss a plant of three connected vessels. (Fig 1-3-7)

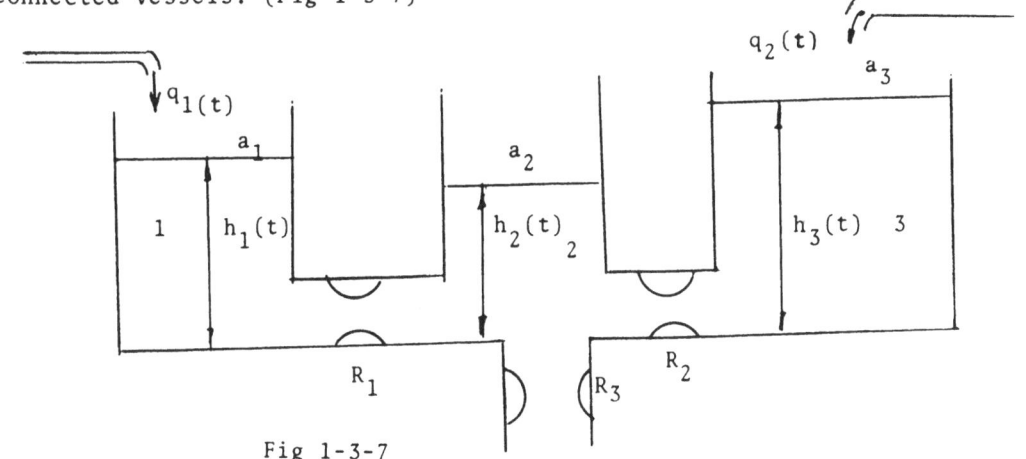

Fig 1-3-7

The inputs of the system are $q_1(t)$ and $q_2(t)$. The outputs are the levels of these vessels $h_1(t)$, $h_2(t)$ and $h_3(t)$. Suppose that the resistences of connection tubes are given by:

$$R = \frac{\Delta h(t)}{q} \qquad (1-3-17)$$

Where Δh is the pressure difference between two terminals and q is the flow through it.

According to material balance, the increase   of liquid volume in any vessel is equal to the volume difference of input flow and output flow .Thus, for these three vessels, we can get:

$$a_1\frac{d}{dt}h_1(t) = q_1(t) - \frac{1}{R_1}(h_1(t)- h_2(t))$$

$$a_2\frac{d}{dt}h_2(t) = \frac{1}{R_1}(h_1(t)-h_2(t)) - \frac{1}{R_2}(h_2(t)-h_3(t)) - \frac{1}{R_3}h_2(t)$$

$$a_3\frac{d}{dt}h_3(t) = q_2(t) + \frac{1}{R_2}(h_2(t)-h_3(t))$$

$$(1-3-18)$$

After arrangement, they become:

$$\dot{h}_1(t) = (-\frac{1}{a_1R_1})h_1(t) +(\frac{1}{a_1R_1})h_2(t) + (\frac{1}{a_1})q_1(t)$$

$$\dot{h}_2(t) = (\frac{1}{a_2R_1})h_1(t)- (\frac{1}{a_2R_1}+\frac{1}{a_2R_2}+\frac{1}{a_2R_3})h_2(t) +(\frac{1}{a_2R_2})h_3(t)$$

$$\dot{h}_3(t) = (\frac{1}{a_3R_2})h_2(t) - (\frac{1}{a_3R_2}) h_3(t) + \frac{1}{a_3}q_2(t)$$

$$(1-3-19)$$

The matrix form is:

$$\dot{X} = AX(t) + BU(t) \qquad (1-3-20)$$

where:

$$X(t) = \begin{bmatrix} h_1(t) \\ h_2(t) \\ h_3(t) \end{bmatrix} \qquad U(t) = \begin{bmatrix} q_1(t) \\ q_2(t) \end{bmatrix} \qquad B = \begin{bmatrix} \frac{1}{a_1} & 0 \\ 0 & 0 \\ 0 & \frac{1}{a_3} \end{bmatrix}$$

$$A = \begin{pmatrix} -\dfrac{1}{a_1 R_1} & -\dfrac{1}{a_1 R_1} & 0 \\[2ex] \dfrac{1}{a_2 R_1} & -\dfrac{1}{a_2}\left(\dfrac{1}{R_1} + \dfrac{1}{R_2} + \dfrac{1}{R_3} \right) & \dfrac{1}{a_2 R_1} \\[2ex] 0 & \dfrac{1}{a_3 R_3} & -\dfrac{1}{a_3 R_2} \end{pmatrix}$$

The state variables are $h_1(t)$, $h_2(t)$ and $h_3(t)$.

The output equation is :

$$Y = CX + DU \qquad (1-3-21)$$

In this example, the output variables are just the state variables, namely:

$$Y = X \qquad (1-3-22)$$

Thus:

$$D = 0 \qquad (1-3-23)$$

$$C = \begin{pmatrix} 1 & 0 & 0 \\ 0 & 1 & 0 \\ 0 & 0 & 1 \end{pmatrix} \qquad (1-3-23)$$

As we know that the state variable analysis method has got very rapid development recently and the modern control theory is just based on it. Especially, in the modern control theory, the analysis of multi-variable systems is a very important subject and a lot of papers and books have been published to discuss this problem, among them the Falb and Wolowich's work certainly is the pioneer.

We can expect that the state variable analysis method is a very promissing method for process control system analysis. But, up to now, the experience of application of this method in process control system analysis is not enough and a lot of work should be done further.

§ 1-4 P-Canonical Plants and V-Canonical Plants[3][5]

In practical MPCS, there is a great variety of coupling cases among variables and they are diverse according to different systems.

But, however, in the control theory, no matter control plants or control systems are researched, we always research the relations among three terms. They are the input, the output and the dynamic characteristics of the plant(or system)by its transfer function. But, in MPCS, multi-inputs and multi-outputs are considered. The disturbances essentially belong to inputs but are not the desired inputs.

Thus, obviously, when we say that coupling among variables exists in MPSC and when the coupling object has been determined (system or the plant and other parts of it) , then there are essentially two kinds of coupling phenomena. One is the coupling of the inputs with the outputs of other channels and the other is the coupling of the outputs with the inputs of other channels. As for the coupling among inputs or outputs themselves, then we can always assign some coupling objects and by which the coupling relations among analogous variables become coupling relations among inputs to outputs or vice versa (§ 1-9,§1-14).

Mesarović at first researched the coupling concepts. He divided the coupling plants with equal inputs and outputs into P-canonical and V-canonical plants.

We must point out that the occurrence of coupling in MPSC mainly due to the coupling in the plants. As for the coupling among manipulated variables or among outputs, we will see later that it can be also considered as a coupling plant. Therefore, in order to research MPSC, we must at first research the control characteristics of the multivariable plants since all problems about coupling are caused from it.

Just because of this, the assortment proposed by Mesarović to the coupling characteristics of MPSC makes the research work on the MPSC be more systematic and more regular and it thus enrich the research contents.

Now, we discuss the mathematic concepts of P-canonical plants and V-canonical plants.

For a plant with n inputs and n outputs , if each output variable C_i (i= 1,2,.... n) of this plant is influenced by all input variables M_i (i=1, 2,.....n), then such a plant is called as a P-canonical plant.

If we denote the transfer function between the Kth input and the ith output as P_{ik}, then for a P-canonical plant, we can express it as follows:

$$\left.\begin{array}{l} C_1 = P_{11}M_1 + P_{12}M_2 + \cdots\cdots + P_{1n}M_n \\ C_2 = P_{21}M_1 + P_{22}M_2 + \cdots\cdots + P_{2n}M_n \\ \cdot\;\;\cdot\;\;\cdot\;\;\cdot\;\;\cdot\;\;\cdot\;\;\;\;\cdot\;\;\cdot\;\;\cdot\;\;\cdot\;\;\cdot\;\;\cdot\;\;\cdot \\ C_n = P_{n1}M_1 + P_{n2}M_2 + \cdots\cdots + P_{nn}M_n \end{array}\right\} \qquad (1\text{-}4\text{-}1)$$

In matrix form, it is:

$$C = PM \qquad\qquad (1\text{-}4\text{-}2)$$

Where C and M are column vectors of n dimensions.

P is a nxn matrix.

$$P = \begin{bmatrix} P_{11} & P_{12} & \cdots\cdots & P_{1n} \\ P_{21} & P_{22} & \cdots\cdots & P_{2n} \\ \cdot & \cdot & \cdots\cdots & \cdot \\ \cdot & \cdot & \cdots\cdots & \cdot \\ P_{n1} & P_{n2} & \cdots\cdots & P_{nn} \end{bmatrix} \qquad (1\text{-}4\text{-}3)$$

A P-canonical plant is illustrated in Fig1-4-1 in both block diagram and transfer function matrix.

It can be seen clearly from Fig 1-4-1 that in the case of many variables, the block diagram is not only difficult to draw, but the relations in it are intricate as well. Thus, in such a case, the transfer function matrix can give simplicity and explicity.

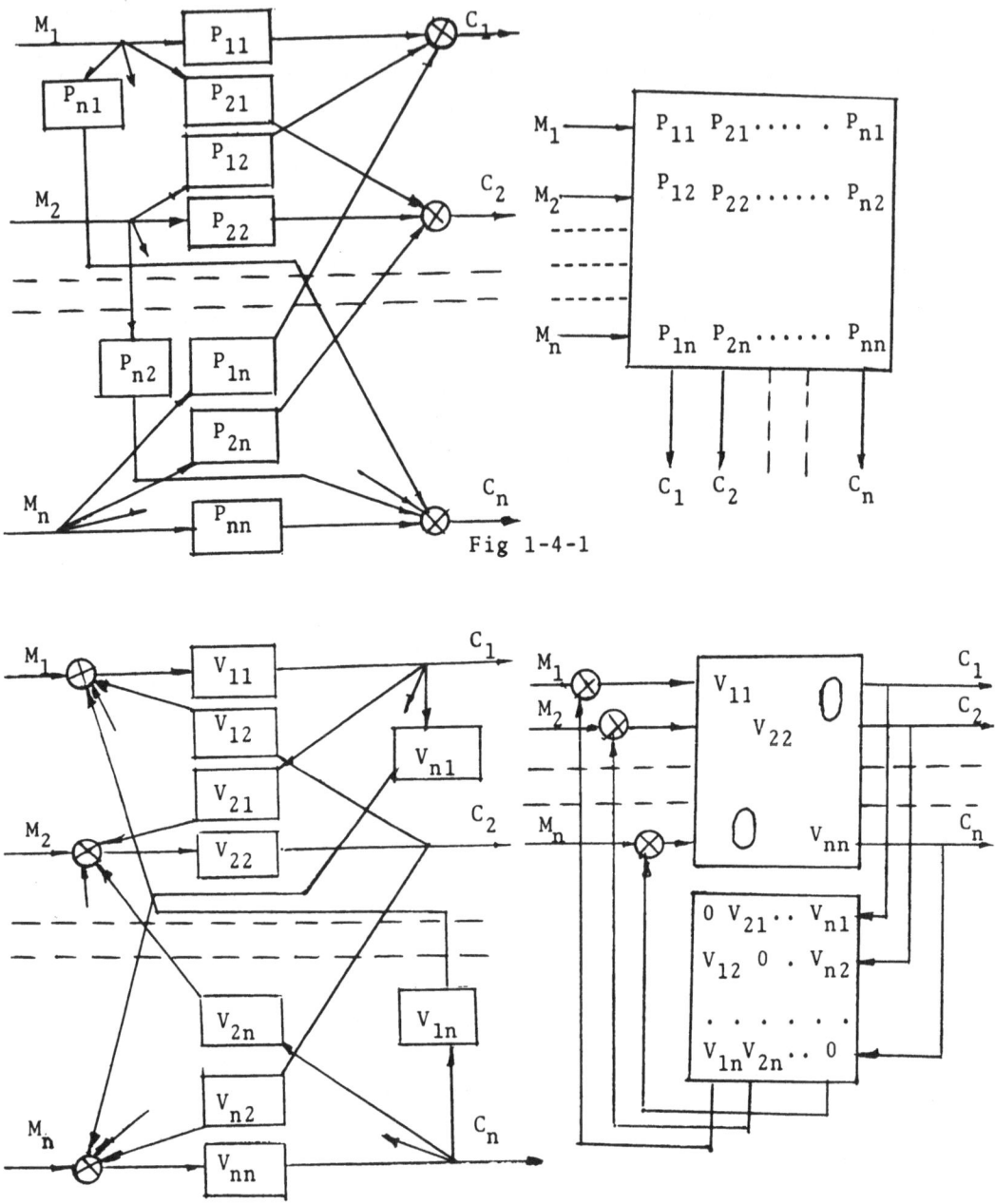

Fig 1-4-1

Fig 1-4-2

The so-called V-canonical plant means: Each output of this plant C_i
is influenced not only by the input of the same channel, but also by all
other outputs through the ith channel. Thus, if the coupling transfer

functions are expressed by V_{ik}, then a V-canonical plant can be expressed mathematically by:

$$\left.\begin{array}{l} C_1 = V_{11}(M_1 + V_{12}C_2 + \cdots\cdots + V_{1n}C_n) \\ C_2 = V_{22}(M_2 + V_{21}C_1 + \cdots\cdots + V_{2n}C_n) \\ :::::::::::::::::::::::::::::::::::::: \\ C_n = V_{nn}(M_n + V_{n1}C_1 + \cdots\cdots\cdots + V_{n,n-1}C_{n-1}) \end{array}\right\} \quad (1\text{-}4\text{-}4)$$

The general form is:

$$C_i = V_{ii}\left(M_i + \sum_{\substack{k=1 \\ k \neq i}}^{n} V_{ik}C_k \right) \qquad (1\text{-}4\text{-}5)$$

The illustration of a V-canonical plant is shown in Fig 1-4-2.

From Fig 1-4-2 we can see that it is impossible to express a V-canonical plant by only one transfer function matrix block.

Let:

$$H = \begin{bmatrix} V_{11} & & & \\ & V_{22} & & \text{\Large O} \\ & & \ddots & \\ \text{\Large O} & & & V_{nn} \end{bmatrix} \qquad (1\text{-}4\text{-}6)$$

and:

$$K = \begin{bmatrix} 0 & V_{12} & V_{13} & \cdots & \cdots & V_{1n} \\ V_{21} & 0 & V_{23} & \cdots\cdots\cdots \\ \cdot & \cdot & \cdot & \cdot & \cdot & \cdot \\ \cdot & \cdot & \cdot & \cdot & \cdot & \cdot \\ V_{n1} & V_{n2} & \cdots & \cdots & \cdot & 0 \end{bmatrix} \qquad (1\text{-}4\text{-}7)$$

then a V-canonical plant can be expressed as:

$$C = HM + HKC \qquad (1\text{-}4\text{-}8)$$

Thus , a V-canonical plant can be also illustrated as Fig 1-4-3:

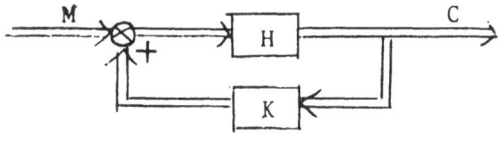

Fig 1-4-3

We should mention three points:

(1) Both these two canonical forms can be found in practice,

(2) These two canonical forms can be transferred to each other equivalently,

(3) We always meet P-canonical forms and in general we are accustomed to analyze them. But, however, in many cases, it would be very valuable to transfer a P-canonical form into a V-canonical form. We will explain these points in detail later on.

What we said above is about the P-canonical plants and V-canonical plants, but if the interaction exists between two systems, the above principles of assortment are also available for system analysis.

For example, Fig 1-4-4 is a V-canonical coupling control system.

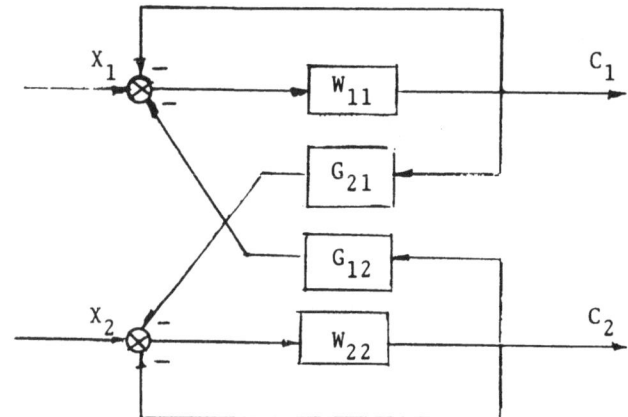

Fig 1-4-4

For this system, we get:

$$C_1(s) = \frac{(1+W_{22})W_{11}X_1}{F} - \frac{W_{11}W_{22}G_{12}X_2}{F} \qquad (1-4-9)$$

$$C_2(s) = \frac{(1+W_{11})W_{22}X_2}{F} - \frac{W_{11}W_{22}G_{21}X_1}{F} \qquad (1-4-10)$$

where:

$$F = (1+W_{11})(1+W_{22}) - W_{11}W_{22}G_{12}G_{21} \qquad (1-4-11)$$

Thus, we see that the characteristic equation of this system is much more complicated than that of a single variable system, so if we did not do decoupling design, then the analysis would be very difficult.

Now, we consider a P-canonical two-variable control system shown in Fig 1-4-5.

For this system, the following equations can be obtained:

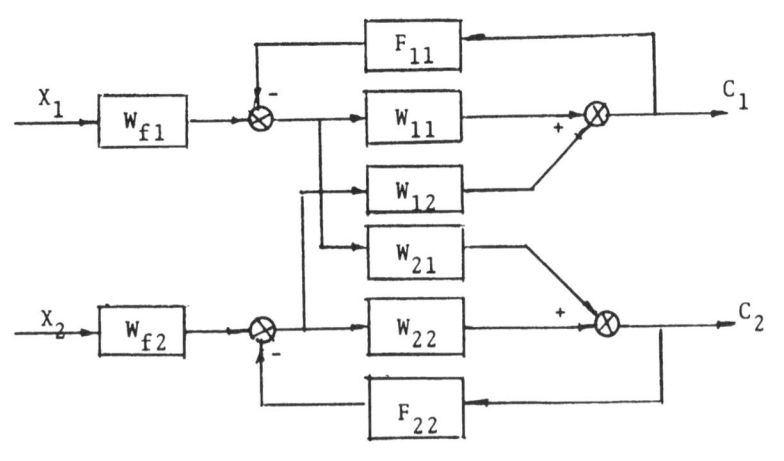

Fig 1-4-5

$$A_{11}C_1 + A_{12}C_2 = B_{11}X_1 + B_{12}X_2 \quad\Bigg\}$$
$$A_{21}C_1 + A_{22}C_2 = B_{21}X_1 + B_{22}X_2 \quad\Bigg\}$$
$$(1\text{-}4\text{-}12)$$

Where:

$$A_{11} = 1 + F_{11}W_{11} \qquad\qquad B_{11} = W_{f1}W_{11}$$

$$A_{12} = F_{22}W_{12} \qquad\qquad B_{12} = W_{f2}W_{12}$$

$$A_{21} = F_{11}W_{21} \qquad\qquad B_{21} = W_{f1}W_{21}$$

$$A_{22} = 1 + F_{22}W_{22} \qquad\qquad B_{22} = W_{f2}W_{22}$$

Solving equation (1-4-12) yields:

$$C_1 = \frac{\begin{vmatrix} B_{11} & A_{1Z} \\ B_{21} & A_{22} \end{vmatrix}}{\begin{vmatrix} A_{11} & A_{12} \\ A_{21} & A_{22} \end{vmatrix}} X_1 + \frac{\begin{vmatrix} B_{12} & A_{12} \\ B_{22} & A_{22} \end{vmatrix}}{\begin{vmatrix} A_{11} & A_{12} \\ A_{21} & A_{22} \end{vmatrix}} X_2 \qquad (1\text{-}4\text{-}13)$$

$$C_2 = \frac{\begin{vmatrix} A_{11} & B_{11} \\ A_{21} & B_{21} \end{vmatrix}}{\begin{vmatrix} A_{11} & A_{12} \\ A_{21} & A_{22} \end{vmatrix}} X_1 + \frac{\begin{vmatrix} A_{11} & B_{12} \\ A_{21} & B_{22} \end{vmatrix}}{\begin{vmatrix} A_{11} & A_{12} \\ A_{21} & A_{22} \end{vmatrix}} X_2 \qquad (1-4-14)$$

Obviously, decoupling could be reached , if we let:

$$B_{12} = B_{21} = A_{12} = A_{21} = 0 \qquad (1-4-15)$$

then:

$$C_1 = \frac{B_{11}}{A_{11}} X_1 = \frac{W_{f1} W_{11}}{1 + W_{11} F_{11}} X_1 \qquad (1-4-16)$$

$$C_2 = \frac{B_{22}}{A_{22}} X_2 = \frac{W_{f2} W_{22}}{1 + W_{22} F_{22}} X_2 \qquad (1-4-16)$$

Theoretically, to connect an element $(-W_{12})$ parallelly in W_{12} chan-nel and an element $(-W_{21})$ parallelly in W_{21} channel could offset the coupling channels and the interactions could be eliminated. Thus, it becomes two independent decoupling systems.

This method is rational and effective from the analysis of block diagrams, but, in the process control engineering practice, is it available practically? It should be analyzed.

In practical process control systems, especially in chemical engineering process control systems, the outputs of these systems always are some parameters of plants with definite capacities (sometimes , these capacities may be very large) , such as temperature, pressure, composition, flow, etc. If there are some coupling channels in them, then that means that some variables will influence some controlled parameters by certain chemical-physical processes. These controlled parameters can be measured by some small physical instruments indeed, but, as we suggested above, the elimination of coupling results of W_{12} and W_{21} is expected by parallel connection of two small compensation elements $(-W_{12})$ and $(-W_{21})$, is it practically realizable?

Obviously, because both $(-W_{12})$ and $(-W_{21})$ are only two small compensation elements with theoretically suitable transfer functions, they can not exert any practical influence on the controlled output variables.

Thus, in the decoupling design of multivariable process control systems , some methods and principles may be rational and effective mathematically, but may be unavailable in practice . This point, perhaps, is especially important for process control engineering.

This means that a really reasonable decoupling design result should be rational not only mathematically, but also physically, i.e. from the view-point of energy and practical capacity it also should be rational.

In this paragraph, we introduced the concepts of P-canonical plants and V-canonical plants. We must point out here that both these canonical forms are not only with mathematical meaning , but also with practical meaning.

This means that we can meet both these two types of plants in process control engineering pactice.

Some practical examples about these two types of plants will be given in the following several paragraphs.

Besides, these two canonical forms can be transferred to each other and this means that a practical plant may be expressed by either a P-canonical form or a V-canonical form.

The principles and methods of the transfer of the two canonical forms will also be discussed below.

§ 1-5 The P-Canonical and V-Canonical Decoupling Elements

The previous narration denotes that for MPCS, suitable measures should be adopted in order to eliminate the interactions among the system variables.

Intuitively say, the following two ways are the simplest : The first way is to cut off the coupling channels, but this way is only meaningful in block diagrams since any real coupling is the expression of some physical (or physical-chemical) process and it is impossible to be cut off by our imagination. The second intuitive way is to combine a compensation channel, which has the same character as the original channel but has the opposite sign, to the coupling channel parallelly and the interaction results will be certainly eliminated . But, we have said before that this way is also only available in block diagrams since the practical system coupling always occurs on the outputs which are some practical parameters of some process with definite capacity and consequently it is futile to expect the elimination of coupling by using small compensation elements.

Therefore, the above two intuitive methods are unavailable in practice indeed and two conclusions can be derived from here:

(1) For any MPCS with coupling, it is necessary to design and to put some decoupling elements into this system in order to realize decoupling,

(2) The decoupling elements are installed in this system as compensation elements . Obviously, they can accept and transfer only quite limited energy, thus they should be installed there , where limited energy can exert influence on the whole system.

This means that the decoupling elements should be installed before plants or on the feedback channels since in the process of signal transfer or comparison among the system elements, the energy through them is always limited but can exert results on the dynamics of the control system.

In control theory, essentially say, what is a decoupling element?

In fact, the decoupling elements are also coupling elements but their coupling results are just to offset the original coupling results. Thus, in this meaning , they belong to compensation elements.

Now that the decoupling elements are coupling elements indeed, then a problem arises naturally: By what coupling manner are they installed in the system?

We have known that for coupling plants there are P-canonical and V-canonical, but from the assortment principles introduced before we can see that these principles may be applied to any coupling object. Consequently, they can be also used to analyze decoupling elements.

In other words, when decoupling elements are inserted in a system, then there may be two decoupling structures—— P-canonical and V-canonical forms.

The two different forms of decoupling elements in a two-variable system are shown in Fig 1-5-1.

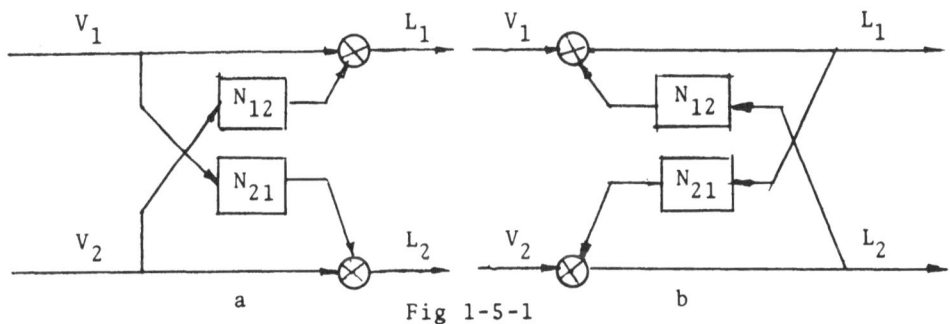

Fig 1-5-1

Fig 1-5-1a is the P-canonical decoupling-element structure with two variables.

Fig 1-5-1b is the V-canonical decoupling —element structure with two variables.

In general, the P-canonical decoupling-element structure can be expressed as:

$$L_1 = V_1 + N_{12}V_2 + N_{13}V_3 + \ldots\ldots + N_{1n}V_n$$

$$L_2 = N_{21}V_1 + V_2 + N_{23}V_3 + \ldots\ldots + N_{2n}V_n$$

$$\vdots\vdots\vdots\vdots\vdots\vdots\vdots\vdots\vdots\vdots\vdots\vdots\vdots\vdots\vdots\vdots\vdots\vdots\vdots\vdots\vdots\vdots\vdots\vdots\vdots\vdots\vdots$$

$$L_n = N_{n1}V_1 + N_{n2}V_2 + \ldots\ldots\ldots + N_{nn}V_n$$

$$(1-5-1)$$

Therefore, the structure matrix of P-canonical decoupling elements can be written as:

$$N_P = \begin{bmatrix} 1 & N_{12} & \cdot & \cdot & \cdot & \cdot & \cdot & \cdot & N_{1n} \\ N_{21} & 1 & \cdot & \cdot & \cdot & \cdot & \cdot & \cdot & N_{2n} \\ \cdot & \cdot & \cdot & \cdot & \cdot & \cdot & \cdot & \cdot & \cdot \\ \cdot & \cdot & \cdot & \cdot & \cdot & \cdot & \cdot & \cdot & \cdot \\ N_{n1} & N_{n2} & \cdot & \cdot & \cdot & \cdot & 1 & \cdot & 1 \end{bmatrix}$$

$$(1-5-2)$$

The general form of the V-canonical decoupling-element structure can be expressed as:

$$L_1 = V_1 + N_{12}L_2 + N_{13}L_3 + \ldots\ldots + N_{1n}L_n$$

$$L_2 = V_2 + N_{21}L_1 + N_{23}L_3 + \ldots\ldots + N_{2n}L_n$$

$$\vdots\vdots\vdots\vdots\vdots\vdots\vdots\vdots\vdots\vdots\vdots\vdots\vdots\vdots\vdots\vdots\vdots\vdots\vdots\vdots\vdots\vdots\vdots\vdots\vdots\vdots$$

$$L_n = V_n + N_{n1}L_1 + N_{n2}L_2 + \ldots\ldots + N_{n,n-1}L_{n-1}$$

$$(1-5-3)$$

The structure matrix of V-canonical decoupling elements can be written as:

$$N_V = \begin{bmatrix} 1 & N_{12} & \cdot & \cdot & \cdot & \cdot & \cdot & N_{1n} \\ N_{21} & 1 & \cdot & \cdot & \cdot & \cdot & \cdot & N_{2n} \\ \cdot & \cdot & \cdot & \cdot & \cdot & \cdot & \cdot & \cdot \\ \cdot & \cdot & \cdot & \cdot & \cdot & \cdot & \cdot & \cdot \\ N_{n1} & N_{n2} & \cdot & \cdot & \cdot & \cdot & \cdot & 1 \end{bmatrix}$$

$$(1-5-4)$$

But, from (1-5-1), we can get:

$$L = N_P V$$

$$(1-5-5)$$

where both L and V are column vectors.

But, in the above expression , we can not replace N_p by N_V direc-
tely.

This means that N_V obtained from (1-5-4) is not the direct transfer matrix.

This is a very important difference between N_p and N_V and when the
V-canonical form is adopted, we should pay great attention to it.

Now, we have introduced both P-canonical and V-canonical decoupling
element structures and when we know the assortment of decoupling elements, naturally we can propose a problem :

For a P-canonical plant , is it absolutely necessary to use the
P-canonical decoupling element structures to realize decoupling ?

Likewise, for a V-canonical plant, is it absolutely necessary to
use the V-canonical decoupling element structures to realize decoupling ?

The answer is negative.

A very important problem in decoupling theory is practically derived from here:

When the coupling form of a plant has been determined(P-canonical
or V-canonical), then which form of decoupling element structures
should be adopted in order to reach the simplest decoupling conditions
and to make the decoupling elements be most easily realizable ?

Obviously, this problem is very important in the decoupling system design and it is closely related to the famous Mesarović ideas
which we will explain in detail later on.

§ 1-6 The Equivalent Transfer of P and V Canonical Forms[5][30]

In the above several paragraphs, at first we discussed P-canonical plants and V-canonical plants and then we discussed P-canonical decoupling-element structures and V-canonical decoupling-element structures. We know that the P-canonical form and V-canonical form are two different concepts. They denote different coupling manners.

For example, the mathematic form of a P-canonical plant is:

$$C = PM \qquad (1-6-1)$$

where, both C and M are n dimensional vectors and P is a nxn matrix.

$$P = \begin{bmatrix} P_{11} & P_{12} & \cdots\cdots & P_{1n} \\ P_{21} & P_{22} & \cdots\cdots & P_{2n} \\ \cdot & \cdot & \cdots\cdots & \\ \cdot & \cdot & \cdots\cdots & \\ P_{n1} & P_{n2} & & P_{nn} \end{bmatrix} \qquad (1-6-2)$$

It denotes that each C_i is determined by all M_i as shown in (1-6-1). But for a V-canonical plant, its mathematic form is given as:

$$C_i = V_{ii}(M_i + \sum_{\substack{k=1 \\ k \neq i}}^{n} V_{ik}C_k) \qquad i=1,2\ldots\ldots n \qquad (1-6-3)$$

Solving the above equation for M_i yields:

$$M_i = \frac{C_i}{V_{ii}} - \sum_{\substack{k=1 \\ k \neq i}}^{n} V_{ik}C_k \qquad i=1,2\ldots\ldots n \qquad (1-6-4)$$

It can be also written in matrix form:

$$M = TC \qquad (1-6-5)$$

where: M and C are n dimensional vectors,

T is a nxn matrix with the following form:

$$
T = \begin{bmatrix}
\dfrac{1}{V_{11}} & -V_{12} & \cdots\cdots\cdots & -V_{1n} \\[2ex]
-V_{21} & \dfrac{1}{V_{22}} & \cdots\cdots\cdots & -V_{2n} \\[2ex]
\cdot & \cdot & \cdots\cdots\cdots & \\
\cdot & \cdot & \cdots\cdots\cdots & \\[1ex]
-V_{n1} & -V_{n2} & \cdots\cdots\cdots & -\dfrac{1}{V_{nn}}
\end{bmatrix}
\qquad (1\text{-}6\text{-}6)
$$

The elements of this matrix can be calculated by following expression:

$$
t_{ik} = \frac{1}{V_{ik}} \delta_{ik} + V_{ik}(\delta_{ik} - 1) \qquad (1\text{-}6\text{-}7)
$$

where, δ_{ik} is the Kronecker operator. It is:

$$
\delta_{ik} = \begin{cases} 0 & \text{when } i \neq k \\ 1 & \text{when } i = k \end{cases} \qquad (1\text{-}6\text{-}8)
$$

(1-6-5) denotes that each M_i is determined by all C_i.

Thus, a P-canonical plant is expressed by (1-6-1) and a V-canonical plant is expressed by (1-6-5); contrarily, what expressed by (1-6-1) is a P-canonical plant and by (1-6-5) is a V-canonical plant.

But, taking (1-6-5) as an example, if T is not a singular matrix,

$$
\det T \neq 0 \qquad (1\text{-}6\text{-}9)
$$

then we can always get:

$$
C = T^{-1}M \qquad (1\text{-}6\text{-}10)
$$

Notice when we get (1-6-10) from (1-6-5), the plant does not change, namely the practical relations between C_i and M_i do not change. But, however, when it is expressed by (1-6-5) , it is a V-canonical plant and when it is expressed by (1-6-10), it is a P-canonical plant. Thus, a V-canonical plant can be transferred to an equivalent P-canonical plant. That is to say if a plant may be expressed by the V-canonical form, then when T is not a singular matrix, it certainly may be expressed by the P-canonical form and vice versa, namely , if a plant may be expressed by the P-canonical form , then when P is not a singular matrix, it certainly may be expressed by the V-canonical form.

Combining (1-6-1) and (1-6-10) and solving, we get:

$$P = T^{-1} \qquad (\det T \neq 0) \qquad (1\text{-}6\text{-}11)$$

and:

$$T = P^{-1} \qquad (\det P \neq 0) \qquad (1\text{-}6\text{-}12)$$

This is the equivalent transfer relation between P-canonical form and V-canonical form of the same plant. Obviously:

$$P = T^{-1} = \frac{adj(T)}{\det T} \qquad (1\text{-}6\text{-}13)$$

If the matrices obtained by crossing off the elements of the ith row and the jth column within matrices P and T are denoted by $\overline{P}_{ik}$ and $\overline{T}_{ik}$, then by (1-6-13) we can get the elements in P :

$$P_{ik} = \frac{\det \overline{T}_{ki}}{\det T} \qquad (1\text{-}6\text{-}14)$$

Notice that there should be a sign $(-1)^{i+k}$ before $\overline{T}_{ki}$, but we omit it for concision. We should not forget it in calculation.

Likewise, we can get:

$$T_{ik} = \frac{\det \overline{P}_{ki}}{\det P} \qquad (1\text{-}6\text{-}15)$$

Therefore, from (1-6-7), we get:

$$V_{ii} = \frac{\det P}{\det \overline{P}_{ii}} \qquad (1\text{-}6\text{-}16)$$

$$V_{ik} = - \frac{\det \overline{P}_{ki}}{\det P} \qquad (1\text{-}6\text{-}17)$$

For instance, a two-variable V-canonical plant is transferred to the following P-canonical forms:

$$P_{11} = \frac{1/V_{22}}{\dfrac{1}{V_{11}}\dfrac{1}{V_{22}} - V_{12}V_{21}} = \frac{V_{11}}{1 - V_{11}V_{22}V_{12}V_{21}}$$

$$P_{22} = \frac{V_{22}}{1 - V_{11}V_{22}V_{12}V_{21}}$$

$$P_{12} = \frac{V_{21}V_{11}V_{22}}{1 - V_{11}V_{22}V_{12}V_{21}} \left.\right\} \quad (1\text{-}6\text{-}18)$$

$$P_{21} = \frac{V_{21}V_{11}V_{22}}{1 - V_{11}V_{22}V_{12}V_{21}}$$

A **two-variable** P-canonical plant is transferred to the following V-canonical forms:

$$V_{11} = \frac{P_{11}P_{22} - P_{12}P_{21}}{P_{22}}$$

$$V_{22} = \frac{P_{11}P_{22} - P_{12}P_{21}}{P_{11}}$$

$$V_{12} = \frac{P_{12}}{P_{11}P_{22} - P_{12}P_{21}} \left.\right\} \quad (1\text{-}6\text{-}19)$$

$$V_{21} = \frac{P_{21}}{P_{11}P_{22} - P_{12}P_{21}}$$

Thus, by $(1\text{-}6\text{-}14)$ — $(1\text{-}6\text{-}17)$, we can transfer a plant described by a V-canonical form into one of the P-canonical form and vice versa.

Now, we can propose a problem: This transfer relation is certainly rational, but is it unique?

No, it is not unique.

We consider the two-variable system again. Suppose that the plant is originally described by the P-canonical form and the control system is shown in Fig 1-6-1.

In this figure, we let:

$$\left.\begin{aligned} V_{11} &= P_{11} \\ V_{22} &= P_{22} \\ P_{11}V_{21}P_{22} &= P_{21} \\ P_{22}V_{12}P_{11} &= P_{12} \end{aligned}\right\} \quad (1\text{-}6\text{-}20)$$

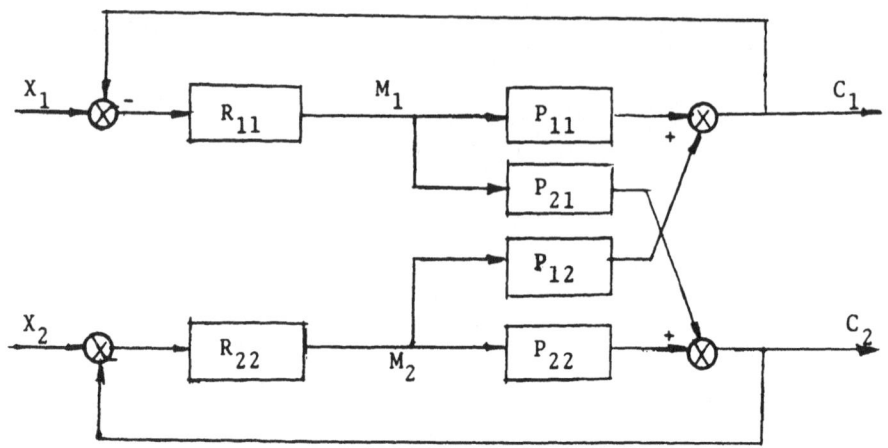

Fig 1-6-1

then we get:

$$V_{11} = P_{11}$$

$$V_{12} = \frac{P_{12}}{P_{11}P_{22}}$$

$$V_{21} = \frac{P_{21}}{P_{11}P_{22}}$$

$$V_{22} = P_{22}$$

(1-6-21)

The system now is shown in Fig 1-6-2.

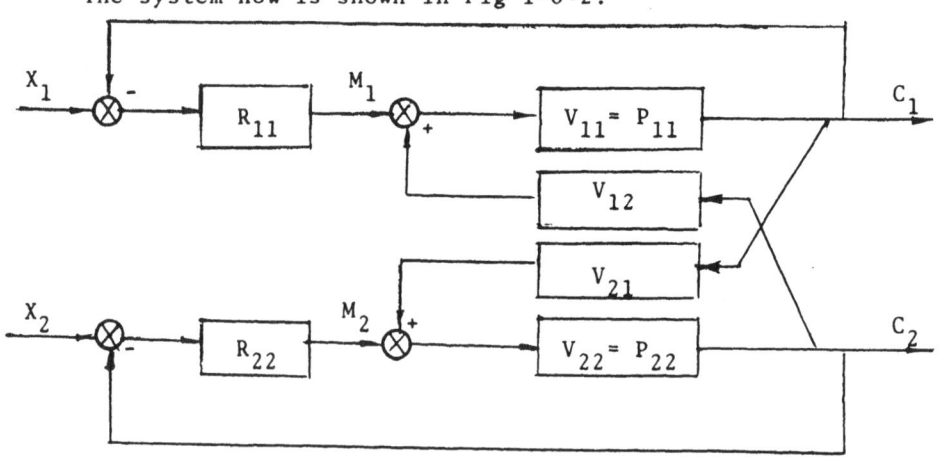

Fig 1-6-2

Obviously, (1-6-21) is different from (1-6-19).

Thus, we know that both P- and V-canonical plants not only can be transferred to each other, but many transfer results can be found as well. What does it mean?

It obviously denotes a fact: It is impossible to determine a plant being P-canonical form or V-canonical form, if only inputs and outputs of this plant, M_1, M_2 and C_1, C_2, are judged. Namely, we can not determine its coupling manner, so we can not get the unique character of each coupling element either.

This is just the first Mesarović idea: For a multivariable plant, it is impossible to determine what form of multivariable plants it is, if only its inputs and outputs are judged.

Notice that this is a conclusion in control theory, and this conclusion does not cover any fact that the researched plant is a P-canonical form or a V-canonical form. This conclusion is only to say that from the view-point of theory , two canonical forms can be transferred to each other.So , in practice, for the plant considered, we can determine the characteristics of its intrinsical channels and coupling channels according to its physical or physical-chemical properties by theory calculation or by experiments and determine which canonical form it is. After we do so, we can transfer, if necessary, to other canonical form for research by the above rules.

From the calculation of transfer function matrices, a V-canonical system is shown in Fig 1-4-3. For it, we get:

$$C = H(M + KC) = HM + HKC \qquad (1\text{-}6\text{-}22)$$

and:

$$(I - HK)C = HM \qquad (1\text{-}6\text{-}23)$$

Therefore:

$$C = (I - HK)^{-1}HM \qquad (1\text{-}6\text{-}24)$$

But a P-canonical plant is:

$$C = PM \qquad (1\text{-}6\text{-}25)$$

Thus, the general formula for a V-canonical form to be transferred to a P-canonical plant is:

$$P = (I - HK)^{-1}H \qquad (1-6-26)$$

Now that the two possible description manners of a plant can be transferred to each other, naturally, the two description manners of the same decoupling-element structure can also be transferred to each other.

We know that the transfer function matrix for a P-canonical decoupling-element structure is :

$$N_p = \begin{bmatrix} 1 & N_{12} & \cdots & \cdots & N_{1n} \\ N_{21} & 1 & \cdots & \cdots & N_{2n} \\ \cdot & \cdot & \cdots & \cdots & \cdot \\ \cdot & \cdot & \cdots & \cdots & \cdot \\ N_{n1} & N_{n2} & \cdots & \cdots & 1 \end{bmatrix} \qquad (1-6-27)$$

and for the V-canonical decoupling-element structure:

$$N_V = \begin{bmatrix} 1 & N_{12} & \cdots & \cdots & N_{1n} \\ N_{21} & 1 & \cdots & \cdots & N_{2n} \\ \cdot & \cdot & \cdots & \cdots & \cdot \\ \cdot & \cdot & \cdots & \cdots & \cdot \\ N_{n1} & N_{n2} & \cdots & \cdots & 1 \end{bmatrix} \qquad (1-6-28)$$

But, not like N_p, N_V does not express a transfer matrix directly. It expresses the following relation:

$$\left. \begin{aligned} L_1 &= V_1 + N_{12}L_2 + N_{13}L_3 + \cdots\cdots + N_{1n}L_n \\ L_2 &= V_2 + N_{21}L_1 + N_{23}L_3 + \cdots\cdots + N_{2n}L_n \\ &\vdots \\ L_n &= V_n + N_{n1}L_1 + N_{n2}L_2 + \cdots\cdots + N_{n,n-1}L_{n-1} \end{aligned} \right\} \qquad (1-6-29)$$

When a V-canonical decoupling-element structure is transferred to a P-canonical decoupling-element structure, equation (1-6-6) can be used. Namely, from (1-6-29) we can get another matrix A , similar to (1-6-6), but $V_{11}=V_{22}= \cdots\cdots = V_{nn}=1$. Then matrix A is:

$$A = \begin{bmatrix} 1 & -N_{12} & \cdots \cdots \cdots & -N_{1n} \\ -N_{21} & 1 & \cdots \cdots \cdots & -N_{2n} \\ \cdot & \cdot & \cdots \cdots \cdots \\ \cdot & \cdot & \cdots \cdots \cdots \\ -N_{n1} & -N_{n2} & \cdots \cdots \cdots & 1 \end{bmatrix} \qquad (1-6-30)$$

Thus, by (1-6-11), when we want to transfer a V-canonical decoupling element structure to a P-canonical structure, we can do by letting:

$$N_p = A^{-1} \qquad (\det A \neq 0) \qquad (1-6-31)$$

The narration of this paragraph shows that in the analysis of MPCS, some problems may have several solution forms, i.e. uncertainty exists.

Then, does this uncertainty also express itself in the decoupling design?

Certainly , it will.

This means that for a coupled multivariable process control system, if only the decoupling design is expected, then several solutions (or more exactely, infinite solutions) may be available for it . But, if besides the demand of decoupling control,there are other special control demands, then the solution may be unique.

We should point out that it is not a bad thing that the decoupling design is always with many solutions because this gives us the possibility to choose the more suitable project for the system considered on the basis of comparison of different possible decoupling projects. We can say that to compare is the most important principle for decoupling design.

About this problem we will discuss in detail in the next several chapters.

§ 1-7 Multivariable Plants and Canonical Plants

Sometimes, multivariable plants are described by differential equation sets, such as:

$$\left.\begin{array}{l} b_{11}C_1 + b_{12}C_2 + \cdots\cdots + b_{1n}C_n = a_{11}M_1 + a_{12}M_2 + \cdots\cdots + a_{1n}M_n \\[8pt] b_{21}C_1 + b_{22}C_2 + \cdots\cdots + b_{2n}C_n = a_{21}M_1 + a_{22}M_2 + \cdots\cdots + a_{2n}M_n \\[8pt] \vdots\vdots\vdots\vdots\vdots\vdots\vdots\vdots\vdots\vdots\vdots\vdots\vdots\vdots\vdots\vdots\vdots\vdots\vdots\vdots\vdots\vdots\vdots\vdots\vdots\vdots\vdots\vdots\vdots\vdots \\[8pt] b_{n1}C_1 + b_{n2}C_2 + \cdots\cdots + b_{nn}C_n = a_{n1}M_1 + a_{n2}M_2 + \cdots\cdots + a_{nn}M_n \end{array}\right\} \quad (1\text{-}7\text{-}1)$$

Where : C_i is the output, M_i is the input,

b_{ik} and a_{ik} are linear differential operator polynomials.
such as : $(1 + T_iS)$, $(1 + 2\zeta w_nS + w_n^2S^2)$.

(1-7-1) can be expressed in matrix form:

$$BC = AM \qquad\qquad (1\text{-}7\text{-}2)$$

Where: A, B are nxn square matrices,

C, M are n-dimensional vectors.

If B is not a singular matrix, then from (1-7-2) we can get:

$$C = B^{-1}AM = PM \qquad\qquad (1\text{-}7\text{-}3)$$

The elements in matrix P are fractions of rational polynomials.

Here, we should notice an important property. Obviously, P is the transfer matrix of this plant and in this matrix, every element is of the same denominator since:

$$P = \frac{(adj\ B)A}{\det B} \qquad\qquad (1\text{-}7\text{-}4)$$

Thus, every element in P has the same denominator $|B|$. In other words, if no offset of zeros to poles is considered, then all elements in matrix P have same poles. For example, it may be as follows:

$$P = \begin{pmatrix} \dfrac{a}{(1 + T_1S)(1 + T_2S)} & \dfrac{1 + bS}{(1 + T_1S)(1 + T_2S)} \\[15pt] \dfrac{c}{(1 + T_1S)(1 + T_2S)} & \dfrac{dS + e}{(1 + T_1S)(1 + T_2S)} \end{pmatrix}$$

So we see that all elements in P have same poles. This is a very important property of transfer matrix P. Obviously, all channels in such a plant are either stable or unstable.

This kind of plants is certainly a multivariable plant and what is the difference between it and the canonical forms ?

The P-canonical plants mentioned before are also multivariable plants, but are different from the plants discussed now.

A P-canonical plant is described by transfer functions:

$$\left.\begin{array}{l} C_1 = P_{11}M_1 + P_{12}M_2 + \cdots\cdots\cdots + P_{1n}M_n \\ C_2 = P_{21}M_1 + P_{22}M_2 + \cdots\cdots\cdots + P_{2n}M_n \\ \vdots\vdots\vdots\vdots\vdots\vdots\vdots\vdots\vdots\vdots\vdots\vdots\vdots\vdots\vdots\vdots\vdots\vdots\vdots\vdots\vdots\vdots \\ C_n = P_{n1}M_1 + P_{n2}M_2 + \cdots\cdots\cdots + P_{nn}M_n \end{array}\right\} \tag{1-7-5}$$

We get:

$$C = PM \tag{1-7-6}$$

In this transfer function matrix, each element is the transfer function of some channel and certainly these channels may be different, therefore in the transfer function matrix of a P-canonical plant, different element may have different poles. The stability of each channel is determined by its own poles.

Thus, the multivariable plant discussed in this paragraph is different from a P-canonical plant. This means if a system is described by (1-7-3) and (1-7-6) separately, then the two transfer matrices are different.

It is not strange at all. This is also an expression of uncertainty of MPCS.

In order to show this difference, we always express a multivariable plant by Fig 1-7-1 , and a P-canonical plant by Fig 1-7-2.

In abstract control theory research, the concept of general multi-variable plants is widely applied, but in process control system research, perhaps, it is more suitable to use the P-canonical plant concept. In this book, only the latter is adopted.

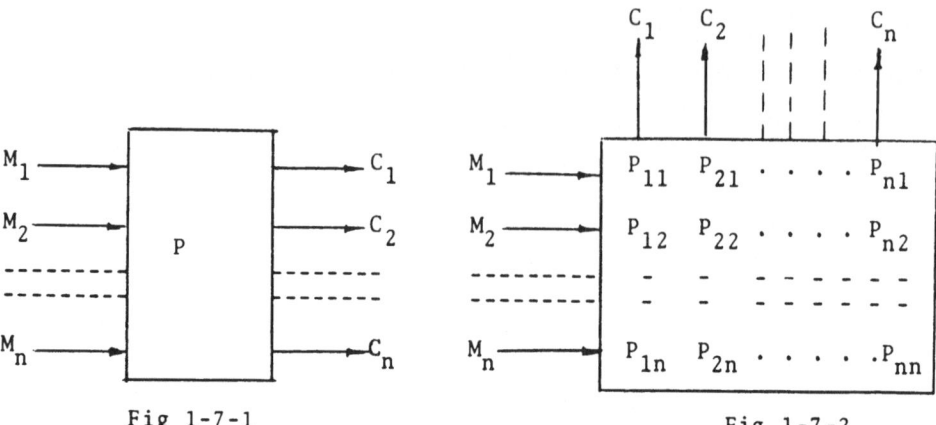

Fig 1-7-1   Fig 1-7-2

If in (1-7-2), B were a unit matrix, then would these two expression forms be the same?

This question is of no meaning since if B were a unit matrix, then
(1-7-1) could not exist for a physical realizable plant.

Now, we discuss the V-canonical plant.

For simplicity, we discuss a two-variable V-canonical plant as
shown in Fig 1-7-3.

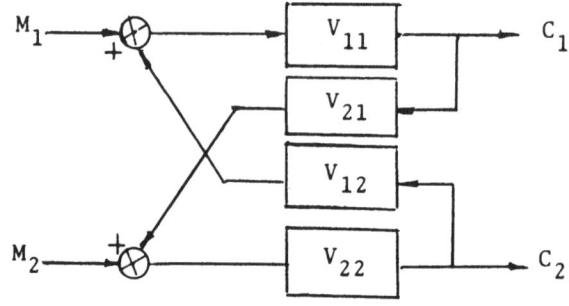

Fig 1-7-3

For the plant in Fig 1-7-3, we can get:

$$\left. \begin{array}{l} C_1 = V_{11}(M_1 + V_{12}C_2) \\ C_2 = V_{22}(M_2 + V_{21}C_1) \end{array} \right\} \qquad (1-7-7)$$

namely:

$$\left. \begin{array}{l} C_1 - V_{11}V_{12}C_2 = V_{11}M_1 \\ -V_{22}V_{21}C_1 + C_2 = V_{22}M_2 \end{array} \right\} \qquad (1-7-8)$$

It yields:

$$
\begin{pmatrix} C_1 \\ \\ C_2 \end{pmatrix} = \begin{pmatrix} \dfrac{V_{11}}{1 - V_{11}V_{22}V_{12}V_{21}} & \dfrac{V_{11}V_{22}V_{12}}{1 - V_{11}V_{22}V_{12}V_{21}} \\ \\ \dfrac{V_{11}V_{22}V_{21}}{1 - V_{11}V_{22}V_{12}V_{21}} & \dfrac{V_{22}}{1 - V_{11}V_{22}V_{12}V_{21}} \end{pmatrix} \begin{pmatrix} M_1 \\ \\ M_2 \end{pmatrix} \qquad (1\text{-}7\text{-}9)
$$

and in matrix form:

$$
C = PM \qquad\qquad (1\text{-}7\text{-}10)
$$

Obviously, every element in P has the same denominator, i.e. with the same poles.

Therefore, the result of description a system by V-canonical form is the same as that described by using the general multivariable form. The essentiality of the V-canonical form is to use feedback to describe coupling, thus in the expression describing a coupling plant by feedback, all elements in the transfer matrix have same poles.

So, sometimes, it is considered that to describe a plant by the V-canonical form is of more general meaning.

But, however, we do not suggest that we should express the plant considered in V-canonical form in every case. We have said that both P-canonical and V-canonical forrms are available for system analysis, so the adoption of either P-canonical plant or V-canoninical plant is determined by the practical situation : Which is more suitable for practical analysis ?

In fact, in the process control engineering practice, in most cases the P-canonical plants are used. This is, perhaps, people are used to using this form and on the other hand the adoption of the P-canonical form can also give satisfactory analysis results.

§ 1-8 Systems with Coupling Manipulated Variables

All the systems discussed above deal with the coupling plants.
But, there is another coupling system and its coupling channels exist
between manipulated variables. Such a coupling system is called as
the system with coupling manipulated variables.

For instance, a two-variable system with coupling manipulated
variables is shown in Fig 1-8-1.

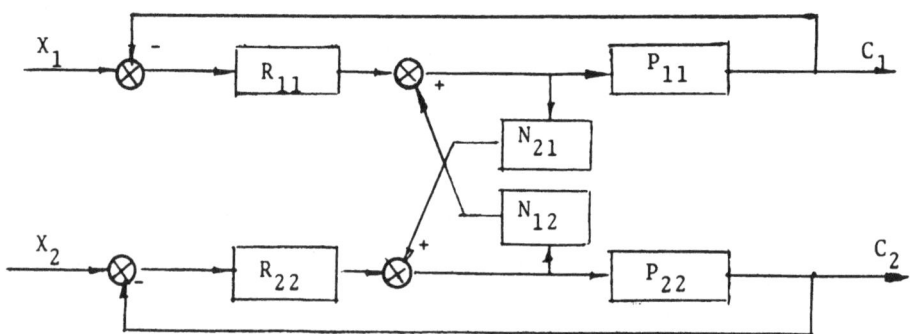

Fig 1-8-1

Obviously, it is not difficult to transfer such a system into
one with a P-canonical plant or a V-canonical plant.

When it is transferred into a system with a P-canonical plant,
the form is:

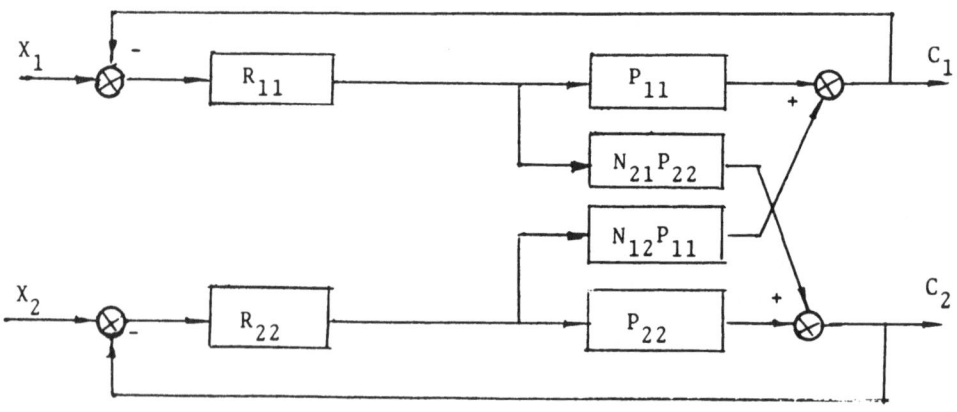

Fig 1-8-2

When it is transferred into a system with a V-canonical plant,
the form is shown in Fig 1-8-3.

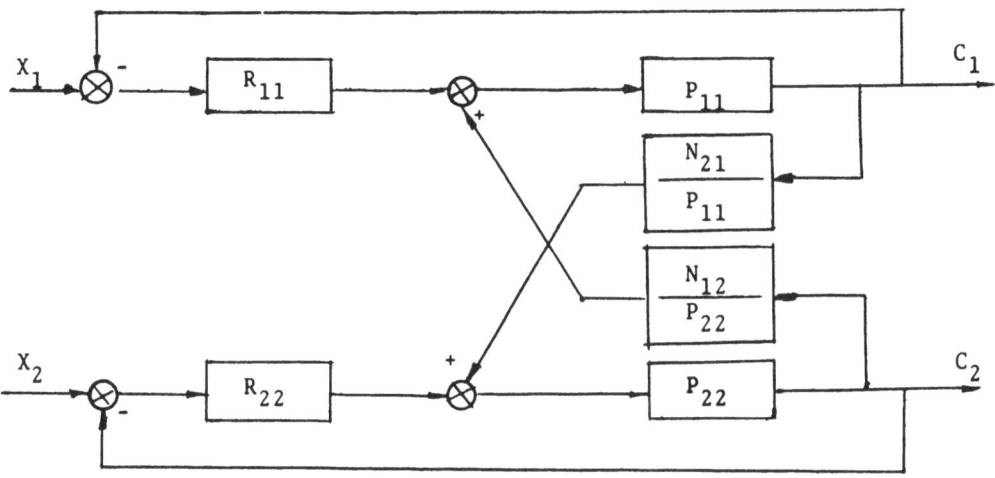

Fig 1-8-3

Thus, a system with coupling manipulated variables can be analyzed either by a P-canonical form or by a V-canonical form.

A special form of systems with coupling manipulated variables should be considered, i.e. the so-called symmetrical system with coupling manipulated variables. Such a system means:

$$\left.\begin{array}{l} R_{11} = R_{22} = R \\ P_{11} = P_{22} = P \\ N_{12} = N_{21} = N \end{array}\right\} \qquad (1-8-1)$$

and is illustrated in Fig 1-8-4.

From this figure, it yields:

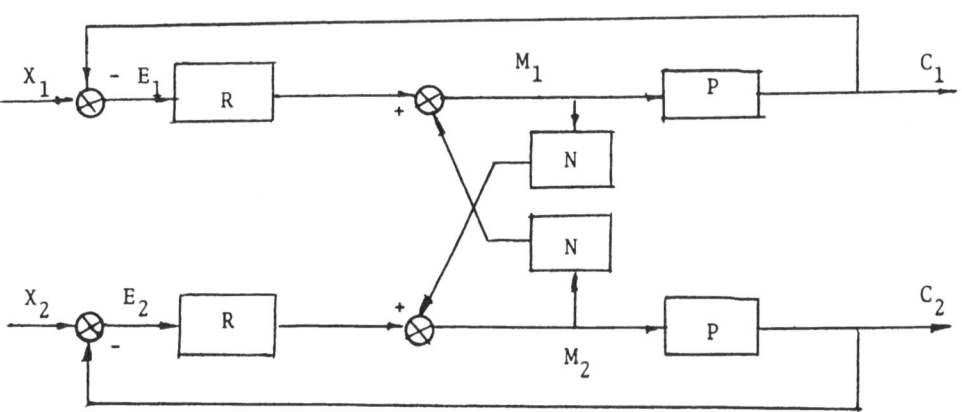

Fig 1-8-4

$$E_1 = X_1 - C_1$$

$$M_1 = E_1 R + M_2 N$$

$$C_1 = M_1 P$$

$$E_2 = X_2 - C_2 \qquad \qquad (1\text{-}8\text{-}2)$$

$$M_2 = E_2 R + M_1 N$$

$$C_2 = M_2 P$$

Let:

$$W = RP \qquad \qquad (1\text{-}8\text{-}3)$$

then, eliminating E_1, E_2, M_1 and M_2, we get:

$$\frac{C_1}{X_1} = \frac{W}{(1+W)^2 - N^2}(1 + W + \frac{X_2}{X_1}N) \qquad (1\text{-}8\text{-}4)$$

$$\frac{C_2}{X_2} = \frac{W}{(1+W)^2 - N^2}(1 + W + \frac{X_1}{X_2}N) \qquad (1\text{-}8\text{-}5)$$

In matrix form:

$$\begin{pmatrix} C_1 \\ C_2 \end{pmatrix} = \begin{pmatrix} 1+W & N \\ N & 1+W \end{pmatrix} \begin{pmatrix} X_1 \\ X_2 \end{pmatrix} \frac{W}{(1+W)^2 - N^2} \qquad (1\text{-}8\text{-}6)$$

Especially, if:

$$X_1 = X_2 \qquad \qquad (1\text{-}8\text{-}7)$$

then:

$$\frac{C_1}{X_1} = \frac{W}{1 + W - N} \qquad \qquad (1\text{-}8\text{-}8)$$

$$\frac{C_2}{X_2} = \frac{W}{1 + W - N} \qquad \qquad (1\text{-}8\text{-}9)$$

The above expressions denote that for a symmetrical system with coupling manipulated variables, the system structure gives the same influence on each output, so the variation of outputs is entirely caused by inputs. Thus, when the inputs are the same, the outputs will be identical. In such a case, this system can be regarded as two independent single loop systems, but coupling is considered since N is included in both denominators of (1-8-8) and (1-8-9).

(1-8-8) and (1-8-9) can be written in matrix form:

$$\begin{pmatrix} C_1 \\ C_2 \end{pmatrix} = \begin{pmatrix} X_1 \\ X_2 \end{pmatrix} \frac{W}{1 + W - N} \qquad (1-8-10)$$

Obviously, when N=1, then:

$$\begin{pmatrix} C_1 \\ C_2 \end{pmatrix} = \begin{pmatrix} X_1 \\ X_2 \end{pmatrix} \qquad (1-8-11)$$

and the system becomes one without any errors. If:

$$X_1 = -X_2 \qquad (1-8-12)$$

then:

$$\frac{C_1}{X_1} = \frac{W}{1 + W + N} \qquad (1-8-13)$$

$$\frac{C_2}{X_2} = \frac{W}{1 + W + N} \qquad (1-8-14)$$

In matrix form:

$$\begin{pmatrix} C_1 \\ C_2 \end{pmatrix} = \begin{pmatrix} X_1 \\ X_2 \end{pmatrix} \frac{W}{1 + W + N} \qquad (1-8-15)$$

Comparing (1-8-13) with (1-8-14), we see that the two systems are identical.

And when:

$$N = -1 \qquad (1-8-16)$$

we get:

$$\begin{pmatrix} C_1 \\ C_2 \end{pmatrix} = \begin{pmatrix} X_1 \\ X_2 \end{pmatrix} \qquad (1-8-16)$$

Thus, the system becomes without any errors.

What is the practical meaning of it?

(1-8-11) denotes when we want to realize a very precise control to a process, i.e. to realize one without errors, since it is impossible to reach by single loop control systems, then we can design two identical systems and connect their manipulated variables, i.e $N=1$, and thus we can realize an ideal control(without errors). Therefore, such a coupling system can be used to realize precise control.

For a control process, the interaction occurs in general in three forms:

(1) Among the outputs and the manipulated variables,

(2) Among the manipulated variables,

(3) Among the outputs.

That means the interaction problem considered now is about the plant variables which are influenced by the outer disturbances and reference inputs.

As for the disturbances and reference inputs, the interaction problem of them is not considered in our analysis because they are signals which can not be controlled by the control system under consideration.

Among the above three types of coupled plants, the interaction analysis of the first case, i.e. the interaction among the outputs and the manipulated variables , is the basic and the essential coupling manner and the other two types can be transferred to the first type.

Therefore, in the research and the discussion of decoupling control system design, main attention is paid to the first type of interaction.

§ 1-9 Full Coupling Systems and Partial Coupling Systems[5]

In the above discussions, the attention was given to the partition of canonical forms to both plants and decoupling-element structures.

Now, there is another problem needed to be discussed. This problem is about the number of coupling channels.

This problem is derived from the fact: When we discuss a coupling system, no matter a system with coupling plants or a system with coupling manipulated variables, the system may be either a full coupling system or a partial coupling system.

A full coupling system means that the channels among coupling variables are perfect, otherwise it is a partial coupling system.

Take a two-variable system as an example, when full coupling exists between two intrinsical channels, the possible connection relations are shown in Fig 1-9-1.

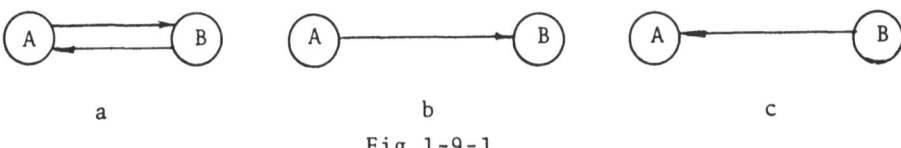

a   b   c

Fig 1-9-1

Fig 1-9-1a is a full coupling system and the others are partial coupling systems. Thus, in a partial coupling system of a two-variable system, always a unilateral channel exists.

The more the number of variables, namely the more the intrinsical channels, the more the partial coupling cases.

Now, take a 3-variable system as an example, when full coupling occurs among the three intrinsical channels A, B, C, the connection relations are shown in Fig 1-9-2. Obviously, there are six coupling channels in it. This is full coupling and how about its partial coupling cases?

We suppose A being the intrinsical channel with the most coupling connections, then we discuss the problem around it.

For a 3-variable coupling system, does it at least have 3 coupling

channels? A 3-variable coupling system may
only have two coupling channels as shown
in Fig 1-9-3.

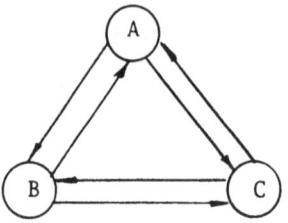

When the system has three coupling
channels , there may be four possible
cases for it as shown in Fig 1-9-**4**.

Fig 1-9-2

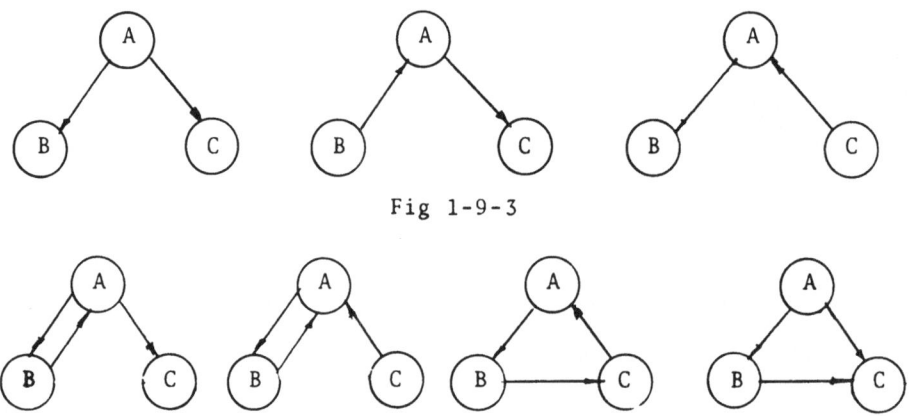

Fig 1-9-3

Fig 1-9-4

When the system has four coupling channels, there may be three possible cases for it as shown in Fig 1-9-**5**.

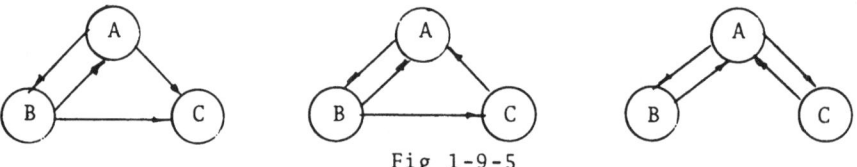

Fig 1-9-5

There is only one possible case for this system with 5 coupling
channels as shown in Fig 1-9-6.

Thus, the possible coupling cases increase
as the number of coupling variables increases.

It is meaningful to understand the number of coupling channels.

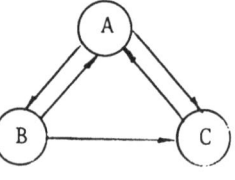

Since for every existing coupling channel

Fig 1-9-6

a corresponding decoupling channel is necessary to offset its coupling
effect, so , in other words, for a decoupled system, the number of its
decoupling elements is no less than the number of the coupling channels
in the system.

Therefore, for a full coupling system with n coupling variables, if
full decoupling is expected, then the number of all decoupling elements
(or decoupling regulators) should be no less than (n^2-n). When the number of regulators of intrinsical channels is also included, then for a
full coupling system with n variables, the number of necessary regulators
for realizing full decoupling is no less than n^2.

So, we see that in the practical control engineering, any coupling
plant with outputs or manipulated variables more than two, the decoupling
system for it will have very complicated structure, for example for a
plant with three outputs 9 decoupling elements are needed for realizing
decoupling control.

Because of this , in process control engineering practice, in most
cases, we design the decoupling control systems for two-variable plants.
If the plants are with more than two outputs, then in general we chose
the two which are the most important variables or are with the most serious
interaction to realize the decoupling design.

Then, certainly, there is a problem : Among many variables of a
plant, how to determine these two which are expected to realize the decoupling control the most ?

This is a very important problem both in theory and in practice
and we will discuss it in detail in Chpter 7.

§ 1-10 Control of Flow Mixing Process——— an Example for P-Canonical Plants[9]

We have introduced different kinds of coupling objects including P- and V-canonical plants and coupling systems with coupled manipulated variables. Certainly, a problem may logically be proposed :
In the process control engineering practice, do all the coupling objects mentioned above exist?

Yes, it is true. All the objective existing coupling systems belong to , or may be transferred to , these cases.

In order to explain explicitly, we take some typical examples from chemical process control engineering to show it .

At first, we discuss the control of flow mixing process. This is an example of P-canonical plants.

Suppose two same liquids with different temperatures θ_1 and θ_2 respectively, and after mixing a liquid with temperature θ is formed.

In process control systems, this is a popular method to enhance temperature of some flow.

Suppose that the controlled variables are the temperature θ after mixing and the total flow Q. Obviously:

$$Q = Q_1 + Q_2 \qquad\qquad (1\text{-}10\text{-}1)$$

Therefore, this is a two-variable control system with two controlled variables, Q and θ, and the manipulated variables are the input flows Q_1 and Q_2 which are controlled by its own flow control system, respectively. The system is shown in Fig 1-10-1.

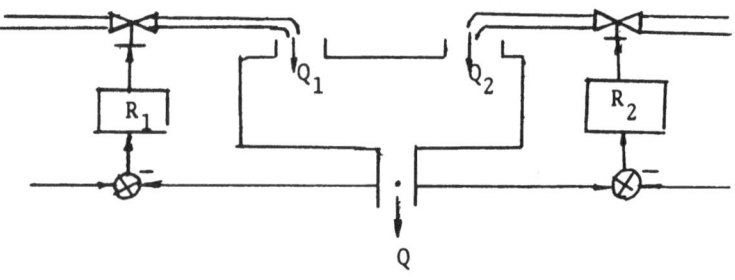

Fig 1-10-1

At the steady state , we have :

$$Q_0 = Q_{10} + Q_{20} \qquad (1\text{-}10\text{-}2)$$

What we want to discuss is the deviation at steady state, i.e.

$$C_1 = \frac{\Delta Q}{Q_0} = \frac{Q_{10}}{Q_0}\frac{\Delta Q_1}{Q_{10}} + \frac{Q_{20}}{Q_0}\frac{\Delta Q_2}{Q_{20}} \qquad (1\text{-}10\text{-}3)$$

Let:

$$\left. \begin{aligned} K_1 &= \frac{Q_{10}}{Q_0} \\[2mm] K_2 &= \frac{Q_{20}}{Q_0} \end{aligned} \right\} \qquad (1\text{-}10\text{-}4)$$

then:

$$K_1 + K_2 = 1 \qquad (1\text{-}10\text{-}5)$$

K_1 and K_2 are the percentages of Q_{10} and Q_{20} in Q_0, respectively.

Thus:

$$C_1 = K_1 q_1 + K_2 q_2 \qquad (1\text{-}10\text{-}6)$$

Here:

$$\left. \begin{aligned} q_1 &= \frac{\Delta Q_1}{Q_{10}} \\[2mm] q_2 &= \frac{\Delta Q_2}{Q_{20}} \end{aligned} \right\} \qquad (1\text{-}10\text{-}7)$$

are normalized flows and are controlled by R_1 and R_2, respectively.

On the other hand, for this process, besides the material balance the energy balance is also held. Thus, if energy loss is not considered, then from heat balance we get:

$$(Q_1 + Q_2)\theta = Q_1 \theta_1 + Q_2 \theta_2 \qquad (1\text{-}10\text{-}8)$$

Here, both θ_1 and θ_2 are considered to be constants and notice that the two liquids are the same in other aspects.

But $\Delta \theta$ may be expressed as:

$$\Delta \theta = \frac{\partial \theta}{\partial Q_1}\Delta Q_1 + \frac{\partial \theta}{\partial Q_2}\Delta Q_2 \qquad (1\text{-}10\text{-}9)$$

Expanding $\Delta \theta$ in Taylor series in (1-10-8), we get:

$$\Delta \theta = \theta - \theta_0 = \frac{Q_{10}Q_{20}}{Q_0^2}(\theta_2 - \theta_1)(\frac{Q_2}{Q_{20}} - \frac{Q_1}{Q_{10}}) \tag{1-10-10}$$

Let :

$$\theta_m = \frac{Q_{10}Q_{20}}{Q_{10}^2}(\theta_2 - \theta_1) \tag{1-10-11}$$

then:

$$C_2 = \frac{\Delta \theta}{\theta_m} = \frac{\Delta Q_2}{Q_{20}} - \frac{\Delta Q_1}{Q_{10}} = q_2 - q_1 \tag{1-10-12}$$

Now, C_1 and C_2 are the controlled variables of this system.

Suppose that the control characteristics of two flow systems are identical, i.e. both are W_F, then the block diagram of this system is:

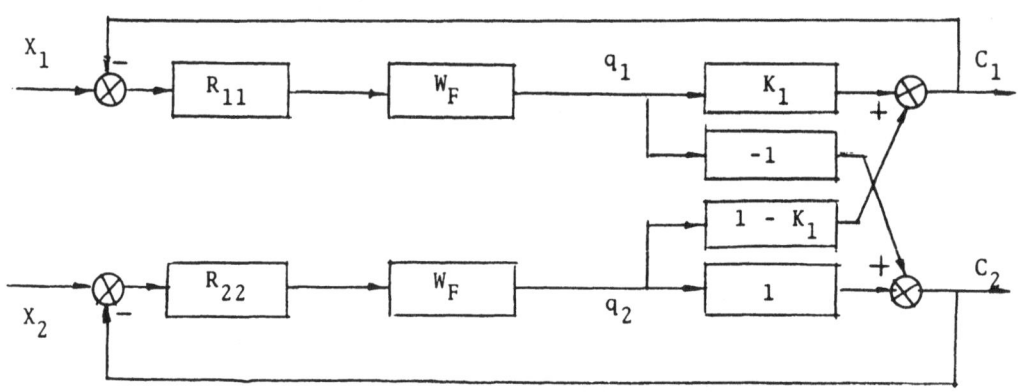

Fig 1-10-2

Obviously, this is a coupling plant of P-canonical form.

For it, the channels of the plant are:

$$\left. \begin{array}{l} \dfrac{C_1}{q_1} = P_{11} = K_1 \\[2em] \dfrac{C_1}{q_2} = P_{12} = 1 - K_1 \\[2em] \dfrac{C_2}{q_1} = P_{21} = -1 \\[2em] \dfrac{C_2}{q_2} = P_{22} = 1 \end{array} \right\} \tag{1-10-13}$$

This system may be also transferred into a V-canonical form. In fact, if we let:

$$
\left.
\begin{aligned}
V_{11} &= P_{11} = K_1 \\
V_{22} &= P_{22} = 1 \\
V_{12} &= \frac{1 - K_1}{K_1} \\
V_{21} &= -\frac{1}{K_1}
\end{aligned}
\right\}
\qquad (1\text{-}10\text{-}14)
$$

then the system becomes a V-canonical form.

But it is essentially a P-canonical system indeed.

We have said that in most cases people prefer to use the P-canonical form to express a coupled plant . Certainly, this is because some people are used to using P-canonical form and on the other hand, some plants , by their physical (or physical-chemical) essentiality, should be expressed by P-canonical forms although they also can be expressed by V-canonical forms mathematically.

Likewise, some plants , by their physical (or physical-chemical) essentiality, should be expressed by V-canonical forms. A practical example is given in the next paragraph.

This means that in practical control engineering, both real P-canonical plants and V-canonical plants can be met and certainly for any practical coupled plant, it can be also transferred equivalently to the other type.

§ 1-11 Flow and Level Control in a Vessel ——an Example for V-Canonical
   Plants

In order to show the V-canonical plants, a very popular control
problem, namely the control of the level and output flow of a vessel,
is considered. The system is illustrated in Fig 1-11-1.

Where, q_i is the input flow and
y_i is the stroke of input valve.

q_c is the output flow and q_c is
the stroke of output control valve.

h is the controlled level.

The vessel is assumed to have
uniform section F.

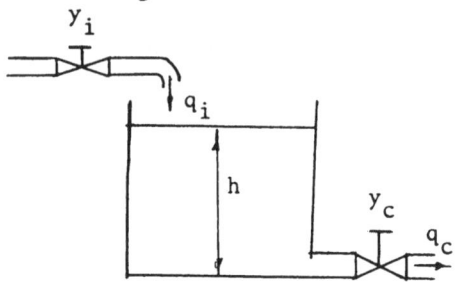

Fig 1-11-1

The variation of output flow q_c is related not only to   the
stroke y_c , but also to the level in the vessel. Thus , we can get:

$$q_c = C_{11} \Delta y_c + C_{12} \Delta h \qquad (1-11-1)$$

Where both C_{11} and C_{12} are positive. It means that the more the
valve opens, the larger the output flow ; at the meantime, the higher
the level, also the larger the output flow.

Now, we consider the change of pondage in the vessel in a very
short period. Obviously, in some period, the difference between input
flow and output flow is the increment of liquid in the vessel, i.e.

$$Fdh = q_i dt - q_c dt \qquad (1-11-2)$$

Therefore, at time t, the level of the vessel is:

$$h = \frac{1}{F} \int_0^t (q_i - q_c)dt + h_0 \qquad (1-11-3)$$

and the variation of level is:

$$\Delta h = \frac{1}{F} \int_0^t (\Delta q_i - \Delta q_c)dt \qquad (1-11-4)$$

But:

$$\Delta q_i = C_i \Delta y_i \qquad (1-11-5)$$

so that:

$$\Delta h = \frac{1}{F}\int_0^t (C_i \Delta y_i - \Delta q_c)dt \qquad\qquad (1\text{-}11\text{-}6)$$

Taking Laplace transform to both (1-11-1) and (1-11-6), we get:

$$\Delta q_c(S) = C_{11}(\Delta y_c(S) + \frac{C_{12}}{C_{11}}\Delta h(S)) \qquad\qquad (1\text{-}11\text{-}7)$$

$$\Delta h(S) = \frac{C_i}{FS}(\Delta y_i(S) - \frac{1}{C_i}\Delta q_c(S)) \qquad\qquad (1\text{-}11\text{-}8)$$

The block diagram is shown in Fig 1-11-2.

Obviously, this is a **V**-canonical plant. Cetrainly, it can be also transferred into a P-canonical plant.

By (1-6-18), its P-canonical form is:

$$\begin{Bmatrix} \Delta q_c \\ \Delta h \end{Bmatrix} = \begin{pmatrix} \dfrac{C_{11}F/C_{12}}{1 + SF/C_{12}} S & \dfrac{C_i}{1 + SF/C_{12}} \\ \dfrac{- C_{11}/C_{12}}{1 + SF/C_{12}} & \dfrac{C_i/C_{12}}{1 + SF/C_{12}} \end{pmatrix} \begin{Bmatrix} \Delta y_c \\ \Delta y_i \end{Bmatrix} \qquad (1\text{-}11\text{-}9)$$

Let:

$$\frac{F}{C_{12}} = T \qquad\qquad (1\text{-}11\text{-}10)$$

then the P-canonical form is shown in Fig 1-11-3.

Notice that the P-canonical form obtained from the V-canonical form has identical poles in all channels.

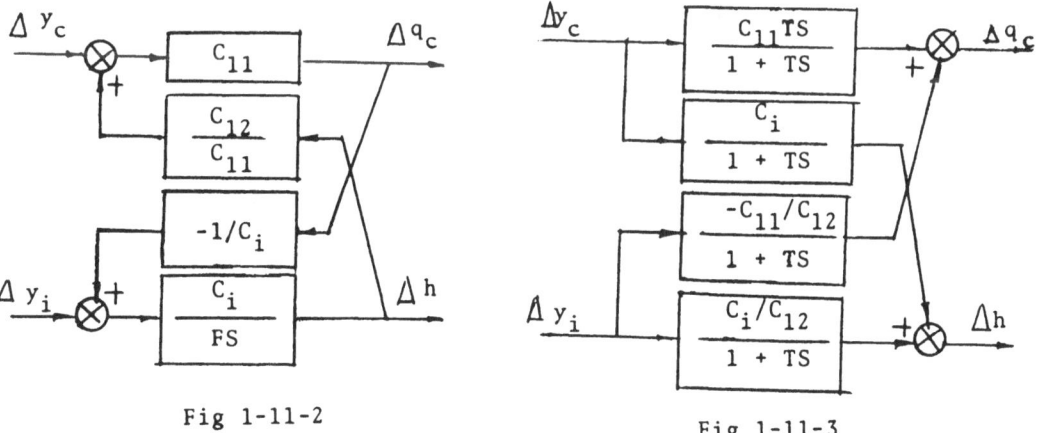

Fig 1-11-2   Fig 1-11-3

§ 1-12 Control of **A** Reactor—An Example **of** Systems with Coupling

   Manipulated Variables

   A reactor is shown in Fig 1-12-1 as an example of systems with coupling manipulated variables.

   There may be a great variety of reactions in such a reactor. From the view-point of chemical dynamic, a reaction may be the first order or the second order.

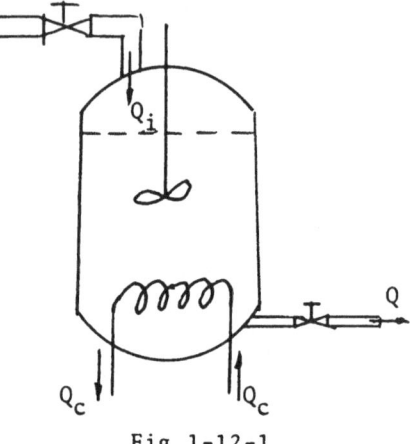

Fig 1-12-1

   For a first order reaction:

   Reactants $\xrightarrow{-\Delta H}$ Products

   For a second order reaction:

   $A + A \xrightarrow{-\Delta H}$ Products

   Suppose that the reaction takes place entirely in the reactor which has definite volume and the reaction is a unilateral heat-release process. In this reaction, quite a lot of heat produced is brought away by the cooling medium and the control system is designed to control the flow of cooling medium directly.

   The basic two principles available to analyze the dynamic characteristics of this process are the balance of material and the balance of energy.

   Owing to the material balance in the reactor during the reaction process, for a first order reaction we can get the following equation (the meaning of symbols are listed at the end of this paragraph) :

$$QA_i = QA + KAV + V\frac{dA}{dt} \tag{1-12-1}$$

or :

$$\frac{dA}{dt} = \frac{Q}{V}(A_i - A) - KA \tag{1-12-2}$$

   For a second order reaction:

$$\frac{dA}{dt} = \frac{Q}{V}(A_i - A) - KA^2 \tag{1-12-3}$$

On the other hand, the heat balance must be held and for a first order reaction, we can get:

$$\rho C_p Q T_i = \rho C_p Q T - KA(-\Delta H)V + \rho C_p V \frac{dT}{dt} + BM\, \Delta T_m \qquad (1\text{-}12\text{-}4)$$

It may be also written as:

$$\frac{dT}{dt} = \frac{Q}{V}(T_i - T) + \frac{KA(-\Delta H)}{\rho C_p} - \frac{BM\, \Delta T_m}{V \rho C_p} \qquad (1\text{-}12\text{-}5)$$

For a second order reaction:

$$\frac{dT}{dt} = \frac{Q}{V}(T_i - T) + \frac{KA^2(-\Delta H)}{\rho C_p} - \frac{BM\, \Delta T_m}{V \rho C_p} \qquad (1\text{-}12\text{-}6)$$

Where, $BM\, \Delta T_m$ is the heat brought away by cooling medium, i.e.

$$BM\, \Delta T_m = Q_c \rho_c C_c (T_2 - T_c) \qquad (1\text{-}12\text{-}7)$$

But the temperature of cooling medium at the entrance and the exit of cooling tube is different, so ΔT_m should be considered as the average of temperature difference between reactants in the reactor and the cooling medium in the cooling tube.

$$\Delta T_m = \frac{(T-T_c) + (T-T_2)}{2} \qquad (1\text{-}12\text{-}8)$$

Thus, if we let:

$$F = \frac{2Q_c \rho_c C_c}{BM} \qquad (1\text{-}12\text{-}9)$$

then ΔT_m may be written as:

$$\Delta T_m = \frac{T - T_c}{1 + 1/F} \qquad (1\text{-}12\text{-}10)$$

Therefore, (1-12-5) and (1-12-6) may be written as:

$$\frac{dT}{dt} = \frac{Q}{V}(T_i - T) - \frac{KA(\Delta H)}{\rho C_p} - \frac{BMF(T - T_c)}{V \rho C_p (1+F)} \qquad (1\text{-}12\text{-}11)$$

$$\frac{dT}{dt} = \frac{Q}{V}(T_i - T) - \frac{KA^2 \Delta H}{\rho C_p} - \frac{BMF(T - T_c)}{V \rho C_p (1+F)} \qquad (1\text{-}12\text{-}12)$$

Equations (1-12-2) and (1-12-11) are the basic dynamic equations for researching a first order reaction and equations (1-12-3) and (1-12-12) are the basic equations for researching a second order reaction.

At the first glance, it seems that (1-12-2) and (1-12-11) are two linear differential equations. But , in fact, the reaction rate coefficient K is not a constant and it relates to the reaction temperature. The relation about these two terms is given by thr well-known Arhenius   formula:

$$K = A_R \, e^{-E/RT} \qquad\qquad (1\text{-}12\text{-}13)$$

Thus, neither (1-12-2) nor (1-12-11) is linear differential equation. Besides, the flow of cooling medium is not a constant either. Therefore, in order to research the control characteristics of the reactor, we must linearize the above non-linear differential equations at some steady points.

The linearization is carried out by expanding the non-linear terms in these equations to Taylor series at some steady points and then take the first two terms of the series as their approximations. Because they are quadratic functions, so we have:

$$f(x_0 + x, \; y_0 + y) = f(x_0, \; y_0) + x\frac{\partial f(x,y)}{\partial x} + y\frac{\partial f(x,y)}{\partial y} \qquad (1\text{-}12\text{-}14)$$

For instance, for KA, we get:

$$KA = K_s A_s + K_s(A - A_s) + \frac{A_s K_s E}{RT_s^2}(T - T_s) \qquad\qquad (1\text{-}12\text{-}15)$$

and for KA^2, we have:

$$KA^2 = K_s A_s^2 + 2K_s A_s(A - A_s) + \frac{A_s^2 K_s E}{RT_s^2}(T - T_s) \qquad\qquad (1\text{-}12\text{-}16)$$

For ΔT_m, it should be linearized to both T and Q_c and the result is:

$$\Delta T_m = \Delta T_{ms} + \frac{2Q_{cs}\,\rho_c C_c}{2Q_{cs}\,\rho_c C_c + BM}\,(T - T_s) +$$

$$+ \frac{BM(T_s - T_c)}{2Q_{cs}^2 \ _cC_c(1 + \frac{1}{F})^2}(Q_c - Q_{cs}) \qquad (1\text{-}12\text{-}17)$$

Denote:

$$\left. \begin{array}{l} \bar{T} = T - T_s \\[4pt] \bar{Q}_c = Q_c - Q_{cs} \\[4pt] \bar{A}_i = A_i \\[4pt] \bar{A} = A - A_s \end{array} \right\} \qquad (1\text{-}12\text{-}18)$$

and:

$$\Delta T_{ms} = 0 \qquad (1\text{-}12\text{-}19)$$

then for a first order reaction, we get:

$$\frac{d\bar{T}}{dt} = \frac{K_s(-\Delta H)}{\rho C_p}\bar{A} + \bar{T}\left[\frac{A_s E K_s(-\Delta H)}{RT_s^2 \rho C_p} - \frac{Q}{V} - \frac{2BMQ_{cs}\rho_c C_c}{V\rho C_p(2Q_{cs}\rho_c C_c + BM)}\right]$$

$$- \frac{B^2 M^2 (T_s - T_c)}{V\rho C_p(2Q_{cs}^2 \rho_c C_c)(1 + 1/F)^2}\bar{Q}_c \qquad (1\text{-}12\text{-}20)$$

$$\frac{d\bar{A}}{dt} = \frac{Q}{V}\bar{A}_i - (\frac{Q}{V} + K_s)\bar{A} - \frac{A_s E K_s}{RT_s^2}\bar{T} \qquad (1\text{-}12\text{-}21)$$

For simplicity, equations (1-12-20) and (1-12-21) may be written as:

$$\frac{d\bar{T}}{dt} + K_1\bar{T} = K_2\bar{A} - K_3\bar{Q}_c \qquad (1\text{-}12\text{-}22)$$

$$\frac{d\bar{A}}{dt} + K_4\bar{A} = K_5\bar{A}_i - K_6\bar{T} \qquad (1\text{-}12\text{-}23)$$

Because linearization is always carried out at steady points, so all initial values are zeros. Thus, taking Laplace transform to the above two equations and combining them, we get:

$$A(S) = \frac{K_5(S + K_1)}{(S+K_1)(S+K_4)+K_2K_6}A_i(S) + \frac{K_3K_6}{(S+K_1)(S+K_4)+K_2K_6}Q_c(S)$$

$$(1\text{-}12\text{-}24)$$

In this expression, we see that K_1, K_3, K_4, K_5 and K_6 all are positive, but k_2 is negative. K_2 denotes the degree of heat release in this reaction, thus, obviously, if:

$$\left| K_2 K_6 \right| > K_1 K_4 \qquad (1\text{-}12\text{-}25)$$

then an unstable plant of second order occurs. That means that the heat produced in this process is more than that removed from it .

(1-12-24) denotes that the variation of the density of outflow is related not only to the variation of the density of the input flow, but also to the variation of the cooling medium flow and both are with quadratic characteristics. In fact, only Q_c can be used as the manipulated variable, consequently A_i is the disturbance and the control system block diagram is shown in Fig 1-12-2.

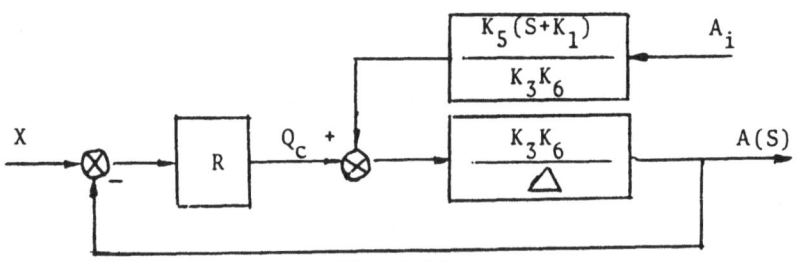

Fig 1-12-2

Likewise, we can get:

$$-T(S) = \frac{K_2 K_5}{(S+K_1)(S+K_4)+K_2 K_6}(-A_i) + \frac{K_3(S+K_4)Q_c}{(S+K_1)(S+K_4)+K_2 K_6} \qquad (1\text{-}12\text{-}26)$$

Similarly, when:

$$\left| K_2 K_6 \right| > K_1 \dot{K}_4 \qquad (1\text{-}12\text{-}27)$$

the plant is unstable. That means when the heat produced in the process can not be removed entirely , then the temperature in the reactor will increase graduately. There is a minus sign between T(S) and Q_c(S) and it denotes when Q_c decreases, then the temperature in the tank increases. Now, combining the flow control system with the composition control system, we get the block diagram as shown in Fig 1-12-3.

Obviously, this is a two-variable control system with coupling manipulated variables. In fact, the identical manipulated variable is

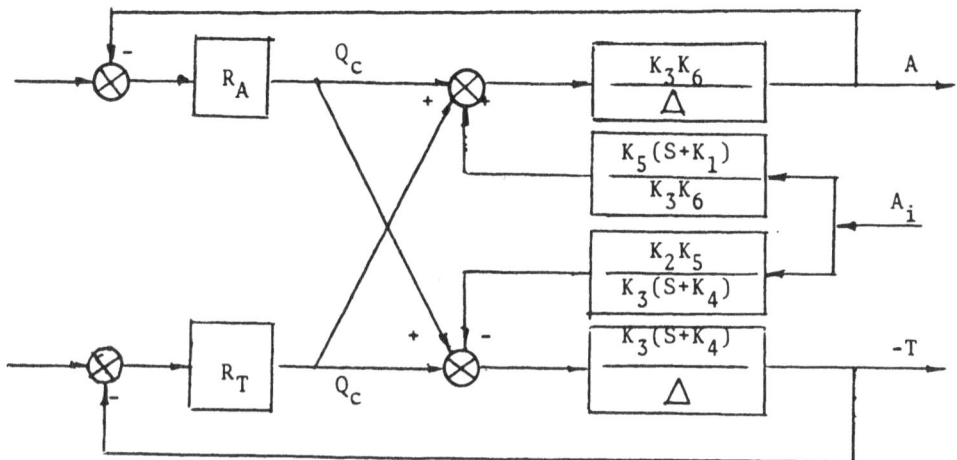

Fig 1-12-3

used for these two systems, thus , any changes of Q_c in either system will cause the change of the output in the other system.

Symbols used in this paragraph:

Q Volume flow of both input and output,

A, A_i Compositions of output and input, respectively.

ρ , ρ_c Densities of reactant and cooling medium, respectively,

C_p, C_c Specific heat of reactant and cooling medium, respectively,

H Heat produced in the process,

T Temperature in the reactor,

V Volume of reactant in the reactor,

B Heat transfer coefficient between reactant and cooling medium,

M Heat transfer surface of cooling medium,

Q_c Flow of cooling medium,

T_c, T_2 Temperature of cooling medium at the entrance and the exit, respectively,

T_i Temperature of input reactant,

E Molecule activity energy,

R Gas constant,

K Reaction rate,

A_r Arhenius frequency factor.

§ 1-13 Control of A Decanter——Neither P-Canonical nor V-Canonical Plant

We have discussed both P-canonical and V-canonical plants in detail. We also analyzed the systems with coupling manipulated variables. Certainly, a problem may be proposed here: Do all practical coupling plants belong to these kinds?

No, it is not.

In order to explain this, we also give a practical example from chemical engineering processes. This example is about the control of a liquid decanter with two liquids of different densities.[31]

Fig 1-13-1 shows a vertical circular decanter.

Suppose that a liquid mixed from two liquids Q_{iu} and Q_{il} of different densities is poured in this decanter in order to separate each one. Certainly, no reaction is assumed here. After separating, two outputs Q_{TO} and Q_{BO} are obtained.

The light liquid takes the upper layer and it has its own level measurement and control to keep a definite output Q_{TO}.

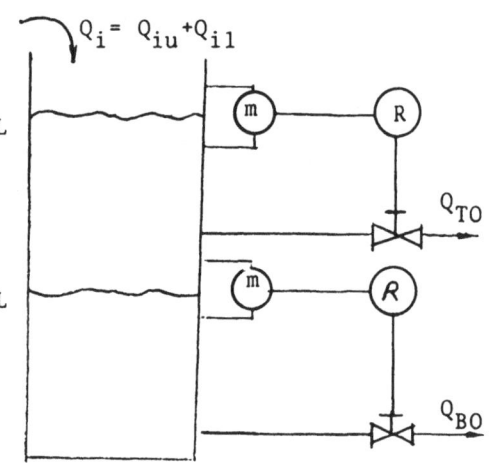

Fig 1-13-1

There is a surface between two liquids. Under the surface there is the heavy liquid and it also has its own level measurement and control to keep a definite output Q_{BO}.

In this system, the change of upper liquid level gives no influence on the control of lower level control, i.e. gives no influence on the output Q_{BO}.

But, however, the change of surface H_{LL} will give influence on both Q_{TO} and Q_{BO}.

So, if we hope that the change of H_{LL} will not give influence on Q_{TO}, then the upper output should not be controlled according to the upper level, but according to $(H_{UL}-H_{LL})$, namely the difference of two levels.

Because the decanter can not hold balance itself, so the plant is with integral character and the block diagram of this system is shown in Fig 1-13-2.

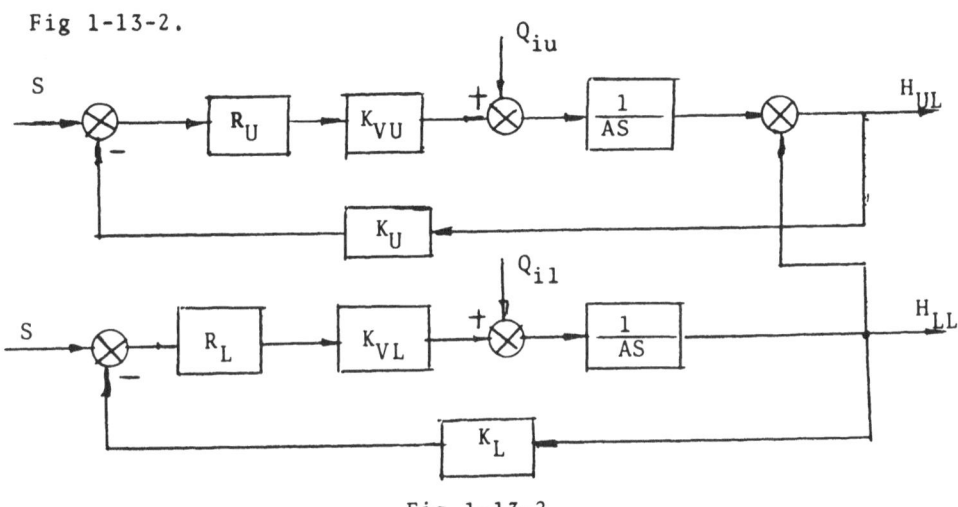

Fig 1-13-2

Where, A is the section area of the decanter,

K_{VU} and K_{VL} are the valve characteristics,

R_U and R_L are two regulators,

K_U and K_L are two measurement devices.

It is clear that this is a partial coupling system since there is only one coupling channel in it.

At the meantime, this is neither a P-canonical plant nor a V-canonical plant. But, we can easily believe that it can be transferred to either a P-canonical plant or a V-canonical plant.

It tells us that some neither P-canonical plants nor V-canonical plants may exist, but they can be transferred to either P-canonical forms or V-canonical forms. Therefore to research the control problems with P-canonical plants or V-canonical plants is with general meaning.

The decoupling design of this system is very simple. If we can make the upper output be controlled according to $(H_{UL}-H_{LL})$, then the influence of H_{LL} on the upper output can be eliminated.

Multiplying the measured value of H_{LL} by K_{1L} and then inputing it into the upper measurement channel, we let:

$$K_U H_{LL}(S) - K_{1L} K_L H_{LL}(S) = 0 \qquad (1-13-1)$$

It yields:

$$K_{1L} = \frac{K_U}{K_L} \qquad (1-13-2)$$

Then, the true measurement value of the upper loop is:

$$K_U H_{UL}(S) - K_{1L} K_L H_{LL}(S) = K_U (H_{UL} - H_{LL}) \qquad (1-13-3)$$

Thus, the upper regulator now only responds the change of the thick of the upper liquid and the change of the lower level H_{LL} no longer gives influence on the upper output.

So the decoupling is realized.

The decoupled system is shown in Fig 1-13-2.

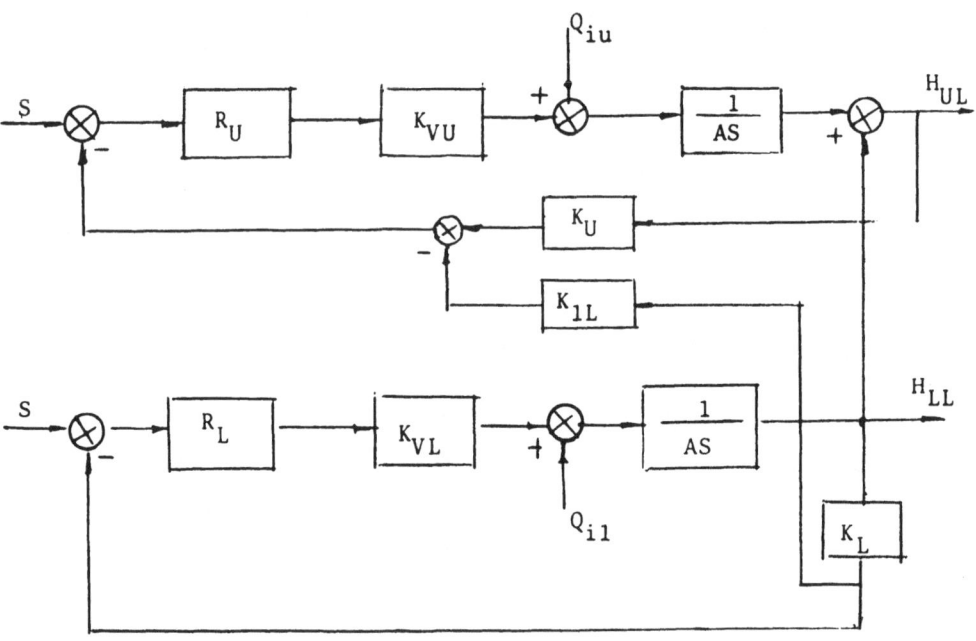

Fig 1-13-3

CHAPTER TWO

DESIGN OF REJECTION TO DISTURBANCES FOR SINGLE VARIABLE
CONTROL SYSTEMS

§ 2-1 Introduction

As well-known, one of the key problems in the design of process control systems is their ability to resist disturbances. Any process control system should have good ability to resist disturbances in order to keep their controlled parameters being held at desired values with some accuracy after certain periods.

If only the resistance to disturbances at steady state is required, then integral control is enough to do so.

But, if the resistance to disturbances is required not only at steady state, but also at transient process, then a system with full ability to resist disturbances is needed. Obviously, this is a kind of process control systems with very high accuracy and to realize such a system is important in both theory and practice.

Recently, a general terminology " Rejection to Disturbances" is widely used for this design and some older terminologies, such as " Invariance Principles " etc, have been ruled out graduately.

We should discuss:

(1) For single variable process control systems, what meathods can be used to realize the design of rejection to disturbances?

(2) For multivariable process control systems, if only the classical control theory is applied, can we realize a system with the ability not only to decouple , but also to reject disturbances ?

These two problems are met with now very frequently in the developments of modern process control engineering theory and practice and we will discuss them in detail in this book.

By the opinion of Cecil Smith, there are five kinds of process control systems practially being considered as " advanced process control systems". They are:[25]

    (1) Cascade control,

    (2) The combination of feedforward and feedback control,

    (3) Smith predictor,

    (4) Adapted control,

    (5) Multivariable decoupling control.

Certainly, the combination of the above five kinds of systems will give more advanced control systems.

What we will study in this book is just the combination of these systems except the fourth. Thus, from the view-point of process control theory, the systems researched here belong to advanced ones and they are the emphatically researched objects in process control engineering now indeed.

In our study, two assumptions are taken:

(1) The systems are with linear constant coefficients,

(2) All disturbances are non-stochastic and measurable.

In fact, the following analysis will show that the first assumption may be unnecessary in some cases.

In addition, we assume that in the system block diagrams, the disturbances have definite input points. Thus, we can make the assortment of the disturbances according to their locations in the block diagrams. And we always start our study from the most basic control systems——the feedback control systems.

We discuss the single variable control systems at first.

Our book is to discuss the decoupling design of MPCS and why should we discuss single variable control systems here?

This is because that the design of rejection to disturbances of single variable control systems is essentially the primary decoupling idea. For any single variable control system, certainly there is a reference and all other inputs are disturbances. Because for a single variable control system, only one reference input and one output are considered, so the decoupling idea has no meaning here. If we want to use this idea here , then it means that the output is only influenced by the reference input; in other words, the system is with the ability to resist disturbances fully.

Therefore, the design of rejection to disturbances for single variable system is the primary idea of decoupling design.

For a single variable system, three kinds of disturbances, i.e. the reference disturbance, the supply disturbance and the load disturbance, should be considered and we will discuss how to realize the design of rejection to each kind of these three disturbances.

The basic ideas of this chapter are not new indeed and most readers are familiar with them. But, however, we will give a systematic discussion on this problem and many important conclusions will be derived .

At the meantime , we should point out here that the general principles discussed here are not difficult in theory , so the problem to realize a system with the ability to reject the disturbances fully is not in theory ,but in practice, for example the measurement of the disturbances , the realization of the compensation elements, etc. And some practical problems are not so easily to be settled , thus sometimes although the system with the ability to reject the disturbances can be design theoretically, yet it can only be realized approximately.

This problem is not only with the single variable systems, but also with the multivariable control systems. We will see in the coming chapters that sometimes we can design a decoupling control for a multivariable system, yet we can only realize it approximately.

§ 2-2 Design of Rejection to Reference Disturbances

We discuss the reference disturbances at first.

This disturbance co-exists with the reference and is imported at the same point. Obviously, it will give the influence on the output in the same manner as the reference does.

We do not consider the high frequency disturbances. If the disturbance is with high frequency, then because of the filter character of the system it will not give remarkable influence on the output. So the disturbances considered here all are in the band width of the system and they can give explicit influence on the system.

Obviously, in order to eliminate the influence caused by the disturbance on the output, it is necessary to take some special measure.

A system with a special function is shown in Fig 2-2-1.

For this system, we get:

$$\frac{C}{U_1} = \frac{W_c W_p + W_p W_f}{1 + W_c W_p W_m} \qquad (2-2-1)$$

Therefore, the condition for realizing rejection to reference disturbances is:

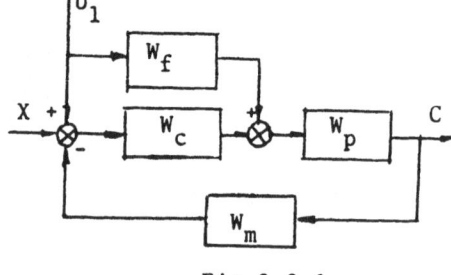

Fig 2-2-1

$$W_f = -W_c \qquad (2-2-2)$$

and U_1 will give no influence on the output at any time.

Because W_c is a physically realizable element, so W_f is easily to be realized.

In practical design, W_f does not include the control valve character , i.e. only the character of the regulator is included, and the output of W_f is added on the output of the regulator.

We should point out that this system is different from the well-known Moore system. The Moore system is shown in Fig 2-2-2.

The difference is: The feedforward channel of the Moore system

is derived from the reference
but the feedforward channel of
Fig 2-2-1 is derived from
the disturbance.

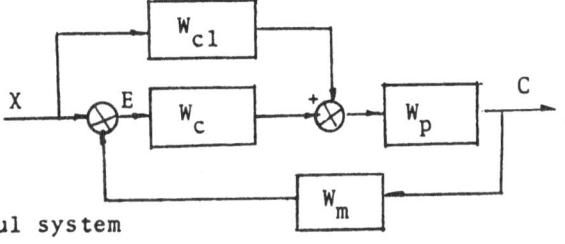

Fig 2-2-2

The Moore system is a very useful system
system and it is a combination of
a feedforward system with a feedback system. When W_{c1} is of different
characters, this system may have various outputs.

From Fig 2-2-2, we get:

$$\left.\begin{array}{l} E = X - CW_m \\ C = EW_cW_p + XW_{c1}W_p \end{array}\right\} \tag{2-2-3}$$

namely:

$$E = X - (EW_cW_p + XW_{c1}W_p)W_m \tag{2-2-4}$$

$$E (1 + W_cW_pW_m) = (1 - W_cW_pW_m)X \tag{2-2-5}$$

$$E = \frac{(1 - W_{c1}W_pW_m)X}{1 + W_cW_pW_m} \tag{2-2-6}$$

We can realize a system without any error, if we let:

$$W_{c1} = \frac{1}{W_pW_m} \tag{2-2-7}$$

When $W_m=1$,

$$W_{c1} = \frac{1}{W_p} \tag{2-2-8}$$

Therefore , the transfer function of its feedforward channel is
$W_{c1}W_p=1$ and we can say that this system utilyzes the feedforward channel
to realize the ideal control model and utilizes the feedback control
to eliminate the influence of different disturbances.

But the system shown in Fig 2-2-1 utilizes the feedback control to
realize its control model and utilizes the feedforward channel to eliminate the influence of the reference disturbance.

For process control systems, because the reference disturbance is not
serious in general, so the design of rejection to reference disturbances
is not very important either.

§ 2-3 Design of Rejection to Supply Disturbances

In process control systems, the most important disturbances are the supply disturbances and the load disturbances.

The so-called supply disturbance occurs with the medium entering the plant. It is also the disturbance of the manipulated variable. So in the block diagram, it enters into the system before the plant; as for the load disturbance, it occurs with the controlled parameters, so it is always added on the output.

Because the supply disturbance is a very popular disturbance, so we will discuss how to design a system with the ability to reject such a disturbance in detail.

The most common method is to use the combination control system to realize such demands. The combination means to combine feedforward control and feedback control.

Fig 2-3-1 shows shch a system.

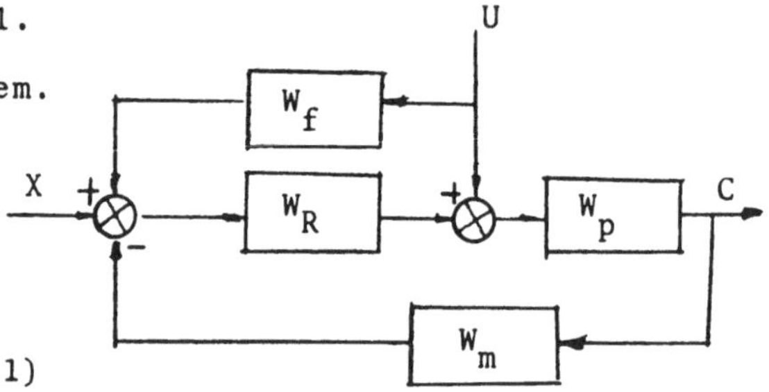

From it we can get:

$$\frac{C}{U} = \frac{W_p + W_f W_R W_m}{1 + W_R W_p W_m}$$

$$(2-3-1)$$

For realizing the rejection to U, it is necessary:

$$W_p + W_f W_R W_m = 0 \qquad (2-3-2)$$

namely:

$$W_f = - \frac{1}{W_R} \qquad (2-3-3)$$

Fig 2-3-1

It seems that the condition is very simple and the structure of the system is not complicated either, then is there anything worth discussing? In fact, some useful conclusions can be obtained here.

(1) As well-known, the basic idea of closed-loop control is to measure the response values of the output and to compare the results measured with the reference in order to get the deviation. This devia-

tion may be caused by different disturbances and the system just adjusts its manipulated variables according to the deviation to perform the control function.

When the feedforward channel is introduced, this channel measures the disturbance itself and gives an inverse influence on the system, thus, the influence of the disturbance can be eliminated without measuring the deviation. Therefore, a feedback control system combined with a feedforward channel can eliminate the influence of the supply disturbance more quickly and better than that without feedforward channel.

(2) From (2-3-1) we know that after introducing the feedforward channel,the characteristic equation of the system remains unchanged; it means that the introducing the feedforward channel does not influence the stability problem of the system. In other words, no matter what element the feedforward element is, it gives no influence on the system stability.

(3) In practical process control systems, the energy level of the compensation signals should be considered. Certainly, it would be better that the energy required for the compensation signals were small. We know that in general the degree of the signal energy levels increases along the direction of the element connection for the main channel. Therefore, the required energy will be the least when the feedforward channel is introduced into the system at the reference import point. But, on the other hand, in which case will the effect of the feedforward channel be the most prominent? In fact, the smaller the lag between the entrance point of feedforward signal and the entrance of the disturbance than the lag of the plant, the better the effect to eliminate the influence of the disturbance. Thus, from this meaning, the feedforward channel should be arranged near the entrance point of the disturbance as close as possible.

Hence, the feedforward channel is always not connected before the regulator, but at the exit of the regulator.

Fig 2-3-2 shows such a system.

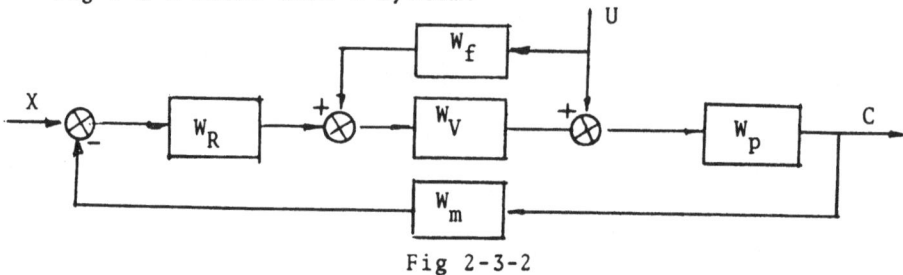

Fig 2-3-2

From this figure, we get:

$$\frac{C}{U} = \frac{W_p + W_f W_V W_p}{1 + W_R W_V W_p W_m} \qquad (2-3-4)$$

Thus, in order to realize rejection to U, it is necessary:

$$W_f = - \frac{1}{W_V} \qquad (2-3-5)$$

Notice thay W_V may not be only the character of the control valve.

In most cases, the W_f obtained from (2-3-3) and (2-3-5) is phy-sically irrealizable , namely the order of the numerator of its trans-fer function is higher than that of its denominator.

This problem will not be very serious in process control enginee-ring. This is because in process control systems, the disturbances are always with low frequency, so we can introduce additional poles in the transfer functions to realize W_f within suitable frequency band.

Now, we discuss a practical example which is a water temperature control system. As we know, in the chemical process, if we want to in-crease the temperature of a stream of cold water, a direct method is to mix it with hot water.

The hot water is heated by a gas boiler and its control character is a first lag. The heated water enters into the mixer to be mixed with the cold water and the character of the mixer is also a first lag. The measurement value of the temperature of the mixed water is compared with the reference and a control system is formed in this manner.

The block diagram is shown in Fig 2-3-3.

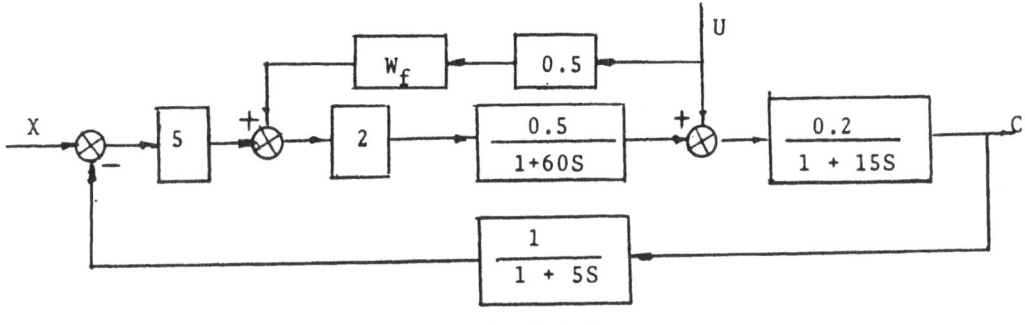

Fig 2-3-3

Suppose the regulator being a propotional regulator with the gain
equal to 5 and the gain of the valve (including the second regulator)
being 2 . The process is performed by adjusting the stroke of the control valve to change the gas flow entering the burning chamber of the
boiler to control the temperature of the hot water. The variation of
the boiler character is always very slow and suppose it with the constant
of 60 seconds. The constant of the mixer is assumed to be 15 seconds
and 5 seconds for the measurement device.

In the figure, C is the final temperature of the mixed water, X is
the desired temperature and U is the disturbance caused by the variation
of the temperature of the cold water.

In order to eliminate the influence of U on the controlled parameter
C, it is necessary to design a system with the ability to reject U. In
fact, it means to determine W_f.

From (2-3-5), we get:

$$0.5W_f = - \frac{1}{W_V} = - \frac{1}{\frac{2 \times 0.5}{1+60S}}$$

namely:

$$W_f = - \frac{1 + 60S}{0.5} = -2(1+60S)$$

Thus, it may be realized by a P+D regulator and its transfer function
is:

$$W_f(S) = - \frac{100}{P}(1 + ST_d)$$

Where P is the propotional band , T_d is the differential time, so it is only necessary to let the propotional band be 50% and T_d be 60 seconds.

(4) For a feedback control system without the feedforward channel, as shown in Fig 2-3-4, its response caused by the disturbance U is:

$$\frac{C}{U} = \frac{W_p}{1 + W_R W_p W_m} = \frac{1}{W_R} \frac{W_R W_p}{1 + W_R W_p W_m} = \frac{G}{W_R} \qquad (2-3-6)$$

Where G is the closed-loop transfer function of the system.

Therefore, for such a system, if we want to weaken the influence of the disturbance, then the gain of the regulator

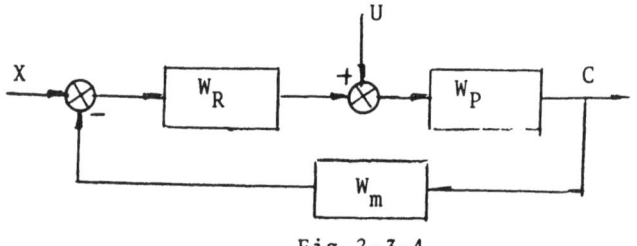

Fig 2-3-4

should be increased and when we want to realize the rejection to the disturbance, theoretically, the gain of W_R should be infinite.

This demand is not only difficult to be realized, but also with the problem of stability, i.e. it will cause unstability.

We have said before when we use feedforward channel to eliminate the influence of U, there is no such a problem as stability . Certainly, this is ideal case, but, however, even for the restriction of physical realizable conditions the feedforward channel could not realize perfect rejection to the disturbance, such a design can weaken the most part of the influence caused by the disturbance   and the remaining part may be weakened by feedback control; for example , we can introduce integral control in the system to eliminate the steady influence of the disturbance. Thus, comparing with the pure feedback control system without feedforward channel, the feedforward-feedback combination control system can reduce the gain of the regulator and it will certainly improve the system stability.

(5) Because the introduction of the feedforward channel eliminates

the most influence of the disturbance, so the frequency band of W_R and W_v can be reduced also and the investment of these elements will also decrease.

On the other hand, owing to the existence of the feedforward chan-nel the failure   of the main regulator will not cause the perfect outage of the whole system and a feedforward control channel still exists , so the manual control can be performed.

Therefore, although the design of rejection to supply disturbances seems very simple, the expounded analysis shows that it contains very abundant contents.

Theoretically, a system shown in Fig 2-3-5 is also capable to reject the disturbance U.

From it, we can get:

$$\frac{C}{U} = \frac{W_f + W_p}{1 + W_R W_p W_m}$$

(2-3-7)

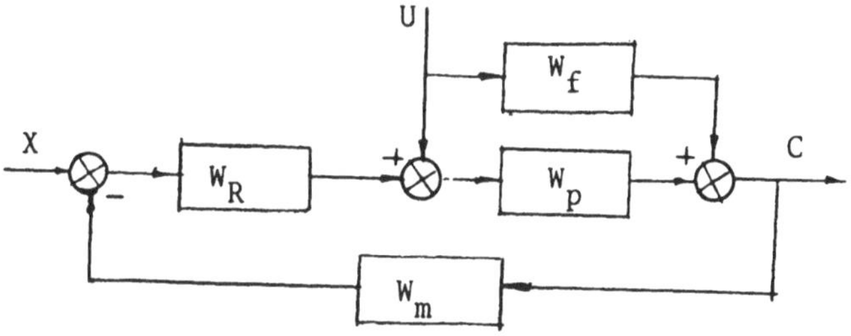

thus, if we let:

$$W_f = - W_p \qquad (2-3-8)$$

Fig 2-3-5

then the full rejection to the disturbance U is realized.

From the analysis of the block diagram, it seems that this project is more rational since W_p is certainly a realizable element for the practical plant, so W_f determined by (2-3-8) is also an easily realizable element.

Does it really mean that this project is better than that of Fig 2-3-1 or Fig 2-3-2 ?

No. It is not true.

The reason we have mentioned before. Because in any practical process control system, especially in chemical process control systems, the system output C always is some parameter of a process with large capacity, such

as temperature, pressure, flow, composition etc, and all these parameters in general may be measured by some small measurement device
(in control systems it is the measurement element located at the
feedback channel), but, however, it is impossible to imagine to influence such parameters by adding some output of small compensation
elements since there is a problem about the quantity degree of energy
and material. For instance, in the above example, how can the output
of the small compensation element W_f influence the temperature of the
mixer ? Obviously, it is impossible. Therefore, we can not expect to
use it to compensate the vaiation of the temperature in the mixer.

Hence, the project of Fig 2-3-5 seems reasonable in block diagram,
but it is unavailable in practice indeed.

The application of the combination of the feedforward control
with the feedback control now is widely seen in industries and a lot
of experience has proved that this is a very effective measure to reject the supply disturbances.

Besides the combination of the feedforward control with the feedback control, another effective way to reduce the influence of the
supply disturbances is the cascade control. Although the cascade control can not eliminate the influences of the supply disturbances entirely, it can reduce them remarkably.

So, if there are several supply disturbances , we can not use the
project introduced here to eliminate all of them because this will result in a very complicated system, and in such a case to combine the
cascade control with the principles discussed here is certainly a good
idea to reduce the influences of the supply disturbances.

We will discuss this idea in the next paragraph.

§ 2-4 Design of Rejection to Supply Disturbances and the Cascade Control

In last paragraph, we discussed the design of rejection to the supply disturbances.

But, we should discuss two problems further:

(1) If there is an auxiliary control loop before the supply disturbance, how will the case be?

(2) If there are two supply disturbances with different characters, how should we deal with this case?

Now, we discuss the first problem and the system is shown below:

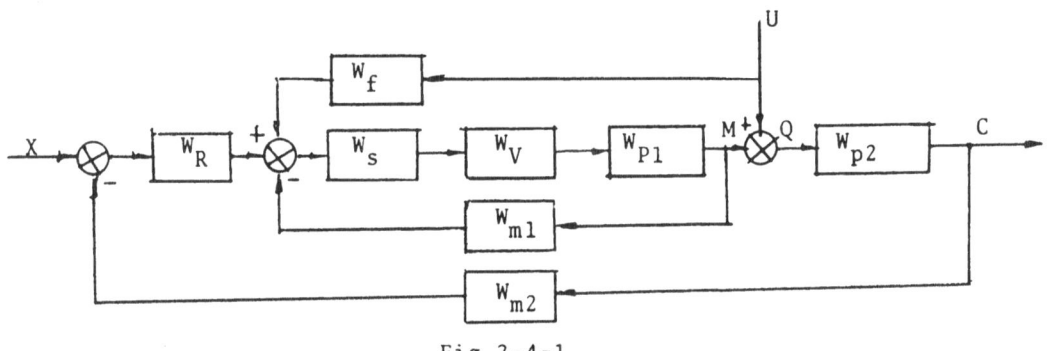

Fig 2-4-1

Because only the influence of the disturbance is considered, so we can let:

$$X = 0 \tag{2-4-1}$$

then from Fig 2-4-1, it yields:

$$M = W_f W_s W_V W_{p1} U - W_{m1} W_s W_V W_{p1} M \tag{2-4-2}$$

It follows:

$$M = \frac{W_f W_s W_V W_{p1} U}{1 + W_{m1} W_s W_V W_{p1}} \tag{2-4-3}$$

where, W_s is the auxiliary regulator ; W_{m1} is the measurement element of the auxiliary loop ; W_{p1} is the plant character of the auxiliary loop.

On the other hand, we have:

$$Q = M + U \tag{2-4-4}$$

If we want to realize the full rejection to U, it is necessary:

$$Q = 0 \qquad\qquad (2-4-5)$$

namely:

$$\frac{W_f W_s W_V W_{p1} U}{1 + W_{m1} W_s W_V W_{p1}} + U = 0 \qquad\qquad (2-4-6)$$

It follows:

$$W_f = - \frac{1 + W_{m1} W_s W_V W_{p1}}{W_s W_V W_{p1}} \qquad\qquad (2-4-7)$$

We should point out that the system shown in Fig 2-4-1 is practically meaningful since it is a combination of a cascade control system with the design of rejection to the supply disturbance. As we know that the cascade control is very capable to eliminate the inluence of the disturbances which enter into the auxiliary loop, but for the disturbances outside the auxiliary loop, its function to eliminate the influence of disturbances is not striking. Thus, for the disturbances outside the auxiliary loop, we should adopt the design of rejection to disturbances to eliminate their influence, i.e. the form of Fig 2-4-1 should be adopted.

That is to say that the principle of realizing rejection to disturbances can be combined with cascade control and it certainly results in improving the control effect.

Naturally, there is a problem: When there are two different kinds of disturbances, and the combination principle mentioned above is used, which one should be weakened by the cascade control?

This problem is difficult to be answered analytically since we can not find a definite mathematical form to express it.

Now, we are going to explain it by an example of the level control of a boiler drum and we can learn some useful experience from it.

The plant is a boiler drum and its input is the fed water. The flow of the fed water is determined not only by the stroke of the regulating valve, but also by the disturbances. Some disturbances show explicit influence on this process and they may be called as substantial

disturbances; some do not express themselves as explicit disturbances,

but they are indeed and thus they can be called as non-substantial .

Now, let us analyze the disturbances.

As we know that the demands on the steam flow depend on the boiler

load. When the load increases, then the demand on the steam will enhance

also. But what does it mean to increase the steam flow? It means more

water in the drum being vaporized and from the view-point of water level

change it corresponds to reducing the fed water.

Therefore, the variation of the steam flow may be considered as a

negative disturbance to the fed water , i.e. a negative supply disturbance.

As a supply distubance of this process, this disturbance is not ex-

plicit, namely we can not detect it by the variation of the fed water since

it does not exert practical influence on the fed water.

On the contrary, the variation of the pressure exerted on the valve

gives an explicit influence on the fed water , so it is a substantial sup-

ply disturbance.

For a substantial supply disturbance, because its influence can be

measured by the fed water, so we can use cascade control to eliminate its

influence; but for the variation of the steam flow, it is not an explicit

disturbance and its influence can only be eliminated by the design of re-

jection   to supply disturbances.

Fig 2-4-2 shows such a system.

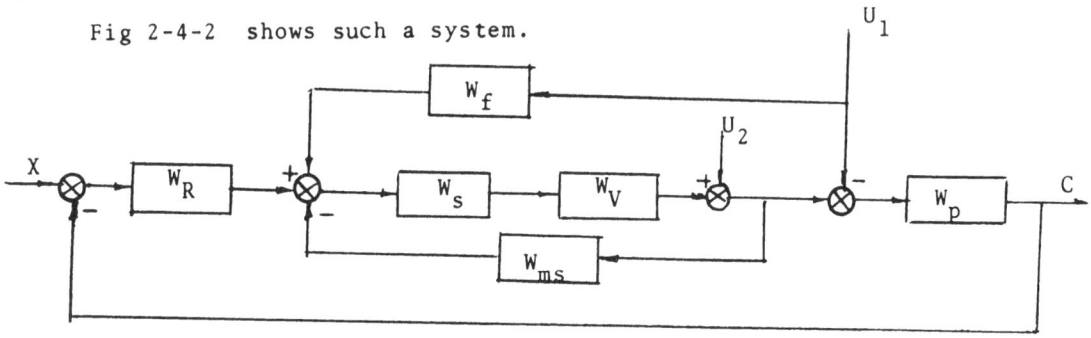

Fig 2-4-2

Where: C is the controlled level,

W_R is the main regulator,

W_s is the auxiliary regulator . Suppose it being P+I form.

W_V is the control valve,

W_p is the plant,

W_{ms} is the measurement element of the auxiliary loop,

W_f is the feedforward element under design.

For the auxiliary loop, its closed-loop character is:

$$G_1 = \frac{W_s W_V}{1 + W_s W_V W_{ms}} \qquad (2-4-8)$$

Because W_s is a P+I regulater, so its gain at low frequency is very high and we get:

$$G_1(S) \approx 1 \qquad (2-4-9)$$

at low frequency.

Then, from (2-3-5), it yields:

$$W_f(S) = 1 \qquad (2-4-10)$$

By using such a feedforward channel , we can eliminate the influence of steam flow change on the control of the level.

Therefore, the project of the combination of feedforward control with the feedback control can be further combined with the cascade control , but, however, some practical problems should be carefully treated because there is no general rule for combination.

We will give more discussion on the design of this system later on.

This example and the discussions below are taken from the British broadcasting course on automatic control.

§ 2-5 How to Utilize Feedback to Simplify the System Design

We have discussed the example of the level control of a boiler. There are two supply disturbances in it. One is explicit (the change of the chamber pressure of the control valve) and the other is implicit (the influence of the variation of the steam flow). We have pointed out that we can use the combination of cascade control and the design of rejection to sypply disturbances to reduce the influence of both disturbances.

In such a design, two regulators are needed. One is the main regulator of the level control and the other is the auxiliary regulator in the inner loop.

Now, let us discuss further. In order to reduce investment, can we use only one regulator to satisfy the control demands?

We return to Fig 2-4-2.

From that figure, we see that the disturbances U_1 and U_2 are sent to the same point on the main channel but with opposite signs. Although it is impossible to measure U_1 how to be input in the system practically, its location in the block diagram is definite.

In addition, in that figure $W_f = 1$, therefore, from the analysis of block diagram, Fig 2-4-2 is entirely corresponding to Fig 2-5-1.

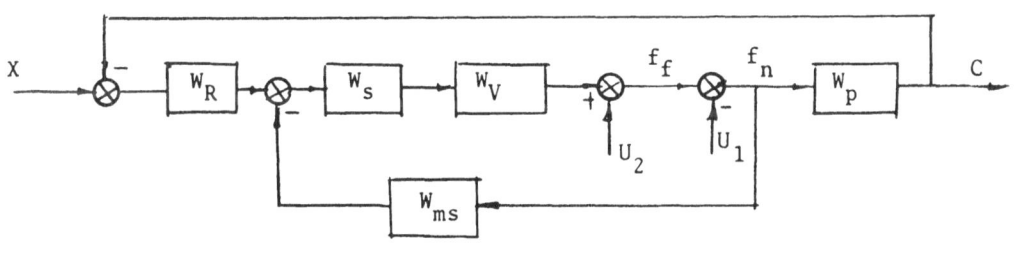

Fig 2-5-1

In this figure, f_f is the practical fed water to the boiler ; f_n is the net fed water obtained from the block diagram with the consideration of U_1. In fact f_n can not be measured but it exists in the block diagram and it should be fed back in the inner loop.

Thus, all disturbances are included in the inner loop and if P+I regulator is adopted in it, then there is no steady error for the step disturbances in the inner loop.

Now, we consider the main loop. The plant is an integral element since the drum can not hold the balance of the level itself. This integral element gives the guarantee that the output response to the step reference is without steady error for the main loop. Therefore, we can choose a propotional regulator for W_R.

Because the main regulator is with propotional character, then the system design may be simplified further.

The method to simplify the design is to utilize the character of the feedback elements.

For example, we can let:

$$W_{ms}(S) = \gamma \qquad\qquad (2-5-1)$$

where, γ is between 0 and 1.

Then , the main regulator may be omitted and the system structure becomes:

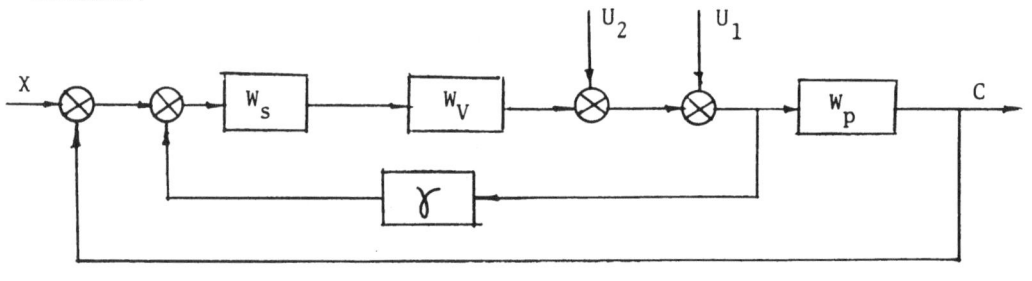

Fig 2-5-2

Why can the main regulator be omitted?

This is because decreasing the feedback gain, i.e. $\gamma < 1$, can increase the whole loop gain of the inner loop and this is equivalent to preset a propotional regulator with suitable gain before the inner loop. Hence, to adjust the value of γ practically may adjust the gain of the whole open system.

In fact, if G_1 is the closed-loop transfer function of the inner loop, then:

$$G_1 = \frac{W_s W_V}{1 + W_s W_V \gamma} = \frac{1}{\gamma + \frac{1}{W_s W_V}} \qquad (2-5-2)$$

Because W_s is a P+I regulator and is with quite large gain at low frequency, therefore at steady state, the closed-loop gain of the inner loop is $1/\gamma$.

Thus, when $\gamma < 1$, then $\frac{1}{\gamma} > 1$ and this corresponds to the closed-loop gain of the inner loop equal to one with a preset propotional regulator (its gain is $\frac{1}{\gamma}$) before it.

The choice of γ should consider to guarantee the stability of the inner loop and the main loop. When γ increases, then the gain of the open loop of the inner loop increases and it is easy to cause the unstability in the inner loop; on the contrary, the decrease of γ will increase the open loop gain of the main loop and will be able to cause the unstability of the main loop, so a balance should be held here on the value of γ.

But, all the above discussions are carried out in the block diagram and we have pointed out for several times that some conclusions may be rational in the analysis of the block diagram but are not available in practice. How about the conclusion now?

In fact, we know that f_n can not be measured and we can only measure f_f, so Fig 2-5-2 is unavailable in practice.

The practically available form is shown in Fig 2-5-3. This is still a combination of cascade control with the design of rejection to supply disturbances. Now , we determine W_f.

The transfer funvtion of the inner loop is:

$$G_1(S) = \frac{K(1 + 1/T_i S)K_V}{1 + K(1 + 1/T_i S)K_V \gamma} = \frac{KK_V(1 + T_i S)}{KK_V \gamma (1+T_i S)+ T_i S} =$$

$$= \frac{KK_V(1 + T_i S)}{KK_V \gamma (1 + T_i S(1 + 1/KK_V \gamma))} = \frac{1 + ST_i}{\gamma (1 + ST_i \alpha)} \qquad (2-5-3)$$

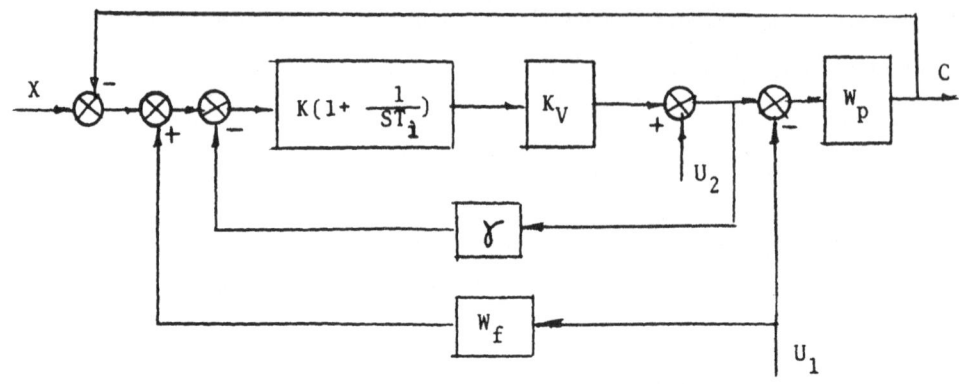

Fig 2-5-3

Where:

$$\alpha = 1 + \frac{1}{KK_V\gamma} \qquad\qquad (2-5-4)$$

Therefore:

$$W_f(S) = \frac{1}{G_1(S)} = \gamma\frac{1 + ST_i\alpha}{1 + ST_i} \qquad\qquad (2-5-5)$$

In $W_f(S)$, the term γ is used to eliminate the steady influence of the disturbances and the term $\dfrac{1 + T_iS\alpha}{1 + ST_i}$ is used to eliminate the dynamic influence of the disturbances.

We notice that there is a γ on the feedback channel and there is also a γ on the feedforward channel of U_1 and both γ are input to the same point of the system, so we can combine them and one amplifier can be saved.

The final system is shown in Fig 2-5-4.

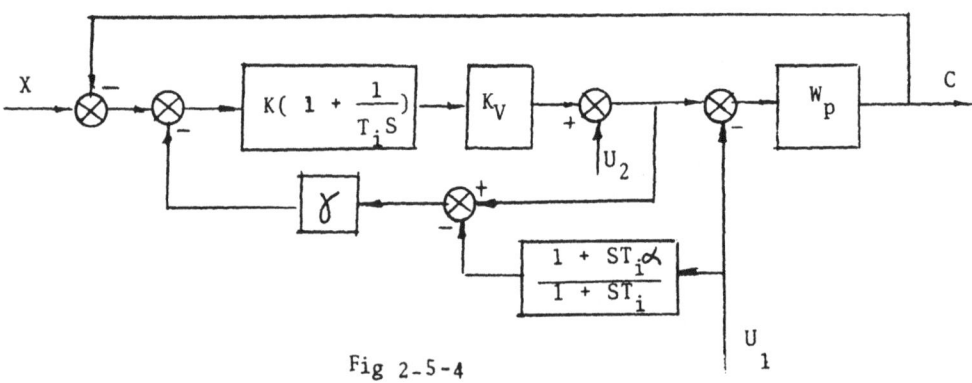

Fig 2-5-4

The practical structure of this system is shown
in Fig 2-5-5.

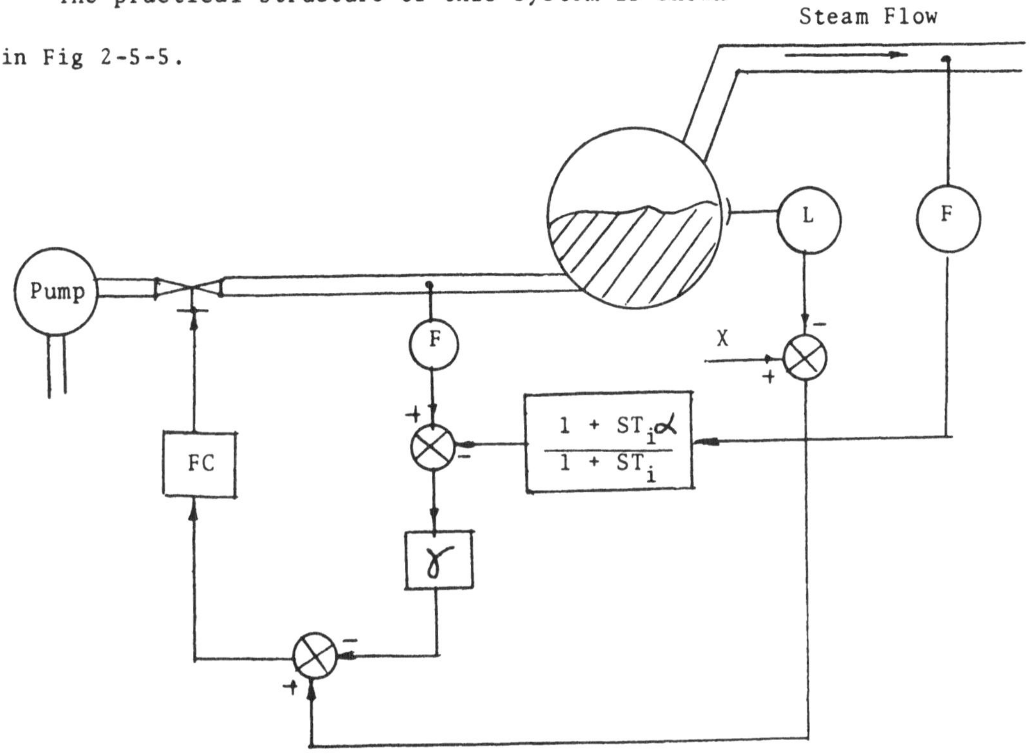

Fig 2-5-5

Up to now, we have expounded the principles of the rejection design to the supply disturbances. We must say that these principles are
available in practice but the project of the feedforward control with
the feedback control is not the unique project to realize the rejection
design.

Another possible project for realizing rejection design will be
given in § 2-8.

§ 2-6 Design of Rejection to Load Disturbances

In process control systems, another important disturbance is the load disturbance occuring on the outputs.

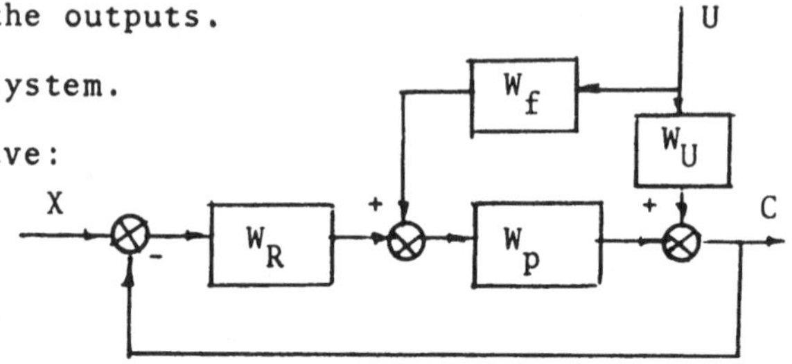

Fig 2-6-1 shows such a system.

From this figure , we have:

$$\frac{C}{U} = \frac{W_U + W_f W_p}{1 + W_R W_p} \qquad (2-6-1)$$

Fig 2-6-1

Therefore, if we want to realize full rejection to disturbance U, then it is necessary:

$$W_f = - \frac{W_U}{W_p} \qquad (2-6-2)$$

And we know:

(1) W_f is related to the character of the plant,

(2) When W_U approximates W_p, then W_f will be simple. In fact, when $W_U = W_p$, then $W_f = 1$.

In addition, when both W_U and W_p are with the same lags, then W_f can be realized by a propotional element.

But, for W_f determined by (2-6-2), there is not only a problem about physical realization mentioned before, i.e. the problem of the numerator being with higher degree than the denominator , but also another physical realization problem.

This is because in chemical process control systems, the plants always have dead time delays, i.e. there is a term $e^{-\tau s}$ in W_p. In such cases, if we realize W_f according to (2-6-2), then certainly W_f will contain the factor $e^{\tau s}$, which is impossible to be realized by such transfer functions.

In such cases, we can expand $e^{-\tau s}$ into fraction form of polynomials by using Padé approximation.

For example, the common Padé approximation terms are shown below:

$$e^{-x}$$

$$\frac{1}{1} \qquad\qquad \frac{1-x}{1} \qquad\qquad \frac{1-x+\frac{1}{2}x^2}{1}$$

$$\frac{1}{1+x} \qquad\qquad \frac{1-\frac{1}{2}x}{1+\frac{1}{2}x} \qquad\qquad \frac{1-\frac{2}{3}x+\frac{1}{6}x^2}{1+\frac{1}{3}x}$$

$$\frac{1}{1+x+\frac{1}{2}x^2} \qquad \frac{1-\frac{1}{3}x}{1+\frac{2}{3}x+\frac{1}{6}x^2} \qquad \frac{1-\frac{1}{2}x-\frac{1}{12}x^2}{1+\frac{1}{2}x+\frac{1}{12}x^2}$$

Expanding $e^{-\tau s}$ by Padé approximation, we can get $W_f(S)$ by using (2-6-2), but now $W_f(S)$ may be a all-pass network.

(2-6-2) shows the condition of full rejection to the disturbance U and we see because the practical character of the plant, sometimes it is difficult to realize W_f, thus, the full rejection to U is not easy to be realized. That means that in general we can only realize partial rejection to the disturbance.

Then, a problem arises: Is there any other method being able to do so? Certainly, there is. For instance, the cascade control is also a good way to reduce the influence of the load disturbances.

Flg 2-6-2 shows a system using cascade control to reduce the influence of the load distubance.

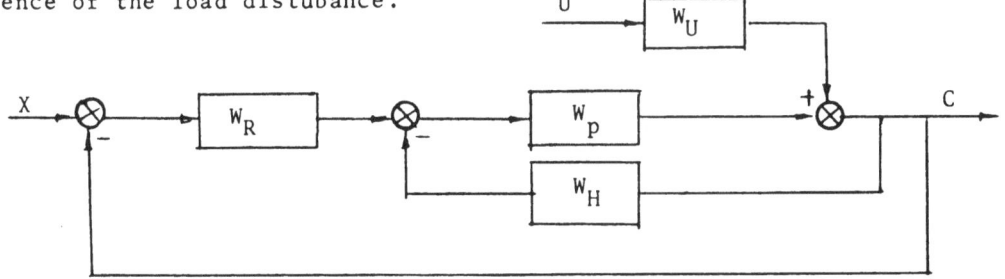

Fig 2-6-2

When the control system is not designed, the relation between the output and the disturbance is:

$$\frac{C}{U} = W_U \qquad (2-6-3)$$

When the above system is adopted but the main channel is broken off, i.e. W_R is broken off, then:

$$\frac{C}{U} = \frac{W_U}{1 + A_m} \qquad (2-6-4)$$

Where:

$$A_m = W_p W_H \qquad (2-6-5)$$

When the main channel is closed, we have:

$$\frac{C}{U} = \frac{W_U}{(1 + A_m)(1 + A_{MC})} \qquad (2-6-5)$$

Where:

$$A_{MC} = \frac{A_{mu}}{1 + A_m} \qquad (2-6-6)$$

$$A_{mu} = W_R W_p \qquad (2-6-7)$$

therefore:

$$\frac{C}{U} = \frac{W_U}{(1 + A_m)(1 + \dfrac{A_{mu}}{1 + A_m})} \qquad (2-6-8)$$

In general, the disturbance is always with low frequency and at low frequency since W_R is a P+I regulator, so A_{mu} is with quite large value and:

$$|A_{MC}| \gg 1 \qquad (2-6-9)$$

then:

$$1 + \frac{A_{mu}}{1 + A_m} \approx \frac{A_{mu}}{1 + A_m} \qquad (2-6-10)$$

It yields:

$$\frac{C}{U} = \frac{W_U}{A_{mu}} = \frac{W_U}{W_R W_p} \qquad (2-6-11)$$

Therefore, when the cascade control is adopted, the influence of the low frequency disturbance is reduced to the degree of $1/A_{mu}$ of the original influence.Notice that this is about the reduction of the dynamic influence, as for the steady influence, since U is approximate to a step disturbance, so its steady influence will be eliminated entirely.

When W_R is a propotional regulator with small gain, i.e. W_R is small, then it may be:

$$\left| A_{MC} \right| < 1 \qquad (2\text{-}6\text{-}13)$$

But, if :

$$\left| A_m \right| \gg 1 \qquad (2\text{-}6\text{-}14)$$

then :

$$1 + \frac{A_{mu}}{1 + A_m} \approx 1 \qquad (2\text{-}6\text{-}15)$$

So :

$$\frac{C}{U} = \frac{W_U}{A_m} \qquad (2\text{-}6\text{-}14)$$

Thus, if the open loop gain of the inner loop is large enough, then the influence of the disturbance may also be reduced. In general, the propotional gain of the auxiliary regulator of the inner loop is quite large, so the condition $\left| A_m \right| \gg 1$ is always held.

For W_f determined by (2-6-2), as we said before, when both W_p and W_U are with same lags and the valve character is omitted, then W_f is a pure propotional element. When the valve is with first lag, the W_f will be a P+D element. All these can be realized by using conventional regulators. But, when W_p and W_U are with different lags, especially when W_p is with dead time delay, then it is difficult to realize W_f.

Recently, some authors suggest to utlize the on-line control to treat such control problems. By experience, in most process control systems, no matter how complicated the characters of the plant and the disturbance channel will be, using:

$$W_f = - \frac{K(1 + \tau_1 s)}{1 + \tau_2 s} \qquad (2\text{-}6\text{-}17)$$

and setting the parameters on-line, i.e. to determine the parameters of

W_f according to the practical measurement of the influence of U on C, we can always get satisfactory effect to reject the disturbance. For example, Shinskey, Nisenfield and others did some research work in this field.[7][50]

Furthermore, some authors, Wood and Pucey, pointed out that for most process control systems, we can let:

$$W_f = -K\frac{1}{1 + \tau s} \qquad (2\text{-}6\text{-}18)$$

and set the parameters on-line, then practically we can get good result to reject the disturbance.

All these denote although by (2-6-2) we can get ideal full rejection to the disturbance, it is difficult to be realized practically. So , we have to use some simplified methods to realize approximate rejection to disturbances and among these methods, the on-line control is a good one.

Up to now, we have introduced the most popular or conventional principles for realizing the rejection design to both supply disturbances and the load disturbances. We see that these principles are not difficult in theory but sometimes are not convenient to be applied in practice. The basic reasons are:

(1) The compensation elements may be difficult to be realized,

(2) There may be several disturbances,

(3) The disturbances may be difficult to be measured,

(4) The disturbances may vary.

Because of these reasons, so in practice only approximate rejection design can be realized.

§ 2-7 Disturbance Analysis and Rejection Design

In the previous several paragraphs, we discussed how to realize the design of rejection to the reference disturbances, supply disturbances and load disturbances. We have learnt that it is possible to take some available measures to eliminate the influence of each disturbance.

Further research will propose such a problem: When several kinds of disturbances co-exist in a process control system, how should we do the rejection design?

In § 2-4, we have said something about it. There, an explicit supply disturbance was reduced by using the cascade control , while an implicit disturbance was treated by the design of rejection. But, however, it was a special case indeed. If two disturbances both are explicit, how should we treat them?

In fact, two problems should be discussed here:

(1) In such a case, whether it is absolutely necessary to adopt different ways introduced before for design? If it is, certainly the final system is very complicated.

(2) When different disturbances co-exist, is it necessary to do full rejection design to each one?

In fact, the essentiality of these two problems is to discuss the characteristics of disturbances and the functions of rejection design.

Now, we discuss the first problem. The key of this problem is: Can some rejection design have several rejection abilities at a time?

It is not impossible.

Let us consider a resolution control system. Such a system is shown in Fig 2-7-1.

Where, f is the resolved medium and U is the resolvent.We hope that in the mixer, the solution can have invariant density. In order to reach this demand, the density control system must be with the ability to reject disturbances.

The flow of the resolved medium can
be easily held invariable,
but the flow of the resolvent
is remarkably influenced
by the variation of pressure
and will change frequently.
So we should design a density
control system with the ability to reject the influence
of the resolvent flow variation.

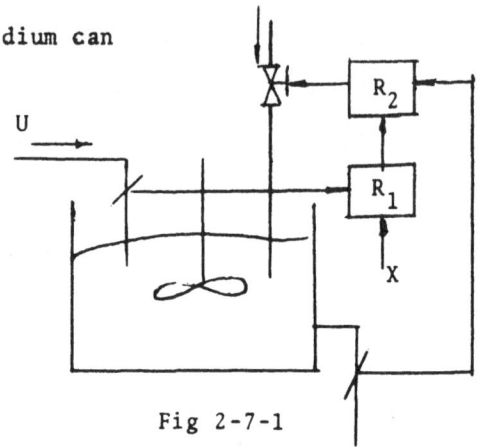

Fig 2-7-1

We suppose that the control valves are with high speed response, i.e. their characters are not considered in the design, then a change of the flow of the resolved medium will require a corresponding change of resolvent with the same sign in order to keep the density in the mixer being invariant.

So, the flow of the resolved medium is the manipulated variable and R_1 and R_2 are two regulators.

There are two plants for this system. They are:

$$W_{p1} = \frac{C(S)}{f(S)} \tag{2-7-1}$$

$$W_{p2} = \frac{C(S)}{U(S)} \tag{2-7-2}$$

The block diagram is shown in Fig 2-7-2.

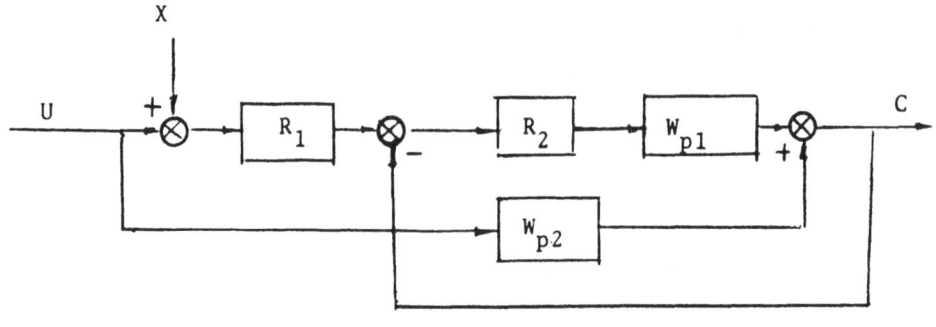

Fig 2-7-2

Obviously, the disturbance enters into the system at two points. One
is at the reference setting point and the other is at the outlet of the
system. By our above analysis, it means that a reference disturbance and
a load disturbance co-exist. In such a case, is it necessary to set two
devices to eliminate the influence of U ?

It is not necessary to do so indeed. Obviously, Fig 2-7-2 can be transferred into the form of Fig 2-7-3.

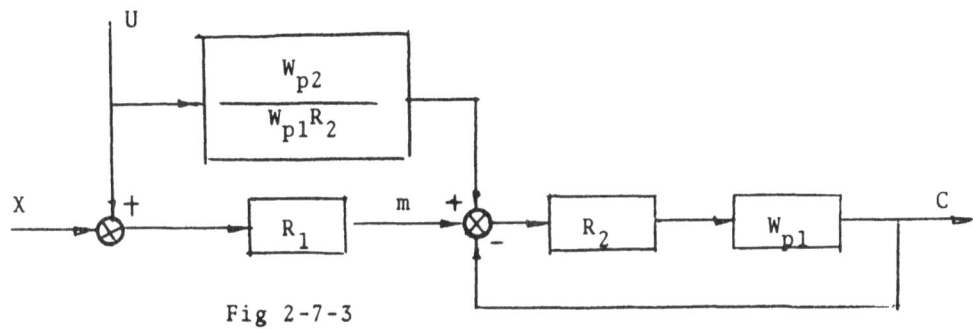

Fig 2-7-3

From Fig 2-7-3 we know that from m to C is a normal single variable
control system and we can design it by conventional method, i.e. because
W_{p1} is known, so it is easy to design R_2.

In addition, from Fig 2-7-3, we get:

$$\frac{C}{U} = \frac{R_2 W_{p1}}{1 + R_2 W_{p1}} \frac{R_1 R_2 W_{p1} + W_{p2}}{R_2 W_{p1}} = \frac{R_1 R_2 W_{p1} + W_{p2}}{1 + R_2 W_{p1}} \qquad (2-7-2)$$

Obviously, if we let:

$$R_1 = - \frac{W_{p2}}{R_2 W_{p1}} \qquad (2-7-3)$$

then C is not influenced by U. That means that only one element com-
pletes the rejection to the disturbances at two points.

Now, we discuss the second problem. It is: When there are several
disturbances in a system, is it necessary to treat each of them with full
rejection design ?

It is not necessary either. In general, if all the disturbances are

explicit, then we should design a full rejection to the most serious
disturbance and for the others which have smaller influence we can reduce them by other methods.

Consider the example of § 2-3 again. The water temperature control system is shown in Fig 2-7-4.

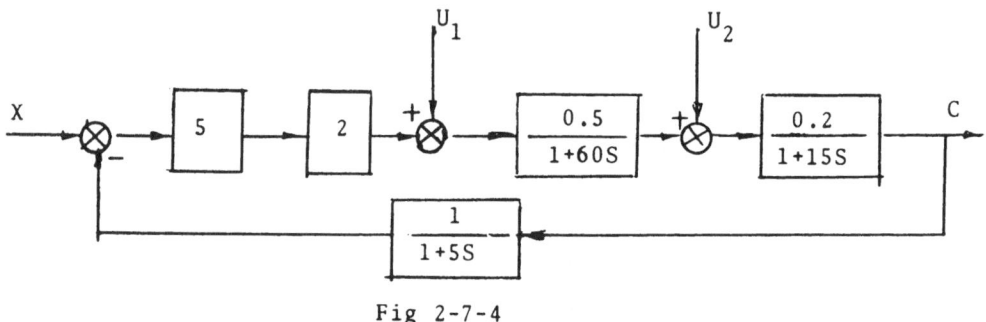

Fig 2-7-4

There are two disturbances in this system. One is the variation
of the pressure of the boiler burning gas and the other is the change
of the temperature of the cold water.

From Fig 2-7-4, we get:

$$\frac{C(S)}{U_2(S)} = \frac{0.2(1+60S)(1+5S)}{(1+60S)(1+15S)(1+5S)+1} \qquad (2-7-4)$$

$$\frac{C(S)}{U_1(S)} = \frac{0.1(1+5S)}{(1+60S)(1+15S)(1+5s)+1} \qquad (2-7-5)$$

Now we discuss which disturbance gives more serious influence on
the system.

At first, from the meaning of the feedback we can know that a signal is produced along the closed loop to eliminate the influence of
the disturbance due to the existence of the feedback (suppose X=0),
so the smaller the time delay between the output and the entrance
point of the disturbance, the faster the correction effect of the
feedback and consequently the smaller the influence of the disturbance.
For example, the peak value of the disturbance response will be reduced.

By this principle we can see that for the above system there are

5 second time delay between C and U_1 and 65 second time delay between C

and U_2, so it is certainly that U_2 will have more serious influence then

U_1 does. It is so from the dynamic analysis and from the static analysis

we can also learn if both U_1 and U_2 are step disturbances, then from

(2-7-4) and (2-7-5),the steady deviation due to U_2 is 0.1 and that due to

U_1 is 0.05, so in both dynamic and static cases, disturbance U_2 is with

more serious influence. Consequently, U_2 should be treated by full rejec-

tion. Then, how to reduce the influence of U_1 ?

The cascade control may be used now and we can design a system shown

in Fig 2-7-5.

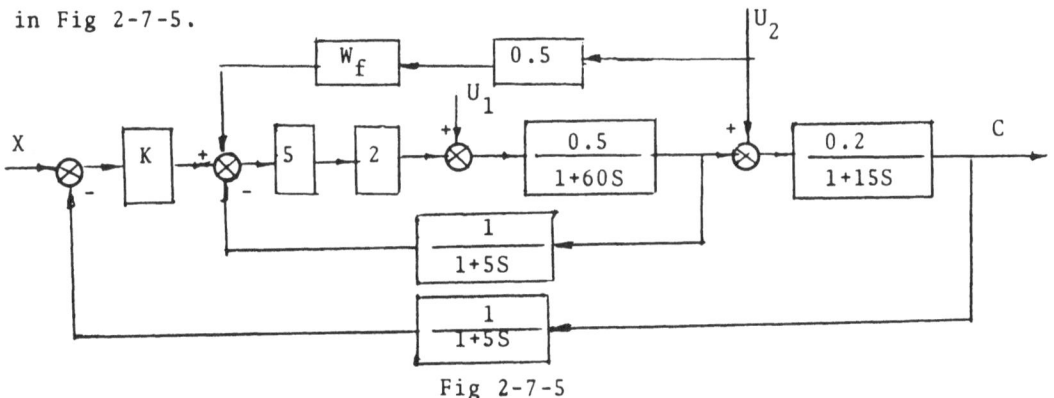

Fig 2-7-5

From (2-3-5), we can get W_f:

$$W_f = - \frac{2}{5} \quad \frac{(1+5S)(1+60S)+5}{1+5S} \qquad (2-7-6)$$

Thus, we combined cascade control with full rejection. In fact,

in the above system, if a P+I regulator is adopted for the main regulator,

then the system is not only with the ability to fully reject to U_2, but

also without steady deviation due to U_1 and this is a very good control

indeed.

So, in general, for supply disturbances, we can use cascade control

to reduce their influence and for the load disturbances, if the realiza-

tion is not very difficult, then it would be better to eliminate their

influence by using full rejection design.

§ 2-8 The Application of State Feedback to Realize the Design of Full

Rejection to Disturbances

The above analysis denotes that for a single variable process

control system, no matter where the disturbance is, we can realize the

full rejection design to disturbances and all the projects used before,

by a special terminology of control, are based on the combined system

by disturbance control.

But, we can propose a question: Is this the unique method for

rejection design?

In most textbooks, there is a common conclusion: It is impossible

to realize the design of full rejection to disturbances by deviation

control. Now , we discuss this conclusion.

As we know that control by deviation is the most popular and basic

control mode.The so-called deviation means the difference between the

reference and the output of the feedback element. From Fig 2-8-1 the

deviation is :

$$E = X - M \qquad (2-8-1)$$

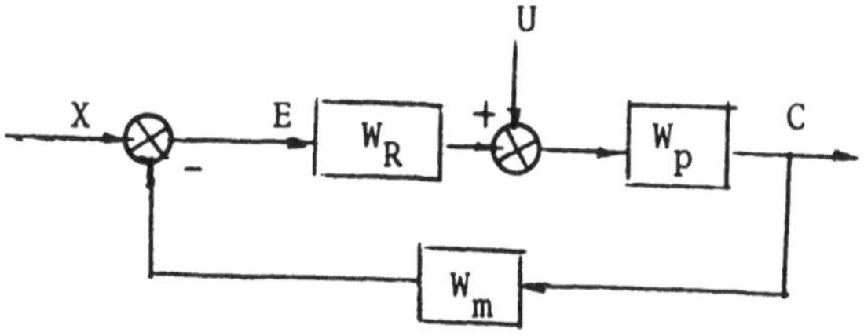

In a single loop control

system, W_m is the measurement

element of the system output C.

Fig 2-8-1

It has been pointed out

in § 2-3 if we want to realize the full rejection to disturbances by

this manner, then the gain of the regulator should be infinite. At first,

it is difficult to do so in practice and, on the other hand, in general

it will cause unstability in the system. Thus, in order to avoid the

unstability problem, cascade control is widely used, namely quite a part

of the propotional gain of the system regulator is set to the auxiliary

regulator in the inner loop. This measure can improve the system ability

to resist disturbances very much, but it can not realize the full rejec-

tion to disturbances yet.

Then, is it really that it is impossible to realize the full rejection design to disturbances by deviation control?

This problem is worth being discussed.

In fact, if we do not consider the element W_f simply as the measurement element of output C, then we can reach another conclusion.

We discuss the state variable feedback control system now. At first, we discuss two simple examples of state variable feedback control systems. Suppose an open loop character :

$$W(S) = \frac{K}{S(S+1)(S+2)} \qquad (2-8-1)$$

and the following closed-loop character is expected:

$$\frac{C}{R} = \frac{50}{(S+2)(S^2+6S+25)} = \frac{50}{S^3+8S^2+37S+50} \qquad (2-8-2)$$

Because in state variable feedback control systems, the state variables are expressed by x_1, x_2,....., so we denote the reference by R here.

Now, we build a state variable control system as shown in Fig 2-8-2.

From the control theory, this system can be transferred into a single loop control system as Fig 2-8-3.

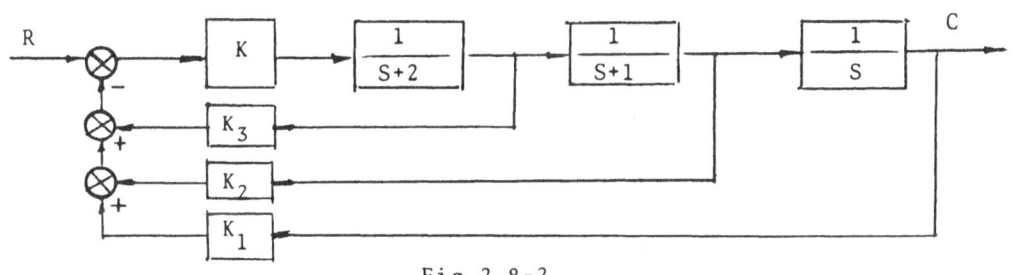

Fig 2-8-2

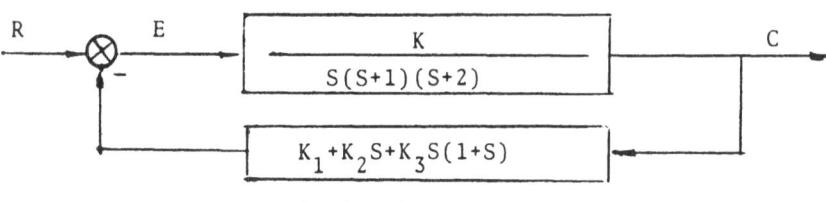

Fig 2-8-3

From Fig 2-8-3, we get:

$$\frac{C}{R}(S) = \frac{K}{S(S+1)(S+2)+K(K_3S^2+(K_3+K_2)S+1)} =$$

$$= \frac{K}{S^3+(3+KK_3)S^2+(2+K(K_2+K_3))S+KK_1} \quad (2-8-3)$$

Equalizing (2-8-2) with (2-8-3) yields:

$$\left. \begin{array}{l} K = 50 \\ KK_1 = 50 \\ 3 + KK_2 = 8 \\ 2 + K(K_2+K_3) = 37 \end{array} \right\} \quad (2-8-4)$$

and we get:

$$K_1 = 1, \ K_2 = 0.6, \ K_3 = 0.1, \ K = 50$$

Therefore, the character of the feedback element is:

$$W_m(S) = K_3S(1+S)+K_2S+K_1 = 0.1(S+2)(S+5) \quad (2-8-5)$$

and:

$$\frac{C}{R}(S) = \frac{K}{S(S+1)(S+2) +0.1(S+2)(S+5)} =$$

$$= \frac{K}{(S+2)(S(S+1)+0.1K(S+5))} = \frac{50}{(S+2)(S^2+6S+25)} \quad (2-8-6)$$

So, the control demand is reached.

The second example is with the following plant :

$$W_p(S) = \frac{1}{S(S+1)(S+10)} \quad (2-8-7)$$

The regulator character is:

$$W_c(S) = \frac{K(S+2)}{S+\alpha} \quad (2-8-8)$$

The following closed-loop character is expected:

$$\frac{C}{R}(S) = \frac{72(S+2)}{(S^2+1.414S+1)(S+9)(S+10)} =$$

$$= \frac{72(S+2)}{S^4+26.4S^3+180.4S^2+229S+144} \quad (2-8-9)$$

Now, we build a state variable control system as shown in Fig 2-8-4 and it can be also turned into a single loop control system as shown in Fig 2-8-5.

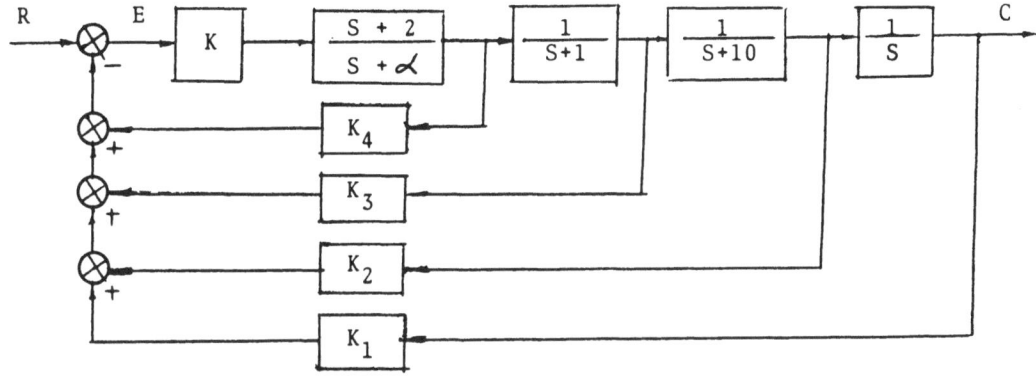

Fig 2-8-4

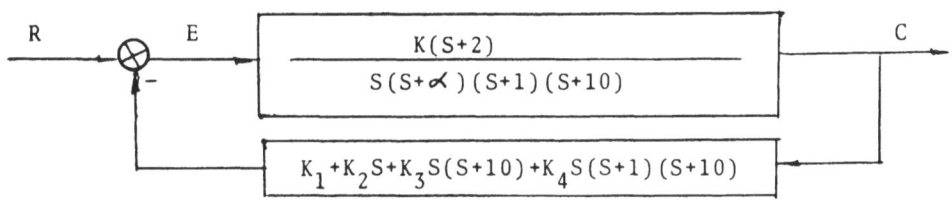

Fig 2-8-5

The coefficients α, K, K_1, K_2, K_3 and K_4 should be determined.

From Fig 2-8-5, we get:

$$\frac{C(S)}{R(S)} = \frac{K(S+2)}{\left\{(KK_4+1)S^4+\left[K(K_3+13K_4)+(11+\alpha)\right]S^3+\left[K(K_2+12K_3+32K_4)+\right.}$$

$$\overline{+(10+11\alpha)\Big]S^2+\Big[K(K_1+2K_2+30K_3+20K_4+10\alpha]S+2KK_1\Big\}} \qquad (2-8-10)$$

Equalizing (2-8-9) with (2-8-10) yields:

$$
\left.
\begin{aligned}
&K = 72\\
&KK_4 + 1 = 1\\
&K(K_3+13K_4)+(11+\alpha) = 26.4\\
&K(K_2+12K_3+32K_4)+(10+11\alpha) = 180.4\\
&K(K_1+2K_2+30K_3+20K_4)+10\alpha = 229\\
&2KK_1 = 144
\end{aligned}
\right\} \qquad (2-8-11)
$$

From it we get:

$$K = 72, \quad K_1 = 1, \quad K_2 = 0.0134,$$

$$K_3 = 0.0014, \quad K_4 = 0, \quad \alpha = 15.3$$

and the character of the regulator is:

$$W_c(S) = \frac{72(S + 2)}{S + 15.3} \qquad\qquad (2\text{-}8\text{-}12)$$

The above examples tell us that we can utilize the state variable feedback to realize control systems with certain demanded merits and these systems are with deviations indeed. So, they should belong to the

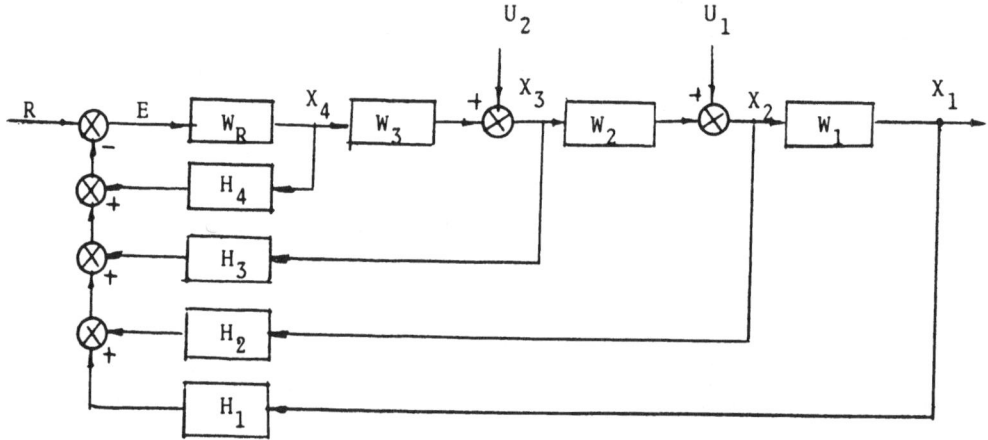

Fig 2-8-6

control by deviation but their feedback element characteristics are with special forms.

Now, let us discuss further whether the state variable feedback can be used to realize the full rejection to disturbances.

Fig 2-8-6 is such a system and we want to realize the full rejection to U_1 and U_2.

It is easily to get the state equations and they can be expressed in the following matrix form:

$$\begin{Bmatrix} 1 & -W_1 & 0 & 0 \\ 0 & 1 & -W_2 & 0 \\ 0 & 0 & 1 & -W_3 \\ W_R H_1 & W_R H_2 & W_R H_3 & 1+W_R H_4 \end{Bmatrix} \begin{Bmatrix} X_1 \\ X_2 \\ X_3 \\ X_4 \end{Bmatrix} = \begin{Bmatrix} U_1 W_1 \\ U_2 W_2 \\ 0 \\ RW_R \end{Bmatrix} \qquad (2\text{-}8\text{-}13)$$

For instance, if the rejection to U_1 is expected, i.e. $X_1 = 0$, then suppose $R=0$ and $U_2=0$ and we get the conditions:

$$-W_1X_2 = U_1W_1$$
$$X_2 - W_2X_3 = 0$$
$$X_3 - X_4W_3 = 0$$
$$W_RH_2X_2 + W_RH_3X_3 + (1+W_RH_4)X_4 = 0$$

$$(2-8-14)$$

From this set of equations, we get:

When $H_3 = H_4 = 0$,

$$H_2 = -\frac{1}{W_RW_2W_3} \qquad (2-8-15)$$

When $H_2 = H_4 = 0$,

$$H_3 = -\frac{1}{W_RW_3} \qquad (2-8-16)$$

When $H_2 = H_3 = 0$,

$$H_4 = -\frac{1}{W_R}. \qquad (2-8-17)$$

Obviously, if any one of (2-8-15),(2-8-16) and (2-8-17) is held, then this system is with full rejection to U_1 and it is realized by deviation control.

H_1 is easily to be determined. For example, when $H_2=H_3=0$, the system transfer function is:

$$\frac{X_1}{R} = \frac{W_RW_1W_2W_3}{1 + W_RH_4 + W_RW_1W_2W_3H_1} \qquad (2-8-18)$$

But :

$$H_4 = -\frac{1}{W_R}$$

so:

$$\frac{X_1}{R} = \frac{1}{H_1} \qquad (2-8-19)$$

This is just ideal control, namely this is the best control the system can reach.

Therefore, if the control demands are given, then it is not difficult to determine H_1.

If $H_1 = 1$, then:

$$X_1 = R \qquad (2-8-20)$$

and there is no deviation in this system.

Thus, by using state variable feedback control system, we can realize full rejection design to disturbances . We need not to measure
the disturbances and , if necessary, we can realize the ideal control
without the deviation at the meantime.

Obviously, in the above analysis, if any one of (2-8-16) and
(2-8-17) is held, then the system is with full rejection to both U_1
and U_2 by deviation control.

In control systems, some state variables (not all) may be measured
more conveniently than disturbances and, by the above analysis, if some
state variable is difficult to be measured, then we can measure another
one , for instance there are three different forms can be adopted for
realizing a system with full rejection to U_1, so the design is quite
flexible . Furthermore, either of (2-8-16) and (2-8-17) gives the full
rejection to both U_1 and U_2 , so it is not necessary to consider two
disturbances separately.

Besides, no special stability problem will arise then, so the
realization of full rejection to disturbances by state variable feedback is an available method.

But, however, this system is physically irrealizable in general,
i.e. the degree of the numerator of H_2, H_3 or H_4 is alway higher than
that of the denominator. This means that differential feedback channels are introduced and the high frequency disturbances will be able
to be fed back. So, when this project is applied, this problem should
be considered carefully.

§ 2-9 The Rejection Design to Disturbances for Smith Predictor

As well-known, in practical process control systems, the plants are often with dead time delays. It means that the transfer functions of plants often contain the term $e^{-\tau s}$.

Because of the existence of the dead time delay, the system will meet troubles in stability. In fact, when τ is quite large, the system is difficult to be stable.

In order to overcome the influence of dead lag, a very effective control model is the Smith predictor.

A typical Smith predictor is shown in Fig 2-9-1.

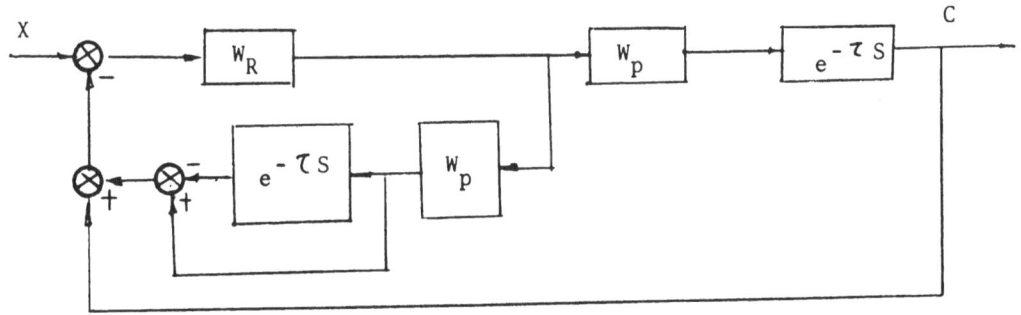

Fig 2-9-1

For this system, the closed-loop transfer function is:

$$\frac{C(S)}{X(S)} = \frac{W_p W_R e^{-\tau s} / (1 + W_p W_R (1- e^{-\tau s}))}{1 + \dfrac{W_p W_R e^{-\tau s}}{1 + W_p W_R (1- e^{-\tau s})}} =$$

$$= \frac{W_p W_R e^{-\tau s}}{1+W_p W_R (1-e^{-\tau s}) +W_p W_R e^{-\tau s}} = \frac{W_p W_R e^{-\tau s}}{1+ W_p W_R} \qquad (2-9-1)$$

Obviously, for this system, the influence on the stability by the dead delay has been eliminated . This is because the compensation element $(W_p - W_p e^{-\tau s})$ is adopted.

Because the Smith predictor has the ability to eliminate the influence of the dead delay on system stability, so it is widely applied in practice and has been considered as an advanced control system.

Now, we discuss the case when the Smith predictor is with disturbances and research whether we can also get full rejection design to
disturbances for it.

The following analysis will show that the prominent merit of the
Smith predictor is: It not only can eliminate the influence of the dead
lag on system stability, but also can reach full rejection design to
disturbances without any measurement to them. In fact, if we observe
Fig 2-9-1 carefully, we can know that the Smith predictor is a state variable control system indeed and we have pointed out   that by using
the state variable feedback control we can realize the full rejection
design to disturbances. So, we will see that the Smith predictor realizes
the full rejection design to disturbances by using state variable feedback control essentially.

Fig 2-9-2 shows such a design.

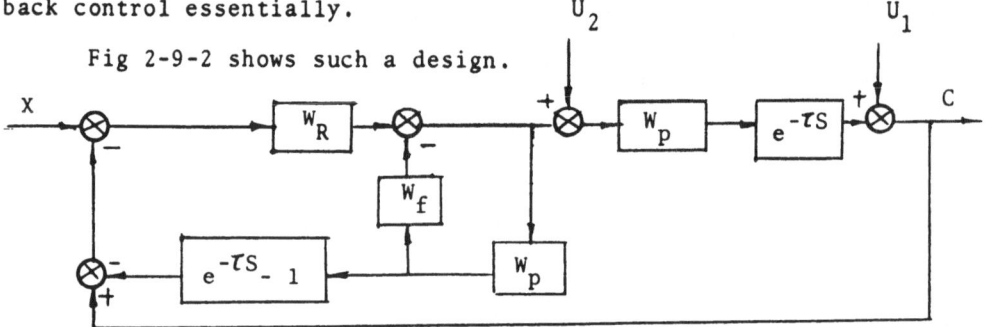

Fig 2-9-2

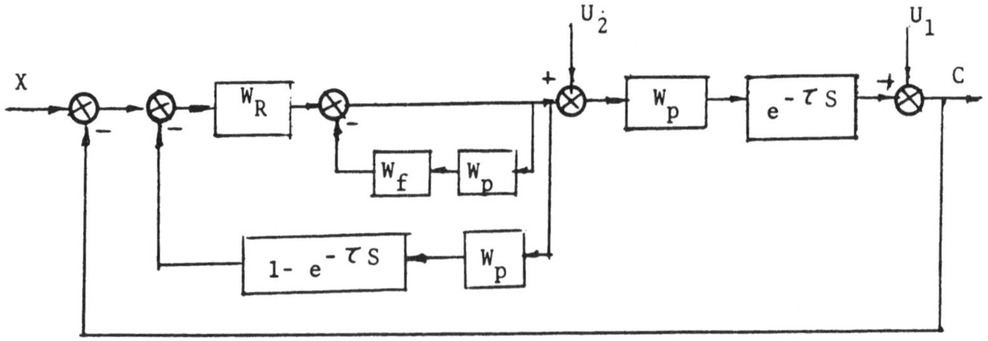

Fig 2-9-3

For convenience, Fig 2-9-2 is transferred into Fig 2-9-3.

From Fig 2-9-3, we get:

$$\frac{C(S)}{X(S)} = \frac{\dfrac{\dfrac{W_R}{1 + W_p W_f + W_R W_p (1-e^{-\tau S})} W_p e^{-\tau S}}{1 + \dfrac{W_R W_p e^{-\tau S}}{1+ W_p W_f+ W_R W_p (1- e^{-\tau S})}}}{} =$$

$$= \frac{W_R W_p e^{-\tau S}}{1 + W_p W_f+ W_R W_p (1- e^{-\tau S})+ W_R W_p e^{-\tau S}} =$$

$$= \frac{W_R W_p e^{-\tau S}}{1 + W_p W_f+ W_R(W_p e^{-\tau S} + W_p(1- e^{-\tau S}))} \qquad (2-9-2)$$

and:

$$\frac{C(S)}{U_1(S)} = \frac{1 + W_f W_p - W_R W_p (e^{-\tau S} - 1)}{1 + W_p W_f + W_R(W_p e^{-\tau S} + W_p(1-e^{-\tau S}))} \qquad (2-9-3)$$

So the output is:

$$C(S) = \frac{W_R W_p e^{-\tau S}X(S) + (1+ W_p W_f- W_R W_p (e^{-\tau S}- 1))U_1(S)}{1 + W_p W_f+ W_R(W_p e^{-\tau S} - W_p(e^{-\tau S} - 1))} \qquad (2-9-4)$$

Thus, if this system is with full rejection to U_1, then it is necessary and sufficient:

$$1 + W_p W_f - W_R W_p (e^{-\tau S} - 1) = 0 \qquad (2-9-5)$$

and it yields:

$$W_f = \frac{W_R W_p (e^{-\tau S}- 1) - 1}{W_p} \qquad (2-9-6)$$

Furthermore, the output of the system then is:

$$C(S) = \frac{W_R W_p e^{-\tau S}}{W_R W_p e^{-\tau S}}X(S) = X(S) \qquad (2-9-7)$$

So, this system is not only with full rejection to U_1, but also without deviations.

This is a very ideal result and it is an important merit of the Smith predictor indeed.

When the disturbance U_2 is considered, we have:

$$C(S) = \frac{W_R W_p e^{-\tau S} X(S) + W_p e^{-\tau S}(1 + W_f W_p - W_R W_p (e^{-\tau S} - 1)) U_2(S)}{1 + W_p W_f + W_R (W_p e^{-\tau S} - W_p (e^{-\tau S} - 1))}$$

$$(2-9-8)$$

and the condition for full rejection to U_2 is:

$$W_f = \frac{W_R W_p (e^{-\tau S} - 1)}{W_p} \qquad (2-9-9)$$

Obviously, both (2-9-6) and (2-9-9) are identical.

That means that the adoption of W_f given by (2-9-6) or (2-9-9) results in full rejection to both U_1 and U_2 and this result has nothing to do with the forms of disturbances and no measurement of disturbances is needed either. Besides, it reachs the ideal control , i.e. without deviations, at the meantime.

When the measurement element is with the character W_m, then the Smith predictor has the following form:

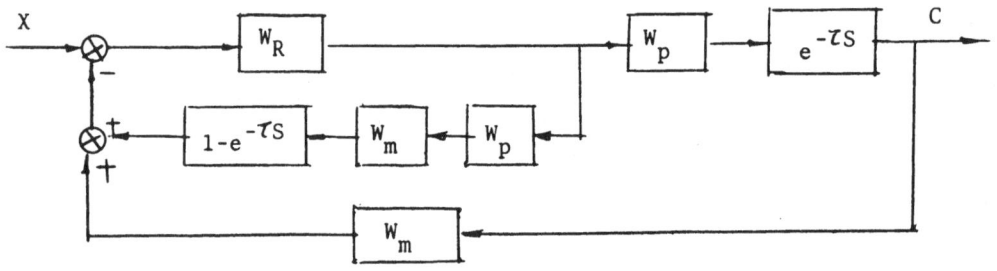

Fig 2-9-4

The closed-loop transfer function of this system is:

$$\frac{C(S)}{X(S)} = \frac{W_R W_p e^{-\tau S}}{1 + W_R W_p W_m} \qquad (2-9-10)$$

And the Smith predictor with the ability to fully reject the disturbances is shown below:

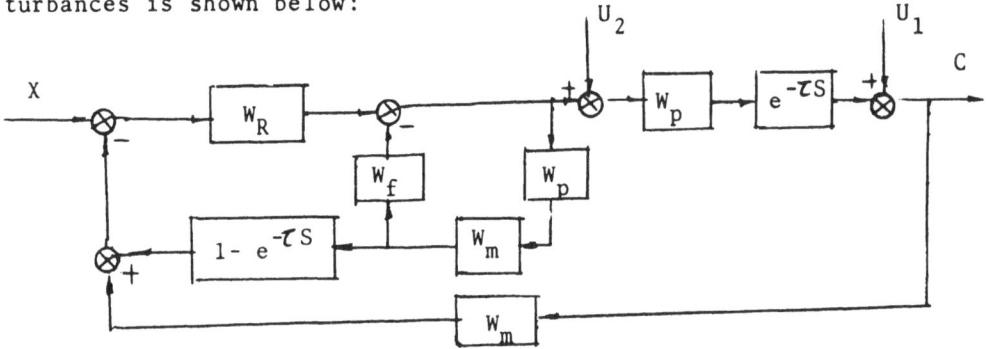

Fig 2-9-5

The system response is: (only U_1 is considered)

$$C(S) = \frac{W_R W_p e^{-\tau S} X(S) + (1+ W_f W_m W_p + W_R W_m W_p (1-e^{-\tau S})) U_1(S)}{1 + W_f W_m W_p + W_R W_m W_p (1-e^{-\tau S}) + W_R W_m W_p e^{-\tau S}} \qquad (2-9-11)$$

If the full rejection to U_1 is expected, then it is necessary:

$$1 + W_f W_m W_p + W_R W_m W_p (1 - e^{-\tau S}) = 0 \qquad (2-9-12)$$

namely:

$$W_f = \frac{W_R W_m W_p (e^{-\tau S} - 1) - 1}{W_m W_p} \qquad (2-9-13)$$

Then, the closed-loop transfer function is:

$$\frac{C(S)}{X(S)} = \frac{W_R W_p e^{-\tau S}}{W_R W_m W_p e^{-\tau S}} = \frac{1}{W_m} \qquad (2-9-14)$$

When the supply disturbance U_2 is considered, the system output is:

$$C(S) = \frac{W_R W_p e^{-\tau S} X(S) + W_p e^{-\tau S} (1+W_f W_m W_p + W_R W_m W_p (1-e^{-\tau S})) U_2(S)}{1 + W_f W_m W_p + W_R W_m W_p (1-e^{-\tau S}) + W_R W_m W_p e^{-\tau S}}$$

$$(2-9-15)$$

The condition for full rejection to U_2 is:

$$W_f = \frac{W_R W_m W_p (e^{-\mathcal{T}S} - 1)}{W_m W_p} \qquad (2-9-16)$$

It is the same as (2-9-13).

So the adoption of a W_f given before can give the full rejection to both U_1 and U_2.

The system is also without deviation then.

When $\mathcal{T} = 0$, then:

$$W_f = -\frac{1}{W_m W_p} \qquad (2-9-17)$$

the channel $1-e^{-\mathcal{T}S}$ is broken off now. That means, for the conventional plant ($\mathcal{T} = 0$), the adoption of an inner loop can result in full rejection to disturbances as shown in Fig 2-9-6.

But this is practically corresponding to infinite open-loop gain.

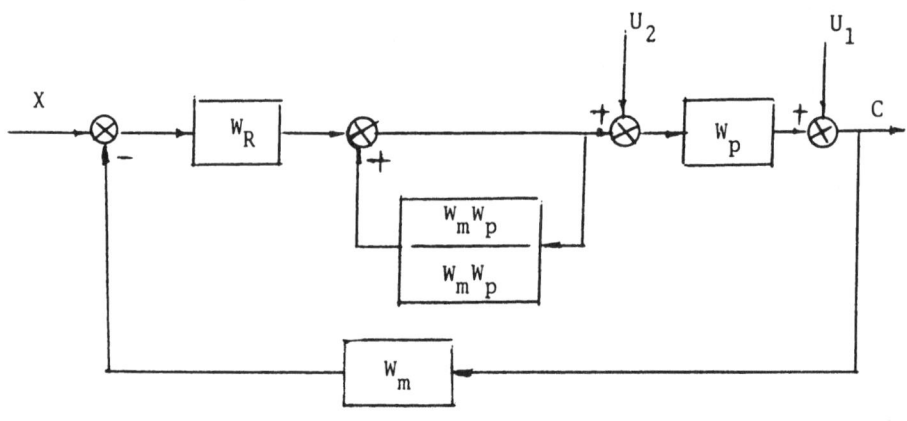

Fig 2-9-6

§ 2-10 The Independence Principle of Rejection Design to Disturbances

Although we did not point out especially in the above discussions, the systems under consideration are assumed to be linear with constant coefficients.

Then, a problem arises: Can the discussed principles of rejection design to disturbances be also available to the non-linear systems or linear systems with time varying coefficients?

Now, we discuss this problem.

In process control systems, the non-linear (or time varing coefficients) cases in general are: either the control system contains non-linear elements or the disturbances are imported into the system through non-linear devices.

Fig 2-10-1 shows such a system.

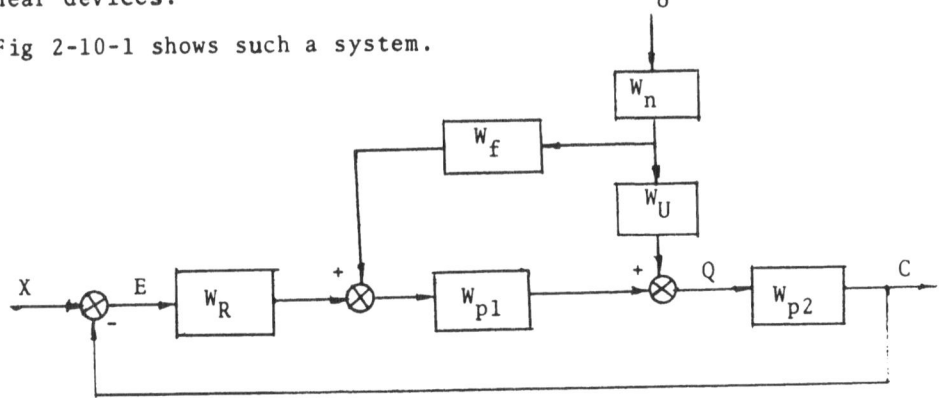

Fig 2-10-1

In this figure, each of W_{p2}, W_n and W_R may be non-linear or time varying. If they are non-linear elements, then they should be expressed by describing functions.

From this figure, we get:

$$C(S) = \frac{(W_f W_{p1} + W_U) W_n W_{p2} U(S)}{1 + W_R W_{p1} W_{p2}} + \frac{W_R W_{p1} W_{p2} X}{1 + W_R W_{p1} W_{p2}} \qquad (2\text{-}10\text{-}1)$$

In order to reach full rejection to the disturbance, it is necessary:

$$W_f W_{p1} + W_U = 0 \qquad (2\text{-}10\text{-}2)$$

namely:

$$W_f = - \frac{W_U}{W_{p1}} \qquad (2\text{-}10\text{-}3)$$

Thus, the condition for full rejection to the disturbance is independent of the forms of W_{p2}, W_R and W_n.

From the analysis of concepts, in order to check the influence of the disturbance we can let R=0 and for a system with full rejection to the disturbance, we get:

$$Q = E = 0 \qquad (2\text{-}10\text{-}4)$$

Therefore, it is not important what forms the regulator W_R and the plant W_{p2} are, i.e. they may be non-linear elements or linear time varying elements.

On the other hand, the output of the system is:

$$C(S) = \frac{(W_f W_{p1} + W_U)W_n W_{p2}U(S)}{1 + W_R W_{p1} W_{p2}} \qquad (2\text{-}10\text{-}5)$$

Now that the condition (2-10-2) gives the guarantee that C(S)=0, so in the above equation W_n may be any form. It means that W_n may also be a non-linear element or a linear time varying element.

Thus, we can say that the methods discussed in this chapter for the design of full rejection to disturbances are universal. They can be applied not only to linear systems, but also to non-linear systems. In other words, it means that the conditions of full rejection to disturbances are independent of the forms of the elements which are not included in these conditions.

§ 2-11 The Disturbance-Rejection Design for a Two-Variable System

   with Only One Controlled Output

   Suppose there is a two-variable system but only one output in it is controlled, then this is also a single variable system. For instance, in the example of § 1-11, if only the level or the flow is controlled, then the system is just one we will discuss now.

   Without doubt, in this case the other manipulated variable will become a disturbance for the controlled channel through the coupling channel. Now , we discuss to do disturbance-rejection design for this system.

   We discuss two cases.

   The first is: If open loop control is carried out for this system, then the disturbance-rejection design is with the following form:

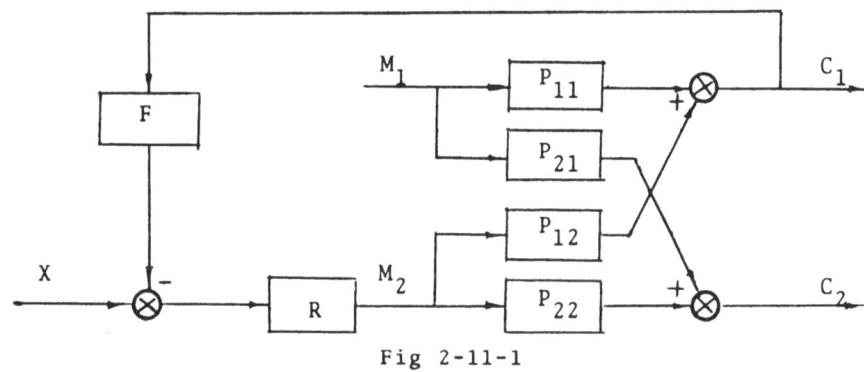

Fig 2-11-1

   In order to consider the influence of the disturbance, we may let X = 0, so the output is:

$$C_2 = M_1 P_{21} + M_1 P_{11} \frac{-FR}{1 + FRP_{12}} P_{22} \qquad (2\text{-}11\text{-}1)$$

Therefore:

$$\frac{C_2}{M_1} = \frac{P_{21} + RF(P_{12}P_{21} - P_{11}P_{22})}{1 + FRP_{12}} \qquad (2\text{-}11\text{-}2)$$

Obviously, if M_1 is expected to have no influence on the controlled output C_2, then it is necessary :

$$F = \frac{P_{21}}{R(P_{11}P_{22} - P_{12}P_{21})} \qquad (2\text{-}11\text{-}3)$$

Obviously, when $P_{21} = 0$, then M_1 is not a disturbance for C_2 and we have consequently $F = 0$.

When $P_{12} = 0$, we have:

$$F = \frac{P_{21}}{RP_{11}P_{22}} \qquad (2\text{-}11\text{-}4)$$

The second case is: The closed-loop control is carried out to C_2 and the system structure is shown in Fig 2-11-2.

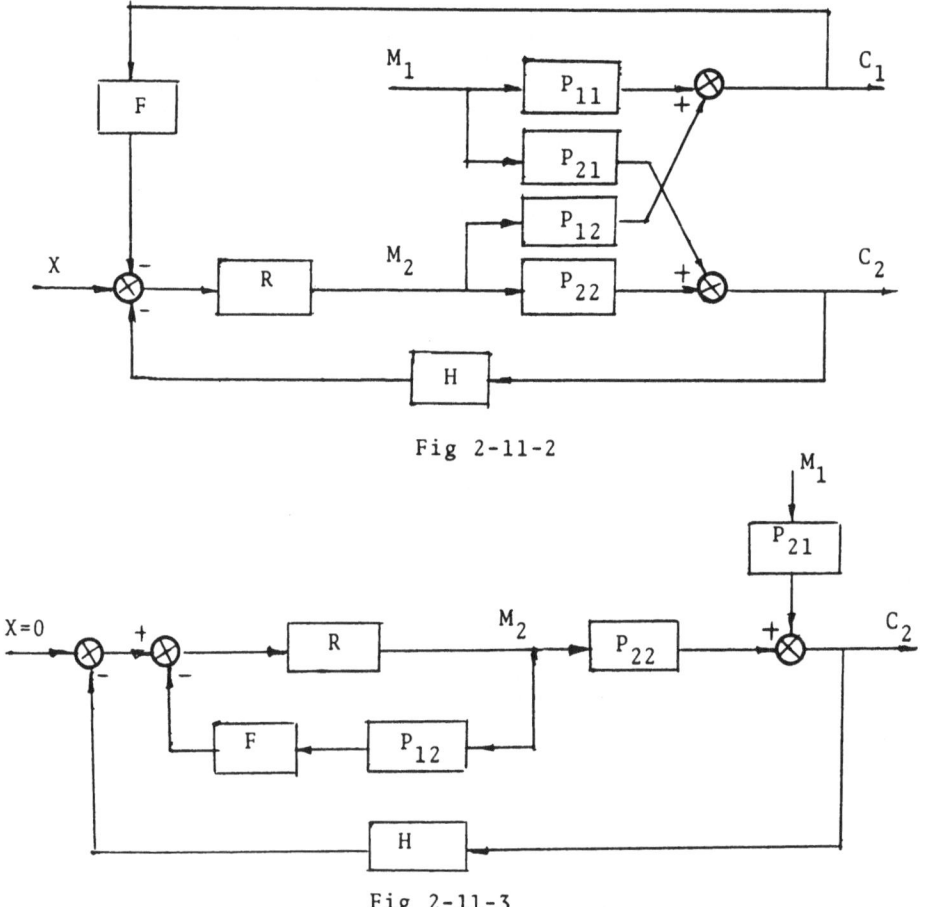

Fig 2-11-2

Fig 2-11-3

In order to get the relation between C_2 and M_1, we let X= 0.

The influence of M_1 on C_2 is exerted through two channels. The first channel is through P_{21} and it is shown in Fig 2-11-3.

From this figure, we get:

$$\frac{C_2}{M_1} = \frac{P_{21}(1 + FRP_{12})}{1 + FRP_{12} + RHP_{22}} \qquad (2-11-5)$$

The second channel is through P_{11} and the system is shown below:

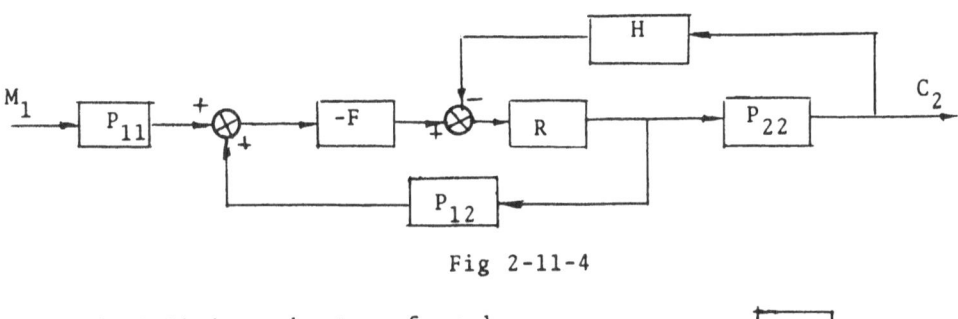

Fig 2-11-4

Fig 2-11-4 can be transferred into Fig 2-11-5.

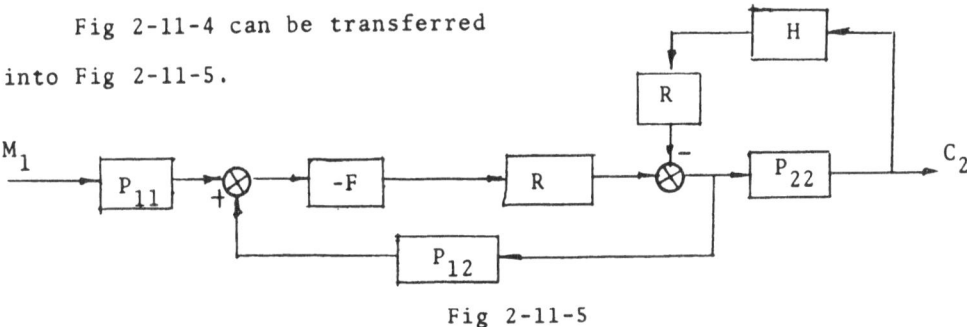

Fig 2-11-5

Fig 2-11-5 can be transferred into Fig 2-11-6 further.

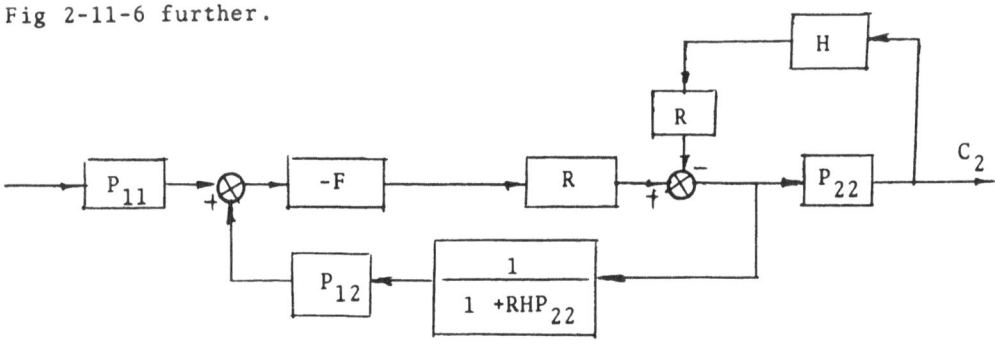

Fig 2-11-6

From Fig 2-11-6 we can get the relation between C_2 and M_1:

$$\frac{C_2}{M_1} = \frac{-P_{11}FR(1+RHP_{22})}{1 + RHP_{22} + FRP_{12}} \cdot \frac{P_{22}}{1 + RHP_{22}} =$$

$$= \frac{-FRP_{11}P_{22}}{1 + RHP_{22} + FRP_{12}} \qquad (2\text{-}11\text{-}6)$$

The final relation between C_2 and M_1 is the sum of (2-11-5) and (2-11-6).

Thus:

$$\frac{C_2}{M_1} = \frac{P_{21} + RF(P_{12}P_{21} - P_{11}P_{22})}{1 + RHP_{22} + RFP_{12}} \qquad (2\text{-}11\text{-}7)$$

If the full rejection to M_1 is expected, then it is necessary:

$$F = \frac{P_{21}}{R(P_{11}P_{22} - P_{12}P_{21})} \qquad (2\text{-}11\text{-}8)$$

It is identical with (2-11-3). It means that no matter the control loop is open or closed, the condition for rejection to M_1 is the same.

We must point out that the conclusions obtained here are only valid when only one variable in this two-variable system is controlled and the other output is free. In such a case , the manipulated variable of the free output may be considered as a disturbance of the controlled system. If, however, both variables are under control, then although the plant is still the same, the system would be a two-variable system and M_1 is no longer able to be considered as a disturbance of the C_2 control loop .

In such a case, the decoupling design principles should be considered for this two-variable control system.

§ 2-12 The Rejection Design to the Disturbance with Ambiguous Input
Channels [38]

In our above discussion, no matter what kind of disturbances is considered, if we want to realize a full rejection design to it, we must know the exact character of the disturbance import channel.

But, however, sometimes the input channel of the disturbance may be very complicated and it can not be expressed by a simple transfer function.

Fig 2-12-1 shows such a system. In this system, U is the system disturbance and we expect that the output C would not be influenced by U.

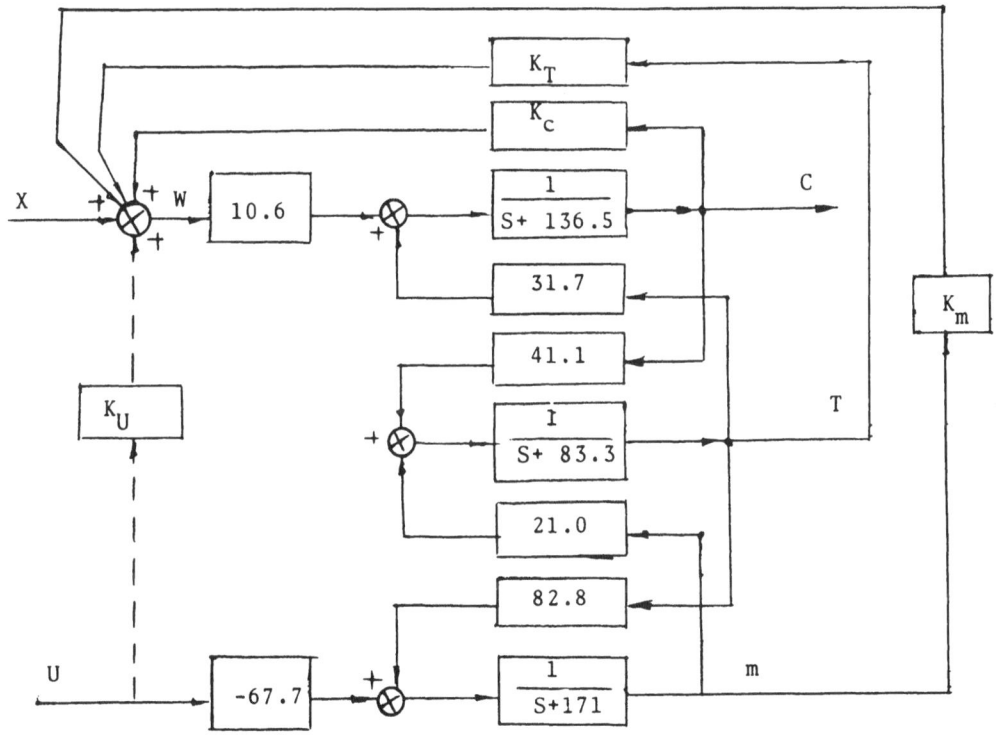

Fig 2-12-1

This is a single variable system but the input channel of the disturbance is not easily to be determined.

In such a case, how to realize the disturbance-rejection design for this system?

Now, we express this system in differential equations:

$$\left.\begin{array}{l} \dfrac{dC}{dt} = -136.5C + 31.7T + 10.6W \\[2mm] \dfrac{dT}{dt} = -83.3T + 41.1C + 21.0m \\[2mm] \dfrac{dm}{dt} = -171m + 82.8T - 67.6U \end{array}\right\} \qquad (2\text{-}12\text{-}1)$$

In order to discuss the influence of the disturbance, let X = 0 and a system with full rejection to **U** gives:

$$\left.\begin{array}{l} \dfrac{dC}{dt} = 0 \\[2mm] C = 0 \end{array}\right\} \qquad (2\text{-}12\text{-}2)$$

Thus, the following three equations are obtained:

$$0 = 31.7T + 10.6W \qquad (2\text{-}12\text{-}3)$$

$$\frac{dT}{dt} = -83.3T + 21.0m \qquad (2\text{-}12\text{-}4)$$

$$\frac{dm}{dt} = -171m + 82.8T - 67.6W \qquad (2\text{-}12\text{-}5)$$

From (2-12-3), we get:

$$\frac{W}{m} = -2.99 = K_T \qquad (2\text{-}12\text{-}6)$$

Subsituting this result into (2-12-4) yields:

$$\frac{W}{m} = -\frac{62.8}{S + 83.3} = K_m \qquad (2\text{-}12\text{-}7)$$

Now, we substitute (2-12-6) and (2-12-7) into (2-12-5) and get:

$$\frac{W}{U} = \frac{4245}{S^2 + 254.3S + 12506} \qquad (2\text{-}12\text{-}8)$$

That means that the satisfaction of anyone of the above three conditions (2-12-6), (2-12-7) and (2-12-8) can result in full rejection to U.

Therefore, it seems that this system is very complicated, but the condition for rejection to the disturbance is easily to be determined.

This is an available method and certainly it can be used in the similar cases.

But there is another method being able to solve this problem.

Take Laplace transform to (2-12-1) and write it into the matrix form:

$$\begin{pmatrix} S+136.3 & -31.7 & 0 & -10.6 \\ -41.1 & S+83.3 & -21 & 0 \\ 0 & -82.8 & S+171 & 0 \end{pmatrix} \begin{pmatrix} C \\ T \\ m \\ W \end{pmatrix} = \begin{pmatrix} 0 \\ 0 \\ -67.6U \end{pmatrix} \qquad (2\text{-}12\text{-}9)$$

Now, we introduce the control equation:

$$W = K_C C + K_T T + K_m m + K_U U \qquad (2\text{-}12\text{-}10)$$

Then, the system equation becomes:

$$\begin{pmatrix} S+136.3 & -31.7 & 0 & -10.6 \\ -41.1 & S+83.3 & -21 & 0 \\ 0 & -82.8 & S+171 & 0 \\ -K_C(S) & -K_T(S) & -K_m(S) & 1 \end{pmatrix} \begin{pmatrix} C \\ T \\ m \\ W \end{pmatrix} = \begin{pmatrix} 0 \\ 0 \\ -67.6U \\ K_U U \end{pmatrix} \qquad (2\text{-}12\text{-}11)$$

Solving for C, we get:

$$C(S) = \begin{vmatrix} 0 & -31.7 & 0 & -10.6 \\ 0 & S+83.3 & -21 & 0 \\ -67.6U & -82.8 & S+171 & 0 \\ K_U(S)U & -K_T(S) & -K_m(S) & 1 \end{vmatrix} \Bigg/ \Delta \qquad (2\text{-}12\text{-}12)$$

where:

$$\Delta = \begin{vmatrix} S+136.3 & -31.7 & 0 & -10.6 \\ -41 & S+83.3 & -21 & 0 \\ 0 & -82.8 & S+171 & 0 \\ -K_C(S) & -K_T(S) & -K_m(S) & 1 \end{vmatrix} \qquad (2\text{-}12\text{-}13)$$

Expanding the numerator of (2-12-12), we get:

$$C(S) = \frac{U(S)\{-(31.7)(21)(67.6)-(10.6)(21)(67.6)K_T(s)-(10.6)(67.6)(S+83.3)K_m(S) + (10.6)[(S+83.3)(S+171)-(21)(82.8)]K_U(S)\}}{\Delta(S)}$$

(2-12-14)

When the rejection to the disturbance is expected, it is necessary that the numerator of (2-12-14) is equal to zero.

There are a lot of methods which can make the numerator be zero. In fact, there are infinite methods indeed. But, however, the following three methods may be the simplest:

$$K_U(S) = K_m(S) = 0, \ K_T(S) = -2.99 \qquad (2\text{-}12\text{-}15)$$

$$K_U(S) = K_m(S) = 0, \ K_m(S) = -\frac{62.8}{S+83.3} \qquad (2\text{-}12\text{-}16)$$

$$\left. \begin{array}{l} K_T(S) = K_m(S) = 0 \\[2em] K_U(S) = \dfrac{4245}{S^2 + 254.3S + 12506} \end{array} \right\} \qquad (2\text{-}12\text{-}17)$$

Substituting (2-12-15),(2-12-16) and (2-12-17) into $\Delta(S)$, respectively , we find $\Delta(S) \neq 0$.

Thus, each of the above three conditions can give the full rejection to the disturbance U.

In fact, they are identical with (2-12-6), (2-12-7) and (2-12-8).

The latter method sometimes is called as the application of the Principle of Invariance.

CHAPTER THREE

DIFFICULTY OF ANALYSIS OF MULTIVARIABLE COUPLED SYSTEMS

§ 3-1 Introduction

Heuristic discussion on the full rejection design to the disturbances for a single variable process control system was given in the last
chapter. The essentiality of this problem is to demand that the system
output be only related to the reference and independent of the disturbances. This also means that there is no coupling effect between the disturbances and the output, so it is a decoupling design problem indeed.

The analysis of the last chapter denotes if we want to get the result of full rejection to disturbances, then some necessary measures
must be adopted, i.e. the rejection design should be taken. The general
structure of such a system is the combination of feedforward control with
feedback control .

Now, we discuss the multivariable processes. A multivariable process
contains several outputs and for process control systems, these outputs
may be measured and influenced or controlled by other variables. Therefore, there must be several channels or loops in such a system.

If the action of a loop can cause a response in another loop, then
we say that coupling exists. The degree of coupling of a system can be
determined by the influence of each other.

In many cases, the coupling of different loops makes the control be
a difficult problem and, in general, in process control systems, a decoupling control is expected.

Why should we realize the decoupling control?

General speaking, it is due to the following reasons:

(1) We have said before that because of the existence of coupling,
the control always becomes a difficult problem,

(2) For a system with coupling, its loops can not be considered separately and the parameter setting must be done many times in order to

get satisfactory results. In fact, in many cases, it is very difficult
to get satisfactory results,

(3) The information and knowledge for the analysis and the design
of a coupling system are much more than those needed for a decoupled
system. For example, for a system with coupling, the coupling degree
of some output with some non-corresponding input should be analyzed
and estimated in order to keep the coupling result not beyond the allowable limit , but for a decoupled system, this analysis is not necessary,

(4) For a decoupled system, it can be designed by standard conventional methods, but for coupling systems, up to now there is no simple
universal design method. Especially, when the number of variables is
large, it is difficult to design in practice,

(5) The parameters of the loops of a decoupled system can be set
on-line, i.e. can be set in closed-loop situation; but for a coupling
system, it can not be set on-line,

(6) Without doubt, the harmful coupling effects are strikingly
weakened by decoupling design.

Thus, for MPCS the decoupling design is always adopted, but, however, some decoupling measures must be taken here and, as a consequence,
some equipments and investment are needed, so the final decision of
adopting decoupling design or not should be determined according to
the practical conditions.

Comparing with the disturbance-rejection design of single variable
systems, the analysis of MPCS, especially the decoupling analysis of
MPCS, has some special characters:

(1) At first, in MPCS, there are several input variables and output variables, so is the channel number. Therefore,in general it is
difficult to analyze such a system by simple transfer function calculation and the transfer function matrices should be adopted,

(2) There are two kinds of coupling cases in MPCS. The first is the coupling between outputs and references and the other is the coupling between outputs and disturbances. Consequently, there are three kinds of decoupled systems: The first is the system with outputs decoupled to the references; the second is the system with outputs decoupled to the disturbances and the third is the system with outputs decoupled to both of them, i.e. the full decoupled system.

(3) For MPCS, the plants may be P-canonical or V-canonical and there is no such a problem in single variable systems,

(4) For single variable systems, even the full rejection design to disturbances is not carried out, they can be analyzed and synthesised by conventional methods, but for MPCS, in many cases(not all, certainly) if the decoupling design were not carried out, it would be quite diffi-cult to analyze and to synthesise them by conventional methods,

(5) We have learnt in the analysis of single variable systems that the full rejection design to disturbances can be realized by either feedfor-ward compensation or feedback compensation(state variable feedback). In other words, the solution of disturbance-rejection design is not unique and this problem is more prominent in the decoupling design of MPCS, i.e. both feedforward and feedback can be used to realize decoupling design. Furthermore, even in feedforward decoupling systems or in feedback decoup-ling systems, there may be different structures available. That means that the solution of decoupling design in MPCS is with uncertainty.

(6) In single variable systems, we have seen that for the disturbance-rejection design, the feedback compensation is with some advantages over the feedforward compensation and how about the case of the decoupling de-sign in MPCS?

This is a very important problem. The analysis of it results in an important idea, i.e. the Mesarović idea. This idea can not be explained by a few words and we will discuss it in detail later on,

(7) Because the transfer function matrices are used, the meaning of decoupling design is very explicit mathematically.

Suppose : A is the system output vector (n-dimensional),

B is the system input vector (n-dimensional),

G is the system transmission matrix (nxn, non-singular)

and:

$$A = GB$$

then the condition for realizing decoupling is: G is a diagonal matrix.

The so-called " Diagonal Matrix Method" means to take some measures (design) to keep G being a diagonal matrix. In addition, we can also demand that the elements on the diagonal be some special forms. The diagonal matrix method is the basic and the most popular decoupling design method indeed, but, however, it is not the unique method.

Essentially, this is a frequency method since all analysis and design procedures are based on the transfer functions.

It seems that this method is very simple. In fact, to let G be a diagonal matrix is only a principle and there are many practical problems associated with it in different system design. Since Boksenbom, Hood and Tsien proposed this idea twenty years ago, this principle has been used widely and successfully to solve a lot of practical control problems and now we can say that by this principle, a systematic and successful theory has been formed.

We will give a discussion on this theory in detail in this book and we will believe that twenty years ago it might be a sophisticated design method but now it has been developed to be a systematic theory.

§ 3-2 The Difficulty of Analysis of Systems with Coupled Plants

For a MPCS, each input of it is related to each ouput in general and if we want to realize non-interaction control, i.e. each input influences only one output and vice versa, then decoupling design is necessary.

If we did not do decoupling design, how would the case be ?

In a MPCS, although there are interaction channels in it, for each reference or input, it has a basic or intrinsical channel by which this input gives the desired influence on some output and this is so-called " Pairing" . The determination of reasonable pairing relations among different variables is a very important problem in multivariable process control system design and we will give a discussion on this problem in detail in Chapter 7.

Now, suppose that the pairing relations have been determined, i.e. the basic channels have been determined, then all connections among these basic channels become coupling channels.

The meaning of decoupling design is to eliminate the effects caused by these coupling channels. Certainly, some necessary measures must be adopted and effcte design methods should be researched and all of these are just the main contents of our book.

If we do not do the decoupling design , then we have to analyze the system as follows:

(1) Imagine that all coupling channels would not exist and break off all coupling channels.Then the system can be designed by its basic channels.

(2) Give the recognition of the existence of coupling channels and do not break them off either. Then try to expand this system on the base of some basic channel. When some basic channel is considered, the other coupling channels will also be concluded in the analysis and all other inputs become the disturbances of this basic channel.

Certainly, the first method is very simple but it is unreasonable. In some special cases, perhaps , we have to do so, namely at first we de-

sign the system without consideration of the coupling channels and then
we measure the influence of coupling effects practically . If the results are not beyond the allowable limits, then the design is available.

The second method is rational, but in general it is very difficult.

In order to explain it, we discuss the simplest two-variable system
shown in Fig 3-2-1.

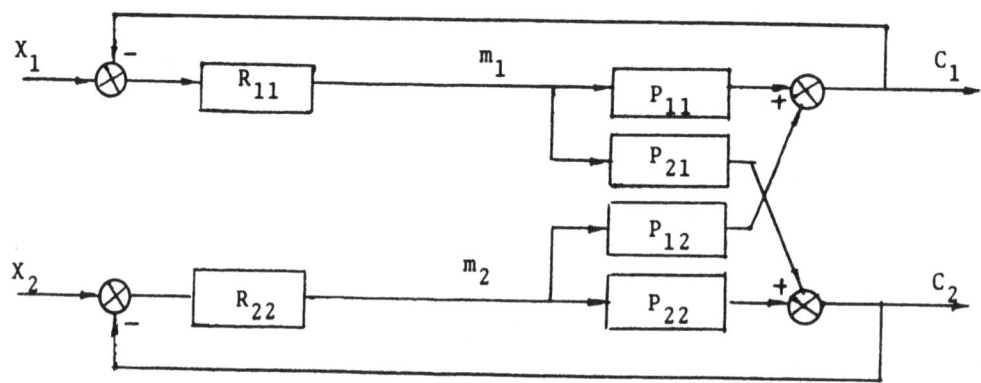

Fig 3-2-1

For this system, we can get:

$$\left.\begin{array}{l} C_1 = P_{11}m_1 + P_{12}m_2 \\ C_2 = P_{21}m_1 + P_{22}m_2 \end{array}\right\} \qquad (3-2-1)$$

and:

$$\left.\begin{array}{l} m_1 = R_{11}(X_1 - C_1) \\ m_2 = R_{22}(X_2 - C_2) \end{array}\right\} \qquad (3-2-2)$$

Eliminating m_1 and m_2 , we get:

$$\left.\begin{array}{l} C_1 = G_{11}X_1 + G_{12}X_2 \\ C_2 = G_{21}X_1 + G_{22}X_2 \end{array}\right\} \qquad (3-2-3)$$

Where:

$$G_{11} = \frac{(1 + R_{22}P_{22})R_{11}P_{11} - R_{11}R_{22}P_{12}P_{21}}{(1+ R_{11}P_{11})(1+ R_{22}P_{22}) - R_{11}R_{22}P_{12}P_{21}} \qquad (3-2-4)$$

$$G_{12} = \frac{P_{12}R_{22}}{(1+ R_{11}P_{11})(1+ R_{22}P_{22}) - R_{11}R_{22}P_{12}P_{21}} \qquad (3-2-5)$$

$$G_{21} = \frac{P_{21}R_{11}}{(1+ R_{11}P_{11})(1+ R_{22}P_{22}) - R_{11}R_{22}P_{12}P_{21}} \qquad (3\text{-}2\text{-}6)$$

$$G_{22} = \frac{(1 + R_{11}P_{11})R_{22}P_{22} - R_{11}R_{22}P_{12}P_{21}}{(1+ R_{11}P_{11})(1+ R_{22}P_{22}) - R_{11}R_{22}P_{12}P_{21}} \qquad (3\text{-}2\text{-}7)$$

In special case, when $P_{12} = P_{21} = 0$, then:

$$\left. \begin{aligned} G_{11} &= \frac{P_{11}R_{11}}{1 + P_{11}R_{11}} \\[2ex] G_{22} &= \frac{P_{22}R_{22}}{1 + P_{22}R_{22}} \\[2ex] G_{12} &= G_{21} = 0 \end{aligned} \right\} \qquad (3\text{-}2\text{-}8)$$

When $P_{12} = 0$ but $P_{21} \neq 0$, i.e. unilateral coupling exists, then:

$$\left. \begin{aligned} G_{11} &= \frac{P_{11}R_{11}}{1 + R_{11}P_{11}} \\[2ex] G_{12} &= 0 \\[2ex] G_{21} &= \frac{R_{11}P_{21}}{(1 + R_{11}P_{11})(1+ R_{22}P_{22})} \\[2ex] G_{22} &= \frac{R_{22}P_{22}}{1 + R_{22}P_{22}} \end{aligned} \right\} \qquad (3\text{-}2\text{-}9)$$

Thus, for the output C_2, the system characteristic equation is :

$$(1 + R_{11}P_{11})(1 + R_{22}P_{22}) = 0 \qquad (3\text{-}2\text{-}10)$$

Therefore, only when both individual single variable systems are stable, then C_2 would be stable.

For (3-2-4) to (3-2-7), the system characteristic equation is:

$$(1 + R_{11}P_{11})(1 + R_{22}P_{22}) - R_{11}R_{22}P_{12}P_{21} = 0 \qquad (3\text{-}2\text{-}11)$$

and the system stability is determined by the roots of this equation.

Notice that equation (3-2-11) is different from (3-2-10). That means when both P_{12} and P_{21} exist, even two basic channels are stable, the whole coupled system may be unstable.

Equation (3-2-11) is corresponding to:

$$1 + W' = 1 + R_{11}P_{11} + R_{22}P_{22} + R_{11}R_{22}(P_{11}P_{22} - P_{12}P_{21}) = 0 \quad (3\text{-}2\text{-}12)$$

Where, W' is the equivalent open loop character. It is:

$$W' = R_{11}P_{11} + R_{22}P_{22} + R_{11}R_{22}(P_{11}P_{22} - P_{12}P_{21}) \quad (3\text{-}2\text{-}13)$$

This form in general is difficult to be expressed by either Nyquist diagram or Bode plots and so is difficult to be analyzed.

For explicity, the channel $X_1 \longrightarrow C_1$ now can be expressed as:

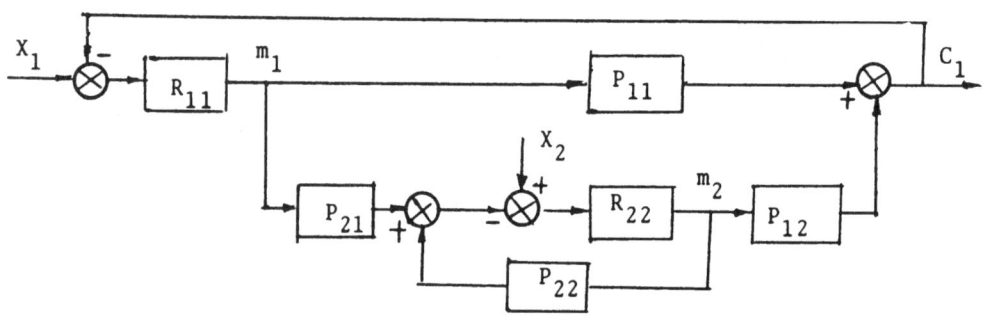

Fig 3-2-2

Obviously, this channel is more complicated than the basic channel. The input X_2 becomes a disturbance of this channel.

If we let $X_2 = 0$, then we can get the equivalent plant character of this channel:

$$W_1(S) = \frac{C(S)}{m_1(S)} = P_{11}\left(1 - \frac{P_{12}P_{21}}{P_{11}P_{22}} \cdot \frac{R_{22}P_{22}}{1 + R_{22}P_{22}}\right) \quad (3\text{-}2\text{-}14)$$

Therefore, the equivalent plant character $W_1(S)$ is more complica-ted than $P_{11}(S)$ and is related to all coupling channels and the other basic channel.

The two variable control system is the simplest multivariable control system and from the above analysis we can know:

(1) It is not easy to transfer Fig 3-2-1 into Fig 3-2-2. In fact, there is only a loop in the plant, namely $P_{12}P_{11} \longrightarrow P_{21}P_{22}$, so the Fig 3-2-1 can be expanded into Fig 3-2-2, when the number of varia-bles is larger than 2, it is impossible to do so.

For example, for a P-canonical plant with three variables, there are five loops in the plant, namely:

$$P_{12}P_{11} \longrightarrow P_{21}P_{22}$$
$$P_{23}P_{22} \longrightarrow P_{32}P_{3}$$
$$P_{31}P_{33} \longrightarrow P_{13}P_{11}$$
$$P_{21}P_{22} \longrightarrow P_{32}P_{33} \longrightarrow P_{13}P_{11}$$
$$P_{12}P_{11} \longrightarrow P_{31}P_{33} \longrightarrow P_{23}P_{22}$$

and for a plant with four variables, there are 20 loops in the plant.

In general, the number of loops in a plant with different variables is shown below:[5]

Number of Variables	Number of Loops in the Plant
2	1
3	5
4	20
5	84
6	409
7	2365
8	16064
9	125664
10	1112073

Thus, in fact, when the number of variables is larger than 2, it is impossible to expand the system into a single loop form.

(2) The equivalent open loop plant character $W_1(S)$, if we can get, is with very complex form and it is difficult to be analyzed by Nyquist diagam, Bode plots or root-locus method,

(3) Certainly, it will be more difficult to analyze the influence of the disturbance X_2.

Therefore, the second method may be available theoretically, but for systems with more than two variables, it is impossible to be used in practice.

That means that in order to analyze multivariable process control systems, decoupling design is necessary.

A MPCS without decoupling is difficult not only to be analyzed , but also to be operated.[17]

Taking a two-variable system as an example, we can show its general form in Fig 3-2-3.

For this system, we have not do decoupling design and P is a 2x2 matrix . R and F both are diagonal matrices of order 2.

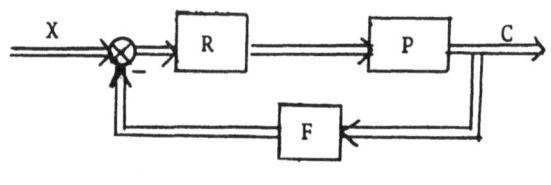

Fig 3-2-3

Certainly, a system without decoupling can also operate. It may have a stable operation within some allowable parameter scope, but its stable operation is always with boundary restrictions and the boundary is related to the elements f_{11} and f_{22} of the feedback matrix F. For example, we can get a rectangular area in the $f_{11} - f_{22}$ plane. When both f_{11} and f_{22} are in this area, the system is stable, but in practice only negative feedback is used, so only the shaded area in this figure is available and the adjustments of both f_{11} and f_{22} should not be beyound this area.

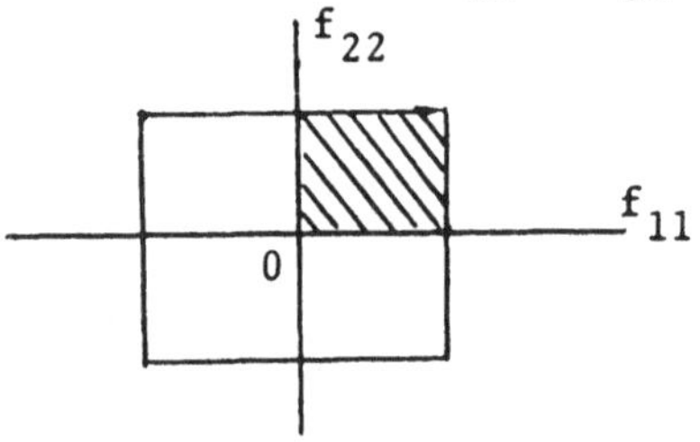

Fig 3-2-4

But, for a two-variable system, the characters of two basic channels in general are different. Suppose that one of them is a conditional stable system, for example channel 1. Then, for smaller f_{11}, channel 1 is stable and when f_{11} becomes larger, it falls in unstable state and will be stable again when f_{11} becomes much larger.

In such a case, for the two-variable system, the stable region is shown in Fig 3-2-5.

We can know that the adjustment of f_{11} should jump over a district and certainly this will bring difficulty for the operation.

But, however, this is not
the worst case since   the
stable region is still regular.

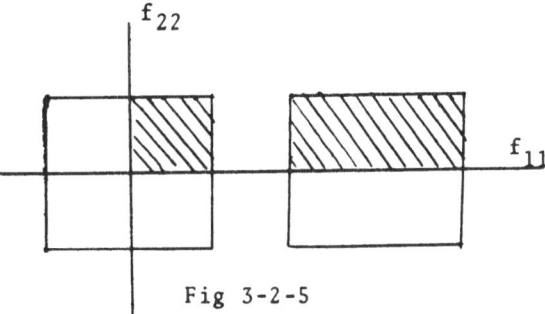

Fig 3-2-5

There may be another case
and in this case the stability
analysis will be more difficult.

For example, the stable region may be not a rectangular area but
an area as shown in Fig 3-2-6.

In such a case, we see that even in the stable region, the change of
f_{11} must be carried out with that of f_{22} at a meantime. For instance,
at the two points A and B, f_{11} is
with different values and the corresponding allowable values of f_{22}
are also different. When $f_{11} = 0$,
f_{22} may vary from 0 to its maximum
value f_{22m} , but as the increase of
f_{11} , the allowable maximum value

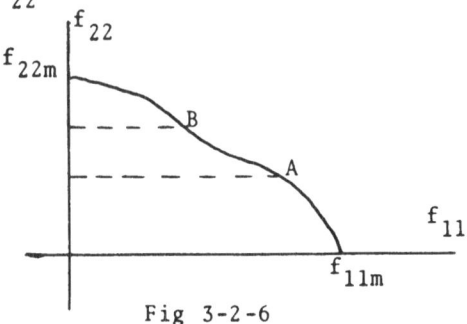

Fig 3-2-6

of f_{22} decreases more and more. That means that the stability is weaken.
When f_{11} reaches its maximum value f_{11m}, it is impossible to find a f_{22}
to have a stable operation. Therefore, in such a case, the system operation is very difficult, for any adjustment of f_{11} or f_{22} should consider
the bond relation between the two.

But,this is not the worst case yet. The worest case is shown in Fig3-2-7.

In this figure, at the point A, where the feedback coefficients for
both channels are f_{11a} and f_{22a}, respectively, the system is stable.

If the system works at this point and everything is in order then, certainly, the situation is available.

But, this stable region denotes if anyone of these two feedback coefficients changes to zero, then the system will soon become unstable.

And this case may occur in practice. f_{11} and f_{22} here represent two feedback elements in these two basic channels, but the measurement elements may fail in normal operation sometimes in practice; furthermore, any channel may be stopped for some reasons. Both the above

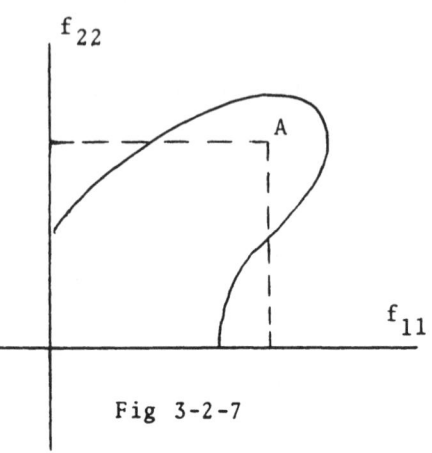

Fig 3-2-7

cases are corresponding to one of these two feedback coefficients being zero and , by Fig 3-2-7, the whole system can not work then.

Certainly, this operation state is not secure and therefore is not desirable.

Consequently, for a system with coupled plant, if we do not carry out the decoupling design, then not only the analysis and design are difficult, but also the operation is not secure.

We have shown that for a multivariable pricess control system, if it is not decoupled, then both the analysis and operation will be difficult. Certainly, the practical difficulties are different for different systems but the above conclusions are always valid. We do not say that it is impossible to analyze a coupled system , but, in general, only some simple cases of coupled systems can be analyzed and designed analytically.

In this chapter, some special cases of coupled systems are discussed and then some general conclusions will be given.

§ 3-3 The Analysis Difficulty of Systems with Coupled Manipulated

Variables

Now, we analyze a system with coupled manipulated variables.

Such a system with two symmetrical variables is shown in Fig 3-3-1.

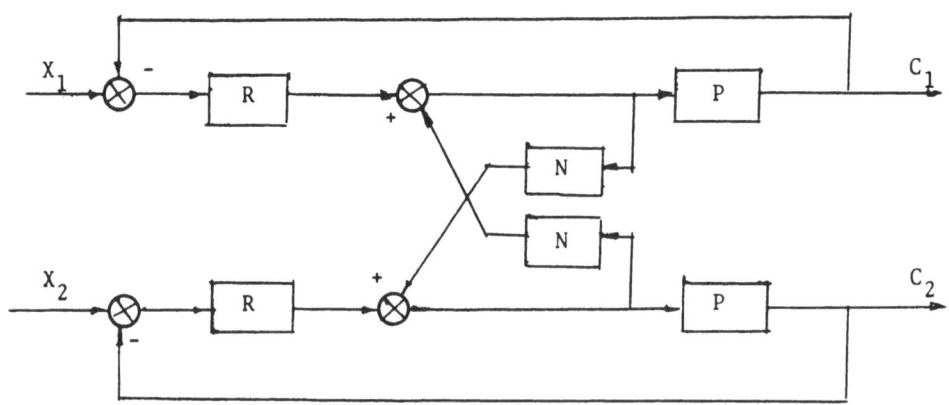

Fig 3-3-1

The basic relation of this system was given in § 1-8 as:

$$\begin{pmatrix} C_1 \\ C_2 \end{pmatrix} = \begin{pmatrix} 1+W & N \\ N & 1+W \end{pmatrix} \begin{pmatrix} X_1 \\ X_2 \end{pmatrix} \frac{W}{(1+W)^2 - N^2}$$
(3-3-1)

where:

$$W = RP$$
(3-3-2)

This is a system without decoupling. When $X_1 = X_2$, the situation

becomes very simple. As pointed out in § 1-8, it can be transferred

into two separate single loop systems then:

$$\frac{C_1}{X_1} = \frac{W}{1+W-N}$$
(3-3-3)

$$\frac{C_2}{X_2} = \frac{W}{1+W-N}$$
(3-3-4)

We must know that this result is obtained merely due to system

symmetry and it is not a decoupling system.

In general, X_1 and X_2 may be different and in such a case this

system is no longer able to be transferred into two single separate

loops and we must research the general formula (3-3-1).

Now, we discuss the stability problem of this system.

In order to discuss stability, we should research the poles of system transfer function.

Now, we prove that the poles of the system transfer function are the zeros of the polynomial $(1 + W)^2 - N^2$.

We let:

$$W = \frac{Z_W(S)}{D_W(S)}$$
$$N = \frac{Z_N(S)}{D_N(S)} \Biggr\}$$

$$(3-3-5)$$

then:

$$C_1 = \frac{X_1 \frac{Z_W}{D_W} (1 + \frac{Z_W}{D_W}) + X_2 \frac{Z_W Z_N}{D_W D_N}}{(1 + \frac{Z_W}{D_W})^2 - \{ \frac{Z_N}{D_N})^2}$$

$$(3-3-6)$$

Expanding yields:

$$C_1 = \frac{X_1 Z_W(D_W + Z_W)D_N^2 + X_2 Z_W Z_N D_W D_N}{(D_W + Z_W)^2 D_N^2 - Z_N^2 D_W^2}$$

$$(3-3-7)$$

But the zeros of $(D_W + Z_W)^2 D_N^2 - Z_N^2 D_W^2$ are just those of $(1+W)^2 - N^2$, so it means that the poles of C_1 are the zeros of $(1+W)^2 - N^2$.

Therefore, in order to research the stability of the system, we may research the distribution of the zeros of $(1+W)^2 - N^2$. Because:

$$(1 + W)^2 - N^2 = 1 + (2W + W^2 - N^2) \qquad (3-3-8)$$

so letting $S = jw$ and drawing the Nyquist diagram for $2W + W^2 - N^2$, we can check the stability of the system.

Obviously, the Nyquist diagram of $2W + W^2 - N^2$ is difficult to be drawn, so the analysis is not easy to be done.

But, for:

$$(1 + W)^2 - N^2 = (1 + W + N)(1 + W - N) \qquad (3-3-9)$$

so the stability research may be transferred into researching the following two equations:

$$1 + W + N = 0$$
$$1 + W - N = 0$$
(3-3-10)

The steps for determination of system stability are:

(1) Draw $W(jw)$ and $N(jw)$ in the complex plane,

(2) Draw curves of $W(jw)+N(jw)$ and $W(jw)-N(jw)$,

(3) By Nyquist criteria, we can judge the stability of $1+ W + N = 0$ and $1 + W - N = 0$,

(4) If both of (3-3-10) are stable, then the original system is stable; if anyone of the two is unstable, then the original coupled system is unstable.

We discuss an example.

The system under considerartion is shown in Fig 3-3-2.

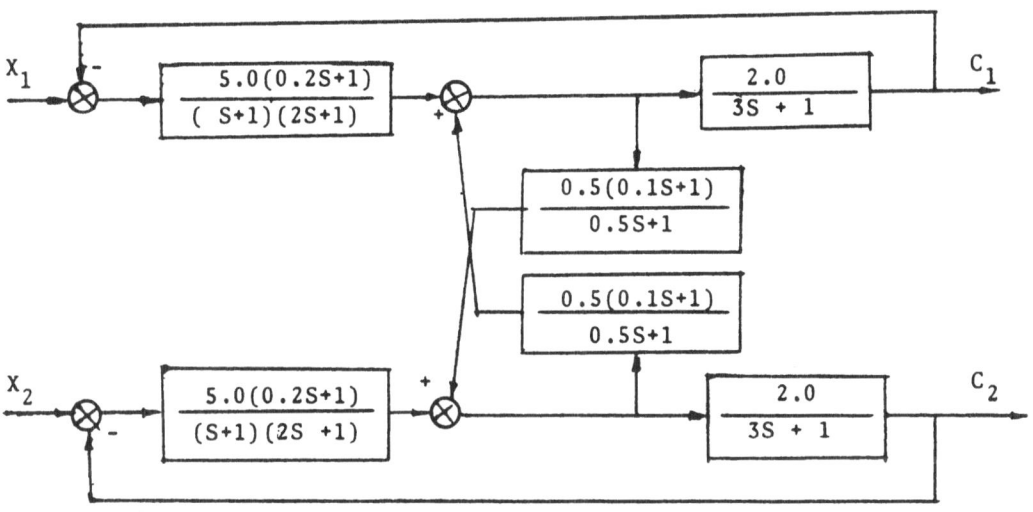

Fig 3-3-2

From this figure, we get:

$$W(S) = \frac{5.0(0.2S+ 1)}{(S+ 1)(2S+1)} \cdot \frac{2.0}{3S+ 1} = \frac{10.0(0.2S+1)}{(S+1)(2S+1)(3S+1)}$$

$$N(S) = \frac{0.5(0.1S+1)}{0.5S + 1}$$

In the complex plane, we can draw W(jw) and N(jw) as shown in Fig 3-3-3.

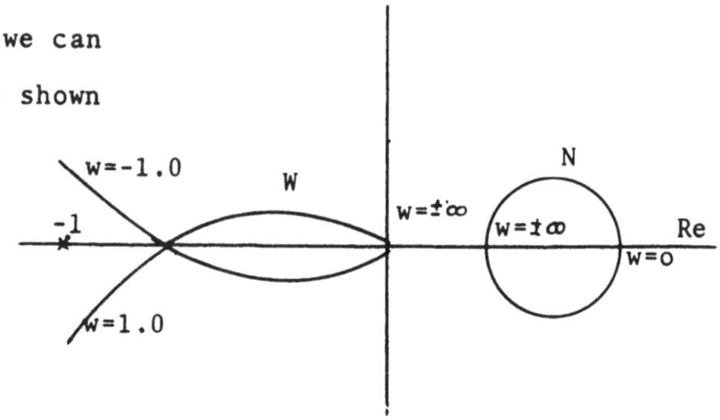

Then we draw the curves of W-N and W+N as shown in Fig 3-3-4 and Fig 3-3-s.

From these figures we can know that the system $1 + W + N = 0$ is stable, but the system $1 + W - N = 0$ is unstable.

Therefore, the whole system is unstable.

If the decoupling design is done and the decoupled system is with the original basic channel model, then from Fig 3-3-3 we can see that it is stable.

So, it means that the coupling makes two stable systems into an unstable system.

Therefore, decoupling design is necessary.

In addition, we see that the analysis of a coupled system must be done according to two steps, so it is not easy.

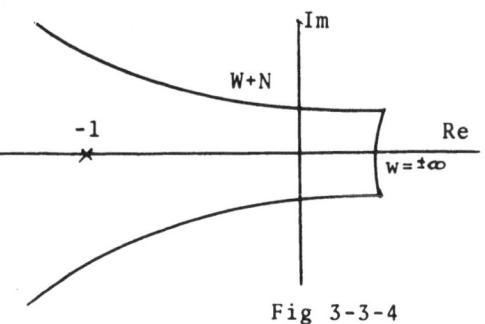

Fig 3-3-3

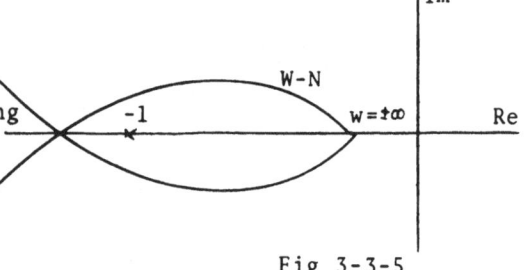

Fig 3-3-4

Fig 3-3-5

§ 3-4 The Coupling Influence and Disturbances

The above analysis denotes that for a coupled system, no matter with a coupled plant or with coupled manipulated variables, the analysis and design are very difficult due to the existence of the coupling.

In addition, from the above analysis we can know that the coupling channels can not be simply considered as the disturbance inputs for separate basic channels. As well-known, the existence of disturbances gives no influence on the stability of single variable control systems (certainly, here we suppose that no cancellation of cascade compensation zeros with the unstable poles of the plants is used in the design).

But, for a multivariable control system with coupling, the above analysis shows that a system with two stable basic channels may be unstable due to the existence of coupled manipulated variables, the coupling channels for any basic channel are not equal to disturbance channels.

On the other hand, when we analyze a basic channel, the disturbances and the reference of the other channels should be considered as the disturbances of the channel considered.

Now, we discuss an example. This example is a boiler control system. It is shown in Fig 3-4-1.

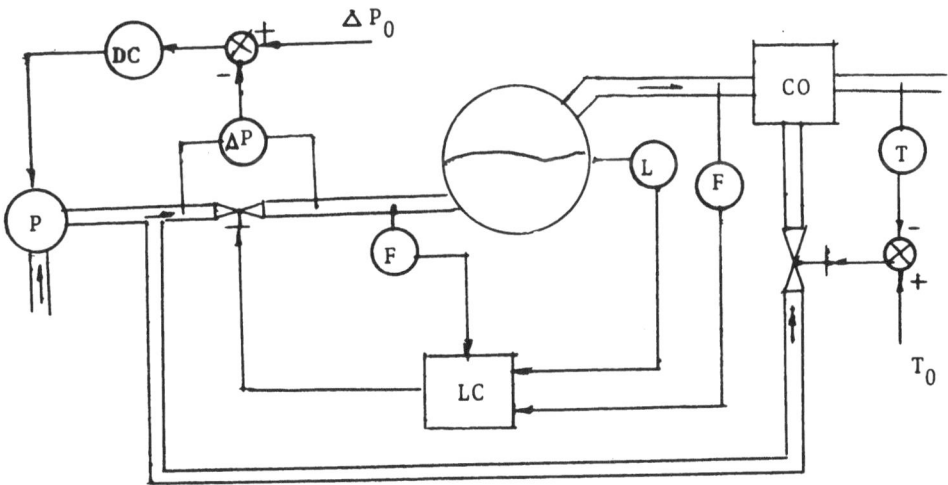

Fig 3-4-1

In this system, fed water is determined by the stroke of the valve and the difference between the output pressure of the pump and that of the boiler drum. When there is a variation of steam flow and it results in a variation of fed water, so the stroke of valve 1 will change but this change causes not only a variation of fed water, but also a variation of pressure drop across the valve. At the meantime, the cooling water for the output steam is also fed by the same pump and by such a way the temperature of the steam led to the turbine is controlled. Thus, the variation of the pressure drop across the valve becomes a harmful influence on the steam temperature control.

Similarly, any change in the steam temperature control system , for example the change of the stroke of valve 2,can cause the variation of the pressure drop across valve 1 and consequently it is a disturbance of the level control system of the bolier drum.

In this figure:

ΔP_0 is the reference of the pressure drop across valve 1,

ΔP is the measurement of the pressure drop,

DC is the rotation speed regulator,

LC is the level regulator of the boiler,

T_0 is the reference of the turbine steam temperature,

CO is the steam cooler,

P is the pump.

In order to overcome the influence of disturbances, the rotation speed of the pump should be controlled to keep the pressure drop across valve 1 being constant and, consequently, a constant pressure can be held for both level regulation and steam temperature regulation.

The pressure drop is measured by a pressure sensor and its output is compared with the reference and the difference between the two is used to control the rotation speed of the pump.

But, the introduction of the pressure control system causes new

coupling.   This coupling takes place between the bolier level control
system and the pressure difference control system. Both feeding valve 1
and the pump are the important parts of these two system simultaneously
and any change of the valve stroke causes not only the variation of fed
water , but also the variation of the pressure drop across the valve;
similarly, any change of pump rotation speed causes not only the variation
of the pressure drop across the valve , but also the variation of the
flow through it.   Then, the coupling is formed.

The block diagram of such a system is shown in Fig 3-4-2.

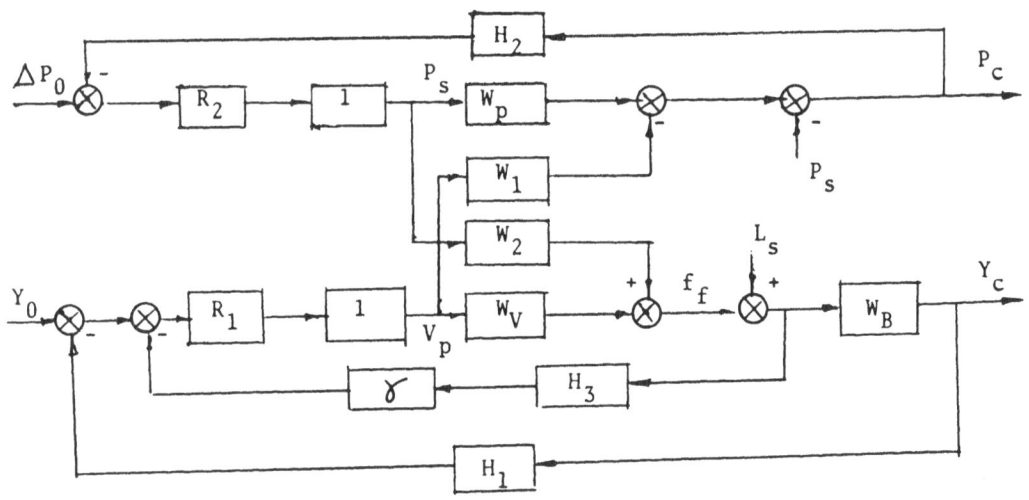

Fig 3-4-2

In this system, the upper part is the pressure drop control system
and the pump speed is control by the difference between ΔP_0 and P_C. We
suppose   that 1% of the change of the regulator output causes 1% of the
change of pump speed. In the figure, P_S is the pump speed.

The lower part of this system is familiar to us and we have discussed it in § 2-5 as a single variable system.

In this system, the relation betweem V_p (the valve stroke position)
and the regulator output is also assumed to be 1. Notice that the coupling is caused by P_S and V_p.

The coupling channels are expressed by W_1 and W_2. Notice that the coupling channel W_1 is with negative coupling result. That means that the larger the valve stroke, the smaller the pressure drop across it.

There are disturbances in both systems.

Now, we discuss the influence of disturbances.

We have said that for a coupled system, it is impossible simply to consider it as two separate independent loops.

In order to explain it, we discuss the lower part of this system.

In general, in a single variable system, the valve character can be considerd as either a propotional element or an element with first lag. Both approximations will not cause serious error. Now, in the case of existence of coupling, especially the coupling just takes place at the two sides of this element, can we still do so?

Now, the change of valve stroke gives influence on the fed water not only through W_V, but also through $W_1 \rightarrow$ the control loop of pressure drop $\rightarrow W_2$. Thus, the character of the pressure drop control system makes the relation between the valve stroke and fed water flow be very complicated. Similarly, the character of the flow control system makes the relation between P_s and output pressure of the pump be very complicated. We have mentioned this problem theoretically in § 3-2 and now we can see more clearly from this example.

By Fig 3-4-2, the relation between V_p and f_f can be drawn as shown in Fig 3-4-3.

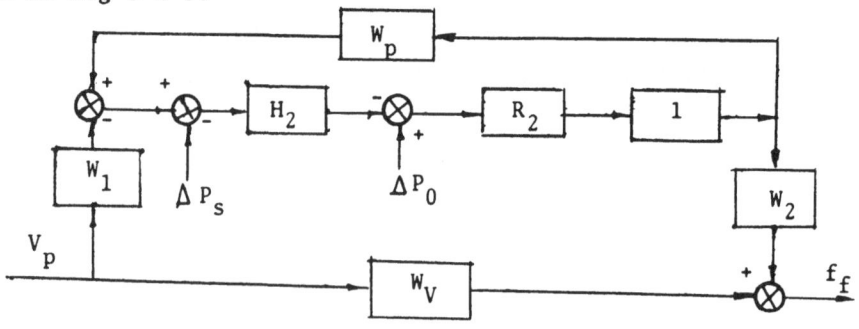

Fig 3-4-3

From this figure, when $\Delta P_s = \Delta P_0 = 0$, we get:

$$\frac{f_f}{V_p} = W_V + W_1 \frac{H_2 R_2}{1 + H_2 R_2 W_p} W_2 \qquad (3-4-1)$$

Obviously, the character of the valve becomes very complicated and it makes the analysis of the level control system be very difficult.

Only when $|W_1|$ and $|W_2|$ are much less than $|W_V|$, then the valve character approximates that of the original single variable loop.

Just like ΔP_s, the reference of pressure drop ΔP_0 becomes a disturbance of level control system. When these two disturbances are considered, the f_f is:

$$f_f = (W_V + W_1 \frac{H_2 R_2}{1 + H_2 R_2 W_p}) V_p + \frac{W_2 R_2}{1 + H_2 R_2 W_p} \Delta P_0 + \frac{W_2 R_2 H_2}{1 + H_2 R_2 W_p} \Delta P_s$$

$$(3-4-2)$$

So, the influence of both ΔP_0 and ΔP_s is weakened by the factor $\frac{1}{1 + H_2 R_2 W_p}$, and the less the $|W_2 R_2|$, the less the influence of the disturbances. Thus, reducing $|R_2|$ or $|W_2|$ is available.

From this example, we can know the reasons why for a coupled system, we can not neglect the coupling channels freely:

(1) The relation between V_p and f_f has been changed and, consequently, the dynamic analysis will change,

(2) The reference and disturbances of the other loop will exist in the expanded loop as distrbances but the import channels of these disturbances are related to the character of the other loop.

Notice that the emergence of these disturbances is not related to W_1 and W_V. This example is also taken from the British broadcasitng course.

Therefore, we know that the existence of coupling channels is not simply equal to the existence of disturbances. It changes the dynamic character of the system. But the reference and disturbances of the other channel are disturbances for the channel considered essentially.

§ 3-5 Singular Coupled Systems [5]

The analysis of § 3-2 denotes that the characteristic equation for the system of two variables shown in Fig 3-2-1 is:

$$Q = 1 + W' = 1 + R_{11}P_{11} + R_{22}P_{22} + R_{11}R_{22} \, (\, P_{11}P_{22} - P_{12}P_{21}) = 0$$

$$(3-5-1)$$

We have pointed out that in general this equation is difficult to be analyzed since it has many terms and so is very complicated.

Now, we discuss two special cases, namely the singular coupled systems and the symmetric coupled systems.

Notice:

$$\left| P(S) \right| = P_{11}P_{22} - P_{12}P_{21}$$

$$(3-5-2)$$

therefore, equation (3-5-1) may be written as:

$$Q = 1 + R_{11}P_{11} + R_{22}P_{22} + R_{11}R_{22} \left| P \right| = 0$$

$$(3-5-3)$$

From (3-5-2), we get:

$$\left| P(S) \right| = P_{11}P_{22} - P_{12}P_{21} = P_{11}P_{22}(\, 1 - \frac{P_{12}P_{21}}{P_{11}P_{22}})$$

$$(3-5-4)$$

Now, we express each transfer function in rational fraction:

$$P_{ij}(S) = \frac{Z_{ij}(S)}{N_{ij}(S)}$$

$$(3-5-5)$$

then (3-5-4) may be written as:

$$\left| P(S) \right| = \frac{Z_{11}Z_{22}N_{12}N_{21} - Z_{12}Z_{21}N_{11}N_{22}}{N_{11}N_{22}N_{12}N_{21}}$$

$$(3-5-6)$$

The so-called singular coupled system means that:

$$\left| P(S) \right| = 0$$

$$(3-5-7)$$

and the system characteristic equation becomes:

$$Q(S) = 1 + R_{11}P_{11} + R_{22}P_{22} = 1 + \frac{Z_{1R}Z_{11}}{N_{1R}N_{11}} + \frac{Z_{2R}Z_{22}}{N_{2R}N_{22}} = 0$$

$$(3-5-8)$$

It is equal to:

$$Q(S) = N_{1R}N_{2R}N_{11}N_{22} + N_{2R}N_{22}Z_{1R}Z_{11} + N_{1R}N_{11}Z_{2R}Z_{22} = 0 \qquad (3\text{-}5\text{-}10)$$

From this equation we can know if both regulators are integral regulators, then both N_{1R} and N_{2R} have a zero at $S = 0$. It corresponds to that $Q(S)$ at least has a zero at $S = 0$. Thus, this system is unstable.

(3-5-9) may be written as:

$$Q(S) = 1 + \frac{Z_{1R}Z_{11}}{N_{1R}N_{11}}\left(1 + \frac{Z_{2R}Z_{22}N_{1R}N_{11}}{Z_{1R}Z_{11}N_{2R}N_{22}} \right) = 0 \qquad (3\text{-}5\text{-}11)$$

We see that $Q(S)$ is with the following form:

$$Q(S) = 1 + F(1 + F_1) = 0 \qquad (3\text{-}5\text{-}12)$$

For such a system, if we want to analyze its characters, we may analyze its root locus. But the root locus can not be obtained directly and we can get it by two steps. At first, we let:

$$Q_1 = 1 + F_1 \qquad (3\text{-}5\text{-}13)$$

By the zeros, poles and the gains of F_1, we can draw the locus expressing the relations between the zeros of Q_1 and the gains of F_1 and this is the first set of root loci.

The gains of F_1 may be given and from the first root locus some points may be determined.

Notice that the zeros of Q_1 are also the zeros of $F(1+F_1)$ and the poles of F_1 are also the poles of $F(1+F_1)$, therefore, from the known zeros of F and Q_1 and the poles of F and F_1 we can draw the second set of root loci for Q. This is also the final root locus of this system.

So , we see that during the analysis, the coupling elements need not be considered but , at the meantime, we can not analyze this system by two separate main channels. That means although the characters of coupling channels do not express themselves in the analysis, it does not mean that they do not exist.

We consider an example. Let:

$$R_{11} = K_1 , \qquad R_{22} = \frac{K_2}{S}$$

$$P_{11}(S) = \frac{1}{S + a_1} \qquad P_{22}(S) = \frac{1}{(S+a_2)(S+b_2)(S+c_2)}$$

and:

$$P(S) = P_{11}P_{22} - P_{12}P_{21} = 0$$

Thus, the characters of coupling channels can be neglected in the analysis and from (3-5-12), the characteristic equation for this system is:

$$1 + \frac{K_1}{S + a_1} \left(1 + \frac{K_2}{K_1} \frac{S+a_1}{S(S+a_2)(S+b_2)(S+c_2)} \right) = 0$$

Now, we draw the first set of root loci. We let:

$$Q_1 = 1 + \frac{K_2}{K_1} \frac{S + a_1}{S(S+a_2)(S+b_2)(S+c_2)}$$

Because the zero of F_1, $-a_1$, and the poles, $(0, -a_2, -b_2, -c_2)$, are known, so it is not difficult to draw the root loci of Q_1 with the parameter K_2/K_1. These loci are shown in Fig 3-5-1.

When the value of K_2/K_1 becomes very large, the loci will extend to the right S plane and $Q_1 = 0$ becomes unstable. Certainly, this is not expected, thus K_2/K_1 should not be too large.

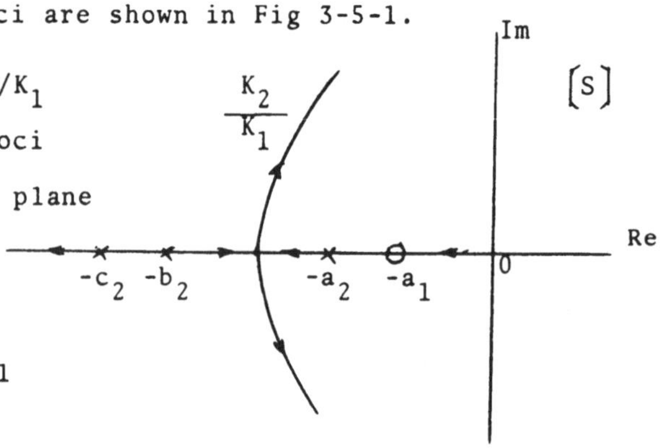

Fig 3-5-1

Therefore, a suitable value of K_2/K_1 can be given to make all root loci of Q_1 be in the left S plane. When the values of K_2/K_1 are given, the zeros of Q_1 are determined and they are also the zeros of $F(1+F_1)$.

Then, from the zeros of F and F_1 and the poles of F and F_1, we can dwaw the final root loci as shown in Fig 3-5-2.

In this figure, z_1, z_2, z_3 and z_4 are zeros determined from

Fig 3-5-1 by given value of K_2/K_1.

These root loci are with the parameter K_1.

Thus, by the dynamic demands we can determine K_1 from system root loci and then from given K_2/K_1, the expected value of K_2 is dtetermined.

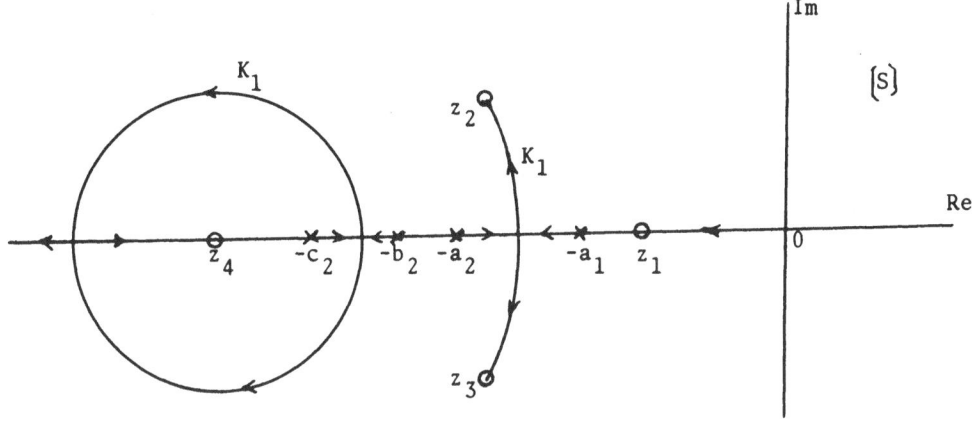

Fig 3-5-2

Obviously, the singular coupled system is a very simple coupled system but even in such a case we see that its analysis is much more difficult than that of single variable systems.

When the number of the variables under control is more than two, we can imagine that the characteristic equation (if it can be derived) will be very complicated and the analysis to such an equation will be more difficult.

No matter the root-locus method or any other conventional design method is applied, the above conclusion is always true and, perhaps, among them, the root-locus method is more easily to be applied because only characteristic equation is analyzed for it.

§ 3-6 Symmetric Coupled Systems

Now, we discuss another type of coupled systems, namely the symmetric coupled systems.

The so-called symmetric coupled system means:

$$\left.\begin{array}{l} P_{12}(S) = aP_{11}(S) \\ P_{21}(S) = bP_{22}(S) \end{array}\right\} \tag{3-6-1}$$

or:

$$\left.\begin{array}{l} P_{12}(S) = bP_{22}(S) \\ P_{21}(S) = aP_{11}(S) \end{array}\right\} \tag{3-6-2}$$

Where, both a and b are constants.

Thus, for it we get:

$$\left| P(S) \right| = P_{11}P_{22} - P_{12}P_{21} = P_{11}P_{22} - abP_{11}P_{22} =$$
$$= (1 - ab)P_{11}P_{22} = KP_{11}P_{22} \tag{3-6-3}$$

Obviously, when:

$$a = b = 1 \tag{3-6-4}$$

or:

$$a = \frac{1}{b} \tag{3-6-5}$$

then:

$$K = 0 \tag{3-6-6}$$

and the system becomes a singular coupled system.

When $K \neq 0$, the system characteristic equation is:

$$Q = 1 + R_{11}P_{11} + R_{22}P_{22} + KR_{11}R_{22}P_{11}P_{22} = 0 \tag{3-6-7}$$

In order to draw root loci, we express all transfer functions in this equation into the forms of rational fractions and we get:

$$1 + \frac{Z_{1R}Z_{11}}{N_{1R}N_{11}}(1 + \frac{Z_{2R}Z_{22}N_{1R}N_{11}}{Z_{1R}Z_{11}N_{2R}N_{22}} (1 + K\frac{Z_{1R}Z_{11}}{N_{1R}N_{11}})) = 0 \tag{3-6-8}$$

Obviously, it is with the following form:

$$1 + F_{1}(1 + F_{2}(1 + F_{3})) = 0 \tag{3-6-9}$$

Therefore, in order to get the system root loci, three sets of loci should be drawn and, consequently, the analysis of this system is even more difficult than that of the singular coupled system.

When we draw the first set of loci, it is with the parameter K. Then a suitable value of K can be given from these loci.

The second set of loci is with the parameter K_2/K_1 and a suitable value of K_2/K_1 can also be given from the second loci.

The third set of loci is with the parameter K_1 and we can determine k_1 by control demands and then we determine K_2 in turn.

Obviously, there are three possible cases:

$$\left. \begin{array}{ll} ab < 1 & K > 0 \\ ab = 1 & K = 0 \\ ab > 1 & K < 0 \end{array} \right\} \qquad\qquad (3\text{-}6\text{-}10)$$

When ab = 1, K = 0, this is just the singular coupled system and the analysis was shown in the last paragraph.

When K $>$ 0, in general the system may be stable if suitable gains are chosen and both regulators may contain integral elements.

When K $<$ 0 and both regulators contain integral elements, the system is always unstable.

In fact, when K $<$ 0, only when the system is with low order and the open loop gain is not large, then the system may be stable.

What does K $<$ 0 mean ?

In fact, it means strong coupling, i.e. ab $>$ 1. The effects of the coupling channels are very evident and the system is very difficult to work with strong coupling unless decoupling design is carried out.

Both singular coupled system and symmetric coupled system are two special kinds of coupled systems and they may be considered as simple ones. But the above analysis denotes that even in these cases, the analysis is difficult.

§ 3-7 The Most Common Coupled Systems of First Order

In practical control engineering, a great number of control systems belongs to the coupled systems of first lag, or at least may be
approximated by such systems.

The so-called coupled system of first lag means that the characters of all plant channels , no matter the main channels or the coupling channels, are with elements of first lag.

Such a system is shown in Fig 3-7-1; where P_{11}, P_{22}, P_{12} and P_{21}
all are elements of first lag.

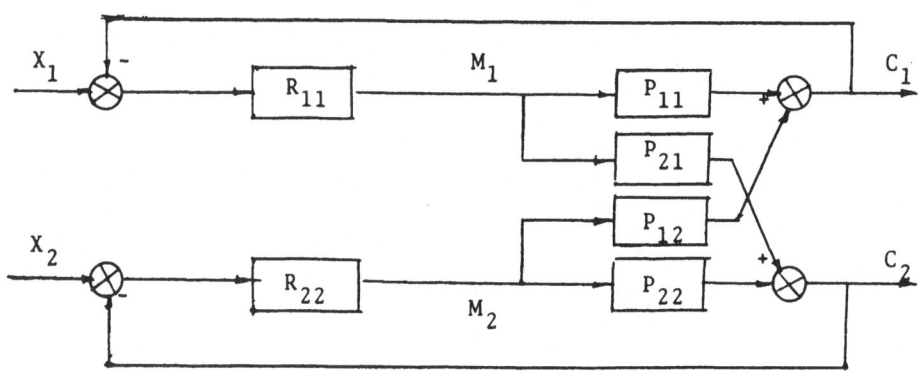

Fig 3-7-1

The characteristic equation of this system is:

$$Q = 1 + R_{11}P_{11} + R_{22}P_{22} + R_{11}R_{22}(P_{11}P_{22} - P_{12}P_{21}) = 0 \quad (3\text{-}7\text{-}1)$$

If both R_{11} and R_{22} contain integral elements, then this equation
will be one of six order, so it is very difficult to analyze.

Now, we discuss two simple cases.

At first, we suppose that P_{11}, P_{12}, P_{21}, and P_{22} are with the same
character, for example:

$$P = \begin{bmatrix} P_{11} & P_{12} \\ P_{21} & P_{22} \end{bmatrix} = \begin{bmatrix} \dfrac{1}{S+1} & \dfrac{1}{S+1} \\ \dfrac{1}{S+1} & \dfrac{1}{S+1} \end{bmatrix} \quad (3\text{-}7\text{-}2)$$

In fact, this is a singular coupled system since :

$$P_{11}P_{22} - P_{12}P_{21} = 0 \quad (3\text{-}7\text{-}3)$$

If no decoupling design is carried out, how will the system work?

We discuss two cases:

The first case is: Suppose that one of the outputs is controlled automatically, while the other is controlled manually, for example C_2 is controlled manually. That means that in the second loop the regulator R_{22} is broken off; thus for C_1, we get:

$$C_1 = \frac{R_{11}P_{11}}{1 + R_{11}P_{11}} X_1 + \frac{P_{12}}{1 + R_{11}P_{11}} M_2 \qquad (3-7-4)$$

Because P_{11} is an element of first lag, so it is easy to make this system stable. That means that in this case, the system is able to be controlled. The conclusion is also true for C_2.

The second case is : Suppose that two output variables are controlled automatically. This case is just as shown in Fig 3-7-1. Then:

$$\left. \begin{array}{l} C_1 = G_{11}X_1 + G_{12}X_2 \\[2mm] C_2 = G_{21}X_1 + G_{22}X_2 \end{array} \right\} \qquad (3-7-5)$$

where G_{11}, G_{12}, G_{21} ,and G_{22} are given by (3-2-4) to (3-2-7).

Now, we substitute the practical forms of P_{11}, P_{12}, P_{21} and P_{22} into (3-2-4) to (3-2-7) and suppose $R_{11} = K_{11}$, $R_{22} = K_{22}$, then we get:

$$G_{11} = \frac{(S + 1)K_{11}}{S^2 + (2 + K_{11}K_{22})S + 1 + K_{11} + K_{22}} \qquad (3-7-6)$$

$$G_{12} = \frac{(S + 1)K_{22}}{S^2 + (2 + K_{11}K_{22})S + 1 + K_{11} + K_{22}} \qquad (3-7-7)$$

$$G_{21} = \frac{(S + 1)K_{11}}{S^2 + (2 + K_{11}K_{22})S + 1 + K_{11} + K_{22}} \qquad (3-7-8)$$

$$G_{22} = \frac{(S + 1)K_{22}}{S^2 + (2 + K_{11}K_{22})S + 1 + K_{11} + K_{22}} \qquad (3-7-9)$$

Obviously:

$$G_{11} = G_{21} \qquad (3-7-10)$$

$$G_{22} = G_{12} \qquad\qquad (3\text{-}7\text{-}11)$$

It denotes although the system is stable, it is uncontrollable in practice. Since the response of C_1 to X_1 is just the same as that of C_2 to X_1, and the response of C_2 to X_2 is just the same as that of C_1 to X_2, so we can not determine which channel is the main one. Thus, for such a system, in practice no channel can be used for control and if we want to get control, then decoupling design is necessary.

In practice, the coupling channels often have opposite signs, such as:

$$P = \begin{pmatrix} \dfrac{1}{S+1} & -\dfrac{1}{S+1} \\[2mm] \dfrac{1}{S+1} & \dfrac{1}{S+1} \end{pmatrix} \qquad\qquad (3\text{-}7\text{-}12)$$

This is a symmetric coupled system indeed, since:

$$K = 1 - ab = 1 + 1 = 2 \qquad\qquad (3\text{-}7\text{-}13)$$

In order to eliminate the static errors, the P+I regulators are adopted (the reasonableness will be proved in § 3-10):

$$R = \begin{pmatrix} K_{11}\dfrac{S+1}{S} & 0 \\[3mm] 0 & K_{22}\dfrac{S+1}{S} \end{pmatrix} \qquad\qquad (3\text{-}7\text{-}14)$$

Substituting the elements of P and R into (3-2-4) to (3-2-7), we get:

$$C_1 = \frac{K_{11}(S+2K_{22})}{S^2+(K_{11}+K_{22})S+2K_{11}K_{22}}\, X_1 - \frac{K_{22}S}{S^2+(K_{11}+K_{22})S+2K_{11}K_{22}} X_2$$

$$(3\text{-}7\text{-}15)$$

$$C_2 = \frac{K_{11}S}{S^2+(K_{11}+K_{22})S+2K_{11}K_{22}}\, X_1 + \frac{K_{22}(S+2K_{11})}{S^2+(K_{11}+K_{22})S+2K_{11}K_{22}} X_2$$

$$(3\text{-}7\text{-}16)$$

Both responses are stable and this corresponds to what we said in the last paragraph that when $K > 0$, even both regulators contain integral elements, the system may be stable still.

Fig 3-7-2 shows some practical responses of this system.

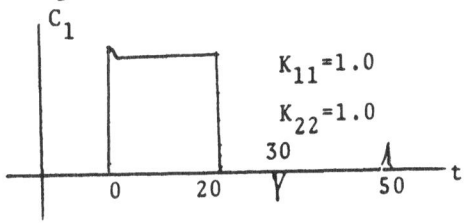

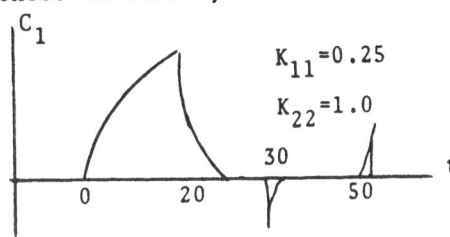

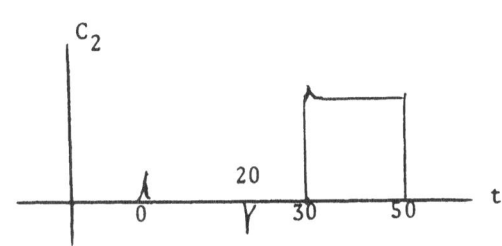

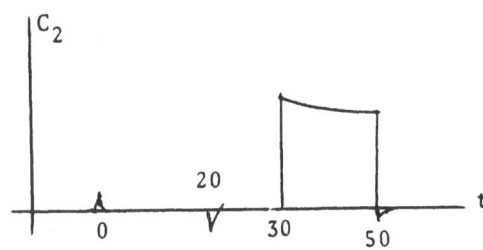

Here, we suppose that X_1 is input 30 seconds prior to X_2.

This figure shows explicitly how C_1 and C_2 being influenced by the other channel input.

We see that the coupling influence is related to the ratio of the gains of two regulators. The larger the gain of the other channel, the stronger the coupling influence from it.

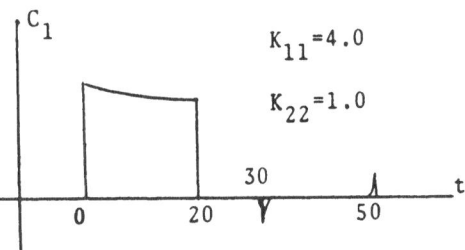

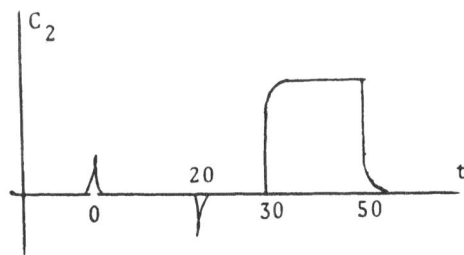

Fig 3-7-2

§ 3-8 The Three-Variable Coupled Systems

The above analysis denotes even for the simplest two-variable control system, the analysis is very difficult.

If the number of variables increases, then the analysis will be more difficult. Now, we discuss a three-variable coupled system and we can see the complication of its analysis.

The general relation for a MPCS is:

$$C = (I + PR)^{-1}PRX \qquad (3-8-1)$$

Now suppose P being a plant with three coupled variables.

No decoupling design is carried out , so R contains only the regulators of the main channels. Thus:

$$PR = \begin{pmatrix} P_{11} & P_{12} & P_{13} \\ P_{21} & P_{22} & P_{23} \\ P_{31} & P_{32} & P_{33} \end{pmatrix} \begin{pmatrix} R_1 & 0 & 0 \\ 0 & R_2 & 0 \\ 0 & 0 & R_3 \end{pmatrix} =$$

$$= \begin{pmatrix} P_{11}R_1 & P_{12}R_2 & P_{13}R_3 \\ P_{21}R_1 & P_{22}R_2 & P_{23}R_3 \\ P_{31}R_1 & P_{32}R_2 & P_{33}R_3 \end{pmatrix} \qquad (3-8-2)$$

and:

$$I + PR = \begin{pmatrix} 1+P_{11}R_1 & P_{12}R_2 & P_{13}R_3 \\ P_{21}R_1 & 1+P_{22}R_2 & P_{23}R_3 \\ P_{31}R_1 & P_{32}R_2 & 1+P_{33}R_3 \end{pmatrix} \qquad (3-8-3)$$

Its determinant is:

$$\begin{aligned}
\Delta = {} & (1 + P_{11}R_1)(1 + P_{22}R_2)(1 + P_{33}R_3) + P_{12}P_{23}P_{31}R_1R_2R_3 \\
& + P_{13}P_{21}P_{32}R_1R_2R_3 - (1 + P_{11}R_1)P_{23}P_{32}R_2R_3 - \\
& - (1 + P_{22}R_2)P_{13}P_{31}R_1R_3 - (1 + P_{33}R_3)P_{12}P_{21}R_1R_2
\end{aligned}$$

$$(3-8-4)$$

We see that it is very complicated.

The inverse matrix is:

$$(\mathbf{I} + PR)^{-1} = \begin{bmatrix} \dfrac{\triangle_{11}}{\triangle} & \dfrac{\triangle_{21}}{\triangle} & \dfrac{\triangle_{31}}{\triangle} \\[2mm] \dfrac{\triangle_{12}}{\triangle} & \dfrac{\triangle_{22}}{\triangle} & \dfrac{\triangle_{32}}{\triangle} \\[2mm] \dfrac{\triangle_{13}}{\triangle} & \dfrac{\triangle_{23}}{\triangle} & \dfrac{\triangle_{33}}{\triangle} \end{bmatrix} \tag{3-8-5}$$

Where:

$$\triangle_{11} = (1 + P_{22}R_2)(1 + P_{33}R_3) - P_{23}P_{32}R_2R_3$$

$$\triangle_{21} = P_{32}P_{23}R_2R_3 - (1 + P_{33}R_3)P_{12}R_2$$

$$\triangle_{31} = P_{12}P_{23}R_2R_3 - (1 + P_{22}R_2)P_{13}R_3$$

$$\triangle_{12} = P_{23}P_{31}R_1R_3 - (1 + P_{33}R_3)P_{21}R_1$$

$$\triangle_{22} = (1 + P_{11}R_1)(1 + P_{33}R_3) - P_{13}P_{31}R_1R_3 \tag{3-8-6}$$

$$\triangle_{32} = P_{13}P_{21}R_1R_3 - (1 + P_{11}R_1)P_{23}R_3$$

$$\triangle_{13} = P_{21}P_{32}R_1R_2 - (1 + P_{22}R_2)P_{31}R_1$$

$$\triangle_{23} = P_{12}P_{31}R_1R_2 - (1 + P_{11}R_1)P_{32}R_2$$

$$\triangle_{33} = (1 + P_{11}R_1)(1 + P_{22}R_2) - P_{12}P_{23}R_1R_2$$

From (3-8-1), $(1+ PR)^{-1}$ and PR, we can get:

$$C_1 = G_{11}X_1 \tag{3-8-7}$$

where:

$$G_{11} = \frac{1}{\triangle}\Big[P_{11}R_1(1 + P_{22}R_2)(1 + P_{33}R_3) - P_{11}P_{23}P_{32}R_1R_2R_3 +$$

$$+ P_{21}P_{32}P_{13}R_1R_2R_3 - (1 + P_{33}R_3)P_{12}P_{21}R_1R_2 + P_{21}P_{32}P_{31}R_1R_2R_3 -$$

$$- (1 + P_{22}R_2)P_{13}P_{31}R_1R_3 \Big] \tag{3-8-8}$$

This is the transfer function of C_1 to X_1 for this three-variable system and we can see that it is very complicated.

But the C_1 obtained from (3-8-7) is not the total and it is only the part caused by X_1. There are another two parts in C_1 caused by X_2 and X_3, respectively, since this is a system without decoupling design.

For example, the part of C_1 caused by X_3 is:

$$C_1 = G_{13}X_3 \tag{3-8-9}$$

where:

$$G_{13} = \frac{1}{\Delta} \left[(1 + P_{22}R_2)(1 + P_{33}R_3)P_{13}R_3 - P_{23}P_{32}P_{13}R_2R_3^2 + \right.$$

$$+ P_{32}P_{13}P_{23}R_2R_3^2 - (1 + P_{33}R_3)P_{12}P_{23}R_2R_3 +$$

$$+ P_{12}P_{23}P_{33}R_2R_3^2 - (1 + P_{22}R_2)P_{13}P_{33}R_3^2 \left. \right] \tag{3-8-10}$$

Similarly, we can determine G_{12}, G_{22}, G_{21}, G_{23}, G_{33}, G_{31} and G_{32}. All these transfer functions have very complicated forms.

Therefore, for a three-variable system without decoupling design, it is impossible to expect to express its dynamic characters by simple transfer functions and when the plant is with higher order, this analysis can not be carried in fact.

We say that not only the three-variable coupled system is difficult to be analyzed, but also the decoupled structure of the three-variabe system is very complicated . So, in general if the number of the variables under control is more than two, we had better choose two of them , which are the main variables or with serious coupling, to form a two-variable system , and the other (or the others) would be treated as a single variable (or single variables).Certainly , this is not an exact method but it can make the analysis be simple.

§ 3-9 Analysis of Coupled V-Canonical Systems [5]

Now, we discuss a coupled V-canonical system shown in Fig 3-9-1.

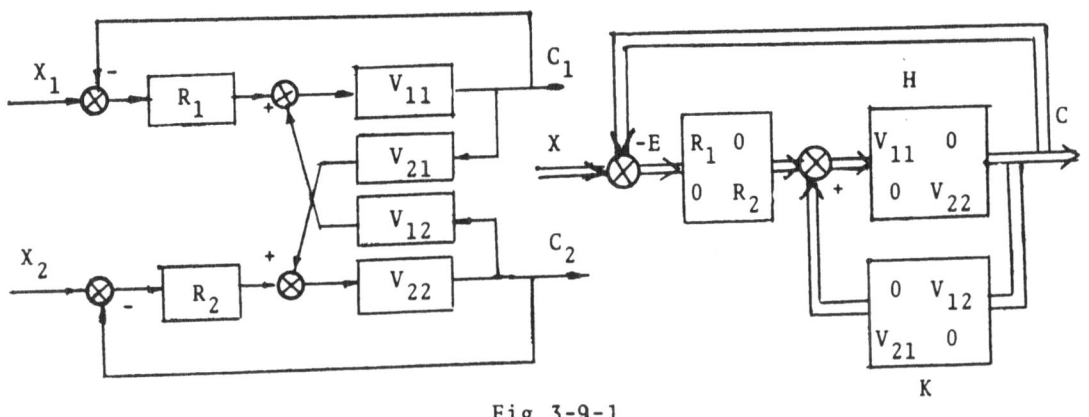

Fig 3-9-1

When a V-canonical plant is transferred into a P-canonical plant, its general form is:

$$P = (I - HK)^{-1}H \qquad (3-9-1)$$

Thus, from Fig 3-9-1, we get the open loop transfer function matrix:

$$F_0(S) = \frac{C(S)}{E(S)} = (I - H(S)K(S))^{-1}H(S)R(S) = (H^{-1}(S)-K(S))^{-1}R(S) \qquad (3-9-2)$$

The system characteristic equation is :

$$\left| I + F_0(S) \right| = \left| I + \frac{C(S)}{E(S)} \right| = 0 \qquad (3-9-3)$$

By the property of determinants, we get:

$$\left| F_0^{-1}(S) \right| \left| I + F_0(S) \right| = \left| F_0^{-1}(S)(I + F_0(S)) \right| = \left| I + F_0^{-1}(S) \right| = 0 \qquad (3-9-4)$$

But:

$$F_0^{-1}(S) = R^{-1}(S)(H^{-1}(S) - K(S)) \qquad (3-9-5)$$

and :

$$\left| F_0^{-1}(S) \right| \neq 0 \qquad (3-9-6)$$

Therefore,

$$F_0^{-1}(S) = \begin{pmatrix} R_1^{-1}V_{11}^{-1} & -R_1^{-1}V_{12} \\ -R_2^{-1}V_{21} & R_2^{-1}V_{22}^{-1} \end{pmatrix} \tag{3-9-7}$$

and:

$$\left| I + F_0^{-1}(S) \right| = \begin{vmatrix} 1 + R_1^{-1}V_{11}^{-1} & -R_1^{-1}V_{12} \\ -R_2^{-1}V_{21} & 1 + R_2^{-1}V_{22}^{-1} \end{vmatrix} = 0 \tag{3-9-8}$$

So , the characteristic equation is:

$$Q_1(S) = (1 + R_1^{-1}V_{11}^{-1})(1 + R_2^{-1}V_2^{-1}) - R_1^{-1}R_2^{-1}V_{12}V_{21} = 0 \tag{3-9-9}$$

We let:

$$Q(S) = Q_1(S)R_1R_2V_{11}V_{22} \tag{3-9-10}$$

then the characteristic equation becomes:

$$Q(S) = (1 + R_1V_{11})(1 + R_2V_{22}) - V_{11}V_{22}V_{12}V_{21} = 0 \tag{3-9-11}$$

Comparing (3-9-11) with (3-2-11), we find that the characteristic equations of both P-canonical systems and V-canonical systems are with same forms, so the analysis principles mentioned above can be also used in the analysis of V-canonical systems.

A coupled plant can be expressed either by the P-canonical form or by the V-canonical form but the practical plant remains unchanged. The form transfer is with mathematic meaning.

So, we can not expected that the analysis difficulty would be avoided because of the transfer of the plant form. That means the analysis difficulty for a P-canonical plant also exists when the plant is transferred into a V-canonical form. This conclusion, certainly, is logical.

§ 3-10 Some General Conclusions About Multivariable Process Control
Systems

We have discussed some general properties of MPCS from different
aspects. The analysis results denote that in general the analysis and
design of a MPCS is very difficult and if the decoupling design is
carried out, then its analysis, design and operation will be easier.
Thus, in most cases, the decoupling design is expected for the multivariable process control systems.

The decoupling design contains a lot of contents and it is the
key of this book. We will discuss it in detail in the future chapters.
But, however, before we discuss the practical steps of decoupling design,
we had better discuss some important general conclusions about a MPCS
and these conclusions are closely related to the following decoupling
design theory indeed.

In order to give the generality we discuss the system shown in
Fig 3-10-1.

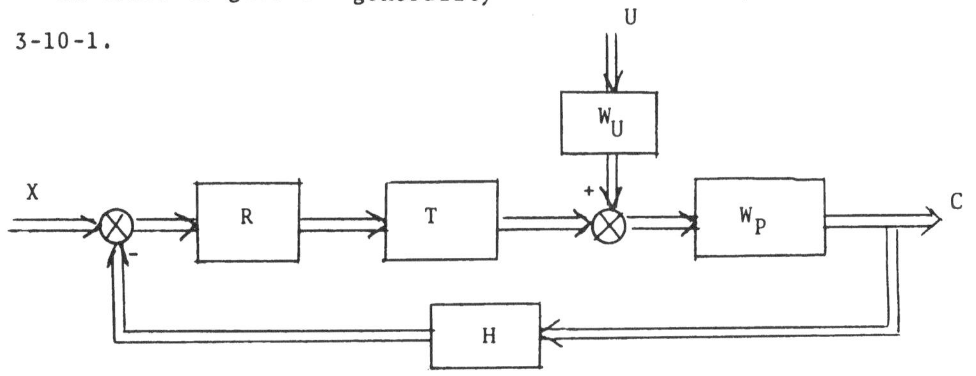

Fig 3-10-1

Where:

C is the output vector,

X is the reference vector,

U is the supply disturbance vector,

R is the regulator transfer function matrix,

W_p is the plant transfer function matrix,

160

H is the feedback transfer function matrix,

T is the valve character matrix,

E is the deviation vector,

W_U is the input transfer function matrix of disturbances.

If the disturbances are not considered and the valve characters are included in the plant matrix, then the system will be shown in Fig 3-10-2. In this figure, $P = W_pT$.

From Fig 3-10-2, we get:

$C(S) = PR(X - B)$

(3-10-1)

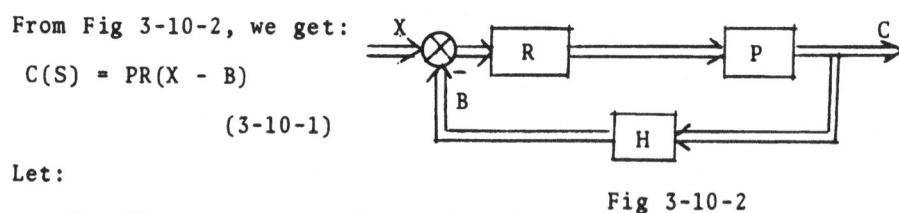

Fig 3-10-2

Let:

$W = PR$ (3-10-2)

then:

$C = W(X - B) = W(X - HC)$ (3-10-3)

It may be written as:

$(I + WH)C = WX$ (3-10-4)

Solving for C, we get:

$$C = (I + WH)^{-1}WX$$ (3-10-5)

Define:

$$G = (I + WH)^{-1}W$$ (3-10-6)

as the closed-loop transfer function matrix of this system and so:

$$C(S) = G(S)X(S)$$ (3-10-7)

is the basic relation for a multivariable process control system.

If $H = I$, i.e. a unit matrix, then:

$WH = W$ (3-10-8)

is called the open loop transfer matrix.

Because this is a coupling system, so the the general form of G is given bellow. Here, we suppose that there are n inputs and n out-puts in this system.

$$G = \begin{pmatrix} G_{11} & G_{12} & - & - & - & - & - & G_{1n} \\ G_{21} & G_{22} & - & - & - & - & - & G_{2n} \\ - & - & - & - & - & - & - & - \\ - & - & - & - & - & - & - & - \\ G_{n1} & G_{n2} & - & - & - & - & - & G_{nn} \end{pmatrix}$$ (3-10-9)

In this matrix, the elements off the diagonal express how the outputs being influenced by the other inputs, i.e. the coupling channels.

If a decoupled system is expected, namely each output is influenced by only one input and every input only influences its corresponding output, then G must be a diagonal matrix, i.e.

$$G_{ij} = 0 \quad \text{for all } i \neq j$$ (3-10-10)

This is the basic idea of diagonal matrix method of decoupling design.

Now, we prove that for a system with unit feedback, if the decoupling control is expected, namely G is expected to be a diagonal matrix, then the necessary and sufficient condition is: The open loop transfer matrix must be a diagonal.

Because $G = (I + W)^{-1} W$, so:

$$(I + W)G = W$$ (3-10-11)

$$G = W(I - G)$$ (3-10-12)

$$W = G(I - G)^{-1}$$ (3-10-13)

Since for a decoupled system G is diagonal, so I-G also is a diagonal matrix and:

$$I - G = \begin{pmatrix} 1-G_{11} & & & & 0 \\ & 1-G_{22} & & & \\ & & \cdot & & \\ & & & \cdot & \\ 0 & & & & 1-G_{nn} \end{pmatrix}$$ (3-10-14)

Its inverse form is:

$$(I - G)^{-1} = \begin{pmatrix} \dfrac{1}{1-G_{11}} & & & \text{\Large 0} \\ & \dfrac{1}{1-G_{22}} & & \\ & & \ddots & \\ \text{\Large 0} & & & \dfrac{1}{1-G_{nn}} \end{pmatrix} \qquad (3\text{-}10\text{-}15)$$

Multiplying it with matrix G yields:

$$W = \begin{pmatrix} \dfrac{G_{11}}{1-G_{11}} & & & \text{\Large 0} \\ & \dfrac{G_{22}}{1-G_{22}} & & \\ & & \ddots & \\ \text{\Large 0} & & & \dfrac{G_{nn}}{1-G_{nn}} \end{pmatrix} \qquad (3\text{-}10\text{-}16)$$

Therefore, W is a diagonal matrix and the elements on its diagonal are:

$$W_{ii} = \frac{G_{ii}}{1 - G_{ii}} \qquad (3\text{-}10\text{-}17)$$

This is the proof of the necessity.

The sufficiency may be clearly seen from $G = (I + W)^{-1}W$ directly. In fact, if W is a diagonal matrix, then $(I + W)^{-1}$ is also a diagonal matrix and so is G.

Thus, W being a diagonal matrix is the necessary and sufficient condition for realizing decoupling design of the closed-loop system.

This is the first property we should explain and it is the base of some decoupling design methods indeed.

If there is a feedback transfer matrix in the system and this feedback transfer matrix is also with **diagonal** form, i.e. H is diagonal, then for a decoupled system:

$$W = \begin{pmatrix} \dfrac{G_{11}}{1-H_{11}G_{11}} & & & 0 \\ & \dfrac{G_{22}}{1-H_{22}G_{22}} & & \\ & & \ddots & \\ 0 & & & \dfrac{G_{nn}}{1-H_{nn}G_{nn}} \end{pmatrix} \qquad (3\text{-}10\text{-}18)$$

So, the above conclusion is still held.

Now, we discuss the second problem: For a MPCS if no decoupling design is considered, i.e. let it operate with coupling, but static deviations are not allowable , how should we treat this demand?

For a unit feedback, the system deviation is:

$$E(t) = X(t) - C(t) \qquad (3\text{-}10\text{-}19)$$

The demand of having no static deviations means:

$$\lim_{t \to \infty} E(t) = 0 \qquad (3\text{-}10\text{-}20)$$

From (3-10-19) , we get:

$$E(S) = X(S) - C(S) = X(S) - G(S)X(S) = (I - G(S))X(S) \qquad (3\text{-}10\text{-}21)$$

By the final value theorem of Laplace transform:

$$\lim_{t \to \infty} E(t) = \lim_{S \to 0} E(S) = 0 \qquad (3\text{-}10\text{-}22)$$

we get:

$$\lim_{S \to 0} G(S) = I \qquad (3\text{-}10\text{-}23)$$

Because for a unit feedback:

$$G = (I + W)^{-1}W \qquad (3\text{-}10\text{-}24)$$

so the above condition is:

$$\lim_{S \to 0} (I + W) = W \qquad (3\text{-}10\text{-}25)$$

Namely:

$$I + W(0) = W(0) \qquad (3\text{-}10\text{-}26)$$

It denotes:

(1) This condition is not related to the elements off the diagonal of matrix W,

(2) This condition demands that all diagonal elements of matrix W be infinite when S ⟶ 0.

It means that in the open loop transfer matrix, every element on the diagonal must at least contain an integral element.

Notice that this conclusion is not related to the decoupling demands and we used this conclusion in the analysis of two-variable systems before.

Now, we discuss the third problem , namely the stability analysis.

In the previous paragraphs, we pointed out the difficulty of the analysis of some practical systems, now we have a general discussion. The system output is:

$$C(t) = \mathcal{L}^{-1}(C(S)) = \mathcal{L}^{-1}(G(S)X(S)) = \mathcal{L}^{-1}((I + WH)^{-1}WX)$$

$$(3-10-27)$$

Because:

$$(I + WH)^{-1} = \frac{adj(I + WH)}{det(I + WH)} \qquad (3-10-28)$$

so every element of the n-dimensional vector $(I + WH)^{-1}WX$ contains a common factor $det(I + WH)$ in its denominator.

Thus, if we want to get the response of C(t), then we should get all roots of :

$$det(I + WH) = 0 \qquad (3-10-29)$$

namely the eigenvalues of the closed-loop system.

For the unit feedback, it is:

$$det(I + W) = 0 \qquad (3-10-30)$$

Therefore, the necessary and sufficient condition for the system stability is that all the closed-loop system eigenvalues are in the left S plane.

All the examples discussed before are special cases of (3-10-30).

For instance, a two-variable system is:

$$\det(I+W) = \begin{vmatrix} 1+W_{11} & W_{12} \\ W_{21} & 1+W_{22} \end{vmatrix} = 1 + W_{11} + W_{22} + W_{11}W_{22} - W_{12}W_{21} = 0$$

$$(3-10-31)$$

but:

$$W = PR = \begin{pmatrix} P_{11} & P_{12} \\ P_{21} & P_{22} \end{pmatrix} \begin{pmatrix} R_{11} & 0 \\ 0 & R_{22} \end{pmatrix} = \begin{pmatrix} P_{11}R_{11} & P_{12}R_{22} \\ P_{21}R_{11} & P_{22}R_{22} \end{pmatrix} \qquad (3-10-32)$$

So equation (3-10-31) becomes:

$$\det(I+W) = 1 + P_{11}R_{11} + P_{22}R_{22} + P_{11}R_{11}P_{22}R_{22} - P_{12}P_{21}R_{11}R_{22} = 0$$

$$(3-10-33)$$

This is just the result of (3-2-11).

In general, when the number of variables is larger than 2, equation (3-10-30) will have very complicated form with high order, thus the stability analysis in general is very difficult.

But, if the system is decoupled, then W becomes a diagonal matrix. Thus:

$$I+W = \begin{bmatrix} 1+W_{11} & & & \\ & 1+W_{22} & & \Large{0} \\ & & \ddots & \\ \Large{0} & & & 1+W_{nn} \end{bmatrix} \qquad (3-10-34)$$

and the system characteristic equation is:

$$\det(I+W) = (1+W_{11})(1+W_{22}) \cdots \cdots (1+W_{nn}) = 0 \qquad (3-10-35)$$

Obviously, in such a case, the stability problem of this coupled system becomes to research n separate single variable systems, namely to determine the stability of each:

$$1 + W_{ii} = 0 \qquad i = 1, 2, \ldots .n \qquad (3-10-36)$$

Certainly, this is much easier than to research (3-10-30).

At last, we discuss the responses of a MPCS to its disturbances.

In the above discussions, the disturbance U was omitted and now when we discuss the results of disturbance influence, the reference X may be neglected.

Then the system is shown in Fig 3-10-3. Here:

$$\left. \begin{array}{l} U'(S) = W_U(S)U(S) \\ W_1(S) =- T(S)R(S)H(S) \end{array} \right\} \quad (3\text{-}10\text{-}37)$$

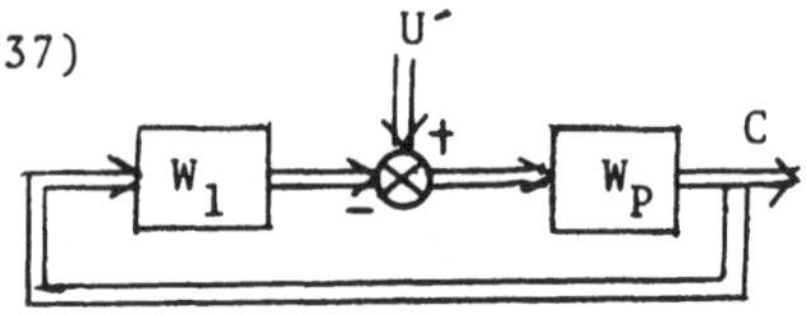

From Fig 3-10-3, we get:

$$C = (I - W_P W_1)^{-1} W_P U' =$$
$$= (I + WH)^{-1} W_P U' \qquad (3\text{-}10\text{-}38)$$

Fig 3-10-3

A very important conclusion can be derived from here: If we realize a decoupling design between C and X, this does not mean to reach a decoupling between C and U at a meantime. This is because when WH is a diagonal matrix , which gives the decoupling between C and X, in general $(I + WH)^{-1} W_P$ is not a diagonal matrix, so the decoupling between C and U can not be reached by the same design.

This conclusion is very meaningful. It relates to a very important concept in the decoupling design of multivariable process control systems, namely the full decoupling design and we will discuss it in detail in the next chapter.

The above four conclusions are the most important properties of multivariable process control systems and it is very useful for us to have a good understanding about them in order to do the further research.

In this chapter, some problems concerning the analysis of general multivariable process control systems are discussed and we see that the analysis of a coupled multivariable control system is really difficult and sometimes it can not be done in practice indeed.

If the system could be decoupled and transferred into several independent subsystems, the analysis would be much simpler and so the decoupling design is very attractive to us.

Since sixties of this century , the decoupling design theory has got very rapid development and a lot of methods have been proposed to solve this problem.

It is impossible for us to introduce and discuss all this methods in this book . Because our main interest is about process control, so in this book only those applied very popularly and successfully in process control engineering are discussed and this does not mean that some other sophisticated methods , for example the Rosenbrock inverse Nyquist array method, the MacFarlane characteristic locus method or the state variable method, are not suitable for process control system design . Yes, all these methods can be used in multivariable process control system design and analysis, but , up to now, the application of these methods are not very popular, so in this book, we will not discuss them since we have not enough experience of application of these methods.

CHAPTER   FOUR

SOME GENERAL PRINCIPLES FOR DECOUPLIMG DESIGN

§ 4-1 Introduction

In the last chapter, we discussed the difficulty of the analysis of multivariable process control systems. In fact, in process control engineering, not only the analysis of the multivariable control
systems is difficult, but, .generally speaking, the practical operation is also difficult.

Therefore, in the process control engineering practice, now we
can say that to realize the decoupling control is the key problem in
the analysis of multivariable process control systems.

Now, we are going to discuss the general theory of realizing
decoupling control.

The basic idea of decoupling control design is very simple, namely let the system transfer matrix be diagonal. We have proved in
the previous chapter when the transfer matrix of the open-loop system
is diagonal, then the transfer matrix of the closed-loop system is
certainly diagonal. Therefore, we can analyze the decoupling problem
with both open-loop transfer matrix and closed-loop transfer matrix.

It seems that this idea is very simple but there are many practical problems which should be considered. Especially for process control systems, there are some special problems worth being discussed.

More exactly speaking, in the decoupling design, the following
basic factors should be considered:

(1) The plant may be P-canonical or V-canonical,

(2) The decoupling element structure also may be P-canonical or
V-canonical,

(3) The decoupling project may be feedforward or feedback,

(4) For feedforward decoupling structure, the decoupling ele-

ment structure may combine with the regulators or locate between the plant and the regulators,

(5) There may be some disturbances in the system and they may be supply disturbances or load disturbances,

(6) The decoupling demands may be different: Perhaps, only the decoupling control between the outputs and the references is expected; but it is also possible that not only the decoupling control between the outputs and the references, but also the decoupling control between the outputs and the references ae well as the disturbances is expected simultaneously, namely the full decoupling control.

(7) For some decoupling structure, it may realize , or can not realize the full decoupling control.

All these problems should be discussed in the decoupling design.

Obviously, the combination of the above terms will result in different decoupling projects. Certainly, there is a problem: Which is the best ?

In order to answer this problem, we should pay attention to:

(1) Are the decoupling conditions easily to be realized ?

(2) Can the system realize the full decoupling ?

If a project is with these two functions, then we can say that it is a good decoupling project. Obviously," best " is a relative concept and we should do comparison.

The analysis of this problem is closely related to the famous Mesarović's idea . It says that the application of V-canonical forms and the feedback decoupling structures will give good decoupling results.

How to embody this idea in our decoupling design is the essential problem discussed in this chapter.

§ 4-2 The Decoupling Design of Open Loop Systems

In general, the process control systems are closed-loop forms and the main contents of the following discussions are about the closed-loop system analysis.

Before we analyze the closed-loop systems, we discuss the decoupling design of open loop systems .

For instance, a V-canonical system of n variables is shown in Fig 4-2-1.

We can know from the figure:

$$C_k(S) = V_{kk}(X_k + \sum_{i=1}^{n} V_{ki}C_i)$$

k = 1,2,..... n

k ≠ i

(4-2-1)

For convenience, we introduce the following matrix:

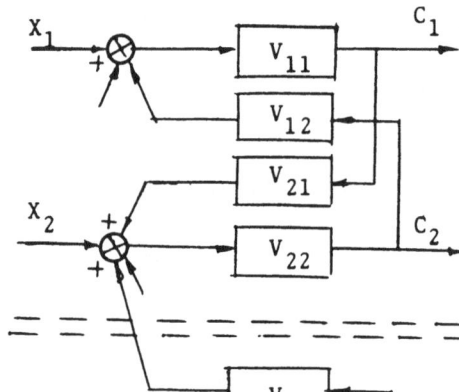

Fig 4-2-1

$$V = \begin{pmatrix} V_{11} & & & 0 \\ & V_{22} & & \\ & & \cdot & \\ 0 & & \cdot & \\ & & & V_{nn} \end{pmatrix}$$

(4-2-2)

$$K = \begin{pmatrix} 0 & V_{12} & - - - - - - & V_{1n} \\ V_{21} & 0 & - - - - - - & V_{2n} \\ - & - & - - - - - - & - \\ - & - & - - - - - - & - \\ V_{n1} & V_{n2} & - - - - - - & 0 \end{pmatrix}$$

(4-2-3)

Then equation (4-2-1) can be written in matrix form:

$$C(S) = V(S)(X(S) + K(S)C(S))$$ (4-2-4)

It yields:

$$C(S) = (I - V(S)K(S))^{-1}V(S)X(S)$$ (4-2-5)

Let:

$$T(S) = (I - V(S)K(S))^{-1} V(S) \qquad (4-2-6)$$

then:

$$C(S) = T(S)X(S) \qquad (4-2-7)$$

$T(S)$ is the system transfer matrix.

The problem is how to get it . From (4-2-1), we have :

$$X_{kk}(S) = \frac{C_k}{V_{kk}} - \sum_{i=1}^{n} V_{ki}C_i \qquad (4-2-8)$$

$$k = 1,2,\ldots\ldots n \qquad k \neq i$$

We introduce another matrix Q with the elements:

$$\left. \begin{array}{l} Q_{kk}(S) = \dfrac{1}{V_{kk}(S)} \\[4mm] Q_{ki}(S) = -V_{ki}(S) \end{array} \right\} \quad \begin{array}{l} k = 1,2,\ldots\ldots n \\[2mm] i = 1,2,\ldots\ldots n \\[2mm] k \neq i \end{array} \qquad (4-2-9)$$

then (4-2-8) may be written as:

$$X(S) = Q(S)C(S) \qquad (4-2-10)$$

In general $Q(S)$ is not a singular matrix, so from (4-2-7) and (4-2-10) we get:

$$T(S) = Q^{-1}(S) \qquad (4-2-11)$$

Thus :

$$T(S) = \frac{adj\ Q}{det\ Q} \qquad (4-2-12)$$

where adj Q is the adjoint matrix of Q and so the elements of $T(S)$ are :

$$T_{ik} = \frac{det\ \overline{Q}_{ki}}{det\ Q} \qquad (4-2-13)$$

Where, $\overline{Q}_{ki}$ is the matrix obtained by obliterating the kth row and the ith column from matrix Q and there should be a sign $(-1)^{k+i}$ before det Q , but it has been omitted for simplicity.

For a two-variable system, we have:

$$T_{11} = \frac{V_{11}}{1 - V_{11}V_{22}V_{12}V_{21}} \qquad (4\text{-}2\text{-}14)$$

$$T_{22} = \frac{V_{22}}{1 - V_{11}V_{22}V_{12}V_{21}} \qquad (4\text{-}2\text{-}15)$$

$$T_{12} = \frac{V_{12}V_{11}V_{22}}{1 - V_{11}V_{22}V_{12}V_{21}} \qquad (4\text{-}2\text{-}16)$$

$$T_{21} = \frac{V_{21}V_{11}V_{22}}{1 - V_{11}V_{22}V_{12}V_{21}} \qquad (4\text{-}2\text{-}17)$$

If decoupling is expected, then it is necessary:

$$T_{12} = T_{21} = 0 \qquad (4\text{-}2\text{-}18)$$

Because neither of V_{11} and V_{22} is zero, so the above demand is corresponding to:

$$V_{12} = V_{21} = 0 \qquad (4\text{-}2\text{-}19)$$

This conclusion is logical since a system shown in Fig 4-2-1 is without any regulation function, so if decoupling is expected for it, certainly all coupling channels should be broken off.

There are two possible ways to break off the coupling channels. The first is to break them off really, but , perhaps, since the coupling channels are objective substance, we can not break them off freely.

The other way is to add compensation channels, For instance, in this example, because both $V_{12}(S)$ and $V_{21}(S)$ are not zeros , so in order to eliminate the coupling effects, we can introduce a pair of $-V_{21}(S)$ and $-V_{12}(S)$ and let:

$$\left.\begin{array}{l} V_{21}(S) - V_{21}(S) = 0 \\ V_{12}(S) - V_{12}(S) = 0 \end{array}\right\} \qquad (4\text{-}2\text{-}20)$$

Thus, the coupling effects are eliminated.

This is the so-called decoupling design. For an open loop control system, we can get the decoupling design visually by setting two opposite channels $-V_{21}(S)$ and $-V_{12}(S)$.

In practice, whether the coupling effects can be eliminated is determined by:

(1) Whether $V_{12}(S)$ and $V_{21}(S)$ describe the coupling characters exactly,

(2) Whether the decoupling channels $-V_{12}(S)$ and $-V_{21}(S)$ can be arranged. Perhaps, this problem is easily to be solved for V-canonical systems , since the coupling channels are from the high-energy-level outputs to the low-energy-level inputs and so it is possible to arrange the decoupling channels. But for P-canonical systems, the coupling channels are from low-energy-level inputs to high-energy-level outputs, in such cases, it is impossible to reach decoupling results by setting small decoupling elements.

The above analysis is for open loop control systems, but for closed-loop systems the decoupling design is much more complicated. For some very simple closed-loop control systems, the decoupling design, perhaps, may be obtained by visual observation, but in most cases analysis should be given in detail. Because of the feedback regulation effects in the closed-loop systems, how to utilize these effects to arrange the decoupling elements in order to get the simplest form and structure of decoupled systems is the key problem which should be discussed in great detail and systematically.

This is just the subject of our future discussion.

§ 4-3 The Decoupling Design of Closed-Loop Systems and Mesarović Ideas

We have pointed out before that the MPCS plants can be divided into two types, namely P-canonical and V-canonical, at the meantime we also said that the decoupling element structure also contains P-canonical and V-canonical. Consequently, a problem arises: In the decoupling design of MPCS, is it necessary to use the P-canonical decoupling element structure for the P-canonical plants or vice versa?

We have mentioned that the answer is negative.

This answer means that for a coupled plant, different ways or structures may be used to realize decoupling.

Then, certainly another problem arises: Which decoupling manner is the best, or at least is better than the others ?

In order to answer this problem we must make clear the meaning of " better". Practically, it contains two aspects. The first means that it results in better decoupling effects and the second means that it is easily to be realized , i.e. the decoupling conditions should be simple . Obviously, the decoupling conditions are certainly express themselves in 'the system structure,so the more complicated the decoupling conditions, the more complicated the system structure and the more difficult the realization of it.

It is impossible to explain this case in a few words and it can be confirmed only by systematic comparison of different design projects.

Now, we explain this problem by the discussion of the decoupling design of a two-variable P-canonical system .

Such a system is shown in Fig 4-3-1. Obviously, it is with a P-canonical plant. For this system, we have:

$$\left.\begin{array}{l} C_1(S) = P_{11}(S)M_1(S) + P_{12}(S)M_2(S) \\ C_2(S) = P_{21}(S)M_1(S) + P_{22}(S)M_2(S) \end{array}\right\} \qquad (4\text{-}3\text{-}1)$$

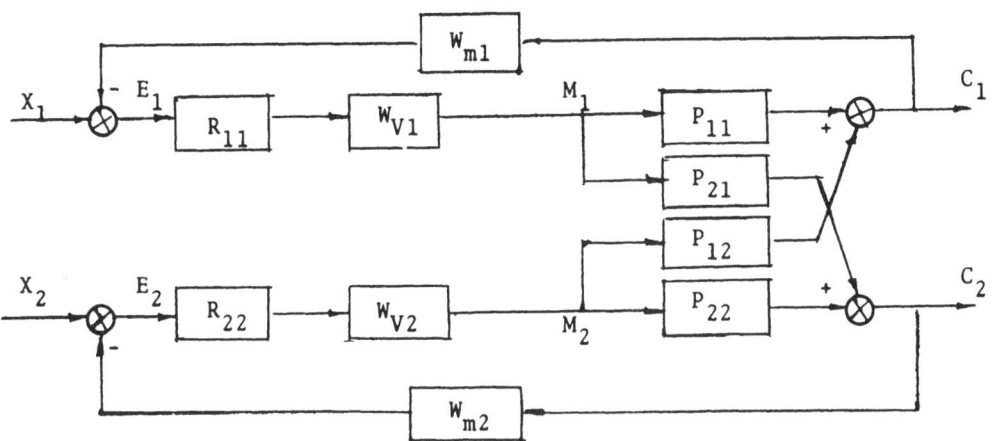

Fig 4-3-1

Writing in matrix form yields:

$$C(S) = P(S)M(S) \tag{4-3-2}$$

The control equations are:

$$\left. \begin{array}{l} M_1(S) = W_{V1}(S)R_{11}(S)E_1(S) \\ M_2(S) = W_{V2}(S)R_{22}(S)E_2(S) \end{array} \right\} \tag{4-3-2}$$

or in matrix form:

$$M(S) = W_V(S)R(S)E(S) \tag{4-3-3}$$

$$E(S) = X(S) - W_m(S)C(S) \tag{4-3-5}$$

Where:

$$W_V(S) = \begin{bmatrix} W_{V1} & 0 \\ 0 & W_{V2} \end{bmatrix} \quad R(S) = \begin{bmatrix} R_{11} & 0 \\ 0 & R_{22} \end{bmatrix} \quad W_m(S) = \begin{bmatrix} W_{m1} & 0 \\ 0 & W_{m2} \end{bmatrix}$$

From the above equations, we can get:

$$C = PW_V RE = WE \tag{4-3-6}$$

The system equation expressed in matrix form is:

$$(I + PW_V RW_m)C = PW_V RX \tag{4-3-7}$$

or:

$$C = (I + PW_V RW_m)^{-1}PW_V WRX \tag{4-3-8}$$

Namely:

$$C = (I + WW_m)^{-1}WX \tag{4-3-9}$$

This system is with coupling and if decoupling control is expected, namely to realize the one-to-one relation between inputs and outputs, then $(I + WW_m)^{-1}W$ should be a diagonal matrix. But, now it is not a diagonal matrix.

Therefore, in order to reach decoupling, we must carry out the decoupling design. An effective method is to replace the regulator matrix $R(S)$ by:

$$R(S) = \begin{pmatrix} R_{11} & R_{12} \\ R_{21} & R_{22} \end{pmatrix} \qquad (4\text{-}3\text{-}10)$$

but the feedback transfer matrix remains unchanged.

This decoupling project is often called as " feedforward decoupling structure" with the combination of regulators and decoupling elements and its block diagram is shown in Fig 4-3-2.

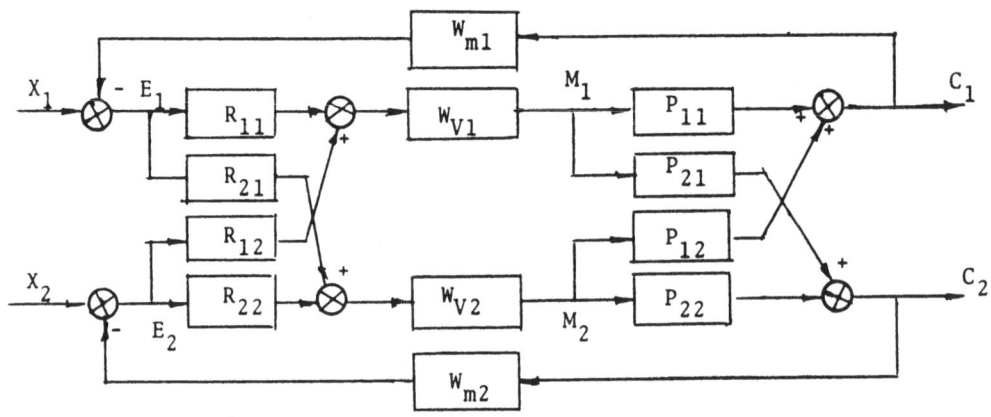

Fig 4-3-2

Substituting $R(S)$, $W_V(S)$ and $P(S)$ into $W(S)$ yields:

$$W(S) = \begin{pmatrix} P_{11}W_{V1}R_{11}(1 + \dfrac{P_{12}W_{V2}R_{21}}{P_{11}W_{V1}R_{11}}) & P_{11}W_{V1}R_{12} + P_{12}W_{V2}R_{22} \\ P_{21}W_{V1}R_{11} + P_{22}W_{V2}R_{21} & P_{22}W_{V2}R_{22}(1 + \dfrac{P_{21}W_{v1}R_{12}}{P_{22}W_{V2}R_{22}}) \end{pmatrix}$$

$$(4\text{-}3\text{-}11)$$

Because both I and W_m are diagonal matrices, so if we want
$(I + W(S)W_m(S))^{-1}W(S)$ being a diagonal matrix, then it is enough that
$W(S)$ is a diagonal matrix as we pointed out in § 3-10.

It demands:

$$\left.\begin{array}{l} P_{21}W_{V1}R_{11} + P_{22}W_{V2}R_{21} = 0 \\[2mm] P_{11}W_{V1}R_{12} + P_{12}W_{V2}R_{22} = 0 \end{array}\right\} \qquad (4\text{-}3\text{-}12)$$

It follows:

$$\left.\begin{array}{l} R_{21} = - \dfrac{P_{21}W_{V1}R_{11}}{P_{22}W_{V2}} \\[6mm] R_{12} = - \dfrac{P_{12}W_{V2}R_{22}}{P_{11}W_{V1}} \end{array}\right\} \qquad (4\text{-}3\text{-}13)$$

These are the decoupling conditions and the decoupling elements
should be realized by these conditions.

This is the case of P-canonical plant with P-canonical decoupling
element structure, and it is one of possible decoupling projects.

Now, we discuss another possible decoupling project shown in
Fig 4-3-3.

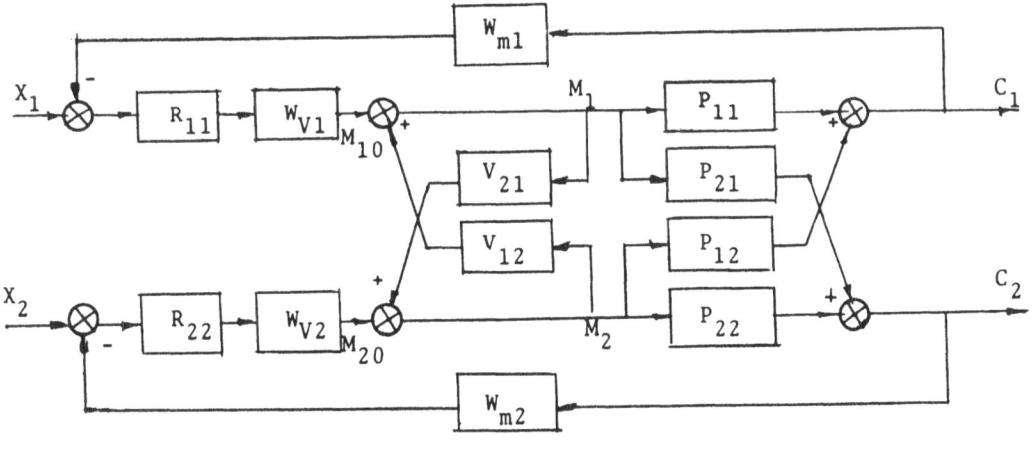

Fig 4-3-3

We see that the difference between Fig 4-3-2 and Fig 4-3-3 is that in the project of Fig 4-3-3 the V-canonical decoupling element structure is used and the decoupling elements do not combine with regulators either. For such a system, we have:

$$M_1 = \frac{M_{10} + V_{12}M_{20}}{1 - V_{12}V_{21}}$$

$$M_2 = \frac{M_{20} + V_{21}M_{10}}{1 - V_{12}V_{21}}$$

$$(4-3-14)$$

Thus:

$$C_1 = \frac{1}{1 - V_{12}V_{21}} ((P_{11} + P_{12}V_{21})M_{10} + (P_{12} + P_{11}V_{12})M_{10})$$

$$C_2 = \frac{1}{1 - V_{12}V_{21}} ((P_{21} + P_{22}V_{21})M_{10} + (P_{22} + P_{21}V_{12})M_{20})$$

$$(4-3-15)$$

Obviously, the decoupling conditions are:

$$P_{12} + P_{11}V_{12} = 0$$
$$P_{21} + P_{22}V_{21} = 0$$

$$(4-3-16)$$

Therefore:

$$V_{12} = - \frac{P_{12}}{P_{11}}$$

$$V_{21} = - \frac{P_{21}}{P_{22}}$$

$$(4-3-17)$$

Comparing (4-3-17) with (4-3-13), we find that in this decoupling project the decoupling elements do not relate to regulators and valve characters , so the characters of (4-3-17) are more easily to be realized than those of (4-3-13) since they only relate to the plant characters. On the contrary, when both regulators and valves are with different characters, the decoupling elements shown in (4-3-13) are with complicated forms and sometimes may be difficult to be realized.

This example tell us explicitly that for the same two-variable P-canonical plant, different decoupling structures may be used to realize decoupling **and** the corresponding decoupling conditions are also different.

Then, when the form of the plant , P-canonical or V-canonical, is determined, which decoupling project is better for decoupling design?

This is a very interesting problem and is worth being researched. In fact, if we did not make it clear theoretically, then we would fall in great blindness in decoupling design. This problem is closely related to the famous Mesarović ideas which say : The V-canonical structures can describe a multivariable control sytem better and, in general, better decoupling effects will be reached if V-canonical structures are adopted **with** feedback decoupling design.

It is not easily to understand this implicit proposition only accor-ding to its narration. Mesarović proposed this proposition from the ge-neral concepts of multivariable control systems and he did not give very explicit proof to it. Thus, when we deal with the decoupling design of multivariable process control systems, we should judge the correctness and the meaning of this proposition from two aspects:

(1) The meaning of " V-canonical structures" contains not only V-canonical plants, but also V-canonical decoupling element structures, then why is it said that the V-canonical structures can describe a mul-tivariable control system better ?

(2) Why the combination of V-canonical structures with feedback de-coupling design can give better decoupling effects. What is the practical meaning of " better" in multivariable process control systems ?

We will discuss these two problems in detail step by step.

§ 4-4 Uncertainty of the Decoupling Design

We have said before that for a P-canonical plant or a V-canonical plant, its mathematical description can be transferred to each other and this does not influence the characters of its inputs and outputs.

What is the physical meaning of this conclusion?

Its physical meaning means: If we stood at the input side or the output side of the plant to observe and knew that this plant is a coupled one,then we could only confirm that this is a coupled plant and could not determine the plant being P-canonical or V-canonical only by the observation results since both canonical forms can transfer to each other. This is an expression of uncertainty of coupling characters of a multivariable control system.

But we must notice here that although we say that we can not determine the exact type of this plant, it does not obstruct us to measure the coupling characters of this plant by experiments with definite manner, for example with P-canonical manner. Our meaning is: When people find the coupling characters of a plant by P-canonical manner, certainly they can say that this is a P-canonical plant , but they , perhaps, do not discover if they measure the coupling characters of the same plant by some special V-canonical manner, they can also get the coupling characters of this plant and in such a case they prefer to say that it is a V-canonical plant.

This is the uncertainty of plant characters.

On the other hand, we said in the last paragraph that for a MPCS, different projects may be adopted to realize decoupling design, for example we may use P-canonical decoupling element structure or V-canonical decoupling element structure. In addition, for each decoupling element structure, there are several available connection (compensation) models for it. In next paragraph, we will introduce the most common four connection models. Thus, it tells us that for a MPCS its

decoupling design is not with a unique definite solution and this is
the uncertainty of the decoupling design.

We will discuss further even when the decoupling element structure
and the connection model have been determined, the solution of the practical parameters of decoupling elements may be not unique. This is also
an expression of uncertainty of decoupling design.

Let us discuss an example.

Fig 4-4-1 shows a coupled system without decoupling design.

Suppose:

$$
\left.
\begin{aligned}
z_1 &= P_{11}R_{11} \\
z_2 &= P_{12}R_{22} \\
z_3 &= P_{21}R_{11} \\
z_4 &= P_{22}P_{22} \\
z_5 &= (1 + z_1)(1 + z_4) - z_2 z_3
\end{aligned}
\right\}
\qquad (4-4-1)
$$

then we get:

$$
C_1 = \frac{(1 + z_4)z_1 - z_2 z_3}{z_5} X_1 + \frac{z_2}{z_5} X_2 \qquad (4-4-2)
$$

$$
C_2 = \frac{(1 + z_1)z_4 - z_2 z_3}{z_5} X_2 + \frac{z_3}{z_5} X_1 \qquad (4-4-3)
$$

Obviously, there is coupling between C_1, C_2 and X_1, X_2.

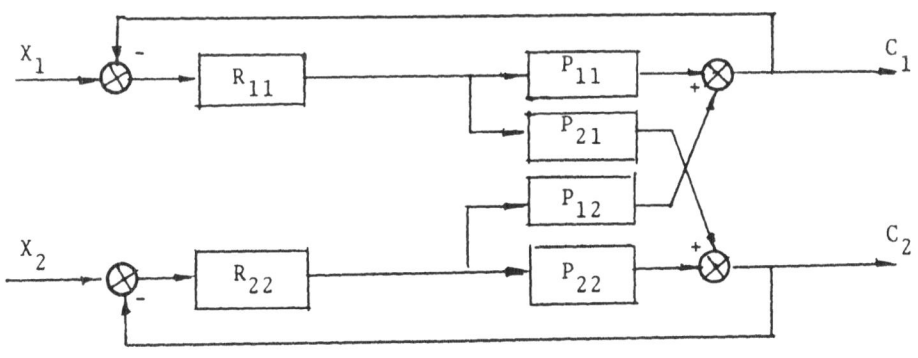

Fig 4-4-1

Now, suppose that P-canonical decoupling element structure is used and the decoupling elements are connected between palnt and regulators.

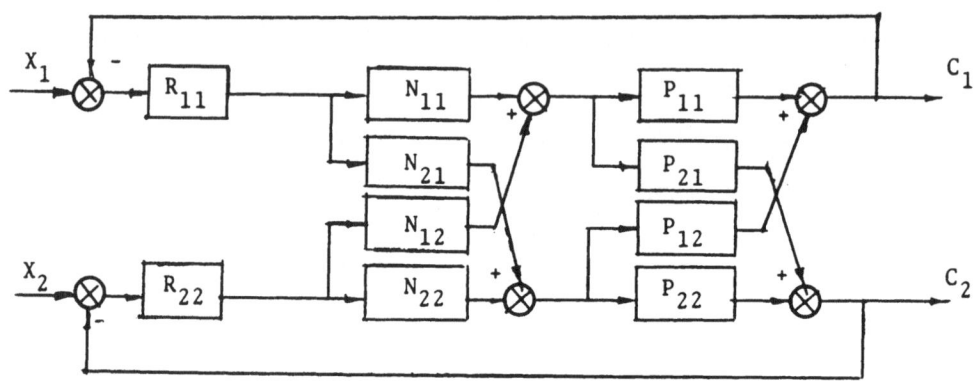

Fig 4-4-2

Comparing two figures, we can get visually:

$$Z_1 = (N_{11}P_{11} + N_{21}P_{12})R_{11}$$

$$Z_2 = (N_{22}P_{12} + N_{12}P_{11})R_{22}$$

$$Z_3 = (N_{11}P_{21} + N_{21}P_{22})R_{11}$$

$$Z_4 = (N_{22}P_{22} + N_{12}P_{21})R_{22}$$

$$Z_5 = (1 + Z_1)(1 + Z_4) - Z_2Z_3$$

(4-4-4)

and we get:

$$C_1 = \frac{(1 + Z_4)Z_1 - Z_2Z_3}{Z_5} X_1 + \frac{Z_2}{Z_5} X_2$$

(4-4-5)

$$C_2 = \frac{(1 + Z_1)Z_4 - Z_2Z_3}{Z_5} X_2 + \frac{Z_3}{Z_5} X_1$$

(4-4-6)

From (4-4-5) and (4-4-6) we can know that the decoupling conditons are:

$$Z_2 = Z_3 = 0$$

(4-4-7)

namely:

$$N_{22}P_{12} + N_{12}P_{11} = 0$$

(4-4-8)

$$N_{11}P_{21} + N_{21}P_{22} = 0 \qquad\qquad (4\text{-}4\text{-}9)$$

We want to determine the practical parameters of the decoupling elements, i.e. the parameters of N_{11}, N_{12}, N_{21} and N_{22}, but there are only two equations giving decoupling conditions, so we can not get a unique set of four parameters from these two equations.

For example, all the following four sets are suitable for the above two equations, so every set is a solution.

$$N_{11} = 1 \;,\; N_{12} = -\frac{P_{12}}{P_{11}} \;,\; N_{22} = 1 \;,\; N_{21} = -\frac{P_{21}}{P_{22}}$$

$$N_{11} = 1 \;,\; N_{12} = 1 \;,\; N_{21} = -\frac{P_{21}}{P_{22}} \;,\; N_{22} = -\frac{P_{11}}{P_{12}}$$

$$N_{11} = -\frac{P_{22}}{P_{21}} \;,\; N_{12} = -\frac{P_{12}}{P_{11}} \;,\; N_{21} = 1 \;,\; N_{22} = 1$$

$$N_{11} = -\frac{P_{22}}{P_{21}} \;,\; N_{12} = 1 \;,\; N_{21} = 1 \;,\; N_{22} = -\frac{P_{11}}{P_{12}}$$

Obviously, the solution is not unique.

Notice that it is not a bad thing that the solution is not unique since just because of this, we get the possibility to choose the better solution which is easily to be realized.

The decoupled system becomes:

$$C_1 = \frac{Z_1}{1 + Z_1} X_1 \qquad\qquad (4\text{-}4\text{-}10)$$

$$C_2 = \frac{Z_4}{1 + Z_4} X_2 \qquad\qquad (4\text{-}4\text{-}11)$$

§ 4-5 The General Decoupling Structures and Calculation Formulas[30]

We have mentioned some problems of decoupling design, for example, the uncertainty of solutions is a salient problem. It means that for a MPCS, different projects may be used to realize decoupling design.

The diagonal matrix method is the basic method for decoupling design. The principle of this method is very evident and is easily to be applied also, but, however, in order to design a successful and rational decoupling system, we must understand the Mesarović ideas.

Therefore, we will discuss the decoupling design theory by two steps. At first, we discuss the general principles and methods of decoupling design and then we discuss the Mesarović ideas.

For a MPCS, the so-called " decoupling" means to realize the one-to-one control relation between outputs and inputs, thus when the system inputs have been determined, the other inputs become disturbances.

Consequently, the decoupling design should have two cases:

(1) The system can realize the one-to-one control relation between outputs and inputs, but can not realize the one-to-one relation between outputs and disturbances,

(2) The system can realize not only the one-to-one control relation between outputs and inputs , but also the one-to-one relation between outputs and disturbances.

Obviously, judging by the results of decoupling, the latter is better than the former.

In general, in process control systems, the decoupling elements are connected into the systems according to the following four manners:

(1) Before the regulators,

(2) Combined with regulators,

(3) Between the plant and regulators,

(4) At the feedback channels.

What we want to discuss is about:

Can all the above manners be used to realize decoupling?

What are their decoupling conditions?

What is the difference of decoupling effects among them?

Which manner should be adopted in given cases?

Only when we understand the above several aspects, we can choose a better decoupling design in practice .

Notice when we discuss the above problems, three kinds of contents are always concerned and they occur at the same time.

The three kinds of contents concerned are:

(1) The plant may be either P-canonical or V-canonical,

(2) The decoupling element structure may be either P-canonical or V-canonical,

(3) The decoupling element structures may be connected into the system according to anyone of the above four manners.

Thus, if each combination gives a set of solutions, then we will have 16 sets of solutions and this is just the expression of uncertainty.

In the follwing discussions the P-canonical decoupling element structure is considered as:

$$
\left.
\begin{aligned}
L_1 &= V_1 + N_{12}V_2 + \cdots\cdots + N_{1n}V_n \\
L_2 &= N_{21}V_1 + V_2 + \cdots\cdots + N_{2n}V_n \\
&\vdots\vdots\vdots\vdots\vdots\vdots\vdots\vdots\vdots\vdots\vdots\vdots\vdots\vdots\vdots\vdots \\
L_n &= N_{n1}V_1 + N_{n2}V_2 + \cdots\cdots + V_n
\end{aligned}
\right\}
\qquad (4\text{-}5\text{-}1)
$$

thus, the P-canonical decoupling matrix is:

$$
N_p = \begin{pmatrix}
1 & N_{12} & - & - & - & - & N_{1n} \\
N_{21} & 1 & - & - & - & - & N_{2n} \\
= & = & = & = & = & = & = \\
N_{n1} & N_{n2} & - & - & - & - & 1
\end{pmatrix}
\qquad (4\text{-}5\text{-}2)
$$

The general   form   of the V-canonical decoupling element structure is :

$$
\left.
\begin{aligned}
L_1 &= V_1 + N_{12}L_2 + N_{13}L_3 + \text{-------} + N_{1n}L_n \\
L_2 &= V_2 + N_{21}L_1 + N_{23}L_3 + \text{-------} + N_{2n}L_n \\
&\vdots\ \vdots\ \vdots\ \vdots\ \vdots\ \vdots\ \vdots\ \vdots\ \vdots\ \vdots\ \vdots\ \vdots\ \vdots\ \vdots\ \vdots\ \vdots\ \vdots\ \vdots\ \vdots \\
L_n &= V_n + N_{n1}L_1 + N_{n2}L_2 + \text{--------}+ N_{n,n-1}L_{n-1}
\end{aligned}
\right\}
\qquad (4\text{-}5\text{-}3)
$$

and the V-canonical decoupling matrix may be written as:

$$
N_V = \begin{pmatrix}
1 & N_{12} & - & - & - & - & - & N_{1n} \\
N_{21} & 1 & & - & - & - & - & N_{2n} \\
\vdots & \vdots & \vdots & \vdots & \vdots & \vdots & \vdots & \vdots \\
N_{n1} & N_{n2} & - & - & - & - & - & 1
\end{pmatrix}
\qquad (4\text{-}5\text{-}4)
$$

but, as we said in § 1-5, N_V is not like N_P and is not a **direct** transfer matrix.

We proved in § 1-6 that if we want to transfer a V-canonical decoupling element structure into a P-canonical one, then we can let:

$$
A = \begin{pmatrix}
1 & -N_{12} & - & - & - & - & - & - & -N_{1n} \\
-N_{21} & 1 & & - & - & - & - & - & -N_{2n} \\
\vdots & \vdots & \vdots & \vdots & \vdots & \vdots & \vdots & \vdots & \vdots \\
-N_{n1} & -N_{n2} & - & - & - & - & - & - & 1
\end{pmatrix}
\qquad (4\text{-}5\text{-}5)
$$

and:

$$
N_P = A^{-1}
\qquad (4\text{-}5\text{-}6)
$$

Now, we discuss the most common case, namely the decoupling element structure is connected between the plant and regulators.

Such a system is shown in Fig 4-5-1.

In this figure, the plant transfer matrix is expressed by S and when the plant is P-canonical , then:

$$
S = P
\qquad (4\text{-}5\text{-}7)
$$

When the plant is V-canonical, then:

$$
S = T^{-1}
\qquad (4\text{-}5\text{-}8)
$$

N is the decoupling element structure matrix and it may be P-canonical, N_p, or V-canonical, N_V.

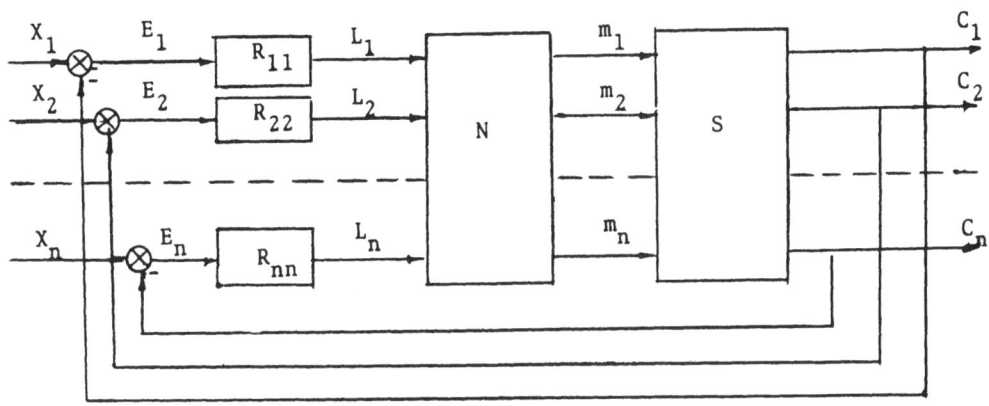

Fig 4-5-1

From this figure, we get:

$$C = SM$$

$$L = RE$$

$$M = NL$$

$$E = X - C$$

(4-5-9)

After necessary transformation, it yields:

$$C = (I + SNR)^{-1}SNRX$$

(4-5-10)

Thus, by the principles of the diagonal matrix method, in order

to realize decoupling, it is necessary and only necessary that

$(I + SRN)^{-1}SNR$ is a diagonal matrix. In other words, SNR should be a

diagonal matrix. That means that the decoupling condition is:

$$SNR = D$$

(4-5-11)

where, D is a diagonal matrix.

Now, we discuss different cases for this project.

At first, we suppose that the decoupling element structure is

P-canonical, i.e. $N = N_p$.

Solving (4-5-11), we get:

$$N_p = S^{-1}DR^{-1}$$

(4-5-12)

Because R is a diagonal matrix, so the above equation can be written

in the element form:

$$N_{ik} = \frac{\det \bar{S}_{ki}}{\det S} \frac{D_{kk}}{R_{kk}}$$

(4-5-13)

When i = k , we get:

$$N_{kk} = \frac{\det \bar{S}_{kk}}{\det S} \frac{D_{kk}}{R_{kk}} \qquad (4-5-14)$$

but, on the other hand, from (4-5-2) we know that $N_{kk} = 1$, so:

$$D_{kk} = \frac{\det S}{\det \bar{S}_{kk}} R_{kk} \qquad (4-5-15)$$

Then, substituting (4-5-15) into (4-5-13) yields:

$$N_{ik} = \frac{\det \bar{S}_{ki}}{\det \bar{S}_{kk}} \qquad (4-5-16)$$

If the plant is P-canonical, then in the above expression, we let: S = P and we get:

$$N_{ik} = \frac{\det \bar{P}_{ki}}{\det \bar{P}_{kk}} \qquad (4-5-17)$$

If the plant is V-canonical, then from (4-5-15) and (1-6-16) we get:

$$D_{kk} = R_{kk} V_{kk} \qquad (4-5-18)$$

Then, from (4-5-13), (1-6-17) and (4-5-18), we get:

$$N_{ik} = - V_{ik} V_{kk} \qquad (4-5-19)$$

Now, we discuss when the decoupling element structure is with V-canonical, namely:

$$N = N_V \qquad (4-5-20)$$

At first, we denote the system decoupling matrix in the form of (4-5-5) and then substitute (4-5-6) into (4-5-11) and solve for A. The result is:

$$A = RD^{-1}S \qquad (4-5-21)$$

In element form, it is:

$$A_{ik} = \frac{R_{ii}}{D_{ii}} S_{ik} \qquad (4-5-22)$$

When $i = k$, from (4-5-5) we know that $A_{kk} = 1$, so from (4-5-22) we get:

$$D_{kk} = R_{kk}S_{kk} \qquad (4-5-23)$$

Subsituting it into (4-5-22) and eliminating R_{ii}, and then from (4-5-5) $A_{ik} = -N_{ik}$, we get finally :

$$N_{ik} = - \frac{S_{ik}}{S_{kk}} \qquad (4-5-24)$$

In this case, if the plant is P-canonical, i.e. $S = P$, then:

$$\left. \begin{array}{l} D_{kk} = P_{kk}R_{kk} \\[2mm] N_{ik} = - \dfrac{P_{ik}}{P_{ii}} \end{array} \right\} \qquad (4-5-25)$$

When the plant is V-canonical, from (1-6-14) we get:

$$P_{ik} = \frac{\det \overline{T}_{ki}}{\det T} \qquad (4-5-26)$$

thus, substituting it into (4-5-24) yields:

$$\left. \begin{array}{l} D_{kk} = \dfrac{\det \overline{T}_{kk}}{\det T} R_{kk} \\[4mm] N_{kk} = - \dfrac{\det \overline{T}_{ki}}{\det \overline{T}_{ii}} \end{array} \right\} \qquad (4-5-27)$$

In summary:

(1) For the P-canonical plant and the P-canonical decoupling element structure, formula (4-5-17) is available,

(2) For the P-canonical plant and V-canonical decouping element structure, formula (4-5-25) is available,

(3) For the V-canonical plant and the P-canonical decoupling element structure, formula (4-5-19) is available,

(4) For the V-canonical plant and the V-canonical decoupling element structure, formula (4-5-27) is available.

For example, a three-variable system with the P-canonical plant and the P-canonical decoupling element structure , then when the decoupling element structure is inserted between the plant and regulators , the decoupling elements are determined by (4-5-17), namely:

$$N_{ik} = \frac{\det \bar{P}_{ki}}{\det \bar{P}_{kk}}$$

This is:

$$N_{12} = \frac{P_{13}P_{32} - P_{12}P_{33}}{P_{11}P_{33} - P_{13}P_{31}}$$

$$N_{13} = \frac{P_{12}P_{23} - P_{13}P_{22}}{P_{11}P_{22} - P_{12}P_{21}}$$

$$N_{21} = \frac{P_{23}P_{31} - P_{21}P_{23}}{P_{22}P_{33} - P_{23}P_{32}}$$

$$N_{23} = \frac{P_{21}P_{13} - P_{11}P_{23}}{P_{11}P_{22} - P_{12}P_{21}}$$

$$N_{31} = \frac{P_{21}P_{32} - P_{22}P_{31}}{P_{22}P_{33} - P_{23}P_{32}}$$

$$N_{32} = \frac{P_{12}P_{31} - P_{11}P_{32}}{P_{11}P_{33} - P_{13}P_{31}}$$

According the same principles mentioned above, we can also discuss the other cases when the location of the decoupling element structure is different. For example, when the decoupling element structure is located before regulators, the system is shown in Fig 4-5-2.

From this figure, it yields:

$$C = (I + SRN)^{-1} SRNX \qquad (4-5-28)$$

If the decoupling control is expected, it is necessary:

$$SRN = D \qquad (4-5-29)$$

is a diagonal matrix.

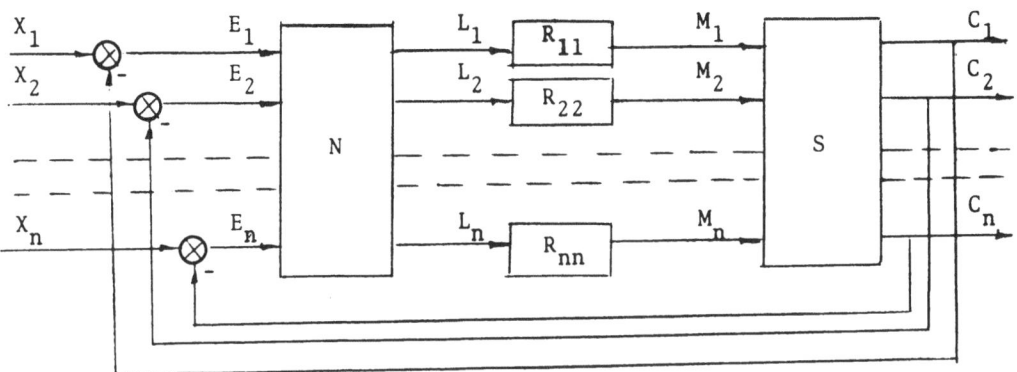

Fig 4-5-2

When the decoupling element structure is combined with the regu-

lators, the system is shown in Fig 4-5-3.

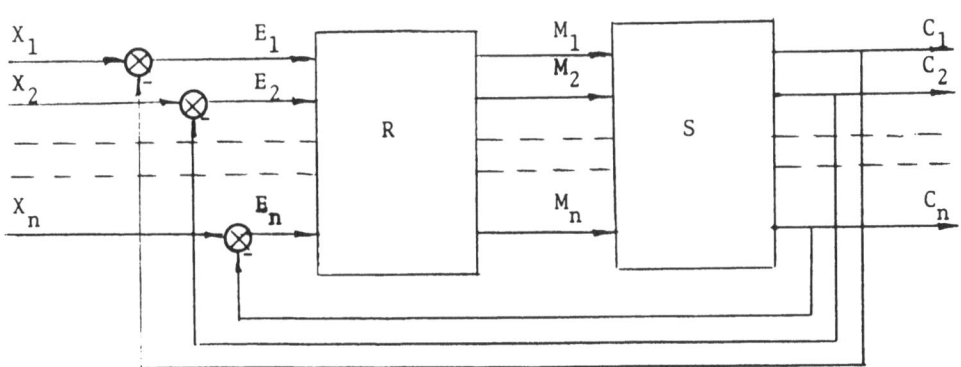

Fig 4-5-3

We have:

$$C = (I + SR)^{-1} SRX \qquad (4-5-30)$$

In order to get decoupling control, it is necessary:

$$SR = D \qquad (4-5-31)$$

is a diagonal matrix.

When the decoupling element structure is located at the feedback

channels, the system is shown in Fig 4-5-4.

For this system, we get:

$$C = (I + SRN)^{-1} SRX \qquad (4-5-32)$$

In order to get decoupling control, it is necessary:

$$(I + SRN)^{-1}SR = D \qquad\qquad (4-5-33)$$

is a diagonal matrix.

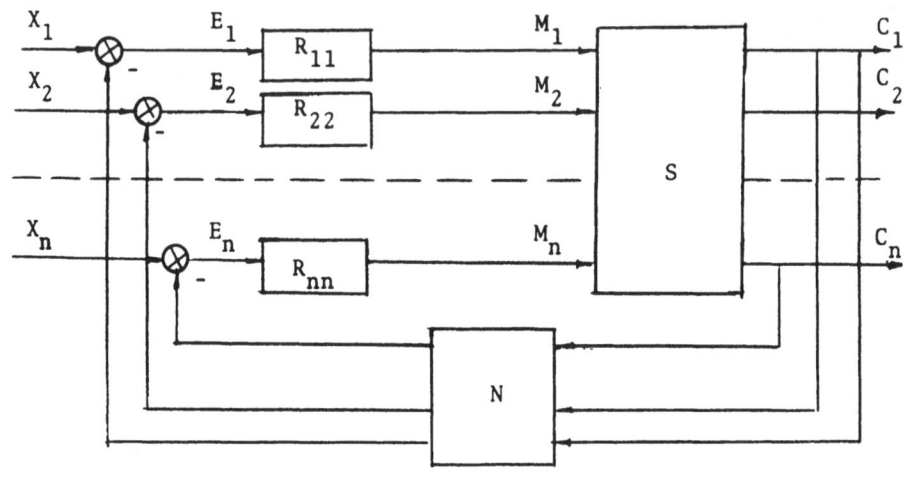

Fig 4-5-4

All the calculation formulas for different cases are listed in the following table.

A problem may be proposed here: We have said before that even the decoupling project has been determined, we can not get the unique solution, but, however, all the solutions in this table are unique.

How to explain it?

There is no contradiction indeed. This is because for all the decoupling projects expressed in (4-5-3) , we have a general assumption, i.e.

$$N_{ii} = 1 \qquad\qquad (4-5-34)$$

Just because of the existence of this assumption, the solution for each case becomes unique. For **instance**, for the example discussed in the last paragraph, when $N_{11} = N_{22} = 1$, the solution is unique.

Decoupling Elements	P-Canonical Plant		V-Canonical Plant	
	P-Canonical	V-Canonical	P-Canonical	V-Canonical
Before Regulators	$N_{ik} = \dfrac{\det \bar{P}_{ki}}{\det \bar{P}_{kk}}\dfrac{R_{kk}}{R_{ii}}$	$N_{ik} = -\dfrac{P_{ik}}{P_{ii}}\dfrac{R_{kk}}{R_{ii}}$	$N_{ik} = -V_{ik}V_{kk}\dfrac{R_{kk}}{R_{ii}}$	$N_{ik} = -\dfrac{\det \bar{T}_{ki}}{\det \bar{T}_{ii}}\dfrac{R_{kk}}{R_{ii}}$
Combined with Regulators	$R_{ik} = \dfrac{\det \bar{P}_{ki}}{\det \bar{P}_{kk}}R_{kk}$	$R_{ik} = -\dfrac{P_{ik}}{P_{ii}}\dfrac{1}{R_{ii}}$	$R_{ik} = -V_{ik}V_{kk}R_{kk}$	$R_{ik} = -\dfrac{\det \bar{T}_{ki}}{\det \bar{T}_{ii}}\dfrac{1}{R_{ii}}$
After Regulators	$N_{ik} = \dfrac{\det \bar{P}_{ki}}{\det \bar{P}_{kk}}$	$N_{ik} = -\dfrac{P_{ik}}{P_{ii}}$	$N_{ik} = -V_{ik}V_{kk}$	$N_{ik} = -\dfrac{\det \bar{T}_{ki}}{\det \bar{T}_{ii}}$
At Feedback Channels	$N_{ik} = -\dfrac{\det \bar{P}_{ki}}{\det P}\dfrac{1}{R_{ii}}$		$N_{ik} = -\dfrac{V_{ik}}{R_{ii}}$	

§ 4-6 The First Practical Meaning of Mesarović Idea

We have discussed how to utilize the diagonal matrix method to perform the decoupling design and the results are shown in the table.

Some conclusions can be reached from this table.

At first, in the first column (P-canonical plant and P-canonical decoupling element structure) and the fourth column (V-canonical plant and V-canonical decoupling element structure), every decoupling element is determined by the ratio of two determinants from the plant character, so when the number of variables is larger than two and the channels are with different characters, the N_{ik} obtained by such expressions are with very complicated forms, but, however, for the second column (V-canonical plant and P-canonical decoupling element structure), every decoupling element is only determined by the ratio or the product of the two transfer functions of the plant or the regulators, so their forms are much simpler. Especially, we should notice that their forms are not related to the number of system variables.

It denotes a very important conclusion in system decoupling design:

For a plant with the given canonical form, only the decoupling element structure of the inverse canonical form is adopted, the decoupling conditions may be simple.

Thus, in order to simplify the realization conditions for decoupling design, the V-canonical form is necessary, i.e. either P-canonical plant and V-canonical decoupling element structure or V-canonical plant and P-canonical decoupling element structure. This is just the first practical meaning of Mesarović idea.

But, at the meantime we can see from this table that not all V-canonical projects are good, for example the decoupling project of V-canonical plant with the V-canonical decoupling element structure is not with simple realization conditions.

Furthermore, from this table we can know that in general the transfer functions of the decoupling elements are related not only to the plant , but also to the regulators. Only when the decoupling elements are located between the plant and the regulators,the transfer functions of decoupling elements are related only to the plant.

That means that in such cases the change of the parameters of the regulators will not give any influence on the decoupling control character, so when the system is set on-line, this project is with great advantage.

In addition, the decoupling realization conditions for each decoupling element are not related to the number of system variables either.

For example, for a two-variable system with a P-canonical plant and a V-canonical decoupling element structure, the decoupling condition is:

$$N_{12} = - \frac{P_{12}}{P_{11}} \qquad (4-6-1)$$

and for a four-variable system with the same structure, this condition remains unchanged, certainly other conditions are added. But, however, this decoupling channel is unchanged, especially, when $P_{12}=0$, then $N_{12}=0$.

For comparison, we discuss a four variable system with a P-canonical plant and a P-canonical decoupling element structure, the corresponding decoupling channel of N_{12} is of the following character:

$$N_{12} = \frac{P_{12}(P_{33}P_{44}-P_{34}P_{43}) - P_{13}(P_{32}P_{44}-P_{34}P_{42}) + P_{14}(P_{32}P_{43}-P_{33}P_{42})}{P_{11}(P_{33}P_{44}-P_{34}P_{43}) - P_{13}(P_{31}P_{44}-P_{34}P_{41}) + P_{14}(P_{31}P_{43}-P_{33}P_{41})}$$

$$(4-6-2)$$

Obviously, this condition is not only very complicated, but also becoming more complicated as the increase of the system variables and even when $P_{12} = 0$, the N_{12} is not zero.

Therefore, the location of the **decoupling** element structure between the plant and the regulators can result in simple decoupling conditions,i.e. they are not related to regulators; and then if
the Mesarović idea is applied, namely the P-canonical plant is with
the V-canonical decoupling element structure or the V-canonical plant
is with the P-canonical decoupling element structure, the decoupling
conditions obtained are the simplest.

Now, we have explained the first practical meaning of the Mesarović idea, as for the second practical meaning of this idea,it is not
easily explained here and we will explain it in the future several
paragraphs.

Another important point is: For the P-canonical decoupling element structure, the energy level of signals is from low to high and
the signals always flow forward . But in control systems, the signals
with high energy level often may be saturated, so when a manipulated
variable connected with the exit of a decoupling element is saturated,
then the system fails to give any compensation to such phenomena. On
the contrary, the V-canonical decoupling element structure is different. Its signals always flow from the high energy level to the low
energy level and when the signal of a manipulated variable is saturared,
it can be sensed by the decoupling element and this phenomenon can
be compensated by the decoupling channels to each other.

The Mesarović idea is with abundant contents which are quite available for decoupling design and we will explain step by step.

§ 4-7 The Decoupling Design of Systems with First Order Elements

In § 3-7, we discussed the coupled systems with first order elements.Now, we discuss the decoupling design of such systems.

Suppose that both plant and decoupling element structure are P-canonical and the decoupling elements are located between the plant and regulators.The system is shown in Fig 4-7-1.

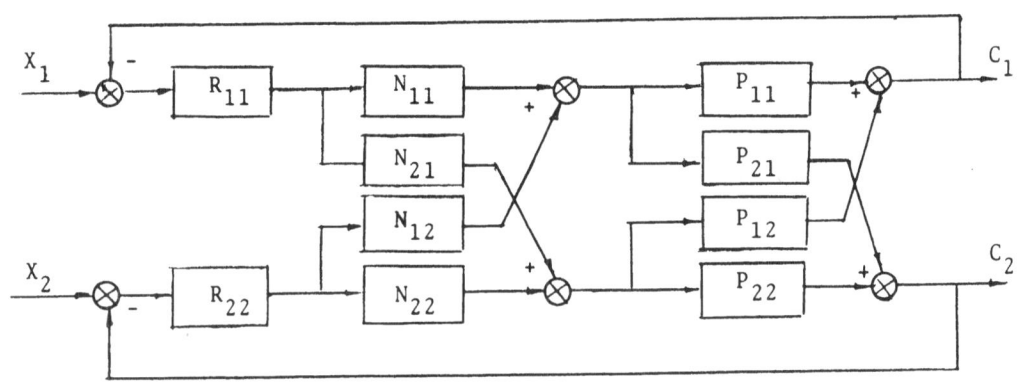

Fig 4-7-1

By the assumption of the last paragraph:

$$N_{11} = N_{22} = 1 \qquad (4-7-1)$$

then for this system, its decoupling conditions are:

$$\left. \begin{aligned} N_{12} &= - \frac{P_{12}}{P_{11}} \\[2em] N_{21} &= - \frac{P_{21}}{P_{22}} \end{aligned} \right\} \qquad (4-7-2)$$

From (3-7-12), we have:

$$\left. \begin{aligned} P_{12} &= - \frac{1}{S + 1} \\[1.5em] P_{21} &= \frac{1}{S + 1} \\[1.5em] P_{11} = P_{22} &= \frac{1}{S + 1} \end{aligned} \right\} \qquad (4-7-3)$$

Thus:

$$N_{12} = 1.0$$

$$N_{21} = -1.0$$

(4-7-4)

Obviously, it is very easy to realize them.

The decoupled outputs are:

$$C_1 = \frac{2K_{11}}{S + 2K_{11} + 1} X_1$$

$$C_2 = \frac{2K_{22}}{S + 2K_{22} + 1} X_2$$

(4-7-5)

where, K_{11} and K_{22} are the gains of the two PI regulators.

The response of the decoupled system is shown in Fig 4-7-2. We see that there is no interaction now.

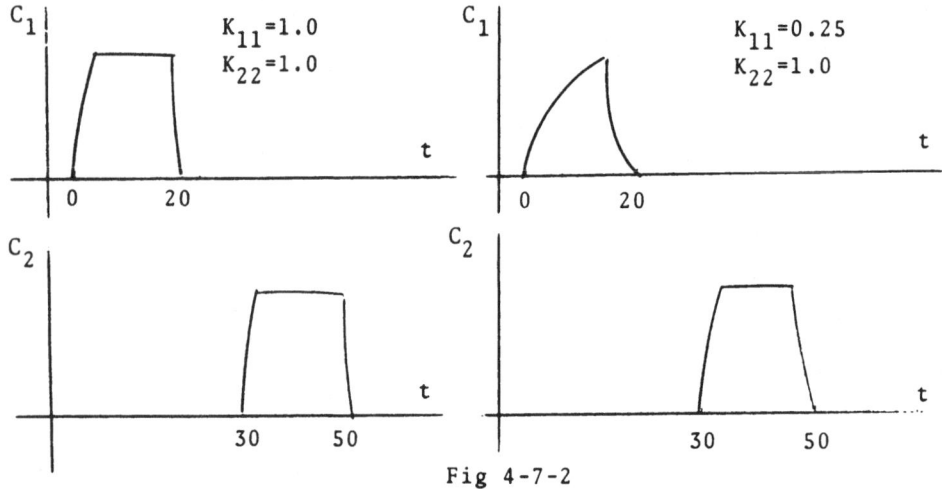

Fig 4-7-2

The above analysis denotes that for the coupled systems with first order plants and all plant channels with same lags, the decoupling elements are propotional links and they are very easily realized.

In general, if:

$$P = \begin{pmatrix} \dfrac{K_{P11}}{T_{11}S+1} & \dfrac{K_{P12}}{T_{12}S+1} \\[3mm] \dfrac{K_{P21}}{T_{21}S+1} & \dfrac{K_{P22}}{T_{22}S+1} \end{pmatrix}$$

(4-7-6)

then for $N_{11} = N_{22} = 1$, the decoupling elements are:

$$N_{12} = - \frac{P_{12}}{P_{11}} = - \frac{K_{P12}}{K_{P11}} \frac{T_{11}S + 1}{T_{12}S + 1} \qquad (4-7-7).$$

$$N_{21} = - \frac{P_{21}}{P_{22}} = - \frac{K_{P21}}{K_{P22}} \frac{T_{22}S + 1}{T_{21}S + 1} \qquad (4-7-8)$$

Thus, both N_{12} and N_{21} can be realized by lead-lag elements.

Because the systems with first order elements are easily decoupled, so in practice, some systems with higher order elements are often approximated by the systems with first order elements in order to get simple decoupling conditions. In such cases, although the decoupling results are not perfect, it can reduce the coupling effects remarkably.

For example, let:

$$P = \begin{pmatrix} \dfrac{1}{(S+1)^2} & -\dfrac{1}{2S + 1} \\[3mm] \dfrac{1}{3S + 1} & \dfrac{1}{(S+1)^2} \end{pmatrix} \qquad (4-7-9)$$

Obviously, the system is with second order elements.

In order to realize the perfect decoupling, the decoupling elements are given by:

$$\left. \begin{aligned} N_{12} &= - \frac{P_{12}}{P_{11}} = \frac{1.0(S + 1)^2}{2S + 1} \\[3mm] N_{21} &= - \frac{P_{21}}{P_{22}} = - \frac{1.0(S + 1)^2}{3S + 1} \end{aligned} \right\} \qquad (4-7-10)$$

These two elements are difficult to be realized.

In order to realize them easily, we take the approximate expressions:

$$\left. \begin{aligned} N_{12} &\approx \frac{2S + 1}{2S + 1} = 1.0 \\[3mm] N_{21} &\approx - \frac{2S + 1}{3S + 1} \end{aligned} \right\} \qquad (4-7-11)$$

So, it can be treated as a system with first order elements and

200

the realization conditions for the decoupling elements are very simple.
Fig 4-7-3 is the response before decoupling design.

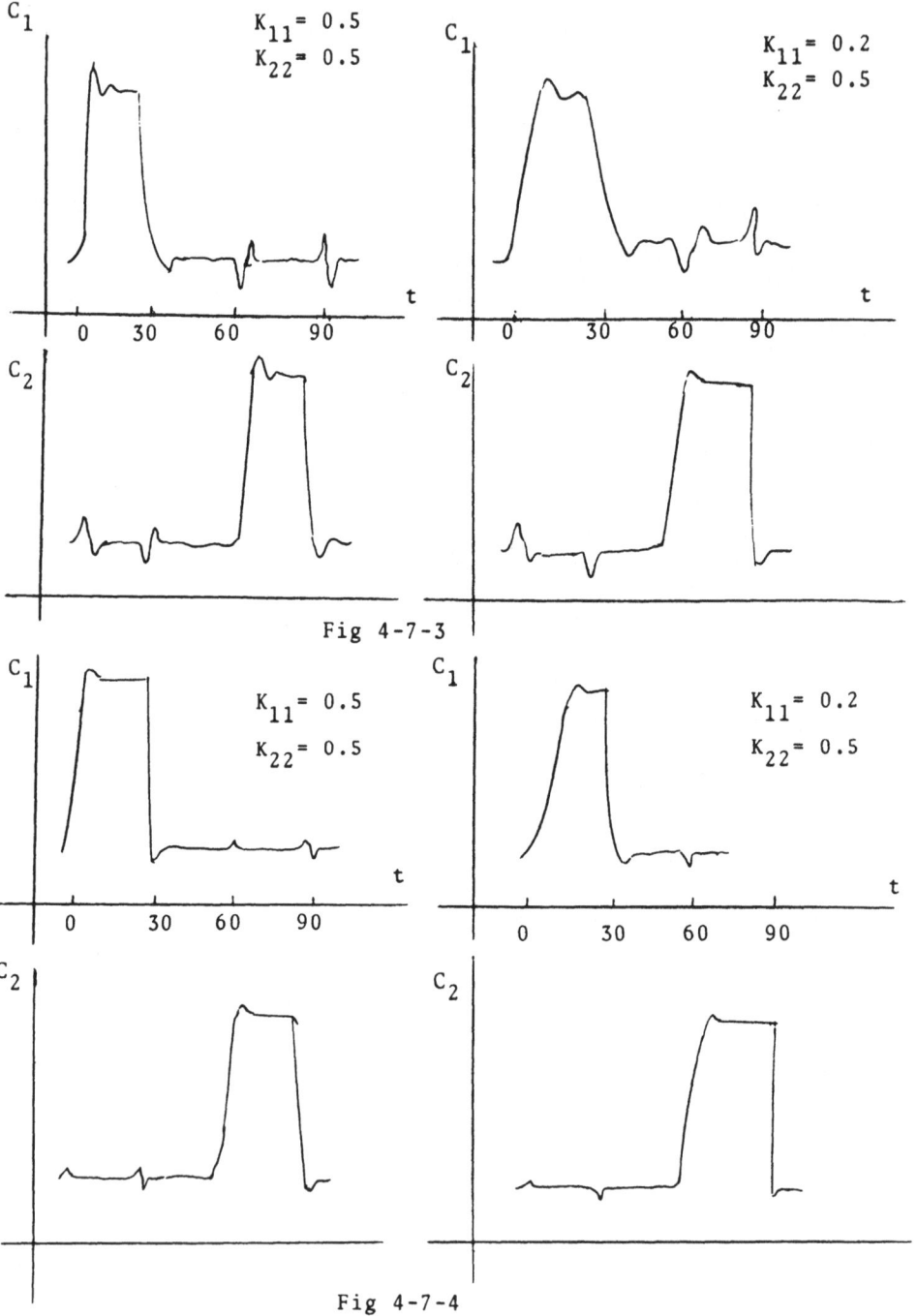

Fig 4-7-3

Fig 4-7-4

Fig 4-7-4 shows the response of the decoupled system by using (4-7-11). Obviously, the interaction between two outputs has been remarkably reduced by the approximate decoupling design. So such an approximate decoupling design may be applied in practice.

Notice that in (4-7-2) and (4-7-11), both N_{12} and N_{21} are independent to each other. That means:

(1) N_{12} or N_{21} may be realized individually,

(2) Even if one of them is not realized, for example N_{21} is not realized, the realization of N_{12} may result in the decoupling of C_1 to X_2.

This character brings great advantage for the tuning of the decoupling elements. If the mathematical forms of the four plant channels are known, certainly the transfer functions of the decoupling elements can be easily determined. If, however, the transfer functions of the plant channels are not known, then the characters of decoupling elements should de determined by experiments.

There are two methods for tuning the decoupling elements by experiments, namely the open loop tuning and the closed-loop tuning.

The open loop tuning means : Both regulators are regulated manually and two step functions are produced from R_{11} and R_{22}. Then, we adjust the parameters of N_{21} in order to keep C_2 not being influenced by the other channel and the parameters of N_{21} obtained by such a way are just the demanded decoupling conditions. Because N_{12} and N_{21} have nothing to do to each other, so both can be set individually. In addition, noting the conclusions of § 4-6, we know that the setting of decoupling elements is not related to regulators either.

The closed-loop tuning means: Closing the two main channels and adjusting the parameters of R_{11} and R_{22}, we can get satisfactory responses of C_1 to X_1 and C_2 to X_2, and then we adjust the parameters of N_{21} to eliminate the influence of X_1 on C_2, thus, we get the demanded decoupling parameters of N_{21}. Similarly, we can determine N_{12}.

§ 4-8 The Properties of Feedforward Decoupling Projects

The so-called feedforward decoupling projects include:

(1) The decoupling element structure is located between the regulators and the plant and we have said that this is a very good decoupling project,

(2) The decoupling element structure is combined with the regulators. This is also a very common decoupling project and a very important advantage of this project is : It will not increase the burden of regulators. The decoupling conditions for this project have
been denoted in the table of § 4-5. Now, we are going to have a discussion in detail for a two-variable system with P-canonical plant.

Fig 4-8-1 shows such a system.

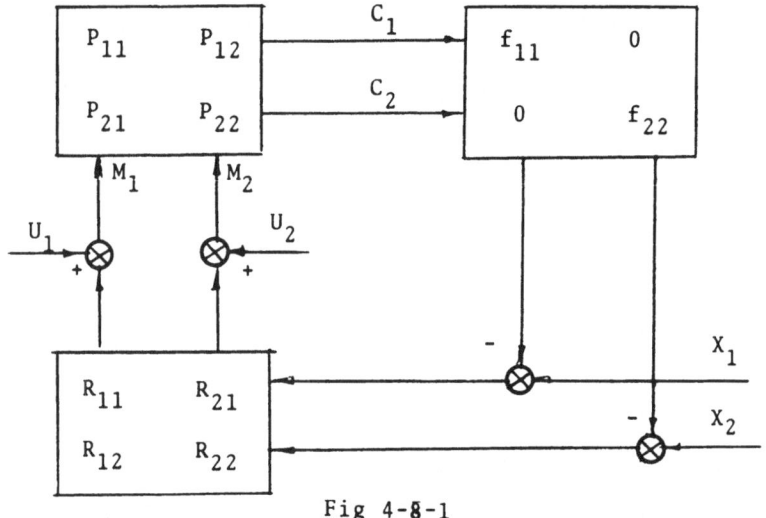

Fig 4-8-1

In this figure, not only the reference inputs , but also the
supply disturbances are introduced. From this figure, we have:

$$C_1 = P_{11}M_1 + P_{12}M_2$$
$$C_2 = P_{21}M_1 + P_{22}M_2$$

$$(4-8-1)$$

or in matrix form:

$$C = PM$$

$$(4-8-2)$$

On the other hand, the following relations are obtained from the figure:

$$M_1 = R_{11}(X_1 - f_{11}C_1) + R_{12}(X_2 - f_{22}C_2) + U_1$$
$$M_2 = R_{21}(X_1 - f_{11}C_1) + R_{22}(X_2 - f_{22}C_2) + U_2$$

$$(4-8-3)$$

or in matrix form:

$$M = R(X - FC) + U \qquad\qquad (4-8-4)$$

Where:

$$M = \begin{pmatrix} M_1 \\ M_2 \end{pmatrix} \quad R = \begin{pmatrix} R_{11} & R_{12} \\ R_{21} & R_{22} \end{pmatrix} \quad F = \begin{pmatrix} f_{11} \\ f_{22} \end{pmatrix} \quad C = \begin{pmatrix} C_1 \\ C_2 \end{pmatrix} \quad U = \begin{pmatrix} U_1 \\ U_2 \end{pmatrix}$$

Subsituting (4-8-4) into (4-8-2), we get:

$$C = PRX - PRFC + PU \qquad\qquad (4-8-5)$$

or:

$$C = (I + PRF)^{-1}(PRX + PU) \qquad\qquad (4-8-6)$$

This is also:

$$C = \frac{(adj(I + PRF))(PRX + PU)}{det (I + PRF)} \qquad\qquad (4-8-7)$$

Obviously, (4-8-7) is with the form of $C = AX + BU$, and it denotes if both A and B are diagonal matrices, then we can realize not only the decoupling between outputs C to references X, but also the decoupling between outputs C and supply disturbances U.

Can we realize it?

We have pointed out in § 3-8 that in general, we can not reach such very ideal control. Now, we discuss it furthermore.

At first , we discuss A. Because F is a diagonal matrix, so it is necessary that PR is a diagonal matrix if A being a diagonal matrix is expected. But:

$$PR = \begin{bmatrix} P_{11}R_{11} + P_{12}R_{21} & P_{11}R_{12} + P_{12}R_{22} \\ P_{21}R_{11} + P_{22}P_{21} & P_{22}R_{22} + P_{21}R_{12} \end{bmatrix} \qquad (4-8-8)$$

thus, in order to make PR be a diagonal matrix, it is necessary:

$$R_{21} = -\frac{P_{21}}{P_{22}} R_{11}$$

$$R_{12} = -\frac{P_{12}}{P_{11}} R_{22}$$

$$(4-8-9)$$

We are very familiar with this result indeed.

Now, let:

$$T = I + PRF \qquad (4-8-10)$$

then:

$$T = \begin{bmatrix} 1 + \dfrac{\triangle PR_{11}f_{11}}{P_{22}} & 0 \\ \\ 0 & 1 + \dfrac{\triangle PR_{22}f_{22}}{P_{11}} \end{bmatrix} \qquad (4-8-11)$$

where:

$$\triangle P = \begin{vmatrix} P_{11} & P_{12} \\ P_{21} & P_{22} \end{vmatrix} = P_{11}P_{22} - P_{12}P_{21} \qquad (4-8-12)$$

Therefore:

$$(\text{adj } T)(PR) = \begin{bmatrix} (1 + \dfrac{\triangle PR_{22}f_{22}}{P_{11}})(\dfrac{\triangle PR_{11}}{P_{22}}) & 0 \\ \\ 0 & (1+\dfrac{\triangle PR_{11}f_{11}}{P_{22}})(\dfrac{\triangle PR_{22}}{P_{11}}) \end{bmatrix}$$

$$(4-8-13)$$

On the other hand:

$$\det(T) = (1 + \frac{\triangle PR_{11}f_{11}}{P_{22}})(1 + \frac{\triangle PR_{22}f_{22}}{P_{11}}) \qquad (4-8-14)$$

The stability conditions are given by $\det(T) = 0$, namely the conditions for realizing:

$$R_{11}f_{11} = -\frac{P_{22}}{\triangle P}$$

$$R_{22}f_{22} = -\frac{P_{11}}{\triangle P}$$

$$(4-8-15)$$

Substituting the above results into (4-8-7) yields:

$$
C = \left(
\begin{array}{cc}
\dfrac{\triangle PR_{11}}{P_{22} + \triangle PR_{11}f_{11}} & 0 \\[4ex]
0 & \dfrac{PR_{22}}{P_{11} + \triangle PR_{22}f_{22}}
\end{array}
\right) X +
$$

$$
+ \left(
\begin{array}{cc}
(1 + \dfrac{\triangle PR_{11}f_{11}}{P_{22}})P_{11} & (1 + \dfrac{\triangle PR_{11}f_{11}}{P_{22}})P_{12} \\[4ex]
(1 + \dfrac{\triangle PR_{22}f_{22}}{P_{11}})P_{21} & (1 + \dfrac{\triangle PR_{22}f_{22}}{P_{11}})P_{22}
\end{array}
\right) U \qquad (4\text{-}8\text{-}16)
$$

Obviously, for a P-canonical two-variable control system, if the control project is given by Fig 4-8-1, namely the P-canonical decoupling element structure is combined with regulators, then this project can realize the decoupling control of the outputs to the reference inputs, but it can not realize the one-to-one influence between outputs and disturbances since the realization of the latter means:

$$
\left.
\begin{array}{l}
1 + \dfrac{\triangle PR_{22}f_{22}}{P_{11}} = 0 \\[4ex]
1 + \dfrac{\triangle PR_{11}f_{11}}{P_{22}} = 0
\end{array}
\right\} \qquad (4\text{-}8\text{-}17)
$$

This is also corresponding to the following relations at any value of S:

$$
\left.
\begin{array}{l}
R_{22}f_{22} = - \dfrac{P_{11}}{\triangle P} \\[4ex]
R_{11}f_{11} = - \dfrac{P_{22}}{\triangle P}
\end{array}
\right\} \qquad (4\text{-}8\text{-}18)
$$

Because these two equations just give the stability conditions of the system, so if these two equations are held at any values of S, then it means that this system is unstable.

That means that this control project can not realize full decoupling control.

When P_{12} and P_{21} are with the same orders of P_{11} and P_{22} and both R_{11} and R_{22} are PI regulators, the decoupling conditions of (4-8-9) are not difficult to be realized.

From (4-8-16) we know:

$$\frac{C_1}{X_1} = \frac{\Delta PR_{11}}{P_{22} + \Delta PR_{11}f_{11}} = \frac{R_{11}\dfrac{\Delta P}{P_{22}}}{1 + \dfrac{\Delta P}{P_{22}}R_{11}f_{11}} \qquad (4\text{-}8\text{-}19)$$

$$\frac{C_2}{X_2} = \frac{\Delta PR_{22}}{P_{11} + \Delta PR_{22}f_{22}} = \frac{R_{22}\dfrac{\Delta P}{P_{11}}}{1 + \dfrac{\Delta P}{P_{11}}R_{22}f_{22}} \qquad (4\text{-}8\text{-}20)$$

Therefore, after decoupling, for the main channels their plant characters are no longer P_{11} and P_{22}. They are now $\Delta P/P_{22}$ and $\Delta P/P_{11}$, respectively.

That means that the meaning of decoupling design is not simply equal to cross out the coupling channels.

But this conclusion is not absolutely true. That means that we can get such a decoupled system with the plant characters P_{11} and P_{22}, the same as those of the main channels of the coupled plant. Such a decoupled system is called ideal decoupling system.

But that is a special case and in general is difficult to be realized. So, in most cases, the above conclusion is valid.

We will discuss this problem in more detail in Chapter 6.

§ 4-9 The Properties of Feedforward Decoupling Projects(Continued)

The analysis of §4-8 denotes that for the case of the combination of the decoupling element structure with the regulators, the project can realize the decoupling control between outputs and reference inputs, but can not realize the one-to-one relations between outputs and the supply disturbances.

Now, we discuss the ability of this project to treat the load disturbances.

We still discuss a two-variable system and when the load distur- bances exist, the system is shown in Fig 4-9-1.

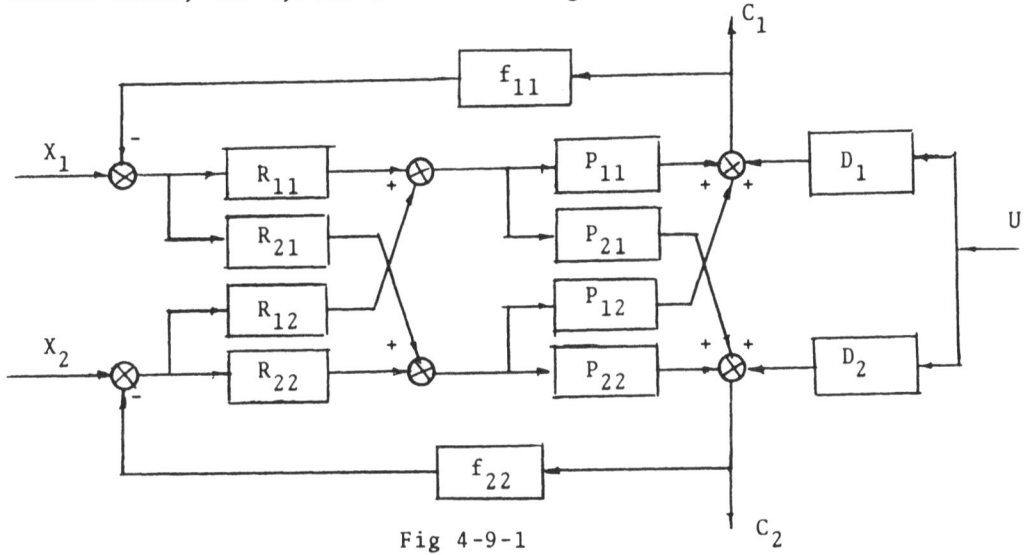

Fig 4-9-1

By the similar analysis of the last paragraph, for this system we can get:

$$C = (I + PRF)^{-1}(PRX + DU) \qquad (4-9-1)$$

Let:

$$W = PR \qquad (4-9-2)$$

then:

$$C = (I + WF)^{-1}(WX + DU) \qquad (4-9-3)$$

The closed-loop transfer function is expressed by:

$$G = (I + WF)^{-1}W \qquad (4-9-4)$$

then:

$$C = GX + GW^{-1}DU \qquad (4-9-5)$$

Thus, if G is a diagonal matrix, then this system can realize the decoupling control between C and X.

On the other hand, in order to make G be a diagonal matrix, WF must be diagonal. Because F is a diagonal matrix, so the above condition means that W should be a diagonal matrix. Hence, a diagonal matrix W gives the guarantee that G is also a diagonal matrix. But, from (4-9-5) we can see when both W and G are diagonal, then $GW^{-1}D$ is also a diagonal matrix.

Thus, that W is a diagonal matrix guarantees not only the decoupling control between outputs and reference inputs, but also the one-to-one relations between outputs and load disturbances.

Let:

$$WF = \begin{bmatrix} \alpha_{11} & \alpha_{12} \\ \alpha_{21} & \alpha_{22} \end{bmatrix} \qquad (4-9-6)$$

where:

$$\alpha_{11} = P_{11}R_{11}F_{11}(1 + \frac{P_{12}P_{21}}{P_{11}R_{11}}) \qquad (4-9-7)$$

$$\alpha_{12} = (P_{11}R_{12} + P_{12}R_{22})F_{22} \qquad (4-9-8)$$

$$\alpha_{21} = (P_{21}R_{11} + P_{22}R_{21})F_{11} \qquad (4-9-9)$$

$$\alpha_{22} = P_{22}R_{22}F_{22}(1 + \frac{P_{21}R_{12}}{P_{22}R_{22}}) \qquad (4-9-10)$$

If the decoupling control is expected, then it is necessary:

$$\alpha_{12} = \alpha_{21} = 0 \qquad (4-9-11)$$

and we get:

$$R_{12} = - \frac{P_{12}R_{22}}{P_{11}} \qquad (4-9-12)$$

$$R_{21} = - \frac{P_{21}R_{11}}{P_{22}} \qquad (4-9-13)$$

This result is the same as (4-8-9).

Substituting (4-9-12),(4-9-13) into (4-9-10) and (4-9-7) yields:

$$\alpha_{11} = R_{11}P_{11}F_{11}\left(1 - \frac{P_{12}P_{21}}{P_{11}P_{22}} \right) \tag{4-9-14}$$

$$\alpha_{22} = R_{22}P_{22}F_{22}\left(1 - \frac{P_{12}P_{21}}{P_{11}P_{22}} \right) \tag{4-9-15}$$

and:

$$W = F^{-1}\begin{bmatrix} \alpha_{11} & 0 \\ 0 & \alpha_{22} \end{bmatrix} = \begin{bmatrix} \alpha_{11}F_{11}^{-1} & 0 \\ 0 & \alpha_{22}F_{22}^{-1} \end{bmatrix} \tag{4-9-16}$$

Thus:

$$G = \left[I + \begin{bmatrix} \alpha_{11} & 0 \\ 0 & \alpha_{22} \end{bmatrix} \right]^{-1} W = \begin{bmatrix} 1 + \alpha_{11} & 0 \\ 0 & 1 + \alpha_{22} \end{bmatrix}^{-1} W =$$

$$= \begin{bmatrix} \dfrac{\alpha_{11}F_{11}^{-1}}{1 + \alpha_{11}} & 0 \\ 0 & \dfrac{\alpha_{22}F_{22}^{-1}}{1 + \alpha_{22}} \end{bmatrix} = \begin{bmatrix} G_{11} & 0 \\ 0 & G_{22} \end{bmatrix} \tag{4-9-17}$$

and we get:

$$\frac{C_1}{X_1} = \frac{\alpha_{11}F_{11}^{-1}}{1 + \alpha_{11}} = \frac{P_{11}\left(1 + \dfrac{P_{12}R_{21}}{P_{11}R_{11}} \right)R_{11}}{1 + P_{11}\left(1 + \dfrac{P_{12}R_{21}}{P_{11}R_{11}} \right)R_{11}} \tag{4-9-18}$$

$$\frac{C_2}{X_2} = \frac{\alpha_{22}F_{22}^{-1}}{1 + \alpha_{22}} = \frac{P_{22}\left(1 + \dfrac{P_{21}R_{12}}{P_{22}R_{22}} \right)R_{22}}{1 + P_{22}\left(1 + \dfrac{P_{21}R_{12}}{P_{22}R_{22}} \right)R_{22}} \tag{4-9-19}$$

namely:

$$\frac{C_1}{X_1} = \frac{\dfrac{P_{11}R_{11} + P_{12}R_{21}}{R_{11}} R_{11}}{1 + \dfrac{P_{11}R_{11} + P_{12}R_{21}}{R_{11}} R_{11}F_{11}} \qquad (4\text{-}9\text{-}20)$$

$$\frac{C_2}{X_2} = \frac{\dfrac{P_{22}R_{22} + P_{21}R_{12}}{R_{22}} R_{22}}{1 + \dfrac{P_{22}R_{22} + P_{21}R_{12}}{R_{22}} R_{22}F_{22}} \qquad (4\text{-}9\text{-}21)$$

Thus, the characters of the main channels of the decoupled system are no longer P_{11} and P_{22}. And:

$$GW^{-1} = \begin{pmatrix} G_{11} & 0 \\ 0 & G_{22} \end{pmatrix} \begin{pmatrix} \dfrac{1}{W_{11}} & 0 \\ 0 & \dfrac{1}{W_{22}} \end{pmatrix} = \begin{pmatrix} \dfrac{G_{11}}{W_{11}} & 0 \\ 0 & \dfrac{G_{22}}{W_{22}} \end{pmatrix}$$

thus: $\qquad\qquad\qquad\qquad\qquad\qquad\qquad\qquad\qquad (4\text{-}9\text{-}22)$

$$\frac{C}{U} = GW^{-1}D = \begin{pmatrix} \dfrac{G_{11}}{W_{11}} & 0 \\ 0 & \dfrac{G_{22}}{W_{22}} \end{pmatrix} \begin{pmatrix} D_1 \\ D_2 \end{pmatrix} =$$

$$= \begin{pmatrix} \dfrac{G_{11}}{W_{11}} D_1 \\ \dfrac{G_{22}}{W_{22}} D_2 \end{pmatrix} = \begin{pmatrix} \dfrac{D_1}{1 + \alpha_{11}} \\ \dfrac{D_2}{1 + \alpha_{22}} \end{pmatrix} \qquad (4\text{-}9\text{-}23)$$

So, this project can realize the decoupling control to load disturbances. When the decoupling element structure is between the plant and the regulators, all the above conclusions are also held since both these two projects belong to the feedforward decoupling system.

In summary, the feedforward decoupling system can very conveniently realize the decoupling control of outputs to reference inputs and outputs to load disturbances, but can not realize the decoupling control of outputs to supply disturbances at the same time.

§ 4-10 The Comparison of Responses to Load Disturbances of Coupled

       Systems and Decoupled Systems with Feedforward Decoupling [40]

       The decoupling projects mentiond above, no matter combined with regulators or located between the plant and regulators, are always before plants and, no matter the decoupling element structures are P-canonical or V-canonical, the decoupling signals are input into the plants in feedforward manners and so such projects are called as feedforward decoupling systems.

       The above analysis has denoted that these projects can realize the decoupling control between outputs and reference inputs. They can also realize the one-to-one influences of load disturbances to outputs but can not get such results for supply disturbances with the same decoupling structures.

       For servomechanism control systems, the inputs always vary and the outputs should vary with the inputs , so the decoupling control between outputs and inputs are very ideal for them.

       But, however, for process control systems the cases are different. In general, the reference inputs for process control systems are some given constants and their main control demands are to keep the outputs being also some desired values (may be not the reference input values) without being influenced by disturbances, thus for any process control system, the ability to reduce the influence of disturbances is always an important control index.

       Although the feedforward decoupling projects can realize the one-to-one relations between outputs and load disturbances, we still want to know whether their ability to reduce the influences of disturbances is better than that of coupled systems.

       Now, we discuss this problem.

       Fig 4-10-1 shows a two-variable system with P-canonical plant and load disturbances.

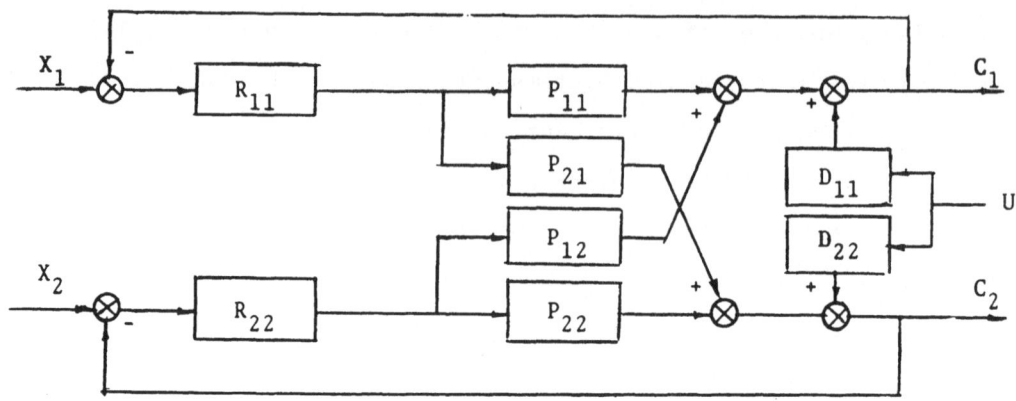

Fig 4-10-1

For this system, we have:

$$\frac{C_1}{U} = \frac{D_1}{1 + P_{11}(1 - KG_2)} \left(1 - \frac{D_2}{D_1} \frac{P_{12}}{P_{22}} G_2 \right) \qquad (4\text{-}10\text{-}1)$$

$$\frac{C_2}{U} = \frac{D_2}{1 + P_{22}(1 - KG_1)} \left(1 - \frac{D_1}{D_2} \frac{P_{21}}{P_{11}} G_1 \right) \qquad (4\text{-}10\text{-}2)$$

where:

$$G_i = \frac{R_{ii}P_{ii}}{1 + R_{ii}P_{ii}} \qquad i = 1, 2 \qquad (4\text{-}10\text{-}3)$$

$$K = \frac{P_{12}P_{21}}{P_{11}P_{22}} \qquad (4\text{-}10\text{-}4)$$

Now, we design a decoupled system and the decoupling element structure is located between the plant and regulators as shown in Fig 4-10-2. This system can realize the one-to-one relations between outputs and load disturbances.

From the table in § 4-5, we know:

$$\left. \begin{aligned} N_{12} &= -\frac{P_{12}}{P_{11}} \\[2ex] N_{21} &= -\frac{P_{21}}{P_{22}} \end{aligned} \right\} \qquad (4\text{-}10\text{-}5)$$

From (4-9-23) we get:

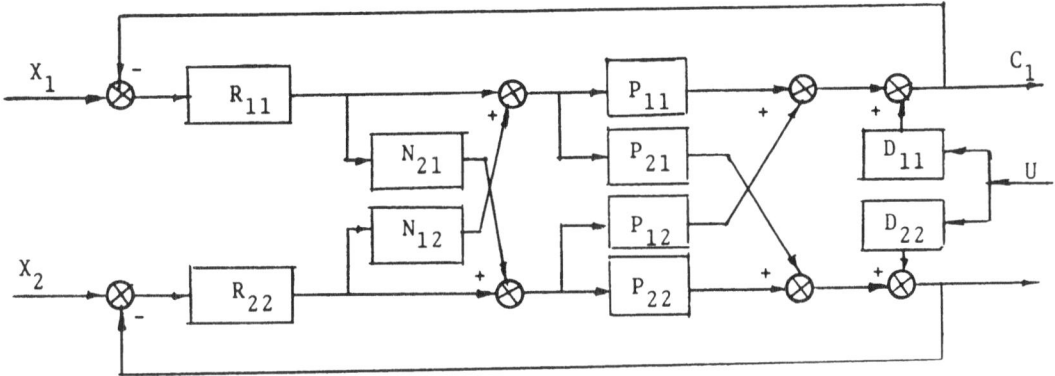

Fig 4-10-2

$$\frac{C_1}{U} = \frac{D_{11}}{1 + P_{11}(1 - K)R_{11}} \qquad (4-10-6)$$

$$\frac{C_2}{U} = \frac{D_{22}}{1 + P_{22}(1 - K)R_{22}} \qquad (4-10-7)$$

In order to judge the system responses to the load disturbance, an estimation index is needed. This index can be expressed by the ratio of deviations, d, which is defined as:

$$d = \frac{\text{Deviation under Control}}{\text{Deviation without Control}} \Bigg|_{X_i = 0} \qquad (4-10-8)$$

It is also:

$$d = \frac{\left| C_1 \text{ or } C_2 \text{ under control} \right|}{\left| C_1 \text{ or } C_2 \text{ without control} \right|} \Bigg|_{X_i = 0} \qquad (4-10-9)$$

The meaning of " under control" means " under decoupling control" and vice versa.

Obviously, the less the deviation ratio, the better the system ability to reduce the influence of disturbances.

For these two systems, namely the coupled system and the decoupled system, it is not difficult to get the deviation ratios.

For the system without decoupling design, we have:

$$d_1 = A_1 B_1 \qquad (4-10-10)$$

where:

$$A_1 = \frac{1}{1 + P_{11}(1 - KG_2)R_{11}} \tag{4-10-11}$$

$$B_1 = 1 - \frac{D_{22}}{D_{11}} \frac{P_{12}}{P_{22}} G_2 \tag{4-10-12}$$

and:

$$d_2 = A_2 B_2 \tag{4-10-13}$$

where:

$$A_2 = \frac{1}{1 + P_{22}(1 - KG_1)R_{22}} \tag{4-10-14}$$

$$B_2 = 1 - \frac{D_{11}}{D_{22}} \frac{P_{21}}{P_{11}} G_1 \tag{4-10-15}$$

For the decoupled system, the deviation ratio is:

$$d_{1n} = \frac{1}{1 + P_{11}(1 - K)R_{11}} \tag{4-10-16}$$

$$d_{2n} = \frac{1}{1 + P_{22}(1 - K)R_{22}} \tag{4-10-17}$$

Now, we compare these two ratios.

Comparing d_1 and d_2 with d_{1n} and d_{2n}, we can find two different points:

(1) The most important difference is about B_1 and B_2. If:

$$\frac{D_{11}(0)}{D_{22}(0)} P_{21}(0) > 0$$

$$\frac{D_{22}(0)}{D_{11}(0)} P_{12}(0) > 0 \tag{4-10-18}$$

then , in most cases B_1 and B_2 are less than 1 for most low frequency scope.

(2) Because $|G_1| < 1$ and $|G_2| < 1$, so in a same frequency scope, A_1 and A_2 are always less than d_{1n} and d_{2n}.

Therefore, we know that in the low frequency scope, which is with practical meaning in process control systems, in general the followimg results are held:

$$d_1 < d_{1n} \atop d_2 < d_{2n} \Big\}\qquad (4\text{-}10\text{-}19)$$

That means that for the ability to reduce the influence of the load disturbances to the outputs, the coupled systems are better than the decoupled systems.

But, however, we prefer to use decoupled systems. This is because after decoupling, every channel can be designed individually and a lot of measures may be adopted in single variable control system design to reduce the influence of disturbances , for example the gains of the regulators may be increased, and , consequently, the influence of the disturbances can be reduced very much. Therefore, for the ability of reducing the influence of disturbances, the decoupled systems are better than coupled systems in practice.

This also means that in general the decoupling design for a multivariable process control system consists of two steps. At the first step, in general only the decoupling demands are considered and when the system is decoupled, the other control demands then can be considered . The above comparison is carried out for the decoupled system at the first step, so the conclusion is not perfect.

Certainly, we can also combine the decoupling design with the disturbance-rejection design (see §5-9) , for such a decoupled system, its ability to reduce the influence of the disturbances to the outputs is certainly better than the coupled systems.

§ 4-11 The Second Practical Meaning of Mesarović Idea

We have said that in the decoupling design, locating the decoupling element structure between the plant and regulators results in simple decoupling conditions.

But, for process control systems, a very important problem is about the influence of disturbances. This problem should be considered not only in single variable system design, but also in MPCS design.

Although we proved in the last paragraph that the coupled systems are with better ability to reduce the disturbance influence than the decoupled systems when the feedforward decoupling projects are adopted, we still hope to use the decoupled systems since we can improve their abilty to reduce the disturbance influence after decoupling.

In Chapter 2, the full rejection design to different disturbances was given in detail and for the design of MPCS, our logical steps are: Because the coupling phenomena exist not only between outputs and reference inputs, but also between outputs and disturbances,so we should design such decoupled systems that they can realize not only the decoupling control between outputs and reference inputs, but also the decoupling control between outputs and disturbances. The decoupled channels obtained by such a design are really influenced by the reference input and disturbances of themselves and then they can be dealt as single variable systems.

So, the ideal decoupling systems should have such functions: They can realize not only the decoupling control between outputs and reference inputs, but also the decoupling control between outputs and different disturbances. This kind of decoupled systems is called as fully decoupled system.

The feedforward decoupling projects are not fully decoupled systems since they can not realize the decoupling control between outputs and supply disturbances.

From the view-point of control theory, any decoupling project with the form as Fig 4-5-2 can not realize the decoupling control between outputs and supply diturbances which exist before the plant and after the decoupling elements. This is because for such projects the cancellation of zeros and poles of the plant and the decoupling elements is adopted and due to this cancellation, some responses caused by the supply disturbances can not be expressed by the transfer functions. Sometimes, when the plant is unstable and the unstable poles are cancelled by the zeros of decoupling elements , the system may be unstable for the disturbance responses. So this is a dangerous case.

Thus, in order to realize full decoupling design, it is impossible to adopt such projects and we should find other more suitable projects.

We still discuss a two-variable system.

Let us consider the decoupling project as shown in Fig 4-11-1.

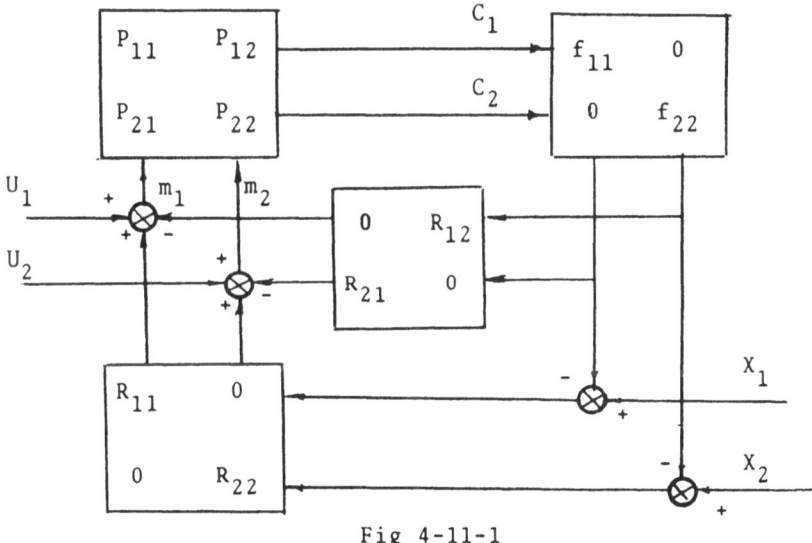

Fig 4-11-1

Here, the decoupling elements are located at the feedback channels. This is the feedback decoupling project with P-canonical plant and P-canonical decoupling element structure.

There are no V-canonical decoupling element structures for feedback decoupling projects since the signals obtained from the feedback decoupling elements are always forward.

For this system , we can get:

$$m_1 = R_{11}(X_1 - f_{11}C_1) - R_{12}f_{22}C_2 + U_1$$
$$m_2 = R_{22}(X_2 - f_{22}C_2) - R_{21}f_{11}C_1 + U_2$$
$$(4-11-1)$$

or in matrix form:

$$M = R_1 X - R_2 FC + U \qquad (4-11-2)$$

where:

$$R_1 = \begin{bmatrix} R_{11} & 0 \\ 0 & R_{22} \end{bmatrix} \qquad R_2 = \begin{bmatrix} R_{11} & R_{12} \\ R_{21} & R_{22} \end{bmatrix}$$

But:

$$C = PM \qquad (4-11-3)$$

thus , subsituting (4-11-3) into (4-11-2) and solving for C yields:

$$C = (I + PR_2 F)^{-1}(PR_1 X + PU) \qquad (4-11-4)$$

namely:

$$C = \frac{(adj(I + PR_2 F))(PR_1 X + PU)}{det (I + PR_2 F)} \qquad (4-11-5)$$

We can see because R_1 is diagonal, so if $(adj(I + PR_2 F))P$ is diagonal, then the outputs of this system are decoupled not only to the reference inputs X, but also to the disturbances U and we get:

$$W = I + PR_2 F = \begin{bmatrix} 1 + (P_{11}R_{11} + P_{12}R_{21})f_{11} & (P_{12}R_{22} + P_{11}R_{12})f_{22} \\ (P_{21}R_{11} + P_{22}R_{21})f_{11} & 1 + (P_{22}R_{22} + P_{21}R_{12})f_{22} \end{bmatrix}$$
$$(4-11-6)$$

Therefore:

$$(adj\ W\ )P\ =\ \begin{cases} \begin{matrix} (1+(P_{21}R_{12}+\ P_{22}R_{22})f_{22})P_{11} \\ -(P_{11}R_{12}+\ P_{12}R_{22})f_{22}P_{21} \end{matrix} & \begin{matrix} (1+(P_{21}R_{12}+\ P_{22}R_{22})f_{22})P_{12} \\ -(P_{11}R_{12}+\ P_{12}R_{22})f_{22}P_{22} \end{matrix} \\ \\ \begin{matrix} (1+(P_{12}R_{21}+\ P_{11}R_{11})f_{11})P_{21} \\ -(P_{22}R_{21}+\ P_{21}R_{11})f_{11}P_{11} \end{matrix} & \begin{matrix} (1+(P_{12}R_{21}+\ P_{11}R_{11})f_{11})P_{22} \\ -(P_{22}R_{21}+\ P_{21}R_{11})f_{11}P_{12} \end{matrix} \end{cases}$$

$$(4\text{-}11\text{-}7)$$

In order to get decoupling control, the above matrix must be diagonal, so we get the decoupling conditions:

$$R_{21}\ =\ \frac{P_{21}}{\Delta Pf_{11}}$$

$$R_{12}\ =\ \frac{P_{12}}{\Delta Pf_{22}}$$

$$(4\text{-}11\text{-}8)$$

where:

$$\Delta P\ =\ P_{11}P_{22}\ -\ P_{12}P_{21} \qquad (4\text{-}11\text{-}9)$$

Notice that this result is in accordance with the result in the table of § 4-5. In § 4-5, we supposed that $f_{11}= f_{22}= 1$ and the decoupling elements are fed back before R_{11} and R_{22}, but here f_{11} and f_{22} are not equal to 1 and they are fed back behind R_{11} and R_{22} and this gives the slight form difference between (4-11-8) and the result in the table of §4-5.

Now:

$$det\ W\ =\ \frac{(P_{11}+\ R_{22}f_{22}\ \Delta P)(P_{22}+\ R_{11}f_{11}\ \Delta P)}{\Delta P} \qquad (4\text{-}11\text{-}10)$$

The stability conditions are expressed by:

$$R_{11}\ =\ -\ \frac{P_{22}}{\Delta Pf_{11}}$$

$$R_{22}\ =\ -\ \frac{P_{11}}{\Delta Pf_{22}}$$

$$(4\text{-}11\text{-}11)$$

For a decoupled system, (4-11-7) becomes:

$$(\text{adj } W)P = \begin{pmatrix} P_{11} + R_{22}f_{22}\Delta P & 0 \\ 0 & P_{22} + R_{11}f_{11}\Delta P \end{pmatrix} \qquad (4\text{-}11\text{-}12)$$

and the system character is :

$$C = \begin{pmatrix} \dfrac{R_{11}\Delta P}{P_{22}+R_{11}f_{11}\Delta P} & 0 \\ 0 & \dfrac{R_{22}\Delta P}{P_{11}+R_{22}f_{22}\Delta P} \end{pmatrix} X + \begin{pmatrix} \dfrac{\Delta P}{P_{22}+R_{11}f_{11}\Delta P} & 0 \\ 0 & \dfrac{\Delta P}{P_{11}+R_{22}f_{22}\Delta P} \end{pmatrix} U$$

$$(4\text{-}11\text{-}13)$$

Obviously, this system has realized the decoupling control to both X and U.

Thus, the comparison of this project with that of Fig 4-5-1 shows that the present project is with better decoupling effects than the feedforward decoupling projects since it can realize the decoupling control to the supply disturbances which , in gereral, are the most important disturbances in process control systems.

In addition, from (4-11- 8) we can see if the decoupling elements are with the following characters:

$$\left. \begin{array}{l} f_{11} = \dfrac{P_{21}}{\Delta P} \\[3mm] f_{22} = \dfrac{P_{12}}{\Delta P} \end{array} \right\} \qquad (4\text{-}11\text{-}14)$$

then we have:

$$R_{12} = R_{21} = 1 \qquad (4\text{-}11\text{-}15)$$

That means that the decoupled system has been realized by using simple signal decoupling and the system is the simplest. In general, in such cases, the differential feedback channels are used.

Then the system becomes two independent single variable control systems as shown in Fig 4-11-2 and their characters are given by the following relation:

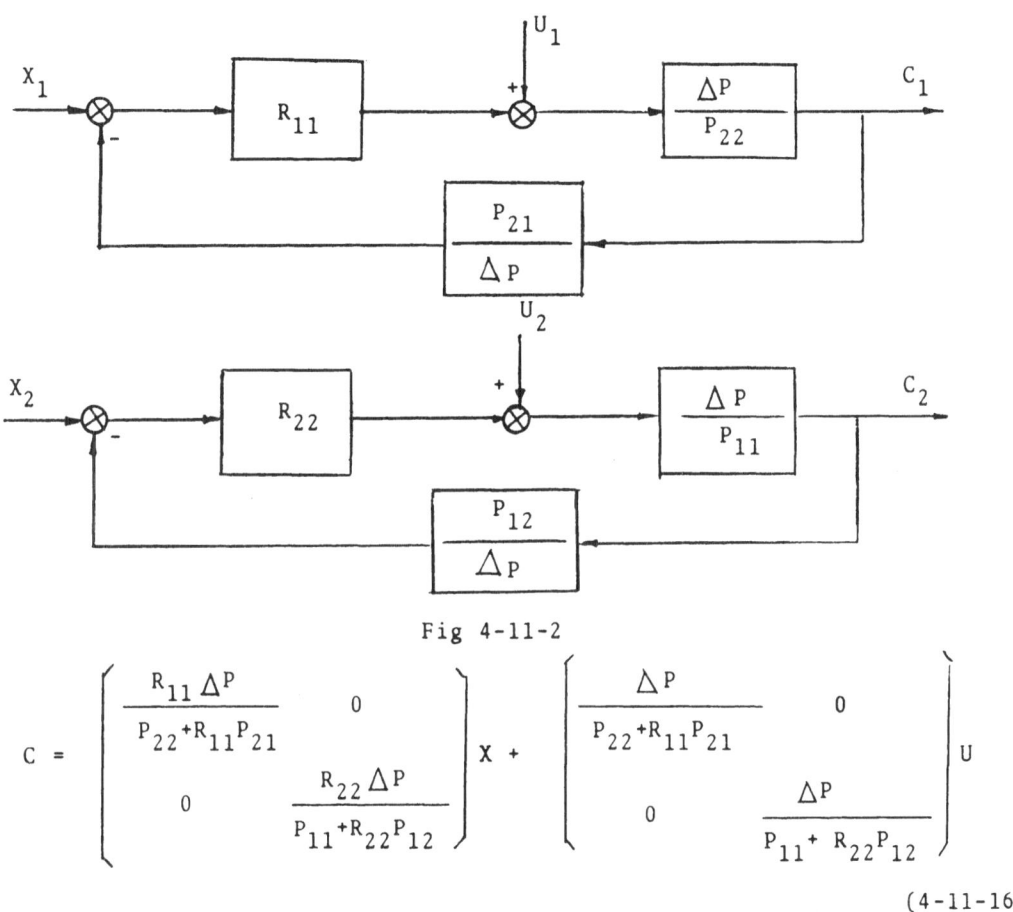

Fig 4-11-2

$$C = \left\{ \begin{array}{cc} \dfrac{R_{11}\Delta P}{P_{22}+R_{11}P_{21}} & 0 \\ 0 & \dfrac{R_{22}\Delta P}{P_{11}+R_{22}P_{12}} \end{array} \right\} X + \left\{ \begin{array}{cc} \dfrac{\Delta P}{P_{22}+R_{11}P_{21}} & 0 \\ 0 & \dfrac{\Delta P}{P_{11}+R_{22}P_{12}} \end{array} \right\} U$$

$$(4-11-16)$$

In summary, we can reach the following conclusion: In the decouplimg design of multivariable process control systems, the feedback decoupling projects are with very excellent decoupling effects, i.e. they can realize the full decoupling to both reference inputs and supply disturbances.

Mesarović idea points out that the application of feedback decoupling structures can get good decoupling results and the analysis here gives the practical meaning of this conclusion.

But, in these cases, the characters of the feedback decoupling elements in general are not very simple. For a two-variable system, they are given by (4-11-8) and for more variable systems, they are:

$$N_{ik} = - \frac{\det \overline{P}_{ki}}{\det P} \frac{1}{R_{ii}} \qquad (4-11-17)$$

Can we find simpler decoupling conditions for feedback decoupling ?

§ 4-12 The Realization of Full Decoupling for General Control Systems
with P-Canonical Plants

In the previous paragraph, we discussed a two-variable system. The analysis denotes that for a system with P-canonical plant, in order to realize the full decoupling   for   outputs to   reference inputs and supply disturbances the feedback decoupling projects should be applied.

Now, we discuss more general systems.

The block diagram for a general MPCS is shown in Fig 4-12-1.

From this figure, we can get the relation between the output and the reference input:

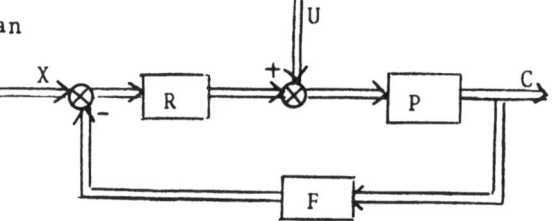

C = PRX - PRFC

(4-12-1)

Fig 4-12-1

Namely:

$$C = (I + PRF)^{-1} PRX = GX \qquad (4-12-2)$$

The relation between the output and the disturbance is:

C = PU - PRFC   (4-12-3)

Namely:

$$C = (I + PRF)^{-1} PU = G_U U \qquad (4-12-4)$$

Obviously, if we want to realize the full decoupling for the output to the reference input and the supply disturbance at the same time, then both matrices:

$$G = (I + PRF)^{-1} PR \qquad (4-12-5)$$

$$G_U = (I + PRF)^{-1} P \qquad (4-12-6)$$

should be diagonal.

In order to satisfy these two conditions, it is necessary:

(1) $(I + PRF)^{-1} P$ is a diagonal matrix,

(2) R is a diagonal matrix.

By this arrangement, a general control system with P-canonical plant can realize the full decoupling for the output to both reference input and supply disturbance.

In the design, the matrix P is known and R is a diagonal matrix. The elements of R may be designed by single variable systems when the system is decoupled.

From (4-12-5) and (4-12-6), we have:

$$G^{-1} = (PR)^{-1} + F \qquad (4-12-7)$$

$$(G_U R)^{-1} = (PR)^{-1} + F \qquad (4-12-8)$$

Because G , G_U and R are diagonal matrices, so the right side of (4-12-8) becomes:

$$(PR)^{-1} + F = \text{Diagonal} \qquad (4-12-9)$$

Thus, we can get the off-diagonal elements of F :

$$F_{ik} = - \frac{\left| \bar{P}_{ki} \right|}{\left| P \right|} \frac{1}{R_{ii}} \qquad (4-12-10)$$

$$i = 1,2,\ldots\ldots n$$

$$k = 1,2,\ldots\ldots n$$

$$i \neq k$$

These are just the decoupling conditions given in the table of §4-5. Namely, these decoupling conditions give the guarantee to realize the full decoupling of C to both X and U.

The diagonal elements of F , namely F_{ii}, can be determined by single loop design.

If the system is arranged as:

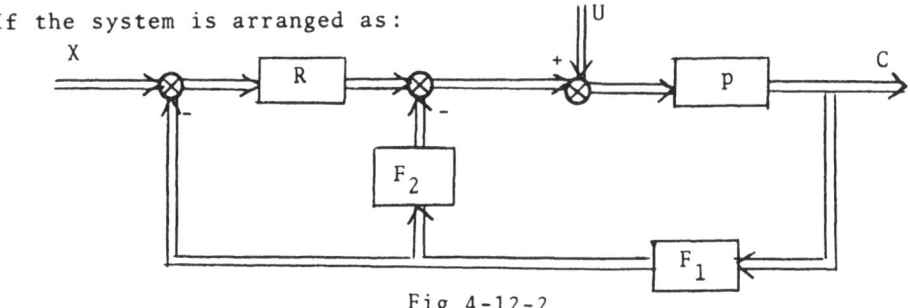

Fig 4-12-2

where:

$$F_1 = \begin{pmatrix} F_{11} & & & 0 \\ & F_{22} & & \\ & & \ddots & \\ 0 & & & F_{nn} \end{pmatrix} \qquad (4\text{-}12\text{-}11)$$

$$F_2 = \begin{pmatrix} 0 & F_{12} & - - - - & F_{1n} \\ F_{21} & 0 & - - - - & F_{2n} \\ \vdots & \vdots & \vdots & \vdots \\ F_{n1} & F_{n2} & - - - - & 0 \end{pmatrix} \qquad (4\text{-}12\text{-}12)$$

then the decoupling conditions expressed by (4-12-10) become:

$$F_{ik} = - \frac{|\overline{P}_{ki}|}{|P|} \frac{1}{F_{kk}} \qquad (4\text{-}12\text{-}13)$$

$$i = 1,2,\ldots\ldots n$$

$$k = 1, 2, \ldots\ldots n$$

$$i \neq k$$

When n=2, i.e. a two-variable system, the results of (4-12-13) are just those of (4-11-8).

This project is better since it is not influenced by the main regulators. In other words, when the parameters of the main regulators are changed, the system decoupling properties are still held.

Logically, a problem may be proposed :

The system shown in Fig 4-12-1 or Fig 4-12-2 can realize the decoupling for C to both X and the supply disturbances, then can it also realize the decoupling between the outputs and the load disturbances at the same time?

When the load disturbances exist, the system is shown in Fig 4-12-3.

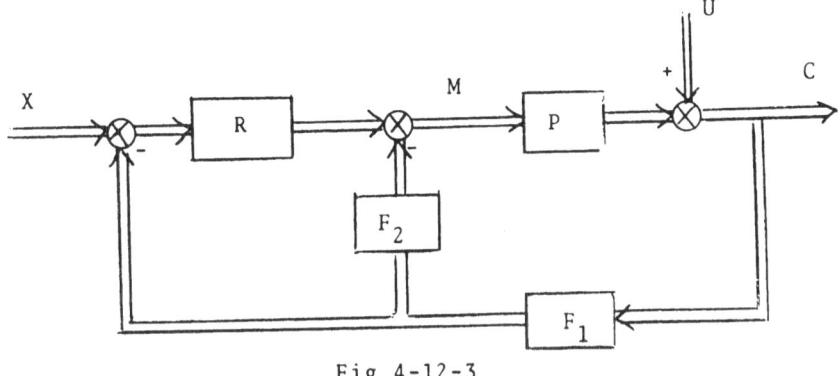

Fig 4-12-3

From this figure, we get:

$$M = RX - RF_1C - F_2F_1C = RX - (RF_1 + F_2F_1)C =$$
$$= RX - (R + F_2)F_1C \qquad (4\text{-}12\text{-}14)$$

Because R is a diagonal matrix and F_2 is with the form (4-12-12),
so (R + F_2) is a nxn matrix. Denote:

$$K = R + F_2 \qquad (4\text{-}12\text{-}15)$$

then:

$$M = RX - KF_1C \qquad (4\text{-}12\text{-}16)$$

On the other hand:

$$C = U + PM \qquad (4\text{-}12\text{-}17)$$

so, solving (4-12-15) and (4-12-16) yields:

$$C = (I + PKF_1)^{-1}(PRX + U) \qquad (4\text{-}12\text{-}18)$$

Thus, if the simultaneous decoupling for C to both X and U is
expected, then both $(I + PKF_1)^{-1}PR$ and $(I + PKF_1)^{-1}$ should be diagonal.
But P is not a diagonal matrix, so these two conditions can not be satisfied simultaneously.

In other words , for the project shown in Fig 4-12-3, when it can
realize the decoupling control between C and the reference input X, then
it can not realize the decoupling control between C and the load disturbance with the same structure.

Combining the above results with the conclusions of § 4-9 , we
get the important conclusion about the full decoupling control for a
MPCS with a P-canonical plant:

226

For a multivariable process control system with a P-canonical plant, if the full decoupling for the outputs to both reference inputs and supply disturbances is expected, then the feedback decoupling projects should be adopted ; if the full decoupling for the outputs to both reference inputs and load disturbances is expected, then feedforward decoupling projects should be adopted.

§ 4-13 The Second Meaning of Mesarović Idea (Continued)

We have discussed the decoupling projects with P-canonical plants, P-canonical decoupling element structures and feedback decoupling channels. We have pointed out that the feedback decoupling projects may have better decoupling effects since they can realize the full decoupling for outputs to both reference inputs and supply disturbances. But, when the system is with P-canonical plant and P-canonical decoupling element structure, the decoupling conditions are not simple.

On the other hand, we pointed out also that in order to realize the full decoupling control for the outputs to both reference inputs and load disturbances, the feedforward decoupling projects should be adopted.

But, the above conclusions are worth being discussed further.

We are going to discuss :

(1) Can the feedforward decoupling projects always realize the full decoupling control for the outputs to both reference inputs and load disturbances ?

(2) On the contrary, are the feedback decoupling projects absolutely not able to realize the full decoupling control for the outputs to both reference inputs and load disturbances?

We still discuss a two-variable system.

The system discussed now is shown in Fig 4-13-1. Here, the feed-forward decoupling project is adopted and the load disturbances are with more complicated input channels.

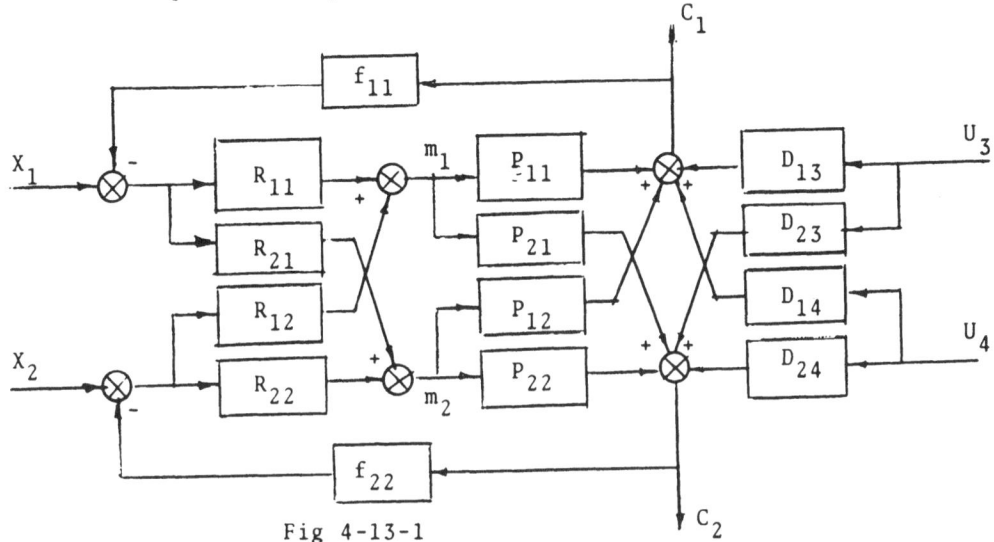

Fig 4-13-1

There are load disturbances in this system, then is it possible to realize the full decoupling control by using this project ?

We have :

$$C = (I + PRF)^{-1}(PRX + DU) \qquad\qquad (4-13-1)$$

Let :

$$W = PR \qquad\qquad (4-13-2)$$

then :

$$C = (I + WF)^{-1}(WX + DU) \qquad\qquad (4-13-3)$$

Denote :

$$G = (I + WF)^{-1}W \qquad\qquad (4-13-4)$$

so :

$$C = GX + GW^{-1}DU \qquad\qquad (4-13-5)$$

In order to realize the decoupling control between C and X, the matrix G should be diagonal, and thus both W and F must be diagonal. Therefore, GW^{-1} is also a diagonal matrix. But D is not a diagonal matrix and is given by:

$$D = \begin{pmatrix} D_{13} & D_{14} \\ \\ D_{23} & D_{24} \end{pmatrix}$$
(4-13-6)

Therefore, $GW^{-1}D$ can not be diagonal when GW^{-1} is a diagonal matrix. Consequently, this system can not realize the full decoupling control for C to both X and the load disturbances U.

Obviuosly, only when the input transfer matrix D is a diagonal matrix, the feedforward decoupling projects can realize the full decoupling control for outputs to both reference inputs and load disturbances. When D is not a diagonal matrix, the above conclusion is unavailable.

We proved before that the feedback decoupling projects have not such decoupling function either, thus we can say when the input transfer matrix of the load disturbances is not a diagonal matrix, no decoupling project discussed before, no matter feedforward or feedback, can realize the full decoupling control for the outputs to both reference inputs and load disturbances.

But, this conclusion should be discussed still further, namely we should discuss the second problem: Are the feedback decoupling projects absolutely not able to realize the full decoupling control for the outputs to both reference inputs and load disturbances?

The above conclusion is valid for systems with P-canonical plants, but by the uncertainty principle, a P-canonical plant can be transferred into an equivalent V-canonical plant.

We know that the influence of m_2 to C_1 is carried by P_{12} and this is a standard P-canonical form. Now, we transfer it into a V-canonical form. We let:

$$P_{22}V_{12}P_{11} = P_{12}$$
(4-13-7)

$$P_{11}V_{21}P_{22} = P_{21}$$
(4-13-8)

Then, we get:

$$V_{12} = \frac{P_{12}}{P_{11}P_{22}}$$

$$V_{21} = \frac{P_{21}}{P_{11}P_{22}}$$

(4-13-9)

The plant remains unchanged in practice but it has been described by V-canonical form.

Our aim is to realize the full decoupling control for the outputs to both reference inputs and load disturbances and now we should discuss whether we can reach such a result.[36]

Let us introduce a feedback channel from C_2 to m_1. Denote this feedback channel as R_{12} and let:

$$R_{12} = - V_{12}$$

(4-13-10)

Obviously, the influence of m_2 to C_1 is eliminated by the introduction of this channel. The scheme is shown in Fig 4-13-2.

Likewise, we can eliminate the influence of m_1 to C_2.

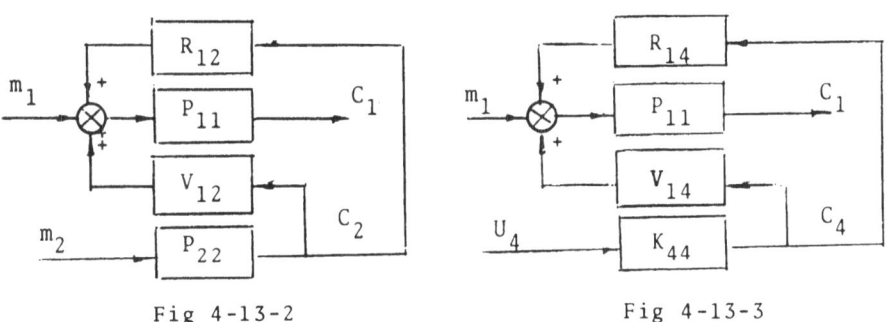

Fig 4-13-2   Fig 4-13-3

Now, let us analyze C_1. It gets the decoupling influence from three aspects, namely from m_2, U_3 and U_4. Now, the influence from m_2 has been eliminated. In order to eliminate the influence of U_4 to C_1, we measure U_4 at first, i.e. we do:

$$C_4 = K_{44}U_4$$

(4-13-11)

Then, we introduce a V-canonical channel expressed as:

$$D_{14} = K_{44}V_{14}P_{11}$$

(4-13-12)

namely:

$$V_{14} = \frac{D_{14}}{K_{44}P_{pp}}$$

(4-13-13)

Introducing a feedback channel from C_4 to m_1 and letting:

$$R_{14} = - V_{14}$$

(4-13-14)

we eliminate the influence of U_4 to C_1 and the scheme is shown in Fig 4-13-3.

Take the same measures to C_2 we can eliminate the influence of m_1 and U_4 to C_2 and the system becomes two separate single variable systems.

This is the project with V-canonical plant, P-canonical decoupling element structure and feedback decoupling channels.

We see that this system has realized the full decoupling control for the output C to both X and U. In addition, the decoupling conditions (4-13-10) and (4-13-14) are very simple and, furthermore, they are not changed with the increase of variable number.

In this system, C_1 now is influenced by X_1 and U_3 and if the full rejection design principle of single variable system is used for it, then the influence of U_3 to C_1 may be eliminated. This design is shown in Fig 4-13-4.

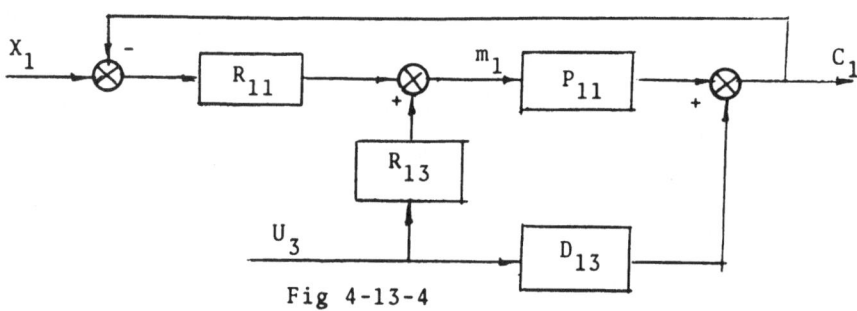

Fig 4-13-4

Because:

$$\frac{C_1}{U_3} = \frac{D_{13} + R_{13}P_{11}}{1 + P_{11}R_{11}}$$

(4-13-15)

so in order to eliminate the influence of U_3 to C_1, it is necessary:

$$R_{13} = - \frac{D_{13}}{P_{11}} \cdots \qquad (4-13-16)$$

Thus, C_1 is only influenced by X_1. Likewise, let:

$$R_{23} = - \frac{D_{23}}{P_{22}} \qquad (4-13-17)$$

then C_2 is only influenced by X_2.

Therefore, this two-variable system has realized not only full de-coupling, but also full rejection to disturbances.

The final structure of such a system is shown in Fig 4-13-5.

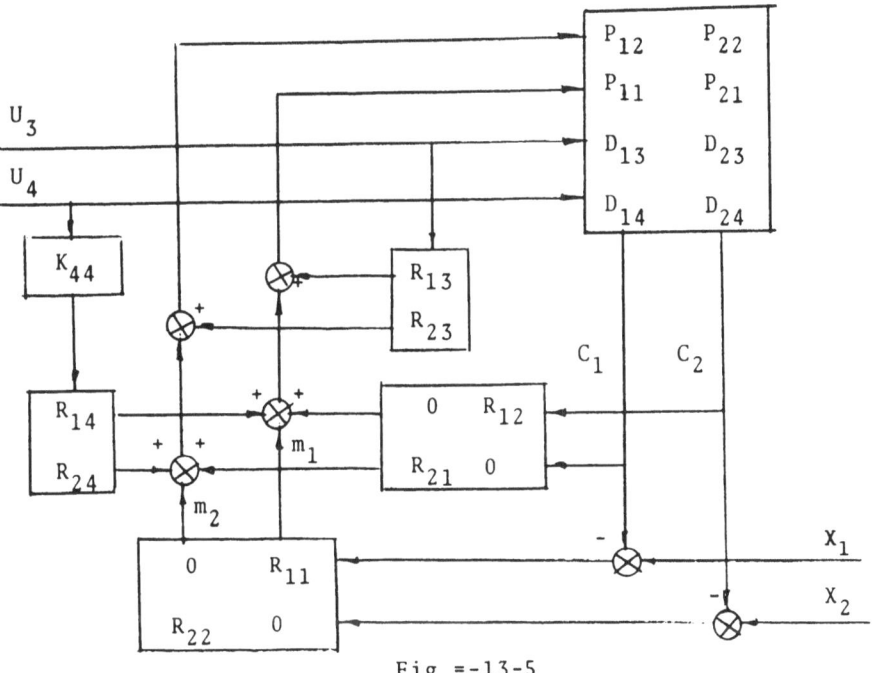

Fig =-13-5

It is clear if :

$$D_{14} = D_{23} = 0 \qquad (4-13-18)$$

namely only one disturbance for each output, then the adoption of feedback decoupling project with V-canonical plant can also eliminate the coupling influence of disturbances.

That means that the adoption of this decoupling project gives the

guarantee to realize the decoupling control for outputs to reference
inputs, load disturbances as well as supply disturbances.

In summary:

(1) When the input transfer matrix of disturbances is diagonal, then the feedback decoupling projects for systems with P-canonical
plants can realize the full decoupling control for outputs to reference
inputs and **supply** disturbances simultaneously,

(2) When the input transfer matrix of the disturbances is diagonal, the feedback decoupling projects for systems with V-canonical
plants can realize the full decoupling control for outputs to reference
inputs, supply disturbances as well as load disturbances,

(3) When the input transfer matrix of the disturbances is diagonal, the **feedforward decoupling** projects with P-canonical plants
and P-canonical decoupling element structures can realize the full decoupling control for outputs to reference inputs and the load disturbances , but can not realize the decoupling control for outputs to
the supply disturbances simultaneously,

(4) When the input transfer matrix of the disturbances is not
diagonal, the conclusion 3 is invalid. In such cases, the plants must
be transferred into V-canonical and take the feedback decoupling projects to the plants and the disturbances simultaneously, then we can
realize the full decoupling control,

(5) For the feedback decoupling projects, the decoupling element structures are always P-canonical since the signals are always
flowing forward.

(6) Especially, we should notice that the decoupling conditions
of the feedback decoupling projects with V-canonical plants are much
simpler than those of the feedback decoupling projects with P-canonical
plants and P-canonical decoupling element structures and are not
changed with the increase of the system variable number.

For the former:

$$N_{ik} = -V_{ik}$$

and for the latter:

$$N_{ik} = \frac{\det \bar{P}_{ki}}{\det P}$$

Thus, the above analysis denotes that the introduction of feedback projects and V-canonical forms can result in good decoupling effects and this is just the essential meaning of Mesarović idea. It says:

In general, to describe the system by V-canonical structure and to adopt feedback decoupling regulators is an effective way to solve the decoupling problems of multivariable control systems.

§ 4-14 The Realization of Full Decoupling Control of Systems with V-Canonical Plants [5]

In the previous several paragraphs, we discussed the practical meanings of the Mesarović idea in multivariable process system decoupling design and we find that the introduction of V-canonical forms and feedback decoupling projects result in good decoupling effects.

In the analysis of the systems with P-canonical plants, we pointed out that no matter the decoupling elements locate between the plant and regulators or combine with the regulators, it is impossible to realize the full decoupling control for outputs to both reference inputs and supply disturbances , i.e. the feedforward decoupling structures have no such full decoupling function. Notice that it also includes the V-canonical decoupling element structures , and if we want to get such decoupling function, we must adopt the feedback decoupling projects.

Then, we discuss the cases when the the plants are V-canonical and with supply disturbances.

The system is shown in Fig 4-14-1. Here, the supply disturbances are considered.

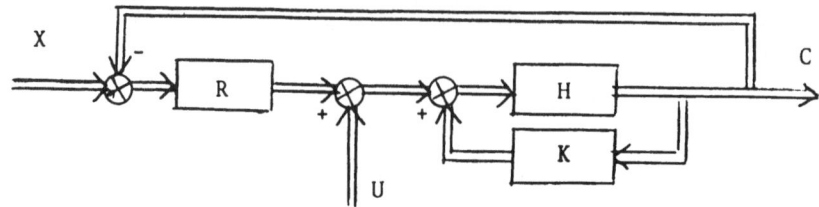

Fig 4-14-1

We have said before that a V-canonical plant can be expressed by two matrices H and K with positive feedback.

From this figure, we get:

$$C = HU + HUX + HKC - HRC \qquad (4-14-1)$$

namely:

$$C = HU + HRX - H(R - K)C \qquad (4-14-2)$$

$$C = (I + H(R - K))^{-1}HU + (I + H(R-K))^{-1}HRX \qquad (4-14-3)$$

In the above expressions, H is a diagonal matrix:

$$
H = \begin{pmatrix}
V_{11} & & & \text{\Large 0} \\
& V_{22} & & \\
& & \ddots & \\
\text{\Large 0} & & & V_{nn}
\end{pmatrix} \qquad (4-14-4)
$$

R is not a diagonal matrix and it contains both main regulators and decoupling elements. K is not a diagonal matrix either. Let:

$$A = R - K \qquad (4-14-5)$$

If A is a diagonal matrix , then $(I + H(R - K)^{-1}H$ is a diagonal matrix and the decoupling control for outputs to supply disturbances is realized.

Because K is:

$$
K \quad = \quad \begin{pmatrix} 0 & V_{12} & - & - & - & - & - & V_{1n} \\ V_{21} & 0 & - & - & - & - & - & V_{2n} \\ - & - & - & - & - & - & - & - \\ - & - & - & - & - & - & - & - \\ V_{n1} & V_{n2} & - & - & - & - & - & 0 \end{pmatrix} \qquad (4\text{-}14\text{-}6)
$$

so the elements of matrix R are:

$$R_{ii} = A_{ii} \qquad i = 1, 2, \ldots \ldots n \qquad\qquad (4\text{-}14\text{-}7)$$

$$R_{ik} = - V_{ik} \qquad \begin{array}{l} i = 1, 2, \ldots \ldots n \\ k = 1, 2, \ldots \ldots n \end{array} \quad i \neq k \qquad (4\text{-}14\text{-}8)$$

Thus, R is not a diagonal matrix and, consequently, the expression $(I + H(R - K))^{-1}HR$ is impossible to be a diagonal matrix.

Therefore , we get the following conclusion: For a system with V-canonical plant and P-canonical decoupling element structure and the decoupling element structure is combined with regulators, it is very easy to realize the decoupling control for its outputs to the supply disturbances, but when the control function is reached, then it is impossible to realize the decoupling control for outputs to its reference inputs simultaneously and vice versa.

Thus, combining this result with the conclusions obtained in the previuos paragraphs, we get the following conclusion: It is impossible to realize the decoupling control for the outputs to the reference ininputs and the supply disturbances simultaneously by feedforward decoupling structures, no matter the plant is P-canonical or V-canonical.

For a system with V-canonical plant, if we want to realize the decoupling control for outputs to reference inputs and supply disturbances simultaneously, two methods may be adopted.

The first possible method is to let the reference inputs be input into the system through a preset network R_x as shown in Fig 4-14-2.

From this figure, we have:

$$C = HU + HRR_xX - HAC \qquad\qquad (4\text{-}14\text{-}9)$$

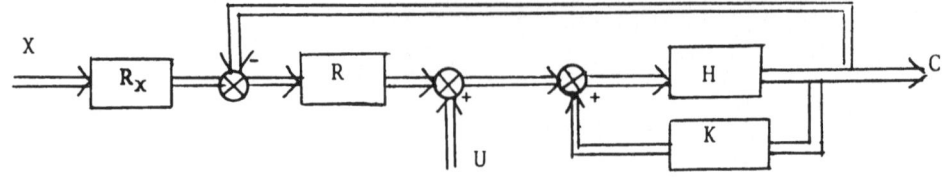

Fig 4-14-2

Because H is a diagonal matrix , so when A is a diagonal matrix, the decoupling control for C to U is realized and when:

$$B = RR_x \qquad\qquad (4\text{-}14\text{-}10)$$

is also a diagonal matrix, then the decoupling control for C to reference inputs X is also realized.

Here, R has been given by (4-14-7) and (4-14-8), so when the diagonal matrix B is given, then the elements of R_x can be determined by:

$$R_{x,ik} = \frac{(\det \bar{R}_{ki})B_{kk}}{\det R} \qquad\qquad (4\text{-}14\text{-}11)$$

Because A, H and K are not difficult to be realized, so R_{ii} and R_{ik} are not difficult to be realized either; and the change of A_{ii} will not give influence on the decoupling control . This is an important advantage of the decoupling design for systems with V-canonical plants.

As for the realization of R_x , it should be determined by practical conditions.

For a two-variable system, these conditions are:

$$\left.\begin{array}{l} R_{11} = A_{11} \\[4pt] R_{22} = A_{22} \\[4pt] R_{12} = -V_{12} \\[4pt] R_{21} = -V_{21} \\[4pt] R_{x,11} = \dfrac{A_{22}B_{11}}{A_{11}A_{22} - V_{12}V_{21}} \\[12pt] R_{x,22} = \dfrac{A_{11}B_{22}}{A_{11}A_{22} - V_{12}V_{21}} \end{array}\right\} \qquad (4\text{-}14\text{-}12)$$

$$R_{x,12} = \frac{V_{12}B_{22}}{A_{11}A_{22} - V_{12}V_{21}}$$

$$R_{x,21} = \frac{V_{21}B_{11}}{A_{11}A_{22} - V_{12}V_{21}}$$

Therefore, for a system with V-canonical plant, the simple feed-forward decoupling project can not realize the full decoupling control for outputs to reference inputs and supply dusturbances simultaneously, but when the reference inputs are input into the system through a pre-set network, then it can reach the desired full decoupling control.

The second possible method is to use the feedback decoupling pro-ject. Such a system is shown in Fig 4-14-3.

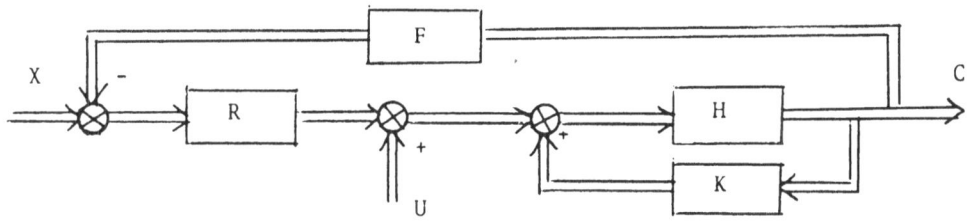

Fig 4-14-3

From this figure, we have:

$$C = HU + HUX + HKC - HRFC \qquad (4-14-13)$$

Let:

$$A = RF - K \qquad (4-14-14)$$

be a diagonal matrix and :

$$C = HU + HRX + H(RF - K)C \qquad (4-14-15)$$

$$C = (I - HA)^{-1}HRX + HU \qquad (4-14-16)$$

Because H, $\dot{A}$ and R all are diagonal matrices, so this system can realize the full decoupling control for the outputs to both reference inputs and supply disturbances.

The elements of F may be determined by (4-14-14):

$$F_{ii} = \frac{A_{ii}}{R_{ii}} \qquad i = 1, 2, \ldots \ldots n \qquad (4\text{-}14\text{-}17)$$

$$F_{ik} = \frac{V_{ik}}{R_{ii}} \qquad \begin{matrix} i = 1, 2, \ldots \ldots n \\ k = 1, 2, \ldots \ldots n \\ i \neq k \end{matrix} \qquad (4\text{-}14\text{-}18)$$

If we let:

$$A_{ii} = R_{ii} \qquad (4\text{-}14\text{-}19)$$

then the system can be simplified as :

$$F_{ii} = 1 \qquad (4\text{-}14\text{-}20)$$

Fig 4-14-4 shows a two-variable system with V-canonical plant and the feedback decoupling project is adopted to realize the full decoupling control for C to both X and U.

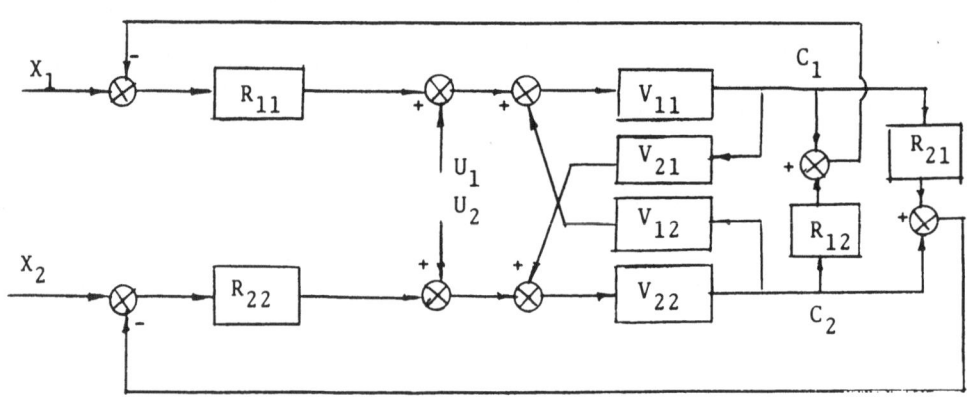

Fig 4-14-4

Where :

$$
\left.
\begin{aligned}
R_{11} &= A_{11} \\
R_{22} &= A_{22} \\
R_{21} &= \frac{V_{21}}{R_{11}} = \frac{V_{21}V_{11}}{W_{11}} \\
R_{12} &= \frac{V_{12}}{R_{22}} = \frac{V_{12}V_{22}}{W_{22}}
\end{aligned}
\right\} \qquad (4\text{-}14\text{-}21)
$$

with:

$$
\left.
\begin{aligned}
W_{11} &= V_{11}R_{11} \\
W_{22} &= V_{22}R_{22}
\end{aligned}
\right\} \qquad (4\text{-}14\text{-}22)
$$

which are the open loop transfer functions for the first channel and the second channel, respectively.

Then, we get:

$$C_1 = \frac{V_{11}U_1 + W_{11}X_1}{1 + W_{11}} \qquad (4\text{-}14\text{-}23)$$

$$C_2 = \frac{V_{22}U_2 + W_{22}X_2}{1 + W_{22}} \qquad (4\text{-}14\text{-}24)$$

From these two expressions, we get the following conclusions:

(1) This system has realized the full decoupling control for the outputs to both reference inputs and supply disturbances, for example, C_1 is only influenced by X_1 and U_1, and so is the C_2 ,

(2) In addition, the decoupled system is exactly corresponding to break off all coupling channels and the two main channels are remained,

(3) From (4-14-21) we can see that both R_{12} and R_{21} are only related to the characters of its own main channel elements and are not related to the other channel . This conclusion is not only true for two-variable systems, but also is true for any multivariable process control system , namely the decouplimg conditions do not change as the increase of the system variable number.

This is just the practical meaning of Mesarović idea, i.e. the application of V-canonical forms and feedback decoupling projects can result in good decoupling effects.

We discuss an example which is taken from Schwarz´s book.

The plant is with P-canonical as follows:

$$P = \begin{bmatrix} (1+ 0.25S)^{-3} & (-(1+ 0.25S)^3(1+ 2S)^2(1+ 3S))^{-1} \\ ((1+ 0.25S)(1+ 2S)(1+ 3S))^{-2} & ((1 + 2S)^2(1+ 3S))^{-1} \end{bmatrix}$$

We transfer it into V-canonical form and the results are:

$$V_{11} = \frac{1}{(1 + 0.25S)^3} - \frac{1}{(1 + 0.25S)^5(1 + 2S)^2(1 + 3S)^2}$$

$$V_{22} = \frac{1}{(1 + 2S)^2(1 + 3S)} + \frac{1}{(1 + 0.25S)^5(1 + 2S)^2(1 + 3S)^3}$$

$$V_{21} = \frac{(1 + 0.25S)^3(1 + 2S)^2(1 + 3S)}{1 + (1 + 0.25S)^2(1 + 2S)^2(1 + 3S)^3}$$

$$V_{12} = \frac{(1 + 0.25S)^2(1 + 2S)^2(1 + 3S)^2}{1 + (1 + 0.25S)^2(1 + 2S)^2(1 + 3S)^2}$$

Suppose that the main channel characters after decoupling are:

$$W_{11} = \frac{K_1}{S} B_1(S)$$

$$W_{22} = \frac{K_2}{S} B_2(S)$$

where, K_1, K_2 and $B_1(S)$, $B_2(S)$ are to be determined. From (4-14-22):

$$R_{11} = \frac{W_{11}}{V_{11}} = \frac{K_1}{S} B_1(S) \frac{(1 + 0.25S)^5(1 + 2S)^2(1 + 3S)^2}{1 + (1 + 0.25S)^2(1 + 2S)^2(1 + 3S)^2}$$

Let:

$$B_1(S) = \frac{1 + (1 + 0.25S)^2(1 + 2S)^2(1 + 3S)^2}{(1 + 0.25S)^5(1 + 2S)^2(1 + 3S)^2}$$

then we get:

$$R_{11} = \frac{K_1}{S}$$

Likewise:

$$R_{21} = -\frac{K_1}{S(1 + 0.25S)^2(1 + 3S)}$$

$$R_{22} = \frac{K_2}{S}$$

$$B_2(S) = \frac{1 + (1 + 0.25S)^2(1 + 2S)^2(1 + 3S)^2}{(1 + 0.25S)^2(1 + 2S)^4(1 + 3S)^3}$$

$$R_{12} = \frac{K_2}{S}$$

Both K_1 and K_2 can be determined by the single variable system design.

Thus, the decoupling elements are not difficult to be determined.

§ 4-15 The General Conclusion on Realizing Full Decoupling Control

We have discussed several cases of realizing full decoupling control.

There is another case: The system is with V-canonical plant and the feedforward decoupling project is adopted, then can this system realize the full decoupling control for outputs to reference inputs and load disturbances ?

The system is shown in Fig 4-15-1.

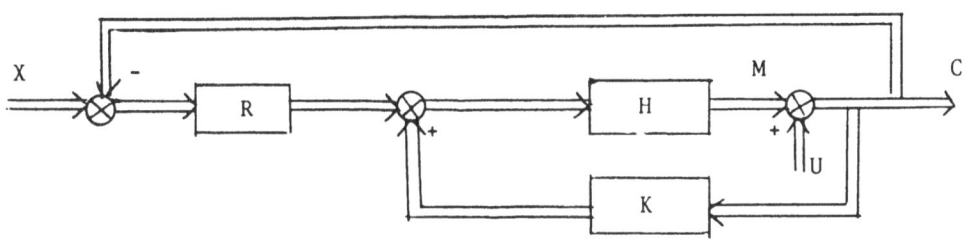

Fig 4-15-1

From the figure, we have:

$$C = HRX - HRC + HKC + U \qquad (4\text{-}15\text{-}1)$$
$$C = (I + (H(R - K)^{-1}HRX + (I + H(R - K))^{-1}U \qquad (4\text{-}15\text{-}2)$$

Because R is not a diagonal matrix, so $(I+ H(R- K))^{-1}HR$ and $(I+ H(R- K))^{-1}$ can not be diagonal simultaneously.

Therefore, this system can not realize the full decoupling control for C to both X and U.

In summary, the full decoupling control for a MPCS is given as:

Demand on Full Decoupling Control	Outputs to Both Reference Inputs and Supply Disturbances		Outputs to Both Reference inputs and Load Disturbances	
Plant Decoupling Project	P- Canonical	V- Canonical	P- Canonical	V- Canonical
Feedforward	No	No	Yes	No
Feedback	Yes	Yes	No	Yes

Suppose the input transfer matrix of disturbances being diagonal.

CHAPTER FIVE

SOME SPECIAL DECOUPLING DESIGN METHODS

§ 5-1 Introduction

For the control system design, decoupling is not the full contents. Besides the decoupling demand, we should determine the parameters of the regulators.

The principles pointed out in the last chapter are: At first, we perform the decoupling design and then the system will be reduced to some subsystems with single variables . Then the regulators can be determined by conventional single loop tuning methods.

But, however, we can propose a problem: Can we combine the regulator tuning with the decoupling design?

Yes, it is possible.

In this chapter, we will introduce some popular and successful methods. Besides, in process control systems, the plants certainly can be divided into P-canonical and V-canonical, but they may be with dead delays and for these plants we also should discuss.

The full decoupling structures mentioned in the last chapter mean that the same structure is used to realize the decoupling demands to both references and disturbances , but they are not systems with full rejection to disturbances. So we should discuss further how to combine the full decoupling design with the full rejection-to-disturbances design .

The consideration of disturbances is a very important problem in process control system design and in the analysis of MPCS because of the application of matrix analysis, sometimes it is very easily to make mistakes due to negligence. So this problem is especially worth being noticed.

In this chapter, the above problem will be discussed.

§ 5-2 The Unit Matrix Method [(32)]

At first, we discuss the application of the unit matrix method which is widely used for the feedforward decoupling projects.

When we discussed the application of feedforward decoupling projects before, we knew that the decoupling element structure may be combined with the main regulators.

Now, we divide the matrix obtained by such a way into two parts, namely:

$$R = R_1 R_2 \qquad (5-2-1)$$

It is also:

$$\begin{pmatrix} R_{11} & R_{12} \\ R_{21} & R_{22} \end{pmatrix} = \begin{pmatrix} R_1' & 0 \\ 0 & R_2' \end{pmatrix} \begin{pmatrix} R_{11}'' & R_{12}'' \\ R_{21}'' & R_{22}'' \end{pmatrix} \qquad (5-2-2)$$

In fact, this means that the decoupling element structure is located between the plant and the regulators.

For the system shown in Fig 4-8-1, then equation (4-8-6) becomes:

$$C = (I + PR_2 R_1 F)^{-1} (PR_2 R_1 X + PU) \qquad (5-2-3)$$

Let:

$$PR_2 = I \qquad (5-2-4)$$

then :

$$C = (I + R_1 F)^{-1} (R_1 X + PU) \qquad (5-2-5)$$

Obviously, because both R_1 and F are diagonal matrices, so this system can realize the decoupling control for outputs to reference inputs , but can not realize the decoupling control for outputs to the disturbances. This conclusion is in accordance with those mentioned in § 4-15.

This design method is called as unit matrix method.

This method now is widely used in decoupling design. Its prominent advantage is : It combines the decoupling element structure with the plant into a unit matrix and , in the control system, this combined matrix can be considered as an extended plant character. Because in this matrix, all diagonal elements are 1, so in the single variable systems obtained after the decoupling design, all the plants are 1, then the system design becomes very simple.

Take the two-variable system as an example. When the decoupling design is done by using the unit matrix method, then from (5-2-4), the decoupling elements are given by:

$$R_2 = \begin{pmatrix} \dfrac{P_{22}}{\Delta P} & -\dfrac{P_{12}}{\Delta P} \\[3mm] -\dfrac{P_{21}}{\Delta P} & \dfrac{P_{11}}{\Delta P} \end{pmatrix} \qquad (5\text{-}2\text{-}6)$$

When no disturbance is considered, the decoupled system is shown in Fig 5-2-1.

Now, the open loop characters of the decoupled single variable systems are simply those of the main regulators. For example, if the PI regulators are

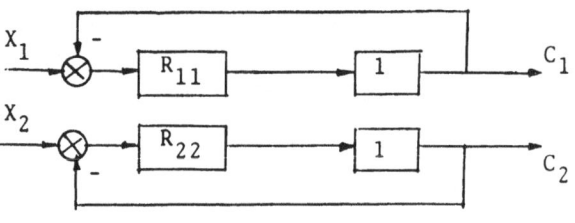

Fig 5-2-1

adopted, then no matter how large the propotional gains they have, the system is always stable. Thus, this design method is with great advantage and when the control demands for the two decoupled systems are different, they can be reached by different regulator characters.

Because of this advantage and flexibility, so this method is widely applied.

But, however, we can not consider that the unit matrix method is as important as the diagonal matrix method. In fact, the diagonal matrix method is   a general principle and the unit matrix method is merely an application of this general principle in a special case.

In the application of the unit matrix method, two points should be noticed:

(1) Equation (5-2-4) denotes that the character of the decoupling element structrue is obtained by full zero-pole cancellation between the
the plant and the decoupling element structure.Because the plant is
always physically realizable, so, consequently, the decoupling element
structure is always physically irrealizable.
(2) Because the unit matrix method is only an application of the diagonal matrix method in a special case, so the application of this method is limited only for the feedforward decoupling projects.

Now, we discuss the application of the unit matrix method to the
systems with V-canonical plants and P-canonical decoupling element
structures. Consider the two-variable system again and the system
block diagram is shown in Fig 5-2-2.

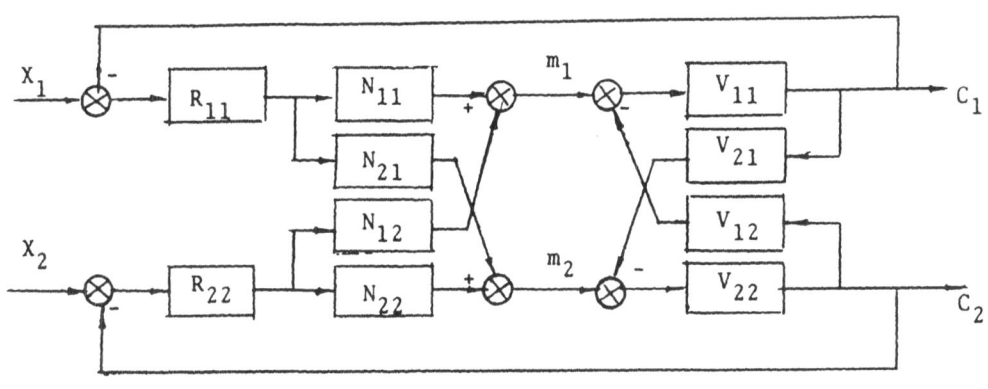

Fig 5-2-2

In order to use the unit matrix method, we introduce the following matrices:

$$D = \begin{Bmatrix} 1 & V_{11}V_{12} \\ V_{22}V_{21} & 0 \end{Bmatrix} \qquad (5-2-8)$$

$$N = \begin{Bmatrix} V_{11} & 0 \\ 0 & V_{22} \end{Bmatrix} \qquad (5-2-9)$$

From Fig 5-2-2, we can get:

$$C_1 = \frac{V_{11}}{1 - V_{11}V_{22}V_{12}V_{21}} m_1 - \frac{V_{11}V_{22}V_{12}}{1 - V_{11}V_{22}V_{12}V_{21}} m_2 \qquad (5\text{-}2\text{-}10)$$

$$C_2 = - \frac{V_{11}V_{22}V_{21}}{1 - V_{11}V_{22}V_{12}V_{21}} m_1 + \frac{V_{22}}{1 - V_{11}V_{22}V_{12}V_{21}} m_2 \qquad (5\text{-}2\text{-}11)$$

or in matrix form:

$$C = D^{-1}HM \qquad (5\text{-}2\text{-}12)$$

By the unit matrix method, it is necessary:

$$D^{-1}HN = I \qquad (5\text{-}2\text{-}13)$$

namely:

$$\frac{\begin{bmatrix} V_{11} & -V_{11}V_{22}V_{12} \\ -V_{22}V_{11}V_{21} & V_{22} \end{bmatrix}}{1 - V_{11}V_{22}V_{12}V_{21}} \; N = I \qquad (5\text{-}2\text{-}14)$$

Let:

$$\Delta = 1 - V_{11}V_{22}V_{12}V_{21} \qquad (5\text{-}2\text{-}15)$$

$$Q = D^{-1}H \qquad (5\text{-}2\text{-}16)$$

then:

$$N = \frac{\text{adj } Q}{\text{det } Q} = \frac{\begin{bmatrix} V_{22} & V_{11}V_{12}V_{22} \\ V_{22}V_{21}V_{11} & V_{11} \end{bmatrix}}{V_{11}V_{22}} = \begin{bmatrix} \dfrac{1}{V_{11}} & V_{12} \\ V_{21} & \dfrac{1}{V_{22}} \end{bmatrix} \qquad (5\text{-}2\text{-}17)$$

Therefore:

$$\left.\begin{aligned} N_{11} &= \frac{1}{V_{11}} \\[6pt] N_{12} &= V_{12} \\[6pt] N_{21} &= V_{21} \\[6pt] N_{22} &= \frac{1}{V_{22}} \end{aligned}\right\} \qquad (5\text{-}2\text{-}18)$$

So, the unit matrix method can be used also for systems with V-canonical plants.

§ 5-3 Design by Given Demands

Although the unit matrix metnod is with great advantage, it is still a two-step design method, namely to decouple the system at first and then to design by single variable system methods.

Now, we discuss such a problem: If the control demands for the decoupled single variable systems are given, can we finish the system design in one step?

This is the so-called " design by given demands".

The given control demands may be:

(1) For the decoupled single variable systems, the closed loop transfer functions , the open loop transfer functions and   the re- gulator characters are given for assumptive decoupled single loops.

That means that for a system shown in Fig 5-3-1 the closed loop transfer function G_i and the system figure are given, so

$$\frac{C_i}{X_i} = G_i = \frac{R_i P_{ii}}{1 + R_i P_{ii}} = \frac{W_i}{1 + W_i} \tag{5-3-1}$$

is given and consequently:

$$W_i = \frac{G_i}{1 - G_i} \tag{5-3-2}$$

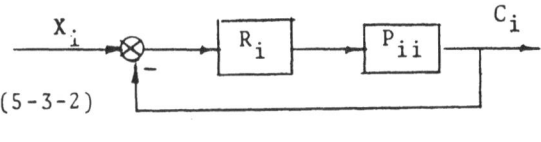

Fig 5-3-1

is known. Thus:

$$R_i = \frac{G_i}{P_{ii}(1 - G_i)} \tag{5-3-3}$$

can be easily determined. Where P_{ii} is the main channel plant character.

So, it seems that the design by given demands is very easy.

But, is this possible?

(2) Only the closed loop control demands are given for the de- coupled single variable systems. This can be done by different me- thods, shch as standard transfer function method, Guillemin-Truxal synthesis method, etc .

That means that in the design the following relation is given:

$$
\begin{Bmatrix} C_1 \\ C_2 \\ \cdot \\ \cdot \\ \cdot \\ C_n \end{Bmatrix} = \begin{bmatrix} G_1 & & & 0 \\ & G_2 & & \\ & & \cdot & \\ 0 & & & G_n \end{bmatrix} \begin{Bmatrix} X_1 \\ X_2 \\ \cdot \\ \cdot \\ \cdot \\ X_n \end{Bmatrix} \qquad (5\text{-}3\text{-}4)
$$

Besides, the plant characters are also known but the characters of the regulators and decoupling elements are not known.

For these two cases, which is possible and realistic?

Now, we discuss an example at first.

The system is shown in Fig 5-3-2 which is a control system of a boiler indeed.

C_1 and C_2 represent the pressure and the level in the drum and C_3 represents the output steam.

The regulation of these parameters forms a coupling system.

Suppose that the output steam is not under control, then the control of the drum pressure and the drum level forms a two-variable system with P-canonical plant, but the output steam becomes the load disturbance of this system.

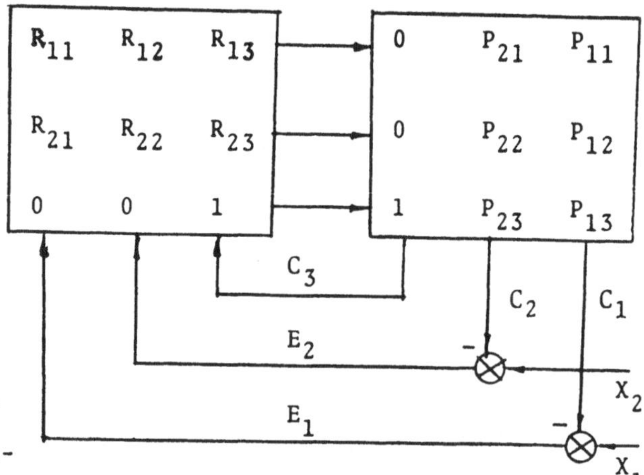

Fig 5-3-2

In this figure, the decoupling element structure is combined with regulators and we have said before that this project can realize the full decoupling control for the outputs to both reference inputs and the load disturbances.

The control demands are:

(1) Not only the full decoupling control, but also the full rejection to the disturbance is expected, namely neither C_1 nor C_2 should be influenced by C_3 ,

(2) The closed loop control characters of C_1 and C_2 are given, namely G_1 and G_2 are known.

For this system, we have:

$$
\begin{pmatrix} C_1 \\ C_2 \\ C_3 \end{pmatrix} = \begin{pmatrix} P_{11} & P_{12} & P_{13} \\ P_{21} & P_{22} & P_{23} \\ 0 & 0 & 1 \end{pmatrix} \begin{pmatrix} R_{11} & R_{12} & R_{13} \\ R_{21} & R_{22} & R_{23} \\ 0 & 0 & 1 \end{pmatrix} \begin{pmatrix} E_1 \\ E_2 \\ C_3 \end{pmatrix}
\tag{5-3-5}
$$

For realization of the full decoupling control and the full rejection to the disturbance, equation (5-3-5) should be with the following form:

$$
\begin{pmatrix} C_1 \\ C_2 \\ C_3 \end{pmatrix} = \begin{pmatrix} \dfrac{G_1}{1 - G_1} & 0 & 0 \\ 0 & \dfrac{G_2}{1 - G_2} & 0 \\ 0 & 0 & 1 \end{pmatrix} \begin{pmatrix} E_1 \\ E_2 \\ C_3 \end{pmatrix}
\tag{5-3-6}
$$

namely:

$$
\begin{pmatrix} C_1 \\ C_2 \\ C_3 \end{pmatrix} = \begin{pmatrix} W_1 & 0 & 0 \\ 0 & W_2 & 0 \\ 0 & 0 & 1 \end{pmatrix} \begin{pmatrix} E_1 \\ E_2 \\ C_3 \end{pmatrix}
\tag{5-3-7}
$$

Therefore, we get:

$$
P_{11}R_{11} + P_{12}R_{21} = W_1
\tag{5-3-8}
$$

$$
P_{12}R_{12} + P_{12}R_{22} = 0
\tag{5-3-9}
$$

$$
P_{11}R_{13} + P_{12}R_{23} + P_{13} = 0
\tag{5-3-10}
$$

and :

$$
P_{21}R_{11} + P_{22}R_{21} = 0
\tag{5-3-11}
$$

$$
P_{21}R_{12} + P_{22}R_{22} = W_2
\tag{5-3-12}
$$

$$P_{21}R_{13} + P_{22}R_{23} + P_{23} = 0 \qquad\qquad (5\text{-}3\text{-}13)$$

Obviously:

$$\left.\begin{array}{l} W_1 \neq P_{11}R_{11} \\[2ex] W_2 \neq P_{22}R_{22} \end{array}\right\} \qquad\qquad (5\text{-}3\text{-}14)$$

thus, the open loop characters of the decoupled single loops are not the same as those of the original main channels. Consequently, the assumption of case 1, namely Fig 5-3-1, is uncorrect.

From (5-3-10) and (5-3-13), we get:

$$P_{11}R_{13} + P_{12}R_{23} = -P_{13} \qquad\qquad (5\text{-}3\text{-}15)$$

$$P_{21}R_{13} + P_{22}R_{23} = -P_{23} \qquad\qquad (5\text{-}3\text{-}16)$$

and it follows:

$$R_{13} = \frac{P_{12}P_{23} - P_{13}P_{22}}{\Delta P} \qquad\qquad (5\text{-}3\text{-}17)$$

$$R_{23} = \frac{P_{21}P_{13} - P_{23}P_{11}}{\Delta P} \qquad\qquad (5\text{-}3\text{-}18)$$

where:

$$\Delta = P_{11}P_{22} - P_{12}P_{21} \qquad\qquad (5\text{-}3\text{-}19)$$

Notice that R_{13} and R_{23} are not needed for decoupling control, but needed for the realization of the full rejection to C_3.

From (s-3-9) and (5-3-12), we get:

$$R_{12} = -\frac{P_{12}W_2}{\Delta P} \qquad\qquad (5\text{-}3\text{-}20)$$

$$R_{22} = \frac{P_{11}W_2}{\Delta P} = \frac{P_{11}}{\Delta P}\frac{G_2}{1 - G_2} \qquad\qquad (5\text{-}3\text{-}21)$$

From (5-3-8) and (5-3-11), we get:

$$R_{11} = \frac{P_{22}W_1}{\Delta P} = \frac{P_{22}}{\Delta P}\frac{G_1}{1 - G_1} \qquad\qquad (5\text{-}3\text{-}22)$$

$$R_{12} = -\frac{P_{21}W_1}{\Delta P} \qquad\qquad (5\text{-}3\text{-}23)$$

Therefore, both R_{11} and R_{22} are different from (5-3-3).

Let us return to (4-8-9). There, the characters of the decoupling elements were obtained by the decoupling demands and are given by:

$$R_{21} = - \frac{P_{21}}{P_{22}} R_{11} \qquad (5-3-24)$$

$$R_{12} = - \frac{P_{12}}{P_{11}} R_{22} \qquad (5-3-25)$$

Substituting R_{11} and R_{22} expressed by (5-3-22) and (5-3-21) into them, we get the same results as (5-3-23) and (5-3-20). That means that as two decoupling elements, the characters of R_{12} and R_{21} are always the same, no matter by decoupling design or by the design with given control demands.

Then, from (5-3-20) to (5-3-25) and by the given closed loop characters G_1 and G_2 (or W_1 and W_2), we can determine all characters of regulators and decoupling elements which satisfy the given control demands. Notice that the solution is unique because there are six independent equations for six unknowns. We can get unique solution here because the given W_1 and W_2 are two restraints.

In general, we have:

$$G = \begin{pmatrix} G_{11} & & & 0 \\ & G_{22} & & \\ & & \cdot & \\ 0 & & \cdot & \\ & & & G_{nn} \end{pmatrix} \qquad (5-3-26)$$

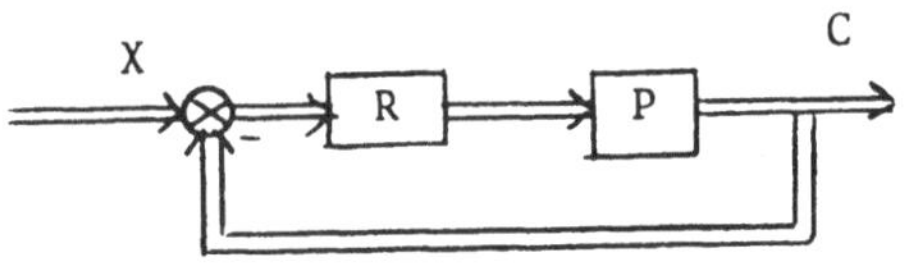

Fig 5-3-3

and:

$$G = (I + W)^{-1} W \qquad (5-3-27)$$

where:

$$W = PR \qquad (5-3-28)$$

Therefore:

$$(I + W)G = W \qquad (5-3-29)$$

or:

$$W = G(I - G)^{-1} \qquad (5-3-30)$$

Therefore:

$$W = G(I - G)^{-1} \qquad\qquad (5-3-31)$$

and R can be obtained by:

$$R = P^{-1}G(I - G)^{-1} \qquad\qquad (5-3-32)$$

For instance, a partial coupling system of two variables is shown in Fig 5-3-4.

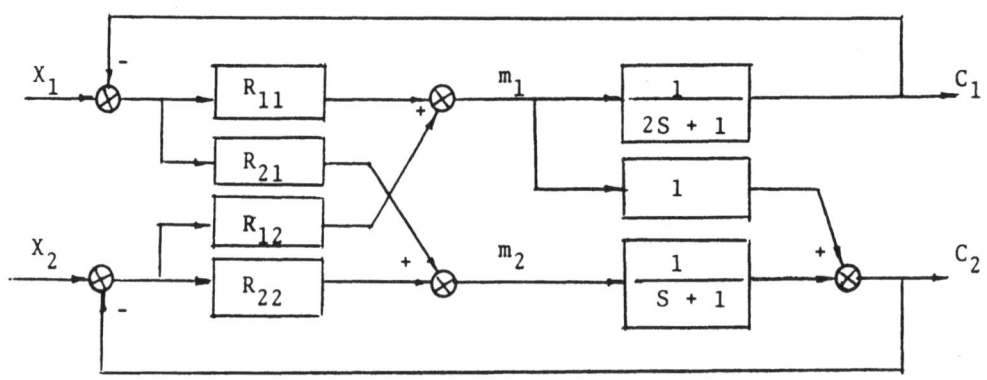

Fig 5-3-4

Suppose the demanded transfer matrix of the closed loop being:

$$G(S) = \begin{bmatrix} \dfrac{1}{S + 1} & 0 \\[3mm] 0 & \dfrac{1}{S + 1} \end{bmatrix} \qquad\qquad (5-3-33)$$

and the parameters of the regulators are under determination.

We have:

$$W = G(I - G)^{-1} = \begin{bmatrix} \dfrac{1}{S + 1} & 0 \\[3mm] 0 & \dfrac{1}{S + 1} \end{bmatrix} \begin{bmatrix} \dfrac{S + 1}{S} & 0 \\[3mm] 0 & \dfrac{S + 1}{5S} \end{bmatrix}$$

$$= \begin{bmatrix} \dfrac{1}{S} & 0 \\[3mm] 0 & \dfrac{1}{5S} \end{bmatrix} \qquad\qquad (5-3-34)$$

On the other hand:

$$\begin{Bmatrix} C_1 \\ C_2 \end{Bmatrix} = \begin{bmatrix} \dfrac{1}{2S+1} & 0 \\ 1 & \dfrac{1}{S+1} \end{bmatrix} \begin{Bmatrix} m_1 \\ m_2 \end{Bmatrix} \qquad (5\text{-}3\text{-}35)$$

$$\begin{Bmatrix} m_1 \\ m_2 \end{Bmatrix} = \begin{bmatrix} R_{11} & R_{12} \\ R_{21} & R_{22} \end{bmatrix} \begin{bmatrix} X_1 - C_1 \\ X_2 - C_2 \end{bmatrix} \qquad (5\text{-}3\text{-}36)$$

So we get:

$$\begin{Bmatrix} C_1 \\ C_2 \end{Bmatrix} = \begin{Bmatrix} \begin{bmatrix} \dfrac{1}{2S+1} & 0 \\ 1 & \dfrac{1}{S+1} \end{bmatrix} \begin{bmatrix} R_{11} & R_{12} \\ R_{21} & R_{22} \end{bmatrix} \begin{bmatrix} X_1 - C_1 \\ X_2 - C_2 \end{bmatrix} \end{Bmatrix} =$$

$$= \begin{Bmatrix} \begin{bmatrix} \dfrac{1}{S} & 0 \\ 0 & \dfrac{1}{5S} \end{bmatrix} \begin{bmatrix} X_1 - C_1 \\ X_2 - C_2 \end{bmatrix} \end{Bmatrix} \qquad (5\text{-}3\text{-}37)$$

Therefore:

$$\begin{bmatrix} R_{11} & R_{12} \\ R_{21} & R_{22} \end{bmatrix} = \begin{bmatrix} \dfrac{1}{2S+1} & 0 \\ 1 & \dfrac{1}{S+1} \end{bmatrix} \begin{bmatrix} \dfrac{1}{S} & 0 \\ 0 & \dfrac{1}{5S} \end{bmatrix} =$$

$$= \begin{Bmatrix} \dfrac{2S+1}{S} & 0 \\ -\dfrac{(S+1)(2S+1)}{S} & \dfrac{S+1}{5S} \end{Bmatrix} \qquad (5\text{-}3\text{-}38)$$

In the application of this method, when the plant is V-canonical, then it should be transferred into a P-canonical plant at first.

§ 5-4 The Boksenbom-Hood Method [1]

   Boksenbom and Hood proposed another design method by given control demands. In their method, at first only the the main channel characters are considered and by the plant characters of the main channels to design the main regulators, then the decoupling design is considered.

   We also consider a two-variable system which is shown in Fig 5-4-1.

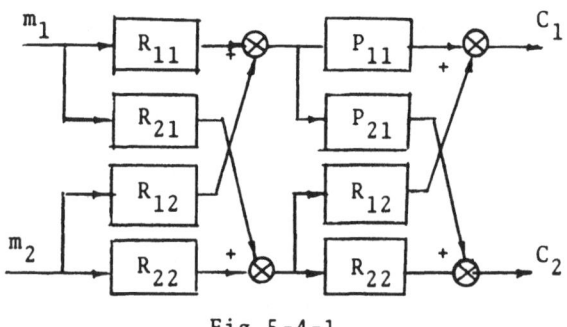

   By this method, we at first design the main regulators according to P_{11} and P_{22} and the results are R_1 and R_2.

      Notice:

$$R_1 \neq R_{11}$$

$$R_2 \neq R_{22}$$

Fig 5-4-1

   Then, we carry out the decoupling design. By the decoupling demands, we have:

$$P_{11}R_{11} + P_{12}R_{21} = P_{11}R_1 \qquad (5-4-1)$$

$$P_{21}R_{11} + P_{22}R_{21} = 0 \qquad (5-4-2)$$

$$P_{12}R_{22} + P_{11}R_{12} = 0 \qquad (5-4-3)$$

$$P_{21}R_{12} + P_{22}R_{22} = P_{22}R_2 \qquad (5-4-4)$$

   From the above four equations, we get:

$$R_{11} = \lambda R_1 \qquad (5-4-5)$$

$$R_{12} = - \frac{P_{12}}{P_{11}} R_{22} \qquad (5-4-6)$$

$$R_{21} = - \frac{P_{21}}{P_{22}} R_{11} \qquad (5-4-7)$$

$$R_{22} = \lambda R_2 \qquad (5-4-8)$$

where:

$$\lambda = \cfrac{1}{1 - \cfrac{P_{12}P_{21}}{P_{11}P_{22}}} \qquad (5\text{-}4\text{-}9)$$

They may be also written as:

$$R_{11} = R_1 \frac{P_{11}P_{22}}{P_{11}P_{22} - P_{12}P_{21}} \qquad (5\text{-}4\text{-}10)$$

$$R_{22} = R_2 \frac{P_{11}P_{22}}{P_{11}P_{22} - P_{12}P_{21}} \qquad (5\text{-}4\text{-}11)$$

Obviously, $R_{11} \neq R_1$, $R_{22} \neq R_2$.

Comparing with (4-8-9) , we know that the forms of the decoupling elements R_{12} and R_{21} remain the same, i.e. the decoupling conditions are not related to the main channel design.

In general, for the systems with n variables, if R_i denotes the regulator of the ith main channel and is obtained by the consideration of the main channel plant character P_{ii}, then , after decoupling design, the corresponding regulator should have the following character:

$$R_{ii} = \cfrac{R_i}{1 + \cfrac{\displaystyle\sum_{k=1}^{n} P_{ik}\det \bar{P}_{ik}}{P_{ii}\det \bar{P}_{ii}}} = \lambda_i R_i \qquad (5\text{-}4\text{-}12)$$

$$k = 1, 2, \ldots \ldots n \qquad k \neq i$$

$$R_{ii} = R_{kk} \frac{\det \bar{P}_{ki}}{\det \bar{P}_{kk}} \qquad (5\text{-}4\text{-}13)$$

where:

$$\lambda_i = \cfrac{1}{1 + \cfrac{\displaystyle\sum_{k=1}^{n} P_{ik}\det \bar{P}_{ik}}{P_{ii}\det \bar{P}_{ii}}} \qquad (5\text{-}4\text{-}14)$$

For example, for a two-variable system:

$$\lambda = \cfrac{1}{1 - \cfrac{P_{12}P_{21}}{P_{11}P_{22}}} \qquad (5\text{-}4\text{-}15)$$

For a three-variable system :

$$\lambda_1 = \cfrac{1}{1 + \cfrac{P_{12}\det \bar{P}_{12} + P_{13}\det \bar{P}_{13}}{P_{11}\det \bar{P}_{11}}} =$$

$$= \cfrac{1}{1 + \cfrac{P_{12}(P_{23}P_{31} - P_{21}P_{33}) + P_{13}(P_{21}P_{32} - P_{22}P_{31})}{P_{11}(P_{22}P_{33} - P_{23}P_{32})}} \qquad (5\text{-}4\text{-}16)$$

$$\lambda_2 = \cfrac{1}{1 + \cfrac{P_{21}\det \bar{P}_{21} + P_{23}\det \bar{P}_{23}}{P_{22}\det \bar{P}_{22}}} =$$

$$= \cfrac{1}{1 + \cfrac{P_{21}(P_{13}P_{32} - P_{12}P_{33}) + P_{23}(P_{12}P_{31} - P_{11}P_{32})}{P_{22}(P_{11}P_{33} - P_{13}P_{31})}} \qquad (5\text{-}4\text{-}17)$$

$$\lambda_3 = \cfrac{1}{1 + \cfrac{P_{31}\det \bar{P}_{31} + P_{32}\det \bar{P}_{32}}{P_{33}\det \bar{P}_{33}}} =$$

$$= \cfrac{1}{1 + \cfrac{P_{31}(P_{12}P_{23} - P_{13}P_{22}) + P_{32}(P_{13}P_{21} - P_{11}P_{23})}{P_{33}(P_{11}P_{22} - P_{12}P_{21})}} \qquad (5\text{-}4\text{-}18)$$

and :

$$R_{11} = \lambda_1 R_1$$

$$R_{22} = \lambda_2 R_2$$

$$R_{33} = \lambda_3 R_3$$

$$R_{12} = R_{22}\frac{P_{13}P_{32} - P_{12}P_{33}}{P_{11}P_{33} - P_{13}P_{31}}$$

$$R_{13} = R_{33}\frac{P_{12}P_{23} - P_{13}P_{22}}{P_{11}P_{22} - P_{12}P_{21}}$$

$$R_{21} = R_{11} \frac{P_{23}P_{31} - P_{21}P_{33}}{P_{22}P_{33} - P_{23}P_{32}}$$

$$R_{31} = R_{11} \frac{P_{32}P_{21} - P_{31}P_{22}}{P_{22}P_{33} - P_{23}P_{32}}$$

$$R_{23} = R_{33} \frac{P_{21}P_{13} - P_{23}P_{11}}{P_{11}P_{22} - P_{12}P_{21}} \qquad (5\text{-}4\text{-}19)$$

$$R_{32} = R_{22} \frac{P_{31}P_{12} - P_{32}P_{11}}{P_{11}P_{22} - P_{12}P_{21}}$$

When the orders of the plant transfer functions are high, this design method may be complicated because in such cases the expression forms of λ will be complicated.

In order to simplify the design procedure, we may let $\lambda_i = 1$, or:

$$\lambda_i = \left. \frac{1}{1 + \dfrac{\displaystyle\sum_{k=1}^{n} P_{ik} \det \bar{P}_{ik}}{P_{ii} \det \bar{P}_{ii}}} \right|_{S=0} \qquad (5\text{-}4\text{-}20)$$

For example, for the two-variable system:

$$\lambda = \frac{1}{1 - \dfrac{P_{12}(0)P_{21}(0)}{P_{11}(0)P_{22}(0)}} \qquad (5\text{-}4\text{-}21)$$

Thus, λ becomes a constant and the design is also simplified.

Then:

$$R_{12} = -\lambda(0) \frac{P_{12}(S)}{P_{11}(S)} R_1(S) \qquad (5\text{-}4\text{-}22)$$

$$R_{21} = -\lambda(0) \frac{P_{21}(S)}{P_{22}(S)} R_2(S) \qquad (5\text{-}4\text{-}23)$$

In general, the right term of (5-4-22) may be written as:

$$\frac{P_{12}(S)}{P_{11}(S)} R_1(S) = \frac{K_1}{S} \frac{\prod_m (1 + T_m S)}{\prod_n (1 + T_n S)} \qquad (5\text{-}4\text{-}24)$$

and it can be reduced to the following approximate form:

$$\frac{P_{12}(S)}{P_{11}(S)} R_1(S) = \frac{K_1}{S} \frac{1 +(\sum_m T_m)S}{1 +(\sum_n \tau_n)S} \qquad (5-4-25)$$

The adoption of this approximate expressions can simplify the system design further. For example, suppose:

$$P = \begin{bmatrix} P_{11} & P_{12} \\ P_{21} & P_{22} \end{bmatrix} = \begin{bmatrix} \dfrac{1}{(1 + 0.025S)^3} & \dfrac{1}{(1 + 0.025S)(1+ 0.1S)} \\ \dfrac{1}{(1 + 0.025S)^2} & \dfrac{-1}{(1+ 0.025S)(1 + 0.1S)^2} \end{bmatrix} \qquad (5-4-26)$$

so:

$$P_{11}(S) = \frac{1}{(1 + 0.025S)^3} = \frac{1}{1 + 0.075S + - - - - -} =$$

$$= \frac{1}{1 + 0.075S} \qquad (5-4-27)$$

$$P_{22}(S) = \frac{1}{(1+ 0.025S)(1+ 0.1S)^2} \approx \frac{1}{1 + 0.225S+ - - -} =$$

$$= \frac{1}{1 + 0.225S} \qquad (5-4-28)$$

Now, we choose:

$$R_1 = \frac{20(1 + 0.075S)}{S} \qquad (5-4-29)$$

$$R_2 = \frac{9(1 + 0.025S)}{S} \qquad (5-4-30)$$

then:

$$\lambda(0) = \frac{1}{1 - \dfrac{P_{12}(0)P_{21}(0)}{P_{11}(0)P_{22}(0)}} = \frac{1}{2} \qquad (5-4-31)$$

and we get:

$$R_{12}(S) = -\frac{1}{2} \frac{(1 + 0.025S)^2}{1 + 0.1S} \frac{9(1 + 0.225S)}{S} \approx -\frac{4.5}{S} \frac{1+0.275S}{S +0.1S} \qquad (5-4-32)$$

Similarly, we can get:

$$R_{21}(S) = \frac{10}{S} \frac{1 + 0.275S}{1 + 0.025S} \qquad (5-4-33)$$

If we want to use the PID regulators to realize R_{12} and R_{21}, then from:

$$\frac{1}{1 + TS} = 1 - TS + T^2S^2 - \cdots \cdots \approx 1 - TS \qquad (5-4-34)$$

we get:

$$R_{12}(S) = -\frac{4.5}{S}(1 + 0.275S)(1 - 0.1S) \approx - \frac{4.5}{S} (1 + 0.175S) \qquad (5-4-35)$$

and:

$$R_{21}(S) = \frac{10}{S}(1 + 0.275S)(1 - 0.1S) = \frac{10}{S}(1 + 0.25S) \qquad (5-4-36)$$

The final characters of the main regulators are:

$$R_{11}(S) = \lambda (0)R_1(S) = 10\frac{1 + 0.075S}{S} \qquad (5-4-37)$$

$$R_{22}(S) = \lambda(0)R_2(S) = 4.5\frac{1 + 0.225S}{S} \qquad (5-4-38)$$

Thus, all regulators and decoupling elements can be realized by PID regulators.

§ 5-5 The Ideal Decoupling Design [55]

We have pointed out before that for the systems with P-canonical plants and P-canonical decoupling element structures located between the plants and the regulators, in general the single variable systems obtained after decoupling design are not equal to those obtained by simply breaking off the coupling channels and the decoupling networks.

Then, is there any possibility that a decoupled system is just equal to that obtained by simply breaking off all coupling and de-coupling channels?

Yes, there is such a possibility.

Now, let us discuss a two-variable system which is shown in Fig 5-5-1.

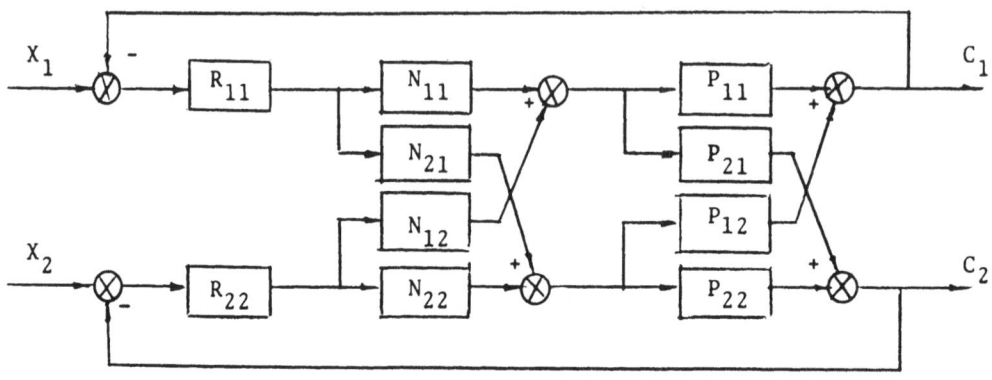

Fig 5-5-1

The system equation is:

$$C = (I + PNR)^{-1}PNRX \qquad (5-5-1)$$

If we demand that the decoupled system be just the original system without any coupling channels, then it means:

$$\frac{C_1}{X_1} = \frac{P_{11}R_{11}}{1 + P_{11}R_{11}} \qquad (5-5-2)$$

$$\frac{C_2}{X_2} = \frac{P_{22}R_{22}}{1 + P_{22}R_{22}} \qquad (5-5-3)$$

This is also:

$$(I + PNR)^{-1}PNRX = \begin{bmatrix} \dfrac{P_{11}R_{11}}{1 + P_{11}R_{11}} & 0 \\ \\ 0 & \dfrac{P_{22}R_{22}}{1 + P_{22}R_{22}} \end{bmatrix} =$$

$$= \begin{bmatrix} \dfrac{1}{1 + P_{11}R_{11}} & 0 \\ \\ 0 & \dfrac{1}{1 + P_{22}R_{22}} \end{bmatrix} \begin{bmatrix} P_{11} & 0 \\ 0 & P_{22} \end{bmatrix} \begin{bmatrix} R_{11} & 0 \\ 0 & R_{22} \end{bmatrix}$$

$$(5-5-4)$$

By the design demands, it is necessary:

$$PN = \begin{bmatrix} P_{11} & 0 \\ 0 & P_{22} \end{bmatrix} = (\text{Diag } P) \qquad (5\text{-}5\text{-}5)$$

thus, we get:

$$N = (P)^{-1}(\text{Diag } P) \qquad (5\text{-}5\text{-}6)$$

That means if we demand that the decoupled system just be the original system without any coupling channels, then the decoupling element structure matrix should be given by (5-5-6).

Such a design method is called as " Ideal Decoupling Design".

There are some differences between this design method and those mentioned before:

(1) When the design is only according to the decoupling demands, the decoupling elements are given by (4-8-9), namely:

$$\left. \begin{array}{l} R_{12} = - \dfrac{P_{12}}{P_{11}} R_{22} \\[3mm] R_{21} = - \dfrac{P_{21}}{P_{22}} R_{11} \end{array} \right\} \qquad (5\text{-}5\text{-}7)$$

It is clear that both R_{12} and R_{21} are related to the main regulators, but in the ideal decoupling design, R_{12} and R_{21} are only related to the plant and do not related to the main regulators,

(2) By the methods mentioned in § 5-3 and § 5-4, the plants of the single variable systems obtained after decoupling design are no longer P_{11} and P_{22}, but in the ideal decoupling design, in the decoupled single variable systems, the plants are still P_{11} and P_{22},

(3) When the Boksenbom-Hood method is used, the final R_{11} and R_{22} are not the original R_1 and R_2, but in the ideal decoupling design, they are the same.

Thus, the ideal decoupling design is different from those methods introduced before.

For the two-variable system, from (5-5-6) we have:

$$
\begin{pmatrix} N_{11} & N_{12} \\ N_{12} & N_{22} \end{pmatrix}
\begin{pmatrix}
\dfrac{P_{11}P_{22}}{P_{11}P_{22}-P_{12}P_{21}} & \dfrac{-P_{22}P_{12}}{P_{11}P_{22}-P_{12}P_{21}} \\[3mm]
\dfrac{-P_{11}P_{21}}{P_{11}P_{22}-P_{12}P_{21}} & \dfrac{P_{11}P_{22}}{P_{11}P_{22}-P_{12}P_{21}}
\end{pmatrix} =
$$

$$
= \dfrac{P_{11}P_{22}}{P_{11}P_{22}-P_{12}P_{21}}
\begin{pmatrix}
1 & -\dfrac{P_{12}}{P_{11}} \\[3mm]
-\dfrac{P_{21}}{P_{22}} & 1
\end{pmatrix} \qquad (5\text{-}5\text{-}8)
$$

Obviously, there are two important properties with this system:

(1) Four decoupling elements are needed, namely $N_{11}, N_{12}, N_{21}, N_{22}$,

(2) $N_{11} = N_{22}$.

But for the non-ideal decoupling systems, for example Fig 4-7-1, only two decoupling elements are needed, namely:

$$
\left.
\begin{aligned}
N_{11} &= N_{22} = 1 \\
N_{12} &= -\dfrac{P_{12}}{P_{11}} \\
N_{21} &= -\dfrac{P_{21}}{P_{22}}
\end{aligned}
\right\} \qquad (5\text{-}5\text{-}9)
$$

The practical scheme of an ideally decoupled system is :

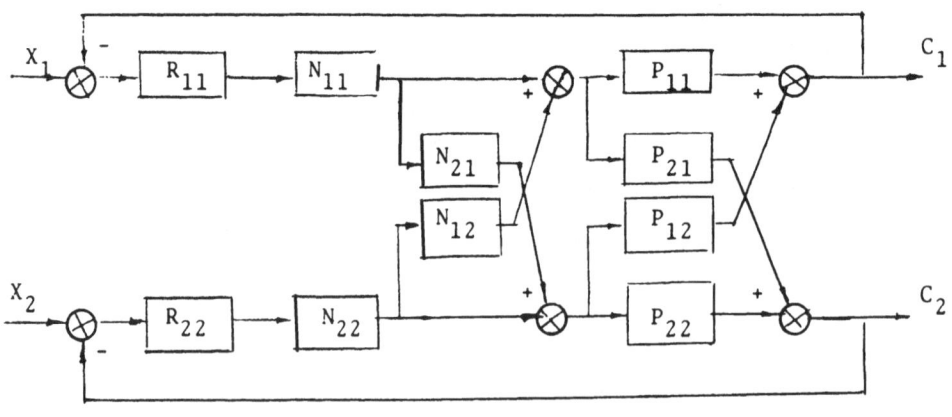

Fig 5-5-2

From this figure we can know:

(1) Four decoupling elements are needed,

(2) The regulators R_{11} and R_{22} should provide necessary signals with energy not only for their own main channels, but also for the decoupling channels,

(3) Because of the additional phase lages of N_{11} and N_{22}, there will be more burden in phase for R_{11} and R_{22}.

Due to the above reasons the ideal decoupling design is not adopted in general. In practice,this kind of decoupled systems is easily to be unstable.

§ 5-6 Non-cancellation Decoupling Design [41]

In the feedforward decoupling system design, we always meet two difficult problems. The first is: The decoupling elements obtained are always physically irrealizable. The second is: Because of the application of the zero-pole cancellation between the plant and the decoupling elements the unstable poles of the plant will result in the occurrence of zeros in the right S plane for the decoupling elements, for example the well-known results:

$$
\left.
\begin{aligned}
N_{12} &= - \frac{P_{12}}{P_{11}} \\[2ex]
N_{21} &= - \frac{P_{21}}{P_{22}}
\end{aligned}
\right\}
\qquad (5\text{-}6\text{-}1)
$$

are very obvious zero-pole cancellation.

At first, these results are difficult to be realized. In addition, in general the design is carried out for once and suitable decoupling elements are obtaind, but, however, the parameters of the plant may vary and the decoupling elements remain unchanged. So, when the full zero-pole cancellation is adopted for an unstable plant, the obtained decoupled system will be unstable. So, this is not a satisfactory design.

The approach that removes the interactions of the coupled system and designs some decoupling elements and regulators for decoupling and the decoupled systems by using the compensators obtained from the plant inverse matrix is straightforward but the following problems arise:

(1) The existence of the plant inverse matrix,

(2) The reliability of the obtained high-degree controllers,

(3) The stability of the designed system when unstable zero-pole cancellation has been used,

(4) The design procedures for high-degree coupled systems is complex.

Thus, when the feedforward decoupling projects are used, we had better find another design approach in order to:

(1) Give the guarantee that the decoupling elements (compensation elements) are certainly able to be realized,

(2) Avoid the adoption of the zero-pole cancellation principle and the unstable poles of the plant are still in the plant transfer functions.

Now, we discuss such an approach.

Suppose the plant being:

$$P = \frac{1}{d_0(S)} B(S) \qquad\qquad (5-6-2)$$

where: P is a nxn matrix,

   $d_0(S)$ is the least common denominator polynomial of P with degree m,

   B(S) is also a nxn matrix.

In order to decouple this system, we use the feedforward decoupling project and the decoupled open loop transfer matrix should be diagonal.

A simple way to reach this aim is to use the following matrix:

$$N_1(S) = adj \ B(S) \qquad\qquad (5-6-3)$$

and let:

$$Q_1(S) = P(S)N_1(S) = \frac{1}{d_0(S)} B(S)B^{-1}(S)det \ B(S) =$$

$$= \frac{1}{d_0(S)} \cdot I \cdot det \ B(S) = diag \ (\frac{m(S)}{d_0(S)}) \qquad (5-6-4)$$

where :

$$m(S) = det \ B(S) \qquad\qquad (5-6-5)$$

Notice that this means the feedforward decoupling project is used.
In the above procedure, we do not use the zero-pole cancellation
principle, but $N_1(S)$ may be physically irrealizable.

In order to let the designed compensation elements be physically
realizable, we may introduce the second compensation structure $N_2(S)$
and because $Q_1(S)$ has been a diagonal matrix, so $N_2(S)$ also should
be diagonal. The application of $N_2(S)$ gives the demanded open loop
transfer matrix as follows:

$$W_d(S) = Q_1(S)N_2(S) = diag \ (\frac{m(S)K_i n_i(S)}{d_0(S)d_i(S)}) \qquad . \qquad (5-6-6)$$

where:

$$N_2(S) = diag \ (\frac{K_i n_i(S)}{d_i(S)}) \qquad\qquad (5-6-7)$$

Here, K_i, $n_i(S)$ and $d_i(S)$ are under determination. The determination of these three terms can give the guarantee not only that
the final compensation elements are realizable, but also that the
decoupled system will meet   the control demands.

In fact, only one decoupling stucture is used and it is divided
into two parts, namely:

$$N(S) = N_1(S)N_2(S) \qquad\qquad (5-6-8)$$

Notice that both $N_1(S)$ and $N_2(S)$ are introduced without using
the cancellation principle.

Thus:

$$N(S) = N_1(S)N_2(S) = adj \; B(S) \cdot diag(\frac{K_i n_i(S)}{d_i(S)}) \qquad (5-6-9)$$

Now, we prove that the zeros of the plant are still remained in the transfer function matrix of the decoupled system. Let:

$$P(S) = \frac{1}{d_0(S)} \; B(S) = N_r(S)D_r^{-1}(S) \qquad (5-6-10)$$

where, both $N_r(S)$ and $D_r(S)$ are matrix polynomials.

The characteristic poles of $P(S)$ are the zeros of $det \; D_r(S) = 0$ and the zeros of $P(S)$ are the zeros of $det \; N_r(S) = 0$.

Equation (5-6-10) may be written as:

$$P(S) = \frac{B(S)}{d_0(S)} = \frac{N_r(S)adj \; D_r(S)}{\triangle(S)} \qquad (5-6-11)$$

where:

$$\triangle(S) = det \; D_r(S) \qquad (5-6-12)$$

Because the determinant of an inverse matrix is equal to the reciprocal of the determinant of the original matrix, i.e:

$$det \; D_r^{-1}(S) = \frac{1}{\triangle} \qquad (5-6-13)$$

and :

$$D_r^{-1}(S) = \frac{adj \; D_r(S)}{\triangle} \qquad (5-6-14)$$

so we get:

$$det \; D_r^{-1}(S) = det \; (\frac{adj \; D_r(S)}{\triangle}) = \frac{1}{\triangle} \qquad (5-6-15)$$

namely:

$$\frac{det(\; adj \; D_r(S) \;)}{\triangle^n} = \frac{1}{\triangle} \qquad (5-6-16)$$

Therefore:

$$det(\; adj \; D_r(S) \;) = \triangle^{n-1} \qquad (5-6-17)$$

Then, take the determinant for the two sides of (5-6-11) and notice the result of (5-6-17) :

$$Det(\frac{B(S)}{d_0(S)}) = \frac{m(S)}{d_0^n(S)} = \frac{det(N_r(S))det(adj \; D_r(S))}{\triangle^n(S)}$$

$$= \frac{\Delta^{n-1}(S)\det N_r(S)}{\Delta^n(S)} = \frac{\det N_r(S)}{\Delta(S)} \qquad (5\text{-}6\text{-}18)$$

From this equation, we get:

$$\frac{m(S)}{d_0(S)} = \frac{d_0^{n-1}(S)}{\Delta(S)} \det N_r(S) \qquad (5\text{-}6\text{-}19)$$

Substituting (5-6-19) into (5-6-6) yields:

$$W_d(S) = \text{diag}\left(\frac{K_i n_i(S) d_0^{n-1}(S) \det N_r(S)}{d_i(S)\Delta(S)} \right) \qquad (5\text{-}6\text{-}20)$$

For the unit feedback, the closed-loop transfer matrix is:

$$G(S) = \text{diag}\left(\frac{K_i n_i(S) d_0^{n-1}(S) \det N_r(S)}{\Delta(S) d_i(S) + K_i n_i(S) d_0^{n-1}(S) \det N_r(S)} \right) \qquad (5\text{-}6\text{-}21)$$

When $\Delta(S)$ and $\det N_r(S)$ have no common factors, all the zeros of the plant remain in the closed-loop transfer functions.

By this design method, the final compensation elements are realizable and the zero-pole cancellation is avoided. In addition, by suitable choice of K_i, $n_i(S)$ and $d_i(S)$ the decoupling design can meet the control demands at the same time.

Now, we discuss a two-variable system.

Suppose the plant being:

$$P(S) = \frac{1}{d_0(S)} \qquad B(S) = \frac{1}{d_0(S)} \begin{pmatrix} B_{11} & B_{12} \\ B_{21} & B_{22} \end{pmatrix}$$

with:

$$d_0(S) = S^4 + 113.2S^3 + 1357.3S^2 + 3503.0S + 2526.9$$

$$B_{11}(S) = 14.9S^2 + 1506.5S + 2543.2$$

$$B_{12}(S) = 95150S^2 + 1132094.7S + 1805947$$

$$B_{21}(S) = 85.2S^2 + 8642.9S + 12268.8$$

$$B_{22}(S) = 124000S^2 + 1492588S + 2525880$$

The control demands are:

(1) Two identical diagonal subsystems decoupled in the closed-loop system,

(2) Unity final values of unit-step responses,

(3) Less than 10-percent maximum overshoot,

(4) The time required for the unit-step response to get the first peak of the overshoot t_p is 0.01 s.

We have:

$$N_1(S) = \text{adj } B(S) = \begin{pmatrix} B_{22} & -B_{12} \\ -B_{21} & B_{11} \end{pmatrix}$$

In this example, we let $n_i(S) = 1$, then:

$$N_2(S) = \begin{pmatrix} \dfrac{K_1}{d_1(S)} & 0 \\ 0 & \dfrac{K_2}{d_2(S)} \end{pmatrix}$$

So the compensation element matrix is:

$$N(S) = N_1(S)N_2(S) = \begin{pmatrix} B_{22} & -B_{12} \\ -B_{21} & B_{22} \end{pmatrix} \begin{pmatrix} \dfrac{K_1}{d_1(S)} & 0 \\ 0 & \dfrac{K_2}{d_2(S)} \end{pmatrix}$$

and the desired open loop transfer matrix is:

$$W_d(S) = \begin{pmatrix} \dfrac{K_1 m(S)}{d_0(S)d_1(S)} & 0 \\ 0 & \dfrac{K_2 m(S)}{d_0(S)d_2(S)} \end{pmatrix}$$

where:

$$m(S) = \det B(S) = -6259180d_0(S)$$

and K_1, K_2, $d_1(S)$ and $d_2(S)$ are under determination.

Because $m(S)$ is negative, so it is difficult to carry out the control if the two diagonal channels of $W_d(S)$ are negative. Therefore, it must be more rational to let:

$$W_{dm} = \begin{pmatrix} \dfrac{-K_1 m(S)}{d_0(S)d_1(S)} & 0 \\ 0 & \dfrac{-K_2 m(S)}{d_0(S)d_2(S)} \end{pmatrix}$$

Then, all the transfer functions of the decoupled open loops will be positive.

In order to reach this result, we post-multiply the matrix B(S) with another matrix N_0 as:

$$B_m(S) = B(S)N_0(S) = \begin{pmatrix} B_{11} & B_{12} \\ B_{21} & B_{22} \end{pmatrix}\begin{pmatrix} 0 & 1 \\ 1 & 0 \end{pmatrix} = \begin{pmatrix} B_{12} & B_{11} \\ B_{22} & B_{21} \end{pmatrix}$$

The result is just to interchange the two columns of B(S).

Then, take the adjoint matrix of B_m and post-multiply it with $N_2(S)$, we get:

$$N_s(S) = (adj B_m)N_2 = \begin{pmatrix} B_{21} & -B_{11} \\ -B_{22} & B_{12} \end{pmatrix}\begin{pmatrix} \dfrac{K_1}{d_1(S)} & 0 \\ 0 & \dfrac{K_2}{d_2(S)} \end{pmatrix}$$

Pre-multiplying the above result with N_0 yields the final compensation element matrix:

$$N_m(S) = N_0(adj B_m)N_2 = \begin{pmatrix} -B_{22} & B_{12} \\ B_{21} & -B_{11} \end{pmatrix}\begin{pmatrix} \dfrac{K_1}{d_1(S)} & 0 \\ 0 & \dfrac{K_2}{d_2(S)} \end{pmatrix}$$

The desired decoupled open loop transfer matrix is:

$$W_{dm} = \begin{pmatrix} \dfrac{-K_1 m(S)}{d_0(S)d_1(S)} & 0 \\ 0 & \dfrac{-K_2 m(S)}{d_0(S)d_2(S)} \end{pmatrix} =$$

$$= \begin{pmatrix} \dfrac{6259180K_1}{d_1(S)} & 0 \\ 0 & \dfrac{6259180K_2}{d_2(S)} \end{pmatrix}$$

In order to satisfy the first control demand, it is enough that:

$$K_1 = K_2 = K$$

$$d_1(S) = d_2(S) = d(S)$$

That means that we will design the single variable system with the plant:

$$W_d(S) = \frac{6259180K}{d(S)}$$

In order to satisfy the second control demand , an integral term should be included in the open loop transfer functions, so we can let:

$$W_d(S) = \frac{6259180K}{S(S+ C)}$$

and the characteristic equation for the closed-loop is :

$$\Delta_d(S) = S^2 + CS + 6259180K = s^2 + 2\zeta w_n S + w_n^2 = 0$$

Therefore:

$$w_n^2 = 6259180K$$

$$C = 2\zeta w_n$$

But:

$$w_n = \frac{\pi}{t_p} = \frac{3.14}{0.01} = 300 \text{ rad/ S}$$

and :

$$M_p = \exp(-\zeta\pi)$$

so:

$$\zeta = -\frac{\ln M_p}{\pi} = -\frac{\ln 0.1}{3.14} = 0.75$$

Thus:

$$C = 2\zeta w_n = 450$$

$$K = 0.01438$$

$$\Delta_d(S) = S^2 + 450S + 90000$$

$$S_{1,2} = -\zeta w_n \pm jw_n\sqrt{1 - \zeta^2} = -225 \pm j198.43$$

The final compensation element matrix is:

$$N_m(S) = \frac{1}{S(S+450)} = \begin{pmatrix} -1783S^2 - 21461.7S - 36319 & 1368S^2 + 16278.3S + 25967.5 \\ 1.23S^2 + 124.3S + 176.4 & -0.214S^2 - 21.7S - 36.6 \end{pmatrix}$$

The decoupled system is:

$$G(S) = \begin{pmatrix} \dfrac{90000}{S^2 + 450S + 90000} \\ \\ \dfrac{90000}{S^2 + 450S + 90000} \end{pmatrix}$$

§ 5-7 The Decoupling Design for Systems with Delay and the Triangle

Matrix Half Decoupling Design

Up to now, all transfer functions under consideration do not contain dead delay which often occurs in process control systems.

Now, we discuss the decoupling design for plants with delay. At first, we must know that all the above decoupling design principles are not related to the practical characters of the plants, i.e. no matter what character the plant has, the above decoupling methods can be used for it.

But, however, for the plants with different properties, the decoupling elements obtained by using the same decoupling design method will have different forms and the problem of realization of these decoupling elements is closely related to the characters of the plants.

Let us discuss a two-variable system of P-canonical plant with dead delay:

$$P(S) = \begin{pmatrix} P_{11} & P_{12} \\ P_{21} & P_{22} \end{pmatrix} = \begin{pmatrix} W_{11}e^{-\tau_1 S} & W_{12}e^{-\tau_2 S} \\ W_{21}e^{-\tau_3 S} & W_{22}e^{-\tau_4 S} \end{pmatrix} \qquad (5-7-1)$$

Because the plant is always realizable, so P_{11}, P_{12}, P_{21} and P_{22} all are with negative delay.

When the P-canonical decoupling element structure is adopted and the decoupling elements are set between the plant and regulators, the characters of the decoupling elements are:

$$N_{12} = - \frac{P_{12}}{P_{11}} = - \frac{W_{12}}{W_{11}} e^{-(\tau_2 - \tau_1)s} \qquad (5-7-2)$$

$$N_{21} = - \frac{P_{21}}{P_{22}} = - \frac{W_{21}}{W_{22}} e^{-(\tau_3 - \tau_4)s} \qquad (5-7-3)$$

We do not consider W_{11}, W_{12}, W_{21} and W_{22} now and from the above two expressions we can soon know when:

$$\tau_1 > \tau_2 \qquad (5-7-4)$$

then it is impossible to realize N_{12} and when:

$$\tau_4 > \tau_3 \qquad (5-7-5)$$

then it is impossible to realize N_{21}.

This is a special problem when the plant is with delay.

Does it mean that in such cases it is impossible to perform the decoupling design?

Let us return to §4-4. We said in §4-4 that for such a system, when the above decoupling structure is adopted, there are four projects capable to perform the decoupling demands, i.e.

(1) $N_{11} = 1$, $N_{12} = -\dfrac{P_{12}}{P_{11}}$, $N_{22} = 1$, $N_{21} = -\dfrac{P_{21}}{P_{22}}$

(2) $N_{11} = 1$, $N_{12} = 1$, $N_{21} = -\dfrac{P_{21}}{P_{22}}$, $N_{22} = -\dfrac{P_{11}}{P_{12}}$

(3) $N_{11} = -\dfrac{P_{22}}{P_{21}}$, $N_{12} = -\dfrac{P_{12}}{P_{11}}$, $N_{21} = 1$, $N_{22} = 1$

(4) $N_{11} = -\dfrac{P_{22}}{P_{21}}$, $N_{12} = 1$, $N_{21} = 1$, $N_{22} = -\dfrac{P_{11}}{P_{21}}$

When $\dfrac{P_{12}}{P_{11}}$ and $\dfrac{P_{21}}{P_{22}}$ are physically irrealizable , then their re-

ciprocals $\dfrac{P_{11}}{P_{12}}$ and $\dfrac{P_{22}}{P_{21}}$ are certainly realizable.

Thus, in the above example, when:

$$\left. \begin{array}{l} \tau_1 > \tau_2 \\ \tau_4 > \tau_3 \end{array} \right\} \qquad (5\text{-}7\text{-}6)$$

then the fourth project should be adopted. When:

$$\left. \begin{array}{l} \tau_2 > \tau_1 \\ \tau_3 > \tau_4 \end{array} \right\} \qquad (5\text{-}7\text{-}7)$$

then the first project should be adopted. When:

$$\left. \begin{array}{l} \tau_2 > \tau_1 \\ \tau_4 > \tau_3 \end{array} \right\} \qquad (5\text{-}7\text{-}8)$$

then the third project should be adopted.

This is just the advantage of the solution uncertainty of the decoupling system design . It permits us to have many possibilities to choose the suitable project.

We should point out here that for the systems with dead delay, it is not suitable to transfer a plant of P-canonical into one of V-canonical. Because when a P-canonical plant is transferred into a V-canonical plant, then we have:

$$\left. \begin{array}{l} V_{11} = P_{11} \\[2mm] V_{12} = \dfrac{P_{12}}{P_{11}P_{22}} \\[4mm] V_{21} = \dfrac{P_{21}}{P_{11}P_{22}} \\[4mm] V_{22} = P_{22} \end{array} \right\} \qquad (5\text{-}7\text{-}9)$$

When:
$$\left. \begin{array}{l} \tau_1 + \tau_4 > \tau_3 \\ \tau_1 + \tau_4 > \tau_2 \end{array} \right\} \qquad (5\text{-}7\text{-}10)$$

both V_{12} and V_{21} are irrealizable. If the feedback decoupling project is adopted, then the decoupling elements are:

$$\left. \begin{array}{l} N_{12} = - V_{12} \\ N_{21} = - V_{21} \end{array} \right\} \qquad (5-7-11)$$

and they are irrealizable either. The Mesarović idea says that the application of V-canonical forms and the feedback decoupling projects can result in good decoupling effects, but if such a system is irrealizable, certainly the Mesarović idea becomes meaningless. So when we apply the Mesarović idea to the systems with delay, we must be very cautious.

For the systems with **dead** delay, not only the realization problem should be considered seriously, but also the rationality of the solution, even it has been realized, should be discussed carefully .

For instance, we discuss a two-variable system with partial coupling and dead delay:

$$\left. \begin{array}{l} P_{11} = K_{11}e^{-\tau_{11}S} \\ P_{12} = 0 \\ P_{21} = K_{21}e^{-\tau_{21}S} \\ P_{22} = K_{22}e^{-\tau_{22}S} \end{array} \right\} \qquad (5-7-12)$$

From (4-4-9) we know if the P-canonical decoupling element structure is adopted, then the decoupling condition is:

$$N_{11}P_{21} + N_{21}P_{22} = 0 \qquad (5-7-13)$$

namely:

$$\frac{N_{11}}{N_{21}} = - \frac{P_{22}}{P_{21}} = - \frac{K_{22}}{K_{21}} e^{-(\tau_{22}-\tau_{21})S} \qquad (5-7-14)$$

Then we can choose:

$$N_{11} = e^{-(\tau_{22}-\tau_{21})S} \qquad (5-7-15)$$

$$N_{21} = - \frac{K_{21}}{K_{22}} \qquad (5-7-16)$$

and we get the following conclusions:

(1) When $\tau_{21} > \tau_{22}$, then (5-7-15) is irrealizable.

In such a case, we should choose another form, for example:

$$
\left.
\begin{aligned}
N_{11} &= e^{-s\tau_{22}} \\
N_{21} &= -\frac{K_{21}}{K_{22}} e^{-s\tau_{21}}
\end{aligned}
\right\}
\tag{5-7-17}
$$

(2) When $\tau_{22} > \tau_{21}$, (5-7-15) may be realized, but when τ_{22} is much larger than τ_{21}, such a control project is irrational in practice.

This is because the decoupling element N_{11} introduces an explicit additional delay ($\tau_{22} - \tau_{21}$) into the first channel and it will retard the response strikingly. Sometimes, the system may be unstable.

In fact, the system character now is:

$$
\frac{C_1}{X_1} = \frac{R_{11}N_{11}P_{11}}{1 + R_{11}N_{11}P_{11}} = \frac{K_{11}R_{11}e^{-(\tau_{22} - \tau_{21} + \tau_{11})s}}{1 + K_{11}R_{11}e^{-(\tau_{22} - \tau_{21} + \tau_{11})s}}
\tag{5-7-18}
$$

Obviously, the delay of the open loop character has increased and when the delay becomes two large, the system will be unstable.

So, for the systems with dead delay when we carry out the decoupling design for them, we must make careful analysis of different results.

Because for the systems with dead delay, there are many practical problems being considered in their decoupling design, so in some cases, we do not adopt the perfect decoupling project and the half decoupling projects are used.

The so-called half decoupling project means for the decoupled system, its open loop transfer matrix is not a diagonal matrix , but a triangle matrix with half elements (upper diagonal or lower diagonal) being zero. Then, for the system variables, one of them   gets the perfect decoupling control and the others get unperfect decoupling control in different degree. When we let the most important controlled variable be under perfect control, then this half decoupling project can also satisfy the main control demands.

For example, for a two-variable system :

$$\begin{pmatrix} C_1 \\ C_2 \end{pmatrix} = \begin{bmatrix} P_{11} & P_{12} \\ P_{21} & P_{22} \end{bmatrix} \begin{pmatrix} m_1 \\ m_2 \end{pmatrix} \tag{5-7-19}$$

where, P_{11}, P_{12}, P_{21} and P_{22} are with dead delay.

By using the triangle matrix decoupling design, it means that:

$$N = \begin{pmatrix} 1 & 0 \\ N_{21} & 1 \end{pmatrix} \tag{5-7-20}$$

then:

$$Q = PN = \begin{bmatrix} Q_{11} & Q_{12} \\ Q_{21} & Q_{22} \end{bmatrix} = \begin{bmatrix} P_{11} & P_{12} \\ P_{21} & P_{22} \end{bmatrix} \begin{bmatrix} 1 & 0 \\ N_{21} & 1 \end{bmatrix} =$$

$$= \begin{bmatrix} P_{11} + P_{12}N_{21} & P_{12} \\ P_{21} + P_{22}N_{21} & P_{22} \end{bmatrix} \tag{5-7-21}$$

Let:

$$P_{21} + P_{22}N_{21} = 0 \tag{5-7-22}$$

then we get an upper triangle matrix.

When:

$$N = \begin{bmatrix} 1 & N_{12} \\ 0 & 1 \end{bmatrix} \tag{5-7-23}$$

then:

$$Q = \begin{bmatrix} Q_{11} & Q_{12} \\ Q_{21} & Q_{22} \end{bmatrix} = \begin{bmatrix} P_{11} & P_{12} \\ P_{21} & P_{22} \end{bmatrix} \begin{bmatrix} 1 & N_{12} \\ 0 & 1 \end{bmatrix} = \begin{bmatrix} P_{11} & P_{11}N_{12} + P_{12} \\ P_{21} & P_{21}N_{12} + P_{22} \end{bmatrix}$$

$$\tag{5-7-24}$$

Let:

$$P_{11}N_{12} + P_{12} = 0 \tag{5-7-25}$$

then we get a lower triangle matrix.

From (5-7-22) and (5-7-25) we have:

$$\left. \begin{array}{l} N_{21} = - \dfrac{P_{21}}{P_{22}} \\[2em] N_{12} = - \dfrac{P_{12}}{P_{11}} \end{array} \right\} \qquad (5\text{-}7\text{-}26)$$

The decoupling conditions are the same as those of the perfect decoupling system.

For example, if:

$$P = \begin{bmatrix} \dfrac{-0.427e^{-1.05S}}{1 + 15S} & \dfrac{0.543e^{-0.5S}}{1 + 11.5S} \\[2em] \dfrac{-0.306e^{-3.15S}}{1 + 21.5S} & \dfrac{0.07e^{-1.05S}}{1 + 11S} \end{bmatrix} \qquad (5\text{-}7\text{-}27)$$

Obviously, N_{12} is irrealizable. So, we have to use the upper triangle matrix to carry out the half decoupling design. Then:

$$N_{21} = -\dfrac{P_{21}}{P_{22}} = 4.43 \ \dfrac{(1 + 11S)e^{-2.10S}}{1 + 21.5S} \qquad (5\text{-}7\text{-}28)$$

Then, by using the table of Pade approximation in § 2-6, $e^{-2.10S}$ can be approximated by:

$$N_{21} = 4.43 \ \dfrac{(1 + 11S)(1 - 1.05S)}{(1 + 21.5S)(1+1.05S)} \qquad (5\text{-}7\text{-}29)$$

By this design, the control of C_2 is perfect decoupling.

We will discuss the practical application of half decoupling design in Chapter 8 about the distillation column control.

§ 5-8 The Multivariable Smith Predictor and Its Decoupling Design[33]

We discussed the Smith predictor in §2-9 and we have known that for single variable plants with dead delay, the application of Smith predictor can effectively eliminate the analysis difficulty caused by the dead delay.

Now, if the multivariable plant under consideration is also with dead delay, can we also use the principle of Smith predictor to eliminate the difficulty in analysis caused by the dead delay?

Yes , it is possible, but, however, its structure will be more complicated than that of the single variable Smith predictor.

Fig 5-8-1 shows a multivariable process control system.

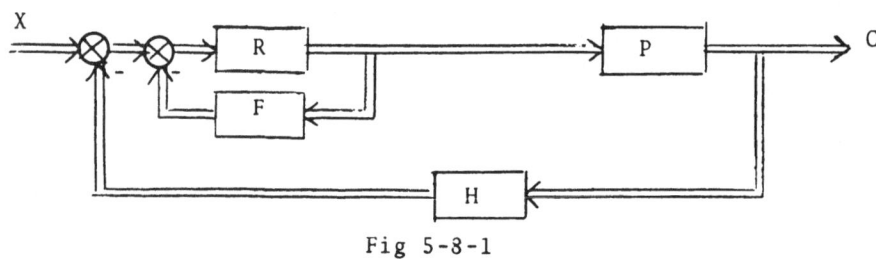

Fig 5-8-1

Here, matrices R, P and H form a conventional control system but the elements of P are with dead delay.

By the principle of Smith predictor, we introduce a compensator F and let:

$$F = H^o P^o - HP \qquad (5-8-1)$$

where, H^o and P^o are obtained from H and P by letting all dead delay terms being zero, respectively.

We calculate the inner loop at first:

$$R^o = (I + RF)^{-1}R \qquad (5-8-2)$$

so for the outer loop, we have:

$$C = (I + PR^o H)^{-1}PR^o X \qquad (5-8-3)$$

The aim of the application of the Smith predictor is to elimi-nate the influence of plant dead delay on the system dynamics and, consequently, higher gains may be adopted for the regulators.

Substituting (5-8-1) and (5-8-2) into (5-8-3) yields:

$$C = (I + PT^{-1}RH)^{-1}PT^{-1}RX \tag{5-8-4}$$

where:

$$T = I + R(H^oP^o - HP) \tag{5-8-5}$$

If P is non-singular, then the following relation is held:

$$(I + PT^{-1}RH)^{-1} = P(T + RHP)^{-1}TP^{-1} \tag{5-8-6}$$

But from (5-8-5) we have:

$$T + RHP = I + RH^oP^o \tag{5-8-7}$$

then (5-8-4) becomes:

$$C = P(I + RH^oP^o)^{-1}RX \tag{5-8-8}$$

Now, we prove that the characteristic equation of this system is:

$$det (I + RH^oP^o) = 0 \tag{5-8-9}$$

At first, we discuss the system without dead delay, i.e. there is no dead delay in P and:

$$C = (I + PRH)^{-1}PRX \tag{5-8-10}$$

Let:

$$A = (I + PRH)^{-1}PR \tag{5-8-11}$$

then if the system is stable , all roots of det (I + PRH) = 0 are in the left S plane and:

$$det (I + PRH) = det (PRA^{-1}) = \frac{det\ A^{-1}}{det\ (PR)^{-1}} \tag{5-8-12}$$

So, det (I + PRH) = 0 is corresponding to:

$$\frac{det\ A^{-1}}{det\ (PR)^{-1}} = 0 \tag{5-8-13}$$

If there is no cancellation of unstable poles and right S plane zeros between P and R, then the system stability is determined by:

$$det\ A^{-1} = 0 \tag{5-8-14}$$

For a system with dead delay, we have:

$$A = P(I + RH^oP^o)^{-1}R \tag{5-8-15}$$

Thus det A^{-1} = 0 means:

$$(\det R^{-1})(\det I+RH^{o}P^{o})(\det P^{-1}) = 0 \qquad (5\text{-}8\text{-}16)$$

namely:

$$\det (I + RH^{o}P^{o}) = 0 \qquad (5\text{-}8\text{-}17)$$

Because all R, H^{o} and P^{o} have no dead delay, so there is no dead delay in the above equation, i.e. the dead delay of the plant no longer occurs in the characteristic equation.

This is the application of the Smith predictor to the multivariable control systems.

For example, a two-variable plant with dead delay is as follows:

$$P = \begin{pmatrix} P_{11}e^{-\tau_{11}s} & P_{12}e^{-\tau_{12}s} \\ P_{21}e^{-\tau_{21}s} & P_{22}e^{-\tau_{22}s} \end{pmatrix} \qquad (5\text{-}8\text{-}18)$$

Therefore:

$$\left. \begin{array}{l} P^{o} = \begin{pmatrix} P_{11} & P_{12} \\ P_{21} & P_{22} \end{pmatrix} \\[2em] R = \begin{pmatrix} R_{11} & 0 \\ 0 & R_{22} \end{pmatrix} \end{array} \right\} \qquad (5\text{-}8\text{-}19)$$

$$I + RH^{o}P^{o} = \begin{pmatrix} 1 + R_{11}P_{11} & R_{11}P_{12} \\ R_{22}P_{21} & 1 + R_{22}P_{22} \end{pmatrix} \qquad (5\text{-}8\text{-}20)$$

and:

$$\det(I+RH^{o}P^{o}) = I + R_{11}P_{11} + R_{22}P_{22} + R_{11}R_{22}(P_{11}P_{22} - P_{12}P_{21}) = 0$$

$$(5\text{-}8\text{-}21)$$

Now, we see that there has been no dead delay in it.

Up to now, what we discussed is the application of Smith predictor to multivariable control systems and the decoupling design was not considered. We must say that the multivariable Smith predictor has been a quite advanced control system and if the decoupling control is further expected, then because of the realization difficulty mentioned in §5-7, the decoupled system will be very complicated and difficult to be realized.

A simple approach to deal this problem is to use static decoupling control by using unit matrix design.

We know that in general the decoupling elements obtained by using the unit matrix design method are difficult to be realized, but if we only demand that the static decoupling control be realized , then the decoupling elements would be easily realized by some propotional networks. Namely, we let:

$$PN = I \qquad\qquad (5-8-22)$$

where N is the decoupling element structure.

Obviously by letting S = 0, it is not difficult to determine N in static state. Then, we let:

$$R' = NR \qquad\qquad (5-8-23)$$

and repeat the design procedure of the multivariable Smith predictor as above with the R being replaced by the R'.

The result will be both Smith predictor and decoupled system.

For example, a two-variable plant is:

$$P = \begin{pmatrix} \dfrac{12.8e^{-S}}{16.7S + 1} & -\dfrac{18.9e^{-3S}}{21.0S + 1} \\[4mm] \dfrac{6.6e^{-7S}}{10.9S + 1} & -\dfrac{19.4e^{-3S}}{14.4S + 1} \end{pmatrix}$$

and the PI regulators are adopted:

$$R = \begin{pmatrix} R_{11} & 0 \\ 0 & R_{22} \end{pmatrix}$$

namely:

$$R_{11} = K_{p1} + \dfrac{K_{i1}}{S}$$

$$R_{22} = K_{p2} + \frac{K_{i2}}{S}$$

If the unit feedback is adopted , then the characteristic equation for the system before the Smith predictor is designed is as follows:

$$\det (I + PR) = 55050S^4 + 14698S^3 + 1219S^2 + 62S + 1 +$$

$$+ (228.9S^2 + 31.9S + 1)\left[R_{11}(12 + 172.8S)e^{-S} - R_{22}(1914 + 323.8S)e^{-3S} - 232.8R_{11}R_{22}e^{-4S}\right] + 124.7(240.5S^2 + 31.1S + 1)R_{11}R_{22}e^{-10S} = 0$$

Obviously, there are some dead delay terms in this equation and they will give influence on system stability. so the values of K_{p1} and K_{p2} can not be very large.

Now, the Smith predictor is designed . Then:

$$P^0 = \begin{pmatrix} \dfrac{12.8}{16.7S+1} & \dfrac{-18.9}{21.0S+1} \\ \dfrac{6.6}{10.9S+1} & \dfrac{-19.4}{14.4S+1} \end{pmatrix}$$

and the system characteristic equation becomes:

$$\det(I + RP^0) = 55050S^4 + (14698 + 39553S - 74117R_{22})S^3 +$$

$$+ (1219 + 8259R_{11} - 14769R_{22} - 23290R_{11}R_{22})S^2 + (62 + 555R_{11} - 942R_{22} - 3546R_{11}R_{22})S + (1 - 108R_{11}R_{22}) = 0$$

We see that there is no dead delay in this equation.

If the decoupling design is carried out, then by (5-8-22) it is not difficult to get:

$$N = \begin{pmatrix} 0.157 & -0.153 \\ 0.053 & -0.1038 \end{pmatrix}$$

Because the matrix F is not related to R, so after the introduction of N, namely after the decoupling design, the system is still a Smith predictor.

Comparing the two characteristic equations, we know that when the system is a Smith predictor, there is no dead delay in its characteristic equation and both the regulators R_{11} and R_{22} may have higher gains.

§ 5-9 The Combination of Decoupling Design with Disturbance-Rejection
    Design

    In the last chapter, we expounded the possibility of realizing
the full decoupling control, i.e. the possibilty of realizing the decoupling control of outputs to both reference inputs and supply disturbances (or load disturbances) with the same decoupling structure.

    When this control demand is reached , then the system is reduced
to some separate independent single variable subsystems. If the full
rejection to the disturbance is further expected, then it can be done
according to the principles mentioned in Chapter 2.

    Can we finish these two designs in one step ?

    For example, for a two-variable plant of P-canonical , if the
feedforward decoupling project is adopted , then by the conclusions
reached in the last chapter it can realize the full decoupling control
of outputs to both reference inputs and load disturbances. Now, suppose that the full rejection to these load disturbances is also expected, how can we finish the design in one step?

    Such a system is shown in Fig 5-9-1.

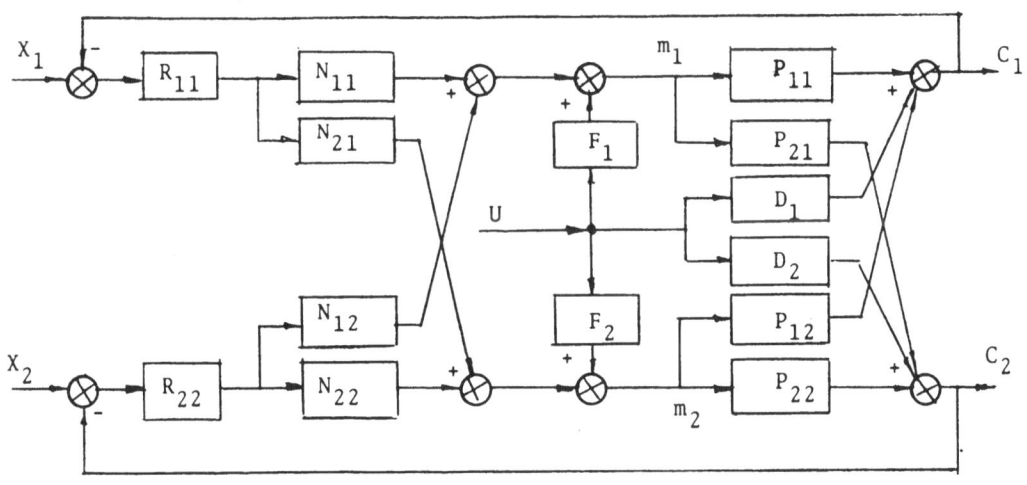

Fig 5-9-1

When $F_1 = F_2 = 0$, for the open loop, we have:

$$\begin{pmatrix} C_1 \\ C_2 \end{pmatrix} = \begin{bmatrix} P_{11} & P_{12} \\ P_{21} & P_{22} \end{bmatrix} \begin{bmatrix} m_1 \\ m_2 \end{bmatrix} + \begin{pmatrix} D_1 \\ D_2 \end{pmatrix} U \qquad (5\text{-}9\text{-}1)$$

and for the closed-loop :

$$\begin{pmatrix} C_1 \\ C_2 \end{pmatrix} = \begin{bmatrix} P_{11} & P_{12} \\ P_{21} & P_{22} \end{bmatrix} \begin{bmatrix} N_{11} & N_{12} \\ N_{21} & N_{22} \end{bmatrix} \begin{bmatrix} R_{11} & 0 \\ 0 & R_{22} \end{bmatrix} \begin{pmatrix} X_1 - C_1 \\ X_2 - C_2 \end{pmatrix} + \begin{pmatrix} D_1 \\ D_2 \end{pmatrix} U \qquad (5\text{-}9\text{-}2)$$

namely:

$$C = PNR(X - C) + DU \qquad (5\text{-}9\text{-}3)$$

If the decoupling control is expected, then PN should be a diagonal matrix. So, from:

$$PN = \begin{pmatrix} P_{11}N_{11} + P_{12}N_{12} & P_{11}N_{12} + P_{12}N_{22} \\ P_{22}N_{21} + P_{21}N_{11} & P_{22}N_{22} + P_{21}N_{21} \end{pmatrix} \qquad (5\text{-}9\text{-}4)$$

we get the decoupling conditions:

$$\left. \begin{array}{l} P_{11}N_{12} + P_{12}N_{22} = 0 \\ P_{22}N_{21} + P_{21}N_{11} = 0 \end{array} \right\} \qquad (5\text{-}9\text{-}5)$$

These are just (4-4-8) and (4-4-9).

That means that the decoupling design is not related to the existence of the disturbances.

We have said that these decoupling conditions also give the decoupling result of outputs to the load disturbances. Now, we want to realize the full disturbance-rejection design.

For this sake, two additional elements F_1 and F_2 are introduced.

Now, we discuss the design of F_1 and F_2. We have:

$$\begin{pmatrix} C_1 \\ C_2 \end{pmatrix} = \begin{bmatrix} P_{11} & P_{12} \\ P_{21} & P_{22} \end{bmatrix} \begin{bmatrix} F_1 \\ F_2 \end{bmatrix} U + \begin{pmatrix} D_1 \\ D_2 \end{pmatrix} U \qquad (5\text{-}9\text{-}6)$$

when only the load disturbance is considered.

If we want to realize the full disturbance-rejection design, then it is necessary:

$$\left. \begin{array}{l} P_{11}F_1 + P_{12}F_2 + D_1 = 0 \\ P_{22}F_2 + P_{21}F_1 + D_2 = 0 \end{array} \right\} \qquad (5\text{-}9\text{-}7)$$

It follows:

$$\begin{pmatrix} F_1 \\ F_2 \end{pmatrix} = - \begin{pmatrix} P_{11} & P_{12} \\ P_{21} & P_{22} \end{pmatrix}^{-1} \begin{pmatrix} D_1 \\ D_2 \end{pmatrix} = - \frac{\begin{pmatrix} P_{22} & -P_{12} \\ -P_{21} & P_{11} \end{pmatrix} \begin{pmatrix} D_1 \\ D_2 \end{pmatrix}}{\begin{vmatrix} P_{11} & P_{12} \\ P_{21} & P_{22} \end{vmatrix}} \qquad (5\text{-}9\text{-}8)$$

and we get :

$$F_1 = \frac{1}{\triangle} (P_{12}D_2 - P_{22}D_1) \qquad (5\text{-}9\text{-}9)$$

$$F_2 = \frac{1}{\triangle} (P_{21}D_1 - P_{11}D_2) \qquad (5\text{-}9\text{-}10)$$

with:

$$\triangle = P_{11}P_{22} - P_{12}P_{21} \qquad (5\text{-}9\text{-}11)$$

We see that the forms of both F_1 and F_2 are not simple.

When $P_{12} = P_{21} = 0$, the above results are reduced to those obtained in Chapter 2.

But, when $P_{12} = 0$, $P_{21} \neq 0$, we have:

$$F_1 = - \frac{D_1}{P_{11}} \qquad (5\text{-}9\text{-}12)$$

$$F_2 = \frac{P_{21}D_1}{P_{11}P_{22}} - \frac{D_2}{P_{22}} \qquad (5\text{-}9\text{-}13)$$

§ 5-10 An Easily Misleading Problem

The application of feedforward decoupling project in decoupling design has been discussed for many times before. Its general form is shown in Fig 5-10-1.

Its basic relation is:

$$C = (I + PR)^{-1}PRX$$
$$(5-10-1)$$

In general , both P and

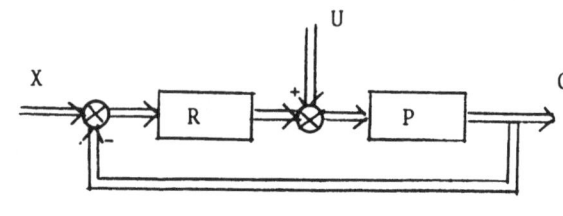

Fig 5-10-1

R are non-singular matrices.

We know that for the matrix calculation the following relation in general is held :

$$PR \neq RP \qquad (5-10-2)$$

so that:

$$I + PR \neq I + RP \qquad (5-10-3)$$

A very easily misleading problem in decoupling design just arises here, namely sometimes PR is written as RP. Thus, great attention must be paid to deal with this matrix relation, especially for those who are not familiar with matrix analysis.

But we should analyze further.For such a system, if a mistake is made as PR being written into RP, what a system will it be ?

Let us discuss a single variable system at first. Such a system is shown in Fig 5-10-2.

For this system, we have:

$$\frac{C}{X} = \frac{PR}{1 + PR}$$
$$(5-10-4)$$

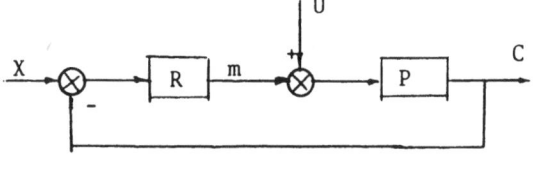

Fig 5-10-2

When the system is drawn as Fig 5-10-3 , then we have:

$$\frac{m}{U} = \frac{-RP}{1 + RP}$$
$$(5-10-5)$$

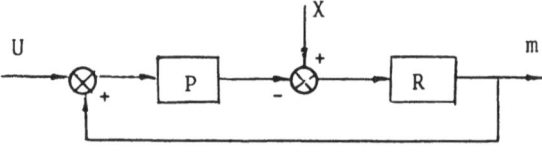

Fig 5-10-3

Notice that these two expressions are for the same system; and there is only one characteristic equation for this system. That means:

$$1 + RP = 1 + PR \qquad (5\text{-}10\text{-}6)$$

Certainly, for the single variable systems, this is true.

Now, let us consider the multivariable control systems.

If (5-10-1) is written as:

$$C = (I + RP)^{-1}RPX \qquad (5\text{-}10\text{-}7)$$

how will the case be?

At first, we discuss the characteristic equation. For (5-10-7), the characteristic equation is:

$$\left| 1 + RP \right| = 0 \qquad (5\text{-}10\text{-}8)$$

but for (5-10-1) , the characteristic equation is:

$$\left| 1 + PR \right| = 0 \qquad (5\text{-}10\text{-}9)$$

Now, both P and R are matrices, so $I + PR \neq I + RP$. But, whether (5-10-8) and (5-10-9) are also different is not known yet.

We can prove that both (5-10-8) and (5-10-9) are identical.

Because both P and R are non-singular, so we can do a matrix $R^{-1}(I + RP)R$ and :

$$R^{-1}(I + RP)R = R^{-1}IR + R^{-1}RPR = I + PR \qquad (5\text{-}10\text{-}10)$$

Thus:

$$\left| R^{-1}(I + RP)R \right| = \left| I + PR \right| \qquad (5\text{-}10\text{-}11)$$

But:

$$\left| R^{-1}(I + RP)R \right| = \left| R^{-1} \right|\left| I + RP \right|\left| R \right| = \left| I + RP \right| \qquad (5\text{-}10\text{-}12)$$

therefore:

$$\left| I + PR \right| = \left| I + RP \right| \qquad (5\text{-}10\text{-}13)$$

It means that even we have a wrong expression (5-10-7), it does not influence the system stability.

This is reasonable. Because for a multivariable control system, we can also write an expression as (5-10-5) , but in matrix form.

$$M = -(I + RP)^{-1}RPU \qquad (5\text{-}10\text{-}14)$$

We notice that both (5-10-14) and (5-10-1) are for the same system, so the characteristic equation from these two expressions must be the same, namely:

$$\left| I + PR \right| = \left| I + RP \right| = 0 \qquad (5\text{-}10\text{-}15)$$

Although the wrong expression (5-10-7) will **give no** influence on the system stability analysis, the decoupling design by using it will give quite different results.

If the decoupling control is expected, then it is necessary:

$$\left.\begin{array}{l} R_{11}P_{12} + R_{12}P_{22} = 0 \\[2ex] R_{21}P_{11} + R_{22}P_{21} = 0 \end{array}\right\} \qquad (5\text{-}10\text{-}16)$$

This is the decoupling condition from (5-10-7). But the correct decoupling condition is:

$$\left.\begin{array}{l} P_{11}R_{12} + P_{12}R_{22} = 0 \\[2ex] P_{21}R_{11} + P_{22}R_{21} = 0 \end{array}\right\} \qquad (5\text{-}10\text{-}17)$$

Obviously, they are different.

Then, if the system were decoupled by (5-10-16), what a system would it be ?

It is also a decoupled system, but the decoupling relation is not between outputs and reference inputs . It realizes the decoupling relation between the manipulated variables and the supply disturbances. This can be well known from (5-10-14).

So, this is a very easily misleading problem and we should pay great attention in system decoupling design.

CHAPTER SIX

SOME REALIZATION PROBLEMS IN DECOUPLING DESIGN

§ 6-1 Introduction

we have expounded the decoupling design ideas and discussed different possible decoupling control projects. We see that the characteristics may be different for different projects.

For any decoupling project designed by the above principles, if no economic problem is considered, all of them should be theoretically realizable at least.

This problem is especially important because many decoupling projects are physically irrealizable in theory.

The " physically realizable " means that for an element if its transfer function is expressed as a fraction of polynomials, then the order of the denominator should not be less than that of its numerator.

In the decoupling design, the realization problem of an element is mainly in two aspects: The realization problem of a plant after transformation from one canonical form to the other; the realization problem of the decoupling elements, especially for the feedforward decoupling structures.

We do not mean that the physically irrealizable decoupling projects (mainly those with irrealizable decoupling elements) could not be used absolutely. In fact, if some high frequency poles are added to their transfer functions, then they will be able to be available.

Another meaning of realization is about the system. For example, what decoupling system is the easiest to be realized ? What form will the system be after decoupling design? What is the condition for static decoupling, etc.

These problems will be discussed in this chapter.

§ 6-2 The Physically Realizable Conditions for V-Canonical Plants

Transferred from the P-Canonical Forms[5]

We have discussed before that both P-canonical and V-canonical plants can be transferred to each other.

In practical control engineering, most plants are P-canonical and all practical plants are certainly physically realizable.

If we transfer these P-canonical plants into V-canonical forms, we always meet a problem, namely the V-canonical plants transferred are with physically irrealizable transfer functions.

The so-called physically **irrealizable** transfer functin means that when the transfer function is expressed in the fraction form of polynomials, the degree of the numerator is higher than that of the denominator.

For example, a P-canonical plant is expressed as:

$$P_{11} = \frac{1}{1 + T_1 S} \qquad\qquad P_{22} = \frac{1}{1 + T_2 S}$$

$$P_{12} = K_1 \qquad\qquad P_{21} = K_2$$

Obviously, all of these transfer functions are physically realizable. Now, if we transfer it into a V-canonical plant, then by (1-6-19), we have:

$$\left.\begin{aligned}
V_{11} &= \frac{1 - K_1 K_2 (1 + T_1 S)(1 + T_2 S)}{1 + T_1 S} \\[2ex]
V_{22} &= \frac{1 - K_1 K_2 (1 + T_1 S)(1 + T_2 S)}{1 + T_2 S} \\[2ex]
V_{12} &= \frac{K_1 (1 + T_1 S)(1 + T_2 S)}{1 - K_1 K_2 (1 + T_1 S)(1 + T_2 S)} \\[2ex]
V_{21} &= \frac{K_2 (1 + T_1 S)(1 + T_2 S)}{1 - K_1 K_2 (1 + T_1 S)(1 + T_2 S)}
\end{aligned}\right\} \qquad (6-2-1)$$

By (1-6-21) the results are:

$$V_{11} = \frac{1}{1 + T_1 S}$$

$$V_{22} = \frac{1}{1 + T_2 S}$$

$$V_{12} = K_1 (1 + T_1 S)(1 + T_2 S)$$

$$V_{21} = K_2 (1 + T_1 S)(1 + T_2 S)$$

(6-2-2)

Obviously, both (6-2-1) and (6-2-2) contain some irrealizable transfer functions.

Now, let us discuss under what conditions the V-canonical plants transferred from P-canonical foms are still physically realizable.

For simplicity, we discuss the two-variable systems but the principles and conclusions are also available for systems with more variables. In addition, we meet the two-variable systems the most in prctical control engineering.

The transfer function of some channel of a two-variable P-canonical plant is expressed as:

$$P_{ik}(S) = \frac{Z_{ik}(S)}{D_{ik}(S)}$$

(6-2-3)

and:

The highest order of Z_{ik} is m_{ik} ,

The highest order of D_{ik} is n_{ik} .

Then the transfer functions of the channels of the V-canonical plant obtained by using (1-6-19) are:

$$V_{11} = \frac{Q}{Z_{11}D_{22}D_{12}D_{21}}$$

(6-2-4)

$$V_{22} = \frac{Q}{Z_{22}D_{11}D_{12}D_{21}}$$

(6-2-5)

$$V_{12} = \frac{Z_{12}D_{11}D_{22}D_{21}}{Q}$$

(6-2-6)

$$V_{21} = \frac{Z_{21}D_{11}D_{22}D_{12}}{Q}$$

(6-2-7)

where:

$$Q = Z_{11}Z_{22}D_{12}D_{21} - Z_{21}Z_{12}D_{11}D_{22} \qquad (6\text{-}2\text{-}8)$$

Because the given P-canonical plant is always realizable, so we have:

$$n_{ik} \geqslant m_{ik} \qquad (6\text{-}2\text{-}9)$$

Now , we demand that V_{ik} be also realizable. It means that in its transfer functions of the channels the order of the denominators are always no lower than that of the numerators.

We discuss this problem in two cases:

(1) Suppose that the lag order of the main channel transfer function of the P-canonical plant is not lower than that of the coupling channels, namely:

$$\left. \begin{array}{ll} n_{11} \geqslant n_{12} & z_{11} \leqslant z_{12} \\[2mm] n_{22} \geqslant n_{21} & z_{22} \leqslant z_{21} \end{array} \right\} \qquad (6\text{-}2\text{-}10)$$

(2) Suppose that the lag order of the main channel transfer function of the P-canonical plant is lower than that of the coupling channels, namely:

$$\left. \begin{array}{ll} n_{11} < n_{12} & z_{11} \geqslant z_{12} \\[2mm] n_{22} < n_{21} & z_{22} \geqslant z_{21} \end{array} \right\} \qquad (6\text{-}2\text{-}11)$$

Then, for the first case, the physically realizable conditions for the V-canonical plant transferred from the P-canonical form are:

$$\left. \begin{array}{c} m_{21} + m_{12} + n_{11} \leqslant m_{11} + n_{12} + n_{21} \\[2mm] m_{21} + m_{12} + n_{22} \leqslant m_{22} + n_{12} + n_{21} \\[2mm] n_{12} = m_{12} \\[2mm] n_{21} = m_{21} \end{array} \right\} \qquad (6\text{-}2\text{-}12)$$

For the second case, these conditions are:

$$\left. \begin{array}{c} m_{22} \leqslant n_{22} \\[2mm] m_{11} \leqslant n_{11} \end{array} \right.$$

$$m_{21} + n_{11} + n_{22} \leq m_{11} + m_{22} + n_{21}$$

$$m_{12} + n_{11} + n_{22} \leq m_{11} + m_{22} + n_{12}$$

(6-2-13)

The above two results are obtained from (6-2-4) to (6-2-7).

In most practical process control systems, for the P-canonical plants, we often have:

$$m_{ik} = 0 \qquad\qquad (6\text{-}2\text{-}14)$$

namely they are some pure lag channels.

Then in the first case, the sum of the lag orders of the two coupling channels must be no less than the order of the higher lag in the two main channels. In fact, from (6-2-12) , it means only when:

$$n_{11} = m_{11}$$
$$n_{22} = m_{22}$$

(6-2-15)

the V-canonical form can be realized.

So when $m_{ik} = 0$, the transferred V-canonical form can not be realized. The example discussed before is just this case.

In the second case, the sum of the lags of the two main channels must be less than the lower lag order of the two coupling channels.

This is the case about the realization conditions of V-canonical plants transferred from P-canonical forms.

As for the P-canonical plants transferred from the V-canonical forms, they are always physically realizable.

§ 6-3 The Physically Realizable Conditions of P-Canonical Decoupling Element Structure (30)

In the last paragraph, we discussed the realization conditions of the plant transfer for the two canonical forms.

Now, we discuss the realizable conditions for the decoupling element structure in decoupling design.

At first, we discuss the systems with P-canonical plants and suppose that the decoupling element structure is located before the plant.

The system is designed by given control demands. That means that
in order to realize decoupling control, it is necessary :

$$PN = A \qquad (6-3-1)$$

where, A is a diagonal matrix with elements given by the control demands and is also called as the extended plant.

Therefore, the decoupling element matrix and the decoupling elements are given by:

$$N = \frac{(adj\ P)A}{det\ P} \qquad (6-3-2)$$

$$N_{ik} = \frac{det\ \bar{P}_{ki}}{det\ P}\ A_{kk} \qquad (6-3-3)$$

$$i = 1,2,\ldots\ldots\ n$$

$$k = 1,2,\ldots\ldots\ n$$

For example, for a two-variable system:

$$N_{11} = \frac{A_{11}P_{22}}{P_{11}P_{22} - P_{12}P_{21}} \qquad (6-3-4)$$

$$N_{22} = \frac{A_{22}P_{11}}{P_{11}P_{22} - P_{12}P_{21}} \qquad (6-3-5)$$

$$N_{12} = \frac{- A_{22}P_{12}}{P_{11}P_{22} - P_{12}P_{21}} \qquad (6-3-6)$$

$$N_{21} = \frac{- A_{11}P_{21}}{P_{11}P_{22} - P_{12}P_{21}} \qquad (6-3-7)$$

Obviously, the realization conditions of N_{11}, N_{12}, N_{13} and N_{22}
are related not only to the plant characters, but also to the properties of A_{11} and A_{22}.

The realization of an element means that all poles of its transfer function must be in the left S plane and the order of its denominator must be no lower than that of the numerator. Let:

$$P_{ij} = \frac{Z_{ij}}{D_{ij}} \qquad (6-3-8)$$

and the orders of Z_{ij} and D_{ij} are m and n , respectively.

For any practical plant, we always have:

$$n \geqq m \qquad (6-3-9)$$

then, (6-3-4) to (6-3-7) can be transferred into:

$$N_{11} = A_{11} \frac{Z_{22} D_{11} D_{12} D_{21}}{R - Q} \qquad (6-3-10)$$

$$N_{22} = A_{22} \frac{Z_{11} D_{22} D_{12} D_{21}}{R - Q} \qquad (6-3-11)$$

$$N_{12} = - A_{22} \frac{Z_{12} D_{11} D_{22} D_{21}}{R - Q} \qquad (6-3-12)$$

$$N_{21} = - A_{11} \frac{Z_{21} D_{11} D_{22} D_{12}}{R - Q} \qquad (6-3-13)$$

where:

$$R - Q = Z_{11} Z_{22} D_{21} D_{12} - Z_{12} Z_{21} D_{11} D_{22} \qquad (6-3-14)$$

Now, we discuss the realization conditions for N_{11}, N_{12}, N_{21} and N_{22}.

Only a simple case is discussed here, namely all transfer functions of this plant are pure lag elements. Thus, all numerators of these functions are constants. A lot of process control systems are with this form indeed.

For such a system, two cases are considered:

(1) Suppose that ideal decoupling control is expected, i.e.

$$\left. \begin{array}{l} A_{11} = P_{11} \\ \\ A_{22} = P_{22} \end{array} \right\} \qquad (6-3-15)$$

In a two-variable plant, the transfer functions of its four channels certainly are given. If in the given plant characters, there is no strict restriction on which two must be main channels and which two must be coupling channels, then we always can choose those two with higher orders of transfer lag being the main channels of the plant, i.e. P_{11} and P_{22} are with higher orders of transfer lag.

In general, for the four plant transfer functions, there are two possible cases:

(1) $n_{11} \geq n_{12}$, $n_{22} \geq n_{21}$,

(2) $n_{11} < n_{12}$, $n_{22} < n_{21}$.

Thus, if P_{11} and P_{22} are determined by the above principle, i.e. $n_{11} \geq n_{12}$, $n_{22} \geq n_{21}$, and let $A_{11} = P_{11}$, $A_{22} = P_{22}$, then all four trans-fer functions of (6-3-10) to (6-3-13) are realizable, namely their de-nominators are always with higher (or equal) order than the numerators.

(2) But, in most cases the ideal decoupling control is not expec-ted , namely A_{11} and A_{22} are not equal to P_{11} and P_{22}, respectively. Nevertheless, both A_{11} and A_{22} are physically realizable and are assu-med with zero order of numerators. The orders of the denominators of A_{11} and A_{22} are n_1 and n_2, respectively.

In such a case, the realizable conditions of the decoupling ele-ments are:

1. When $n_{11} \geq n_{12}$, $n_{22} \geq n_{21}$:

$$\left.\begin{aligned} n_1 + n_{22} &\geq n_{12} + n_{21} \\ n_2 + n_{11} &\geq n_{12} + n_{21} \\ n_1 &\geq n_{12} \\ n_2 &\geq n_{21} \end{aligned}\right\} \qquad (6\text{-}3\text{-}16)$$

2. When $n_{11} < n_{12}$, $n_{22} < n_{21}$:

$$\left.\begin{aligned} n_1 &\geq n_{11} \\ n_2 &\geq n_{22} \\ n_1 + n_{21} &\geq n_{11} + n_{22} \\ n_2 + n_{12} &\geq n_{11} + n_{22} \end{aligned}\right\} \qquad (6\text{-}3\text{-}17)$$

From the above realization conditions, the following conclusions can be reached:

(1) For a coupled plant, if its main channels are always with higher lag orders than the coupling channels, then in the decoupled extended plant, the lag order of any diagonal element transfer function should be at least equal to that of the corresponding coupling channel transfer function of the original coupled plant,

(2) For a coupled plant, if its main channels are always with lower lag orders than the coupling channels, then in the decoupled extended plant, the lag order of any diagonal element transfer function should be at least equal to that of the corresponding main channel transfer function of the original coupled plant,

(3) As a summary, for a realizable decoupled system, the lag order of the diagonal element transfer functions in the decoupled extended plant must be at least equal to the lowest lag order of the transfer functions of the original coupled plant.

Therefore, the decoupling elements obtained by using unit matrix decoupling method are always irrealizable because all these elements do not satisfy the above conditions.

For the systems designed not by given demands, the decoupling elements are given by:

$$N_{12} = - \frac{P_{12}}{P_{11}} = - \frac{Z_{12}D_{11}}{D_{12}Z_{11}}$$

$$N_{21} = - \frac{P_{21}}{P_{22}} = - \frac{Z_{21}D_{22}}{D_{21}Z_{22}}$$

(6-3-18)

So, the realization conditions are determined by the relations between Z_{ik} and D_{ik}.

§ 6-4 The Realization Conditions of V-Canonical Decoupling Element

Structure for P-Canonical Plants [5]

In the last paragraph, we discussed the realization conditions
for the P-canonical decoupling element structure applied in the systems
with P-canonical plants. Now, we discuss the case when V-canonical decoupling element structure is applied.

Such a system is shown in Fig 6-4-1.

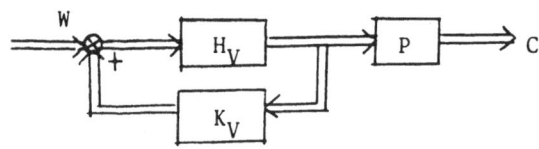

Fig 6-4-1

Here, H_V and K_V are the characters of V-canonical decoupling element structure. We have:

$$C(S) = P(S) (I - H_V K_V)^{-1} H_V W(S) = F(S) W(S) \qquad (6-4-1)$$

When the decoupling control is realized, then:

$$F(S) = P(S)(I - H_V K_V)^{-1} H_V \qquad (6-4-2)$$

is a diagonal matrix.

From (6-4-2) we get:

$$F^{-1}(S) = H_V^{-1}(S)(I - H_V K_V)P^{-1}(S) \qquad (6-4-3)$$

$$H_V^{-1}(S) - K_V(S) = F^{-1}(S)P(S) \qquad (6-4-4)$$

Thus, we get the following element relations:

$$(H_V^{-1}(S) - K_V(S))_{ki} = (F^{-1}(S)P(S))_{ki} \qquad (6-4-5)$$
$$k = 1,2,\ldots\ldots n$$
$$i = 1,2,\ldots\ldots n$$

Notice that $H_V(s)$ is a diagonal matrix and $K_V(S)$ is a matrix with
zero diagonal elements. Therefore, we get:

$$(H_V(S))_{kk} = P_{kk}^{-1} F_{kk} \qquad (6-4-6)$$
$$k = 1,2,\ldots\ldots\ldots n$$

$$(K_V(S))_{ki} = - P_{ki} F_{kk}^{-1} \qquad (6-4-7)$$
$$k = 1,2,\ldots\ldots n \quad k \neq i$$
$$i = 1,2,\ldots\ldots n$$

Denote:

$$P_{kk} = \frac{Z_{kk}}{N_{kk}} \qquad F_{kk} = \frac{Z_k}{N_k}$$

then we get:

$$\left.\begin{array}{c} (H_V)_{kk} = \dfrac{N_{kk}}{Z_{kk}} \dfrac{Z_k}{N_k} \\[2mm] k = 1,2,\ldots\ldots\, n \\[4mm] (K_V)_{ki} = - \dfrac{Z_{ki}}{N_{ki}} \dfrac{N_k}{Z_k} \\[2mm] k = 1,2,\ldots\ldots\, n \qquad k \neq i \\[1mm] i = 1,2,\ldots\ldots\, n \end{array}\right\} \qquad (6\text{-}4\text{-}8)$$

Therefore, the realizable conditions for $(H_V)_{kk}$ are:

$$n_k + m_{kk} \geq n_{kk} + m_k \qquad\qquad (6\text{-}4\text{-}9)$$
$$k = 1,2,\ldots\ldots\, n$$

and the realizable conditions for $(K_V)_{ki}$ are:

$$n_{ki} + m_k \geq n_k + m_{ki} \qquad\qquad (6\text{-}4\text{-}10)$$
$$k = 1,2,\ldots\ldots\ldots\, n$$
$$i = 1,2,\ldots\ldots\ldots\, n$$
$$k \neq i$$

From (6-4-9) and (6-4-10) we can get further:

$$n_{ki} - m_{ki} \geq n_k - m_k \geq n_{kk} - m_{kk} \qquad\qquad (6\text{-}4\text{-}11)$$
$$k = 1,2,\ldots\ldots\, n$$
$$i = 1,2,\ldots\ldots\, n$$
$$k \neq i$$

That means that the difference of the numbers of the poles and the zeros of the coupling channels must be no less than that of the main channels in the coupled plant. This is the realization condition for the V-canonical decoupling element structure.

§ 6-5 The Realization Conditions of P-Canonical Decoupling Element

Structure for V-Canonical Plants[5]

Now, we discuss the realization conditions of P-canonical decoupling element structure when it is applied to the system with a V-canonical plant.

The V-canonical plant can be expressed as:

$$C_i = V_{ii}(m_i + \sum_{k=1}^{n} V_{ik}C_k)$$

$$(6-5-1)$$

$$i = 1,2,\ldots\ldots n$$

Denote:

$$H = \begin{pmatrix} V_{11} & & & 0 \\ & V_{22} & & \\ & & \ddots & \\ 0 & & & V_{nn} \end{pmatrix}$$

$$(6-5-2)$$

$$K = \begin{pmatrix} 0 & V_{12} & \cdots\cdots & V_{1n} \\ V_{21} & 0 & \cdots\cdots & V_{2n} \\ \vdots & \vdots & \vdots\vdots\vdots\vdots\vdots & \vdots \\ V_{n1} & V_{n2} & \cdots\cdots & 0 \end{pmatrix}$$

$$(6-5-3)$$

then:

$$C = HM + HKC \qquad (6-5-4)$$

When the decoupling element structure is designed, then the system is shown in Fig 6-5-1 and we have:

Fig 6-5-1

$$C = HNW + HK\frac{HM}{I-HK} =$$

$$= (I + \frac{HK}{I- HK})HNW = (I - HK)^{-1}HNW$$

$$(6-5-1)$$

In order to realize decoupling control, it is necessary:

$$(I - HK)^{-1}HN = A$$

$$(6-5-2)$$

where A is a diagonal matrix.

For analysis convenience, we let:

$$(I - HK)^{-1}H = P_E \qquad (6-5-7)$$

and this means that the relation between C and M is transferred into
a P-canonical plant. Therefore:

$$A = P_E N \qquad (6-5-8)$$

and now the determination of the decoupling element structure is just
the same as we we discussed in § 6-4. We know:

$$N = P_E^{-1}A \qquad (6-5-9)$$

and from (1-6-11):

$$P_E^{-1} = T \qquad (6-5-10)$$

namely:

$$N = TA \qquad (6-5-11)$$

where T is determined by (1-6-6), i.e.

$$T = \begin{pmatrix} \dfrac{1}{V_{11}} & -V_{12} & - & - & - & - & - & -V_{1n} \\ -V_{21} & \dfrac{1}{V_{22}} & - & - & - & - & - & -V_{2n} \\ - & - & - & - & - & - & - & - \\ - & - & - & - & - & - & - & - \\ -V_{n1} & -V_{n2} & - & - & - & - & - & \dfrac{1}{V_{nn}} \end{pmatrix} \qquad (6-5-12)$$

Therefore, we get the decoupling elements :

$$\left. \begin{array}{l} N_{kk} = \dfrac{A_k}{V_{kk}} \\[3mm] N_{ik} = -V_{ik}A_k \end{array} \right\} \qquad (6-5-13)$$

$$\begin{array}{l} i = 1,2,\ldots\ldots n \\ k = 1,2,\ldots\ldots n \end{array} \qquad i \neq k$$

Then, denote:

$$\left. \begin{array}{l} V_{ik} = \dfrac{Z_{ik}}{D_{ik}} \\[3mm] A_k = \dfrac{Z_k}{D_k} \end{array} \right\} \qquad (6-5-14)$$

and we get:

$$N_{kk} = \frac{Z_k D_{kk}}{D_k Z_{kk}} \qquad K = 1,2,\ldots\ldots n \qquad (6\text{-}5\text{-}15)$$

$$N_{ik} = -\frac{Z_{ik} Z_k}{D_{ik} D_k} \qquad \begin{array}{l} i = 1,2,\ldots\ldots n \\ k = 1,2,\ldots\ldots n \\ i \neq k \end{array} \qquad (6\text{-}5\text{-}16)$$

Now, we can discuss their realization conditions.

In order to let N_{kk} and N_{ik} be physically realizable, it is necessary:

$$n_k + m_{kk} \geqq m_k + n_{kk}$$
$$n_k + n_{ik} \geqq m_k + m_{ik} \qquad (6\text{-}5\text{-}17)$$

These are the general conditions. For a two-variable system, if all plant channels are lag elements, then:

$$m_{ik} = m_{kk} = 0 \qquad (6\text{-}5\text{-}18)$$

and suppose that A_k also contains lag elements, i.e.

$$m_k = 0 \qquad (6\text{-}5\text{-}19)$$

then the realization conditions are:

$$\left.\begin{array}{l} n_1 \geqq n_{11} \\ n_2 \geqq n_{22} \\ n_{12} + n_2 \geqq 0 \\ n_{21} + n_1 \geqq 0 \end{array}\right\} \qquad (6\text{-}5\text{-}20)$$

The latter two conditions certainly can be satisfied, so the conditions become:

$$\left.\begin{array}{l} n_1 \geqq n_{11} \\ n_2 \geqq n_{22} \end{array}\right\} \qquad (6\text{-}5\text{-}21)$$

Thus, in order to let all decoupling elements be realizable, for the extended plant the lag orders of the transfer functions of the diagonal elements should be at least no lower than those of the main channel transfer functions of the original coupled plant.

§ 6-6 The Realization Conditions of V-Canonical Decoupling Element

Structure for V-Canonical Plants [5]

We have discussed the realization conditions of P-canonical decoupling elements for V-canonical plants . Now, we discuss the realization conditions of V-canonical decoupling elements for V-canonical plants.

Such a system is shown in Fig 6-6-1.

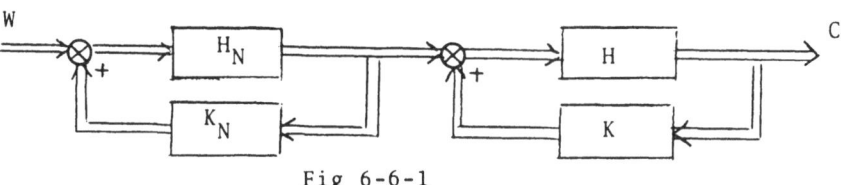

Fig 6-6-1

where H and K express the plant ; H_N and K_N express the V-canonical decoupling element structure.

From the figure, we have:

$$C = (I - HK)^{-1} H (I - H_N K_N)^{-1} H_N W \qquad (6-6-1)$$

and the open loop transfer matrix is:

$$F = (I - HK)^{-1} H (I - H_N K_N)^{-1} H_N \qquad (6-6-2)$$

In order to realize decoupling control, F must be a diagonal matrix. Taking the inverse matrices for the two sides of the above equation, we get:

$$F^{-1} = H_N^{-1} (I - H_N K_N) H^{-1} (I - HK) =$$
$$= (H_N^{-1} - K_N)(H^{-1} - K) \qquad (6-6-3)$$

Thus:

$$H_N^{-1} - K_N = F^{-1} (H^{-1} - K)^{-1} \qquad (6-6-4)$$

Notice that both H and H_N are diagonal matrices and K_N and K are
matrices with zero diagonal elements.

Thus:

$$(H_N)_{kk} = F_{kk} \frac{\det (H^{-1} - K)}{\det (H^{-1} - K)_{kk}} \qquad (6-6-5)$$
$$k = 1, 2, \ldots\ldots\ldots n$$

$$(K_N)_{ki} = - F_{kk}^{-1} \frac{\det (H^{-1} - K)_{ik}}{\det (H^{-1} - K)} \qquad (6-6-6)$$

$$k = 1,2,\ldots\ldots\ldots n$$

$$i = 1,2,\ldots\ldots\ldots n$$

$$i \neq k$$

For a two-variable system, from (6-6-4) and (6-6-5) we get:

$$(H_N)_{11} = F_{11} \frac{V_{11}^{-1}V_{22}^{-1} - V_{12}V_{21}}{V_{22}^{-1}} =$$

$$= \frac{Z_1}{D_1} \frac{D_{11}D_{22}D_{12}D_{21} - Z_{11}Z_{22}Z_{12}Z_{21}}{Z_{11}D_{22}D_{12}D_{21}}$$

$$(H_N)_{22} = F_{22} \frac{V_{11}^{-1}V_{22}^{-1} - V_{12}V_{21}}{V_{11}^{-1}} =$$

$$= \frac{Z_2}{D_2} \frac{D_{11}D_{22}D_{12}D_{21} - Z_{11}Z_{22}Z_{12}Z_{21}}{Z_{22}D_{11}D_{12}D_{21}}$$

$$(K_N)_{12} = - F_{11}^{-1} \frac{V_{12}}{V_{11}^{-1}V_{22}^{-1} - V_{12}V_{21}} =$$

$$= - \frac{D_1}{Z_1} \frac{Z_{11}Z_{22}Z_{12}D_{21}}{D_{11}D_{22}D_{12}D_{21} - Z_{11}Z_{22}Z_{12}Z_{21}}$$

$$(K_N)_{21} = - F_{22}^{-1} \frac{V_{21}}{V_{11}^{-1}V_{22}^{-1} - V_{12}V_{21}} =$$

$$= - \frac{D_2}{Z_2} \frac{Z_{11}Z_{22}Z_{21}D_{12}}{D_{11}D_{22}D_{12}D_{21} - Z_{11}Z_{22}Z_{12}Z_{21}}$$

$$(6-6-6)$$

Certainly, the plant is realizable, so:

$$m_{ik} \leq n_{ik} \tag{6-6-7}$$

and the realization conditions for the decoupling elements are:

$$n_1 - m_1 \geq n_{11} - m_{11}$$

$$n_2 - m_2 \geq n_{22} - m_{22}$$

$$n_1 - m_1 \geq n_{11} - m_{11} + n_{22} - m_{22} + n_{12} - m_{12}$$

$$n_2 - m_2 \geq n_{11} - m_{11} + n_{22} - m_{22} + n_{21} - m_{21}$$

$$(6-6-8)$$

§ 6-7 The Most Easily Realizable Decoupled System

    In practice,the most popular decoupled system is with P-canonical

plant, P-canonical decoupling element structure and the decoupling ele-

ments are located between the regulators and the plant.

    In § 4-6, we have discussed the advantages of application of such

projects. But, however, even for these systems, the decoupling elements

sometimes are also difficult to be realized.

    For example, for the system shown in Fig 6-7-1:

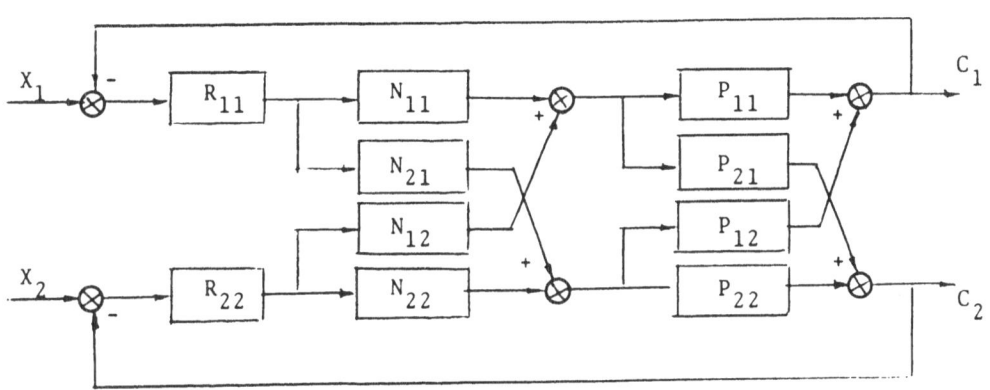

Fig 6-7-1

if we let:

$$PN = I \qquad (6\text{-}7\text{-}1)$$

namely, the unit matrix method is applied, then in general we can get

good control effects but :

$$N = P^{-1} \qquad (6\text{-}7\text{-}2)$$

is irrealizable. If we want to realize the ideal decoupling control,

then we have:

$$\left.\begin{array}{l} \dfrac{C_1}{X_1} = \dfrac{R_{11}P_{11}}{1 + R_{11}P_{11}} \\[3mm] \dfrac{C_2}{X_2} = \dfrac{R_{22}P_{22}}{1 + R_{22}P_{22}} \end{array}\right\} \qquad (6\text{-}7\text{-}3)$$

    We have pointed out in § 6-3 that for a two-variable system with

P-canonical structures, the decoupling elements expressed by:

$$
\begin{pmatrix} N_{11} & N_{12} \\ \\ N_{21} & N_{22} \end{pmatrix} = \begin{pmatrix} \dfrac{P_{11}P_{22}}{P_{11}P_{22} - P_{12}P_{21}} & \dfrac{-P_{22}P_{12}}{P_{11}P_{22} - P_{12}P_{21}} \\ \\ \dfrac{-P_{11}P_{21}}{P_{11}P_{22} - P_{12}P_{21}} & \dfrac{P_{11}P_{22}}{P_{11}P_{22} - P_{12}P_{21}} \end{pmatrix}
$$

$$(6-7-4)$$

are not easily to be realized when P_{11}, P_{12}, P_{21} and P_{22} are not with simple forms.

But, however, sometimes these decoupling elements may be easily realized. For example, in § 4-7 we got a conclusion that when all P_{11}, P_{12}, P_{21} and P_{22} are first lag elements and are with the same constants, then the decoupling elements will be very simple. In fact, in such cases, they can be realized by propotional elements.

Certainly, for the realization of decoupled systems, the most ideal realization conditions for the decoupling elements are that they can be realized by propotional elements with the demanded decoupling control in both dynamic and static states.

The problem is in what cases we can get these most ideal decoupling conditions.

From Fig 6-7-1 we know that from the regulator R_{11} the control character for C_1 is:

$$N_{11}P_{11} + N_{21}P_{12} = A_{11} \qquad (6-7-5)$$

and because decoupling control is expected, so the control character of C_2 from R_{11} is:

$$N_{11}P_{21} + N_{21}P_{22} = 0 \qquad (6-7-6)$$

Similarly, we can get:

$$N_{22}P_{22} + N_{12}P_{21} = A_{22} \qquad (6-7-7)$$

$$N_{22}P_{12} + N_{12}P_{11} = 0 \qquad (6-7-8)$$

Thus, we get:

$$N_{11} = \frac{A_{11}P_{22}}{P_{11}P_{22}-P_{12}P_{21}} = \frac{A_{11}K_{22}W_{22}}{K_{11}K_{22}W_{11}W_{22} - K_{12}K_{21}W_{12}W_{21}} \qquad (6-7-9)$$

$$N_{22} = \frac{A_{22}P_{11}}{P_{11}P_{22} - P_{12}P_{21}} = \frac{A_{22}K_{11}W_{11}}{K_{11}K_{22}W_{11}W_{22} - K_{12}K_{21}W_{12}W_{21}} \qquad (6\text{-}7\text{-}10)$$

$$N_{21} = \frac{-A_{11}P_{21}}{P_{11}P_{22} - P_{12}P_{21}} = \frac{- A_{11}K_{21}W_{21}}{K_{11}K_{22}W_{11}W_{22} - K_{12}K_{21}W_{12}W_{21}} \qquad (6\text{-}7\text{-}11)$$

$$N_{12} = \frac{-A_{22}P_{12}}{P_{11}P_{22} - P_{12}P_{21}} = \frac{- A_{22}K_{12}W_{12}}{K_{11} K_{22}W_{11}W_{22} - K_{12}K_{21}W_{12}W_{21}} \qquad (6\text{-}7\text{-}12)$$

Here:

$$P_{ij} = K_{ij}W_{ij} \qquad (6\text{-}7\text{-}13)$$

K_{ij} is the static gain and W_{ij} is the dynamic character.

The easiest realization conditions mean that all N_{11}, N_{12}, N_{21} and N_{22} are propotional elements. This demand is corresonding to:

(1) The static gain of A_{11} is K_{c1} and the dynamic character is W_{11}:

$$A_{11} = K_{c1}W_{11} \qquad (6\text{-}7\text{-}14)$$

(2) Similarly:

$$A_{22} = K_{c2}W_{22} \qquad (6\text{-}7\text{-}15)$$

(3) Besides:

$$\left. \begin{array}{l} W_{11} = W_{12} \\[2mm] W_{22} = W_{21} \end{array} \right\} \qquad (6\text{-}7\text{-}16)$$

or :

$$W_{11}W_{22} = W_{12}W_{21} \qquad (6\text{-}7\text{-}17)$$

Then, we get:

$$N_{11} = \frac{K_{c1}K_{22}}{K_{11}K_{22} - K_{12}K_{21}} \qquad (6\text{-}7\text{-}18)$$

$$N_{22} = \frac{K_{c2}K_{11}}{K_{11}K_{22} - K_{12}K_{21}} \qquad (6\text{-}7\text{-}19)$$

$$N_{21} = - \frac{K_{c1}K_{21}}{K_{11}K_{22} - K_{12}K_{21}} \qquad (6\text{-}7\text{-}20)$$

$$N_{22} = - \frac{K_{c2}K_{12}}{K_{11}K_{22} - K_{12}K_{21}} \qquad (6\text{-}7\text{-}21)$$

and we see that all of them are propotional elements.

What does it mean?

(6-7-16) denotes that for each controlled variable, it has the same response to every manipulated variable.

(6-7-14) and (6-7-15) denote that the dynamic control characters of the decoupled main channels are the same as those of the main channels of the coupled plant.

Then we get the following conclusions:

For a multivariable process control system, if for each controlled variable, its responses to every manipulated variables are the same, then we can choose some propotional elements given by (6-7-18) to (6-7-21) as the decoupling element characters for this decoupled system. These decoupling elements give the decoupling effects in both static and dynamic states and the characters of the decoupled channels are the same as those of the main channel characters of the coupled plant.

This is the most easily realizable decoupled system.

Obviously, the case discussed in § 4-7 is only a special case of this general conclusion.

For example, for (4-7-7) and (4-7-8), by the above conclusion, it is necessary:

$$\left.\begin{array}{l} T_{22} = T_{21} \\ T_{11} = T_{12} \end{array}\right\} \qquad (6-7-22)$$

and we get:

$$\left.\begin{array}{l} N_{12} = - \dfrac{K_{p12}}{K_{p22}} \\[3mm] N_{21} = - \dfrac{K_{p21}}{K_{p11}} \end{array}\right\} \qquad (6-7-23)$$

and both are propotional elements.

In other words, for the standard decoupling structure with $N_{11} = N_{22} = 1$, if for each controlled variable, its responses to every mani-

pulated variable have the same time constant, the the decoupling elements are some most easily realizable propotional elements.

On the contrary, let us discuss (6-7-14) and (6-7-15). We know that
just due to the application of the two conditions (6-7-14) and (6-7-15)
so we obtained the results of (6-7-18) to (6-7-21) which are the most
easily realizable conditions. This means that for the characters of the
decoupled subsystems, we had rather taking them as some dynamic expression forms than taking them as 1. Because the ideal character 1 means
difficult to be realized and (6-7-18) to (6-7-21) are very easy to be
realized. This is also to say that for the decoupling design most important attention is given to the decoupling demands and realization
conditions   as for the control demands of the decoupled sybsystems we
can adjust the gains of the regulators to meet.

In some cases, it is possible that for each manipulated variable
it has the same responses to all controlled variables, i.e.

$$\left. \begin{aligned} W_{11} &= W_{21} \\ W_{22} &= W_{12} \end{aligned} \right\} \qquad (6\text{-}7\text{-}24)$$

then:

$$\left. \begin{aligned} A_{11} &= K_{c1}W_{11} = K_{c1}W_{21} \\ A_{22} &= K_{c2}W_{22} = K_{c2}W_{12} \end{aligned} \right\} \qquad (6\text{-}7\text{-}25)$$

The characters of the decoupling elements are:

$$\left. \begin{aligned} N_{11} &= \frac{K_{c1}K_{22}}{K_{11}K_{22} - K_{12}K_{21}} \\[2ex] N_{22} &= \frac{K_{c2}K_{11}}{K_{11}K_{22} - K_{12}K_{21}} \\[2ex] N_{12} &= \frac{-K_{c1}K_{21}}{K_{11}K_{22} - K_{12}K_{21}} \frac{W_{21}}{W_{12}} \\[2ex] N_{21} &= \frac{-K_{c2}K_{12}}{K_{11}K_{22} - K_{12}K_{21}} \frac{W_{12}}{W_{21}} \end{aligned} \right\} \qquad (6\text{-}7\text{-}26)$$

Among them, N_{11} and N_{22} are propotional elements and the other two are not.

§ 6-8 The Forms of the Decoupled Systems

When a multivariable process control system is decoupled, it is reduced to several separate subsystems and the design of these decoupled systems can be done according to the single variable control system theory. This is just the logical procedure of decoupling design discussed before.

But, what are the forms of the decoupled subsystems ? Are they obtained by simply breaking off all coupling channels and decoupling channels in the systems?

We happened to meet such a problem before and now we are going to give a special discussion.

We still discuss a two-variable system.

In §4-4, we discussed a system with P-canonical plant and decoupling element structure and the decoupling elements are located between the regulators and the plant. The decoupled subsystems are:

$$
\left. \begin{array}{l}
C_1 = \dfrac{Z_1}{1 + Z_1} X_1 \\[3mm]
C_2 = \dfrac{Z_4}{1 + Z_4} X_2
\end{array} \right\}
\qquad (6-8-1)
$$

where:

$$
\left. \begin{array}{l}
Z_1 = (N_{11}P_{11} + N_{21}P_{12})R_{11} \\[3mm]
Z_4 = (N_{22}P_{22} + N_{12}P_{21})R_{22}
\end{array} \right\}
\qquad (6-8-2)
$$

Obviously, the open loop characters of the decoupled subsystems are not the same as those of the main channels of the coupled system :

$$Z_1 \neq N_{11}P_{11}R_{11}$$
$$Z_2 \neq N_{22}P_{22}R_{22}$$

(6-8-3)

In other words, the decoupled subsystems are not equal to those wchich are obtained by simply breaking off the coupling channels and decoupling channels in this system. This means that , taking N_{21} as an example, the aim of introduction of such a channel is to eliminate the coupling effect of the first channel to the second channel and this aim is reached indeed, but, however, it provides an additional channel for the first main channel at the meantime, i.e. $N_{11}P_{12}$. This additional channel should be considered in the analysis of decoupled subsystem characters.

Now, we discuss the case when the decoupling element structure is combined with the regulators. Such a system is shown in Fig 6-8-1.

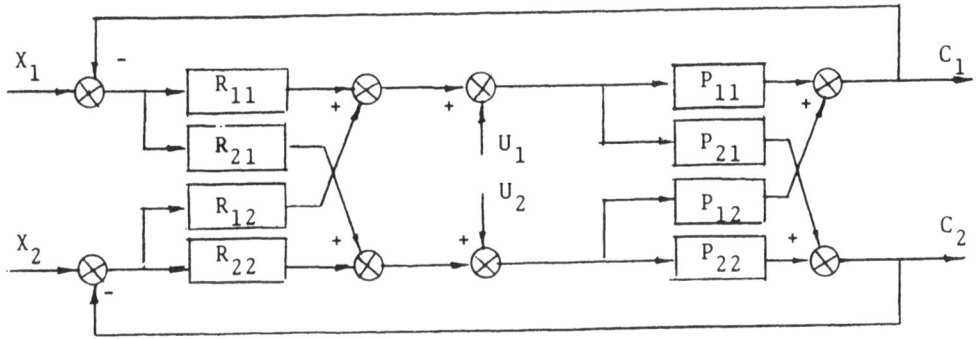

Fig 6-8-1

We know that for this system it can realize the decoupling control between outputs and reference inputs but can not realize the decoupling relations between outputs and supply disturbances with the same decoupling structure. Thus, we have:

$$C_1 = P_{11}U_1 + P_{12}U_2 + (P_{11}R_{11} + P_{12}R_{21})(X_1 - C_1) \quad (6-8-4)$$
$$C_2 = P_{22}U_2 + P_{21}U_1 + (P_{22}R_{22} + P_{21}R_{12})(X_2 - C_2) \quad (6-8-5)$$

Let:

$$P_{11}R_{11} + P_{12}R_{21} = A_{11}$$
$$P_{22}R_{22} + P_{21}R_{12} = A_{22}$$

(6-8-6)

then we get:

$$C_1 = \frac{P_{11}U_1 + P_{12}U_2 + A_{11}X_1}{1 + A_{11}} \qquad (6-8-7)$$

$$C_2 = \frac{P_{22}U_2 + P_{21}U_1 + A_{22}X_2}{1 + A_{22}} \qquad (6-8-8)$$

From these two expressions, we know:

(1) $A_{11} \neq R_{11}P_{11}$, $A_{22} \neq R_{22}P_{22}$. This means that the decoupled subsystems are not equal to those obtained by simply breaking off all coupling channels and decoupling channels,

(2) In C_1 there is a term caused by U_2 and in C_2 there is a term caused by U_1 . This means that in this decoupled system, the coupling influence of the supply disturbances still exists. This is in accordance with the conclusions obtained before.

In summary, for the systems with P-canonical plants and P-canonical decoupling element structures , the decoupled subsystems obtained by using feedforward decoupling projects in general are not equal to those obtained by simply breaking off all coupling channels and decoupling channels in the original coupled systems.

But, in some special cases, these two results may be equal. For example, the ideal control is so because the ideal decoupling system is just designed as that obtained by simply breaking all coupling channels and decoupling channels.

In this case, the decoupling elements must be:

$$\begin{pmatrix} N_{11} & N_{12} \\ N_{21} & N_{22} \end{pmatrix} = \begin{pmatrix} \dfrac{P_{11}P_{22}}{P_{11}P_{22} - P_{12}P_{21}} & \dfrac{-P_{22}P_{12}}{P_{11}P_{22} - P_{12}P_{21}} \\ \dfrac{-P_{11}P_{21}}{P_{11}P_{22} - P_{12}P_{21}} & \dfrac{P_{11}P_{22}}{P_{11}P_{22} - P_{12}P_{21}} \end{pmatrix}$$

$$(6-8-9)$$

Now, we discuss another case: The system is with a P-canonical plant but the decoupling element structure is V-canonical. Suppose that the feedforward decoupling project is adopted and the system is shown in Fig 6-8-2.

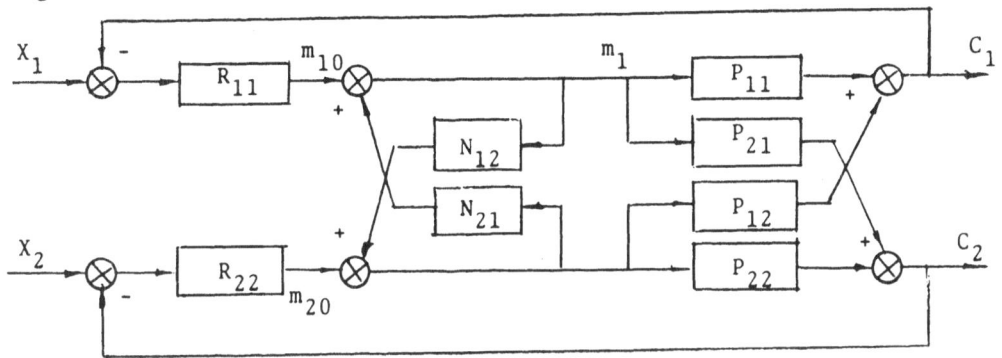

Fig 6-8-2

For it, we have:

$$m_1 = \frac{m_{10} + N_{12}m_{20}}{1 - N_{12}N_{21}} \tag{6-8-10}$$

$$m_2 = \frac{m_{20} + N_{21}m_{10}}{1 - N_{12}N_{21}} \tag{6-8-11}$$

Therefore:

$$C_1 = \frac{1}{1 - N_{12}N_{21}} ((P_{11} + P_{12}N_{21})m_{10} + (P_{12} + P_{11}N_{12})m_{20}) \tag{6-8-12}$$

$$C_2 = \frac{1}{1 - N_{12}N_{21}} ((P_{21} + P_{22}N_{21})m_{10} + (P_{22} + P_{21}N_{12})m_{20}) \tag{6-8-13}$$

and the decoupling conditions are:

$$\left. \begin{array}{l} P_{12} + P_{11}N_{12} = 0 \\[2mm] P_{21} + P_{22}N_{21} = 0 \end{array} \right\} \tag{6-8-14}$$

It follows:

$$N_{12} = - \frac{P_{12}}{P_{11}} \tag{6-8-15}$$

$$N_{21} = - \frac{P_{21}}{P_{22}} \tag{6-8-16}$$

Then, for the decoupled subsystems, we have:

$$\frac{C_1}{m_{10}} = \frac{P_{11} + P_{12}N_{21}}{1 - N_{12}N_{21}} = \frac{P_{11} + P_{12}(-\dfrac{P_{21}}{P_{22}})}{1 - (-\dfrac{P_{12}}{P_{11}})(-\dfrac{P_{21}}{P_{22}})} =$$

$$= \frac{\dfrac{1}{P_{22}}(P_{11}P_{22} - P_{12}P_{21})}{\dfrac{1}{P_{11}P_{22}}(P_{11}P_{22} - P_{12}P_{21})} = P_{11} \qquad (6\text{-}8\text{-}17)$$

similarly:

$$\frac{C_2}{m_{20}} = P_{22} \qquad (6\text{-}9\text{-}18)$$

Thus, for the systems with P-canonical plants , V-canonical decoupling element structures and feedforward decoupling projects, the
decoupled subsystems are just equal to those obtained by simply breaking off all coupling channels and decoupling channels.

The decoupled system of the discussed two-variable system is
shown in Fig 6-8-3.

Take the flow control
system of Fig 1-10-2 as an
exmple; when the above decoupling design is carried
out to it, then the system
block diagram is shown bellow.

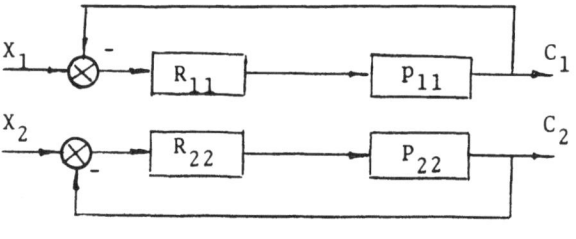

Fig 6-8-3

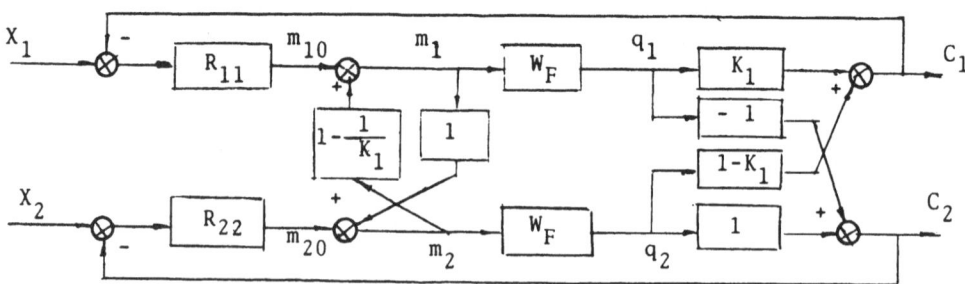

Fig 6-8-4

By (6-8-15) and (6-8-16), the decoupling elements are:

$$N_{12} = - \frac{P_{12}}{P_{11}} = - \frac{1 - K_1}{K_1} = 1 - \frac{1}{K_1}$$

$$N_{21} = - \frac{P_{21}}{P_{22}} = 1$$

(6-8-19)

and the decoupled subsystems are:

$$\frac{C_1}{m_{10}} = K_1 W_F$$

$$\frac{C_2}{m_{20}} = W_F$$

(6-8-20)

where, C_1 and C_2 are flow and temperarure, respectively.

From (1-10-5) we know $K_1 + K_2 = 1$, so neither K_1 nor K_2 is larger than 1 and in order to control the flow effectively, we should choose K_1 larger than 0.5.

The control operation of these two decoupled subsystems is carried out so: When the flow is expected to change, i.e. there is a change of X_1, then two control valves will open (or close) in the same direction and when the temperature is expected to change, i.e . there is a change in X_2 , then due to the negative value of $1 - \frac{1}{K_1}$ the two valves will move in opposite directions.

This means that even the system is decoupled and two separate subsystems are formed, but the control operations of each subsystem are still related to the other, so in this sense the decoupled subsystems are not some simple isolated systems.

Now, we discuss the systems with V-canonical plants.

We have proved in §4-14 that for the systems with V-canonical plants and feedback decoupling projects, the decoupled subsystems are just equal to those obtained by simply breaking off all coupling channels and decoupling channels. The scheme is shown in Fig 6-8-5.

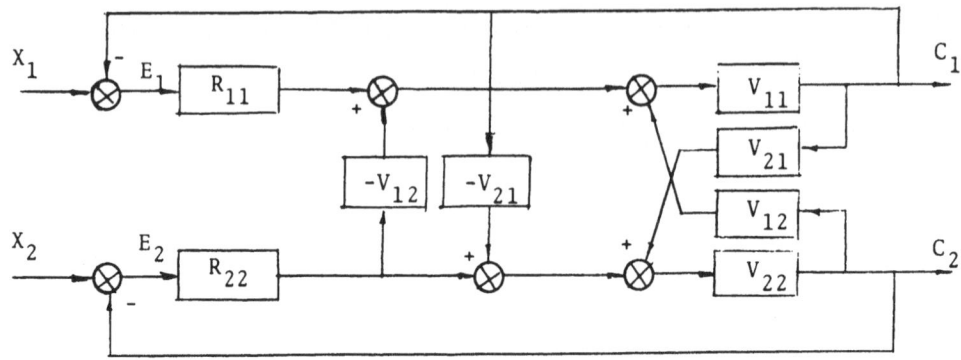

Fig 6-8-5

For the decoupled subsystems, we have:

$$\frac{C_1}{E_1} = R_{11}V_{11}$$

$$\left.\begin{array}{c}\\\\\\\\\end{array}\right\} \qquad (6\text{-}8\text{-}21)$$

$$\frac{C_2}{E_2} = R_{22}V_{22}$$

Therefore , they are just those obtained by simply breaking off all coupling channels and decoupling channels.

From this paragraph we get a conclusion : For all systems with V-canonical stuctures, no matter V-canonical plants or V-canonical de-coupling structures, the decoupled subsystems may be those obtained by simply breaking off coupling channels and decoupling channels.

This is also a practical meaning of Mesarović idea.

§ 6-9 The Realization Conditions of Static Decoupling[21]

All the contents discussed above are available to both dynamic decoupling and static decoupling. Certeinly, it is our desire that we can realize the dynamic decoupling control. But, however, the above discussions show two problems met very often:

(1) The decoupling elements may be physically irrealizable.

(2) Even though they may be realizable, their transfer functions

may have very complex forms. When the variable number is larger than 2, the case is more evident.

So, sometimes we have to use the static decoupling control. Certainly, this means that the control demands have been depressed , i.e. the dynamic decoupling control is not expected and only the static decoupling control is demanded, but for many process control systems, it is enough to realize the static decoupling control.

Obviously, decoupling elements are also needed for realizing static decoupling control, but the realization conditions for the static decoupling control are less and simpler than those for dynamic decoupling control.

Then, how to realize the static decoupling control?

We analyze a single variable system at first. For such a system, we have:

$$C(S) = G(S)X(S) \qquad (6-9-1)$$

where G(S) is the system transfer function.

If the input is a step function, then the static value of the output is:

$$C(t)\Big|_{t \to \infty} = \lim_{S \to 0} SG(S)X(S) = G(0) \qquad (6-9-2)$$

Thus, in the single variable control systems, the static values of the system responses can be obtained by setting S=0 in their transfer functions.

Is this principle also available in multivariable process control systems ?

In fact, we used such a conclusion before, but we did not give any proof.

This means that we do not search any other design method for realizing static decoupling control , but get it by setting S= 0 in the dynamic decoupling elements (the integral terms are not included).

Two problems should be discussed here:

(1) For the dynamic decoupling element matrices, if we set S=0 in them (the integral terms are not included), are the results certainly available for static decoupling control ?

(2) What systems can realize static decoupling control?

We will not give strict proof on these problems here because it is beyond the scope of our book and readers can find the proof in Wolowich's work. Wolovich proved these problems by using state variable method.

His results are:

If there are no zeros at S=0 for the diagonal elements of the closed-loop system transfer matrix satisfying the dynamic decoupling control demands, then the system can realize the static decoupling control by setting S = 0 in this matrix.

The diagonal elements of the closed-loop transfer matrix with zeros at S = 0 means to realize differential control, but, in process control engineering practice, we never expect to realize differential control, so the above conclusion is available in practice.

§ 6-10 The General Realization Conditions for Multivariable Feedforward Control Systems (34)

In Chapter 2, we expounded the application of the feedforward control projects to the single vaiable systems. The research results show if the disturbances are measurable, then the feedforward control systems can be adopted to eliminate the influence of the disturbances on the outputs.

Because most practical process control systems are closed-loop, so the application of feedforward control principles is often combined with feedback control systems.

In § 5-9, we discussed the combinaton of decoupling design with feedforward control projects to perform the decoupling control with full distubance-rejection for a two-variable system.

Now, we discuss the more general problems of the application of feedforward control projects.

At first, we discuss a multivariable plant. For such a plant, it may accept three kinds of inputs, i.e.

(1) Some unknown disturbances and they can not be measured either. Suppowe that there are N such disturbances.

(2) Some known disturbances but they can not be regulated by this control system. There are K of them.

(3) Some manipulated variables and they can be regulated by this control system and, consequently, they are the direct factors to influence the outputs. There are M of them.

For a multivariable system, all of these three plant inputs are expressed by vectors as U_{Ux1} , K_{Kx1} and M_{Mx1}, respectively.

The output of the plant is also a vector with the form of C_{Cx1}.

The control character of the plant is a matrix with C outputs and (U + K + M) inputs: $P_{Cx(U+K+M)}$.

Therefore, the output of the plant can be written as:

$$C_{Cx1} = P_{Cx(U+K+M)} \begin{pmatrix} U_{Ux1} \\ \hline K_{Kx1} \\ \hline M_{Mx1} \end{pmatrix}_{(U+K+M)x1} \qquad (6\text{-}10\text{-}1)$$

where dotted lines show that the matrix is blocked.

The relation can be illustrated by Fig 6-10-1.

Now, we discuss how to eliminated the influence of disturbances to system outputs.

In order to do so, the feedforward control projects are adopted.

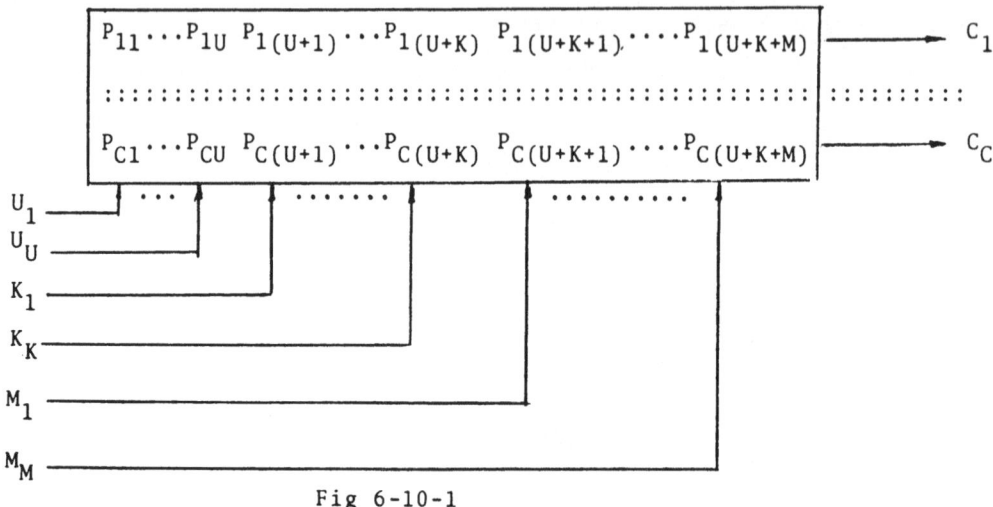

Fig 6-10-1

Because the disturbances K_{Kx1} are measurable, so the feedforward channels can be derived from K_{Kx1}.

Now, suppose that the manipulated variables M_{Mx1} are just
obtained from the disturbances K_{Kx1}
through the feedforward channels
F_{MxK} , namely:

$$M_{Kx1} = F_{MxK}K_{Kx1} \qquad (6-10-2)$$

then (6-10-1) becomes:

$$C_{Cx1} = P_{Cx(U+K+M)} \begin{bmatrix} U_{Ux1} \\ ---------- \\ K_{Kx1} \\ ---------- \\ F_{MxK}K_{Kx1} \end{bmatrix}_{(U+K+M)x1} \qquad (6-10-3)$$

The general form of Fig 6-10-2 then becomes Fig 6-10-3.

Now, we divide the plant matrix
$P_{Cx(U+K+M)}$ into three sub-matrices,
i.e. $\mathbf{P_{CxU}}$, P_{CxK} and P_{CxM}. They
accept the inputs U_{Ux1}, K_{Kx1} and
M_{Mx1}, respectively.

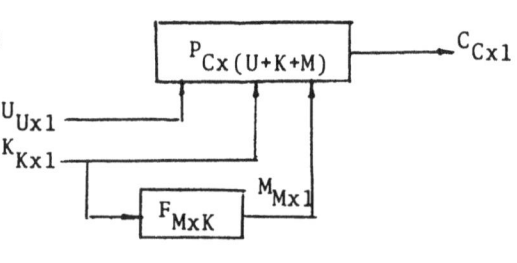

Fig 6-8-3

Then (6-10-3) may be written as:

$$C_{Cx1} = (\ P_{CxU}U_{Ux1} + P_{CxK}K_{Kx1} + P_{CxM}F_{MxK}K_{Kx1}\ )_{Cx1} =$$

$$= (\ P_{CxU}U_{Ux1} + (\ P_{CxK} + P_{CxM}F_{MxK})K_{Kx1}\ )_{Cx1} =$$

$$= (\ P_{CxU} \mid P_{Cxk} + P_{CxM}F_{MxK}\ )\begin{pmatrix} U_{Ux1} \\ \text{------} \\ K_{Kx1} \end{pmatrix}_{Cx1} \qquad (6\text{-}10\text{-}4)$$

Therefore, Fig 8-10-3 can be reduced to Fig 6-10-4.

Let:

$$P_{Cx(U+K)}^{\sim} = (\ P_{CxU}^{\sim} \mid P_{CxK}\ ) =$$

$$= (\ P_{CxU} \mid P_{Cxk} + P_{CxM}F_{MxK}\ )$$

$$\qquad\qquad (6\text{-}10\text{-}5)$$

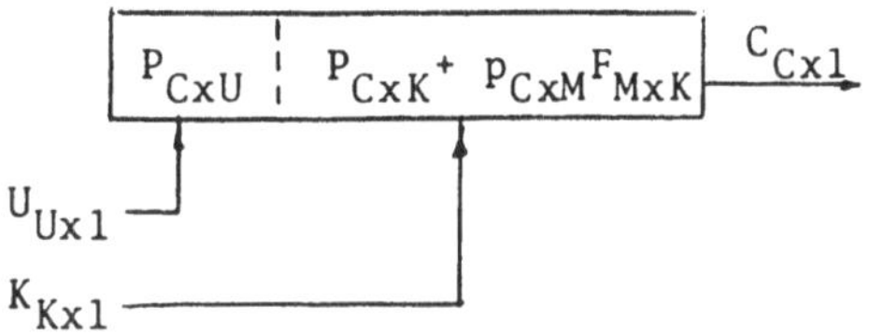

Fig 6-10-4

then from (6-10-4) and (6-10-5) we get:

$$C_{Cx1} = P_{Cx(U+K)}^{\sim}\begin{pmatrix} U_{Ux1} \\ \text{-------} \\ K_{Kx1} \end{pmatrix}_{(U+K)x1} \qquad\qquad (6\text{-}10\text{-}6)$$

and Fig 6-10-4 is reduced to Fig 6-10-5 further.

(6-10-6) denotes the influence results of the disturbances U_{Ux1} and K_{Kx1} to the system when the feed-forward compensation is adopted.

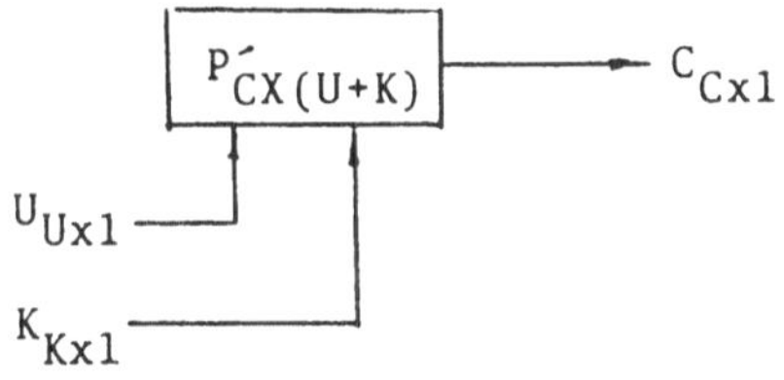

Fig 6-10-5

At first, we see :

$$P_{CxU} = P_{CxU}^{\sim} \qquad\qquad (6\text{-}10\text{-}7)$$

and this means that the feedforward compensation gives no influence on the responses caused by the unknown disturbances. Certainly, this conclusion is logical and reasonable. But:

$$P_{CxK}^{\sim} = P_{CxK} + P_{CxM}F_{MxK} \qquad\qquad (6\text{-}10\text{-}8)$$

and this means that the feedforward compensation will give remarkable influence on the responses caused by the measurable disturbances K_{Kx1}.

The most ideal control is to make $P_{Cxk}^{\sim}$ be a zero matrix, then the influence of the measurable disturbances K_{Kx1} on the system responses will be eliminated. Because of (6-10-8) this is possible.

Let us consider an example. Suppose:

$$\begin{pmatrix} C_1 \\ C_2 \end{pmatrix} = \begin{pmatrix} \dfrac{1}{T_1 S + 1} & \dfrac{-K_1}{(T_1 S+1)(T_2 S+1)} & \dfrac{K_2 - K_1 K_3 + K_2 T_2 S}{(T_1 S+1)(T_2 S+1)} & \dfrac{K_4}{T_1 S+1} \\[2ex] 0 & \dfrac{K_5}{T_2 S + 1} & \dfrac{K_3 K_5}{T_2 S + 1} & 0 \end{pmatrix} \begin{pmatrix} q_1 \\ q_2 \\ q_3 \\ q_4 \end{pmatrix}$$

$$(6-10-9)$$

and: $K_1 > 0$, $K_2 > 0$, $K_3 < 0$, $K_4 > 0$, $K_5 > 0$.

If $U_{Ux1} = 0$, then:

$$K_{Kx1} = \begin{pmatrix} q_1 \\ q_2 \end{pmatrix} \qquad M_{Mx1} = \begin{pmatrix} q_3 \\ q_4 \end{pmatrix}$$

The feedforward compensation matrix is assumed to be:

$$F_{MxK} = \begin{pmatrix} 0 & -\dfrac{1}{K_3} \\[2ex] -\dfrac{1}{K_4} & \dfrac{K_2}{K_3 K_4} \end{pmatrix}_{2x2} \qquad (6-10-10)$$

We will explain later why the feedforward compensation matrix should be with this form.

Substituting the above expressions into (6-10-8), we get:

$$P'_{CxM} = (P_{CxK} + P_{CxM} F_{MxK}) =$$

$$= \begin{pmatrix} \dfrac{1}{T_1 S + 1} & \dfrac{-K_1}{(T_1 S + 1)(T_2 S + 1)} \\[2ex] 0 & \dfrac{K_5}{T_2 S + 1} \end{pmatrix} +$$

$$+ \begin{pmatrix} \dfrac{K_2 - K_1 K_2 + K_1 T_2 S}{(T_1 S+1)(T_2 S+1)} & \dfrac{1}{T_1 S + 1} \\[2ex] \dfrac{K_3 K_5}{T_2 S + 1} & 0 \end{pmatrix} \begin{pmatrix} 0 & \dfrac{-1}{K_3} \\[2ex] \dfrac{-1}{K_4} & \dfrac{K_2}{K_3 K_4} \end{pmatrix} =$$

$$= \begin{pmatrix} 0 & 0 \\ 0 & 0 \end{pmatrix} \qquad (6\text{-}10\text{-}11)$$

Therefore, when such a feedforward compensation is adopted, the influence of the disturbances K_{Kx1} on the outputs is eliminated. That is to say that the feedforward compensation can be effectively used to eliminate the influence of the measurable disturbances.

Now, we suppose that in these disturbances, q_2 is an unmeasurable disturbance. Thus, the feedforward compensation matrix F_{MxK} becomes F_{2x1} because only the measurable disturbance can provide necessary information.

We have:

$$F_{2x1} = \begin{pmatrix} 0 \\ -\dfrac{1}{K_4} \end{pmatrix} \qquad (6\text{-}10\text{-}12)$$

and $U_{Ux1} = q_2$, $K_{Kx1} = q_1$.

Substituting them into (6-10-5) yields:

$$P_{Cx(U+K)}^{-} = \left[\left[\begin{pmatrix} -\dfrac{K_1}{(T_1S+1)(T_2S+1)} \\ \dfrac{K_5}{T_2S+1} \end{pmatrix} \middle| \left\{ \begin{pmatrix} \dfrac{1}{T_1S+1} \\ 0 \end{pmatrix} \right. \right. \right. +$$

$$+ \begin{pmatrix} \dfrac{K_2-K_1K_3+K_2T_2S}{(T_1S+1)(T_2S+1)} & \dfrac{K_4}{T_1S+1} \\ \dfrac{K_1K_3}{T_2S+1} & 0 \end{pmatrix} \left. \begin{pmatrix} 0 \\ -\dfrac{1}{K_4} \end{pmatrix} \right\} \right] = \begin{pmatrix} \dfrac{-K_1}{(T_1S+1)(T_2S+1)} & 0 \\ \dfrac{K_5}{T_2S+1} & 0 \end{pmatrix}$$

$$\qquad (6\text{-}10\text{-}13)$$

and:

$$C_{Cx1} = \begin{pmatrix} \dfrac{-K_1}{(T_1S+1)(T_2S+1)} & 0 \\ \dfrac{K_5}{T_2S+1} & 0 \end{pmatrix} \begin{pmatrix} q_2 \\ q_1 \end{pmatrix} \qquad (6\text{-}10\text{-}14)$$

Thus, the influence of the measurable disturbances has been eliminated by the feedforward compensation channels, but the influence of the
unmeasurable disturbances is remained and the feedforward compensation
channels gives no effects on these disturbances.

The condition of realizing full rejection to the measurable disturbances is:

$$P\acute{C}_{CxK} = P_{CxK} + P_{CxM}F_{MxK} = 0_{CxK} \tag{6-10-15}$$

namely the result is a zero matrix.

In process control systems, in general C = M, i.e. the number of the
outputs is equal to the number of manipulated variables, and when P_{CxM}
is a non-singular matrix, we can soon get F_{MxK} :

$$F_{MxK} = - (P_{CxM})^{-1}P_{CxK} \tag{6-10-16}$$

For the above example, because C = M and:

$$\left| P_{CxM} \right| = \begin{vmatrix} \dfrac{-K_2 - K_1K_3 + K_2T_2S}{(T_1S + 1)(T_2S + 1)} & \dfrac{K_4}{T_1S + 1} \\ \dfrac{K_3K_5}{T_2S + 1} & 0 \end{vmatrix} \neq 0 \tag{6-10-17}$$

so we have:

$$F_{MxK} = - \begin{Bmatrix} 0 & \dfrac{T_2S + 1}{K_3K_5} \\ \dfrac{T_1S + 1}{K_4} & \dfrac{-K_2 - K_1K_3 + K_2T_2S}{-K_3K_4K_5} \end{Bmatrix} \begin{Bmatrix} \dfrac{1}{T_1S + 1} & \dfrac{-K_1}{(T_1S+1)(T_2S+1)} \\ 0 & \dfrac{K_5}{T_2S + 1} \end{Bmatrix}$$

$$= \begin{Bmatrix} 0 & -\dfrac{1}{K_3} \\ -\dfrac{1}{K_4} & \dfrac{K_2}{K_3K_4} \end{Bmatrix} \tag{6-10-18}$$

This is just the result of (6-10-10).

When the number of the manipulatecd variables is not equal to that of the outputs, then (6-10-16) is unavailable. If the manipulated variables are less than the outputs, then it is impossible to realize the full rejection to the disturbances and when the manipulated variables are more than the outputs, then there are infinite solutions for this problem.

For example, in the above example suppose:

$$U = 0 \ , \ K = 2 \ , \ M = 2 \ , \ C = 1.$$

then:

$$P_{Cx(K+M)} = \left[\frac{1}{T_1 S + 1} \quad \frac{-K_1}{(T_1 S+1)(T_2 S+1)} \quad \frac{K_2 - K_1 K_3 + K_2 T_2 S}{(T_1 S+1)(T_2 S+1)} \quad \frac{K_4}{T_1 S + 1} \right]$$

$$(6-10-19)$$

and:

$$K_{Kx1} = \begin{bmatrix} q_1 \\ q_2 \end{bmatrix} \qquad M_{Mx1} = \begin{bmatrix} q_3 \\ q_4 \end{bmatrix} \qquad C_{Cx1} = C_1$$

Because $C \neq M$, so (6-10-18) is unavailable and:

$$P_{CxM} = \left[\frac{K_2 - K_1 K_3 + K_2 T_2 S}{(T_1 S + 1)(T_2 S + 1)} \quad \frac{K_4}{T_1 S + 1} \right] \qquad (6-10-20)$$

The influences of q_1 and q_2 on C_1 are exerted through the first two terms of $P_{Cx(K+M)}$ and the influences of two manipulated variables on C_1 are through the latter two terms of $P_{Cx(K+M)}$, therefore if the manipulated variables are caused by the disturbances q_1 and q_2 through the feedforward compensation elements: f_{11}, f_{12}, f_{21} and f_{22} and let:

$$\frac{K_2 - K_1 K_3 + K_2 T_2 S}{(T_1 S+1)(T_2 S+1)} f_{11} + \frac{K_4}{T_1 S + 1} f_{21} = - \frac{1}{T_1 S + 1} \qquad (6-10-21)$$

$$\frac{K_2 - K_1 K_3 + K_2 T_2 S}{(T_1 S+1)(T_2 S+1)} f_{11} + \frac{K_4}{T_1 S + 1} f_{22} = - \frac{K_1}{(T_1 S+1)(T_2 S+1)} \qquad (6-10-22)$$

then the influences of the disturbances q_1 and q_2 on the output are eliminated.

Here, f_{11} , f_{12}, f_{21} and f_{22} form a feedforward compensation element matrix:

$$F_{MxK} = \begin{pmatrix} f_{11} & f_{12} \\ f_{21} & f_{22} \end{pmatrix} \qquad (6\text{-}10\text{-}23)$$

From (6-10-21) and (6-10-22) we can see that there are four unknowns but only two equations, so there are infinite solutions.

We can choose two of them freely, for example let:

$$f_{11} = f_{12} = 0 \qquad (6\text{-}10\text{-}24)$$

then :

$$f_{21} = -\frac{1}{K_4} \qquad (6\text{-}10\text{-}25)$$

$$f_{22} = \frac{K_1}{K_4(T_2S + 1)} \qquad (6\text{-}10\text{-}24)$$

§ 6-11 The General Realization Principles for Multivariable Feedforward-Feedback Combined Control Systems [34]

The above analysis denotes that the feedforward control projects can eliminate the influences of the measurable disturbances on system outputs but they can not eliminate the influences caused by the unmeasurable disturbances, in fact these projects have no effects on unmeasurable disturbances. In addition, the elimination of the influences of the measurable disturbances is obtained by strict conditions and when these conditions are destroied, then the influences of the measurable disturbances still exist.

In order to get more credible control, we can introduce feedback and design the feedforward-feedback combined control systems.

In such a system, the outputs caused by the disturbances are measured and fed back through a feedback transfer matrix B_{MxC}. Each element in this matrix is an independent feedback transfer function and all feedback elements are connected with the manipulated variables which cause the outputs.

Then, the transfer matrix of the manipulated variables becomes:

$$M_{Mx1} = F_{MxK}K_{Kx1} + B_{MxC}C_{Cx1} \qquad (6\text{-}11\text{-}1)$$

Substituting (6-11-1) into (6-10-1) yields:

$$C_{Cx1} = P_{Cx(U+K+M)} \begin{pmatrix} U_{Ux1} \\ \hline K_{Kx1} \\ \hline F_{MxK}K_{Kx1} + B_{MxC}C_{Cx1} \end{pmatrix}_{(U+K+M)x1} \qquad (6\text{-}11\text{-}2)$$

It is illustrated in Fig 6-11-1.

It denotes that the manipultated variables are influenced by disturbances through F_{MxK} and outputs through B_{MxC}.

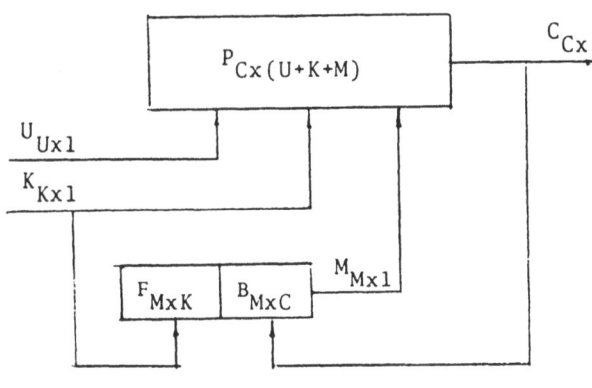

Fig 6-11-1

Expanding (6-11-2) yields:

$$C_{Cx1} = P_{CxU}U_{Ux1} + P_{CxK}K_{Kx1} + P_{CxM}F_{MxK}K_{Kx1} + P_{CxM}B_{MxC}C_{Cx1} \qquad (6\text{-}11\text{-}3)$$

It can be reduced further to:

$$C_{Cx1} = \left[P_{CxU} \mid P_{CxK} + P_{CxM}F_{MxK} \right] \begin{pmatrix} U_{Ux1} \\ \hline K_{Kx1} \end{pmatrix}_{(U+K)x1} +$$

$$+ P_{CxM}B_{MxC}C_{Cx1} \qquad (6\text{-}11\text{-}4)$$

and:

$$C_{Cx1} = \left[I_{CxC} - P_{CxM}B_{MxC} \right]^{-1} \left[P_{CxU} \mid P_{CxK} + P_{CxM}F_{MxK} \right] \begin{bmatrix} U_{Ux1} \\ ----- \\ K_{Kx1} \end{bmatrix}_{(U+K)x1}$$

$$(6-11-5)$$

We still define:

$$P'_{Cx(U+K)} = \left[P'_{CxU} \mid P'_{CxK} \right] = \left[P_{CxU} \mid P_{CxK} + P_{CxM}F_{MxK} \right] \qquad (6-11-6)$$

then:

$$C_{Cx1} = P''_{CxC}P'_{Cx(U+K)} \begin{bmatrix} U_{Ux1} \\ -------- \\ K_{Kx1} \end{bmatrix}_{(U+K)x1} =$$

$$= P'''_{Cx(U+K)} \begin{bmatrix} U_{Ux1} \\ ------- \\ K_{Kx1} \end{bmatrix}_{(U+K)x1} \qquad (6-11-7)$$

where:

$$P''_{CxC} = \left[I_{CxC} - P_{CxM}B_{MxC} \right]^{-1} \qquad (6-11-8)$$

$$P'''_{Cx(U+K)} = P''_{CxC}P'_{Cx(U+K)} \qquad (6-11-9)$$

(6-10-4),(6-11-5) and (6-11-9) are illustrated in Fig 6-11-2, Fig 6-11-3 and Fig 6-11-4, respectively.

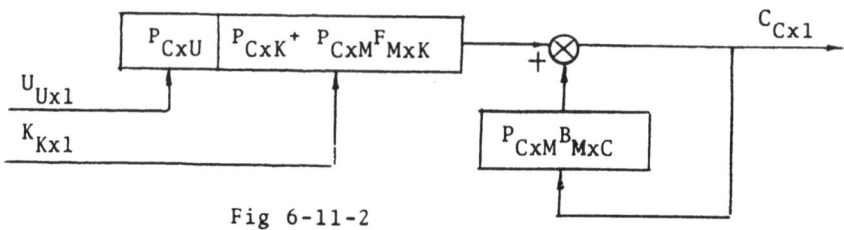

Fig 6-11-2

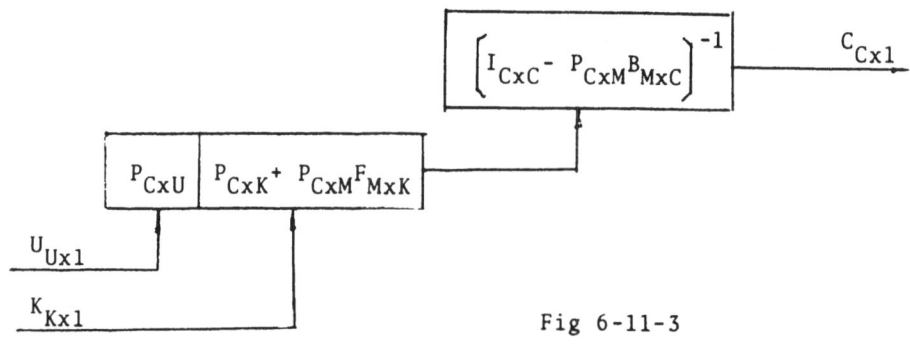

Fig 6-11-3

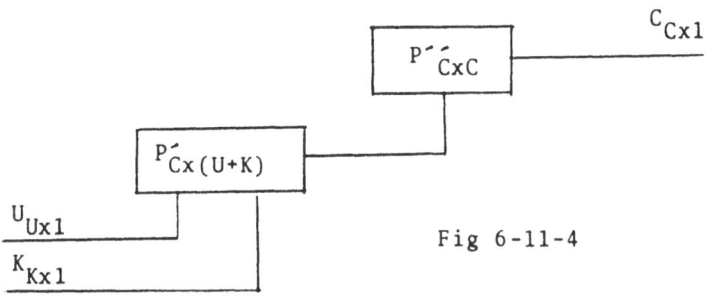

$$C_{Cx1}$$

$$P''_{CxC}$$

$$P'_{Cx(U+K)}$$

$$U_{Ux1}$$

$$K_{Kx1}$$

Fig 6-11-4

From Fig 6-11-4 we can see that the relation between U and C is no longer the original plant transfer matrix and becomes the serial connection of P''_{CxC} and $P'_{Cx(U+K)}$. This means that the relation between U and C has changed but that it will increase the influence of U or decrease the influence of U should be determined by the practical design. Now, we discuss the example of §6-10 again. Suppose that in this example, the feedback transfer matrix is:

$$B_{MxC} = \begin{pmatrix} 0 & B_{12} \\ B_{21} & -B_{12}\dfrac{K_2 - K_1 K_3 + K_2 T_2 S}{K_4(T_2 S + 1)} \end{pmatrix}_{2x2} \qquad (6\text{-}11\text{-}10)$$

where both B_{12} and B_{21} are under determination.

By the definition of P'' , we have :

$$P''_{CxC} = \left[\left(\begin{bmatrix} 1 & 0 \\ 0 & 1 \end{bmatrix} - \begin{pmatrix} \dfrac{K_2-K_1 K_3 + K_2 T_2 S}{(T_1 S+1)(T_2 S+1)} & \dfrac{K_4}{T_1 S + 1} \\ \dfrac{K_3 K_5}{T_2 S + 1} & 0 \end{pmatrix} \right. \right. \times$$

$$\left. \left. \times \begin{pmatrix} 0 & B_{12} \\ B_{21} & -B_{12}\dfrac{K_2 - K_1 K_3 + K_2 T_2 S}{K_4(T_2 S + 1)} \end{pmatrix} \right)^{-1} \right] =$$

$$= \begin{pmatrix} 1 - B_{21}\dfrac{K_4}{T_1 S + 1} & 0 \\ \\ 0 & 1 - B_{12}\dfrac{K_3 K_5}{T_2 S + 1} \end{pmatrix}^{-1} = \begin{pmatrix} \dfrac{1}{1 - B_{21}\dfrac{K_4}{T_1 S + 1}} & 0 \\ \\ 0 & \dfrac{1}{1 - B_{12}\dfrac{K_3 K_5}{T_2 S + 1}} \end{pmatrix}$$

$$(6\text{-}11\text{-}11)$$

In addition, $P'_{Cx(U+K)}$ is given by (6-10-13).

Then, substituting (6-11-11) and (6-10-13) into (6-11-9) yields:

$$P''_{Cx(U+K)} = \begin{pmatrix} \dfrac{T_1 S + 1}{T_1 S + 1 - B_{21} K_4} & 0 \\ \\ 0 & \dfrac{T_2 S + 1}{T_2 S + 1 - B_{12} K_3 K_5} \end{pmatrix} \begin{pmatrix} \dfrac{-K_1}{(T_1 S+1)(T_2 S+1)} & 0 \\ \\ \dfrac{K_5}{T_2 S + 1} & 0 \end{pmatrix} =$$

$$= \begin{pmatrix} \dfrac{-K_1}{T_1 T_2 S^2 + (T_2 - T_2 B_{21} K_4 + T_1)S + (1 - B_{21} K_4)} & 0 \\ \\ \dfrac{K_5}{T_2 S + 1 - B_{12} K_3 K_5} & 0 \end{pmatrix} \quad (6\text{-}11\text{-}12)$$

Therefore, for the measurable disturbances, the full-rejection control is still held. This is because the feedforward compensation channels are designed by the full rejection principles.

How about the case of the unmeasurable disturbances?

From (6-11-12) we know the system stability conditions are given by :

$$\left. \begin{array}{l} B_{12} > \dfrac{1}{K_3 K_5} \\ \\ B_{21} < \dfrac{1}{K_4} \end{array} \right\} \qquad (6\text{-}11\text{-}13)$$

since $K_3 K_5 < 0$.

When B_{21} is negative with very large absolute value, then P''_{11} $\longrightarrow$ 0 and when B_{12} is negative with very large abolute value, then $P''_{12} \longrightarrow$ 0.

This means that if the feedback elements are with high gains, then the influences of the unmeasurable disturbances will be reduced remarkably.

Thus, reasonable application of feedforward compensation can eliminate the influences of the measurable disturbances and reasonable application of feedback compensation can reduce the influences of the unmeasurable disturbances remarkably. This principle is valid not only in single variable control system analysis, but also in the analysis of multivariable control systems.

CHAPTER   SEVEN

THE   BRISTOL-SHINSKEY   METHOD

§ 7-1 Introduction

Up to now, we have known the principles and the practical methods
for decoupling design.

But there are still some problems we have not discussed : (1) How
to determine the degree of interaction analytically ? (2) In a multivariable system, there may be many possible variable pairing (output-
manipulated variable pairing) relations, how to determine the interaction effects of different variable pairing relations ?(3) How to choose
the best variable pairing ? (4) Generally speaking, a multivariable
system should be decoupled in order to avoid the analysis difficulty,
but, is there any possibility that the interaction can be neglected ?
If any, what is the theory basis for determining this possibility ?

The essentiality of the above problems is : Before the decoupling
control is designed, how to determine the interaction degree for some
variable pairing relations ? If we can solve this problem , then we
will be able to find out the best variable pairing relations for this
system and to determine among which variables the most serious interaction exists. That means that we should give quantity analysis of the
system interaction and certainly this analysis is the straightforward
basis for the determination of the necessity of decoupling design.

Bristol proposed a very sophisticated and effective method to
solve the above problems and the key of his method is the relative gain
analysis. Bristol´s method has wun great success in process control engineering and has been developed by many authors, for instance Shinskey,
MaCvoy , Nisenfeld,etc. Especially Shinskey applied this method successfully to the distillation column control and his success makes this method more attractive. So, now this method is also called as Bristol-
Shinskey method. Its general concepts are discussed in this chapter.

§ 7-2 Determination of Coupling Degree by Direct Measuremenet

In the analysis of a coupled multivariable system, at first we must know the coupling degree among the variables and then we can determine whether the decoupling design is needed and how to do it.

So, we should know how to determine the coupling degree in a coupled system, especially the static coupling degree.

The most direct method is to analyze the system block diagram because the block diagram shows the relations among different variables in this system.

Let us consider a simple example which is also taken from the British broadcasting course on automatic control.

Suppose a coupled system given as Fig 7-2-1:

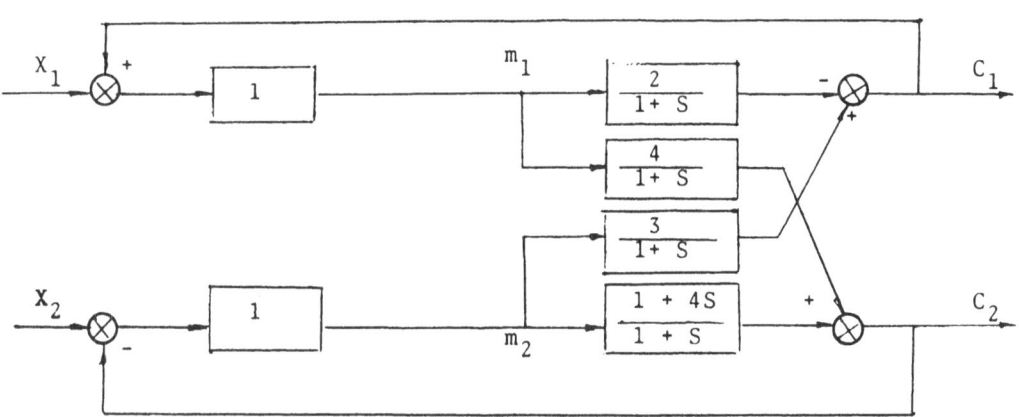

Fig 7-2-1

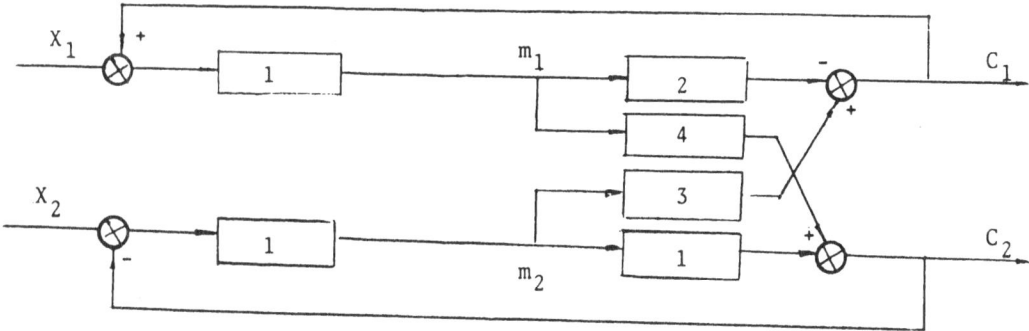

Fig 7-2-2

Because there are no integral terms in this block diagram, so we can let S = 0 for the steady state analysis and the system is reduced to Fig 7-2-2.

From Fig 7-2-2, we get:

$$m_1 = X_1 + C_1 \qquad\qquad (7\text{-}2\text{-}1)$$

$$m_2 = X_2 - C_2 \qquad\qquad (7\text{-}2\text{-}2)$$

$$C_1 = -2m_1 + 3m_2 \qquad\qquad (7\text{-}2\text{-}3)$$

$$C_2 = 4m_1 + m_2 \qquad\qquad (7\text{-}2\text{-}4)$$

Substituting (7-2-1) and (7-2-2) into (7-2-3) yields:

$$C_1 = -2X_1 - 2C_1 + 3X_2 - 3C_2 \qquad\qquad (7\text{-}2\text{-}5)$$

namely:

$$3C_1 = -2X_1 + 3X_2 - 3C_2 \qquad\qquad (7\text{-}2\text{-}6)$$

Substituting (7-2-1) and (7-2-2) into (7-2-4) yields:

$$2C_2 = 4X_1 + X_2 + 4C_1 \qquad\qquad (7\text{-}2\text{-}7)$$

Then, we substitute (7-2-7) into (7-2-6):

$$3C_1 = -2X_1 + 3X_2 - \frac{3}{2}(4X_1 + X_2 + 4C_1) \qquad\qquad (7\text{-}2\text{-}8)$$

$$6C_1 = -4X_1 + 6X_2 - 3(4X_1 + X_2 + 4C_1) \qquad\qquad (7\text{-}2\text{-}9)$$

$$18C_1 = -16X_1 + 3X_2 \qquad\qquad (7\text{-}2\text{-}10)$$

namely:

$$C_1 = - \frac{8}{9} X_1 + \frac{1}{6} X_2 \qquad\qquad (7\text{-}2\text{-}11)$$

Therefore, in the steady state, C_1 is mainly determined by X_1 but is still related to X_2. The ratio of C_1 to X_2 is:

$$\frac{C_1}{X_2} = \frac{1}{6} \qquad\qquad (7\text{-}2\text{-}12)$$

If we substitute (7-2-6) into (7-2-7), then we get:

$$2C_2 = 4X_1 = X_2 + \frac{4}{3}(-2X_1 + 3X_2 - 3C_2) \qquad\qquad (7\text{-}2\text{-}13)$$

$$6C_2 = 12X_1 + 3X_2 - 8X_1 + 12X_2 - 12C_2 \qquad\qquad (7\text{-}2\text{-}14)$$

$$18C_2 = 4X_1 + 15X_2 \qquad\qquad (7\text{-}2\text{-}15)$$

namely:

$$C_2 = \frac{2}{9} X_1 + \frac{5}{6} X_2 \qquad\qquad (7\text{-}2\text{-}16)$$

Therefore, in the steady state C_2 is mainly determined by X_2 but is still related to X_1 . The ratio of C_2 to X_1 is:

$$\frac{C_2}{X_1} = \frac{2}{9} \qquad (7-2-17)$$

We hope that the system would not have coupling. Certainly , to perform the decoupling design is the most effective way. But, however, if we do not perform the decoupling design, are there any other ways to reduce the coupling ?

Yes, there are.

For example, an effective way is to increase the gains of the re-gulators and this will reduce the system coupling.

Now, suppose that the gains of both regulators are increased from 1 to 4, then by the similar steps mentioned above, we can get:

$$C_1 = -\frac{232}{237} X_1 + \frac{12}{237} X_2 \qquad (7-2-18)$$

$$C_2 = \frac{16}{237} X_1 + \frac{228}{237} X_2 \qquad (7-2-19)$$

From these two equations we can know that in the steady state, most part of C_1 is determined by X_1 and most part of C_2 is determined by X_2. Although coupling still exists, it has been weakened very much. For example, now:

$$\left.\begin{array}{l} \dfrac{C_1}{X_2} = \dfrac{12}{237} \approx \dfrac{1}{20} \\[4mm] \dfrac{C_2}{X_1} = \dfrac{16}{237} \approx \dfrac{1}{15} \end{array}\right\} \qquad (7-2-20)$$

So, the more closely the control ratios $\dfrac{C_1}{X_1}$ and $\dfrac{C_2}{X_2}$ appro-ach to one, then also the more closely the coupling degrees $\dfrac{C_1}{X_2}$ and $\dfrac{C_2}{X_1}$ approach to zero.

Theoretically speaking, more increase of the regulator gains can reduce the coupling degree further, but the regulator gains can not be infinite because they are limited by the control indexes and stability demands. Besides, the PI regulators can only eliminate the steady state coupling and the dynamic coupling still exists.

There is another effective method capable of improving the coupling control. That is to choose more reasonable variable pairing.

In Fig 7-2-1, the output C_1 is controlled by m_1 and C_2 by m_2. Now, let us change the pairing relation of the variables , namely let C_1 be controlled by m_2 and C_2 by m_1 . Then the system block diagram will be changed to Fig 7-2-3.

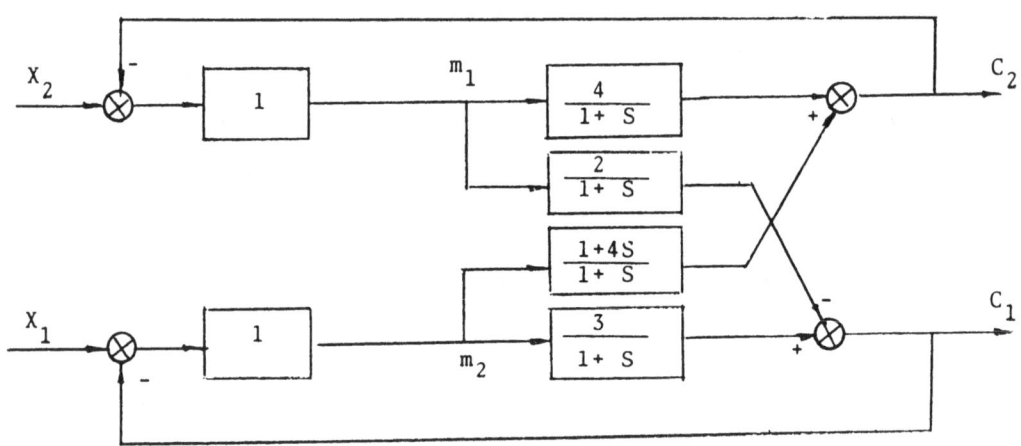

Fig 7-2-3

In steady state, this figure is reduced to Fig 7-2-4.

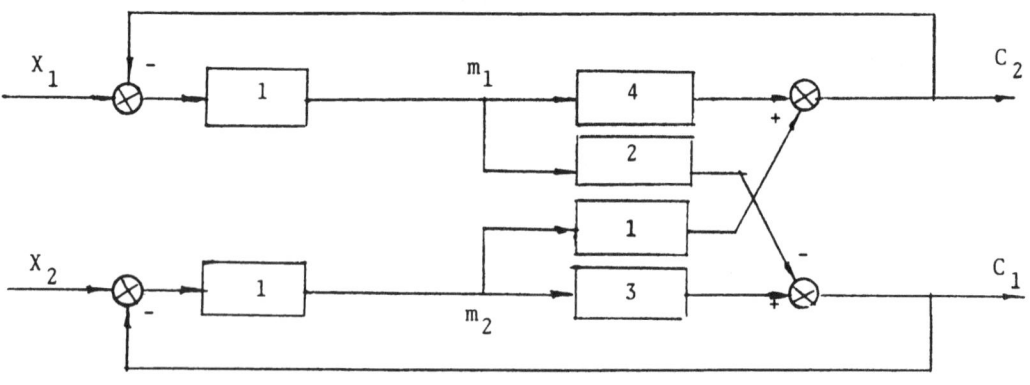

Fig 7-2-4

Similarly, we have:

$$m_1 = X_2 - C_2 \qquad\qquad (7\text{-}2\text{-}21)$$

$$m_2 = X_1 - C_1 \qquad\qquad (7\text{-}2\text{-}22)$$

$$C_2 = 4m_1 + m_2 \qquad\qquad (7\text{-}2\text{-}23)$$

$$C_1 = -2m_1 + 3m_2 \qquad\qquad (7\text{-}2\text{-}24)$$

therefore:

$$C_1 = -2X_2 + 2C_2 + 3X_1 - 3C_1 \qquad\qquad (7\text{-}2\text{-}25)$$

namely:

$$4C_1 = 3X_1 - 2X_2 + 2C_2 \qquad\qquad (7\text{-}2\text{-}26)$$

Likewise:

$$C_2 = 4X_2 - 4C_2 + X_1 - C_1 \qquad\qquad (7\text{-}2\text{-}27)$$

namely:

$$5C_2 = X_1 + 4X_2 - C_1 \qquad\qquad (7\text{-}2\text{-}28)$$

Substituting (7-2-28) into (7-2-26) yields:

$$4C_1 = 3X_1 - 2X_2 + \frac{2}{5}(X_1 + 4X_2 - C_1) \qquad\qquad (7\text{-}2\text{-}29)$$

$$20C_1 = 15X_1 - 10X_2 + 2X_1 + 8X_2 - 2C_1 \qquad\qquad (7\text{-}2\text{-}30)$$

$$22C_1 = 17X_1 - 2X_2 \qquad\qquad (7\text{-}2\text{-}31)$$

then:

$$C_1 = \frac{17}{22} X_1 - \frac{2}{22} X_2 \qquad\qquad (7\text{-}2\text{-}32)$$

By the same way, we can get:

$$C_2 = \frac{1}{22} X_1 + \frac{18}{22} X_2 \qquad\qquad (7\text{-}2\text{-}33)$$

Comparing (7-2-32) and (7-2-33) with (7-2-11) and (7-2-16) , we see that $\dfrac{C_1}{X_2}$ has been reduced from $\dfrac{1}{6}$ to $\dfrac{1}{11}$, and $\dfrac{C_2}{X_1}$ from $\dfrac{2}{9}$ to $\dfrac{1}{22}$. Both $\dfrac{C_1}{X_1}$ and $\dfrac{C_2}{X_2}$ also decrease , but just a little.

Thus, from the point of view of decreasing coupling, the system shown in Fig 7-2-3 is better than that shown in Fig 7-2-1.

It denotes that for a multivariable process control system, its coupling degree is closely related to the variable pairing and thus the correct choice of variable pairing is one of the important research contents of multivariable process control systems. A conclusion is also reached here that it is not necessary to take decoupling design for any coupled system since sometimes the correct choice of variable pairing can reduce the coupling degree remarkably and the decoupling design may be not needed.

In addition, for the system shown in Fig 7-2-3, if the gains of the regulators are increased further, then certainly the coupling degree will be decreased further, too. Thus, the correct choice of variable pairing with suitable regulator gains sometimes is an effective way to reduce the system coupling indeed.

We should point out here that although the above analysis is about the steady state, all the conclusions are also valid to dynamic state.

Comparing Fig 7-2-1 and Fig 7-2-3, we can see that the reduction of coupling degree is due to the fact that the gains of the coupling channels are decreased. In general, the less the ratio of the coupling channel gain to the main channel gain, the less the coupling degree. This fact is very heuristic for us to have a correct variable pairing.

The above analysis tells us that for a coupled multivariable process control system we should analyze its coupling degree carefully and analyze which measures can be taken to reduce the system coupling degree. The block diagram analysis method is a direct method and it can be used only to a practical system when the block diagram of this system has been obtained. So, by this method we can not derive more general conclusions on the coupling degree analysis and, consequently, the application of this direct method is quite limited.

But, however, there is a universal method capable of analyzing the system coupling degree. This is the Bristol-Shinskey method and we will

introduce it very soon . The explanation of Bristol-Shinskey method
and the discussion on its application are the main contents of the last
two chapters of this book.

§ 7-3 Relative Gain Matrices [42]

We will discuss the Bristol-Shinskey method step by step.

For a multivariable process control system, it has many channels.
Suppose that C_i is one of its controlled variables and m_i is a manipulated variable, then all controlled variables (measured variables) may
be arrayed in a matrix C and all manipulated variables are arrayed in
a matrix M.

Bristol defined a matrix relation as:

$$C = \Phi M \qquad\qquad (7-3-1)$$

and the static value of an element φ_{ij} in matrix Φ is called as the
first gain coefficient of the channel $m_j \longrightarrow C_i$ .In fact, in a coupled
system, this is the steady state gain of the channel between m_j to C_i
when the observed manipulated variable has a change $\triangle m_j$ and all other
manipulated variables m_r ($r \neq j$) remain unchanged. Thus, the first gain
coefficient is nothing else but the steady state gain of the channel
$m_j \longrightarrow C_i$ when only this channel is under operation and all other channels are broken off.

Then, Bristol defined another matrix P and the static value of an element P_{ij} in this matrix is called as the second gain coefficient of the
channel $m_j \longrightarrow C_i$. In fact, in a coupled system, we can measure the
change of the controlled variable C_i(it is obtained when only the manipulated variable m_j has a change and all other controlled variables
remain unchanged), and then the ratio of the steady state change of C_i
to the change of m_j is the second gain coefficient of this channel. This

means that except the $m_j \longrightarrow C_i$ channel all other channels are closed and are with ideal control (then all C_r remain unchanged) and under this condition, the steady state gain of the channel $m_j \longrightarrow C_i$ is its second gain coefficient.

By the above definitions we can know that it is not difficult to determine the first gain coefficients. In fact, they are the static coupling coefficients of different channels in normal measurement conditions . Because when we measure the coupling results of different channels in normal manner, we always break off all other channel regulators and then give a change to a manipulated variable and measure the responses of system outputs caused by this manipulated variable. Thus, the measured results are just the first gain coefficients of corresponding channels.

As for the second gain coefficients, how can we measure them by the definition given above?

This problem is rather complicated and we will discuss it in detail later on.

From matrices Φ and P, Bristol defined the third matrix $\wedge$.

In this matrix, all elements are the ratio of the corresponding elements of the above two matrices, namely:

$$\lambda_{ij} = \frac{\varphi_{ij}}{P_{ij}} \qquad (7\text{-}3\text{-}2)$$

and this ratio is called as the relative gain of the channel $m_j \longrightarrow C_i$.

So, $\wedge$ is called as the relative gain matrix.

The analysis of the relative gain matrices is the key of the Bristol-Shinskey method and we will expound it in the future context.

Obviously, φ_{ij} and P_{ij} may be written as:

$$\varphi_{ij} = \left. \frac{\partial C_i}{\partial m_j} \right|_{m_r = \text{constant}} \qquad (7\text{-}3\text{-}3)$$

$$P_{ij} = \left. \frac{\partial c_i}{\partial m_j} \right|_{C_r = \text{constant}} \qquad (7\text{-}3\text{-}4)$$

so the relative gain is often written as:

$$\lambda_{ij} = \frac{\left. \dfrac{\partial c_i}{\partial m_j} \right|_m}{\left. \dfrac{\partial c_i}{\partial m_j} \right|_C} \qquad (7\text{-}3\text{-}5)$$

§ 7-4 The Determination of the Second Gain Coefficient

The analysis of the last paragraph denotes that in order to determine the relative gains of a coupled system, we must determine the
first and the second gain coefficients at first.

It is not difficult to determine the first gain coefficients because they can be easily measured by their definition.

But the second gain coefficient is not easily to be measured.

In order to explain how to determine the second gain coefficient,
we discuss two examples.

A two-variable control system is shown in Fig 7-4-1.

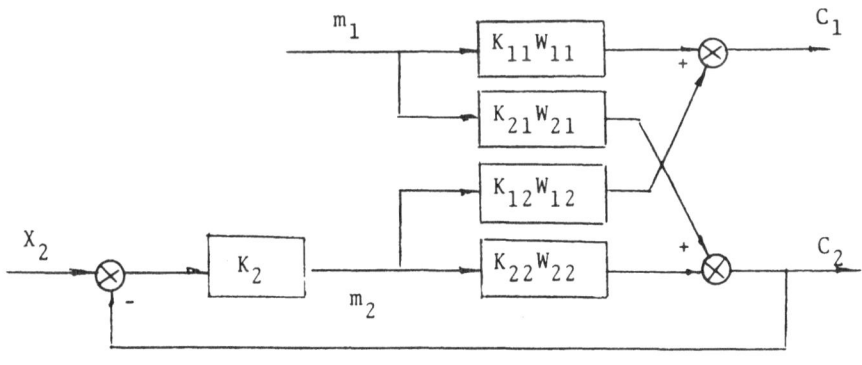

Fig 7-4-1

From this figure, we know:

$$\Phi = \begin{bmatrix} \varphi_{11} & \varphi_{12} \\ \varphi_{21} & \varphi_{22} \end{bmatrix} = \begin{bmatrix} K_{11}W_{11} & K_{12}W_{12} \\ K_{21}W_{21} & K_{22}W_{22} \end{bmatrix} \qquad (7\text{-}4\text{-}1)$$

where, K_{ij} is the static gain and W_{ij} is the dynamic character.

The transfer function of the channel $m_1 \longrightarrow C_1$ can be determined easily from this figure:

$$\frac{C_1}{m_1} = K_{11}W_{11} + K_{21}W_{21}\frac{-K_2}{1 + K_2 K_{22}W_{22}} K_{12}W_{12} =$$

$$= \frac{K_{11}W_{11} + K_2(K_{11}K_{22}W_{11}W_{22} - K_{21}K_{12}W_{12}W_{21})}{1 + K_2 K_{22}W_{22}} \qquad (7\text{-}4\text{-}2)$$

Two cases will be considered:

(1) $K_2 = 0$, then:

$$\frac{C_1}{m_1} = K_{11}W_{11} \qquad (7\text{-}4\text{-}3)$$

The static gain is just K_{11} and it is also the first gain coefficient of the channel $m_1 \longrightarrow C_1$.

(2) The second case is that the ideal control is performed for C_2. What is the meaning of ideal control ? In process control theory, the realization of ideal control means the open loop with infinite gain, namely $K_2 \longrightarrow \infty$ and then we have:

$$\lim_{K_2 \longrightarrow \infty} \frac{C_1}{m_1} = \frac{K_{11}W_{11}K_{22}W_{22} - K_{12}W_{12}K_{21}W_{21}}{K_{22}W_{22}} \qquad (7\text{-}4\text{-}4)$$

and in the steady state, we have:

$$\lim_{K_2 \longrightarrow \infty} \frac{C_1}{m_1} = \frac{K_{11}K_{22} - K_{12}K_{21}}{K_{22}} \qquad (7\text{-}4\text{-}5)$$

This is the second gain coefficient of the channel $m_1 \longrightarrow C_1$.

This conclusion can be extended to more general case: If the plant transfer property is expressed by a nxn matrix and feedback signals are provided to n-1 input terminals and keep the (n-1) corresponding outputs being unchanged, namely the ideal control is performed, then the steady state gain between the nth output and the free input is the second gain coefficient of this channel.

In theory , this method for determining the second gain coefficients is available , but it is difficult to be performed in practice since it is not easy to make the open loop gain be infinite in any case. So, we should discuss further : When the first gain coefficients are known, can we get the second gain coefficients from them directly by calculation?

This is possible.

We consider a general two-variable plant shown in Fig 7-4-2.

For this plant, the following relations are evident:

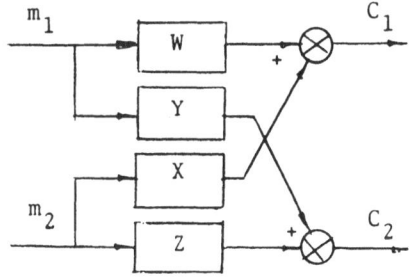

Fig 7-4-2

	m_1	m_2
C_1	W	X
C_2	Y	Z

namely:

$$C_1 = Wm_1 + Xm_2$$
$$C_2 = Ym_1 + Zm_2$$

$$(7-4-6)$$

Now, we introduce the second gain coefficients as follows:

	m_1	m_2
C_1	$\dfrac{1}{p}$	$\dfrac{1}{r}$
C_2	$\dfrac{1}{q}$	$\dfrac{1}{s}$

namely:

$$C_1 \qquad\qquad C_2$$

$$m_1 \qquad p \qquad\qquad q$$

$$m_2 \qquad r \qquad\qquad s$$

Now, we explain why $\dfrac{1}{p}$, $\dfrac{1}{r}$, $\dfrac{1}{q}$ and $\dfrac{1}{s}$ are the second gain coefficients.

From the above array, we get:

$$\left.\begin{array}{l} m_1 = pC_1 + qC_2 \\[2mm] m_2 = rC_1 + sC_2 \end{array}\right\} \qquad\qquad (7\text{-}4\text{-}7)$$

When C_2 is held to be unchanged, namely $\Delta C_2 = 0$, then:

$$\frac{\Delta C_1}{\Delta m_1} = \frac{1}{p} \qquad\qquad (7\text{-}4\text{-}8)$$

$$\frac{\Delta C_1}{\Delta m_2} = \frac{1}{r} \qquad\qquad (7\text{-}4\text{-}9)$$

When C_1 is held to be unchanged, namely $\Delta C_1 = 0$, then:

$$\frac{\Delta C_2}{\Delta m_1} = \frac{1}{q} \qquad\qquad (7\text{-}4\text{-}10)$$

$$\frac{\Delta C_2}{\Delta m_2} = \frac{1}{s} \qquad\qquad (7\text{-}4\text{-}11)$$

The four expressions of (7-4-8) to (7-4-11) satisfy the definition of the second gain coefficient, so they are the second gain coefficients.

From (7-4-6) and (7-4-7) we get:

$$C_1 = W(pC_1 + qC_2) + X(rC_1 + sC_2) \qquad\qquad (7\text{-}4\text{-}12)$$

$$C_2 = Y(pC_1 + qC_2) + Z(rC_1 + sC_2) \qquad\qquad (7\text{-}4\text{-}13)$$

namely:

$$1 = Wp + Wq\frac{C_2}{C_1} + Xr + Xs\frac{C_2}{C_1} \qquad\qquad (7\text{-}4\text{-}14)$$

$$1 = Yp\frac{C_1}{C_2} + Yq + Zr\frac{C_1}{C_2} + Zs \qquad (7\text{-}4\text{-}16)$$

Notice that all measurable terms in these equations are with the form of increments, so C_2 being unchanged means $C_2 = 0$ in the above equations and consequently: ($C_1 \neq 0$)

$$1 = Wp + Xr \qquad (7\text{-}4\text{-}17)$$

$$0 = Yp + Zr \qquad (7\text{-}4\text{-}18)$$

When C_1 is unchanged, namely $C_1 = 0$, $C_2 \neq 0$, it yields:

$$0 = Wq + Xs \qquad (7\text{-}4\text{-}19)$$

$$1 = Yq + Zs \qquad (7\text{-}4\text{-}20)$$

The above four equations can be written in matrix form as follows:

$$I = \begin{pmatrix} 1 & 0 \\ 0 & 1 \end{pmatrix} = \begin{pmatrix} W & X \\ Y & Z \end{pmatrix}\begin{pmatrix} p & q \\ r & s \end{pmatrix} \qquad (7\text{-}4\text{-}21)$$

and we get:

$$\begin{bmatrix} p & q \\ r & s \end{bmatrix} = \frac{adj\begin{bmatrix} W & X \\ Y & Z \end{bmatrix}}{det\begin{bmatrix} W & X \\ Y & Z \end{bmatrix}} = \frac{\begin{bmatrix} Z & -X \\ -Y & W \end{bmatrix}}{WZ - XY} \qquad (7\text{-}4\text{-}22)$$

$$\begin{aligned}
p &= \frac{Z}{WZ - XY} & \frac{1}{p} &= \frac{WZ - XY}{Z} \\
q &= \frac{-X}{WZ - XY} & \frac{1}{q} &= -\frac{WZ - XY}{X} \\
r &= \frac{-Y}{WZ - XY} & \frac{1}{r} &= -\frac{WZ - XY}{Y} \\
s &= \frac{W}{WZ - XY} & \frac{1}{s} &= \frac{WZ - XY}{W}
\end{aligned} \qquad (7\text{-}4\text{-}23)$$

Now, we introduce another matrix ψ and it is given by:

$$\psi = \begin{bmatrix} p & r \\ q & s \end{bmatrix} = \left(\begin{bmatrix} W & X \\ Y & Z \end{bmatrix}^{-1}\right)^T = (\Phi^{-1})^T \qquad (7\text{-}4\text{-}24)$$

It means that the matrix ψ is the transpose of the inverse matrix of the first gain coefficient matrix Φ .

The reciprocals of the elements of the matrix ψ are just the second gain coefficients.

Therefore, if we know the first gain coefficient matrix Φ , then we can get the matrix ψ by calculation and the second gain coefficients are obtained . By this way, it is not necessary to measure the second gain coeffients by the procedure mentioned above and consequently it will simplify the system analysis.

When both the first gain coefficients and the second gain coefficients are obtained, the calculation of relative gains is straightforward, for example for the two-variable system we have:

$$
\left.
\begin{aligned}
\lambda_{11} &= \frac{K_{11}K_{22}}{K_{11}K_{22} - K_{12}K_{21}} \\[2mm]
\lambda_{12} &= \frac{-K_{12}K_{21}}{K_{11}K_{22} - K_{12}K_{21}} \\[2mm]
\lambda_{21} &= \frac{-K_{12}K_{21}}{K_{11}K_{22} - K_{12}K_{21}} \\[2mm]
\lambda_{22} &= \frac{K_{11}K_{22}}{K_{11}K_{22} - K_{12}K_{21}}
\end{aligned}
\right\}
\qquad (7-4-25)
$$

§ 7-5 The Properties of Relative Gain Matrices [42][44][45][46]

Now, we discuss the properties of the relative gain matrices in detail.

We have said that the matrix ψ can be determined by the first gain coeffiencient matrix Φ and each element in ψ is the reciprocal of the corresponding second gain coefficient, namely:

$$\psi_{ij} = \frac{1}{p_{ij}} \qquad (7-5-1)$$

thus, the relative gain is :

$$\lambda_{ij} = \varphi_{ij}\psi_{ij} \qquad (7-5-2)$$

We define a matrix relation:

$$\Lambda = \Phi * \psi \qquad (7-5-3)$$

where the asterisk $*$ denotes the following calculation relation being

carried out in (7-5-3):

$$\lambda_{ij} = \varphi_{ij}\psi_{ij} \qquad (7-5-4)$$

and ψ_{ij} is the ratio of the cofactor Φ_{ij} to the determinant Φ.

So , (7-5-3) may be written as:

$$\Lambda = \begin{bmatrix} \varphi_{11} & \cdots & \varphi_{1n} \\ & \varphi_{ij} & \\ \varphi_{n1} & \cdots & \varphi_{nn} \end{bmatrix} * \begin{bmatrix} \Phi_{11} & \cdots & \Phi_{1n} \\ & \Phi_{ij} & \\ \Phi_{n1} & \cdots & \Phi_{nn} \end{bmatrix} \frac{1}{|\Phi|}$$

and:

$$\qquad (7-5-5)$$

$$\lambda_{ij} = \varphi_{ij} \frac{\Phi_{ij}}{|\Phi|} \qquad (7-5-6)$$

What does the relative gain λ_{ij} mean ?

In fact, it means the coupling degree of two variables.

Taking the two-variable system again as an example, for it we can

get the following relative gains:

$$\lambda_{11} = \varphi_{11} \frac{\varphi_{22}}{\varphi_{11}\varphi_{22} - \varphi_{12}\varphi_{21}} = \lambda_{22} \qquad (7-5-7)$$

$$\lambda_{12} = - \frac{\varphi_{21}\varphi_{12}}{\varphi_{11}\varphi_{22} - \varphi_{12}\varphi_{21}} = \lambda_{21} \qquad (7-5-8)$$

Obviously, when $\varphi_{12} = \varphi_{21} = 0$, then:

$$\lambda_{12} = \lambda_{21} = 0 \qquad\qquad (7\text{-}5\text{-}9)$$

and $\varphi_{12} = \varphi_{21}$ means that there is no coupling between channel 1 and channel 2. That is to say when there is no coupling between two subsystems , then for each subsystem its own relative gain is 1 and their mutual relative gains are zero.

Obviously, when φ_{12} and φ_{21} are large, then λ_{12} and λ_{21} are also large . That means that serious coupling exists between two channels.

From (7-5-7) and (7-5-8), we can find another important proper-ty of relative gains:

$$\left.\begin{array}{l} \lambda_{11} + \lambda_{12} = 1 \\[2mm] \lambda_{11} + \lambda_{21} = 1 \end{array}\right\} \qquad\qquad (7\text{-}5\text{-}10)$$

It denotes that in a relative gain matrix the sum of all ele-ments in the same row or in the same column is one.

Thus, the relative gain matrix may be also written as:

$$\Lambda = \begin{bmatrix} \lambda_{11} & 1 - \lambda_{11} \\[2mm] 1 - \lambda_{11} & \lambda_{11} \end{bmatrix} \qquad\qquad (7\text{-}5\text{-}11)$$

where:

$$\lambda_{11} = \cfrac{1}{1 - \cfrac{K_{12}K_{21}}{K_{11}K_{22}}} \qquad\qquad (7\text{-}5\text{-}12)$$

and K_{ij} is the static gain of the channel $m_j \longrightarrow C_i$.

We have known that for a system without coupling its relative gain matrix is a diagonal matrix. Then, how about its contrary propo-sition? The contrary proposition is: If the system relative gain matrix is a diagonal matrix, is this a system without any coupling ?

No. The answer is negative.

Consider the two-variable system again. From (7-5-7) and (7-5-8) we know that either K_{12} or K_{21} equal to zero makes the system relative gain matrix be diagonal ($K_{12} = 0$, $K_{21} \neq 0$ or $K_{12} \neq 0$, $K_{21} = 0$). So, for example, when $K_{12} = 0$, $K_{21} \neq 0$, then there is no influence of m_2 on C_1 but the influence of m_1 on C_2 still exists through K_{21} and this is still a coupled system, even though its relative gain matrix is diagonal. But, however, such a system can be considered to be two separate systems indeed because for the control of C_2 , the coupling signal from m_1 can be considered as an independent disturbance. In such a way, the two systems are divided.

In addition, " diagonal matrix" is a mathematical terminology and it denotes such a matrix that all elements of the main diagonal are 1 and all other elements are zero. But, by the above analysis of the relative gain matrix we can know that both the following matrices:

$$\begin{bmatrix} 1 & 0 \\ 0 & 1 \end{bmatrix} \text{ and } \begin{bmatrix} 0 & 1 \\ 1 & 0 \end{bmatrix}$$

denote systems without coupling . Although the latter can not be called a diagonal matrix, in fact if we change the orders of the manipulated variables or the controlled variables, then we get a diagonal matrix for the relative gains.

Notice that the first gain coefficients may be positive or negative and this will give great influence on the relative gains.

If the positive number of the first gain coefficients is odd, then all relative gains are in the scope $0 \longrightarrow 1$. When two manipulated variables or two controlled variables are not similar to each other, then the case is just like this. For example, the pressure and the flow of the same tube are controlled by two serial valves is the case with unsimilar controlled variables and that the top product and the bottom product of a distillation column are controlled by material balance and energy balance, respectively is the case with unsimilar manipulated variables. In both cases, the relative gains are in the scope of $0 \longrightarrow 1$.

Now, we consider the first example.

Suppose that the pressure and the flow in a tube are controlled by two serial valves. The scheme is shown in Fig 7-5-1.

The common arrangement is using valve 1 to control the pressure and using valve 2 to control the flow.

But, in fact, any change of the stroke of either valve will influence the pressure and the flow simultaneously. So, logically, a problem arises: Is this scheme reasonable and how about the another possible control scheme ?

Because for a valve we have:

$$Q^2 = KB\triangle P \tag{7-5-13}$$

where K is a value related to the density of medium ; B is the opening of the valve and $\triangle P$ is the pressure difference across this valve , so we can get the same relation for two serial valves:

$$Q^2 = m_1(P_0 - P_1) = m_2(P_1 - P_2) \tag{7-5-14}$$

It yields:

$$P_1 = \frac{m_0 P_0 + m_2 P_2}{m_1 + m_2} \tag{7-5-15}$$

Substituting it into (7-5-14) and letting $Q^2 = F$, we get:

$$F = \frac{m_1 m_2 (P_0 - P_2)}{m_1 + m_2} \tag{7-5-16}$$

From this expression, we can get the first gain coefficients:

$$\frac{\partial F}{\partial m_1}\bigg|_{m_2} = \frac{m_2(P_0 - P_2)}{m_1 + m_2} - \frac{m_1 m_2(P_0 - P_2)}{(m_1 + m_2)^2} =$$

$$= (P_0 - P_2) (\frac{m_2}{m_1 + m_2})^2 \tag{7-5-17}$$

and the second gain coefficient:

$$\frac{\partial F}{\partial m_1}\bigg|_P = P_0 - P_1 = (P_0 - P_2)\frac{m_2}{m_1 + m_2} \qquad (7\text{-}5\text{-}18)$$

Therefore, we can get the relative gain λ_{Fm_1} :

$$\lambda_{Fm_1} = \frac{\dfrac{\partial F}{\partial m_1}\bigg|_{m_2}}{\dfrac{\partial F}{\partial m_1}\bigg|_P} = \frac{(P_0 - P_2)(\dfrac{m_2}{m_1 + m_2})^2}{(P_0 - P_2)\dfrac{m_2}{m_1 + m_2}} = \frac{m_2}{m_1 + m_2} =$$

$$= \frac{P_0 - P_1}{P_0 - P_2} \qquad (7\text{-}5\text{-}19)$$

Similarly, we can get :

$$\lambda_{Fm_2} = \frac{P_1 - P_2}{P_0 - P_2} \qquad (7\text{-}5\text{-}20)$$

If the relation:

$$P_1 = P_0 - \frac{F}{m_1} = P_2 + \frac{F}{m_2} = \frac{m_1 P_0 + m_2 P_2}{m_1 + m_2} \qquad (7\text{-}5\text{-}21)$$

is applied and the above procedure is repeated, then we can get the relative gains $\lambda_{P_1 m_1}$ and $\lambda_{P_1 m_2}$.

At last, we get the following relative gain array:

	m_1	m_2
F	$\lambda_{Fm_1} = \dfrac{P_0 - P_1}{P_0 - P_2}$	$\lambda_{Fm_2} = \dfrac{P_1 - P_2}{P_0 - P_2}$
P_1	$\lambda_{P_1 m_1} = \dfrac{P_1 - P_2}{P_0 - P_2}$	$\lambda_{P_1 m_2} = \dfrac{P_0 - P_2}{P_0 - P_2}$

Because P_0 is larger than P_2, so in all elements of this matrix the denominator is larger than the numerator and, consequently, all the relative gains are in the scope of $0 \longrightarrow 1$.

As for the reasonable variable pairing, it depends on the magnitudes of $(P_0 - P_1)$ and $(P_1 - P_2)$. If $(P_0 - P_1) > (P_1 - P_2)$, then $\lambda_{Fm_1} > \lambda_{Fm_2}$ so it would be better to use valve 1 to control the flow and if $(P_0 - P_1) < (P_1 - P_2)$, then $\lambda_{Fm_1} < \lambda_{Fm_2}$, so in this case we should use valve 2 to control the flow. When $P_0 - P_1 = P_1 - P_2$, then two schemes are the same, namely we can use any valve to control the flow or the pressure.

When the positve number of the first gain coefficients is even, then in the relative gain matrix, λ_{11} is either larger than 1 or less than zero and, consequently, the other relative gain in the same row or in the same column is either less than zero or larger than 1, respectively. When two controlled variables or two manipulated variables are similar, the case is just like this.

For example, a mixed liquid is with three compositions. One of them is water. The density and the viscosity of the mixed liquid are under control. Any change of the other two compositions will give influence on the controlled density and viscosity. Suppose the mathematical models being:

$$\rho = \frac{Am_1 + Bm_2}{F}$$
$$\mu = \frac{Cm_1 + Dm_2}{F} \tag{7-5-22}$$

and all A,B,C and D are positive ; m_1 and m_2 are controllable flows and F is the total flow without control.

By the calculation principles of relative gains, we can get the following results:

	m_1	m_2
ρ	$\dfrac{AD}{AD - BC}$	$\dfrac{-BC}{AD - BC}$
μ	$\dfrac{-BC}{AD - BC}$	$\dfrac{AD}{AD - BC}$

Because A,B,C and D all are positive, so in the above relative gain array, two elements must be negative . Which two relative gains will be negative is determined by the magnitude of (AD-BC).

For instance, if A = B = C = 0.5 and D = 1.0, then the relative gain matrix is :

$$
\begin{array}{ccc}
 & m_1 & m_2 \\
\rho & 2 & -1 \\
\mu & -1 & 2
\end{array}
$$

From this array we can see that ρ can not be controlled by m_2 and μ can not be controlled by m_2 . If μ were controlled by m_1 , that means that μ should increase when m_1 increases; but the relative gain is negative, so the contrary control result is obtained, namely the larger the m_1, the less the μ . When μ becomes less, the control demands want m_1 to be larger, so , as a result, the control valve will move to the opposite direction with full range and no effective control is obtained. This means that the variable pairing with negative relative gains will result in unstable control process.

In order to explain this result , we consider another example. Suppose that a pump feeds water to two parallel tubes with constant total flow. The scheme is shown in Fig 7-4-2.

When m_j is controlled manually, then any increase of m_i will result in the increase of flow F_i and the decrease of flow F_j simultaneously.

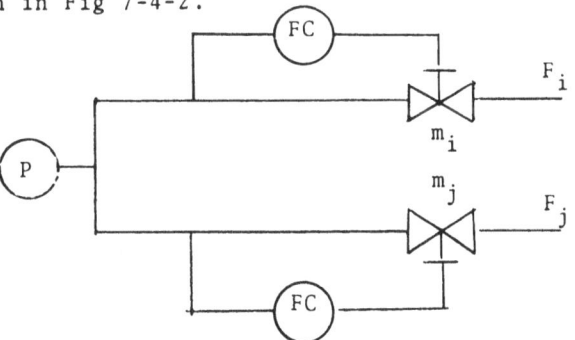

Fig 7-5-2

We have:

$$F_i = A_{ii}m_i - A_{ij}m_j \qquad (7-5-23)$$

and in general:

$$A_{ii} > A_{ij} \tag{7-5-24}$$

If both tubes are the same, then:

$$F_j = A_{ii}m_j - A_{ij}m_i \tag{7-5-25}$$

and the relative gains are:

$$\lambda_{ii} = \lambda_{jj} = \frac{A_{ii}^2}{A_{ii}^2 - A_{ij}^2} \tag{7-5-26}$$

Because $A_{ii} > A_{ij}$, so that:

$$\lambda_{ii} = \lambda_{jj} > 1 \qquad \lambda_{ji} < 0 \tag{7-5-27}$$

What does it mean ? It means if F_j were controlled by m_i, then the larger (or the less) the m_i , the less (or the larger) the F_j. Therefore , a contradictory control result is obtained and the valves will move to the opposite direction in full ranges.

Obviously, such a variable pairing is unavailable in practice.

In general, for a pair of a manipulated variable and a controlled variable, if the relative gain of this pair approaches to 1 , for example $0.8 < \lambda < 1.2$, then it means this channel is influenced by other channels very little , namely in (7-5-12) both K_{12} and K_{21} are small, so this channel can be closed by its own regulator without special decoupling design.

When the relative gain is lower than zero or approaches to zero, then this channel can not be closed by its own regulator because it is impossible to get good control in this case. This is the case of uncorrect choice of variable pairing relations and we should choose other more suitable pairing relations.

When the relative gains are in the scope of 0.3 to 0.7 or larger than 1.5, then it means that very serious coupling exists in the system and decoupling design should be considered.

Because of these impotant properties of the system relative gain matrix, so when we design a multivariable process control system in order to judge coupling degrees among different channels we should calculate the relative gain matrix at first.

For example, for a system with five variables if we get its relative gain matrix as follows:

$$\begin{pmatrix} \lambda_{11} & \lambda_{12} & \lambda_{13} & 0 & 0 \\ \lambda_{21} & \lambda_{22} & \lambda_{23} & 0 & 0 \\ \lambda_{31} & \lambda_{32} & \lambda_{33} & 0 & 0 \\ 0 & 0 & 0 & 1 & 0 \\ 0 & 0 & 0 & 0 & 1 \end{pmatrix}$$

What does it mean ?

For the fourth row (and column) and the fifth row (and column) , the two elements on the diagonal are one and the others are zero. This means that the fourth variable and the fifth variable are not related to other channels , i.e. there is no coupling about the fourth channel and the fifth channel. Thus, in the system decoupling design it is not necessary to consider these two variables and in such a way a system with five variables is reduced to one with only three variables. Consequently, the system analysis will be simplified.

Now, we consider another practical calculation example.

Suppose a three-variable system with the following character:

$$\begin{pmatrix} C_1 \\ C_2 \\ C_3 \end{pmatrix} = \begin{pmatrix} \dfrac{-1.0e^{-1.5S}}{(1+0.5S)(1+5S)} & 0 & \dfrac{1.6e^{-2S}}{1+12S} \\ \dfrac{-1.0e^{-2S}}{(1+5S)(1+12S)} & \dfrac{-1.1e^{-2S}}{(1+S)(1+2S)} & \dfrac{2.5e^{-2S}}{1+4S} \\ \dfrac{-1.6}{S(1+0.2S)} & 0 & \dfrac{1.4}{S(1+0.5S)} \end{pmatrix} \begin{pmatrix} m_1 \\ m_2 \\ m_3 \end{pmatrix}$$

$$(7-5-28)$$

In order to use the Bristol principles, we consider the steady state and the system steady state transfer matrix is:

$$
= \begin{pmatrix} -1.0 & 0 & 1.6 \\ -1.0 & -1.1 & 2.5 \\ \dfrac{-1.6}{S} & 0 & \dfrac{1.4}{S} \end{pmatrix} \qquad (7\text{-}5\text{-}29)
$$

Because $\psi = (\Phi^{-1})^T$, so we get:

$$
\psi = \begin{pmatrix} \dfrac{1.5}{S} & \dfrac{2.6}{S} & \dfrac{1.7}{S} \\ 0 & \dfrac{1}{S} & 0 \\ -1.7 & 0.9 & -1.1 \end{pmatrix} \dfrac{S}{1.1} \qquad (7\text{-}5\text{-}30)
$$

and the relative gain matrix is :

$$
\Lambda = \Phi * \psi = \begin{pmatrix} -1.4 & 0 & 2.4 \\ 0 & 1 & 0 \\ 2.4 & 0 & -1.4 \end{pmatrix} \qquad (7\text{-}5\text{-}31)
$$

It tells us that C_2 is only related to m_2 and thus this channel
need not be considered in the decoupling design. On the other hand,
we see that λ_{13} is 2.4 and λ_{11} is -1.4. We have said before that
the negative relative gain is not suitable for variable pairing. Thus,
if both C_1 and C_2 want to have a good control, then the above variable
pairing is not suitable and we can change the pairing relations, i.e.

let C_1 be controlled by m_3 and C_3 be controlled by m_1. Then, for the
re-arranged system, its relation is:

$$
\begin{Bmatrix} C_1 \\ C_3 \end{Bmatrix} = \begin{pmatrix} 1.6 & -1.0 \\ \dfrac{1.4}{S} & -\dfrac{1.6}{S} \end{pmatrix} \begin{Bmatrix} m_3 \\ m_1 \end{Bmatrix} \qquad (7\text{-}5\text{-}32)
$$

and the decoupling design now can be done for this two-variable system.

The analysis shows the prominent advantages of the Bristol relative gain principles : From (7-5-28) or its P-canonical block diagram
we can not detect that in the steady state the channel $m_2 \longrightarrow C_2$ is

not influenced by the other channels and we can not find either that
the original peiring relations are not suitable for the control of C_1
and C_3 . When the Bristol relative gain analysis is applied, we soon
get the above important conclusions and, certainly, it will make the
further decoupling design much easier.

§ 7-6 The Direct Measurement of the Relative Gains from the System
Responses

We have discussed how to calculate the first and the second gain
coefficients and how to determine the   relative gains from these coefficients.

When the transfer functions of all channels are known, it is very
convenient to determine the relative gains by this way. But, however,
in many process control systems, sometimes we do not know the channel
transfer functions and in such a case we should determine the relative
gains from a practical plant.

Certainly, by the definitions of the first and the second gain
coefficients we can perform some operations to determine these two coefficients and by the obtained informations we can get the relative
gains. But, this procedure is not allowed to be performed for any
practical system in any case.

Therefore, we hope that we can determine the relative gains only
by some practical measured parameters obtained under system normal ope-
ration.We say that this is possible in some cases and we do not say
that it is possible in any case.

Now, we discuss a possible case.

Fig 7-6-1 shows a control system of a mixer. Two mediums A and

B are mixed in a tank and then pumped out. The output flow Q and its composition C are under control.

Where :

$$Q = Q_A + Q_B \tag{7-6-1}$$

$$C = \frac{Q_A}{Q_A + Q_B} = \frac{Q_A}{Q} \tag{7-6-2}$$

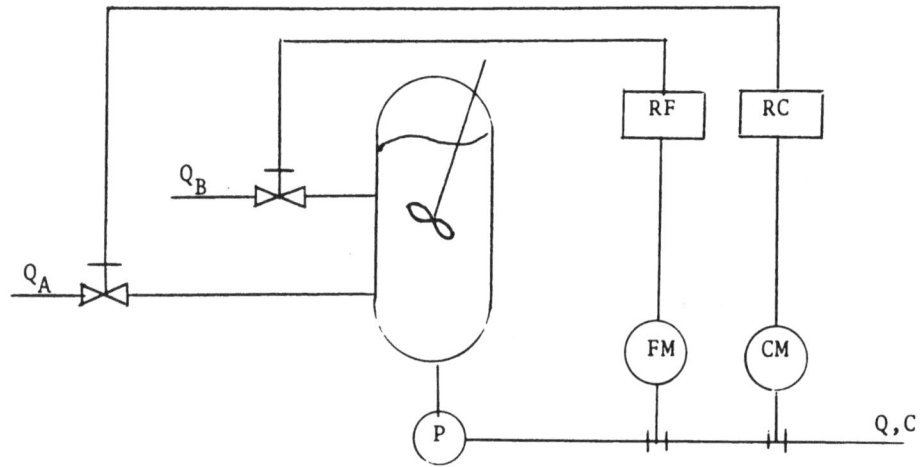

Fig 7-6-1

In this system, we suppose that C and Q are controlled by Q_A and Q_B , respectively.

Obviously, this is a coupled system, namely any change in either Q_A or Q_B will give influence on both Q and C. The block diagram is shown in Fig 7-6-2.

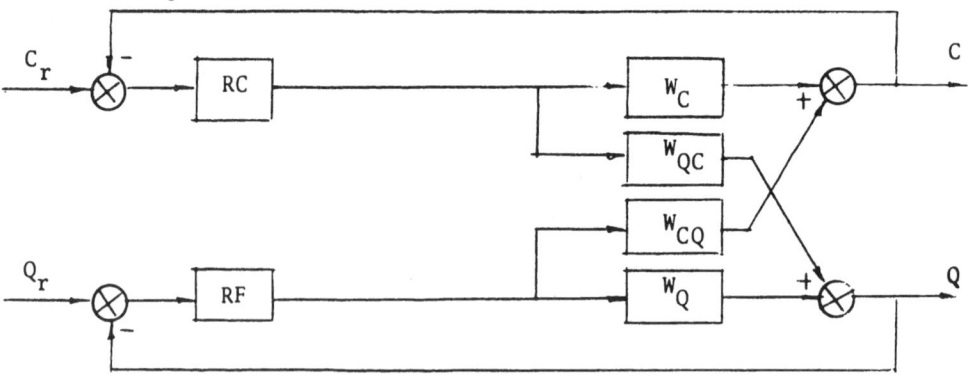

Fig 7-6-2

If all W_C, W_{QC}, W_{CQ} and W_Q are known, then we can determine the relative gains by the principles mentioned before and estimate the coupling degrees between two channels.

But, if all these channel functions are unknown, how can we determine the relative gaines?

The definition of the first gain coefficient shows that it is the ratio of the observed output to its corresponding manipulated variable (all are in increments) when only this manipulated variable is changed and other manipulated variables remain unchanged. So, we have:

$$\varphi_{11} = \left. \frac{\partial C}{\partial Q_A} \right|_{Q_B = \text{Constant}} \qquad (7\text{-}6\text{-}3)$$

From (7-6-2), it yields:

$$\varphi_{11} = \frac{\partial C}{\partial Q_A} = \frac{Q_B}{(Q_A + Q_B)^2} = \frac{1 - C}{Q} \qquad (7\text{-}6\text{-}4)$$

The definition of the second gain coefficient shows that it is the ratio of the observed output to its corresponding manipulated variable (all are in increments) when all other outputs are kept unchanged. So, we have:

$$P_{11} = \left. \frac{\partial C}{\partial Q_A} \right|_{Q_B = \text{Constant}} \qquad (7\text{-}6\text{-}5)$$

and from (7-6-2) we get:

$$P_{11} = \frac{\partial C}{\partial Q_A} = \frac{1}{Q} \qquad (7\text{-}6\text{-}6)$$

Therefore, we can get the relative gain:

$$\lambda_{11} = \frac{\varphi_{11}}{P_{11}} = \frac{1 - C}{Q} \bigg/ \frac{1}{Q} = 1 - C \qquad (7\text{-}6\text{-}7)$$

and the system relative gain array is:

	C	Q
Q_A	1 - C	C
Q_B	C	1 - C

This means that by the measured value of C under normal operation we can determine the system relative gains and, consequently, the coupling degrees between two channels are also determined.

Obviously, when the value of C is not large, the coupling degree between two channels (it is the same value for two channels to each other) is not serious and the scheme of Fig 7-6-1 is available.

When C increases, then the coupling effects become serious more and more and when C = 0.5, we have:

	C	Q
Q_A	0.5	0.5
Q_B	0.5	0.5

and the coupling becomes the most serious now.

When C $\longrightarrow$ 1, it means that C should be controlled by Q_B and Q by Q_A.

This example shows that in some cases we can determine system relative gains by practical measured values under normal operation, but this does not mean that this method can be carried out to any system in any case. In fact, only by practical analysis to the systems considered we can determine whether we can use this method.

§ 7-7 Further Discussion on the Application of Relative Gains and the Meaning of the Variable Pairing

Now, we have a further discussion on the example about the mixer control system mentioned in the last paragraph.

The controlled variables are the output flow Q and the composition C, namely:

$$Q = Q_A + Q_B \qquad\qquad (7\text{-}7\text{-}1)$$

$$C = \frac{Q_A}{Q_A + Q_B} \qquad\qquad (7\text{-}7\text{-}2)$$

We have got the relative gain array for this system:

	C	Q	(Table 7-7-1)
Q_A	1 - C	C	
Q_B	C	1 - C	

We know that in the relative gain array , when all relative gains are in the scope 0——— 1 , then the largest one means the most reasonable variable pairing.

For example, when:

C = 0.2 , then C should be controlled by Q_A ,

C = 0.8 , then C should be controlled by Q_B .

The most serious interaction occurs when C = 0.5 and in this case either Q_A or Q_B can be used to control C.

By the above principle, when the largest relative gain is used to pair the variables,then the coupling degree in the system is the least.

When we want to eliminate all coupling effects, then decoupling design is needed and special decoupling elements should be set in the system.

Now, let us have a discussion: For such a system,if we do not perform the decoupling design, can we use other ways to realize (at least, partially) decoupling control ?

(7-7-1) and (7-7-2) now are rewritten as:

$$\mathscr{L} = Q_A + Q_B \qquad\qquad (7\text{-}7\text{-}3)$$

$$\eta = \frac{Q_A}{Q_A + Q_B} \qquad (7-7-4)$$

These two **expressions** show if composition C is controlled by η and the output flow Q is controlled by ξ, then there is no coupling between these two control systems.

If the composition C is still controlled by Q_A but the output flow Q is controlled by ξ, then the flow control is not influenced by the composition control but the composition control is still influenced by the flow control. This means that half decoupling control is realized.

Fig 7-7-1 is such a half-decoupled system. In this system, no decoupling elements are used.

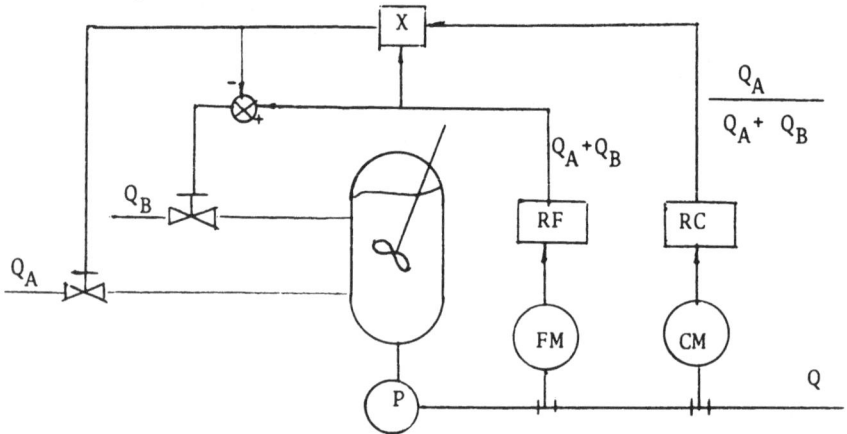

Fig 7-7-1

Now, let us have a further discussion on the system variable pairing relations because the correct vaiable pairing is a necessary condition to realize reasonable control.

Consider the above example again. Let the relative gain array be:

	Q_A	Q_B	(Table 7-7-2)
C	0.75	0.25	
Q	0.25	0.75	

Obviously, the largest relative gain is 0.75 so we say the most reasonable control project is C being controlled by Q_A and Q being controlled by Q_B.

Now, if we have a change:

	Q_A	Q_B	(Table 7-7-3)
C	0.25	0.75	
Q	0.75	0.25	

then the rational project is to let C be controlled by Q_B. Although Q_A now still gives influence on C, the control effects of Q_B is three times of those of Q_A.

This means that, take Table 7-7-2 as an example, if there are 0.75 units of changes with C, then one unit change of Q_A is needed for the compensation of C. On the other hand, one unit change of Q_A will cause 0.25 units of the change of Q simultaneously and thus there must be a change of Q_B to keep the total flow Q being unchanged. The necessary change of Q_B can be calculated as:

$$\Delta Q_B = (\frac{\Delta C}{\lambda_{CQ_A}})(\frac{\lambda_{QQ_A}}{\lambda_{QQ_B}}) \qquad (7\text{-}7\text{-}5)$$

For the above example, we have:

$$\Delta Q_B = (\frac{0.75}{0.75})(\frac{0.25}{0.75}) = 0.333 \qquad (7\text{-}7\text{-}6)$$

Then, this change of Q_B will cause the change of C so in order to keep C being unchanged, a necessary change of Q_A is needed and it can be calculated as:

$$\Delta Q_A = \Delta Q_B (\frac{\lambda_{CQ_B}}{\lambda_{CQ_A}}) \qquad (7\text{-}7\text{-}7)$$

Substituting (7-7-5) and (7-7-6) into (7-7-7), we get:

$$\Delta Q_A = (\frac{\Delta C}{\lambda_{CQ_A}})(\frac{\lambda_{QQ_A}}{\lambda_{QQ_B}})(\frac{\lambda_{CQ_B}}{\lambda_{CQ_A}}) = 0.333 \times \frac{1}{3} = 0.111 \qquad (7\text{-}7\text{-}8)$$

Therefore the coupling effects are decaying with the same ratio for each circle.

The decay factor is just the ratio of the relative gains. From the above expression we can see that the first decay factor is the ratio of the initial deviation to λ_{CQ_A} and from then on the decay ratio is $\frac{1}{3}$.

The numerator λ_{QQ_A} of the second term is the change of the output flow Q caused by the effects of the first term due to the coupling, so it is a kind of disturbance results and the denominator of the second term is a kind of control actions needed to eliminate the disturbance result due to the coupling.

This is the case when correct variable pairing is adopted.

Now, we discuss the results when the uncorrect variable pairing is adopted.

We still take Table 7-7-2 as an example. Now, we suppose that C is controlled by Q_B and Q by Q_A.

Obviously, when there are 0.25 units of changes with C, then one unit change is necessary for Q_B to compensate the change of C. But one unit change of Q_B will cause 0.75 units change of Q and in order to eliminate this change of Q, some change of Q_A is needed, so this is a circulative process.

The change of Q_B is :

$$\Delta Q_B = (\frac{\Delta C}{\lambda_{CQ_B}}) \ (\frac{\lambda_{QQ_B}}{\lambda_{QQ_A}}) \ (\frac{\lambda_{CQ_A}}{\lambda_{CQ_B}}) \qquad (7\text{-}7\text{-}9)$$

Substituting the values of Table 7-7-2 in it, we get:

$$Q_B = (\frac{0.25}{0.25})(\frac{0.75}{0.25})(\frac{0.75}{0.25}) = 1 \times 3 \times 3 = 9 \qquad (7\text{-}7\text{-}10)$$

So, when at the beginning Q_B has one unit change, after two circles 9 units of changes are needed to restore the control.

Therefore, this is an unstable system.

This example shows that the variable pairing is with very important meaning in coupled system analysis. So when we treat a multivariable process control system design, we should choose proper variable pairing relations.

The relative gain analysis method is the most effective method for choosing correct variable pairing relations.Sometimes, if we do not use the relative gain to determine the correct variable pairing relations but only by some simple observations , the uncorrect variable pairing relations may be resulted in.

For example,Fig 7-7-3 is a flow mixing system with three liquids.

Suppose that the liquids through V_1 and V_3 are with the temperature of 100° F and that through V_2 is with the temperature of 200° F.

The arrangement of this system is symmetrical and the liquids through the three valves are mixed in the two side tubes. We want to control the temperature of the two side tubes and the total flow.

To control the temperature means to con- trol the heat. For example, the heat H_{11} comes from the liquids through valves V_1 and V_2. Suppose that the pressure and specific heat are the same for the three

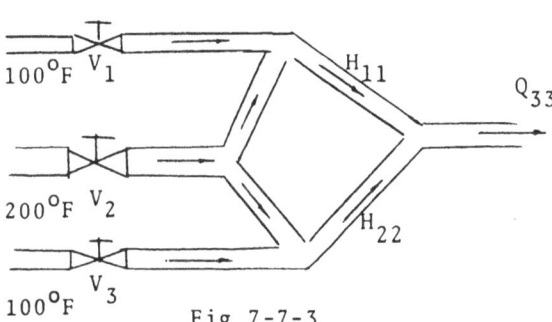

Fig 7-7-3

input liquids and all valves are linear, then the heat H_{11} can be ex- pressed as:

$$H_{11} = 100 \times \frac{V_1}{100} + 0.5 \times 200 \times \frac{V_2}{100} = V_1 + V_2 \qquad (7\text{-}7\text{-}11)$$

Similarly, H_{22} can be expressed as:

$$H_{22} = 100 \times \frac{V_3}{100} + 0.5 \times 200 \times \frac{V_2}{100} = V_2 + V_3 \qquad (7\text{-}7\text{-}12)$$

The total output flow can be expressed as:

$$Q_{33} = \frac{V_1}{100} + \frac{V_2}{100} + \frac{V_3}{100} \qquad (7\text{-}7\text{-}13)$$

or:

$$Q_{33}' = 100Q_{33} = V_1 + V_2 + V_3 \qquad (7\text{-}7\text{-}14)$$

Now, we discuss how to choose suitable variable pairing relations for this system. We see that there are six possible pairing relations for this system.

Controlled Varibles		H_{11}	H_{22}	Q_{33}'
1		V_1	V_2	V_3
2	Manipulated Variable	V_1	V_3	V_2
3		V_2	V_1	V_3
4		V_2	V_3	V_1
5		V_3	V_1	V_2
6		V_3	V_2	V_1

But, which is the most suitable pairing?

If we do not analyze the pairing relations by relative gain analysis and only by simple observation, then in general we will think that the second pairing relation is suitable because the system is symmetrical and this pairing relation is just in accordance with the symmetrical structure.

But, is it true in practice ?

Now, let us analyze the relative gains.

The first gain coefficient matrix of this system is :

$$
\Phi = \begin{bmatrix} \dfrac{\partial H_{11}}{\partial v_1} & \dfrac{\partial H_{11}}{\partial v_2} & \dfrac{\partial H_{11}}{\partial v_3} \\[2mm] \dfrac{\partial Q_{33}}{\partial v_1} & \dfrac{\partial Q_{33}}{\partial v_2} & \dfrac{\partial Q_{33}}{\partial v_3} \\[2mm] \dfrac{\partial H_{22}}{\partial v_1} & \dfrac{\partial H_{22}}{\partial v_2} & \dfrac{\partial H_{22}}{\partial v_3} \end{bmatrix} = \begin{bmatrix} 1 & 1 & 0 \\ 1 & 1 & 1 \\ 0 & 1 & 1 \end{bmatrix} =
$$

$$
= \begin{bmatrix} \varphi_{11} & \varphi_{12} & \varphi_{13} \\ \varphi_{21} & \varphi_{22} & \varphi_{23} \\ \varphi_{31} & \varphi_{32} & \varphi_{33} \end{bmatrix} \tag{7-7-15}
$$

and the inverse matrix is:

$$
\Phi^{-1} = \begin{bmatrix} 0 & 1 & -1 \\ 1 & -1 & 1 \\ -1 & 1 & 0 \end{bmatrix} \tag{7-7-16}
$$

So:

$$
(\Phi^{-1})^T = \begin{bmatrix} 0 & 1 & -1 \\ 1 & -1 & 1 \\ -1 & 1 & 0 \end{bmatrix} = \begin{bmatrix} \psi_{11} & \psi_{12} & \psi_{13} \\ \psi_{21} & \psi_{22} & \psi_{13} \\ \psi_{31} & \psi_{32} & \psi_{33} \end{bmatrix} \tag{7-7-17}
$$

and the relative gain matrix is:

$$
\Lambda = \begin{bmatrix} \varphi_{11}\psi_{11} & \varphi_{12}\psi_{12} & \varphi_{13}\psi_{13} \\ \varphi_{21}\psi_{21} & \varphi_{22}\psi_{22} & \varphi_{23}\psi_{23} \\ \varphi_{31}\psi_{31} & \varphi_{32}\psi_{32} & \varphi_{23}\dot\psi_{33} \end{bmatrix} = \begin{bmatrix} 1\times0 & 1\times1 & 1\times(-1) \\ 1\times1 & 1\times(-1) & 1\times1 \\ 0\times(-1) & 1\times1 & 1\times0 \end{bmatrix} =
$$

$$
= \begin{bmatrix} 0 & 1 & 0 \\ 1 & -1 & 1 \\ 0 & 1 & 0 \end{bmatrix} \tag{7-7-18}
$$

It means:

	V_1	V_2	V_3
H_{11}	0	1	0
Q_{33}	1	-1	1
H_{22}	0	1	0

Now, we can see which pairing is the most suitable.

We have said that by simple observation we will choose V_1 to control H_{11} and V_3 to control H_{22}. But, if we choose this pairing relation, then the relative gain array is:

	V_1	V_2	V_3
H_{11}	0		
Q_{33}		-1	
H_{22}			0

and we see that it is the worst control scheme indeed because two relative gains are zero and the third is -1 , so that none of the variables can be controlled well.

If we adopt:

	V_1	V_2	V_3
H_{11}	0		
Q_{33}			1
H_{22}		1	

or:

	V_1	V_2	V_3
H_{11}		1	
Q_{33}			1
H_{22}	0		

then both schemes are better than the above one.

Thus, for some multivariable process control systems, the application of relative gain analysis can discover some imperceptible intrinsical control properties.

Now , we discuss why the scheme which seems rational by observation is not reasonable in practice.

It is not difficult to understand. Fig 7-7-4 is such a scheme.

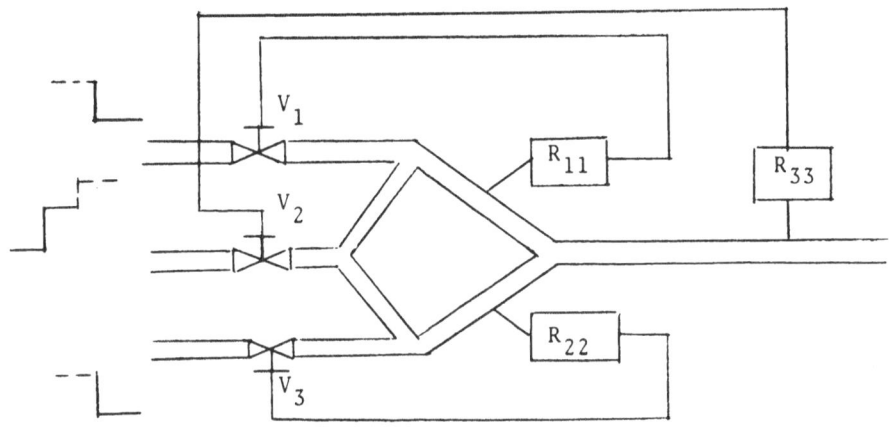

Fig 7-7-3

When there is a step increment in V_2 , both H_{11} and H_{22} will increase and thus the two regulators R_{11} and R_{22} will act on V_1 and V_3 to decrease these two input flows. But, because both V_1 and V_3 decrease simultaneously, then Q_{33} will also decrease. The decrease of Q_{33} will make regulator R_{33} act on V_2 to increase V_2 further. So, this is an unstable circle and the system is an unstable system. This is because uncorrect variable pairing is adopted.

§ 7-8 Coupling Indices[51]

The above analysis shows that for a multivariable system because of the different choice of variable pairing relations, sometimes the coupling process decays more and more, but, on the contrary, sometimes it may be serious more and more ,i.e a divergent process.

No matter convergent or divergent, the circles repeat with the equal ratio in the process.

When the common ratio is less than 1, then the process is convergent and is a **divergent** process when the common ratio is larger than 1.

This common ratio expressed by D in the furture is called as the coupling index and it denotes the coupling results being convergent or divergent.

Now, let us discuss (7-7-5):

$$\Delta Q_B = (\frac{\Delta C}{\lambda_{CQ_A}})(\frac{\lambda_{QQ_A}}{\lambda_{QQ_B}})(\frac{\lambda_{CQ_B}}{\lambda_{CQ_A}})$$ (7-8-1)

What can we know from this expression ?

It denotes when there is a change ΔC with C,then through λ_{CQ_A} a corresponding change of Q_A occurs to keep C being unchanged and this is half a circle. Then, due to the change of Q_A , through λ_{QQ_A} a change in Q occurs and it further causes a change of Q_B through λ_{QQ_B} and this is the second half circle . The change of Q_B will cause the change of C through λ_{CQ_B} and it will further cause the change of Q_A through λ_{CQ_A}. This is the third half circle and so on.

For a two-variable system, the following relation is always held:

$$D = \frac{\lambda_{QQ_A}}{\lambda_{QQ_B}} = \frac{\lambda_{CQ_B}}{\lambda_{CQ_A}}$$ (7-8-2)

As we said in the last paragraph, when:

$D = \frac{1}{3}$,the process is convergent,

$D = 3$, the process is divergent.

So, in general, when:

$D < 1$, the process is convergent, stable,

$D > 1$, the process is divergent, unstable.

Therefore, if the change of some manipulated variable is denoted as m and its initial deviation is ε , then from the above analysis, we can know:

$$m = \varepsilon D^{(N-1)} \qquad\qquad (7-8-3)$$

where, N is the number of the half circles under consideration.

So, when we analyze the variable pairing relations for a multivariable process control system, we can use the coupling indices. We see when the coupling index approaches zero, then the coupling results become less and less and this means that this system is easily to be controlled. Thus the magnitudes of the coupling indices denote the properties of a coupled system. For the above example, if Q is controlled by Q_A , then the coupling index is 3 and the process is unstable. If Q is controlled by Q_B , then the coupling index is 0.333 and the coupling results decay more and more and, consequently, in this system the reasonable variable pairing relations should be $Q_A \longleftrightarrow C$ and $Q_B \longleftrightarrow Q$.

In a two-variable control system, there are only two possible pairing relations, so one of them will give a convergent process and the other will give a divergent process.

Certainly, the following case may also exist:

	Q	C
Q_A	0.5	0.5
Q_B	0.5	0.5

and in this case, no matter which pairing relation is adopted the coupling index is always 1 and this means that the coupling process is a uniform oscillation. This oscillation process is going continuosly and so it can be considered as a **serious** couplng process.

For a convergent process, we often want to know how many half circles are needed for reaching the control demands.

In other words, it means that m, ε and D are given and N should be determined.

It is not difficult to determine N. Taking logarithms to each
side of (7-8-3), we get:

$$\ln m = \ln \mathcal{E} + (N-1)\ln D \qquad\qquad (7\text{-}8\text{-}4)$$

It follows:

$$N = \frac{\ln m - \ln \mathcal{E}}{\ln D} + 1 \qquad\qquad (7\text{-}8\text{-}5)$$

Certainly, only integral results are available.

Obviously, when $D \longrightarrow 1$, then $N \longrightarrow \infty$.

All the above analysis is done for a process with coupling. We
see that for such a process there are three possible cases: decaying
(convergent), divergent and oscillation with equal amptitude. Obviously,
for the practical application, there are also three possible cases:
available, unavailable and permissible for some improvement.

The available process means : 1. the variable pairing relations
are correct, 2. the coupling indices are satisfactory,3. the value of
N is small enough. If the above three demands are satisfied, then the
system can be used without special decoupling design.

For the unavailable system, perhaps at first the uncorrect variable pairing relations are chosen and the coupling indices are larger
than 1 and a divergent process is obtained . So, in this case, we must
change the variable pairing relations at first.

But, sometimes the variable pairing relations may be correct
and for a practical process, the coupling indices may be not suitable,
for example less than 1 but close to 1. This is the case permissible
for some improvement. In other words, decoupling design is needed in
order to get better control effects.

If there is no possibility for choosing suitable variable pairing relations and the system is with large coupling indices then certainly decoupling design is needed and this means to use additional

measures to reduce the coupling results.

§ 7-9 Dynamic Relative Gains [61]

The relative gains introduced above are available for steady states. Now, let us discuss the dynamic case. Can we also find some similar relative gains for dynamic states? If any, what practical meaning do they have ?

We discuss a two-variable P-canonical plant shown in Fig 7-9-1.

We have:

$$C_1 = m_1 P_{11}(S) + m_2 P_{12}(S) \quad (7\text{-}9\text{-}1)$$

$$C_2 = m_1 P_{21}(S) + m_2 P_{22}(S) \quad (7\text{-}9\text{-}2)$$

We can also define a dynamic relative gain :

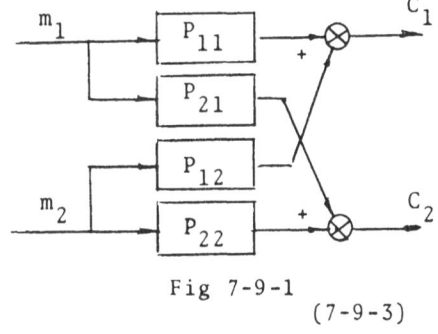

Fig 7-9-1

$$\lambda_{C_1 m_1} = \frac{\left(\dfrac{\partial C_1}{\partial m_1}\right)\Big|_{S, m_2 = 0}}{\left(\dfrac{\partial C_1}{\partial m_1}\right)\Big|_{S, C_2 = 0}} \quad (7\text{-}9\text{-}3)$$

where, S is considered as a constant.

$m_2 = 0$ and $C_2 = 0$ mean that there are no changes in m_2 and C_2 because all expressions are in increment forms.

Then from (7-9-1) and (7-9-3), we get:

$$\lambda_{C_1 m_1} = \frac{P_{11}}{P_{11} - \dfrac{P_{12} P_{21}}{P_{22}}} = \frac{1}{1 - \dfrac{P_{12} P_{21}}{P_{11} P_{22}}} \quad (7\text{-}9\text{-}4)$$

Denote:

$$K = \frac{P_{12} P_{21}}{P_{11} P_{22}} \quad (7\text{-}9\text{-}5)$$

By the similar method, we can get $\lambda_{C_1 m_2}$, $\lambda_{C_2 m_1}$ and $\lambda_{C_2 m_2}$.

Then, we can get the following dynamic relative gain array:

$$
\begin{array}{ccc}
 & m_1 & m_2 \\
C_1 & \dfrac{1}{1-K} & -\dfrac{K}{1-K} \\
\\
C_2 & \dfrac{-K}{1-K} & \dfrac{1}{1-K}
\end{array}
$$

Just like the static relative gain array, in the above array the sum of the elements of every row , or column , is equal to 1.

We have:

$$\lambda_{C_1 m_1} = \frac{1}{1-K} \tag{7-9-6}$$

so:

$$K = \frac{\lambda_{C_1 m_1} - 1}{\lambda_{C_1 m_1}} \tag{7-9-7}$$

Now, we discuss the meaning of $\lambda_{C_1 m_1}$.

At first, we know that in the dynamic analysis, $\lambda_{C_1 m_1}$ is meaningful within some frequency domain. Let $S = jw$, then $\lambda_{C_1 m_1}$ is a quantity with both amplitude and phase.

We discuss the amplitude at first. We can explain its meaning by the same manner adopted for the explanation of the static relative gains. So, it is a ratio of two gain coefficients ($m_i \longrightarrow C_j$) obtained in two cases ($m_k = 0$, $k \neq i$ and $C_k = 0$, $k \neq j$) at some definite frequency. For $\lambda_{C_1 m_1}$, these two cases mean that the second channel is open and the second channel has realized ideal control at that frequency, respectively. Thus, $\lambda_{C_1 m_1}$ is a measurement of coupling degree of m_1 and C_1 at some definite frequency.

The meaning of the phase of $\lambda_{C_1 m_1}$ is rather difficult to be understood. In fact, it is a measurement of time which is needed for the disturbance transferring from one channel to another. Thus, it denotes whether the disturbance is transferred from one channel to another in suitable time and it is also able to be an indirect measurement of the coupling effects.

We give our stress on the meaning of different values of $\lambda_{C_1 m_1}$.

Obviously, when $\lambda_{C_1 m_1} = 1$, then there is no coupling in the system because $K = 0$. So, in this case , either P_{12} or P_{21} is equal to zero . Although in this case, unilateral coupling channels may still exist, this case can be considered as an independent disturbance entering a channel and the whole system can be transferred into two subsystems without coupling.

$\lambda_{C_1 m_1} = 0.5$ denotes the most serious coupling.

Notice that $\lambda_{C_1 m_1}$ may be larger than 1. When K is in the scope of $0.5 \longrightarrow 1.0$, then $\lambda_{C_1 m_1}$ becomes a large positive number N and the relative gain array is:

	m_1	m_2
C_1	N	1 - N
C_2	1 - N	N

The large value N for $\lambda_{C_1 m_1}$ means that the channel m_1 to C_1 is with very weak control action , so this is not suitable for control either.

Now, we discuss an example. The plant is:

$$C_1 = \frac{K_{11} e^{-\tau_{11} S}}{T_{11} S + 1} m_1 + \frac{K_{12} e^{-\tau_{12} S}}{T_{12} S + 1} m_2 \qquad (7\text{-}9\text{-}8)$$

$$C_2 = \frac{K_{21} e^{-\tau_{21} S}}{T_{21} S + 1} m_2 + \frac{K_{22} e^{-\tau_{22} S}}{T_{22} S + 1} m_2 \qquad (7\text{-}9\text{-}9)$$

Substituting all these to (7-9-5), we get:

$$K = (\frac{K_{12} K_{21}}{K_{11} K_{22}})(\frac{T_{11} S + 1}{T_{22} S + 1})(\frac{T_{12} S + 1}{T_{21} S + 1}) e^{-(\tau_{12} + \tau_{21} - \tau_{11} - \tau_{22})S}$$

$$(7\text{-}9\text{-}10)$$

K denotes the coupling degree of coupling and we see that it is related with K_{ij}, T_{ij} and τ_{ij}.

That means that these three terms will give influence on the coupling degree.

Because K is a complex number, so from (7-9-10) we know that $\mathcal{T}_{ij}$ will not give influence on the amplitude of K. $\mathcal{T}_{ij}$ denotes the transfer time of coupling signals from one channel to another. In general, when the sum of ($\mathcal{T}_{12}+\mathcal{T}_{21}-\mathcal{T}_{11}-\mathcal{T}_{22}$) is large, the coupling results are always harmful.

The amplitude of K is easily to be understood. When only steady state is considered, we have:

$$K = \frac{K_{12}K_{21}}{K_{11}K_{22}} \qquad (7-9-11)$$

and:

$$\lambda_{C_1 m_1} = \frac{1}{1 - \dfrac{K_{12}K_{21}}{K_{11}K_{22}}} \qquad (7-9-12)$$

T_{ij} gives the frequency influence on K and λ, for example, if:

$$P_{11} = P_{22} = \frac{2e^{-S}}{10S + 1} \qquad (7-9-13)$$

$$P_{12} = P_{21} = \frac{0.5e^{-S}}{S + 1} \qquad (7-9-14)$$

for different frequencies, the results of. K and $\lambda_{C_1 m_1}$ are given as:

w	K	$\lambda_{C_1 m_1}$
0	0.0625	1.065
0.1	0.125	1.14
0.2	0.301	1.43
0.3	0.573	2.34
0.4	0.917	12.05

If we use the steady state results to research the variable pairing, then the follwing relative gain array is:

	m_1	m_2
C_1	1.065	-0.065
C_2	-0.065	1.065

So, the reasonable control project is to use m_1 to control C_1 and m_2 to control C_2.

But, from the above table we can see although this variable pairing is responsible for steady state, it will cause serious coupling results in the high frequency cases.

That means when the inputs are step functions($w = 0$), we can get good variable pairing relations. But,when these variable pairing relations have been determined and the inputs become sine functions , then the coupling problem will be serious as the increase of the frequency and decoupling design is needed.

Therefore, whether the decoupling design is needed is related not only to the variable pairing, but also to the frequency scope.

But in process control systems, in general the inputs can be considered as step functions, so in fact to consider the relative gain array in steady state is enough.

§ 7-10 Relative Gains in Time Domain [61]

We have introduced the relative gains of steady states and dynamic states. When we discussed the dynamic relative gains , they were obtained at different frequencies.

But there is another meaning about dynamic relative gains, i.e. the meaning in time domain.

Any response takes place in time domain and the steady state is only a special case, i.e. $t \longrightarrow \infty$. Then, certainly, we can propose a question: How about the coupling cases in the time domain, is it the same at any time? If not, then at different times, how can we estimate the coupling results?

In the study of coupling results in time domain, the input can be considered as a step function.

The principles and the steps of the study of coupling results in time domain are the same as those taken for the research of steady state gains, namely the variable pairing is taken one by one while the other variables remain unchanged.

Suppose that m_1 is paired with C_1 and then there is a step change with m_1. The change of C_1 caused by that of m_1 in the period $0 \longrightarrow t$ is:

$$\Delta C_1 = \int_0^t (C_1 - C_s) d\theta \qquad (7\text{-}10\text{-}1)$$

where, C_s is the steady state value of C_1 and m_2 remains unchanged.

Likewise, we can get(when m_2 is paired with C_2) :

$$\Delta C_2 = \int_0^t (C_2 - C_s) d\theta \qquad (7\text{-}10\text{-}2)$$

Then, we get the following matrix:

$$M = \begin{bmatrix} (\dfrac{\Delta C_1}{\Delta m_1})_{m_2} & (\dfrac{\Delta C_2}{\Delta m_1})_{m_2} \\ \\ (\dfrac{\Delta C_1}{\Delta m_2})_{m_1} & (\dfrac{\Delta C_2}{\Delta m_2})_{m_1} \end{bmatrix} \qquad (7\text{-}10\text{-}3)$$

What do the elements of this matrix mean ?

Obviously, they are the first gain coefficients in time domain.

So, by the method of getting the relative gain matrix we calculate:

$$\psi = (M^{-1})^T \qquad (7\text{-}10\text{-}4)$$

and:

$$\lambda_{ij} = M_{ij} \psi_{ij} \qquad (7\text{-}10\text{-}5)$$

Then we get the relative gain matrix:

$$\Lambda = \begin{bmatrix} \lambda_{11} & 1 - \lambda_{11} \\ 1 - \lambda_{11} & \lambda_{11} \end{bmatrix} \qquad (7\text{-}10\text{-}6)$$

where:

$$\lambda_{C_1 m_1} = \cfrac{1}{1 - \cfrac{(\dfrac{\Delta C_2}{\Delta m_1})_{m_2} (\dfrac{\Delta C_1}{\Delta m_2})_{m_1}}{(\dfrac{\Delta C_1}{\Delta m_1})_{m_2} (\dfrac{\Delta C_2}{\Delta m_2})_{m_2}}} \qquad (7\text{-}10\text{-}7)$$

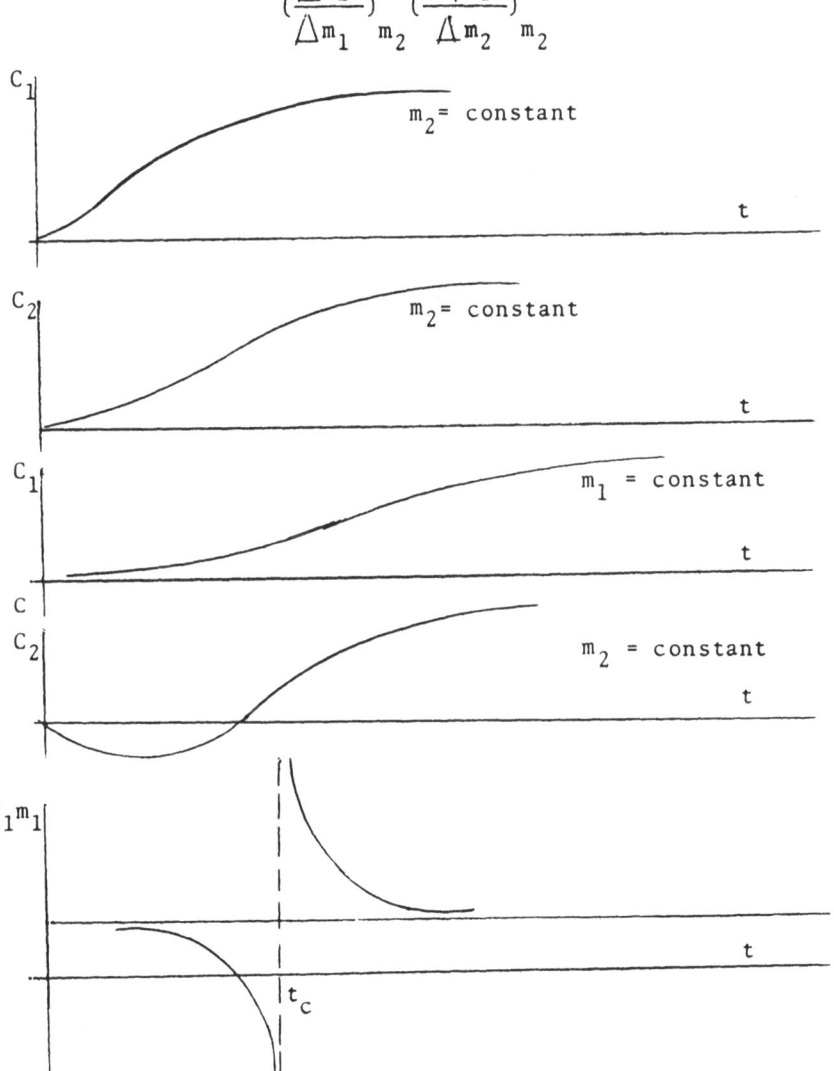

Fig 7-10-1

A typical system is shown in Fig 7-10-1.

When t $\longrightarrow \infty$, all curves are towards determinate values and:

$$\lambda_{C_1 m_1} = \cfrac{1}{1 - \cfrac{K_{12}K_{21}}{K_{11}K_{22}}} \tag{7-10-8}$$

where, K_{ij} is the steady gain of the channel m_j to C_i.

From 7-10-1 we can see that the coupling results are very serious at the beginning step and this is because the existence of the inverse response of $(\Delta c_2 / \Delta m_2)_{m_1}$.

The $\lambda_{C_1 m_1}$ decreases as the time increases and at some time t_c,

$\lambda_{C_1 m_1}$ is towards $-\infty$, and in the interval $t > t_c$, $\lambda_{C_1 m_1}$ varies from positive infinite to a steady value. So, before the steady state, this system is with serious coupling.

This means that some definite variable pairing relation can not be expected to be satisfactory in each case for a system when the dynamic coupling results are also considered.

§ 7-11 The Application of Relative Gain Method to General Decoupling Design [7]

We have said how to use the Bristol relative gain matrix to judge the coupling degrees of system variables in the steady state. Then, by this judgement, the system can be reduced to the simplest and most reasonable form.

The next step is the decoupling design.

The decoupling design can be carried out by the methods intro-

duced in the previous chapters. But, the unit matrix method should not
be confounded with the unit relative gain matrix. They are different
concepts but are with relations indeed. That means that the last relative gain matrix of the system designed by using the unit matrix method
or other methods should be a diagonal matrix.

For example, for a two-variable P-canonical plant, when P-canonical
decoupling element structure is adopted and is arranged between the
plant and the regulators, the system block diagram is shown below:

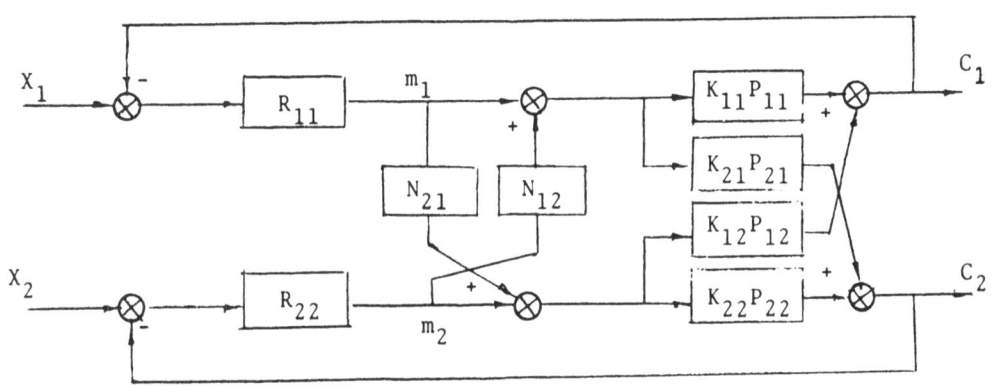

Fig 7-11-1

Obviously, the system will be decoupled, if the following relations are satisfied:

$$N_{12} = - \frac{K_{12}P_{12}}{K_{11}P_{11}} \qquad (7-11-1)$$

$$N_{21} = - \frac{K_{21}P_{21}}{K_{22}P_{22}} \qquad (7-11-2)$$

The relative gain between m_1 and C_1 is:

$$\lambda_{11} = \frac{1}{1 - \frac{(K_{21} + n_{21}K_{22})(K_{12} + n_{12}K_{11})}{(K_{22} + n_{12}K_{21})(K_{11} + n_{21}K_{12})}} \qquad (7-11-3)$$

where n_{12} and n_{21} are the steady gains of N_{12} and N_{21}.

Obviously, when:

$$n_{21} = - \frac{K_{21}}{K_{22}}$$

$$n_{12} = - \frac{K_{12}}{K_{11}}$$

$$(7-11-4)$$

then:

$$\lambda_{11} = 1 \qquad\qquad (7-11-5)$$

and very good decoupling control is reached.

But, when:

$$n_{12} = - \frac{K_{22}}{K_{21}}$$

$$n_{21} = - \frac{K_{11}}{K_{12}}$$

$$(7-11-6)$$

then $\lambda_{11} = 0$, and the system is beyond control entirely.

When:

$$n_{12} n_{21} = 1.0 \qquad\qquad (7-11-7)$$

then :

$$\lambda_{11} = \infty \qquad\qquad (7-11-8)$$

and the system is unstable then and so it is also out of control.

Thus, the gains of decoupling elements N_{12} and N_{21} must be chosen carefully in order to get good decoupling control and unsuitable choice of n_{12} and n_{21} may result in the failure of control.We see that these results can be easily obtained by the application of Bristol relative gain method. (7-11-1) and (7-11-2) only give the decoupling conditions but can not show what will hapen when these conditions are divagated.

Then, how to determine the parameters of the decoupling elements? There are two decoupling elements, should we determine their parameters one by one ?

We need not do so. In order to determine the regulator parameters, we let:

$$n_{21} = -K \frac{K_{21}}{K_{22}} \qquad\qquad (7\text{-}11\text{-}9)$$

$$n_{12} = -K \frac{K_{12}}{K_{11}} \qquad\qquad (7\text{-}11\text{-}10)$$

From the above analysis we know when $K = 1$, then the above two conditions are just (7-11-1) and (7-11-2), i.e. the decoupling control is realized.

From the view-point of decoupling, certainly the perfect decoupling is the best, but when we consider the dynamic responses of the system, the perfect decoupling control may be not the best and in general,

$$K = 0 \longrightarrow 0.7 \qquad\qquad (7\text{-}11\text{-}11)$$

is the scope for choice. That means that K should not be too large and a slight coupling in the system is available.

On the other hand, from (7-11-7) we know when $n_{12}n_{21} = 1.0$, the system is out of control and it corresponds to:

$$K_{\infty} = \sqrt{\frac{K_{11}K_{22}}{K_{12}K_{21}}} \qquad\qquad (7\text{-}11\text{-}12)$$

For example, suppose :

$$K_{11} = 0.673 , \quad K_{21} = 0.462 ,$$
$$K_{12} = -0.573, \quad K_{22} = -0.488$$

then from (7-11-12) we get:

$$K_{\infty} = 1.1 \qquad\qquad (7\text{-}11\text{-}13)$$

namely, when K takes this value , then $\lambda_{11} \longrightarrow \infty$ and the system is out of control.

For the above values of K_{11} to K_{22} , several typical values of λ_{11} are given below.

Fig 7-11-2 illustrates the change of λ_{11} as K varies.

n_{12}	n_{21}	λ_{11}
0	0	5.23
0.854	0.947	1.00
1.056	1.170	0.00
1.000	1.000	∞

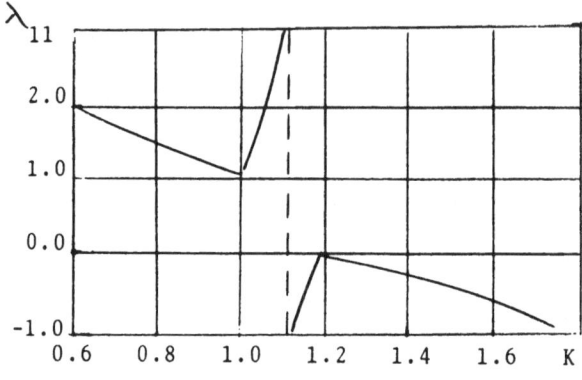

Fig 7-11-2

From the figure we know that λ_{11} is never in the scope $0 \longrightarrow 1$, no matter what value K takes.

Why does it happen ?

The relative gain of the original plant is:

$$\lambda_{11p} = \frac{1}{1 - \dfrac{K_{12}K_{21}}{K_{11}K_{22}}} \qquad (7\text{-}11\text{-}14)$$

Substituting it into (7-11-12), we get:

$$K_{\infty} = \sqrt{\frac{\lambda_{11p}}{\lambda_{11p} - 1}} \qquad (7\text{-}11\text{-}15)$$

Obviously, when λ_{11p} is larger than one and incerases, then $K_{\infty} \longrightarrow 1$. In such a case, we can use decoupling elements to re- duce the system deviation , i.e. to improve the system properties. Then it is possible to provent K_{∞} from taking some real value because k_{∞} taking some real value means the system being out of control. When λ_{11p} is in the scope $0 \longrightarrow 1$, then K_{∞} is an imaginary

number and this means that no matter what value K takes, no real value
of K_∞ will exist; in other words , $n_{12}n_{21}$ will not equal one and
λ_{11} will not be towards infinite either. Therefore, such a coupled
plant is very easily to realize decoupling control because no   value of
K will cause the system out of control and we can choose suitable K to
get some desired λ_{11}.

Thus, for the plants with $|\lambda_{11}| > 1$, it is possible to choose some
K to make $|\lambda_{11}|$ be the least and it is also possible that the system
is out of control because of unsuitable choice of K.

For the plants with $|\lambda_{11}| < 1$, no value of K can cause the system
out of control and suitable choice of K can make λ_{11} be in the scope
$0 \longrightarrow 1$.

For example,

$$K_{11} = 0.185 \qquad K_{21} = -0.241$$

$$K_{12} = 0.100 \qquad K_{22} = -0.071$$

then $\lambda_{11p} = 0.35$.

We can get the following calculation results:

K	λ_{11}
0	0.35
0.5	0.89
1.0	1.00
1.5	0.97
∞	0.35

Obviously, comparing with the cases of K = 0 and K = ∞ , any value of K can improve the relative gain and avails to reducing coupling.
When K = 1.0 , the decoupling effects are the best.

§ 7-12 Decoupling Design using Triangle Matrices [7][44][89]

Certainly it is an ideal control if a multivariable process control system can realize perfect decoupling. But, however, it is not possible in any case and, on the other hand, sometimes it is also not necessary.

Some decoupling elements are necessary for realizing decoupling control. The least number of the decoupling elements including the main regulators is the square of the number of the controlled variables.

Obviously, the more the number of the controlled variables, the more complicated the decoupling element structure. Consequently, the realization problem of decoupling elements and the practical arrangement also become more difficult. In fact, in some chemical process, not all controlled variable are with the same importance. Sometimes, one of the controlled variables is necessary to be controlled precisely, for example, in a distillation column the composition of one terminal is the most important controlled variable. Owing to this fact in many chemical processes, Shinskey suggested to use the half-decoupling design and he proposed the triangle matrix design **idea** including both upper triangle matrices and lower matrices.

The general meaning of half decoupling design by using triangle matrices has been introduce in § 5-7 and now we will give a further discussion on it.

We know when the feedforward decoupling projects are used to realize decoupling control , if the diagonal matrix method is adopted, then the plant transfer matrix should be multiplied by the decoupling element structure transfer matrix to form a diagonal matrix; if the unit matrix method is adopted, then a unit matrix is formed. Likewise, the result may be an upper triangle matrix or a lower triangle matrix and the half decoupling control is obtained.

Take a three-variable system as an example and its block dia-

387

gram is shown in Fig 7-12-1.

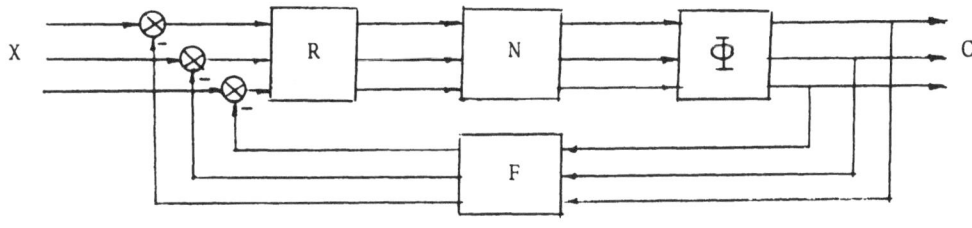

Fig 7-12-1

In order to be in accordance with the notations used in the Bristol method, the plant transfer matrix here is denoted by Φ.

The design principle is to multiply Φ with the decoupling element structure matrix N and the product should be an upper triangle matrix or a lower triangle matrix.

But the multiplication of two matrices Φ and N will result in different products for different orders of Φ and N, namely they are different for pre-multiplying and post-multiplying.

That matrix Φ is post-multiplied by matrix N means that the decoupling element structure is arranged between the plant and the regulators just as shown in Fig 7-12-1. That matrix Φ is pre-multiplied by matrix N means that the decoupling element structure is arranged after the plant. In practical process control engineering, the post-multiplying scheme is reasonable.

Thus, neither the upper triangle matrix nor the lower triangle matrix means the relative gain matrix. In fact, any relative gain matrix can not be an upper triangle matrix or a lower triangle matrix. The triangle matrix discussed here is the product of matrices Φ and N.

Thus, in such a system, at least one of the controlled variables is decoupled with other variables. Notice that in order to get the triangle matrix product, then matrix N must be triangular.

For example, for the system shown in Fig 7-12-1, we have:

$$Q = \Phi \, N \qquad\qquad\qquad (7\text{-}12\text{-}1)$$

namely:

$$Q = \begin{bmatrix} \varphi_{11} & \varphi_{12} & \varphi_{13} \\ \varphi_{21} & \varphi_{22} & \varphi_{23} \\ \varphi_{31} & \varphi_{32} & \varphi_{33} \end{bmatrix} \begin{bmatrix} 1 & 0 & 0 \\ N_{21} & 1 & 0 \\ N_{31} & N_{32} & 1 \end{bmatrix} = \begin{bmatrix} q_{11} & q_{12} & q_{13} \\ q_{21} & q_{22} & q_{23} \\ q_{31} & q_{32} & q_{33} \end{bmatrix}$$

$$(7\text{-}12\text{-}2)$$

In order to let Q be an upper triangle matrix, it is necessary:

$$\left. \begin{aligned} q_{21} &= \varphi_{21} + \varphi_{22}N_{21} + \varphi_{23}N_{31} = 0 \\ q_{31} &= \varphi_{31} + \varphi_{32}N_{21} + \varphi_{33}N_{31} = 0 \\ q_{32} &= \varphi_{32} + \varphi_{33}N_{32} = 0 \end{aligned} \right\} \qquad (7\text{-}12\text{-}3)$$

Because all φ_{ij} are known, so we can determine N_{ij} and then N is determined.

Then, each subsystem can be designed independently, namely to close F_{11}, F_{22} and F_{33} individually. In general, the adverse order is better. Because now C_1 is the controlled variable related to three manipulated variables, so at first we make some suitable arrangement for it and then C_2 and C_3. Notice that in this system C_3 has been decoupled with the other variables, so the closing order is adverse.

Now, we discuss the example of § 7-5. The three-variable system there after using the relative gaing matrix analysis is reduced to (7-5-32):

$$\Phi = \begin{bmatrix} \dfrac{1.6e^{-2S}}{1 + 12S} & \dfrac{-1.0e^{-1.5S}}{(1 + 0.5S)(1 + 5S)} \\[3ex] \dfrac{1.4}{S(1 + 0.5S)} & \dfrac{-1.6}{S(1 + 0.2S)} \end{bmatrix} \qquad (7\text{-}12\text{-}4)$$

We perform the half decoupling design to it, i.e. multiply it with a triangle matrix N.

When the pre-multiplying and the post-multiplying are applied to it, we obtain four possible cases:

1. $\Phi \begin{bmatrix} 1 & 0 \\ N & 1 \end{bmatrix}$. When $N = \dfrac{1.4}{1.6}$, we get $Q = \begin{bmatrix} 0.7 & -1.0 \\ 0 & -\dfrac{1.6}{S} \end{bmatrix}$

2. $\Phi \begin{bmatrix} 1 & N \\ N & 1 \end{bmatrix}$. When $N = \dfrac{1.4}{1.6}$, we get $Q = \begin{bmatrix} 1.6 & 0 \\ \dfrac{1.4}{S} & -\dfrac{0.7}{S} \end{bmatrix}$

3. $\begin{bmatrix} 1 & 0 \\ N & 1 \end{bmatrix} \Phi$. When $N = -\dfrac{1.4}{1.6S}$, we get $Q = \begin{bmatrix} 1.6 & -1.0 \\ 0 & -\dfrac{0.7}{S} \end{bmatrix}$

4. $\begin{bmatrix} 1 & N \\ 0 & 1 \end{bmatrix} \Phi$. When $N = -\dfrac{S}{1.6}$, we get $Q = \begin{bmatrix} 0.7 & 0 \\ \dfrac{1.4}{S} & -\dfrac{1.6}{S} \end{bmatrix}$

All these are steady states. As for its dynamic characters, take the third case as an example, it is:

$$N(S) = -\frac{1.4}{S(1+0.5S)} \frac{1 + 12S}{1.6e^{-2S}} = -\frac{0.9(1 + 12S)e^{2S}}{1 + 0.5S} \qquad (7\text{-}12\text{-}5)$$

Because e^{2S} is physically irrealizable, so we need not consider this case.

When the first case is considered, we have:

$$N(S) = \frac{1.4}{S(1 + 0.5S)} \frac{S(1 + 0.2S)}{1.6} = \frac{0.9(1 + 0.2S)}{1 + 1.5S}$$

$$(7\text{-}12\text{-}6)$$

This is realizable . So if we choose N(S) as (7-12-6) , then the half decoupling control with an **upper triangle transfer matrix** is obtained. In fact, in §7-5 we have analyzed this system and we know that C_2 has no coupling by the original analysis and now C_3 is decoupled with m_3 (notice (7-5-32)) , so only C_1 is coupled with m_2 and m_1. That means that for a three-variable system, two controlled variables have got de-coupling control and we can say that in general it has been quite satis-factory in practice.

The above principles of half decoupling design can be easily ex-tended to more multivariable systems.

At first, the system should be analyzed by the Bristol relative gain matrix in order to get the simplest and the most reasonable form.

For example, at last we get a four-variable system and the vari-able pairing relations have been arranged. We want to realize perfect decoupling control for channel Φ_{44} and the other channels can be arranged by their importance orders.

The upper triangle matrix obtained by post-multiplying design is:

$$
\begin{bmatrix} \varphi_{11} & \varphi_{12} & \varphi_{13} & \varphi_{14} \\ \varphi_{21} & \varphi_{22} & \varphi_{23} & \varphi_{24} \\ \varphi_{31} & \varphi_{32} & \varphi_{33} & \varphi_{34} \\ \varphi_{41} & \varphi_{42} & \varphi_{43} & \varphi_{44} \end{bmatrix} \begin{bmatrix} 1 & 0 & 0 & 0 \\ N_{21} & 1 & 0 & 0 \\ N_{31} & N_{32} & 1 & 0 \\ N_{41} & N_{42} & N_{43} & N_{44} \end{bmatrix} =
$$

$$
= \begin{bmatrix} q_{11} & q_{12} & q_{13} & q_{14} \\ 0 & q_{22} & q_{23} & q_{24} \\ 0 & 0 & q_{33} & q_{34} \\ 0 & 0 & 0 & q_{44} \end{bmatrix} \qquad (7\text{-}12\text{-}7)
$$

and from this equation we soon get:

$$
\begin{bmatrix}
\varphi_{22} & \varphi_{23} & \varphi_{24} & 0 & 0 & 0 \\
\varphi_{32} & \varphi_{33} & \varphi_{34} & 0 & 0 & 0 \\
\varphi_{42} & \varphi_{43} & \varphi_{44} & 0 & 0 & 0 \\
0 & 0 & 0 & \varphi_{33} & \varphi_{34} & 0 \\
0 & 0 & 0 & \varphi_{43} & \varphi_{44} & 0 \\
0 & 0 & 0 & 0 & 0 & \varphi_{44}
\end{bmatrix}
\begin{bmatrix}
N_{21} \\ N_{31} \\ N_{41} \\ N_{32} \\ N_{42} \\ N_{43}
\end{bmatrix}
= -
\begin{bmatrix}
\varphi_{21} \\ \varphi_{31} \\ \varphi_{41} \\ \varphi_{32} \\ \varphi_{42} \\ \varphi_{43}
\end{bmatrix}
\qquad
\begin{array}{l} 4\times4 \\[3em] 3\times3 \\[1.5em] 2\times2 \end{array}
$$

$$(7\text{-}12\text{-}8)$$

We can get N_{ij} from the above matrix equation and we see that the lower order system equations are always included in those of the higher order systems.

When the post-multiplying matrix is upper triangular, then Q obtained is a lower triangle matrix and in such a design, channel φ_{11} is perfectly decoupled and C_4 is with the most serious coupling control. We have then:

$$
\begin{bmatrix}
\varphi_{11} & 0 & & & & \\
0 & \varphi_{11} & \varphi_{12} & & & \\
& \varphi_{21} & \varphi_{22} & & & \\
& & & \varphi_{11} & \varphi_{12} & \varphi_{13} \\
& & & \varphi_{21} & \varphi_{22} & \varphi_{23} \\
& & & \varphi_{31} & \varphi_{32} & \varphi_{33}
\end{bmatrix}
\begin{bmatrix}
N_{12} \\ N_{13} \\ N_{23} \\ N_{14} \\ N_{24} \\ N_{34}
\end{bmatrix}
= -
\begin{bmatrix}
\varphi_{12} \\ \varphi_{13} \\ \varphi_{23} \\ \varphi_{14} \\ \varphi_{24} \\ \varphi_{34}
\end{bmatrix}
\qquad
\begin{array}{l} 2\times2 \\[3em] 3\times3 \\[3em] 4\times4 \end{array}
$$

The matrix equation for systems with more variables can be obtained by similar steps.

CHAPTER   EIGHT

DISTILLATION COLUMN CONTROL

§ 8-1 Introduction

In the petrolum and chemical industry, distillation columns are
not only very popular separation processes, but also the operation
units which expend energy the most. In U.S.A. people have surveyed and
got the conclusions that nearly 40 to 50 persents of energy in the petrolum and chemical industries are exhausted in the distillation units.
Thus, people have to pay great attention to the control problems of
distillation columns. We can say that the problems of distillation column control have occupied very important positions in both process
control theory and practice.

In order to save energy, we always hope to increase the efficiency of distillation processes. But, no matter we perform any improvement
in technology , the distillation column, as a perfect separation process , can not get high effiency , if no suitable control system is designed for it.

But the control of a distillation column is a rather difficult
problem. In the past quite a long period, people designed the distillation column control systems mainly by experience. For example, the most
popular control project adopted before is : to control the temperature
of the top tray by the reflux and to control the temperature of the bottom tray by up vapor or the steam of the reboiler. This project now is
called as conventional control project. It seems rational from the view-
point of experience. When the temperature of the top tray enhances ,
increasing the reflux rate can reduce the top temperature and when the
temperature of bottom tray becomes lower, then increasing the reboiler
steam rate can enhance the temperature of the bottom trays. But, however, people discovered also from the experience that the control results are not very good when it is used to control the compositions of

two terminals. Quite obvious interaction exists and sometimes the control even can not be realized. But only by experience people can not make clear where is the key of the problem. Thus, sometimes some people even asserted that it would not be able to realize the two-terminal composition control simultaneously.

The common reasons which cause the difficulty of distillation column control are owing to the following items:

(1) The control response of a distillation column with many trays is always very slow and it can be considered as a plant with dead delay,

(2) There are many factors influencing separation, thus many control loops are needed and there are always interactions among these loops and different variables,

(3) The dynamic theory research on a column is very complicated due to the numurous parameters, influencing factors of different kinds and the great number of trays. So, it is very difficult to get the suitable theory results which can be used in practice. Thus, we have to measure the column dynamics one by one and, consequently, we often find difficult to get some general properties of control plants,

(4) A distillation column, for example a product column, is often the eventual operational unit of a chemical process. Thus, many different influences of the previous units can be concentrated in this last unit,

(5) There are always a lot of variables in a distillation column and this fact causes the complexity of pairing the manipulated variables and the controlled variables. We have said that in the decoupling design of a multivariable process control system the correct choice of variable pairing is very important and in the distillation column control this problem is also very important and we can see later on that it is not easy to determine a proper paring of variables in distillation columns,

(6) Sometimes we find difficult to express different factors which

influence separation in control terminology. For example, there are always some constraint conditions in a distillation column and they are
not easily to be expressed in control terminology and control demands.

All the above items make the control of distillation columns be
difficult. Certainly, in different cases, the reasons are different
according to practical conditions.

However, from the middle of sixties, a breakthrough was achieved
in the distillation column control engineering both in theory and in
practice and Shinskey offered his prominant contributions to it. Using
an entirely new design method, Shinskey and others successfully designed
a series of complicated control systems for distillation columns and
got very satisfactory results. By the words of Shinskey, the appearance
of this new method is a " revolution in the distillation column control".

The essentiallity of this new method is to solve the most difficult
problem in distillation column control system design, namely the pairing
of variables , by using the sensitivities and the Bristol relative gain
as the main analyzing basis. Because when the rational pairing of variables is reached, then the design of control systems becomes easily to
be solved.

By using this method, we can judge theoretically that the conventional control project mentioned above is not a good project in fact
for the control of the compositions of the two terminals and we can
point out also how to analyze the system interaction. We can see that
the compositions of the two terminals can be controlled simultaneously
and there are some better control projects than the conventional project indeed.

To sum up, the application of Shinskey's method to distillation
column control can be concentrated into three design rules expressed
as follows:

(1) In the case of controlling the product quality of one terminal,

the product quality should be controlled by using material-balance con-

trol mode,

(2) In the case of controlling the product quality of one terminal,

the flow rate of the product which is the minor between the products of

two terminals should be chosen as the manipulated variable to control

the product quality,

(3) In the case of controlling the product quality of two terminals,

in general , the terminal, whose products are of less pure products and

more impurities, should be controlled by using the material-balance mo-

de and the other terminal, whose products are of pure products and less

impurities , should be controlled by using the energy-balance control

mode.

The so-called material-balance control mode and the energy-balance

control mode are: When either the top product flow rate(distillation

rate) D or the bottom rate B is chosen as the manipulated variable, then

this is the material-balance control mode ; when either the top reflux

rate or the reboiler steam is chosen as the manipulated variable, then

this is the energy-balance control mode.

In fact, the third Shinskey's design rule is always used by combi-

nation with the judgement of using the Bristol's relative gains.

The above three Shinskey's design rules have got remarkable succes-

ses in distillation column control practice. This is well-known now.

But, the three design rules are not very easily to be understood.

The Shinskey's design idea expressed mainly by the above three rules

is now considered as a kind of advanced ideas. That means that this de-

sign idea is rational. Then, certainly, people can propose the following

problems: Why are these three rules reasonable? Are they always reaso-

nable? On what bases did Shinskey propose these three rules , only from

the summary of experience ?

This is just what we want to discuss in the last chapter of this book. In fact, if we could not explain the above questions , then we would not be able to believe the above design rules or would use them blindly and even would not dare to use them. Thus, in order to avoid failure of application of Shinskey's design rules in practice, we must get a good understanding about them.

In fact, the Shinskey's three design rules are of their own theory bases. This is the most successful application of the Bristol-Shinskey method introduced in the last chapter in practical control engineering.

We should point out that the problem of determining the proper control projects of distillation columns, as a developing process, has endured three stages. The first stage is to determine the control project by experience and the conventional control project is the most popular. In the practical application for a long period, many shortages of using this project have been exposed,so this project is no longer the emphysised one. The second stage is to determine the proper control project by using Shinskey's ideas . The Shinskey's ideas have got widespread approval now and we can say that the control technique of distillation columns now is just entering into this stage. The third stage is to determine the control project by controllong some reflux ratio or by controlling the separation factor. Some of these projects (not all) may be better than Shinskey's projects in theory , but the practical systems by using these projects are rather complicated in general, thus they are still at the step of discussion and under experiment.

So, to design control systems of distillation columns by using Shinskey's design rules is worth being advocated the most now because it has the direct industry meaning.

The references will not be cited for each paragraph and readers can find all of them at the end of this book.

§ 8-2 Some Basic Hypotheses on Distillation Column Control

Now, we are going to discuss the control problems of distillation columns. There is a great variety of distillation columns and each of them has its own characteristics. In order to make the essentiality of the problems be more clear, we should do some general hypotheses on distillation column control and we are sure that these hypotheses are closely in accordance with many practical cases.

These hypotheses are:

(1) The products mean the products at the top and at the bottom, we do not consider any side products now,

(2) Both the rate and the compositions of the feed may vary, but we do not consider it as a problem of the distillation column control. The task of distillation column control is to control the relavent conditions of distillation flow and the bottom flow (including both rate and compositions) and the operation conditions in the column, for example the reflux system, reboiler, etc.

(3) The pressure in the column is held being constant by using a definite pressure control system, for example by control the flow of the cooling water, and thus it is an independent control system and we can design it by normal procedure without paying special consideration to it. In other words, in the whole design of distillation column control systems, the control of the pressure in the column can be considered as independent relatively and is dealt individually,

(4) We only consider binary distillation. If it is not a binary column, how should we treat it ? We can also treat it as a binary column, namely we take the lightest composition as the light composition and all the others are considered as the heavy composition.

In the analysis, the composition, or the quality, means the composition of the top flow and the bottom flow and are expressed as Y and X, respectively,

(5) For a given pressure, the temperature of some top tray is closely related to the compositions of the distillation flow. But, in any
practical system, the measurement of the temperature is much easier
than that of the compositions, so we can treat the measurement of the
temperature as the measurement of the compositions. Certainly, there
are some corresponding relations for calculation between them but it
does not influence control. So, in the following analysis, when we consider the pairing problems among variables, no need is considered for
the temperature control.

§ 8-3 The Possible Pairing Relations of Variables in Distillation Co-
    lumn Control

Owing to the hypotheses adopted above, there are still four variables being controlled in a column:

The composition of the distillation flow Y ,

The composition of the bottom flow   X ,

The level of the reflux accumulator   A ,

The level of the column bottom R .

and the manipulated variables which can be adopted now are:

The rate of the distillation flow   D ,

The rate of the bottom flow   B   ,

The reflux flow rate   L   ,

The up steam rate   V   (or the corresponding rate V^* of the medium flow in the reboiler) .

Thus, for the control of a distillation column, the possible
states of variable pairing are 4 != 24 .

Notice that the manipulated variables only can be chosen from
the above variables. Certainly, such as $\frac{D}{F}$ and $\frac{B}{F}$ are also avai-

lable because we have made the feed rate F be constant, so $\frac{D}{F}$ and $\frac{B}{F}$ are still corresponding to D and B, respectively. But it is absolutely not allowed to choose such $\frac{D}{V}$, $\frac{L}{V}$ to be manipulated variables, because such cases are beyond Shinskey's projects.

The all possible variable pairing states are shown in list 1.

Number	Manipulated Variable of A	Manipulated Variable of R	Manipulated Variable of Y	Free Variable
1	D	L	B	V
2	D	L	V	B
3	D	V	L	B
4	D	V	B	L
5	D	B	V	L
6	D	B	L	V
7	L	D	V	B
8	L	D	B	V
9	L	V	D	B
10	L	V	B	D
11	L	B	D	V
12	L	B	V	D
13	B	D	L	V
14	B	D	V	L
15	B	L	D	V
16	B	L	V	D
17	B	V	L	D
18	B	V	D	L
19	V	D	L	B
20	V	D	B	L
21	V	L	D	B
22	V	L	B	D
23	V	B	D	L
24	V	B	L	D

We can see that if we did not pre-assume that the control of the pressure in the column is treated independently and considered it into the variable pairing, then the possible states of variable pairing would be 5 != 120 and the analysis would become more difficult.

The difficulty of the distillation column control is in a quite large degree expressed here.We should find out a reasonable project from the above 24 possible projects for the practical control system design of a distillation column. In fact, the essential core of Shinskey's three design rules is just to determine a reasonable principle which can be used to solve the problem of project determination.

Table 1 is very important since it contains all the possible projects and is the basis of the following discussion.

§ 8-4 The Basic Principles Applied to Determine the Reasonable Control Project

For any practical distillation column, it is not easy to pick out the most reasonable and applicable project from the above 24 possibilities. Experience certainly is important for us to get a satisfactory answer but a lot of facts show that sometimes some problems are not easily to be solved by experience , for example the failure of the application of the conventional project in some cases is an obvious evidence of the above statement.

Thus, we must build up a logical procedure by which we can get a logical and reasonable result from the above 24 projects.

So, at first we should solve the following problem:

By what principles to determine the reasonable control project?

The general principles can be expressed as:

When we determine the most sensitive pairing between the manipulated variables and the controlled variables, at the meantime we should strive to make the interaction between the material-balance control and the energy-balance control be the minimum.

It is too abstract to say so. In practice, it contains the following contents:

(1) The quality control of the designed product is the most important problem considered here. It is more important than the other items. So, when we determine the reasonable variable pairing relations, we should at first consider the control of the designed product quality, i.e. to determine the variable pairing for the designed product quality control at first,

(2) The static sensitivity of the compositions of the controlled product to the change of the chosen manipulated variable should be large enough,

(3) The response speed of the composition change of the controlled product to the change of the chosen manipulated variable should be high enough,

(4) The interaction between control loops should be weak. Especially for the main controlled variables, the influence by the interaction with other controlled loops should be weak enough. It should be solved at first by correct variable pairing. If the correct variable pairing can not get good results yet , then the decoupling design is necessary,

(5) Under the promise that the above demands are satisfied, the facilities of the control system should be simple and easy to be realized, i.e. to take the near-by pairing as soon as possible.

We must know that in the above 24 projects no one can express itself the degree of satisfying the above five demands. Thus, we can see that in the design of the distillation column control systems a very important design step is to compare. That means that the most reasonable project can be obtained only by comparison among these projects.

We have pointed out the bases of the comparison but we still should determine the practical comparison steps and this problem will be discussed very soon.

If only one terminal product composition is controlled, e.g. the top
product composition is controlled, then the problem is simpler. We first
determine the most reasonable manipulated variable for the control of
that composition, then the manipulated variables for the control of two
levels (the levels of the reflux accumulator and the bottom of the column) can be determined by the response speed. This is **the so-called**
near-by pairing. After these two manipulated variables are determined,
the left one can be used to control the composition of the other terminal. Sometimes, the composition of the other terminal does not need to
be controlled or the left manipulated variable is not suitable for the
control of that composition, then this manipulated variable becomes a
self-adjusted free variable.

§ 8-5 The Calculation of Sensitivities

　　Now, we begin to discuss the practical procedure to determine the
most reasonable control project for a distillation column.

　　We have pointed out that the basic idea for modern distillation
column control is to analyze the sensitivities and the relative gains.
So , at first we should solve the problem to calculate the sensitivities
in a distillation column.

　　In the static state, the following material balance relations are
held for any column:

$$F = D + B \qquad\qquad (8-5-1)$$

$$FZ = DY + BX \qquad\qquad (8-5-2)$$

where Z,Y and X are the **light** compound compositions in feed, distillation flow and the bottom flow, respectively.

　　From the above equations, we get:

$$\frac{D}{F} = \frac{Z - X}{Y - X} \qquad (8-5-3)$$

$$\frac{B}{F} = \frac{Y - Z}{Y - X} \qquad (8-5-4)$$

In the above two expressions, both F and Z are beyond control, i.e. they are not controlled in our discussion scope, but X and Y must be controlled.

These two equations denote when the composition in the feed, i.e. Z, is constant, then we can control the compositions of the top product and the bottom product by material balance. From (8-5-3) and (8-5-4) we get:

$$Y = \frac{F}{D} (Z - X) + X \qquad (8-5-5)$$

$$1 - X = \frac{F}{B} (Y - Z) + (1 - Y) \qquad (8-5-6)$$

In general, X is very small and Y approaches 1.

From the above equations we can see that $\frac{D}{F}$ or $\frac{F}{B}$ is the most important factor to determine Y and X. That means that the relation of the material balance is the basic relation in distillation column control. Both $\frac{D}{F}$ and $\frac{F}{B}$ are effective control measures, for decreasing D (corresponding to increasing B) will enhance both Y and X; on the other hand, decreasing B will cause reduction of X and Y.

Thus, when Z is unchanged, Y may be controlled by $\frac{D}{F}$ but X must be held as unchanged. But all the above expressions are related to each other. This means that Y and X are not suitable to be controlled at the meantime by D and B. Otherwise, owing to the constraint of F = D + B , the regulators should be very sensititive and may be unrealizable in practice. In order to avoid serious interaction, then if Y is controlled by D or $\frac{D}{F}$, X should be held to be constant by other ways.

On the other hand , the separation factor of a distillation column is difined as:

$$S = \frac{Y_L / Y_H}{X_L / X_H} = \frac{Y / (1 - Y)}{X / (1 - X)} = \frac{Y(1 - X)}{X(1 - Y)} \qquad (8-5-7)$$

where, Y_L , Y_H are the moles of the light and the heavy compositions in
the distillation flow, respectively and X_L, X_H are the moles of the
light and the heavy compositions in the bottom flow, respectively.

When the states of the feed are definite, S may be expressed as:

$$S = f(\alpha , n , \frac{V}{F} , E , n_f) \qquad (8-5-8)$$

where:

E is the efficiency of trays,

n_f is the location of the feed-in tray,

$\frac{V}{F}$ is the ratio of up steam rate to feed rate ,

α is the average volatility,

n is the theory number of trays.

For a built-up column, α , n , n_f, and E are known and are constants, thus:

$$S = f(\frac{V}{F}) \qquad (8-5-9)$$

Shinskey pointed out that the above expression can be expressed
in the following form:

$$\frac{V}{F} = \beta \ln S \qquad (8-5-10)$$

where, β is a positive constant.

From the above several expressions we can see that D is a function of Y, S and X(Y,S). Namely:

$$D = D(Y, S, X(Y,S)) \qquad (8-5-11)$$

When S holds unchanged, we differentiate D to Y and get :

$$\left. \frac{\partial D}{\partial Y} \right|_S = \frac{\partial D}{\partial Y} + \frac{\partial D}{\partial X} \left. \frac{\partial X}{\partial Y} \right|_S \qquad (8-5-12)$$

But from (8-5-3) , we have:

$$\frac{\partial (D/F)}{\partial Y} = - \frac{Z - X}{(Y - X)^2} \qquad (8-5-13)$$

$$\frac{\partial (D/F)}{\partial X} = - \frac{Y - Z}{(Y - X)^2} \qquad (8-5-14)$$

On the other hand, from (8-5-7) we have:

$$\frac{\partial X}{\partial Y}\bigg|_S = \frac{X(1 - X)}{Y(1 - Y)} \qquad (8-5-15)$$

Substituting (8-5-13),(8-5-14) and (8-5-15) into (8-5-12), we get:

$$\frac{\partial (D/F)}{\partial Y}\bigg|_S = - \frac{Z - X}{(Y - X)^2}\left[1 + \frac{(Y - X)X(1 - X)}{(Z - X)Y(1 - Y)}\right] \qquad (8-5-16)$$

If Y is controlled by D and X by V (now, we only deem it as a possible case), then by the definition of the Bristol relative gain, the
relative gain between $\frac{D}{F}$ and Y is:

$$\lambda_{YD} = \left(\frac{\partial Y}{\partial \frac{D}{F}}\right)_V \bigg/ \left(\frac{\partial Y}{\partial \frac{D}{F}}\right)_X \qquad (8-5-17)$$

From (8-5-10) we know that V being unchanged is just the same as
S being unchanged. Thus:

$$\left(\frac{\partial Y}{\partial \frac{D}{F}}\right)_V = \left(\frac{\partial Y}{\partial \frac{D}{F}}\right)_S \qquad (8-5-18)$$

and then:

$$\lambda_{YD} = \left(\frac{\partial Y}{\partial \frac{D}{F}}\right)_S \bigg/ \left(\frac{\partial Y}{\partial \frac{D}{F}}\right)_X \qquad (8-5-19)$$

This means:

$$\left(\frac{\partial Y}{\partial \frac{D}{F}}\right)_S = \lambda_{YD}\left(\frac{\partial Y}{\partial \frac{D}{F}}\right)_X = -\frac{(Y-X)^2}{Z-X}\lambda_{YD} \tag{8-5-20}$$

Comparing (8-5-16) with (8-5-20), we get:

$$\lambda_{YD} = \cfrac{1}{1 + \cfrac{(Y-Z)X(1-X)}{(Z-X)Y(1-Y)}} \tag{8-5-21}$$

Thus, the relative gain of the variable pair Y and D can be calculated from the known F, D and B which are the compositions of the three rates and the measurements are not needed.

When V is held unchanged, we have:

$$-\frac{\partial Y}{\partial \frac{D}{F}}\bigg|_V = \frac{\partial Y}{\partial \frac{B}{F}}\bigg|_V = \frac{\partial Y}{\partial \frac{L}{F}}\bigg|_V = \frac{(Y-X)^2}{Z-X}\lambda_{YD} \tag{8-5-22}$$

$$-\frac{\partial X}{\partial \frac{D}{F}}\bigg|_V = \frac{\partial X}{\partial \frac{B}{F}}\bigg|_V = -\frac{\partial Y}{\partial \frac{V}{F}}\bigg|_V = \frac{(Y-X)^2}{Y-Z}(1-\lambda_{YD}) \tag{8-5-23}$$

Similarly, when L is held unchanged, we have:

$$-\frac{\partial Y}{\partial \frac{D}{F}}\bigg|_L = \frac{\partial Y}{\partial \frac{B}{F}}\bigg|_L = -\frac{\partial Y}{\partial \frac{Y}{F}}\bigg|_L = \frac{1}{\beta}Y(1-Y)(\lambda_{YL}-1) \tag{8-5-24}$$

$$-\frac{\partial X}{\partial \frac{D}{F}}\bigg|_L = \frac{\partial X}{\partial \frac{B}{F}}\bigg|_L = -\frac{\partial X}{\partial \frac{V}{F}}\bigg|_L = \frac{1}{\beta}X(1-X)\lambda_{YL} \tag{8-5-25}$$

where:

$$\lambda_{YL} = \left[1 + \frac{\beta(Y-X)^2}{Y(1-Y)(Z-X)}\right]\lambda_{YD} \tag{8-5-26}$$

is the relative gain between Y and L when Y is controlled by L and X is controlled by V.

When the distillation flow is held unchanged (the bottom flow is also unchanged simultaneously), we have:

$$\left. \frac{\partial Y}{\partial \frac{V}{F}} \right|_D = \left. \frac{\partial Y}{\partial \frac{L}{F}} \right|_D = \frac{1}{\beta} Y(1 - Y)(1 - \lambda_{YD}) \qquad (8-5-27)$$

$$-\left. \frac{\partial X}{\partial \frac{V}{F}} \right|_D = -\left. \frac{\partial X}{\partial \frac{L}{F}} \right|_D = \frac{1}{\beta} X(1 - X)\lambda_{YD} \qquad (8-5-28)$$

What do the above partial differentials mean?

Obviously, they are sensitivities. Namely, suppose one variable being unchanged and the change of some controlled variable caused by the change of some manipulated variable may be expressed by one of the above partial differentials. Thus, they are sensitivities.

The above results denote a very important fact : The important basis for determination of the variable pairing in a distillation column, namely sensitivities, may be expressed by the compositions of the column. That means when a distillation column has been designed out , then its designed compositions are known and its sensitivities are also easily to be determined.

That result brings us a great convenience for analysis.

§ 8-6 The Choice of Control Project when Only One Terminal Product
        Is Controlled

We have discussed the sensitivities of the distillation columns and a conclusion is reached. That is: The sensitivities of a distillation column can be calculated by the designed compositions.

Now, we are going to discuss further: What is the usage of the sensitivities?

We will see when the quality of only one terminal product is controlled, the analysis of the sensitivities is the most powerful basis to determine the reasonable control project.

In order to explain this statement we discuss it with a practical example.

The following table shows the parameters of a methanol recovery column in steady state.

Steady State Conditions for a Methanal Recovery Column

	Feed	Distillate	Residue	Reflux	Vapor
Flow-rate (Kg-mol/hr)	400	17.5	382.5	568.5	586

Mole Fraction

Methanol	0.046= Z	0.986= Y	0.0032= X
Formaldehyde	0.196 ⎫	0.005 ⎫	0.205 ⎫
Water	0.758 ⎬ 1-Z	0.008 ⎬ 1-Y	0.792 ⎬ 1-X

In the feed, there are methanol, formaldehyde and water and we want to get the recovery of the methanol.

The control demands are: The composition of the top product must be controlled strictly; as for the composition of the residue , it is enough to keep it within an allowable scope. That means that the control demands on the residue composition are weaker than those of the top product.and in fact this is one terminal product control.

Now, let us determine the reasonable control project.

The key is to determine the suitable variable pairing relations and this means that we should find out the most resonable control project from the 24 possible projects shown in Table 8-3-1.

We calculate sensitivities.

Substituting X,Y and Z into (8-5-21), we get:

$$\lambda_{YD} = 0.165 \qquad\qquad (8\text{-}6\text{-}1)$$

and $\quad S = 1938.5 \,, \quad \beta = 0.1466 \quad, \quad \lambda_{YL} = 39.605.$

From (8-5-22) we get:

$$-\left.\frac{\partial\,Y}{\partial\,\frac{D}{F}}\right|_V = \left.\frac{\partial\,Y}{\partial\,\frac{B}{F}}\right|_V = -\left.\frac{\partial\,Y}{\partial\,\frac{L}{F}}\right|_V = 3.7 \quad (8\text{-}6\text{-}2)$$

It denotes when the up steam is unchanged (or similar with the constant rate V´ of the heating medium in the reboiler) , then an increment of the ratio of the distillation flow to the feed flow will cause 3.7 increments of the composition of the distillation flow.

Similarly, from (8-5-24) we get:

$$-\left.\frac{\partial\,Y}{\partial\,\frac{D}{F}}\right|_L = \left.\frac{\partial\,Y}{\partial\,\frac{B}{F}}\right|_L = -\left.\frac{\partial\,Y}{\partial\,\frac{V}{F}}\right|_L = 3.6 \quad (8\text{-}6\text{-}3)$$

When the distillation flow D and the bottom flow B are held being constants, then from (8-5-27) we get:

$$\left.\frac{\partial\,Y}{\partial\,\frac{V}{F}}\right|_D = \left.\frac{\partial\,Y}{\partial\,\frac{L}{F}}\right|_D = 0.079 \quad (8\text{-}6\text{-}4)$$

Let us compare the results of the sensitivities obtained in (8-6-2) (8-6-3) and (8-6-4) and try to get some conclusions.

The difference between (8-6-2) and (8-6-3) is not serious, but the result of (8-6-4) is remarkably different from those of (8-6-2) and (8-6-3). By the second general principle of determination of the reasonable control project, namely the static sensitivity of the composition of controlled product to the change of the chosen manipulated variable should be large enough, we can see that the result of (8-6-4) shows that this case is not suitable to be used as a control project and only the projects expressed by (8-6-2) and (8-6-3) can be used to control. That the projects expressed by (8-6-4) fail to be adopted means that any project with definite B or definite D (namely the self-adjust system of B or D) is not applicable. Thus, in Table 8-3-1, the projects 2,3,7,12,16,17,19 and 24 all should be ruled out.

On the other hand, because F = D + B and F is definite, so it is impossible to use, for instance, D to control Y , when the other vari-able B is self-adjusted. This is because any change of D absolutely causes the change of B, so the self-adjustment of B will loss its mea-ning. Thus, in Table 8-3-1, the projects 9,10,21 and 22 all should be ruled out. This is just what we said before that X and Y can not con-trolled by D and B simultaneously.

Therefore, only 12 projects are left and all of them are just ex-pressed by (8-6-2) and (8-6-3).

They are shown in Table 8-6-1.

Table 8-6-1

Manipulated Variable		Definited Variable		Project Number
Distillation	D	Up Steam	V	11
Distillation	D		V	15
Bottom Flow	B		V	1
Bottom Flow	B		V	8
Reflux Flow	L		V	6
Reflux Flow	L		V	13
Distillation	D	Reflux	L	18
Distillation	D		L	23
Bottom Flow	B		L	4
Bottom Flow	B		L	20
Up Steam	V		L	5
Up Steam	V		L	14

Now, we take comparison among the above 12 possible projects. In according to the same conditions, we compare them pair by pair.

At first, project 11 is compared with project 15. It is obviously that project 15 is irrational. Because by the fifth general principle, namely the principle of near-by pairing, A should be controlled by L and R should be controlled by B. Thus, project 15 is ruled out.

Then, we compare project 1 with project 8. Project 8 is irrational. Because D is with small value(17.5), it is difficult to use this small value to control the bottom level of a large column. Thus, project 8 should be ruled out.

Comparing project 6 with project 13, we see that project 13 is obviously not in accordance with the principle of near-by pairing and so project 13 is ruled out.

Because the level of the column bottom is influenced by V directly, it is difficult to be controlled by a small flow D and should be controlled by V directly, so the comparison between project 4 with project 20 shows that project 20 should be ruled out.

At last, we compare project 5 with project 14. Obviously, project 14 is not in accordance with the principle of near-by pairing, so project 14 is ruled out.

Thus, by comparison we ruled out 6 projects and still 6 projects are left. They are shown in Table 8-6-2.

Table 8-6-2

Manipulated Variable	Definited Variable		Number of Project
Distillation flow D	Up Steam	V	11
Bottom flow B		V	1
Reflux flow L		V	6
Distillation flow D	Reflux	L	23
Bottom flow B		L	4
Up steam V		L	5

Now, we will continue to compare further. We want to find out the best project from the 6 projects left.

At first, we discuss which variable should be used to control Y? D or B ?

For the control of Y, the response speed in the case of being controlled by the change of D is much larger than that of being controlled by the change of B.

On the other hand, from (8-6-2) and (8-6-3) we know that the sensitivities of the change of Y to the change of D and the change of B are the same,then for $\triangle D = \triangle B$, the caused $\triangle Y$ are the same. This point is very important . In addition, notice that in this example D = 17.5, B = 382.5, thus , the control valves applied are quite different. When a precise composition control is reached, the $\triangle Y$ varies very small and thus both $\triangle D$ and $\triangle B$ are not large. For D=17.5 , B=382.5, suppose $\triangle D = \triangle B = 0.5$, which manipulated variable can realize the above control demands more easily? Obviously, $\triangle D$ is more suitable to be used to realize the control because the relative open degree of $\triangle D$ to the control valve full range is much larger than that of $\triangle B$ to its own control valve. Therefore, the control of $\triangle Y$ by adoption of the change of D is more convenient than by adoption of the change of B.

This is just the Shinskey's second design rule. Namely, the flow rate of the product which is the minor between the products of two terminals, should be chosen as the manipulated variable to control the product quality.

Notice that the reasonableness of this design rule is just on the base of equal sensitivities and the hypothesis that D is much less than B.

Therefore, we can see that this Shinskey's design rule is not all from experience. The key is that the changes of the   two flows to the change of the composition of the controlled product are with the same sensitivities.

Thus, we know that in the six candidate projects in Table 8-6-2, project 1 and project 4 should be ruled out.

Now, only four projects are left and we compare project 11 with

project 23. In both these two projects, Y is controlled by D. In order
to compare these two projects, we should discuss something about the
level control problem of the reflux accumulator at the top of the column. The level control here is unlike the common level control in general tanks. That is to say that the aim of the level control of the
reflux accumulator in a distillation column is not to control the
fluctuation of the level in the container.Its main aim is to provide
a feedback result to maintain the material balance in the column. For
example, owing to some reason the quantity of the up steam arriving
at the top is over the demanded value but the distillation flow is definite , then the function of the level controller will increase the
reflux rate in order to maintain the material balance in the column.
For some uncontrolled factors, for instance temperature, it is related
to the composition of the top product and gives influences on the distillation states at the meantime, so if there were no reflux control,
the damage of the material balance in the column would be discovered
till the composition of the distillation flow changes when the temperature varies. Thus, the reflux control is a very effective measure
to hold the material balance in the column. Now, we discuss project
23. In this project, the level of the reflux accumulator is controlled
by V and the reflux rate L is not utilized. Obviously, project 23 is
irrational and it should be ruled out.

Now, only projects 5, 6 and 11 are left.

In fact, according to the above analysis, we should control the
level of the reflux accumulator by reflux rate L and we see that neither project 5 nor project 6 satisfies this demand and thus both of
them should be ruled out. But, however, we can discusss this problem
in another way.

Take project 5 ae an example. The manipulated variable here is
the up steam rate V. This is also corresponding to use heating rate

V′ in the reboiler as the manipulated variable. We have pointed out that the composition of the bottom flow only needs to be controlled in a certain scope and the control demand on it is much looser than that on the top composition. Thus, if the composition of the bottom flow is controlled by V , then it can use the manual control and if the automatic control is adopted, the control operation is allowed to be slow and the loop gain need not be large. The reason for adopting slow control operation and small loop gain is to reduce the interaction between the bottom flow composition control and the top distillation flow composition control. But if we adopt project 5, namely the composition of the the distillation flow is controlled by the up steam; the level of the column bottom is controlled by B and the the level of the reflux accumulator is controlled by D, then the composition of the bottom flow would be controlled, if need, by L. We have pointed out when the composition of the distillation flow is controlled by L and the composition of the bottom flow is controlled by V, i.e. project 6, then the relative gain of the system is :

$$\lambda_{YL} = 39.605 \qquad\qquad (8\text{-}6\text{-}5)$$

But for a relative gain matrix:

	L	V
Y	λ_{YL}	λ_{YV}
X	λ_{XL}	λ_{XV}

we have:

$$\left. \begin{aligned} \lambda_{YL} + \lambda_{YV} &= 1 \\ \lambda_{YL} + \lambda_{XL} &= 1 \end{aligned} \right\} \qquad\qquad (8\text{-}6\text{-}6)$$

Therefore:

$$\lambda_{XL} = \lambda_{YV} = 1 - 39.605 = -38.605 \qquad\qquad (8\text{-}6\text{-}7)$$

and we know when project 6 is adopted, $\lambda_{YL} = 39,605$ and when project 5 is adopted, $\lambda_{YV} = -38.605$.

We know when the relative gain is larger than 1.5 (absolute value), it means that decoupling design is needed for such systems. Even X is not controlled now, in projects 5 and 6, a slight change of the free manipulated variable will give serious influence on the control loop of the top product and the top product composition is expected to have precise and strict control and is not expected to be influenced by other loops or variables, so neither project 5 nor project 6 is available.

In such a way, by the analysis of sensitivities and relative gains we can see that in the 24 possible projects, 23 projects of them should be ruled out reasonably   and only project 11 is left. Project 11 has no shortcomings of the other projects, for instance it is not a project with definite D and B;it adopts the reflux flow to control the level of the reflux accumulator; all variable pairing relations of it are in accordance with the near-by pairing principle ; the control sensitivity of D to Y is high (3.7) and the disturbance degree of V to Y is small (0.079), so project 11 is the most reasonable control project.

This project is: The composition of the distillation flow is controlled by the distillation flow rate ; the level of the reflux accumulator is controlled by the reflux rate; the level of the column bottom is controlled by the bottom flow rate and the heating steam of the reboiler is self-adjusted.

This is just the result of Shinskey´s first and second design rules : In the case of controlling the product quality of one terminal, the product quality should be controlled by using material-balance control mode and the flow rate of the product which is the minor between the products of two termonals should be chosen as the manipulated variable to control the product quality. By our words, it means that D should be controlled by Y.

Therefore, Shinskey´s design rules are not fully from experience. By the above analysis to sensitivities we can see clearly the theory basis of Shinskey's design rules. Thus, when we design the control system for a distillation column, we should combine the sensitivity analysis with Shinskey's design rules and in general the results are in accordance to each other.

Figure 8-6-1 shows the system scheme of the reasonable control project.

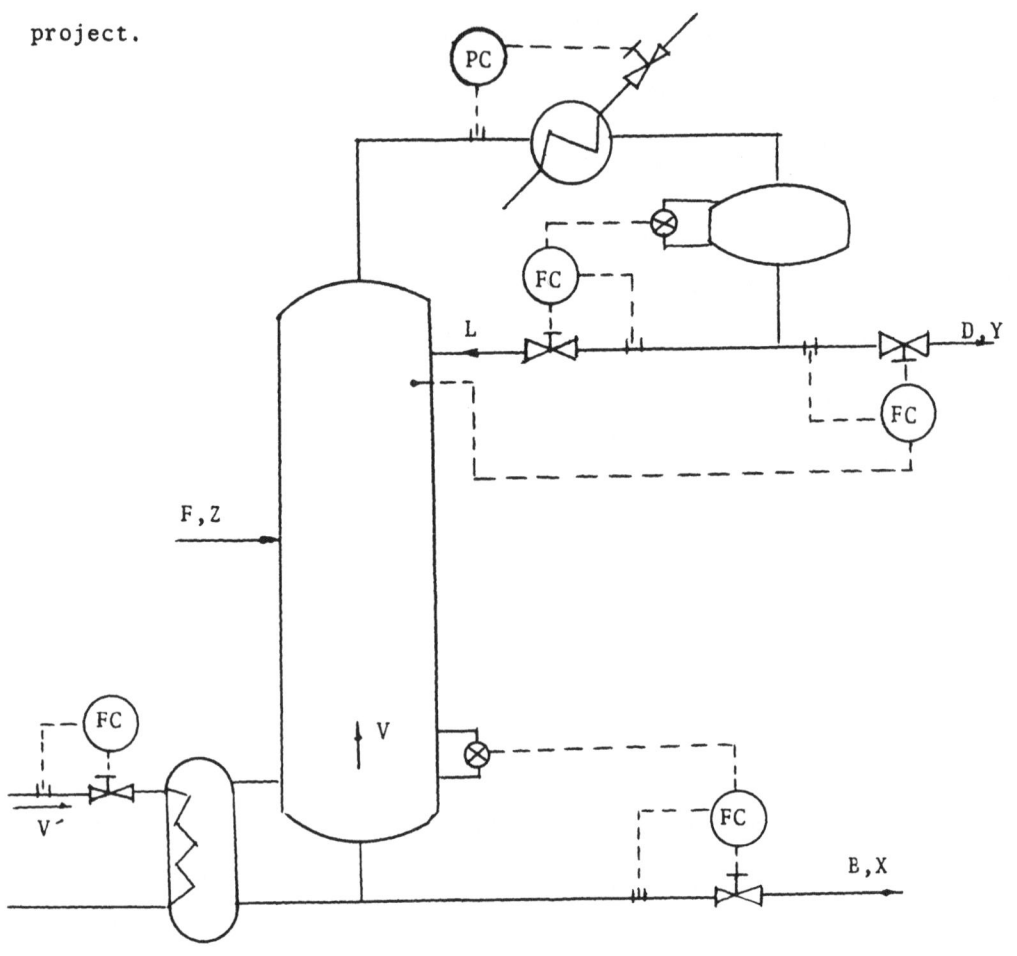

Fig 8-6-1

§ 8-7 The General Discussion on the Reasonableness of Project 11

In the last paragraph, we got a very exact judgement by the analysis of sensitivities that the reasonable control project of the discussed distillation column should be project 11 and this result is fully in accordance with Shinskey's two design rules.

But, however, capable readers will soon discover that in practice
not only the above discussed example should use project 11, but many
other examples shown in different references or met in industries also
use project 11.

Does it mean that for the control of the top product composition,
project 11 is with general reasonableness ?

This problem is worth being discussed.

Now, we discuss this problem. Because we are going to discuss its
general reasonableness, so we can not calculate the practical sensitivities and we should discuss it from some general principles.

When a distillation column has been designed out , then only the
manipulated variables can be used to control and to compensate the
variation of the product composition. Essentially speaking, there are two
kinds of operation conditions giving influences on the product composition. One is the variation of $\frac{V}{F}$ and the other is the variation
of $\frac{D}{F}$. In fact, the variation of $\frac{V}{F}$ means the problem of heat balance and the variation of $\frac{D}{F}$ means the material balance.

That is to say that between these two operation conditions, we
can definite anyone and change the other. Both possible operation conditions are able to exert control function.

Why the variation of these two operation conditions can influence
and control the product composition ?

We discuss $\frac{V}{F}$ at first. For a distillation column, the higher
the $\frac{V}{F}$, the less the demanded theoretical number of trays. But when
we design control systems, the column has been designed out and thus

the number of the trays is definite. Therefore, the higher the $\dfrac{V}{F}$, the purer the product composition. From:

$$\frac{V}{F} = \beta \ln S \qquad\qquad (8\text{-}7\text{-}1)$$

we know that the higher the $\dfrac{V}{F}$, the higher the separation factor S. Certainly, there are some restricts on the increase of $\dfrac{V}{F}$, for instance the flood over the top is not allowed.

How does the variation of $\dfrac{D}{F}$ give influence on the product composition? Obviously, when $\dfrac{D}{F} = 1.0$, then the composition of the distillation flow is equal to that of the feed and when $\dfrac{D}{F}$ is small, then from:

$$\frac{D}{F} = \frac{Z - X}{Y - X} \qquad\qquad (8\text{-}7\text{-}2)$$

we know that Y must be quite large. Thus, the variation of $\dfrac{D}{F}$ can influence the composition of the distillation flow remarkably.

Therefore, control by $\dfrac{D}{F}$ and control by $\dfrac{V}{F}$ are two basic control modes. Fig 8-6-1 and Fig 8-7-1 are the typical schemes of these two control modes. Fig 8-6-1 is the project we analyzed before and it is controlled by $\dfrac{D}{F}$. Fig 8-7-1 is the mode of control by $\dfrac{V}{F}$. In this figure, the column bottom level is controlled by the bottom flow B ; the level of the reflux accumulator is controlled by the reflux flow; the distillation flow is self-adjusted, so the composition of the distillation flow is controlled by V. In fact, this is project 12 in Table 8-3-1.

Now that both modes can be used to control the product composition, then from the general meaning, which one is better ?

We are sure that at least the $\dfrac{D}{F}$ control mode is of the following advantages:

(1) In a distillation column, both reflux flow and up steam are with very large quantities but the distillation flow in general is not

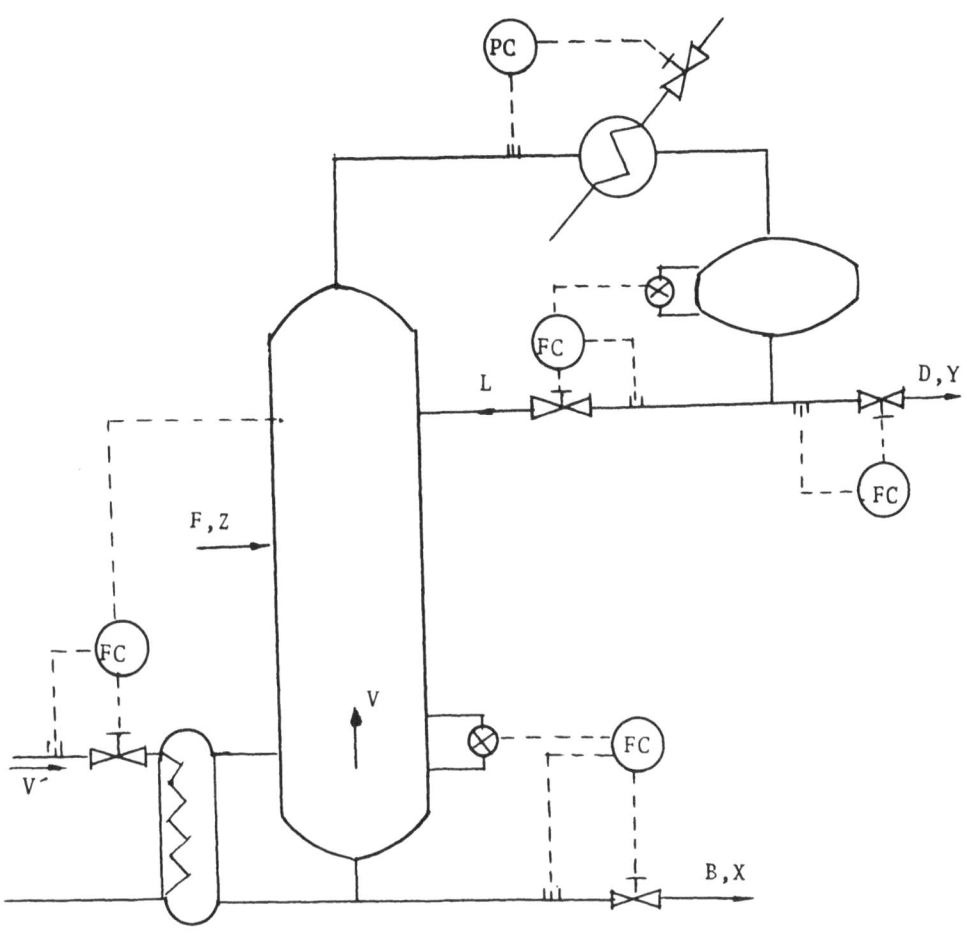

Fig 8-7-1

large. Therefore, comparing with controlling the reflux flow or the up steam, to control distillation flow is more convenient and more exact, for example the sensitivity of the valve stroke to the change of distillation flow may be high enough and, consequently, it will realize the composition control precisely.

(2) Due to the adoption of the $\frac{D}{F}$ control mode, it is not necessary to vary the input heat and thus the up steam and the level in the column can be kept unchanged generally. This fact makes it possible to avoid the occurrence of the flood over the top, so this operation condition can guarantee the operation security.

(3) Another important advantage is , as we pointed out in the previous paragraph, that the sensitivity of the $\frac{D}{F}$ control mode

which is corresponding to V being unchanged is much higher than that of the $\frac{V}{F}$ control mode which is corresponding to D being unchanged. In fact, the former may be several decade times of the latter. This conclusion is correct not only for the example discussed in §8-6, but also for the general columns we meet in practice. Sometimes, it may be several hundred times. That means when some disturbance in the column causes some change of the distillation flow composition, then if $\frac{D}{F}$ mode is adopted, a slight change of D can update the variation of the composition; but if $\frac{V}{F}$ mode is adopted, V or V´ should have a change with a quit large percentage.

Therefore, generally speaking, we can say that the $\frac{D}{F}$ control mode is better than the $\frac{V}{F}$ control mode. The understanding of this point is very helpful for us to determine the control project.

Now, we discuss how to determine the practical control project.

The general principles for determination of the reasonable control project are still those mentioned in § 8-4.

By the third principle, namely the response speed of the composition change of the controlled product to the change of the chosen manipulated variable should be high enough, we can see because to control the column bottom level by using the reflux flow L or the distillation flow D always forms a very slow process, so that such projects are not suitable for control.

In such a way, in Table 8-3-1, the projects 1,2,7,8,13,14,15,16, 19,20,21 and 22 with the sum of 12 should be ruled out, i.e, half of these projects is ruled out. Notice that the measure and reason for ruling out some projects adopted here are different from those adopted in the previous paragraph. In §8-6, we also ruled out 12 projects at the first step , but they are different from those ruled out now in this paragraph.

Likewise, it is also a slow process to control the level of the reflux accumulator by the variation of the bottom flow, thus both projects
17 and 18 should be ruled out. Another similar case is to control the
level of the reflux accumulator by the change of the up steam, i.e. projects 23 and 24. They are also corresponding to a slow process and thus
should be ruled out.

By the comparison of $\frac{V}{F}$ control mode and $\frac{D}{F}$ mode , we know that
the $\frac{V}{F}$ control mode is not suitable for control and, consequently,
both projects 12 and 3 should be ruled out. Notice that project 3 is
analogous to the $\frac{V}{F}$ control mode.

Obviously, project 10 is irrational since in this project Y is not
controlled by D , but by B and on the other hand D is not utilized. We
know that the rate of B is much larger than that of D, so it is much
less convenient to control Y by B than by D and thus project 10 should
be ruled out.

Similarly, project 9 is also irrational since to control the bottom
level by the bottom flow B is more directly than by the up steam , but
in this project B is not utilized and R is controlled by V . Therefore,
project 9 should be ruled out.

In such a way, only four projects are left , namely projects 4,5,
6 and 11. Now, we should choose the most suitable project from them.

In the operation of control systems, certainly the disturbances
caused by measurements should be considered. For example, when the bottom level is controlled by the up steam, due to the circular process
through the reboiler the level of the bottom fluctuates very much and
because of this fluctuation (more exactly, jumping), the measurement
results in general are not exact. For the heavy load cases, the control
action will not be in time since the measurements can not reflect the
real level and this will be able to cause danger because a distillation
column normally works near the flood-point , so the control action not

in time may cause flood over the top. Besides, the plant character is difficult to be determined when the bottom level is controlled by the up steam and it is also difficult to get tuning for the loop regulators. Because of the above reasons, project 4 is not suitable for adoption.

Now, still projects 5, 6 and 11 are left.

We make the judgement by the reflux control. In the previous paragraph we have said that to control the level of the reflux accumulator by the reflux flow is an effective measure to keep the material balance in the column. We consider another example to explain this statement. Suppose that some disturbance occurs in the condenser, for instance because of very cold wind or water , the condensed liquid increases and, consequently, the level of the accumulator will enhance. If the level is controlled by the reflux flow, then the reflux flow will increase. The reflux flow pours to the top trays of the column and it causes the change of the heat exchange . As a result, the steam entering the condenser will decrease and thus the flow entering the accumulator will also decrease. In other words ,the results caused by the disturbance will not transfer in the column further and a new balance is reached very soon. This is the remarkable advantage of the adoption of controlling the accumulator level by the reflux flow. Thus, to adopt the reflux flow to control the accumulator level is a quite ideal control project and we should adopt it whenever possible since it can reduce the results caused by disturbances.

Obviously, in the three projects left, only project 11 satisfies this demand and thus project 11 is the most rational control project.

In this paragraph, we did not use practical sensitivity calculation and by the the general principles and demands of the distillation column control , we got the same conclusion as that of the previous paragraph.

Therefore, when only the   composition of the top product is controlled, project 11 is of the general reasonableness , namely the control scheme with direct material-balance control and automatic reflux flow control is a very good control project.

Similarly, by the analogous analysis we can know when only the composition of the bottom product is controlled, project 3 is the most reasonable project.

§ 8-8 The Choice of the Control Project When Two Terminal Products
    Are Controlled

What we discussed before is about the case when only one terminal product is controlled strictly. If both top and bottom products are expected to be controlled strictly, the case will be quite different.

Certainly, at first we should ask : Can the results obtained for the case of one terminal product control be also used for the two terminal product control ?

Generally speaking, it is impossible.

We still consider the example of §8-6. If the project determined for the one terminal product control with proved reasonableness now is used for the two terminal product control, what will happen ?

At first, we see that:

$$- \left(\frac{\partial X}{\partial \frac{D}{V}} \right)_V = 0.82 \tag{8-8-1}$$

It means if this project is used for two terminal product control, the sensitivity of using D to control Y is high (3.7) indeed, but the variation of X caused by the change of D can not be neglected either.

In other words, the control of X is seriously interacted with the control loop of Y. Because the two terminal product compositions are expected to have **precise** control, so serious interaction is not allowed.

In project 11, the free variable is V. Now that the bottom product composition is also expected to be controlled , then X should be controlled by V.

When X is controlled by V, how is the sensitivity ? We calculate (8-5-28) and get:

$$- (\frac{\partial X}{\partial \frac{V}{F}})_D = 0.0036 \tag{8-8-2}$$

Obviously, the control ability of V to X is very weak and:

$$(\frac{\partial Y}{\partial \frac{V}{F}})_D = 0.79 \tag{8-8-3}$$

So, the influence of V on Y is stronger than the control action of V to X. It means that this pairing, i.e. Y is controlled by D and X is controlled by V , will cause serious interaction between two terminal product control systems. In fact, from the relative gain matrix:

$$
\begin{array}{cc}
 & \begin{array}{cc} D & V \end{array} \\
\begin{array}{c} Y \\ X \end{array} & \begin{pmatrix} \lambda_{YD} & \lambda_{YV} \\ \lambda_{XD} & \lambda_{XV} \end{pmatrix}
\end{array}
=
\begin{array}{cc}
 & \begin{array}{cc} D & V \end{array} \\
\begin{array}{c} Y \\ X \end{array} & \begin{pmatrix} 0.165 & 0.835 \\ 0.835 & 0.165 \end{pmatrix}
\end{array}
$$

we can know that for the two terminal product composition control, project 11 in this example is not a good project.

Then, by the observation to the relative gain matrix, if we exchange the variable pairing relations, namely let X be controlled by D and Y be controlled by V, will we get a successful project ? In fact, this result has become project 12.

The answer is negative.

The exchange of variable pairing relations can result in a suitable relative gain matrix, but then Y is controlled by V and X is controlled by D. Obviously both manipulated variables are far apart to their controlled variables and certainly the system responses will be very slow. Therefore, this project is not suitable.

We should point out that it is not to say that project 11 is not suitable for two terminal product control in any cases. From:

$$\lambda_{YD} = \cfrac{1}{1 + \cfrac{(Y - Z)X(1 - X)}{(Z - X)Y(1 - Y)}} \tag{8-8-4}$$

we can see when the top product becomes pure and pure, i.e. $Y \longrightarrow 1$, then λ_{YD} approaches 0 more and more. When λ_{YD} is larger than 0.5, project 11 is available for two terminal product control, namely the less the purity of the top product, the more suitable the adoption of project 11 for two terminal product control. But in the discussed example, $\lambda_{YD} = 0.165$, namely the top product is quite pure, so project 11 is not available here.

Then, in such a case what variable pairing relations should be adopted? How can we make judgement ?

In fact, it is not difficult .

The first step: Checking project 11. If $\lambda_{YD} > 0.5$, then project 11 can be considered to be adopted. If $\lambda_{YD} < 0.5$, neither project 11 nor project 12 can be adopted,

The second step : From ((-5-26) we know:

$$\lambda_{YL} = \left[1 + \frac{\beta (Y - X)^2}{Y(1 - Y)(Z - X)} \right] \lambda_{YD} \tag{8-8-5}$$

This means that Y is controlled by L and X is controlled by V, namely the conventional project.

In general , Y is always with high value and thus $(1 - Y)$ is quite small and the higher the value of Y, i.e. the product purity is higher, the more the (1 - Y) approaches zero. Thus, in general, λ_{YL} is quite large, for instance in our example λ_{YL} is as high as 39.605. Consequently, λ_{XV} = -38.605 , so this project is with serious interaction when it is used for two terminal product composition control and decoupling design should be done for it. This case is well known to us and it gives a conclusion that the conventional project is not suitable for two terminal product composition control. This means that both projects 6 and 5 are not suitable for two terminal product composition control unless decoupling design is carried out. But, however, even so sometimes people prefer to use this conventional project and this is because it has quite high se. sitivities, for instance in our example:

$$
(\frac{\partial Y}{\partial \frac{L}{F}})_V = 3.7
$$

$$
(\frac{\partial X}{\partial \frac{V}{F}})_L = -0.86
$$

(8-8-6)

so the sensitivities are not low . This is an important advantage of the conventional project but from the view-point of interaction, the conventional project is not a good one.

The third step: We have:

$$
\lambda_{YD} = (\frac{\partial Y}{\partial \frac{D}{F}})_V \left/ (\frac{\partial Y}{\partial \frac{D}{F}})_X \right.
$$

(8-8-7)

and this means that Y is controlled by D and X is controlled by V.

But:

$$
\frac{B}{F} = 1 - \frac{D}{F}
$$

(8-8-8)

so:

$$
\frac{\partial B}{\partial F} = - \frac{\partial D}{\partial F}
$$

(8-8-9)

It yields:

$$\lambda_{YD} = \lambda_{YB} \qquad (8\text{-}8\text{-}10)$$

Therefore, if the project of Y controlled by D and X controlled by B is not suitable for two terminal product control, then this conclusion is also valid for the project of Y controlled by B and X controlled by X or L.

But, because $\lambda_{YD} = \lambda_{YB}$, then by the characteristics of the relative gain matrix it is certainly that:

$$\lambda_{XB} = 1 - \lambda_{YB} = 1 - \lambda_{YD} \qquad (8\text{-}8\text{-}11)$$

Thus, when λ_{YD} is not suitable, then λ_{XD} must be suitable. But we have said before that the project of X controlled by D and Y controlled by V is not available. Now, consider λ_{YB}. When λ_{YB} is not suitable, then λ_{XB} must be suitable because both λ_{YD} and λ_{YB} are always less than 1. In our example:

$$\lambda_{XB} = 1 - \lambda_{YB} = 1 - 0.165 = 0.835 \qquad (8\text{-}8\text{-}12)$$

That means that from the relative gain analysis, it is available to use B to control X.

Because both X and B are at the bottom of the column, so the response is certainly quite fast. Then , how about its sensitivities?

We have:

$$\left(\frac{\partial X}{\partial \frac{D}{F}}\right)_V = -\left(\frac{\partial X}{\partial \frac{B}{F}}\right)_V = -0.82 \qquad (8\text{-}8\text{-}13)$$

$$\left(\frac{\partial X}{\partial \frac{D}{F}}\right)_L = -\left(\frac{\partial X}{\partial \frac{B}{F}}\right)_L = \left(\frac{\partial X}{\partial \frac{V}{F}}\right)_L = -0.86 \qquad (8\text{-}8\text{-}14)$$

Obviously, in both cases the absolute values of the sensitivities are larger than $\left|\left(\dfrac{\partial X}{\partial \frac{V}{F}}\right)_D\right| = 0.0036$.

Therefore, when project 11 is unavailable for two terminal product control, i.e. the project of Y controlled by D and X controlled by V is unavailable, then the project of X controlled by B is certainly available and Y may be controlled by up steam V or reflux flow L. From the dynamic analysis , the difference is slight but from the consideration of the bottom level control, it is more suitable to be controlled by V and thus L is chosen as the manipulated variable for the control of Y.

The project is: Y is controlled by L; X is controlled by B; A is controlled by D and R is controlled by V. In fact, this is project 3.

For this project, its relative gains are suitable, i.e. the interaction is not serious, and decoupling design is not necessary; the responses at two terminals are with satisfactory speed because all variable pairing relations are in accordance with the near-by principle , so this project is reasonable. In this project, the material-balance control is carried out to the bottom composition and the energy-balance control is carried out to the top composition.

The scheme of such a system is shown in Fig 8-8-1.

In this example, the impurity ratio of the bottom composition is $\frac{0.0032}{0.205}$ = 1.55% and the impurity of the top composition is $\frac{0.005}{0.986}$ = 0.6%, thus the top product has less impurity and is purer and the bottom product has larger impurity and is less pure.Now, at the top , Y is controlled by L, i.e. the energy-balance control is applied, and at the bottom, X is controlled by B, i.e. the material-balance control is applied. This is just the Shinskey's third design rule:

In the case of controlling the product compositions of two terminals, in general, the terminal, whose products are of less pure products and more impurities, should be controlled by using the material-balance mode and the other terminal, whose products are of purer products and less impurities , should be controlled by using the energy-balance control mode.

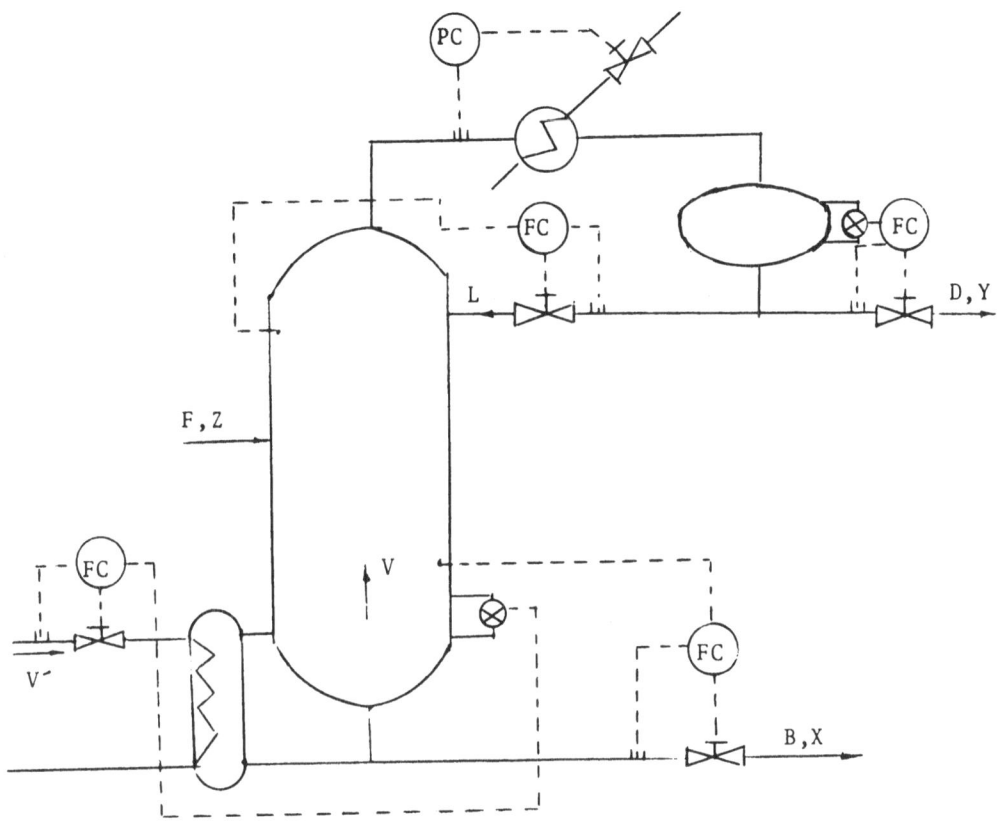

Fig 8-8-1

Therefore, the Shinskey´s third design rule is not proposed only by
experience and in fact it is obtained by the analysis of sensitivities
and relative gains as well as the summary of many practical examples.
We can say now when the two terminal product compositions are expected
to be controlled , in order to get a suitable control project with the
least interaction, the relative gain analysis is the most effective basis for correct determination and , in general, the Shinskey´s third design rule is in accordance with this analysis.

More exactly, the conclusion is:

When the top product is with lower purity, i.e. $\lambda_{YD} > 0.5$, then
project 11 is still available. By project 11, the top composition is controlled by D, namely the material-balance control mode is applied, and
the bottom product now has less impurity and by this project it should

be controlled by V, namely the terminal with less impurity is controlled by the energy-balance mode. When the top product is with higher
purity,i.e. $\lambda_{YD} < 0.5$, then project 11 is no longer available and
project 3 should be adopted. By project 3, the bottom composition is
controlled by B, namely the terminal with less purity is controlled by
the material-balance mode,and in this project the top composition is
controlled by L, namely the terminal with less impurity is controlled
by the energy-balance mode. Therefore, for the two terminal product
composition control, we can choose the reasonable project according to
different cases , the result is project 11 or project 3. Both results
are in accordance with the Shinskey´s third design rule.

Now, we can say that we have given expounded explanation to the
Shinskey´s three design rules which are used in the distillation column control system design widely more and more.

§ 8-9 Is the Shinskey´s Project the Best ?

We have analyzed Shinskey´s three design rules and we know that
in general the control project determined by using Shinskey´s rules is
reasonable and available.

Certainly, we can propose a problem : We are sure that the control project determined by using Shinskey´s rules is reasonable, but
in all distillation column control systems, is this project the best?
Especially when two terminal product composition control is considered.

We do not discuss the optimum control here. The optimum control
system design is carried out to satisfy some special index and then to
find out some measure or structure to realize this design.

What we are going to discuss is to determine the most suitable
variable pairing project which results in the least interaction , or

the ideal relative gains approaching 1.

In our above analysis , we have proved that project 3 is the best, then what will we still discuss ? This conclusion is correct indeed, but it is obtained on the basis of choosing the best one from the possible 24 projects. The 24 possible projects mean that the controlled variables are Y,X,A and R and the manipulated variables are D,B,L and V.

Now, we can ask : Besides these possible variable pairing relations, are there any other possible variable pairing relations which can also be used for distillation column control ?

Yes, there are some and even some of them can result in better projects than those we discussed before.

Let us discuss it from the beginning. Before Shinskey proposed his material-balance control mode idea for distillation column control, the popular control project used then was the conventional control project, namely Y is controlled by L and X is controlled by V and this is the energy-balance control mode.For this control project, people have known quite early from experience that the interaction is very serious in such a project. We have pointed out theoretically that for this project λ_{YL} and λ_{XV} are very large , so in general such a project is not suitable for two terminal product composition design unless decoupling design is carried out.

Then, from the analysis of sensitivities and relative gains, Shinskey proposed his control projects by material-balance control modes, namely Y is controlled by D and X is controlled by V (project 11) or Y is controlled by L and X is controlled by B (project 3). We have known that both project 11 and project 3 are without strong interaction between two terminals and the decoupling design is not necessary. This is the basic reason why these two control projects gain special attention recently and are adopted in practice widely more and more.

But, however, there are some shortages with Shinskey´s project.

From the above analysis we can see when $\lambda_{YD} > 0.5$, the project 11 is available, i.e. Y is controlled by D and X is controlled by V, and $\left| \dfrac{\partial X}{\partial \frac{L}{F}} \right| = 0.0036$. This means that the sensitivity of controlling

X by V is very low. When $\lambda_{YD} < 0.5$, then project 3 is available, i.e. Y is controlled by L and X is controlled by B, and:

$$\left| \frac{\partial Y}{\partial \frac{L}{F}} \right| = 0.079$$

it is also very small.

Therefore, the control project determined by using the Shinskey's third design rule is without strong interaction indeed, but the channel using energy-balance control is always with quite low sensitivity,i.e. the plant gain is not high enough and this fact will bring some trouble for the control system. Obviously, in such a case in order to get remarkable control effcts, the valve stroke should be large and the manipulated variable would have large variation which may cause serious change of energy equilibrium status in the column and does not avail to the distillation process.

Because of this shortage , so other new projects were proposed. We may point out some famous from them:

(1) The Ryskamp project (87). Its scheme is : Y is controlled by $\dfrac{D}{V}$ and X is controlled by V,

(2) The Rijnsdrop project (77). It is analogous to the Ryskamp project, namely Y is controlled by $\dfrac{L}{V}$ and X is controlled by V.

By the reports of some references, both these projects can give good control effects.

(3) The Macvoy project (70). Its idea is: From the Rijnsdrop project the principle of Y controlled by $\dfrac{L}{V}$ is adopted and from the Shinskey project the priciple of X controlled by B is adopted, namely

to combine the reflux ratio control with the material-balance control. Some analyses denote that this project is with less interaction and faster responses and some authors consider that this project would be promising.

(4) The Waltz project(85) . Its idea is : Y is controlled by D and this is still the Shinskey´s material-balance control mode but V will be used not to control B, but to control S.

Why this project is available?

We know that:

$$\frac{V}{F} = \beta \ln S$$

so if this relation is always held, then it means that S is only related to V. Thus, the relative gain between the channel Y-D and the channel S-V is 1, i.e. no interaction and when both Y and S are under control , then, consequently, X is under control. Therefore, this control idea is reasonable.

This control project has got attention.

So, in the distillation column composition control, besides the Shinskey projects, there are other available projects and some of them may be better than Shinskey´s projects.

But, however, although some of them may be better than Shinskey projects in control effects, all of them are with more complicated structures than those of Shinskey projects and, on the other hand, they are still at the experiment and discussion step . So, in this meaning Shinskey projects now are the most practical and available projects and Shinskey´s design ideas are still advanced.

In summary, the general situation of distillation column composition control now is : For only one terminal product composition control, the application of the Shinskey project is spread wider and wider ; for the two terminal product composition control, both Shinskey´s project and

the conventional project are popular but the Shinskey's project has wun
attention more and more and for the conventional project , in general
the decoupling design should be accompanied.

§ 8-10 The Relative Gains of Some Popular Control Projects

We have said that the analysis of relative gains is the basis for
determination of suitable control projects of distillation columns.

We have introduced how to calculate the relative gains for some
projects. Now, we make a summary here.

In the distillation column composition control, the most popular
control projects are:

(1) Y—— D , X—— V ,

(2) Y—— B , X—— V ,

(3) Y—— L , X—— V ,

(4) Y—— L , X—— B.

Now, we discuss the calculation of relative gains one by one.

(1) Y—— D , X—— V .

$$\lambda_{YD} = (\frac{\partial Y}{\partial \frac{D}{F}})_V \Big/ (\frac{\partial Y}{\partial \frac{D}{F}})_X \qquad (8-10-1)$$

From:

$$\frac{\partial D/F}{\partial Y}\Big|_S = \frac{\partial D/F}{\partial Y} + \frac{\partial D/F}{\partial X}\frac{\partial X}{\partial Y}\Big|_S \qquad (8-10-2)$$

where:

$$\frac{\partial D/F}{\partial Y} = -\frac{Z - X}{(Y - X)^2} \qquad (8-10-3)$$

$$\frac{\partial D/F}{\partial Y} = -\frac{Y - Z}{(Y - X)^2} \qquad (8-10-4)$$

435

$$\frac{\partial X}{\partial Y}\bigg|_S = \frac{X(1-X)}{Y(1-Y)} \qquad (8\text{-}10\text{-}5)$$

we get:

$$\frac{\partial D/F}{\partial Y}\bigg|_S = \frac{\partial D/F}{\partial Y}\bigg|_V = -\frac{Z-X}{(Y-X)^2}\left(1 + \frac{(Y-Z)X(1-X)}{(Z-X)Y(1-Y)}\right) =$$

$$= \left(\frac{\partial D/F}{\partial Y}\right)_X \frac{1}{\lambda_{YD}} \qquad (8\text{-}10\text{-}6)$$

Thus:

$$\lambda_{YD} = \frac{1}{1 + \dfrac{(Y-Z)X(1-X)}{(Z-X)Y(1-Y)}} \qquad (8\text{-}10\text{-}7)$$

and:

$$\left.\begin{array}{l}\lambda_{YV} = 1 - \lambda_{YD} \\[4pt] \lambda_{XV} = \lambda_{YD} \\[4pt] \lambda_{XD} = 1 - \lambda_{YD}\end{array}\right\} \qquad (8\text{-}10\text{-}8)$$

(2) Y——B , X——V.

$$\lambda_{YB} = \left(\frac{\partial Y}{\partial \frac{B}{F}}\right)_V \bigg/ \left(\frac{\partial Y}{\partial \frac{B}{F}}\right)_X \qquad (8\text{-}10\text{-}9)$$

Because :

$$-\frac{\partial B}{\partial F} = \frac{\partial D}{\partial F} \qquad (8\text{-}10\text{-}10)$$

so that:

$$\lambda_{YB} = -\left(\frac{\partial Y}{\partial \frac{D}{F}}\right)_V \bigg/ -\left(\frac{\partial Y}{\partial \frac{D}{F}}\right)_X = \lambda_{YD} \qquad (8\text{-}10\text{-}11)$$

and :

$$\left.\begin{array}{l}\lambda_{YV} = 1 - \lambda_{YD} \\[4pt] \lambda_{XB} = 1 - \lambda_{YD} \\[4pt] \lambda_{XV} = \lambda_{YD}\end{array}\right\} \qquad (8\text{-}10\text{-}12)$$

(3) Y——L , X——V.

From:

$$L = V - D \tag{8-10-13}$$

when V is held unchanged , i.e. S does not change, then we get:

$$\frac{\partial \ L/F}{\partial \ Y}\bigg|_{V} = - \ \frac{\partial \ D/F}{\partial \ Y}\bigg|_{S} \tag{8-10-14}$$

But:

$$\frac{\partial \ D/F}{\partial \ Y} = - \ \frac{D/F}{Y - X} \tag{8-10-15}$$

on the other hand:

$$\frac{\partial \ V/F}{\partial \ Y}\bigg|_{X} = \frac{\partial \ V/F}{\partial \ Y}\bigg|_{X} - \frac{\partial \ D/F}{\partial \ Y}\bigg|_{X} \tag{8-10-16}$$

where:

$$\frac{\partial \ L/F}{\partial \ Y}\bigg|_{X} = \frac{d \ V/F}{dS} \ \frac{\partial \ S}{\partial \ Y}\bigg|_{X} \tag{8-10-17}$$

Now:

$$\frac{\partial \ S}{\partial \ Y}\bigg|_{X} = \frac{S}{Y(1 - Y)} \tag{8-10-18}$$

$$\frac{d \ V/F}{d \ S} = \frac{\beta}{S} \tag{8-10-19}$$

thus:

$$\frac{\partial \ L/F}{\partial \ Y}\bigg|_{X} = \frac{\beta}{Y(1 - Y)} + \frac{D/F}{Y - X} \tag{8-10-20}$$

When Y is controlled by L and X is controlled by V, the relative gain of this project is:

$$\lambda_{YL} = \frac{\dfrac{\partial \ L/F}{\partial \ Y}\bigg|_{X}}{\dfrac{\partial \ L/F}{\partial \ Y}\bigg|_{V}} = \frac{\dfrac{\beta}{Y(1 - Y)} + \dfrac{D/F}{Y - X}}{- \dfrac{\partial \ D/F}{\partial \ Y}\bigg|_{S}} \tag{8-10-21}$$

But what is the term $\dfrac{\partial \ D/F}{\partial \ Y}\bigg|_{S}$?

In fact, it is the total derivative of D/F with respect to Y.

$$\frac{d\ D/F}{dY} = \left.\frac{\partial\ D/F}{\partial\ Y}\right|_X + \left.\frac{\partial\ D/F}{\partial\ X}\right|_Y \left.\frac{\partial\ X}{\partial\ Y}\right|_S \tag{8-10-22}$$

Where:

$$\left.\frac{\partial\ D/F}{\partial\ Y}\right|_X = -\ \frac{D/F}{Y\ -\ X} \tag{8-10-23}$$

$$\left.\frac{\partial\ D/F}{\partial\ X}\right|_Y = \frac{D/F\ -\ 1}{Y\ -\ X} \tag{8-10-24}$$

$$\left.\frac{\partial\ X}{\partial\ Y}\right|_S = \frac{X(1\ -\ X)}{Y(1\ -\ Y)} \tag{8-10-25}$$

so that :

$$\frac{d\ D/F}{dY} = -\ \frac{D/F}{Y\ -\ X}\ -\ \frac{1\ -\ D/F}{Y\ -\ X}\ \frac{X(1\ -\ X)}{Y(1\ -\ Y)} \tag{8-10-26}$$

and:

$$\frac{D}{F} = \frac{Z\ -\ X}{Y\ -\ X} \tag{8-10-27}$$

Substituting (8-10-26) and (8-10-27) into (8-10-21), we get:

$$\lambda_{YL} = \frac{1\ +\ \dfrac{\beta\ (Y\ -\ X)^2}{Y(1\ -\ Y)(Z\ -\ X)}}{1\ +\ \dfrac{(Y\ -\ Z)X(1\ -\ X)}{(Z\ -\ X)Y(1\ -\ Y)}} \tag{8-10-28}$$

Namely:

$$\lambda_{YL} = \left[1\ +\ \frac{\beta\ (Y\ -\ X)^2}{Y(1\ -\ Y)(Z\ -\ X)}\right]\lambda_{YD} \tag{8-10-29}$$

All terms at the right side are positive and in general $(1 - Y)$ is quite small, so λ_{YL} is always very large.

The other relative gains are:

$$\left.\begin{array}{l} \lambda_{XV} = \lambda_{YL} \\ \lambda_{YV} = 1\ -\ \lambda_{YL} \\ \lambda_{XL} = 1\ -\ \lambda_{YL} \end{array}\right\} \tag{8-10-30}$$

Let us have a comparison.

When Y is controlled by D and X is controlled by V, we can get the following relative equations:

$$Y = \lambda_{YD}D + (1 - \lambda_{YD})V$$
$$X = (1 - \lambda_{YD})D + \lambda_{YD}V$$

(8-10-31)

But:

$$D + L = V$$

(8-10-32)

so the above equation can be transferred to:

$$\left.\begin{array}{l} Y = - \lambda_{YD}L + V = K_{11}L + K_{12}V \\ X = (\lambda_{YD} - 1)L + V = K_{21}L + K_{22}V \end{array}\right\}$$

(8-10-33)

From the relative gain equation we get:

$$\lambda_{YL} = \frac{K_{11}K_{22}}{K_{11}K_{22} - K_{12}K_{21}} = - \frac{\lambda_{YD}}{1 - 2\lambda_{YD}}$$

(8-10-34)

There are some practical results:

λ_{YD}	0	0.25	0.5	0.75	1.0
λ_{YL}	0	-0.5	$-\infty$	1.5	1.0

Therefore, we can see that except $\lambda_{YD} = 0$ and 1.0, λ_{YL} is always worse than λ_{YD}. That means that the pairing relations Y—— L, X—— V are worse than the pairing relations Y—— D, X—— V.

(4) Y—— L , X—— B.

$$\lambda_{YB} = (\frac{\partial Y}{\partial \frac{B}{F}})_L \bigg/ (\frac{\partial Y}{\partial \frac{B}{F}})_X$$

(8-10-35)

From (8-5-24):

$$(\frac{\partial Y}{\partial \frac{B}{F}})_L = \frac{1}{\beta} Y(1 - Y)(\lambda_{YL} - 1)$$

(8-10-36)

We have said that in general λ_{YL} is very large, so :

$$(\frac{\partial Y}{\partial \frac{B}{F}})_L \approx \frac{1}{\beta} Y(1 - Y)\lambda_{YL}$$

(8-10-37)

and:

$$\lambda_{YL} = \left[1 + \frac{\beta (Y - X)^2}{Y(1 - Y)(Z - X)} \right] \lambda_{YD} \approx \frac{\beta (Y - X)^2 \lambda_{YD}}{Y(1 - Y)(Z - X)}$$

$$(8-10-38)$$

Thus:

$$\left(\frac{\partial Y}{\partial \frac{B}{F}} \right)_L \approx \frac{1}{\beta} Y(1 - Y) \frac{\beta (Y - X)^2}{Y(1 - Y)(Z - X)} \lambda_{YD} = \frac{(Y - X)^2}{Z - X} \lambda_{YD}$$

$$(8-10-39)$$

But:

$$\left(\frac{\partial Y}{\partial \frac{B}{F}} \right)_X = - \left(\frac{\partial Y}{\partial \frac{D}{F}} \right)_X = \frac{(Y - X)^2}{Z - X}$$

$$(8-10-40)$$

Therefore from (8-10-35) we get:

$$\lambda_{YB} = \lambda_{YD}$$

$$(8-10-41)$$

and:

$$\left. \begin{array}{l} \lambda_{XB} = 1 - \lambda_{YD} \\ \lambda_{YL} = 1 - \lambda_{YD} \\ \lambda_{XL} = \lambda_{YD} \end{array} \right\}$$

$$(8-10-42)$$

§ 8-11 The Columns with Side Products[8]

All the distillation columns discussed before are considered only with two terminal products, i.e. the top product and the bottom product. No side products are considered up to now.

When the side products are considered, the analysis will become quite complicated.

For example, for a column with three products the most volatile composition is designated a and the least volatile composition is de-

signed c. In general, three products may contain three compositions
but for simplicity we suppose there are no c and a in the top product
and the bottom product, respectively, and the column scheme is shown
in Fig 8-11-1.

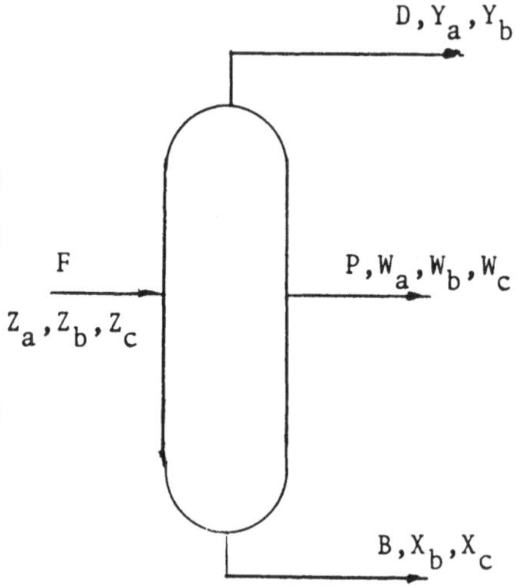

D, Y_a, Y_b

Therefore, the material balance
equations of this column are:

$$F = D + P + B \qquad (8\text{-}11\text{-}1)$$

$$FZ_a = DY_a + PW_a \qquad (8\text{-}11\text{-}2)$$

$$FZ_b = DY_b + PW_b + BX_b$$
$$(8\text{-}11\text{-}3)$$

F

Z_a, Z_b, Z_c

P, W_a, W_b, W_c

$$FZ_c = PW_c + BX_c \qquad (8\text{-}11\text{-}4)$$

The separate factors for this
column are:

B, X_b, X_c

$$S_{ab} = \cfrac{Y_a / Y_b}{W_a / W_b} \qquad (8\text{-}11\text{-}5)$$

Fig 8-11-1

$$S_{bc} = \cfrac{W_b / W_c}{X_b / X_c} \qquad (8\text{-}11\text{-}6)$$

$$\frac{V}{F} = \beta_{ab} \ln S_{ab} = \beta_{bc} \ln S_{bc} \qquad (8\text{-}11\text{-}7)$$

(8-11-7) denotes although the relative volatility between components a and b differs from that between b and c and, consequently,
the numbers of trays in the two sections are also different, yet both
separation factors vary in the same way with V/F.

In the above equations, we can eliminate B,P or B,D and get:

$$\frac{D}{F} = \frac{W_a(Z_b - X_b) - Z_a(W_b - X_b)}{W_a(Y_b - X_b) - Y_a(W_b - X_b)} \qquad (8\text{-}11\text{-}8)$$

$$\frac{P}{F} = \frac{Y_a(Z_b - X_b) - Z_a(Y_b - X_b)}{Y_a(W_b - X_b) - W_a(Y_b - X_b)} \qquad (8\text{-}11\text{-}9)$$

Certainly, we can get the partial differentials from these two expressions and these partial differentials are the system sensitivities and then we can calculate the relative gains. But, in this case the partial differentials will have very complicated forms.

So , perhaps, it would be better to get the sensitivities and the relative gains by experiements.

For example, for a column with $\dfrac{V}{F} = 3.0$ and the other parameters are:

	Z	Y	W	X
a	0.80	0.95	0.01	
b	0.10	0.05	0.94	0.02
c	0.10		0.05	0.98

We define a matrix as:

$$\Phi = \begin{bmatrix} (\dfrac{\partial Y_a}{\partial D})_{PV} & (\dfrac{\partial W_a}{\partial D})_{PV} & (\dfrac{\partial X_b}{\partial D})_{PV} \\[3mm] (\dfrac{\partial Y_a}{\partial P})_{DB} & (\dfrac{\partial W_a}{\partial P})_{DB} & (\dfrac{\partial X_b}{\partial P})_{DB} \\[3mm] (\dfrac{\partial Y_a}{\partial V})_{PD} & (\dfrac{\partial W_a}{\partial V})_{PD} & (\dfrac{\partial X_b}{\partial V})_{PD} \end{bmatrix} \qquad (8\text{-}11\text{-}10)$$

We can do experiments for this column. For example, let $\Delta Y_a = \Delta W_b = \Delta X_b = 0.001$ and get:

$$\Phi = \begin{array}{c} D \\ P \\ V \end{array} \begin{bmatrix} -1.12 & -15.9 & 885 \\ 1.06 & 15.0 & -9.26 \\ 0.117 & -0.026 & -0.046 \end{bmatrix} \qquad (8\text{-}11\text{-}11)$$

with columns headed Y_a, W_a, X_b.

In order to get the relative gains, we must know the inverse matrix of Φ and it is:

$$
\Phi^{-1} = \begin{bmatrix}
-6 \times 10^{-4} & 1.5 \times 10^{-2} & 8.41 \\
6.6 \times 10^{-4} & 6.6 \times 10^{-2} & -0.594 \\
1.1 \times 10^{-3} & 1.2 \times 10^{-3} & 3.3 \times 10^{-3}
\end{bmatrix} \tag{8-11-12}
$$

Transposing it, we get:

$$
(\Phi^{-1})^T = \begin{bmatrix}
-6 \times 10^{-4} & 6.6 \times 10^{-4} & 1.1 \times 10^{-3} \\
1.5 \times 10^{-2} & 6.6 \times 10^{-2} & 1.2 \times 10^{-3} \\
8.41 & -0.594 & 3.3 \times 10^{-3}
\end{bmatrix} \tag{8-11-13}
$$

Multiplying the elements φ_{ij} of Φ with the corresponding elements of (8-11-13), we get the following relative gain matrix :

$$
\begin{array}{cccc}
 & D & P & V \\
Y_a & -6.7 \times 10^{-4} & 1.6 \times 10^{-2} & \underline{0.984} \\
\Lambda = W_a & -1 \times 10^{-2} & \underline{0.99} & 1.5 \times 10^{-2} \\
X_b & \underline{0.974} & -1.1 \times 10^{-2} & 1.5 \times 10^{-4}
\end{array} \tag{8-11-14}
$$

Obviously, from this relative gain matrix we can know that for this column the most suitable variable pairing relations are:

$$
D \longrightarrow X_b \quad, \quad P \longrightarrow W_a \quad, \quad V \longrightarrow Y_a \quad.
$$

If in this column, some product is not under control then the column becomes a one with two products.

But, sometimes we can not get suitable variable pairing relations for the remained two product column. For example, if X_b is not under control and the separate factors are not changed , then from:

$$
\left.
\begin{aligned}
S_{bc} &= \frac{W_b \,/\, W_c}{X_b \,/\, X_c} \\[2mm]
S_{ab} &= \frac{Y_a \,/\, Y_b}{W_a \,/\, W_b}
\end{aligned}
\right\} \tag{8-11-15}
$$

we know that the uncontrolling of X_b is nothing to do with Y_a and W_a, so we get:

	Y_a	W_a
D	-1.12	-15.9
P	1.06	15.0

and the relative gain is:

$$\lambda_{YD} = \frac{(-1.12)(15.0)}{(-1.12)(15.0) - (15.9)(1.06)} = -311 \qquad (8\text{-}11\text{-}16)$$

Thus, neither $D \longrightarrow Y_a$, $P \longrightarrow W_a$ nor $P \longrightarrow Y_a$, $D \longrightarrow W_a$ is suitable for the column control.

It means that for a three product column if some product is uncontrolled, then it is not absolutely possible that the remained two product column can be controlled well. So in such a case, we should analyze very carefully.

§ 8-12 Non-Binary Distillation Columns[8]

In the last paragraph, we discussed the columns with three products but did not pay attention to the three compositions.

In fact, up to now the columns under consideration are dealt with as binary , namely the mixed material in the column can be divided into the light component and the heavy component.

But, in practice, few separations are truely binary. In general, there are more than two components in a column, for example a depropanizer has the following compositions : Ethane , Propane , Isobutane and Water.

The distillation problem may be about two components and one of them is the light component and the other is the heavy component , but besides these two, there are other compositions.

For the two compositions under separation, the separate factor is defined as:

$$S = \frac{Y_L / Y_H}{X_L / X_H} \qquad (8\text{-}12\text{-}1)$$

where L and H denote the light composition and the heavy composition, respectively.

The general composition relations for this column are:

$$Y_L = 1 - Y_H - Y_{LL} \qquad (8\text{-}12\text{-}2)$$

$$X_H = 1 - X_L - X_{HH} \qquad (8\text{-}12\text{-}3)$$

where LL denotes all compositions lighter than L and HH denotes all compositions heavier than H.

Substituting (8-12-2) and (8-12-3) into (8-12-1) and taking the partial differential , we get:

$$\left.\frac{\partial X_H}{\partial Y_L}\right|_S = - \frac{(Y_L + Y_H)X_L X_H}{(X_L + X_H)Y_L Y_H} \qquad (8\text{-}12\text{-}4)$$

Comparing with the binary case:

$$\left.\frac{\partial X}{\partial Y}\right|_S = \frac{X(1 - X)}{Y(1 - Y)} \qquad (8\text{-}12\text{-}5)$$

we see that they are different and when $Y_{LL} = X_{HH} = 0$, then (8-12-4) is reduced to (8-12-5).

Because $dX_H = - dX_L$, $dY_L = -dY_H$ (when Y_{LL} and X_{HH} are not changed) , so (8-12-4) can be also written as:

$$\left.\frac{\partial X_H}{\partial Y_H}\right|_S = \left.\frac{\partial X_L}{\partial Y_L}\right|_S = \frac{(Y_L + Y_H)X_L X_H}{(X_L + X_H)Y_L Y_H} \qquad (8\text{-}12\text{-}6)$$

and the relative gains will be also different from those of the binary columns.

The following relations are still valid for this column:

$$\left.\begin{array}{l} F = D + B \\ FZ_H = DY_H + BX_H \\ FZ_L = DY_L + BX_L \end{array}\right\} \qquad (8\text{-}12\text{-}7)$$

It yields:

$$\frac{D}{F} = \frac{Z_H - X_H}{Y_H - X_H} \qquad (8-12-8)$$

and from this expression we can get:

$$\frac{\partial (D/F)}{\partial Y_H}\bigg|_{X_H} = -\frac{D/F}{Y_H - X_H} \qquad (8-12-9)$$

$$\frac{\partial (D/F)}{\partial X_H}\bigg|_{Y_H} = \frac{D/F - 1}{Y_H - X_H} \qquad (8-12-10)$$

These are the same as those of the binary columns and:

$$\frac{\partial (D/F)}{\partial Y_H}\bigg|_S = \frac{\partial D/F}{\partial Y_H}\bigg|_{X_H} + \frac{\partial D/F}{\partial X_H}\bigg|_{Y_H}\frac{\partial X_H}{\partial Y_H}\bigg|_S \qquad (8-12-11)$$

Subsituting (8-12-9) and (8-12-10) into it, we get:

$$\frac{\partial (D/F)}{\partial Y_H}\bigg|_S = -\frac{D/F}{Y_H - X_H} - \frac{(1 - D/F)(Y_L + Y_H)X_L X_H}{(Y_H - X_H)(X_L + X_H)Y_L Y_H} \qquad (8-12-12)$$

and the relative gain is :

$$\lambda_{Y_H D} = \frac{\dfrac{\partial Y_H}{\partial D/F}\bigg|_S}{\dfrac{\partial Y_H}{\partial D/F}\bigg|_X} = \frac{\dfrac{\partial D/F}{\partial Y_H}\bigg|_X}{\dfrac{\partial D/F}{\partial Y_H}\bigg|_S} = \frac{\dfrac{\partial D/F}{\partial Y_H}\bigg|_X}{\dfrac{\partial D/F}{\partial Y_H}\bigg|_V} =$$

$$= \frac{1}{1 + \dfrac{(Y_H - Z_H)(Y_L + Y_H)X_L X_H}{(Z_H - X_H)(X_L + X_H)Y_L Y_H}} \qquad (8-12-13)$$

This is corresponding to the pairing relation: Y_H —— D and X_H — V

Because:

$$\frac{Y_H - Z_H}{Z_H - X_H} = \frac{B}{D} = \frac{Y_L - Z_L}{Z_L - X_L} \qquad (8-12-14)$$

$$\lambda_{Y_L D} = \cfrac{1}{1 + \cfrac{(Y_L - Z_L)(Y_L + Y_H)X_L X_H}{(Z_L - X_L)(X_L + X_H)Y_L Y_H}} \qquad (8-12-15)$$

so there is only one λ_{YD} for both Y_H and Y_L when they are all controlled by D.

For example, a depropanizer is with the following parameters:

	Feed %	Distillate %	Bottoms %
Ethane	1.2	2.9	
Propane	39.4 (Z_L)	95.5 (Y_L)	0.4 (X_L)
Isobutane	14.0 (Z_H)	1.6 (Y_H)	22.6 (X_H)
Water	45.4		77.0

The distillation control problem is considered between the propane and the isobutane and we can get:

$$\lambda_{YD} = \cfrac{1}{1 + \cfrac{(95.5 - 39.4)(95.5 + 1.6)0.4 \times 22.6}{(39.4 - 0.4)(0.4 + 22.6)95.5 \times 1.6}} = 0.736 \qquad (8-12-16)$$

so the relative gain is suitable and that means that Y may be controlled by D.

Likewise, when Y is controlled by L and X is controlled by V, we can get:

$$\lambda_{YL} = \left[1 + \frac{\beta(Y_L - X_L)^2}{Z_L - X_L} \left(\frac{1}{Y_L} + \frac{1}{Y_H} \right) \right] \lambda_{YD} \qquad (8-12-17)$$

and λ_{YL} is always larger than λ_{YD}.

The analysis of the non-binary column control in general is similar with that of the binary columns if the two compositions under consideration are determined, but the formulas for calculating relative gaings are different from those for binary columns.

§ 8-13 Decoupling Design of Distillation Column Control Systems

We have got the conclusion if project 11 or project 3 is used for the two terminal product control, then in general the interaction problem is not very serious and the decoupling design may be unnecessary.

But if the conventional control project (project 6) is adopted, namely Y is controlled by L ; X is controlled by V ; R is controlled by B and A is controlled by D, then this system is certainly with serious interaction and we have proved this statement theoretically. In a word, this is because λ_{YL} is always very large and numerous practical examples also give proofs on this conclusion.

Although the conventional project has serious interaction in the control process, yet we can see that in many cases this project is still adopted and the reason for this is, as we said before, that the conventional project always has quite high sensitivities.

People have reached a general opinion that decoupling design should be carried out when the conventional project is adopted.

If, however, we did not do the decoupling design for the conventional project, namely the interaction effects were neglected and both the top channel and the bottom channel were designed independently, would it be available ?

No, it is unavailable.

This is because in fact the plant now is a P-canonical plant and the system is with the scheme as shown in Fig 8-13-1.

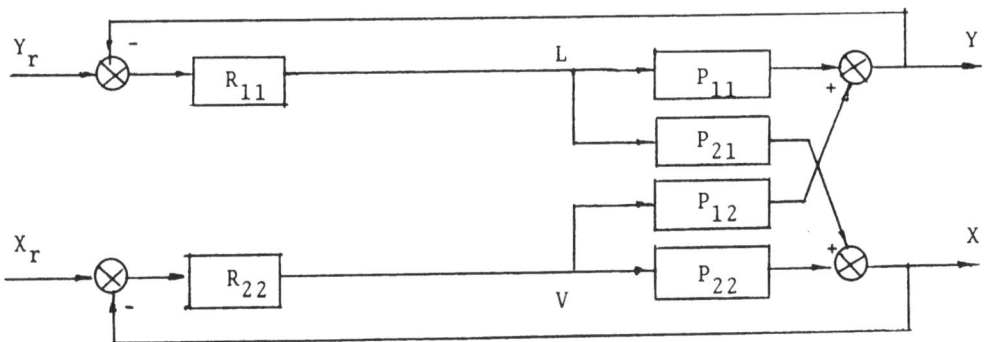

Fig 8-13-1

For this system :

$$\frac{Y}{L} = P_{11} - \frac{R_{22}P_{12}P_{21}}{1 + R_{22}P_{22}} \tag{8-13-1}$$

$$\frac{X}{V} = P_{22} - \frac{R_{11}P_{12}P_{21}}{1 + R_{11}P_{11}} \tag{8-13-2}$$

Obviously:

$$\frac{Y}{L} \neq P_{11} \quad , \quad \frac{X}{V} \neq P_{22}$$

so, if we despise the existence of the practical interaction and neg-lect it without any reason, then the calculation results are quite dif-ferent from the practical system. Therefore, we can not do so.

Wood and Berry pointed out that the conventional project is not suitable for two terminal composition control unless decoupling design is carried out . Their conclusions are :[59]

(1) If the control system design is carried out in spite of the existence of the system interaction, then   the design results are unavailable for the practical systems,

(2) Because of the interaction, the tuning of regulators in ge-neral is very difficult,

(3) The system responses in general are very slow or with serious oscillations.

Therefore, in order to apply the conventional project to the two terminal composition control, the decoupling design is always necessary.

Then, how to do the decoupling design ?

There are a lot of reports on this problem but the Luyben's re-sults are especially worth being discussed.[55]

Luyben researched two kinds of decoupling systems, namely the ideal decoupling design and the simplified decoupling design.

Let us remember the ideal decoupling design mentioned in §5-5.

The decoupling system is shown in Fig 8-13-2.

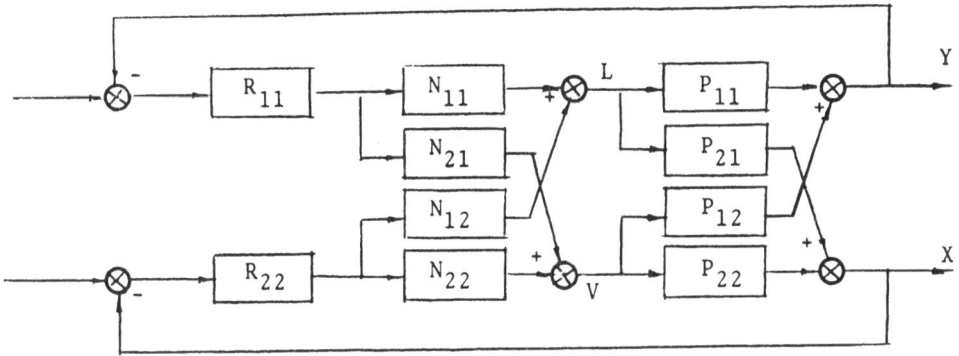

Fig 8-13-2

The so-called ideal decoupling means that the plant characteristics after decoupling design are just the same as the main channel plant characteristics before decoupling design, namely:

$$\frac{Y}{L} = P_{11}$$

$$\frac{X}{V} = P_{22}$$

$$\left.\begin{array}{c} \\ \\ \end{array}\right\} \qquad (8-13-3)$$

For **ideal** decoupling design, the characteristics of the decoupling elements are:

$$\begin{Bmatrix} N_{11} & N_{12} \\ \\ N_{21} & N_{22} \end{Bmatrix} = \frac{P_{11}P_{22}}{P_{11}P_{22} - P_{12}P_{21}} \begin{pmatrix} 1 & -\dfrac{P_{12}}{P_{11}} \\ \\ \dfrac{-P_{21}}{P_{22}} & 1 \end{pmatrix}$$

$$(8-13-4)$$

We have said before that the **ideal** decoupling design seems very good, but in practice the regulators R_{11} and R_{22} should provide necessary signals with energy not only for their own main channels, but also for the decoupling channels and this will give more burden to R_{11} and R_{22}. In general, the system is difficult to be realized and is easily to be unstable.

Then , how is it used for the distillation column control ?

·Luyben´s research results denote that the ideal decoupling design can be used for the distillation column control but when the percentages of Y and X differ,namely the purity changes, then the characters of the plant change very seriously and, consequently, the characters of the regulators also change very much. When $Y > 0.98$, the gains of N_{12} and N_{21} increase remarkably and the system becomes unstable.

Luyben´s measurement results are:

$$Y = 0.98 \quad X = 0.02 \qquad\qquad Y = 0.95 \quad X = 0.5$$

$$N_{11} = N_{22} \qquad \frac{10.62}{12.5S + 1} \qquad\qquad 3.298\left(\frac{1.5S + 1}{5S + 1}\right)$$

$$N_{12} \qquad \frac{10.08}{12.5S + 1} \qquad\qquad 2.697\left(\frac{1.5S + 1}{5S + 1}\right)$$

$$N_{21} \qquad \frac{10.14}{12.5S + 1} \qquad\qquad \frac{2.809}{(2S + 1)^2}$$

Obviously, when Y increases, the static gains of N_{11}, N_{22}, N_{12} and N_{21} all increase.

For different values of Y, Luyben´s results are:

X	Y	$N_{11} = N_{22}$	N_{12}	N_{21}
0.05	0.95	3.30	2.70	2.81
0.02	0.98	10.62	10.08	10.14
0.01	0.99	33.80	33.28	33.31
0.005	0.995	126.74	126.24	126.23

From this table we can see that the gains of the decoupling elements increase very quickly as Y increases.

Therefore, Luyben´s conclusion is : The ideal decoupling project only can be used within a limit and the purer the top product, the more difficult the realizing the ideal decoupling control.

In fact, this conclusion is easily to be understood. For:

$$\lambda_{YL} = \left[1 + \frac{\beta (Y - X)^2}{Y(1 - Y)(Z - X)}\right]\lambda_{YD} \qquad (8-13-5)$$

When the purity of the top product increases, then $(1 - Y)$ approaches zero more and, consequently, λ_{YL} becomes larger. That means that the interaction becomes more serious. So, if not only the decoupling control is expected, but also all coupling results should be eliminated, namely the ideal decoupling control is expected, then certainly the compensation function of the decoupling elements should be strenghthened , i.e. the gains of the decoupling elements should be increased.

Therefore, the ideal decoupling control is not easily to be realized and Luyben researched another decoupling project, namely the simplified decoupling project.

The structure of the simplified decoupling control system is shown in Fig 8-13-3.

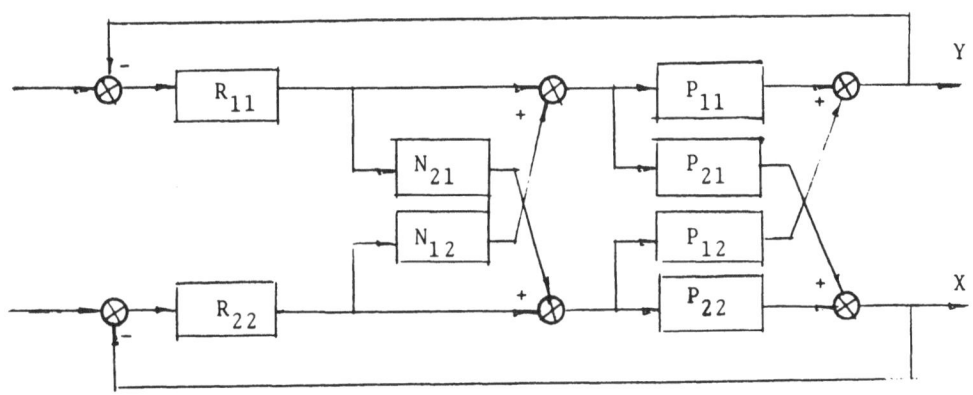

Fig 8-13-3

The characteristic equations for this decoupled system are:

For the top channel:

$$1 + R_{11}(\frac{P_{11}P_{22} - P_{12}P_{21}}{P_{22}}) = 0 \qquad (8-13-6)$$

For the bottom channel:

$$1 + R_{22} \left(\frac{P_{11}P_{22} - P_{12}P_{21}}{P_{11}} \right) = 0 \qquad (8\text{-}13\text{-}7)$$

But for the ideal decoupled system, the characteristic equations are:

For the top channel:

$$1 + R_{11}P_{11} = 0 \qquad (8\text{-}13\text{-}8)$$

For the bottom channel:

$$1 + R_{22}P_{22} = 0 \qquad (8\text{-}13\text{-}9)$$

Therefore, although both systems can get the decoupling control effects, yet their dynamic characters are different and in the simple decoupling system , some coupling results are still reflected in its dynamic responses.

The decoupling conditions for the simplified decoupling system are:

$$\left. \begin{aligned} N_{12} &= - \frac{P_{12}}{P_{11}} \\[2em] N_{21} &= - \frac{P_{21}}{P_{22}} \end{aligned} \right\} \qquad (8\text{-}13\text{-}10)$$

Notice that in this control project, P_{21} is always with dead delay because the influence of the reflux change on the bottom composition should be transferred from the top to the bottom.

Luyben's practical measurement results are:

	Y= 0.98 X= 0.02	Y= 0.95 X= 0.05
N_{21}	$\dfrac{0.9547e^{-1.5S}}{0.4S + 1}$	$\dfrac{0.8515e^{-1.5S}}{0.4S + 1}$
N_{12}	0.9488	0.8180

and the static gains of both N_{12} and N_{21} approach zero as Y increases, namely they do not increase as Y increases.

Therefore, this simplified decoupling system is with simple struc-

X	Y	Gain of N_{21}	Gain of N_{12}
0.05	0.95	0.8518	0.8180
0.02	0.98	0.9547	0.9488
0.01	0.99	0.9856	0.9846
0.005	0.995	0.9960	0.9961

ture and without unstable results. So , this simplified decoupling system is available for practice.

Theoretically speaking,

$$\left. \begin{array}{l} P_{11} = \left(\dfrac{\partial Y}{\partial \dfrac{L}{F}} \right)_D = \dfrac{1}{\beta} Y(1 - Y)(1 - \lambda_{YD}) \\[24pt] P_{12} = \left(\dfrac{\partial Y}{\partial \dfrac{V}{F}} \right)_D = \dfrac{1}{\beta} Y(1 - Y)(1 - \lambda_{YD}) \\[24pt] P_{22} = \left(\dfrac{\partial X}{\partial \dfrac{V}{F}} \right)_D = - \dfrac{1}{\beta} X(1 - X) \lambda_{YD} \\[24pt] P_{21} = \left(\dfrac{\partial X}{\partial \dfrac{L}{F}} \right)_D = - \dfrac{1}{\beta} X(1 - X) \lambda_{YD} \end{array} \right\} \qquad (8\text{-}13\text{-}11)$$

thus:

$$\left. \begin{array}{l} P_{11} = P_{12} \\[8pt] P_{22} = P_{21} \end{array} \right\} \qquad (8\text{-}13\text{-}12)$$

and :

$$\left. \begin{array}{l} N_{12} = - \dfrac{P_{12}}{P_{11}} = -1 \\[24pt] N_{21} = - \dfrac{P_{21}}{P_{22}} = -1 \end{array} \right\} \qquad (8\text{-}13\text{-}13)$$

It means that theoretically the gains of both N_{12} and N_{21} should be 1. But, in practice, D can not be kept entirely unchanged, so P_{11}

454

and P_{12}, P_{22} and P_{21} can not be equal entirely and thus both N_{12} and N_{21} approach 1. Therefore, Luyben's measurement results are reasonable and this simplified decoupling system is available in practice.

In the application of this project, all signals through the decoupling elements are provided by two regulators and this will certainly gives more burden to the regulators . In order to reduce the burden on two regulators, the following scheme can be used:

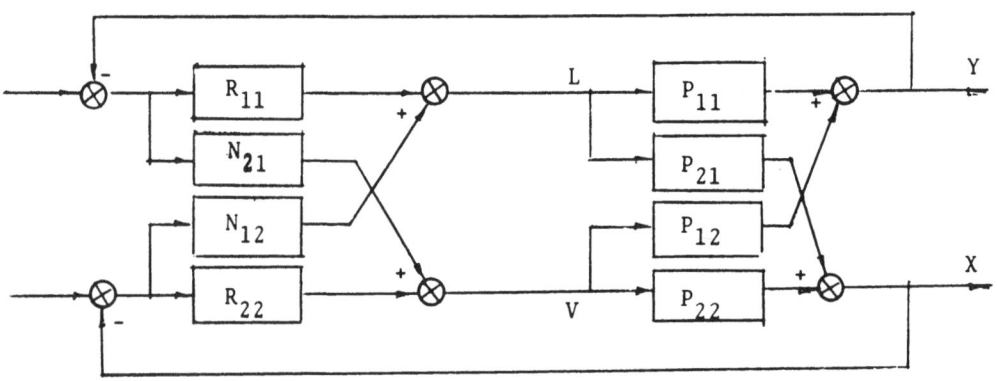

Fig 8-13-4

and in this structure, the regulators only provide the necessary signals for their own channels. But the parameters of regulators should be stable because in this case the characters of the decoupling elements are related to the regulators.

(8-13-12) denotes that in the ideal case, we have $P_{11} = P_{12}$ and $P_{22} = P_{21}$. In fact, this ideal case can not be expected in practice, but, however, in this control project, they are approximately equal to each other and this conclusion has been proved by many practical examples.

For instance, a separate column of methanol-water with 10 trays is with the following practical measurement characters:

$$P_{11} = \frac{-10.8(1 + 3.08S)}{2.13S^2 + 2.04S + 1}$$

$$P_{12} = \frac{0.52(1 + 3.125S)}{1.78S^2 + 1.87S + 1}$$

$$P_{22} = \frac{1.84}{1.87S^2 + 2.19S + 1} \Bigg\}$$ (8-13-14)

$$P_{21} = \frac{-28.14e^{-0.65S}}{1.90S^2 + 2.21S + 1}$$

In the measurements of these characters, the manipulated variable of the bottom composition is the heating medium in the reboiler but not the up steam, so there are obvious differences between the static gains of P_{11} and P_{12} as well as P_{21} and P_{22} and this is not strange at all. If the manipulated variable of the bottom product composition were the up steam, the differences of the gains between P_{11} and P_{12} as well as P_{22} and P_{21} would not be very large. Even so, we see that in the above practical measurement results, the dynamic characters of P_{11} and P_{12} as well as P_{22} and P_{21} are quite similar.

The decoupling elements are:

$$N_{21} = -R_{11}\frac{P_{21}}{P_{22}}$$ (8-13-15)

$$N_{12} = -R_{22}\frac{P_{12}}{P_{11}}$$ (8-13-16)

Substituting the above results into (8-13-15) and (8-13-16), we get:

$$N_{21} = -R_{11}(-\frac{28.14}{1.84})(\frac{1 + 2.19S + 1.87S^2}{1 + 2.21S + 1.90S^2})e^{-0.65S}$$ (8-13-17)

$$N_{12} = -R_{22}(-\frac{0.52}{10.8})(\frac{1 + 1.312S}{1 + 3.08S})(\frac{1 + 2.04S + 2.13S^2}{1 + 1.87S + 1.78S^2})$$ (8-13-18)

Because the dynamic characters are similar, so we can get approximately:

$$N_{21} = -R_{11}(-15.28e^{-0.65S}) \qquad\qquad (8-13-19)$$

$$N_{12} = -R_{22}(-0.048) \qquad\qquad (8-13-20)$$

and the realization problem becomes simple.

If both regulators are propotional types , then both Y and X control loops will have steady deviations but N_{12} and N_{21} are very easily
to be realized.

If both regulators are P+I types :

$$R_{11} = K_{11} \frac{1 + T_1 S}{T_1 S} \qquad\qquad (8-13-21)$$

$$R_{22} = K_{22} \frac{1 + T_2 S}{T_2 S} \qquad\qquad (8-13-22)$$

then :

$$N_{21} = \frac{15.28 K_{11}(1 + T_1 S)e^{-0.65S}}{T_1 S} \qquad\qquad (8-13-23)$$

$$N_{12} = 0.048 K_{22} \frac{1 + T_2 S}{T_2 S} \qquad\qquad (8-13-24)$$

When S $\longrightarrow$ 0 , both N_{12} and N_{21} approach infinite and this denotes that they have enough ability to eliminate the steady coupling
influences.

Now that the ideal decoupling design is not easily to be realized
and the simplified decoupling design is available, then certainly we
can use the simplified decoupling control. But, however, are there any
shortages with the simplified decoupling systems ?

For both ideal decoupling system (Fig 8-13-2) and simplified decoupling system(Fig 8-13-3), two independent control loops are obtained after decoupling design. Taking the top composition control as
an example, we get two loops, respectively. They are shown in Fig 8-
13-5.

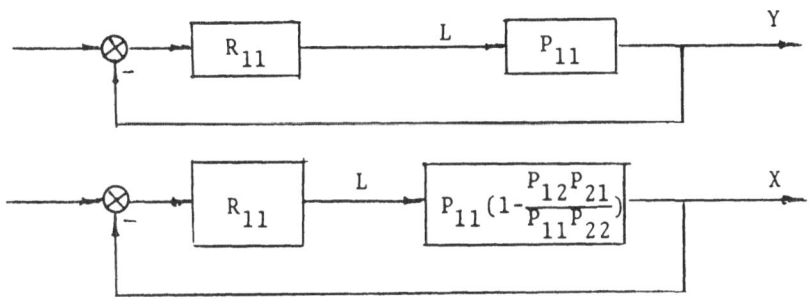

Fig 8-11-5

For the simplified decoupling system, the static gain of the plant is :

$$\frac{Y}{L} = K_{11}(1 - \frac{K_{12}K_{21}}{K_{11}K_{22}})$$ (8-13-25)

but the relative gain between Y and L is :

$$\lambda_{YL} = \frac{1}{1 - \dfrac{K_{12}K_{21}}{K_{11}K_{22}}}$$ (8-13-26)

thus:

$$\frac{Y}{L} = \frac{K_{11}}{\lambda_{YL}}$$ (8-13-27)

We know that the purer the top product, the more serious the interaction and , consequently, the larger the λ_{YL} . Thus, the steady gain of the plant of the simplified decoupling system becomes less and less. In other words, if the adoption of R_{11} for the ideal decoupling system (the plant character is P_{11}) can result in good control effects, then for the simplified decoupling system, the same R_{11} will result in slow response because the plant gain has decreased and this is an important shortage of the simplified decoupling control system.

Then, a problem arises here: It is well known that the conventional control project is with serious interaction and the reason for adopting this project in some cases is just because it has high sensitivities . But, the above analysis denotes that this advantage of the conventional control project can be held only in the ideal decoupling design and when the simplified decoupling design is applied, the plant gain decreases remarkably , namely the sensitivities decrease, thus the original advantage no longer exists and in order to increase the response speed, we have to increase the regulator gains and this is also just the shortage of the Shinskey's projects. But the application of Shinskey's projects does not need decoupling design . Thus, whether the conventional project should be adopted should be determined according to the practical calculation results and practical comparison of different projects.

Besides, when the conventional project is applied, although to increase the regulator gains is an available measure to speed up the response, yet there is a danger for doing so. That is : when some decoupling element fails in the operation, namely one of N_{12} and N_{21} is broken off, then because of the high gain of the regulator, some control loop becomes unstable. In order to avoid this danger, the regulators are not allowed to have very high gains.

Another applicable method to avoid this danger is to adopt the half decoupling design. For example, the top product is expected to be not influenced by the bottom control loop and we design:

$$N_{12} = - \frac{P_{12}}{P_{11}} \qquad (8-13-28)$$

but the bottom product is allowed to bear interaction and thus N_{21} is not necessary. The system equations now are:

$$Y = P_{11}L \qquad (8-13-29)$$

$$X = P_{21}L + P_{22}(1 - \frac{P_{12}P_{21}}{P_{11}P_{22}}) \qquad (8-13-30)$$

and the block diagram is shown in Fig 8-13-6. Obviously, there is no N_{21} channel in this system.

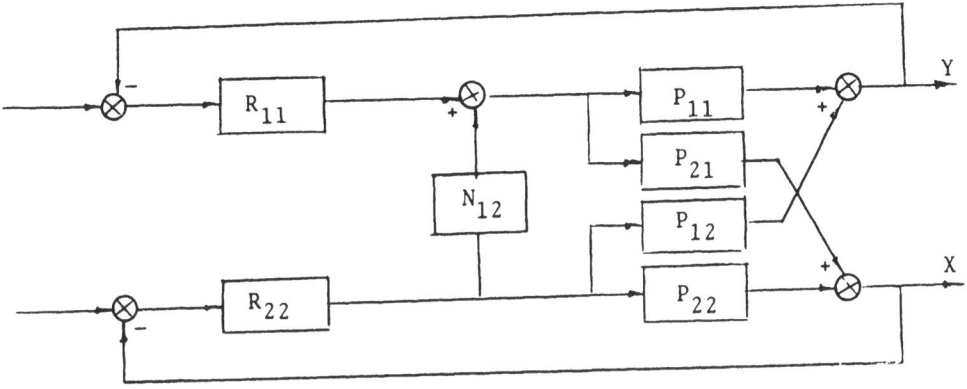

Fig 8-13-6

Although the bottom product is still influenced by the top loop,
the top product (in general it is the most important product in a
column) has been decoupled with the bottom loop. Besides, we see that
the top loop is corresponding to an ideal decoupling loop and thus it
can keep quite high sensititivities. The reliability of the system operation now is twice of that of the simplified decoupling system, so
this is also an available project.

This is just the triangle decoupling design. We know that for the
triangle decoupling design, there are upper triangle decoupling control and lower triangle decoupling control.

For the upper triangle decoupling design, it means that:

$$Q(S) = \begin{bmatrix} P_{11} & P_{12} \\ P_{21} & P_{22} \end{bmatrix} \begin{bmatrix} 1 & 0 \\ N_{21} & 1 \end{bmatrix} = \begin{bmatrix} P_{11} + P_{12}N_{21} & P_{12} \\ P_{21} + P_{22}N_{21} & P_{22} \end{bmatrix}$$

$$(8\text{-}13\text{-}31)$$

should be an upper triangle matrix and it is enough if:

$$P_{21} + P_{22}N_{21} = 0 \qquad\qquad (8\text{-}13\text{-}32)$$

namely:

$$N_{21} = -\frac{P_{21}}{P_{22}} \qquad\qquad (8\text{-}13\text{-}33)$$

For the lower triangle decoupling design, it means that:

$$Q(S) = \begin{bmatrix} P_{11} & P_{12} \\ \\ P_{21} & P_{22} \end{bmatrix} \begin{bmatrix} 1 & N_{12} \\ \\ 0 & 1 \end{bmatrix} = \begin{bmatrix} P_{11} & P_{11}N_{12} + P_{12} \\ \\ P_{21} & P_{21}N_{12} + P_{22} \end{bmatrix}$$

$$(8\text{-}13\text{-}34)$$

should be a lower triangle matrix and it is enough if:

$$P_{11}N_{12} + P_{12} = 0 \qquad\qquad (8\text{-}13\text{-}35)$$

namely:

$$N_{12} = - \frac{P_{12}}{P_{11}} \qquad\qquad (8\text{-}13\text{-}36)$$

The system shown in Fig 8-13-6 is just the lower triangle decoupling project.

We should point out that in the distillation column control, we can not expect that the lower triangle decoupling system can be realized in every case. The lower triangle decoupling system gives the guarantee that the top product composition is not influenced by the bottom control loop but the interaction to the bottom control loop is not eliminated. We say that this demand is not realized at any time, but on the contrary, the upper triangle decoupling control project is realizable in most cases.

This is because the control of the distillation column in general is to control a process with large capacities. The four plant characters P_{11} , P_{12}, P_{21} and P_{22} are often with different dead delays. Among them, the influence of the change of the reflux flow on the bottom composition occurs in the liquid-phase and is transferred from the top to the bottom, so this process, i.e. P_{21}, is always with the largest dead delay and thus:

$$N_{21} = - \frac{P_{21}}{P_{22}}$$

is always with negative dead delay and is realizable. This means that the upper triangle decoupling control is always realizable, namely

the decoupling control of the bottom product composition is always realizable.

But, for a column with small reflux flow and a few trays,   the
variation of the top tray temperature (it is a measurement of the top
product composition) due to the change of the up steam occurs in vapor-
phase and may have higher speed than that due to the change of the reflux flow, namely the dead delay of P_{12} is less than that of P_{11}.

Thus:

$$N_{12} = - \frac{P_{12}}{P_{11}}$$

is with positive dead delay and it is impossible to be realized , i.e.
the lower triangle decoupling design sometimes may be irrealizable.

§ 8-14 Why Should Two Terminal Products Be Controlled ?

Now that the two terminal product composition control is with
a lot of problems and some of them are even difficult to be solved,then
certainly we should ask : Why should two terminal product compositions
be controlled ? If only   one terminal composition were controlled,
we would not meet so many problems .

The basic reason to control the two terminal product compositions
simultaneously is to save energy.

When the feed composition is with large variation and the purity
of the top product is not very high, the two terminal composition control
can save energy very   remarkably. We have pointed out at the beginning
of this chapter that the distillation column is the most important unit
to expend energy in the chemical industry, so to save energy is a very

important goal for distillation column design.

When only one terminal product is controlled, then at the other terminal either V or L is kept unchanged and the practical $\frac{V}{F}$ is always larger than that necessary for keeping the product quality of this terminal. This means that more energy is expended because V is caused by the outer energy.

The variation of the feed composition is the most important disturbance in the distillation column control, therefore a good control project should be so, that during the variation of F , the value $\frac{V}{F}$ always is the least among different projects.

Luyben researched this problem and got the conclusion that the two terminal composition control project is the best.

For $\frac{Y}{X} = \frac{0.95}{0.05}$, $\alpha = 1.2$, Luyben got the following different results.

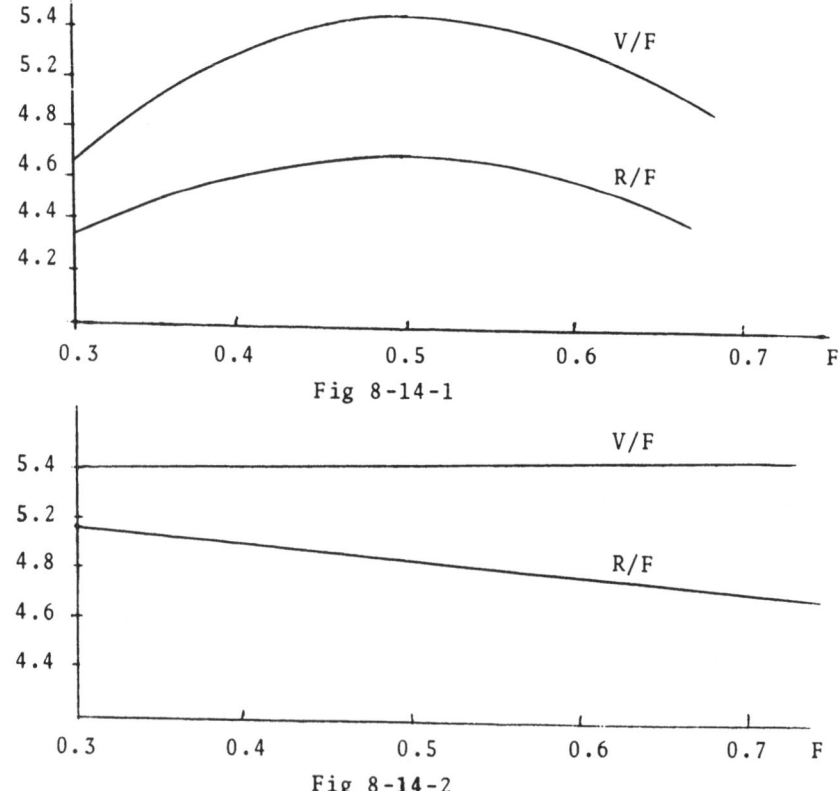

Fig 8-14-1

Fig 8-14-2

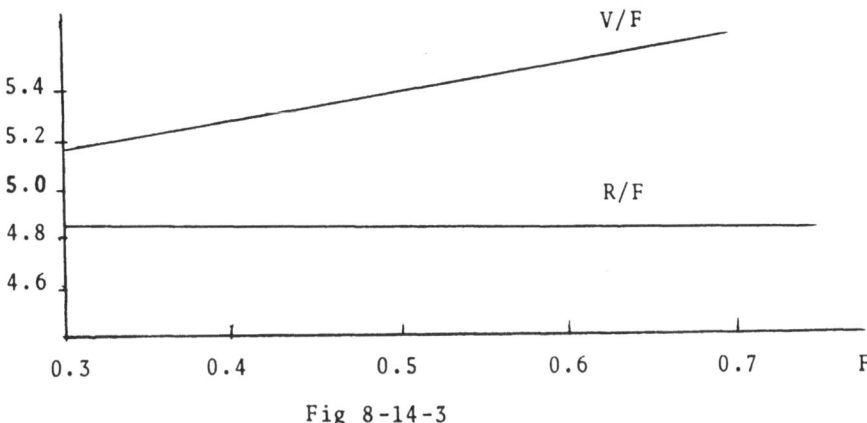

Fig 8-14-3

Fig 8-14-1 shows the two terminal control project, namely Y is controlled by L and X by V. We see that V/F and R/F change with F and when F = 0.5, both V/F and R/F get their largest values.

Fig 8-14-2 is the case that V/F is definite and one terminal product is controlled by L. The V/F value here must be the largest value of Fig 8-14-1 in order to be suited for all F. From this figure we can see that both V/F and R/F are larger than the corresponding values of Fig 8-14-1 no matter F is larger than 0.5 or is less than 0.5 and this means that more energy is expended.

Fig 8-14-3 is the case that R/F is definite and one terminal product is controlled by V . Just like Fig 8-14-2, the value R/F here is the largest of Fig 8-14-1. We also see that both V/F (especially when F > 0.5) and R/F are larger than the corresponding values of Fig 8-14-1 and certainly more energy is expended in this case. Notice that larger reflux demands larger up steam and, consequently, more energy.

Therefore, in general the two terminal composition control can save energy. This is true especially for the columns with lower relative volatility , not high product purity and remarkable change of feed composition.

§ 8-15 The Control of Azeotropic Distillation [50]

Water cannot be economically stripped from an aqueous solution of acetic acid by conventional distillation, because acetic acid and water form an azeotrope consisting of 97% water. Azeotropic distillation must be used to produce satisfactory separation.

In azeotropic distillation, a solvent is added that forms a minimum boiling azeotrope with one of the components to be separated (water in this example) . This minimum boiling azeotrope leaves the column as a vapor that condenses and separates into two layers (the azeotrope is heterogeneous) with the solvent floating to the top. The organic or solvent layer is used as reflux and is manipulated to maintain the correct solvent inventory in the rectification section of the column. The aqueous layer is discarded and the extra solvent in the reflux accumulator is also discarded. The pure acetic acid is obtained from the bottom flow.

The scheme is shown in Fig 8-15-1.

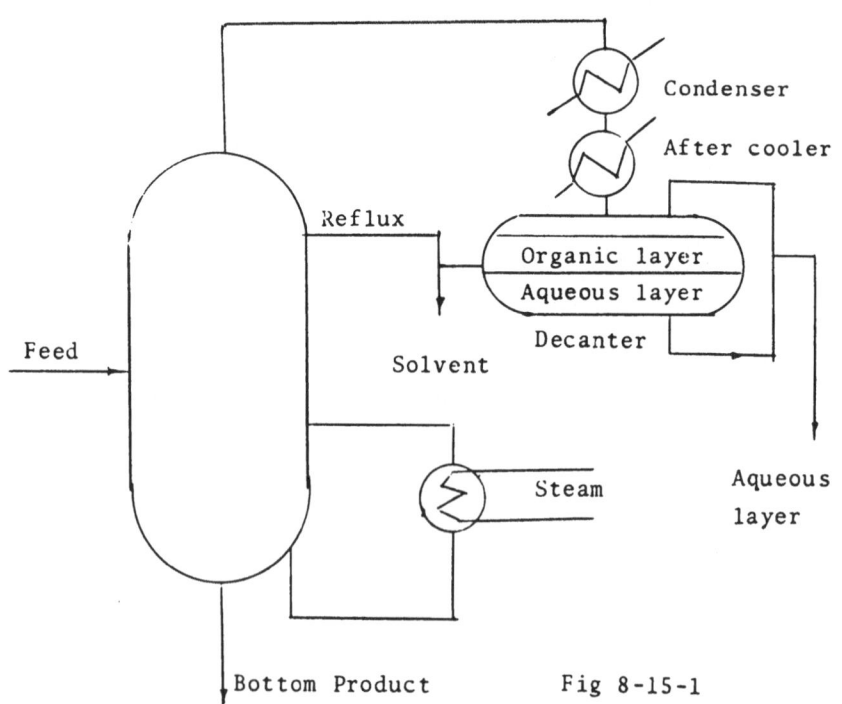

Fig 8-15-1

For this column, the condition of material balance gives:

$$V = D + L \qquad (8\text{-}15\text{-}1)$$

where , V is the up steam; D is the distillates (the total overflow of both water and solvent) and L is the reflux rate.

Suppose that 100% of the acetic acid is recovered in the bottoms and that 100% of the solvent and water are recovered in the overhead , then the combined flow of distillate D can be expressed :

$$D = F (Z_1 + Z_2) \qquad (8\text{-}15\text{-}2)$$

where F is the feedrate; Z_1 is the weight fraction of solvent in the feed and Z_2 is the weight fraction of water in the feed.

From (8-15-1) and (8-15-2) , we get:

$$\frac{V}{F} - \frac{L}{F} = Z_1 + Z_2 \qquad (8\text{-}15\text{-}3)$$

For the solvent, the material balance condition gives:

$$VY - LW = FZ_1 \qquad (8\text{-}15\text{-}4)$$

where, Y is the weight fraction of solvent in the vapor and W is the weight fraction of solvent in the reflux.

From these equations we can get:

$$L = F \frac{Y(Z_1 + Z_2) - Z_1}{W - Y} \qquad (8\text{-}15\text{-}5)$$

$$V = F \frac{W(Z_1 + Z_2) - Z_1}{W - Y} \qquad (8\text{-}15\text{-}6)$$

The controlled variables of this column are Y and X where X is the total impurities in the acetic acid product. The manipulated variables are L and V.

In this column, the reflux must be manipulated to maintain the solvent inventory at the proper level. If reflux is too low, the vapors will be composed of solvent-water azeotrope and water-acid azeotrope , since not enough solvent is available to combine with water. If reflux is too high, solvent works its way down the column and steam consumption becomes excessive because of the increased heat load.

X is controlled by the heating steam . If the impurities in the acid , X, are too high , then the steam flow must be increased in order to boil the excess contaminants away. Conversely, if X is too low,then steam is being wasted to make a needlessly pure product.

The interaction is obvious in this column control . For example, if it is necessary to increase reflux to correct the vapor composition, there is a larger head load on the reboiler.Steam must be increased to prevent the greater internal reflux from upsetting bottoms composition. But this increase in steam flow cancels part of the effects that the previously changed reflux exerted on vapor composition , so reflux must change again. Thus, the circle continues and this is just the interaction. Theoretically , this interaction will eventually settle out if the correct variable pairing relations are adopted. Obviously, if the interaction is too serious, the control, perhaps, must be operated manually.

We should discuss :

(1) Are the variable pairing relations Y — L and X — V suitable for the control of this column ? Namely , can the interaction circle eventually be stopped by using these variable pairing relations?

(2) If these variable pairing relations are available, how long time will the circle continue ?

(8-15-5), (8-15-6) and (8-15-4) can be rewritten as:

$$Y = \frac{W(\ L/F\ ) + Z_1}{Z_1 + Z_2 + L/F} \tag{8-15-7}$$

$$Y = W - (\ \frac{W(\ Z_1 + Z_2\ ) - Z_1}{V/F}\ ) \tag{8-15-8}$$

$$Y = \frac{Z_1 + WL/F}{V/F} \tag{8-15-9}$$

From these relations , we get:

$$\frac{\partial Y}{\partial \frac{L}{F}}\Bigg|_X = \frac{W - Y}{Z_1 + Z_2 + L/F} \qquad (8\text{-}15\text{-}10)$$

$$\frac{\partial Y}{\partial \frac{L}{F}}\Bigg|_{V/F} = \frac{W}{\frac{V}{F}} \qquad (8\text{-}15\text{-}11)$$

and the relative gains are:

$$\lambda_{YL} = \frac{\partial Y}{\partial \frac{L}{F}}\Bigg|_{V/F} \Bigg/ \frac{\partial Y}{\partial \frac{L}{F}}\Bigg|_X = \frac{W(Z_1 + Z_2 + L/F)}{\frac{V}{F}(W - Y)} \qquad (8\text{-}15\text{-}12)$$

Suppose: $Y = 0.935$, $V/F = 1.55$, $L/F = 0.63$, then from:

$$\frac{V}{F} Y - \frac{L}{F} W = Z_1 \qquad (8\text{-}15\text{-}13)$$

and (8-15-3) we can get Z_1 and Z_2 and then from (8-15-12) we get:

$$\lambda_{YL} = 27.7 \qquad (8\text{-}15\text{-}14)$$

Thus, the relative gain matrix is :

	L	V
Y	27.7	-26.7
X	-26.7	27.7

Obviously, both λ_{LX} and λ_{YV} are negative, so the pairing relations of Y——— V and X——— L are unavailable.

The pairing relations of Y——— L and X——— V can be used but serious interaction can be found in this system.

Now, we analyze the interaction.

The interaction index of this system is:

$$D_I = \frac{\lambda_{XL}}{\lambda_{YL}} = \frac{-26.6}{27.7} = -0.96 \qquad (8\text{-}15\text{-}15)$$

We know when $|D_I| < 1$,the interaction process is convergent and so
this interaction process is stable.

What does the interaction index mean ?

For the azeotropic column, the interaction index means that a 10-deg increase in bottoms temperature (due to an increase in steam flow) will increase the top temperature by 9.6 deg, i.e. 10 deg. multilpied by the absolute value of the interaction index. Then, if reflux is increased to lower the top temperature by 9.6 deg, the bottoms temperature will fall by 9.2 deg, i.e. 9.6 deg. multiplied by the absolute value of the interaction index. The next reaction would be an increase in steam to raise the bottoms temperature; and the result would be an increase in the top temperature of 9.2 times 0.96, or 8.8 deg.

And the circle is so continued. We see that the process is convergent.

Then, when will the circle end ?

Theoretically speaking, it will continue without end.

Now, if the allowed eventual deviation is m and the initial deviation is $\mathcal{E}$, then by (7-8-3) :

$$m = \mathcal{E} \, D_I^{(N-1)} \qquad\qquad (8\text{-}15\text{-}16)$$

where N is the number of the half interaction circles.

From it, we get:

$$N = \frac{\ln m - \ln \mathcal{E}}{\ln D_I} + 1 \qquad\qquad (8\text{-}15\text{-}17)$$

For example, if m= 2° C , namely the allowed temperature deviation.

Then, if the initial temperature deviation is 10° C, the necessary number of the half interaction circles for reaching 2°C deviation is:

$$N = \frac{0.69 - 2.303}{-0.40} + 1 = 41.3 \qquad\qquad (8\text{-}15\text{-}18)$$

Therefore, the number of the circles is 21.

For an azeotropic column, in general a circle takes 40 minutes. Thus, it will take the column about 14 hours to line out after an upset. The column certainly cannot tolerate such a period of off-specification operation. In other words, the decoupling control is necessary.

REFERENCES

(1) Boksenbom, A.S and Hood, R. " General Algebraic Method to Control
    Analysis of Complex Engine Types "
    NACA-TR-930, Washington,D.C. 1949.

(2) Tsien, H. S. " Engineering Cybernetics "
    McGraw-Hill Book Company New york , 1954.

(3) Mesarovic, M.D. " The Control of Multivariable Systems "
    New york — London , John Wiley, 1960.

(4) A.J. Fossard. " Multivariable System Control "
    New York , North-Holland, 1977.

(5) Helmut Schwarz." Mehrfachregelungen " (Band I)
    Springer-Verlag , Berlin/Heideberg/ New York , 1967.

(6) M . V. Meerov. " Multivariable Control Systems "
    Isral Program for Scientific Translation Ltd , 1968.

(7) F. G. Shinskey. " Process Control Systems "
    McGraw-Hill book Company 1967, Second Edition 1979.

(8) F. G. Shinskey. " Distillation Control"
    McGraw-Hill Book Company New York 1977.

(9) Leonhard , A. " Introduction to Control Engineering and Linear
    Control Systems " Springer-Verlarg. Berlin.

(10) M. S. Feder and R. Hood. " Analysis for Control Application
     of Dynamic Characteristics of Turboject Engine with Tail-Pipe
     Burning " NACA Tech Note 2183 Washington.D.C. Sept. 1950.

(11) H, Freemen . " A Synthesis Method of Multipole Control Systems"
     AIEE. Trans. Appl. Ind. Vol 76, Pt II, pp. 28-31, March . 1957.

(12) H. Freemen . " Stability and Physical Realizebility Considera-
     tions in the Synthesis of Multipole Control Systems"
     AIEE. Tran. Appl. Ind. Vol. 77. Pt II. pp. 1-5. March. 1958.

(13) R.J. Kavanagh. " Noninteracting Controls in Linear Multivari-
     able Systems "
     AIEE. Trans. Appl. Ind. Vol 76. Pt II. pp.95-99. May. 1957.

(14) R.J. Kavanagh. " Multivariable Control System Synthesis"
     AIEE. Trans. Appl. Ind. Vol 77. Pt II. pp.425-429. Nov. 1958.

(15) R.J. Kavanagh. " The Application of Matrix to Multivariable
     Control Systems " J. Franklin. Inst. 262(1957) pp. 349-367.

(16) H.H. Rosenbrock. " Design of Multivariable Control Systems
     Using Inverse Nuquist Array"
     Pro. IEE. Vol.116. No.11. pp.1929-1936. Nov. 1969.

(17) H.H. Rosenbrock . " Computer-Aided Design of Multivariable Control Systems " Proc. Second Advanced Control Conference.

(18) MacFarlane.A.G.   " A survey of Some Recent Results in Linear Multivariable Feedback Theory" Automitica . Vol.8 .pp.455-492.

(19) A.G. MacFarlane and Belletrutti. J.J . " The Characteristic Locus Design Method " Automatica. Vol.9. No.5. pp.575-558. 1973.

(20) Falb.P.L and W.A.Wolovich. " Decoupling in the Design and Synthesis of Multivariable Control Systems "
IEEE. Trans. Automatic Control. Vol AC-12 .pp.651.659.Dec. 1967.

(21) Wolovich.W.A. " Static Decoupling "
IEEE Trans. Automatic Control. Vol AC-18. October. 1973.

(22) Gilbert.E.G. " The Decoupling of Multivariable Systems by State Feedback " SIAM,J. Control. Vol.7 pp.50-63. 1969.

(23) Gilbert.E.G. " Controllability and Obserability in Multivariable Control Systems " SIAM,J. Control. No.2. 1963.

(24) Morgan.B.S. " The Synthesis of Linear Multivariable Systems by State-Variable Feedback"
IEEE. Trans. Automatic Control. Vol.Ac-9.pp.405-411. Oct.1964.

(25) C.L. Smith. " Automatic Process Control —— Where Are We ?"
Advance in Instrumentation Vol. 28. Pt I. 1973.

(26) H. Schwarz. " Vorschläge Zur Elimination Von Kopplungen in Mehrfachregelkreisen " Regelungstechnik . 1962. s.439.

(27) H. Schwarz. " Zur Autonomisierung Mehrfachgeregelter Systeme"
Regelungstechnik . 13. 1965. Heft 6 und 8.

(28) H. Schwarz. " Das Atabilitätsverhalten Entkoppelter Zweifachregelkreise" Messen— Steuern— Regeln . Heft 2, 1967.

(29) Beuchelt,R. " Vermeidung von Kopplungen in Zweifachregelkreisen"
Regelungstechnik . Heft 5, 1964.

(30) W. Engel. " Grundlegende Untersuchungen über die Entkopplung von Mehrfachregelkreisen " Regelungstechnik. (14).1966. Heft 12.

(31) P.S. Buckley. " Multivariable Control in the Process Industries"
Proc. Second Advanced Control Conference.

(32) Zalkind . C.S. " Practical Approach to Non-Interacting Control"
Instruments and Control Systems. March-April . 1967.

(33) O. Ray. " Multivariable Control Design for Linear Systems Having Multiple Time Delays " AIChE . Vol.25. 1978. No.6. Nov.

(34) R. E. Bollinger and D.E. Lamb. " Multivariable Systems: Analysis and Feedforward Control Synthesis " I&EC Fundamentals. No.4.1962.

(35) Bolinger.R.E and D.E.Lamb."The Design of a Combined Feedforward-Feedback Control System "
Chem Eng Progr Sys Ser No.55.61.66. 1965.

(36) Foster. R.D and W.F. Stevens. " A Method for the Noninteracting Control of Linear Multivariable Processes"
AIChE.J. 13 . 1967.

(37) Greenfield. G.G. and T.J. Ward. " Feedforward and Dynamic Uncoupling Control of Linear Multivariable Systems "
AIChE.J.14. 1968.

(38) Haskins. D.E. and C.M. Sliepcevich. " The Invariance Principle of Control for Chemical Processes"
Ind Eng Chem Fundamentals . Vol 4. 1965.

(39) S.G. Lloyd. " Basic Concepts of Multivariable Control"
Instrumentation Technology. 1973. December. pp.31-37.

(40) Niederlinski . A. " Two Variable Distillation Control Decouple or not Decouple " AIChE.J. 17. No.5. pp.1261-1263 . 1971.

(41) Leang-San Shieh, Ying-Jyi Paul.Wei and R.E. Yates. " A Modified Direct-Decoupling Method for Multivariable Control System Design"
IEEE Trans. Ind.Electronic & Control Instrumentation. Vol IECI-28. No.1. Feb. 1981. pp. 1-9.

(42) Bristol.E.H. " On a New Measure of Interaction for Multivariable Process Control" IEEE. Trans. Automatic Control. Vol.AC-11. No.1 pp. 133-134. 1966.

(43) Bristol.E.H. " What Happens when You Decouple? —— A Qualitative Analysis" Proc. Second Advanced Control Conference. pp.111-119.

(44) Stainthorp.F.P. " A simple Method of Arriving at Control Structure for Multivariable Systems "
Measurement and Control. Vol.5. July. 1972.

(45) F.G. Shinskey. " Interaction Between Control Loops"
Instruments and Control Systems. Vol.49. 1976. No.5,6,7.

(46) F.G. Shinskey. " Basic Concept of Multivariable Control"
Instrumentation Technology 1973. Vol.20. No.4.

(47) F.G. Shinskey. " Stable Distillation Control Through Proper Pairing of Variables " ISA Trans. Vol.10. No.4. 1971. pp.403-407.

(48) F.G. Shinskey. " Material Balance Control on Multi-Product Towers " Oil and Gas Journal. July. 1969.

(49) Nisenfeld . A.E and Schultz. H.M. " Interaction Analysis Applied to Control System Design"
Instrumentation Technology 1971. April. pp.51-57.

(50) Niesenfeld .A.E. and Stravinski. C.A. " Feedforward Control for Azeotropic Distillation " Chemical Engineering .1968.Sept. pp. 169-177.

(51) Nisenfeld.A.E and Schultz.H.M. " Interaction Analysis in Control System Design" Advances in Instrumentation Vol.25. Pt.I. 70-562.

(52) Nisenfeld. A.E. " Reflux or Distillate —— Which to Control " Chem Eng. 76(21) .1969. October. pp.169-171.

(53) J.A. Conover , A.E. Nisenfeld and R.K.MiYasaki. " Initial Response of a Distillation Column to Load Changes" ISA Trans. Vol.10. No.4. 1971. pp. 395-402.

(54) L.C. McCane and P.W.Gallier. " Digital Simulation : A Tool for the Analysis and Design of Distillation Controls " ISA Trans. Vol.12. No.3. 1973. pp.193-207.

(55) W.L. Luyben." Distillation Decoupling " AIChE .J. Vol.16. No.2. 1970. pp.198-203.

(56) W.L. Luyben. " Distillation, Feedforward control with Intermediate Feedback Control trays" Chem Eng Sci Vol.24. 997. (1969)

(57) Dahlin.E.B. " Interactive Control of Paper Machines" Control Engineering . January. 1970. pp.76-81.

(58) Juantorena .R and Romeo.R.T. " Application of the Relative Gain Matrix to a Distillation Column" Instrunentation in the Chemical and Petroleum Industies, 7. 1971.

(59) Wood. R.K. and Berry.M.W. " Terminal Composition Control of a Binary Distillation Column" Chem. Eng. Sci. Vol. 28. 1707. (1973)

(60) C.O. Schwanke, T.F.Edgar and J.O.Hougen. " Development of Multivariable Control Strategies for Distillation Columns " ISA. Trans. Vol.16. No.4. pp.69-81. 1977.

(61) M. F. Witcher and T.J. MaCvoy. " Interacting Control Systems: Steady State and Dynamic Measurement of Interaction" ISA Trans. Vol.16. No.3. pp.36-41. 1977.

(62) Tung,L.S, Edgar,T.F. " Analysis of Control-Output Interaction in Dynamic Systems" The 71 Annual AIChE Meeting. Miami. Nov. 1978.

(63) Gagnepain,J.P and Seborg.D.E. An Analysis of Process Interactions with Applications to Multiloop Control System Design" The 72nd Annual AIChE Meeting, San Francisco. November.1979.

(64) Kominek,K.W. and Smith.C.L. " Analysis of System Interaction" The 86th National AIChE Meeting, Houston, April.1979.

(65) E.H.Bristol. " Recent Results in Interaction in Multivariable Process Control " The 71st Annual AIChE Meeting, Miami.Nov.1978.

(66) W.L.Luyben . " Steady-State Energy Conservation Aspects of
Distillation Column Control " IEC, Fund. Vol.14,1975, p.321.

(67) F.G. Shinskey. " The Stabitity of Interacting Control Loops
with and Wothout Decoupling " Proc. IFAC. Multivariable
Technological Systems Conf. 4th International Symposium. 1977.

(68) Wang.J.C. " Relative Gain Matrix for Distillation Control — A
Rigorous Computational Procedure "
Proc. 1979 ISA Spring Conference. Vol. 15. New Orleans. April.
1979. pp. 61-70.
Or: ISA Trans. 1981. Vol.20. No.1 . pp.3-12.

(69) Wang.J.C. " Compute Relative Gain Matrices for Better Distillation Control " Instrumentation Technology. Vol.27. Mar. 1980
pp. 40-44,

(70) T.J. McAvoy. " Interacting Control Systems : Steady State Treat-
ment of Dual Composition Control in Distillation Columns "
ISA Trans. Vol.16. No.4. 1977. pp.83-90,

(71) T.J. McAvoy : " Steady State Decoupling Sensitivity with Application to Distillation Control " Paper . No. 36f. Proc. American
Inst Chem Eng. Houston Texas . April. 1979,

(72) T.J. McAvoy and K. Weischedel. " A Dynamic Comparison of Material
Balance versus Conventional Control of Distillation Columns "
The VIII IFAC Congress. Kyoto. Japan. August. 1981.

(73) T.J. McAvoy. " On the Difference Between Distillation Column
Control Problems " The second Engineering Fundation Conference o
on Chemical Process Control. Sea Island. GA. Tanuary. 1981,

(74) T. J. McAvoy. " Relative Gain Expressions for Dual Composition
Control" 1981. Joint Automatic Control. Vol.1. WP-7B,

(75) Jafarey,A., McAvoy, T.J. and Douglas,J.M. " Analytical Relation-
ships for the Relative Gain for Distillation Control "
IEC Fund . Vol .18. 1979. pp. 181-187,

474

(76) Weischedel,K. and McAvoy,T.J. " Feasibility of Decoupling in Conventionally Controlled Distillation Columns " IEC Fund. Vol. 19. 1980. P.379,

(77) Rijsdrop,J.E. " Interaction in Two-Variable Control Systems for Distillation Columns " Automatica. 1965.Oct. Pt I,II. pp.15-52,

(78) Rijinsdorp, J.E., Van Kampen,J.A. and Bollen, H. " Automatic Feedback Control of Two Product Questions of A Distillation Column" Paper.32b. Third IFAC. London. 1966,

(79) K.V. Waller, L.G. Hammarström. and K.C. Fagervik. " A Comparison of Six Control Approaches for Two-Product Control of Distillation " Report 80-2 of the Process Control Lab. ÅBO Akademi,

(80) K.V. Waller . " 1981: University Research on Dual Composition Control of Distillation : A Review " The Second Engineering Fundation Conference on Chemical Process Control. Sea Island.GA.

(81) K.V. Waller. " Impressions of Chemical Process Control Education and Research in the USA" Kemia-Kemi , Vol. 7. 1980, p.85,

(82) K.C. Fagervik.,K.V.Waller and L.G.Hammarström. " One-Way and Two-way Decoupling in Distillation" Report 81-3 of the Process Control Lab. ÅBO Akademi,

(83) P. Scholander. " Computer Control of a Pilot Plant Stripping Column " Proc 4th IFAC/IFIP Conference on Digital Computer Application to Process Control. Zurich. 1974,

(84) Miller,J.A., Murrill,P.W and L.L.Smith. " How to Apply Feedforward Control" Hydrocarbon Process. Vol.48. No.7. 1969.p.165,

(85) A.J. Waltz. " Separation Factor Control " Advances in Instrumentation. 1979. Vol.34. Pt.I pp.55-67,

(86) A.J. Waltz. " Using Separation Factor for Dual Composition Control " Instrumentation Tech . 1980. Vol.27. No.8. pp.41.44,

(87) Ryskamp.C. " New Strategy Improves Dual Composition Column Control" Hydrocarbon Prod. Vol.59. January. 1980,

(88) Shinya Ochiai." A Guide for Quickly Designing Distillation Column Control Systems " 1980.Joint Auto.Con. Vol.1. TA7-B.

(89) Liu Chen Hui ." On the Bristol-Shinskey Method" Automation and Instruments in Chemical Engineering (Chinese) 1981. NO.9. Sept.

(90) Liu Chen Hui and Yin Chao Ban " The Distillation Column Control And Shinskey´s Three Design Rules " To be published in Automation and Instruments in Chemical Engineering (Chinese). 1982.

Lecture Notes in Control and Information Sciences

Edited by A. V. Balakrishnan and M. Thoma

Lecture Notes in Control and Information Sciences

Edited by A. V. Balakrishnan and M. Thoma